Lecture Notes in Computer Science 9146

More information about this series at http://www.springer.com/series/7409

Francesco Ricci · Kalina Bontcheva
Owen Conlan · Séamus Lawless (Eds.)

User Modeling, Adaptation and Personalization

23rd International Conference, UMAP 2015
Dublin, Ireland, June 29 – July 3, 2015
Proceedings

Editors
Francesco Ricci
Free University of Bozen-Bolzano
Bozen-Bolzano
Italy

Kalina Bontcheva
University of Sheffield
Sheffield
UK

Owen Conlan
Trinity College Dublin
Dublin
Ireland

Séamus Lawless
Trinity College Dublin
Dublin
Ireland

ISSN 0302-9743 ISSN 1611-3349 (electronic)
Lecture Notes in Computer Science
ISBN 978-3-319-20266-2 ISBN 978-3-319-20267-9 (eBook)
DOI 10.1007/978-3-319-20267-9

Library of Congress Control Number: 2015940991

LNCS Sublibrary: SL3 – Information Systems and Applications, incl. Internet/Web, and HCI

Springer Cham Heidelberg New York Dordrecht London

Printed on acid-free paper

Springer International Publishing AG Switzerland is part of Springer Science+Business Media
(www.springer.com)

Preface

The 23rd International Conference on User Modeling, Adaptation, and Personalization (UMAP 2015) was held in Dublin, Ireland, from June 29 to July 3, 2015. UMAP is the premier international conference for researchers and practitioners working on systems that adapt to their individual users or to groups of users. UMAP is the successor of the biennial User Modeling (UM) and Adaptive Hypermedia and Adaptive Web-based Systems (AH) conferences that were merged in 2009. It is organized under the auspices of User Modeling Inc. The conference spans a wide scope of topics related to user modeling, adaptation, and personalization. UMAP 2015 was focused on bringing together cutting-edge research from user interaction and modeling, adaptive technologies, and delivery platforms. UMAP 2015 had the theme "Contextualizing the World," highlighting the significance and impact of user modeling and adaptive technologies on a large number of everyday application areas such as: intelligent learning environments, recommender systems, eCommerce, advertising, personalized information retrieval and access, digital humanities, eGovernment, cultural heritage, and personalized health.

The conference included high-quality peer-reviewed papers of three kinds: research, experience, and industry. The research papers present substantive new research results on user modeling, adaptation, and/or personalization. The experience papers present innovative applications of user modeling, adaptation, and personalization, exploring the benefits and challenges of applying user modeling techniques and adaptation technology in real-life applications and contexts. The industry papers showcase mature and solid use of user modeling, adaptation and personalization, clearly illustrating the benefits and challenges of applying user modeling techniques and adaptation technology in commercial contexts.

The international Program Committee consisted of 118 leading members of the user modeling and adaptive hypermedia communities as well as highly promising young researchers. They were assisted by 20 additional reviewers. There were 112 submissions, each submission received three reviews; program chairs facilitated consensus achievement when needed. In all, 25 submissions (28 % acceptance rate) were accepted for long presentation at the conference, another seven papers were accepted for short presentation at the conference (30 % acceptance rate), and one paper was accepted in the industry track. The overall acceptance rate was 29 %. The papers addressed well-established as well as emerging topics in user modeling, adaptation, and personalization. Among these are: recommender systems, group decision making, user personality and emotions, tracking user actions, social network analysis, eye tracking, intelligent tutoring systems, mobile guides, gaming, privacy, context awareness, student modeling, and exploratory search.

Three distinguished researchers gave plenary invited talks on related topics, illustrating prospective directions for the field. Jaime Teevan is a senior researcher at Microsoft Research and an affiliate assistant professor at the University of Washington.

Working at the intersection of human–computer interaction, information retrieval, and social media, she studies people's information-seeking activities. Ed H. Chi is a research scientist at Google. Previously, he was the area manager and a principal scientist at Palo Alto Research Center's Augmented Social Cognition Group. He led the group in understanding how Web2.0 and Social Computing systems help groups of people to remember, think, and reason. Dr Eoin O'Dell is an associate professor of law and chair of the fellows in Trinity College Dublin. He researches and publishes primarily in the fields of freedom of expression, and private and commercial law, and especially where they overlap in IP, IT, and cyberlaw.

The conference also included a doctoral consortium that provided an opportunity for doctoral students to explore and develop their research interests under the guidance of a panel of distinguished scholars. This track received seven submissions of which four were accepted as full presentations.

The UMAP2015 program included the following workshops:

- Deep Content Analytics Techniques for Personalized and Intelligent Services: organized by Lora Aroyo, Geert-Jan Houben, Pasquale Lops, Cataldo Musto, and Giovanni Semeraro
- Personalization Approaches in Learning Environments: organized by Milos Kravcik, Olga C. Santos, Jesus G. Boticario, Maria Bielikova, and Tomas Horvath
- Personalization and Adaptation in Technology for Health: organized by Cecile Paris, Floriana Grasso, Matt Dennis, and Kirsten Smith
- Personalization in eGOVernment and Smart Cities — Smart Services for Smart Territories: organized by Nikolaos Loutas, Fedelucio Narducci, Adegboyega Ojo, Matteo Palmonari, Cécile Paris, and Giovanni Semeraro

We would like to acknowledge the excellent work and great help from the UMAP 2015 Organizing Committee listed herein. We would also like to acknowledge Lucy Moffatt's help with compiling the proceedings of UMAP 2015 and thank her for her efforts. We also gratefully acknowledge our sponsors who helped us with funding and organizational expertise: User Modeling Inc., U.S. National Science Foundation, Microsoft Research, and Springer. Finally, we want to acknowledge the use of EasyChair for the management of the review process.

May 2015

Kalina Bontcheva
Francesco Ricci
Owen Conlan
Séamus Lawless

Organization

UMAP 2015 was organized by the Knowledge and Data Engineering Group at the School of Computer Science and Statistics, Trinity College, Dublin, Ireland, under the auspices of User Modeling Inc. The conference took place from June 29 to July 3, 2015, in Dublin, Ireland.

Organizing Committee

General Co-chairs

Séamus Lawless	Trinity College Dublin, Ireland
Owen Conlan	Trinity College Dublin, Ireland

Program Co-chairs

Kalina Bontcheva	The University of Sheffield, UK
Francesco Ricci	Free University of Bozen-Bolzano, Italy

Doctoral Consortium Co-chairs

Vincent Wade	Trinity College Dublin, Ireland
Robin Burke	DePaul University, USA
Alexander O'Connor	Trinity College Dublin, Ireland

Demo and Poster Co-chairs

Nava Tintarev	University of Aberdeen, UK
Alexandra Cristea	University of Warwick, UK

Workshop Co-chairs

Alan Said	Delft University of Technology, The Netherlands
Judith Masthoff	University of Aberdeen, UK

Tutorial Co-chairs

Christina Gena	University of Turin, Italy
Rosta Farzan	University of Pittsburgh, USA

Industrial Showcases Co-chairs

Ben Steichen	Santa Clara University, USA

Project Liaison Co-chairs

Christoph Trattner	Graz University of Technology, Austria
Dhavalkumar Thakker	University of Leeds, UK

Publicity Co-chairs

Laura Grehan	Dublin City University, Ireland
Kevin Koidl	Trinity College Dublin, Ireland

Local Organizing and Web Chair

Yvette Graham	Trinity College Dublin, Ireland

Student Volunteers Chair and Web Chair

Rami Ghorab	Trinity College Dublin, Ireland

Program Committee

PC Members for Conference Papers

Kenro Aihara	National Institute of Informatics, Japan
Harith Alani	The Open University, UK
Omar Alonso	Microsoft Research, USA
Liliano Ardissono	University of Turin, Italy
Lora Aroyo	VU University of Amsterdam, The Netherlands
Hideki Asoh	National Institute of Advanced Industrial Science and Technology, Japan
Ryan Baker	Teachers College, Columbia University, USA
Linas Baltrunas	Telefonica Research, Spain
Mathias Bauer	mineway GmbH, Germany
Shlomo Berkovsky	NICTA, Australia
Sara Bernardini	King's College London, UK
Mária Bieliková	Slovak University of Technology in Bratislava, Slovak Republic
Pradipta Biswas	University of Cambridge, UK
John Breslin	NUI Galway, Ireland
Derek Bridge	University College Cork, Ireland
Peter Brusilovsky	University of Pittsburgh, USA
Robin Burke	DePaul University, USA
Iván Cantador	Universidad Autónoma de Madrid, Spain
Giuseppe Carenini	University of British Columbia, Canada
Pablo Castells	Universidad Autónoma de Madrid, Spain
Federica Cena	University of Turin, Italy
Li Chen	Hong Kong Baptist University, Hong Kong, SAR China
Keith Cheverst	Lancaster University, UK
Min Chi	North Carolina State University, USA
David Chin	University of Hawaii, USA
Mihaela Cocea	University of Portsmouth, UK
Paolo Cremonesi	Politecnico di Milano, Italy
Alexandra Cristea	University of Warwick, UK

Sidney D'Mello	University of Notre Dame, USA
Elizabeth M. Daly	IBM Research, Ireland
Paul De Bra	Eindhoven University of Technology, The Netherlands
Marco De Gemmis	University of Bari, Italy
Michel Desmarais	Ecole Polytechnique de Montreal, Canada
Ernesto Diaz-Aviles	IBM Reseach, Ireland
Vania Dimitrova	University of Leeds, UK
Peter Dolog	Aalborg University, Denmark
Benedict Du Boulay	University of Sussex, UK
Casey Dugan	IBM T.J. Watson Research Center, USA
Jill Freyne	CSIRO, Australia
Séamus Lawless	Trinity College Dublin, Ireland
Fabio Gasparetti	Roma Tre University, Italy
Mouzhi Ge	Free University of Bozen-Bolzano, Italy
Cristina Gena	University of Turin, Italy
Rosella Gennari	Free University of Bozen-Bolzano, Italy
Werner Geyer	IBM T.J. Watson Research Center, USA
M. Rami Ghorab	Trinity College Dublin, Ireland
Bradley Goodman	The MITRE Corporation, USA
Ido Guy	Yahoo Labs, Israel
Conor Hayes	DERI, Ireland
Eelco Herder	L3S Research Center, Germany
Jesse Hoey	University of Waterloo, Canada
Andreas Hotho	University of Würzburg, Germany
Geert-Jan Houben	TU Delft, The Netherlands
Eva Hudlicka	Psychometrix Associates, USA
Giulio Jacucci	Helsinki Institute for Information Technology, Finland
Dietmar Jannach	TU Dortmund, Germany
Robert Jäschke	L3S Research Center, Germany
W. Lewis Johnson	Alelo Inc., USA
Marius Kaminskas	University College Cork, Ireland
Alexandros Karatzoglou	Telefonica Research, Spain
Judy Kay	University of Sydney, Australia
Styliani Kleanthous	Open University of Cyprus, Cyprus
Bart Knijnenburg	University of California, USA
Alfred Kobsa	University of California, USA
Joseph Konstan	University of Minnesota, USA
Antonio Krueger	DFKI, Germany
Tsvi Kuik	The University of Haifa, Israel
Bob Kummerfeld	University of Sydney, Australia
H. Chad Lane	University of Southern California, USA
Neal Lathia	University of Cambridge, UK
James Lester	North Carolina State University, USA
Pasquale Lops	University of Bari, Italy
Bernd Ludwig	Univeristy of Regensburg, Germany

Judith Masthoff	University of Aberdeen, UK
Gordon McCalla	University of Saskatchewan, Canada
Kathleen Mccoy	University of Delaware, USA
Alessandro Micarelli	Roma Tre University, Italy
Tanja Mitrovic	University of Canterbury, New Zealand
Riichiro Mizoguchi	Japan Advanced Institute of Science and Technology, Japan
Bamshad Mobasher	DePaul University, USA
Kasia Muldner	Arizona State University, USA
Elena Not	FBK-irst, Italy
Aditya Pal	IBM Research, USA
Georgios Paliouras	NCSR Demokritos, Greece
Alexandros Paramythis	Contexity AG, Switzerland
Paolo Petta	Austrian Research Institute for Artificial Intelligence, Austria
Luiz Augusto	Octosocial Labs, Australia
Katharina Reinecke	University of Zurich, Switzerland
Lior Rokach	Ben-Gurion University, Israel
Cristobal Romero	University of Cordoba, Spain
Matthew Rowe	Lancaster University, UK
Giancarlo Ruffo	University of Turin, Italy
Alan Said	TU Delft, The Netherlands
George Samaras	University of Cyprus, Cyprus
Olga C. Santos	UNED, Spain
Markus Schedl	Johannes Kepler University, Austria
Giovanni Semeraro	University of Bari, Italy
Bracha Shapira	Ben-Gurion University, Israel
Amit Sharma	Cornell University, USA
Barry Smyth	University College Dublin, Ireland
Marcus Specht	Open University of the Netherlands, The Netherlands
Myra Spiliopoulou	University of Magdeburg, Germany
Ben Steichen	University of British Columbia, Canada
Loren Terveen	University of Minnesota, USA
Dhavalkumar Thakker	University of Leeds, UK
Nava Tintarev	University of Aberdeen, UK
Marko Tkalcic	Johannes Kepler University, Austria
Christoph Trattner	TU-Graz, Austria
Julita Vassileva	University of Saskatchewan, Canada
Jian Wang	LinkedIn Corporation, USA
Stephan Weibelzahl	Private University of Applied Sciences Göttingen, Germany
Martin Willemsen	Eindhoven University of Technology, The Netherlands
Kalina Yacef	The University of Sydney, Australia
Michael Yudelson	Carnegie Learning, Inc., USA
Markus Zanker	Alpen-Adria-Universität Klagenfurt, Austria
Jie Zhang	Nanyang Technological University, Japan

Yong Zheng	DePaul University, USA
Ingrid Zukerman	Monash University, Australia

PC Members for Doctoral Consortium

Mária Bieliková	Slovak University of Technology in Bratislava, Slovak Republic
Robin Burke	DePaul University, USA
Alexander O'Connor	Trinity College, Ireland
Vincent Wade	Trinity College, Ireland

Additional Reviewers

Marios Belk
Annalina Caputo
Matt Dennis
Guibing Guo
Benjamin Heitmann
Tomáš Kramár
Mirko Lai
Corrado Mencar
Cataldo Musto
Fedelucio Narducci
Dimitris Pierrakos
Amon Rapp
Shaghayegh Sahebi
Giuseppe Sansonetti
Shitian Shen
Kirsten Smith
Zhu Sun
Dimitrios Vogiatzis
Guojing Zhou
Floriano Zini

Contents

Long Presentations

Short Presentations

Doctoral Consortium

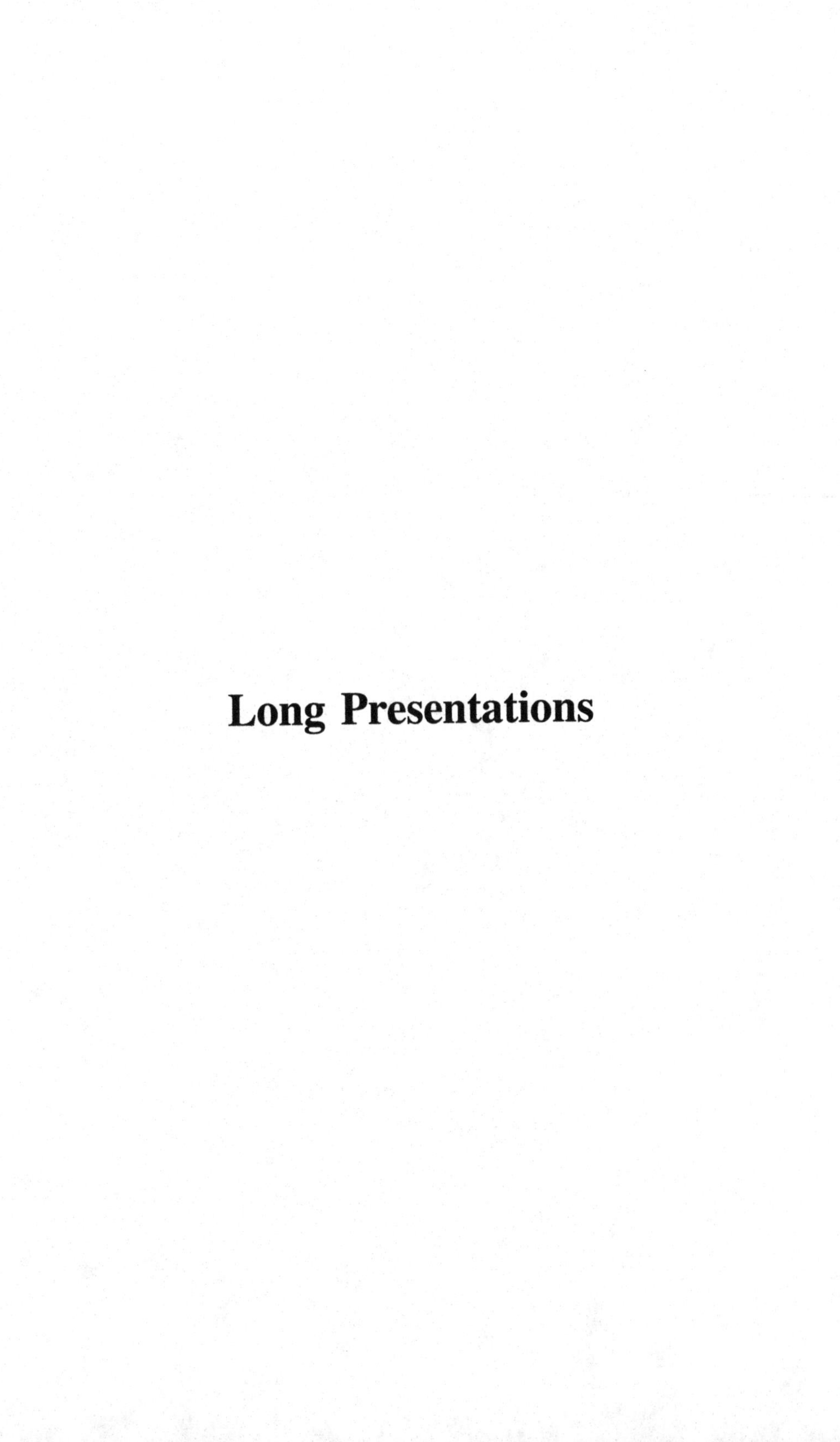

Long Presentations

Exploring the Potential of User Modeling Based on Mind Maps

Joeran Beel[1(✉)], Stefan Langer[1], Georgia Kapitsaki[2], Corinna Breitinger[1], and Bela Gipp[3]

[1] Docear, Magdeburg, Germany
{beel,langer,breitinger}@docear.org
[2] Department of Computer Science, University of Cyprus, Nicosia, Cyprus
gkapi@cs.ucy.ac.cy
[3] Department of Computer and Information Science, University of Konstanz, Konstanz, Germany
bela.gipp@uni-konstanz.de

Abstract. Mind maps have not received much attention in the user modeling and recommender system community, although mind maps contain rich information that could be valuable for user-modeling and recommender systems. In this paper, we explored the effectiveness of standard user-modeling approaches applied to mind maps. Additionally, we develop novel user modeling approaches that consider the unique characteristics of mind maps. The approaches are applied and evaluated using our mind mapping and reference-management software Docear. Docear displayed 430,893 research paper recommendations, based on 4,700 user mind maps, from March 2013 to August 2014. The evaluation shows that standard user modeling approaches are reasonably effective when applied to mind maps, with click-through rates (CTR) between 1.16% and 3.92%. However, when adjusting user modeling to the unique characteristics of mind maps, a higher CTR of 7.20% could be achieved. A user study confirmed the high effectiveness of the mind map specific approach with an average rating of 3.23 (out of 5), compared to a rating of 2.53 for the best baseline. Our research shows that mind map-specific user modeling has a high potential, and we hope that our results initiate a discussion that encourages researchers to pursue research in this field and developers to integrate recommender systems into their mind mapping tools.

Keywords: Mind map · User modeling · Recommender systems

1 Introduction

Mind mapping is a visual technique to record and organize information, and to develop new ideas. As such, mind-maps are used for tasks like brainstorming, knowledge management, note taking, presenting, project planning, decision-making, and career planning. Originally, mind mapping was performed using pen and paper, but since the 1980s, more than one hundred software tools for aiding users in creating mind maps have evolved. These tools are used by an estimated two million users who create

F. Ricci et al. (Eds.): UMAP 2015, LNCS 9146, pp. 3–17, 2015.
DOI: 10.1007/978-3-319-20267-9_1

around five millions mind-maps every year [1]. Mind-maps received attention in various research fields. They have been used to implement a lambda calculator [2], to filter search results from Google [3], to present software requirements [4], to research how knowledgeable business school students are, and there are numerous studies about the effectiveness of mind-maps as a learning tool [5]. In the field of document engineering and text mining, mind maps were created automatically from texts [6], and have been utilized to model XML files [7].

In the field of user-modeling and recommender-systems research, mind maps have thus far received no attention. However, mind-maps typically contain structured information that reflects the interests, knowledge, and information needs of their users. In this regard, the content of mind-maps is comparable to the content of emails, web pages, and research articles [1]. Hence, we believe that mind maps should be equally well suited for user modeling as are other documents, such as emails [8], web-pages [9], and research articles [10].

We assume that the reader is familiar with the idea behind mind mapping, and provide only a brief example of a mind-map, which we created using the mind-mapping and reference-management software *Docear* (Figure 1). For more information about mind maps, please refer to [11]. The mind map in Figure 1 was created to manage academic PDFs and references. We created categories reflecting our research interests ("Academic Search Engines"), subcategories ("Google Scholar"), and sorted PDFs by category and subcategory. Docear imported annotations (comments, highlighted text, and bookmarks) made in the PDFs, and clicking a PDF icon opens the linked PDF file. Docear also extracts metadata from PDF files (e.g. title and journal name), and displays metadata when the mouse hovers over a PDF icon. A circle at the end of a node indicates that the node has child nodes, which are collapsed. Clicking the circle unfolds the node, i.e. make its child nodes visible.

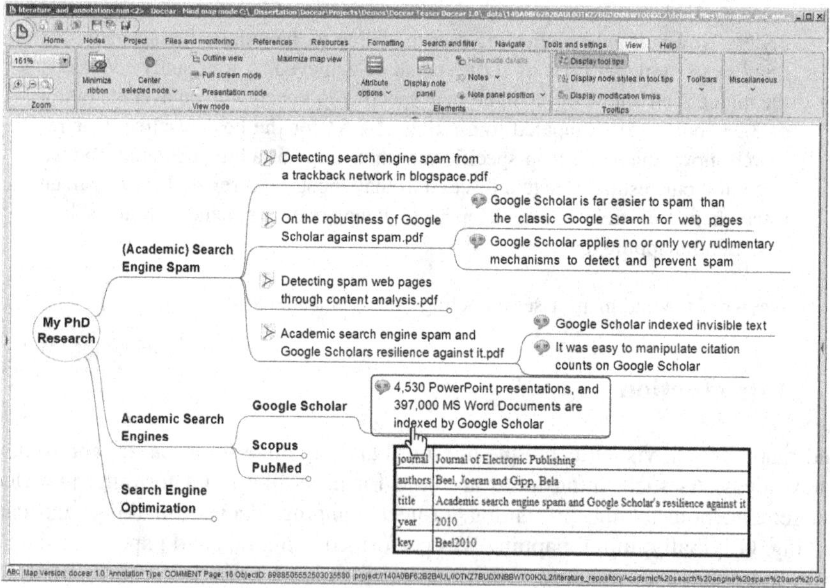

Fig. 1. Screenshot of a mind-map in Docear

As mentioned, we are the first to research the potential of mind-maps for user modeling and recommender systems. However, in industry the companies *Mind-Meister* and *Mindomo* already have utilized mind-maps for user modeling, more precisely for personalized advertisements. MindMeister extracted terms from the node that a user created or edited most recently, and used these terms as the user model. MindMeister sent this user model, i.e. the terms, to Amazon's Web Service as a search query. Amazon returned book recommendations that matched the query, and MindMeister displayed the recommendations in a window next to the mind-map.

Mindomo applied a similar concept in which Google AdSense was used instead of Amazon. Both companies have since abandoned their user modeling systems, although they still actively maintain their mind mapping tools. In an email, Mindomo explained that "people were not really interested" in the advertisements [1]. We were surprised about Mindomo's statement, because we expected mind-maps to be an effective source for user modeling.

To explore the effectiveness of mind map-based user modeling, we re-implemented MindMeister's approach, and used it in our mind mapping and reference management software Docear to recommend research papers [1]. Instead of using Amazon's Web Service or Google AdSense, we built our own corpus of recommendation candidates and used Apache Lucene to match candidates with user models. MindMeister's approach, i.e. utilizing the terms from the most recently edited or created node, achieved click-through rates (CTR) between 0.2% and around 1%. Compared to other recommender systems [12], such a CTR is disappointing, which might explain why Mindomo and MindMeister abandoned their recommender systems.

MindMeister's user modeling approach is one of three content-based filtering (CBF) approaches that we consider rather obvious to use with mind maps. The second approach is to build user models based on terms contained in the users' *current* mind map. The third approach is to utilize terms from *all* mind maps a user ever created. We implemented the second and third approach as well [1]. With Docear, both approaches achieved CTRs of around 6%, which is a reasonable performance and significantly better than the first approach. We were surprised that rather similar user modeling approaches differed in their effectiveness by a factor of six. Apparently, small differences in the algorithms – such as whether to utilize terms from a single node or from the entire mind-map – have a significant impact on user-modeling performance. The question arises if, and how, the effectiveness can further be increased by adjusting the user modeling approach to the unique characteristics of mind-maps.

Therefore, our main research goal is to identify variables that influence the effectiveness of user-modeling approaches based on mind maps. Identifying these variables allows the development of a mind map-specific user modeling approach that should perform significantly better than the trivial user-modeling approaches that we already implemented. From such a mind map-specific user modeling approach, millions of mind mapping users could benefit [1].

2 Methodology

In a brainstorming session, we identified 28 variables that might affect the effectiveness of user modeling based on mind maps. Due to time restrictions, we implemented and evaluated only a few variables that we considered most promising, and for which an evaluation with Docear was feasible. The variables we focused on included the number of mind maps to analyze, the number of nodes to utilize, the size of the user model, whether to use only visible nodes, and different mind map-specific weighting schemes.

From March 2013 to August 2014, Docear's recommender system delivered 45,208 recommendation sets, with 430,893 recommendations to 4,700 users. Recommendations were displayed as a list of ten research papers, for which the titles were shown. A click on a recommendation opened the paper in the user's web browser. The publication corpus used for recommendations included around 1.8 million documents from various languages, and various research fields. For more details on the recommender system please refer to [13].

Each set of recommendations was created with a randomly assembled algorithm. That means, whenever recommendations were requested, a random value was chosen for each variable. For instance, one algorithm might have utilized *visible* nodes from the *2* most recently modified mind-maps, and stored the *25* highest weighted terms in the user model. Another algorithm might have used the *250* most recently modified nodes (*visible and invisible)* among all mind-maps, weighted the *citations* of these nodes, and stored the *5* highest weighted citations in the user model.

To measure effectiveness and identify the optimal values for the variables, we compared click-through rates (CTR), which describe the ratio of delivered recommendations by those that were clicked. For instance, to evaluate whether a user model size of *ten* or *100* terms was more effective, CTR of all algorithms with a user model size of ten was compared to CTR of all algorithms with a user model size of 100. There is a lively discussion about the meaningfulness of CTR and online evaluations and its alternatives, i.e. offline evaluations and user studies. We do not discuss this issue here but refer to a recent publication, in which we showed that online evaluations are preferable over offline evaluations, and that CTR seems to be the most sensible metric for our purpose [14]. In that publication we also explain why showing only the title of the recommended papers is sufficient for our evaluation, instead of showing further information such as author name and publication year.

After finding the optimal values for each variable, we combined the optimal values in a single algorithm and compared this algorithm against four baselines to analyze whether this mind-map-specific user modeling performed better than the baselines. Effectiveness was again measured with CTR but we additionally conducted a user study based with 182 users who rated 491 recommendation sets on a five-star scale.

One baseline was the stereotype approach. Stereotyping is one of the earliest user modeling and recommendation classes [15]. In stereotyping, one assumes that users will like what their peer group is enjoying. For Docear we generalized that all Docear users are researchers, and that all researchers would be interested in literature about academic writing. Hence, when the stereotype approach was chosen, a list of ten papers relating to academic writing was recommended. These papers were manually selected by the Docear team. The second, third, and fourth baselines were those CBF variations that are rather obvious and that we already used in our initial study [1]: a) the approach of MindMeister, in which only terms of the most recently modified node are analyzed for the user model ('modified' means created, edited or moved); b) all terms of the user's current mind-map are used for the user model; **c)** all terms of all mind maps that the user ever created are utilized for the user model.

Our methodology has a limitation, since determining the optimal values for each variable separately ignores potential dependencies. For instance, only because a user model size of 100 terms is most effective on average, and analyzing 500 nodes is most effective on average, does not mean that analyzing 500 nodes *and* having a user model size of 100 terms is the optimal combination. In the ideal case, we would have evaluated all possible variations to find the single best variation. However, for some variables, there are up to 1,000 possible values, and combining all these variables and values leads to millions of possible variations. Evaluating this many variations was not feasible for us. The second best option would have been a multivariate statistical analysis to identify the impact of the single variables. However, also for such an analysis we did not have enough data. Therefore, our methodology was the third best option. It will not lead to a single optimal combination of variables, but as our result shows, our methodology leads to a significantly better algorithm than the baselines, and the results help understanding the factors that affect effectiveness in mind map-based user modeling.

We analyzed the effects of the variables for both CBF based on citations and CBF based on terms, and expected that the optimal values for the variables would differ for terms and citations. A "citation" is a reference or link in a mind-map to a research paper. In Figure 1, nodes with a PDF icon, link to a PDF file, typically a research article. If such a link exists, this is seen as a citation for the linked research article. A citation is also made when a user added bibliographic data, such as title and author to a node.

For the term-based CBF variations, all reported differences are statistically significant ($p<0.05$), if not reported otherwise. Significance was calculated with a two tailed t-test and χ^2 test where appropriate. Results for citation based CBF are mostly not statistically significant, because the approach was implemented only a few months ago, and not all users cite research papers in their mind maps. Therefore, insufficient citation-based recommendations were delivered to produce significant results. Consequently, the focus of this paper lies on the term-based CBF variations. We also report runtimes in the charts for informative reasons, but do not discuss the data in this paper. It should be noted that runtimes could significantly differ with different implementations, or on different hardware.

Please note: Most of the data that we used for our analysis is publicly available [13]. The data should allow replicating our calculations, and performing new analyses beyond the results that we presented in this paper. To foster further research on mind map-specific user modeling, we invite other scientists to join us, and cooperate on the development and research of Docear's recommender system.

3 Results

3.1 Mind-Map and Node Selection

When utilizing mind maps for user modeling, one central question is *which mind maps* to analyze, and *which parts* of the mind maps to analyze. We experimented with a few variables to answer this question.

We hypothesized that analyzing all mind maps of a user is not the most effective approach. If the mind maps analyzed are too many or too old, this could introduce noise into the user model. To test this hypothesis, Docear's recommender system randomly used the *x* most recently modified mind maps, regardless of *when* they were modified. For users who created at least eight mind maps, no statistically significant difference could be found for the number of utilized mind maps (Figure 2). Judging by these numbers, it seems that the number of the most recently modified mind maps is not an effective variable to optimize the user modeling process.

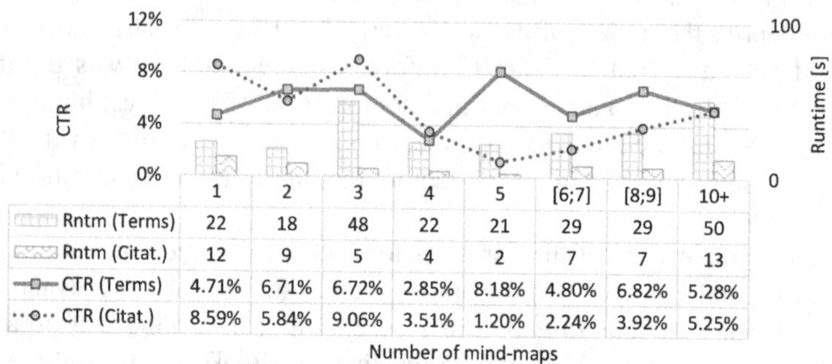

	1	2	3	4	5	[6;7]	[8;9]	10+
Rntm (Terms)	22	18	48	22	21	29	29	50
Rntm (Citat.)	12	9	5	4	2	7	7	13
CTR (Terms)	4.71%	6.71%	6.72%	2.85%	8.18%	4.80%	6.82%	5.28%
CTR (Citat.)	8.59%	5.84%	9.06%	3.51%	1.20%	2.24%	3.92%	5.25%

Fig. 2. CTR by the number of mind-maps to analyze (for users with 8+ mind-maps)

As an alternative to using the *x* most recently modified *mind maps*, Docear analyzed the *x* most recently modified *nodes*. For example, if *x=50*, the terms (or citations) that are contained in the 50 most recently modified nodes were used for user modeling. The intention is that users might be working in different sections of several mind maps, and only those actively edited sections are relevant for user modeling. For users who have created at least 1,000 nodes, saturation appears (Figure 3). When the 50 to 99 most recently created nodes are used, CTR is highest (7.50%). When more nodes are analyzed, CTR decreases. We did the same analysis for other user groups, and results were always the same – using only the 50 to 99 most recently modified nodes led to the highest CTRs on average. With regard to citations the results slightly change. For users with 1,000 or more nodes, using the most recent 10 to 49 citations is most effective (8.36% vs. 7.32% for using 1 to 9 citations).

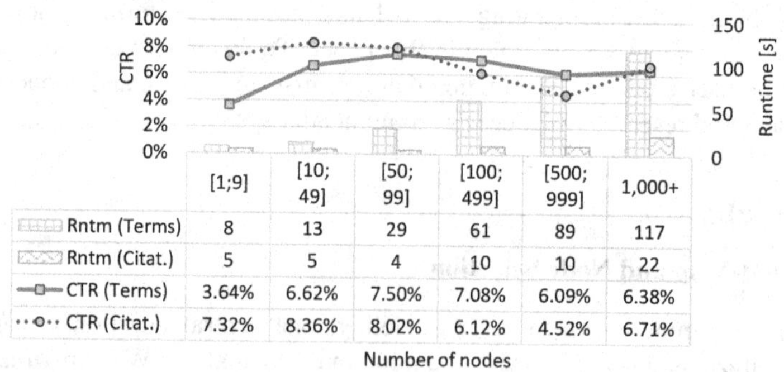

	[1;9]	[10; 49]	[50; 99]	[100; 499]	[500; 999]	1,000+
Rntm (Terms)	8	13	29	61	89	117
Rntm (Citat.)	5	5	4	10	10	22
CTR (Terms)	3.64%	6.62%	7.50%	7.08%	6.09%	6.38%
CTR (Citat.)	7.32%	8.36%	8.02%	6.12%	4.52%	6.71%

Fig. 3. CTR by the number of nodes to analyze (for users with 1,000+ nodes)

Selecting a fix number of nodes might not be the most effective criteria. The most recent, for example, 100 nodes could include nodes that were modified some years ago. Such nodes would probably not represent a user's current information needs any more. Therefore, Docear's recommender system randomly used all nodes that were modified within the past *x days* (Figure 4). When the recommender system utilized only those nodes that were modified on the current day, CTR was 3.81% on average for users who used Docear for at least 360 days. When nodes from the last two or three days were utilized, CTR increased to 5.52%. CTR was highest, when nodes modified during the past 61 to 120 days were used (7.72%), and remained high when nodes of the past 121 to 180 days were used. When nodes were used that were modified more than 180 days ago, CTR began to decrease. Apparently, the interests of Docear's users change after a few months.

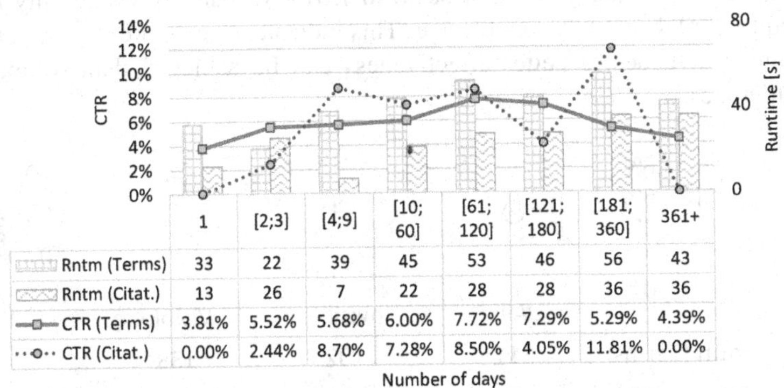

	1	[2;3]	[4;9]	[10; 60]	[61; 120]	[121; 180]	[181; 360]	361+
Rntm (Terms)	33	22	39	45	53	46	56	43
Rntm (Citat.)	13	26	7	22	28	28	36	36
CTR (Terms)	3.81%	5.52%	5.68%	6.00%	7.72%	7.29%	5.29%	4.39%
CTR (Citat.)	0.00%	2.44%	8.70%	7.28%	8.50%	4.05%	11.81%	0.00%

Fig. 4. CTR for nodes analyzed in the past *x* days (for users being registered 360+ days)

Another variable we tested was the node modification type (Figure 5). The recommender system chose randomly, whether to utilize only nodes that were newly *created*, nodes that were *moved*, nodes that were *edited*, or nodes with any type of *modification* (created, edited, *or* moved). Utilizing moved nodes only, resulted in the highest CTR (7.40%) on average, while the other modification types achieved CTRs around 5%.

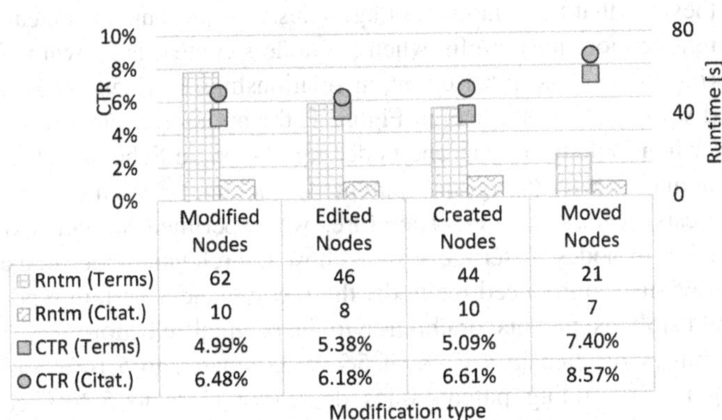

	Modified Nodes	Edited Nodes	Created Nodes	Moved Nodes
Rntm (Terms)	62	46	44	21
Rntm (Citat.)	10	8	10	7
CTR (Terms)	4.99%	5.38%	5.09%	7.40%
CTR (Citat.)	6.48%	6.18%	6.61%	8.57%

Fig. 5. Node modification type

We find this interesting, because this result indicates that the evolution of a mind-map might be important for user modeling, and certain actions (e.g. moving nodes) indicate a higher importance of certain nodes. We have only experimented with a binary selection scheme, i.e. selecting or not selecting a node based on actions such as editing or moving nodes. It might also be interesting to weight nodes based on the user's action. For instance, the user modeling process could utilize all nodes but weight moved nodes stronger than newly created nodes.

Most mind-mapping tools allow folding a node, i.e. to hide its children. In Docear, this is indicated by a circle at the end of node (Figure 1). We hypothesized that nodes that are hidden, are currently not relevant for describing the user's information need. Therefore, Docear's recommender system randomly chose whether to use only *visible* nodes, *invisible* nodes, or *all* nodes. When using visible nodes only, CTR increased from 6.00% (analyzing all nodes) to 7.61% (Figure 6). Using only invisible nodes led to a CTR of 4.89% on average. This indicates once more that by selecting a few meaningful nodes, a better effectiveness can be achieved than by examining simply all nodes.

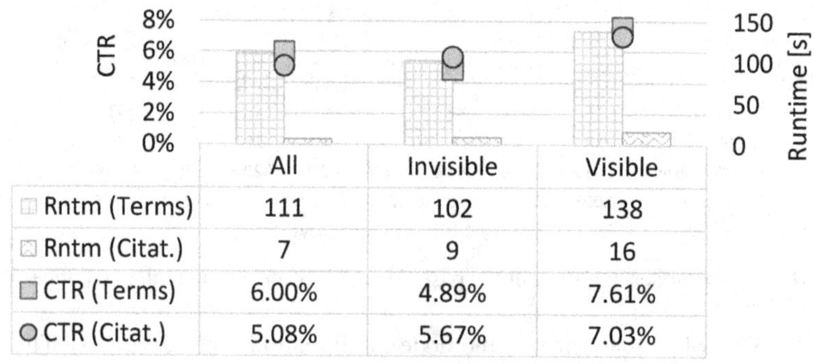

	All	Invisible	Visible
Rntm (Terms)	111	102	138
Rntm (Citat.)	7	9	16
CTR (Terms)	6.00%	4.89%	7.61%
CTR (Citat.)	5.08%	5.67%	7.03%

Node visibility

Fig. 6. Node visibility as selection criteria (at least 100 nodes analyzed)

We hypothesized that the relation among nodes is important. This means the terms of a node might be more meaningful when the node's context is known with regard to the neighboring nodes. The most common relationships in mind maps are *parents*, *children*, and *siblings*. For instance, in Figure 1, the author's information needs seem rather vague when looking only at one node, e.g., "Google Scholar indexed invisible text". In combination with the (grand) parent "(Academic) Search Engine Spam" the author's interests become clearer. Therefore, we experimented with extending the original selection of nodes. After the system chose the relevant nodes to examine with one of the previously introduced methods, the recommender system randomly chose whether to add siblings, parents, or children to the original selection.

Adding siblings resulted in a CTR of 5.73% compared to 5.10% for not adding siblings (Figure 7). Adding parent-nodes decreased CTR to 5.36% compared to 5.46% for not adding parent-nodes. Adding children increased CTR from 5.22% to

5.61%. All differences are small but statistically significant. In addition, when the recommender system combined all factors, i.e. adding siblings and children but ignoring parents, CTR was 6.18% on average, which was a significant improvement, compared to not extending nodes (4.84%). One might suspect that extending the original node selection was only more effective because the extension caused more nodes to be used and the more nodes are used, the higher CTR becomes in general. However, this suspicion is not correct. For instance, when 100 to 499 nodes were selected, and no children or siblings were added, CTR was 5.15% on average. When 10 to 50 nodes were selected and after adding children and siblings 100 to 499 nodes were used, CTR was 5.45%. This indicates that selecting a few recently modified nodes, and extending them with their siblings and children, is more effective than selecting simply more nodes based only on the modification date.

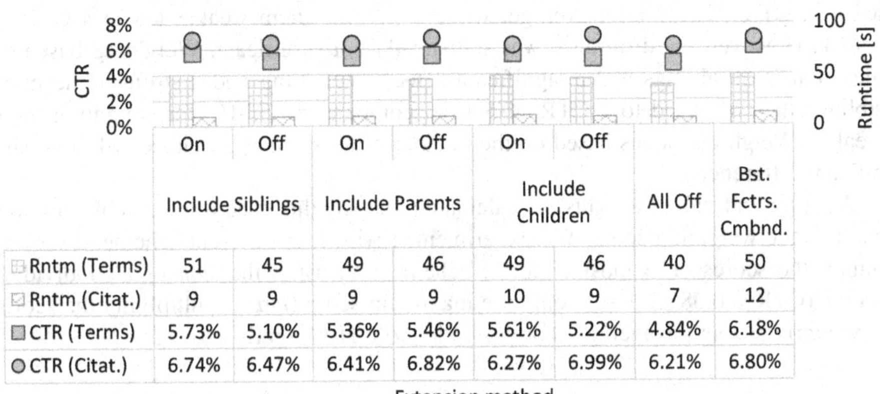

	Include Siblings: On	Include Siblings: Off	Include Parents: On	Include Parents: Off	Include Children: On	Include Children: Off	All Off	Bst. Fctrs. Cmbnd.
Rntm (Terms)	51	45	49	46	49	46	40	50
Rntm (Citat.)	9	9	9	9	10	9	7	12
CTR (Terms)	5.73%	5.10%	5.36%	5.46%	5.61%	5.22%	4.84%	6.18%
CTR (Citat.)	6.74%	6.47%	6.41%	6.82%	6.27%	6.99%	6.21%	6.80%

Fig. 7. Extending the original node selection

3.2 Node Weighting

Often, user modeling applications weight features (e.g. terms) that occur in a certain document field (e.g. in title) stronger than features occurring in other fields (e.g. the body text). Mind maps have no fields for title, abstract, headings, or body text. Instead, mind maps have nodes, which have a certain *depth*, i.e. their distance from the root node. We hypothesized that the depth of a node might indicate the importance of the node. For instance, in Figure 1, the node “Scopus” has a depth of 2, and we would assume that this term describes the user’s interests with a different accuracy than the node “Academic Search Engines” that has a depth of 1.

To test the hypothesis, Docear’s recommender system randomly chose whether to weight terms of a node stronger or weaker, depending on its depth. If the nodes were to be weighted stronger the deeper they were, the weight of a node (1 by default) was multiplied with **a)** the absolute depth of the node; **b)** the natural logarithm of the depth; **c)** the common logarithm of the depth; or **d)** the square root of the depth. If the resulting weight was lower than 1, e.g., for ln (2), then the weight was set to 1.

If nodes were to receive less weight the deeper they were, then the original weight of 1 was multiplied with the reciprocal of the metrics a) – d). If the resulting weight was larger than 1, e.g., for ln(2), the weight was set to 1. In the following charts, we provide CTR for the mentioned metrics. However, the differences among the metrics are not statistically significant. Hence, we concentrate on comparing the overall CTR, i.e. the CTR of weighting nodes stronger or weaker the deeper they are regardless of the particular metric.

Results show that when nodes are weighted stronger the deeper they are in a mind map, CTR increases. Weighting them stronger, led to a CTR of 5.61% on average, while weighting them weaker led to a CTR of 5.12% on average. We also experimented with other metrics that are based on the number of children, the number of siblings, and the number of words contained in a node. It appears that weighting nodes stronger the more children a node has, increases CTR. Weighting them stronger led to a CTR of 5.17% on average, while weighting them weaker led to a CTR of 4.97%. However, the difference was statistically not significant. Weighting based on the number of siblings had a significant effect. Weighting nodes stronger the more siblings they have led to a CTR of 5.40%, compared to 5.01% for weighting them weaker. Weighting nodes based on the number of terms they contained led to no significant differences.

After the individual weights are calculated, the weights need to be combined into a single node weighting score. We experimented with four different schemes for combining the scores. The most effective scheme was using the *sum* of all individual scores (CTR = 6.38%). Using only the maximum score (*max*), multiplying the scores (*product*) or using the average score (*avg*) led to CTRs slightly above 5%.

3.3 User Model Size

Just because utilizing, e.g. the 50 most recently moved nodes is most effective, does not mean that necessarily *all* features of these nodes need to be stored in the user model. Therefore, Docear's recommender system randomly selected to store only the *x* highest weighted features in the user model. For user modeling based on at least 50 nodes, CTR is highest (8.81%) for user models containing the 26 to 50 highest weighted terms (Figure 8). User models containing less, or more, terms achieve significant lower CTRs. For instance, user models with one to ten terms have a CTR of 3.92% on average. User models that contained more than 500 terms have a CTR of 4.84% on average. Interestingly, CTR for citations continuously decreases the more citations a user model contains[1]. Consequently, a user model size between 26 and 50 seems most sensible for terms, and a user model size of ten or less for citations.

[1] The high CTR for user models with 501 and more citations is statistically not significant.

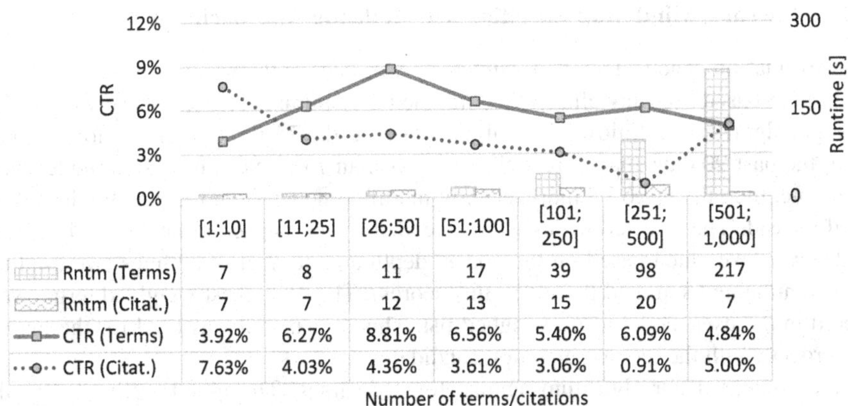

	[1;10]	[11;25]	[26;50]	[51;100]	[101; 250]	[251; 500]	[501; 1,000]
Rntm (Terms)	7	8	11	17	39	98	217
Rntm (Citat.)	7	7	12	13	15	20	7
CTR (Terms)	3.92%	6.27%	8.81%	6.56%	5.40%	6.09%	4.84%
CTR (Citat.)	7.63%	4.03%	4.36%	3.61%	3.06%	0.91%	5.00%

Fig. 8. CTR by user model size (feature weight not stored)

The previous analysis was based on un-weighted lists of terms and citations, i.e. the user model contained only a list of the features without any weight information. If the weights were stored in the user model, and used for the matching process, the picture changes (Figure 9). In this case, CTR has a peak for user models containing between 251 and 500 terms (8.13%). Interestingly, this CTR is similar to the maximum CTR for the optimal non-weighted user model size (8.81% for 26 to 50 terms). We find this surprising, because we expected weighted lists to be more effective than un-weighted lists. The results for weighted citations are also surprising – CTR varies and shows no clear trend. We have no explanation for this result and believe that further research is necessary[2].

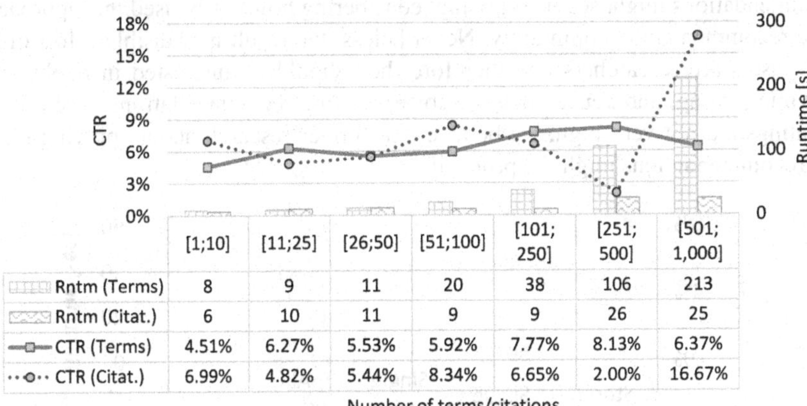

	[1;10]	[11;25]	[26;50]	[51;100]	[101; 250]	[251; 500]	[501; 1,000]
Rntm (Terms)	8	9	11	20	38	106	213
Rntm (Citat.)	6	10	11	9	9	26	25
CTR (Terms)	4.51%	6.27%	5.53%	5.92%	7.77%	8.13%	6.37%
CTR (Citat.)	6.99%	4.82%	5.44%	8.34%	6.65%	2.00%	16.67%

Fig. 9. CTR by user model size (feature weight stored)

[2] We double-checked all data and the source code, and are quite confident that there are no flaws in the user modeling process.

3.4 Docear's Mind Map-Specific User Modeling Approach

The evaluation made clear that numerous variables influence the effectiveness of mind map-based user modeling. We combined the optimal values of these variables in a single algorithm as follows: The algorithm used the 75 most recently moved nodes from the past 90 days that were visible. If less than 75 moved and visible nodes were available, then the up to 75 most recently modified nodes from the past 90 days were used instead. The selected nodes were extended by all their children and siblings. All nodes were weighted based on the nodes' depth and number of siblings (we used the ln weighting and summed the individual scores). The 35 highest weighted terms were stored in the user model as un-weighed list. This user model was used for the matching process with the recommendation candidates.

We compared our algorithm against four baselines. The four baselines were the stereotype approach, and the three "obvious" CBF approaches (using terms from a single node, from a single mind map, or from all mind maps).

Among the baselines, using all terms from all mind maps and from a single mind map performed alike in terms of CTR (Figure 10) and ratings. Using terms from only one node – the approach that MindMeister applied – resulted in the lowest CTR (1.16%) and ratings (1.63). Stereotype recommendations performed comparably reasonable with a CTR of 3.08% and a rating of 1.97 on average. Overall, CTR of the baselines tends to be lower than in our previous evaluation [1]. However, since our previous evaluation, we added several new variables, and some might have decreased CTR on average. In addition, Docear's Web Spider was not running in the past couple of months. This means, no new recommendation candidates were added to the corpus. Hence, long-time users probably often received recommendations they had received previously, which decreases average CTR. The reasonable effectiveness of stereotype recommendations might seem surprising, considering how rarely used this approach is in the recommendation community. Nevertheless, the result is plausible. Most of Docear's users are researchers and therefore they should be interested in books about academic writing, and hence click the corresponding recommendations. Even though the ratings are not very high, we believe that further research about applying stereotype recommendations might be promising.

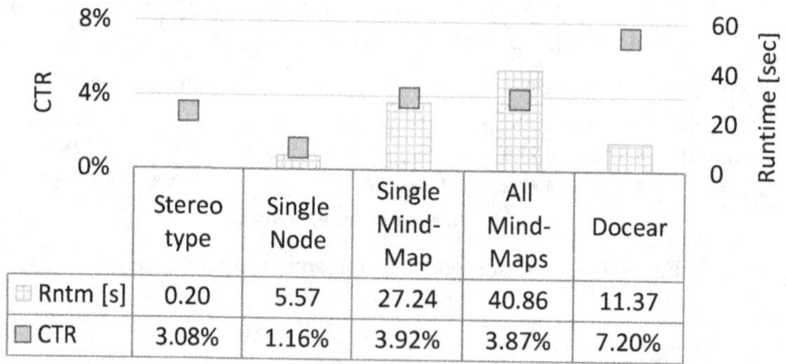

	Stereo type	Single Node	Single Mind-Map	All Mind-Maps	Docear
Rntm [s]	0.20	5.57	27.24	40.86	11.37
CTR	3.08%	1.16%	3.92%	3.87%	7.20%

Fig. 10. Docear's mind map-specific approach vs. Baselines (CTR and Runtime)

Docear's mind map-specific user modeling algorithm significantly outperformed all baselines and achieved a CTR of 7.20% on average (Figure 10). This is nearly twice as high as the best performing baseline and six times as high as MindMeister's approach, the only approach that had been applied in practice thus far. User ratings also show a significantly higher effectiveness for Docear's approach (3.23) than for the best performing baseline (2.53). Because we experimented only with a few variables, and the experiments were of relative basic nature, we are convinced that more research could further increase the effectiveness.

4 Discussion and Summary

We explored the effectiveness of user modeling based on mind maps. Our goal was to learn whether this is a promising field of research, and whether users could benefit from mind map-specific user modeling systems. We examined how effective standard user modeling approaches are when applied to mind maps, and how to enhance these approaches by taking into account the characteristics of mind maps. We implemented a mind map based research paper recommender system, and integrated it into our mind mapping software Docear. The recommender system displayed 430,893 recommendations to 4,700 users from March 2013 to August 2014, and recommendations were created with several variations of content-based filtering (CBF), of which some considered different characteristics of mind maps. The evaluation of the different user modeling approaches revealed the following results.

First, standard user modeling approaches can be reasonably effective when applied to mind maps. However, the effectiveness varied depending on which standard approach was used. When user models were based on all terms of users' mind maps, the click-through rate (CTR) was around 4%. When only terms from the most recently modified node were used, CTR was 1.16%. These results led us to the conclusion that user modeling based on mind maps is not trivial, and minor differences in the approaches lead to significant differences in the effectiveness of the user modeling.

Second, user modeling based on mind maps can achieve significantly higher CTRs when the characteristics of mind maps are considered. Based on our research, the following variables should be considered: **a)** the number of analyzed nodes. It seems that the terms of the most recently modified 50 to 99 nodes are sufficient to describe the users' information needs. Using more, or less, nodes decreased the average CTR **b)** Time restrictions were important. It seems that utilizing nodes that were created more than four months ago, decreased CTR. **c)** CTR increased when only nodes were used that were recently *moved* by a user, instead of using nodes that were created or edited. **d)** Using only nodes that are visible in the mind map also increased effectiveness compared to using both visible and invisible nodes. **e)** Extending the originally selected nodes by adding siblings and children increased average CTR slightly and statistically significantly. This indicates that the full meaning of nodes becomes only clear when their neighbor nodes are considered. **f)** We also found that weighting nodes, and their terms, based on node depth and the number of siblings increased CTR. The deeper a node, the more siblings it has, and possibly the more children it has, the more relevant are its terms to describe the users' information needs. The separate weights should be combined by their sum. **g)** The final user model should contain the highest weighted 26 to 50 terms, if the user model is stored as unweighted list. If weights are stored, it seems that larger user models are sensible. However, more research is needed to clarify this.

Third, when the variables were combined in their favorable way, this mind map specific user modeling approach outperformed standard user modeling approaches applied to mind maps by a factor of nearly two (CTR of 7.20% vs. 3.92%). Compared to the approach that was applied in practice by MindMeister (using only the last modified node), our approach increased effectiveness by a factor of six (CTR of 7.20% vs. 1.16%).

Our research has a few limitations. So far, the values for the variables are only rough suggestions. For instance, the finding that the optimal user model size is between 26 and 50 terms is still rather vague. Hence, more research is required to specify the optimal values of the variables. There are also more potential variables that we have not yet analyzed but which might be promising. For instance, the evolution of mind maps over time might enhance the effectiveness of mind map-specific user modeling. We could imagine that weighting nodes by the intensity of use (e.g. how often a node was edited, opened, or moved) might provide valuable information. We also advocate research on the differences of content and the structure of mind maps that were created for different purposes, such as brainstorming or literature management. This might provide valuable insights on the characteristics of mind maps. More research is needed to explore dependencies among the variables. This requires more advanced statistical analyses of the variables, which in turn requires research using large-scale recommender systems that have significantly more users than Docear. It should also be noted that our research was based only on Docear, which is a unique mind mapping software, because it focuses on academic users. Additional research with other mind mapping tools seems desirable. This is particularly true because most mind mapping tools focus on certain groups of users and it would be interesting to explore whether there is *one* mind map-specific user modeling approach that suits all mind mapping applications, or whether each application needs to apply a different approach. Most of our results with regard to citations were statistically not significant. It would also be interesting to research in more detail how citations, or hyperlinks, could be exploited. In addition, we only evaluated the algorithms using CTR. For future research, user studies might also be desirable to evaluate the algorithms.

Overall, the results of our research reinforced our astonishment that mind-maps are being disregarded by the user modeling and recommender system community. We believe that this paper showed the potential of mind map-specific user modeling, and we hope that it initiates a discussion, which encourages other researchers to do research in this field. We believe there is a lot of interesting work that could further increase the effectiveness of mind map-specific user modeling. We also hope that our results encourage developers of mind mapping tools to integrate recommender systems into their software. The results of our paper will help with implementing a suitable user modeling approach. This would benefit mind mapping users or, in case of personalized advertisement, generate revenues that are presumably higher than those that could be achieved with the user modeling approaches of MindMeister and Mindomo.

References

1. Beel, J., Langer, S., Genzmehr, M., Gipp, B.: Utilizing Mind-Maps for Information Retrieval and User Modelling. In: Dimitrova, V., Kuflik, T., Chin, D., Ricci, F., Dolog, P., Houben, G.-J. (eds.) UMAP 2014. LNCS, vol. 8538, pp. 301–313. Springer, Heidelberg (2014)
2. Chien, L.-R., Buehre, D.J.: A Visual Lambda-Calculator Using Typed Mind-Maps. In: International Conference on Computer and Electrical Engineering, pp. 250–255 (2008)
3. Zualkernan, I.A., AbuJayyab, M.A., Ghanam, Y.A.: An alignment equation for using mind maps to filter learning queries from Google. In: 2006. Sixth International Conference on Advanced Learning Technologies, pp. 153–155 (2006)
4. Contó, J.A.P., Godoy, W.F., Cunha, R. H.E., Palácios, C.G., LErario, A., Domingues, A.L., Gonçalves, J.A., Duarte, A.S., Fabri, J.A.: Applying Mind Maps at Representing Software Requirements. Contributions on Information Systems and Technologies, 1 (2013)
5. Holland, B., Holland, L., Davies, J.: An investigation into the concept of mind mapping and the use of mind mapping software to support and improve student academic performance (2004)
6. Kudelic, R., Malekovic, M., Lovrencic, A.: Mind map generator software. In: Proceedings of the 2nd IEEE International Conference on Computer Science and Automation Engineering (CSAE), pp. 123–127 (2012)
7. Bia, A., Muñoz, R., Gómez, J.: Using Mind Maps to Model Semistructured Documents. In: Lalmas, M., Jose, J., Rauber, A., Sebastiani, F., Frommholz, I. (eds.) ECDL 2010. LNCS, vol. 6273, pp. 421–424. Springer, Heidelberg (2010)
8. Ha, Q.M., Tran, Q.A., Luyen, T.T.: Personalized Email Recommender System Based on User Actions. In: Bui, L.T., Ong, Y.S., Hoai, N.X., Ishibuchi, H., Suganthan, P.N. (eds.) SEAL 2012. LNCS, vol. 7673, pp. 280–289. Springer, Heidelberg (2012)
9. Göksedef, M., Gündüz-Ögüdücü, S.: Combination of Web page recommender systems. Expert Systems with Applications **37**(4), 2911–2922 (2010)
10. Zarrinkalam, F., Kahani, M.: SemCiR - A citation recommendation system based on a novel semantic distance measure. Program: Electronic Library and Information Systems **47**(1), 92–112 (2013)
11. Buzan, T.: The Mind Map Book (Mind Set). BBC (BBC Active) (2006)
12. Hofmann, K., Schuth, A., Bellogın, A., de Rijke, M.: Effects of Position Bias on Click-Based Recommender Evaluation. In: de Rijke, M., Kenter, T., de Vries, A.P., Zhai, C., de Jong, F., Radinsky, K., Hofmann, K. (eds.) ECIR 2014. LNCS, vol. 8416, pp. 624–630. Springer, Heidelberg (2014)
13. Beel, J., Langer, S., Gipp, B., Nürnberger, A.: The Architecture and Datasets of Docear's Research Paper Recommender System. D-Lib Magazine - The Magazine of Digital Library Research 20(11/12) (2014)
14. Beel, J., Langer, S.: A Comparison of Offline Evaluations, Online Evaluations, and User Studies in the Context of Research-Paper Recommender Systems. Under Review (2014). Pre-print available at http://www.docear.org/publications/
15. Rich, E.: User modeling via stereotypes. Cognitive Science **3**(4), 329–354 (1979)

Modeling Motivation in a Social Network Game Using Player-Centric Traits and Personality Traits

Max V. Birk[1(✉)], Dereck Toker[2], Regan L. Mandryk[1], and Cristina Conati[2]

[1] Department of Computer Science, University of Saskatchewan, 110 Science Place, Saskatoon, SK S7N 5C9, Canada
{max.birk,regan.mandryk}@usask.ca

[2] Department of Computer Science, University of British Columbia, 2366 Main Mall, Vancouver, BC V6T 1Z4, Canada
{dtoker,conati}@cs.ubc.ca

Abstract. People are drawn to play different types of videogames and find enjoyment in a range of gameplay experiences. Envisaging a representative game player or persona allows game designers to personalize game content; however, there are many ways to characterize players and little guidance on which approaches best model player behavior and preference. To provide knowledge about how player characteristics contribute to game experience, we investigate how personality traits as well as player styles from the BrianHex model moderate the prediction of player motivation with a social network game. Our results show that several player characteristics impact motivation, expressed in terms of enjoyment and effort. We also show that player enjoyment and effort, as predicted by our models, impact players' in-game behaviors, illustrating both the predictive power and practical utility of our models for guiding user adaptation.

Keywords: User modeling · Personality · Player experience · Social network game · Linear regression · Moderation · Motivation

1 Introduction

Game designers often envisage a representative player of their game, and can benefit from making design decisions with this illustrative player in mind. These archetypal players – or 'player personas [6] – can be created from many factors, including demographic characteristics (e.g., age, sex), expertise with a system (e.g., novices), gameplay goals or aspirations (e.g., to pass the time), personality traits (e.g., extroverted), or what motivates a player to enjoy a game (e.g., sensation seeker). Player-centric models can help designers tailor their games to a specific type of player with specific play preferences. For example, Orji et al [18], showed that tailoring serious games for health to specific player types may increase their efficacy.

Although there are different approaches for characterizing players, there is little knowledge about which characterizations are most informative for predicting player experience and for guiding design decisions accordingly. For example, the five-factor model (FFM), an approach of describing personality according to five traits [14], is a

F. Ricci et al. (Eds.): UMAP 2015, LNCS 9146, pp. 18–30, 2015.
DOI: 10.1007/978-3-319-20267-9_2

robust and well-studied model; however, personality has not been shown to be consistently effective in predicting player experience [e.g., 5,12,13,21,27]. In an attempt to uncover candidates for "robust traits that could be used for a player instrument" [3], Bateman and Nacke created the BrainHex model [17], which characterizes people along seven dimensions specific to the game play experience (Achiever, Conqueror, Mastermind, Daredevil, Survivor, Seeker, Socialiser). Although BrainHex has successfully been used in some game studies (e.g., to model how different types of players respond to various persuasive strategies in serious games [18]), it is not as stable, as theoretically grounded, or as well studied as the FFM.

The goal of this paper is to provide a better understanding of if and how player personality and the BrainHex player-centric traits can serve as characterizations of player experience to guide personalized game design. Similar to previous work [e.g. 5,16, 22,24], we characterize player experience in terms of invested effort and enjoyment in game play, two key aspects defining a player's intrinsic motivation to play, a well-established construct for evaluating player experience [5]. We then build models to ascertain how personality and player-centric traits interact with known predictors of invested effort and game enjoyment: satisfaction of needs such as competence, autonomy, relatedness, presence, and intuitive control [24]. Investigating the moderating effect of personality traits and player typologies on well-established player experience measures – i.e., need satisfaction and intrinsic motivation – is important to understand how individual differences enhance or diminish the experience of playing a video game. With a personalized understanding of player experience, designers could create engaging experiences tailored to a specific play style, and consider individual needs/interests to create more compelling experiences.

To build the models, we collected data from over 3400 players of the social network game Pot Farm (Eastside Games Studio, 2010). Social network games are games played online that take advantage of a player's social network, supporting the impulsive use of social network services [19]. We collected player-centric and personality traits along with validated measures of player experience [24] and logs of in-game behaviors. A moderated regression analysis [11] based on this data shows that both FFM and BrainHex factors impact the well-established influence of need satisfaction on player enjoyment and effort, showing that these traits should be considered in combination with the satisfaction of needs to predict player motivation in game play. Furthermore, we show that our models can also predict in-game player behavior.

The importance of our results is two-fold. They contribute to our understanding of game and play experience, adding richness to the theoretical models of player characterization that can be leveraged for more informed, personalized game design. They also reveal how differences in player experience are reflected in players' in-game behaviors. These findings are important for designing adaptive game elements aimed at improving player motivation, since they can help identify which behaviors are worth encouraging for which users in real-time during game play.

2 Related Work

The use of player archetypes to describe a fictional and representative player derives from the persona framework developed by Cooper [7] in the context of human-computer interaction, in which personas are described as detailed user archetypes to inform a product's design. Applying this approach to play, Canossa and Drachen [6] created play personas, defined as "[…] clusters of preferential interaction (what) and navigation (where) attitudes, temporally expressed (when), that coalesce around different kinds of inscribed affordances in the artifacts provided by game designers".

Player-centric models are new approaches to differentiate player preferences and help designers to build games addressing a diverse audience. Different typologies have been proposed to classify players. One of the first was Bartle's Test of Gamer Psychology [2], which divides players into four classes: killer, achiever, socializer, and explorers [1]. Building on Bartle's work, Yee et al. [31] applied principal component analysis (PCA) to survey data and identified Achievement (finding enjoyment in progression and completion), Social (the enjoyment of socializing in the game world), and Immersion (finding enjoyment in dwelling in a game environment) as the three driving factors of motivation in Massively Multiplayer Online Role-Playing Games.

Integrating concepts from previous methodologies, the BrainHex model [17] distinguishes between 7 types of players: *Achievers* are goal-oriented and are motivated by completing tasks or collecting things. *Conquerors* enjoy defeating difficult opponents, and overcoming challenges. *Daredevils* are excited by the thrill of taking risks and enjoy playing on the edge. *Masterminds* enjoy solving puzzles, and devising strategies. *Seekers* enjoy exploring things, sense-stimulating activities and discovering their surroundings. *Socialisers* enjoy interacting with others. *Survivors* love the experience associated with terrifying scenes and the thrill of escaping from scary situations. Based on the BrainHex questionnaire [4], players are characterized by how much they associate with each of the groups. There is promising evidence that this model can be leveraged to understand the connection between player type and experience; for instance, it was successfully used to model how different types of players respond to various persuasive strategies in serious games [18].

Whereas player-centric models are specific to video games, researchers have also investigated player models built on the more general construct of personality. Most of this work relied on the well-established Five Factor Model of personality, (FFM) [14], which categorizes personality types along the five dimensions of Extraversion, Neuroticism, Agreeableness, Conscientiousness, and Openness. For instance, Johnson et al. [13] showed that conscientiousness is negatively correlated with flow, suggesting that planning and goal orientation might interfere with the flow experience in games. The relevance of personality for genre preference is also under investigation: Peever et al. [20] demonstrate that personality can be used to predict player preference for certain genres, whereas Park et al. [20] found the opposite. It is still an open question how personality can be leveraged to improve player modeling. However, research on player motivation and personality indicates relevance for Games User Research (GUR) and the evaluation of player experience [5,20].

A few efforts have been made to compare personality and player-centric models (e.g., [16,17]), however, there is no clear indication of which is more relevant to predict player experience [23]. We perform a moderation analysis [11], with the established link between need satisfaction and player motivation, operationalized as enjoyment and effort, moderated by personality (FFM) and player type (BrainHex). The original aspect of our work is that we explore if and how player traits models moderate the effect of well-known predictors of effort and enjoyment associated with the satisfaction of a variety of player needs: autonomy (accepting challenge under one's own volition); competence (experiencing success and failure based on one's own skills); relatedness (experiencing relations to others); presence (a sense of immersion in the game) and intuitive control (the natural mapping of control to action) [24].

3 Data Collection and Modeling

In order to carry out our evaluation of player type and personality in terms of gameplay enjoyment, we leveraged a real-world case study using an established online social game. The players in our data set were gathered from the free-to-play Facebook game 'Pot Farm', which currently has over 600,000 monthly active users. Pot Farm is a marijuana-themed 'Ville style farming simulation where users plant and harvest crops, complete quests, collect gold, and level up (see [26] for an overview of 'Ville style design patterns, and themes). We chose a farming simulation because it is among the most popular types of social network games [25].

We administered surveys to Pot Farm players over one week using a mechanism that prompted players via an in-game pop-up message. Players could complete the survey for a reward of in-game content or they could decline. To ensure broad coverage, surveys were administered randomly across several ranges of play-experience – from brand new players to those who had been playing the game for several months; however, survey respondents had to have played the game at least once within the past week. We also collected data on age, sex, and level, as well as game-based attributes (i.e., telemetry) of game events such as coins, quests, and achievements.

Players were surveyed using the following validated scales: *Player-Centric Traits* were measured using the 21-item BrainHex instrument [4]. FFM *Personality Traits* were assessed using the Ten-Item-Personality-Inventory (TIPI) [10], which has been used in games research [12]. *Enjoyment and Effort* were assessed using the 5-item and 4-item subscales interest-enjoyment and effort-importance of the intrinsic motivation inventory (IMI) [15]. *Need Satisfaction* was assessed using the 21-item Player Experience of Need Satisfaction (PENS) questionnaire [24].

For each user, we recorded in-game actions logged during their time spent playing Pot Farm. The game events are reported as daily totals, and because the amount of play-time varied across users, we take the average over the last five played days (for new users it consists of the values for their first day of play). The set of play experience items we consider are: neighbour visits (i.e., farms visited of Facebook friends who also play Pot Farm), social claims (i.e., claiming the reward for an advanced achievement that a neighbour has achieved), logins, coin events (i.e., coins added to the player's inventory), quests completed (i.e., in-game tasks completed), achievements unlocked (i.e., completion of a more or less difficult series of tasks), and contraptions (i.e., objects created by combining other in-game items).

We obtained 3486 completed surveys; however, 1477 participants were removed if 3 or more of their factors were 2 standard deviations from the mean, or if they had zero variance across a construct. We removed more than 40% of the original sample from our analysis to remove participants who clicked through the questionnaires without considering the answers in order to quickly earn the premium currency reward for survey completion. The majority of removed participants was due to zero variance across the survey, which indicates that the response to each item was the same within and between constructs, e.g. indicating "strongly agree" to all items independent of the survey questions (e.g., "I enjoy the game very much", "The game does not hold my attention"). Next, we randomly subsampled remaining players across different amounts of play-time to produce an even distribution across player experience. For the resulting 1172 participants, each attribute is z-standardized [9], to allow for comparisons between scales across and within models. Ages of the 1176 players (33.9% female) ranged from 18 to 65, with the majority (33.1%) being 18-24.

Because the link between need satisfaction and motivation has been established [24], our goal is to see how this link is moderated by personality or player traits. We use moderated multiple regression analysis [11], which is similar to a traditional multiple regression but includes interactions between pairs of individual predictors. Using SPSS, we constructed 20 models, 10 for each of our motivational factors, enjoyment and effort (*outcome variables*), based on the path diagram show in Figure 1. Each model consists of one of the five needs, along with either the set of personality traits (FFM) or player-centric traits (BrainHex). These traits appear individually as predictors in the model, and also as moderators with each need satisfaction item. Three *control variables* (age, sex, game level) are also included in all models.

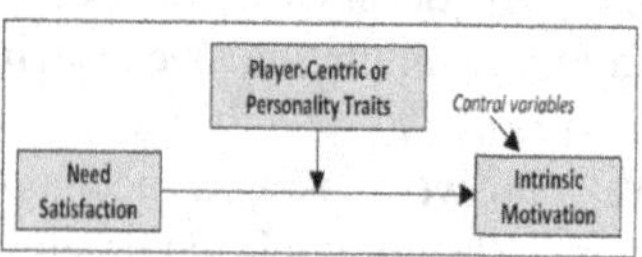

Fig. 1. Structure of Moderated Multiple Regression Model

4 Results of Moderation Analysis

We organize the presentation of the results by the motivation variables being predicted, i.e., enjoyment and effort. However, we summarize results for the control variables here because they had similar trends across all 20 models. Game level was always the only significant control variable (*mean-p* < .001; *mean-β* = .17), with players at higher levels being more motivated.

4.1 Predicting Enjoyment

The fit of the models (adjusted R^2) and the β values for the moderator (player-centric or personality trait), the predictor, (need), and the interaction between the moderator and the predictor (i.e., the effect of moderation) are shown in Table 1. Each of the 5 need satisfaction predictors (i.e., PENS Item) are always a significant predictor of enjoyment, with β values that are always positive, confirming previous work that greater satisfaction of any of the five needs predicts higher enjoyment [24].

Player-centric traits show significant main effects on enjoyment across models for mastermind and achiever. Personality traits also show main effects across all models for conscientiousness and openness (see Table 1). These results reveal that two of the personality traits and two of the BrainHex traits have predictive value for player enjoyment. However, most notably there are additional cases where personality or player traits moderate the influence of needs satisfaction on player enjoyment. We follow up on these significant moderation effects with a simple slopes analysis, which considers the regression of the predictor on the dependent measure for low, average, and high levels of the moderating variable [9]. Comparing the slopes in terms of their significance and the value and direction of beta allows us to interpret the moderating influence of traits on the value of needs for predicting motivation. All relevant slopes are depicted in Figure 2.

Table 1. Simple and moderated effects on enjoyment. Adjusted R^2 for all effects are presented at the top of each column. *T = Player Centric Traits; T*N = Moderation of T and Need Satisfaction.* ^{X} indicates an effect significant at the .05 level, * indicates significance at the .01 level, ** indicates significance at .001.

	Competence		*Autonomy*		*Relatedness*		*Presence*		*Intuitive Control*	
Enjoyment	T (β)	T*N (β)	T (β)	T*N (β)	T (β)	T*N (β)	T (β)	T*N (β)	T (β)	T*N (β)
	Model R^2= 0.22		Model R^2= 0.27		Model R^2= 0.14		Model R^2= 0.16		Model R^2= 0.24	
PENS Item	**0.32****	n/a	**0.39****	n/a	**0.09****	n/a	**0.19****	n/a	**0.35****	n/a
Seeker	**0.07^X**	0.04	0.05	0.02	**0.09***	-0.02	**0.09***	-0.03	0.07	0.04
Survivor	-0.02	-0.01	-0.04	-0.04	-0.05	-0.04	-0.07^X	0.00	-0.04	-0.03
Mastermind	**0.09***	-0.09^X	**0.10***	0.02	**0.14****	0.04	**0.14****	0.02	**0.09***	-0.03
Conqueror	-0.01	0.07	-0.03	-0.05	-0.02	-0.05	-0.01	-0.08^X	-0.02	-0.02
Socializer	0.03	-0.03	0.04	0.01	0.03	0.03	0.03	0.04	0.04	0.03
Daredevil	-0.04	0.00	-0.04	0.01	-0.03	-0.04	-0.04	-0.02	-0.02	0.07^X
Achiever	**0.16****	0.02	**0.16****	0.01	**0.17****	0.09^X	**0.17****	0.06	**0.14****	0.00
	Model R^2= 0.23		Model R^2 0.28		Model R^2 0.16		Model R^2 0.19		Model R^2= 0.25	
PENS Item	**0.31****	n/a	**0.39****	n/a	**0.12****	n/a	**0.22****	n/a	**0.34****	n/a
Extraversion	0.02	-0.01	0.01	-0.01	0.02	0.00	0.03	0.04	0.04	-0.06*
Agreeableness	0.05	0.02	**0.06^X**	-0.01	0.05	0.01	**0.07^X**	0.03	0.06	0.00
Conscientiousness	**0.15****	-0.01	**0.14****	-0.02	**0.17****	0.02	**0.16****	0.00	**0.13****	0.04
Emotional Stability	0.03	-0.05	0.03	-0.02	0.04	0.03	0.05	-0.03	0.01	0.00
Openness	**0.15****	-0.06^X	**0.16****	-0.02	**0.19****	-0.01	**0.21****	-0.02	**0.14****	-0.05^X

Competence: There are moderations of mastermind and openness on the influence of competence on enjoyment. For both, the steepness of the slope is higher for people with low value of the traits (β_{mast}=.38, β_{open}=.37, $p<.001$), as compared to medium (β_{mast} =.34, β_{open} =.32, $p<.001$), and high (β_{mast} =.30, β_{open} =.27, $p<.001$). These progressions indicate that competence becomes a weaker predictor of enjoyment as players increase in ratings for mastermind or openness.

Relatedness: There is a moderation of relatedness by achiever: Relatedness only predicts enjoyment for medium (β=.09, p<.001) and high (β=.15, p<.001) achievers.

Presence: There is a moderation of presence on enjoyment by conqueror; the steepness of the slope is higher for low conqueror (β=.23, p<.001), as compared to medium (β=.18, p<.001), and high conqueror (β=.13, p<.01), indicating that presence becomes a weaker predictor of enjoyment as players increase in ratings for conqueror.

Intuitive Control: There are moderations of daredevil, extraversion and openness on the influence of intuitive control on enjoyment. The moderations of extraversion and openness are similar: the steepness of the slope is higher for low measures of these traits (β=.44 for extraversion, β=.39 for openness, p<.001), as compared to medium (β=.39 for extraversion, β=.35 for openness, p<.001), and high values (β=.34 for extraversion, β=.31 for openness, p<.001). Thus, intuitive control becomes a weaker predictor of enjoyment as players increase in ratings for extroversion or openness.

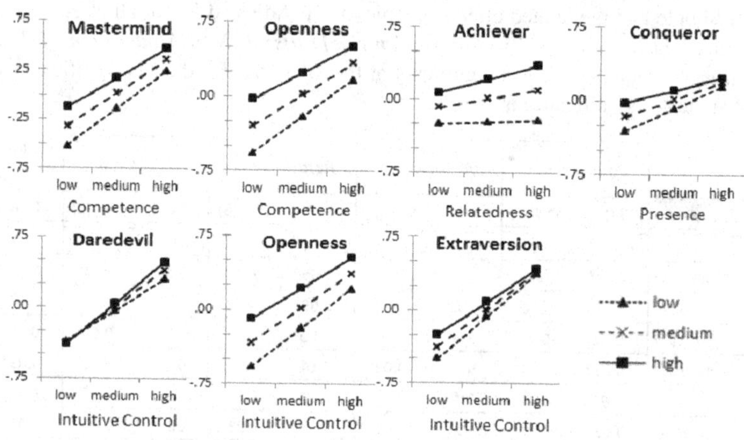

Fig. 2. Follow up simple slopes analysis for the discovered significant effects of need satisfaction on *enjoyment*, moderated by player traits (refer to Table 1)

Daredevil has the opposite moderating effect on the influence of intuitive control on enjoyment: the steepness of the slope is lower for low daredevil (β=.33, p<.001), as compared to medium (β=.39 p<.001), and high daredevil (β=.44, p<.001); intuitive control is a weaker predictor of enjoyment as players decrease in ratings for daredevil.

4.2 Predicting Effort

In terms of predicting effort, seven significant moderators were discovered using the same analysis described the previous subsection. Due to space limitations, we only show the final directionalities in Figure 3.

Notably, as was the case for enjoyment, there is no moderating effect of traits on autonomy, but there are effects for the other four needs. These effects, however, involve different traits (with the exception of mastermind on competence) showing that the two motivational factors of enjoyment and effort should be treated separately when it comes to leveraging player type for personalized game designed.

Our results show two different ways in which personality and player-centric traits moderate the influence of need satisfaction on effort: (1) the trait affects whether or not there is a predictive relationship of need satisfaction on motivation; (2) the relationship is present throughout the models; however, the predictive power of the need changes depending on the level of the player-trait moderator (see Table 1).

We found three examples of the first moderation type: achiever determines whether or not relatedness predicts enjoyment, whereas mastermind and agreeableness predict whether or not relatedness predicts effort. All other moderation effects scale the influence of need satisfaction on the prediction of enjoyment or effort.

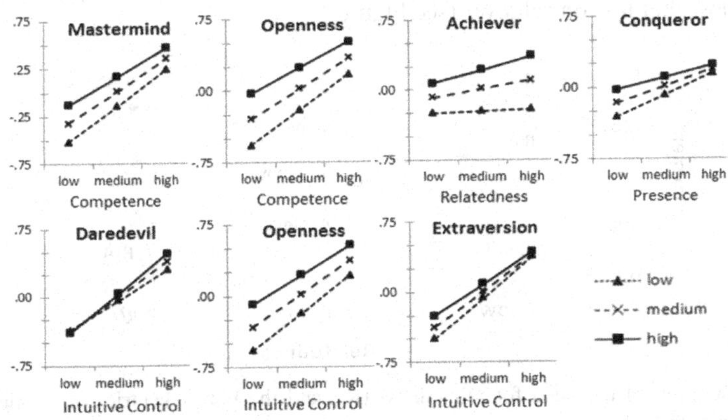

Fig. 3. Follow up simple slopes analysis for the discovered significant effects of need satisfaction on *effort*, moderated by player traits

4.3 Summary of Results for Predicting Motivation

Both types of moderation are interesting because they show how the influence of user traits can identify instances where an increase in need satisfaction does not necessarily lead to a substantial increase in player motivation. This is important because it can guide designers to focus on improving player motivation by meeting the needs of players with specific traits only when it will actually matter (e.g., for improving player motivation, it is worthwhile to understand how to improve relatedness for high achievers, whereas it has no impact on motivation for low achievers).

5 How Player Traits are Expressed in Game Data

The models of how player traits moderate the satisfaction of needs on motivation have application beyond contributing to our theoretical understanding. In particular, because we can predict how different players experience enjoyment and effort in games, we should be able to use the models to predict how these various players will express motivation differences through their in-game behaviors. That is, the models should inform designers on how players will behave in the game as measured through logs of in-game actions. Making this connection would allow for customization of game experience by allowing designers to identify in-game behaviors that are worth encouraging because they a`rȩ known to increase motivation for certain player types.

To illustrate this point, we apply one of the moderated regression models presented earlier to make hypotheses about how groups of players, differentiated by their traits and their needs satisfaction, behave in the game. We chose the achiever-relatedness-enjoyment model as a representative example from the type (1) of moderated relationships as discussed in the previous section (Figure 4). We created four groups: R^+A^+ were high on both relatedness and achiever ratings; R^-A^- were low on both relatedness and achiever; R^-A^+ were low on relatedness but high on achiever, and R^+A^- were high on relatedness, but low on achiever (see Figure 4).

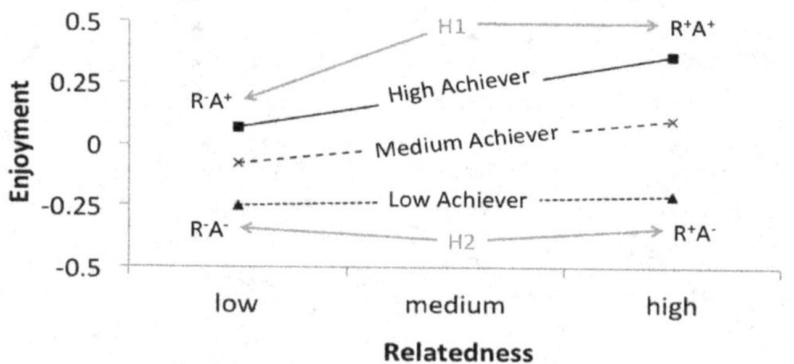

Fig. 4. Moderation of the need for relatedness (R), and the player centric trait achiever (A), predicting enjoyment

Because our model predicts that levels of relatedness make a difference only for high achievers and not for low achievers, our hypotheses are:

- *H1. Members of R+A+ exhibit more in-game behaviors than members of R-A+.*
- *H2. Members of R+A- will not exhibit more in-game behaviors than R-A-.*

A MANOVA with group (4 levels: R^+A^+, R^-A^-, R^+A^-, R^-A^+) as a between-subjects factor on in-game behaviors showed a significant effect of group membership. In particular, there were differences for social claim ($F_{3,289}$=8.8, p<.001, η^2=.08), logins ($F_{3,289}$=3.5, p=.016, η^2=.04), coin events ($F_{3,289}$=2.9, p=.029, η^2=.03), and contraptions ($F_{3,289}$=2.8, p=.038, η^2=.03). We used pairwise comparisons with the Holm-Bonferroni correction (α=0.05) to test the planned comparisons in our two hypotheses. Table 2 shows a summary of game behavior according to the four groups.

H1. As expected, members of R^+A^+ had significantly higher social claims, daily logins, and coin events than members of R^-A^+ (although there was no significant difference in the number of contraptions), confirming H1.

H2. As expected, there were no differences in any in-game behavior measures between R^+A^- and R^-A^-, confirming H2.

Table 2. Mean (m) and standard error (SE) for game data for combinations of high/low achiever and high/low relatedness

	R^+A^+		R^-A^-		R^+A^-		R^-A^+	
Actions (daily sum)	m	(SE)	m	(SE)	m	(SE)	m	(SE)
Neighbour Visits	5	(1.5)	2.7	(0.6)	2.8	(0.8)	2.3	(0.4)
Social Claims	75	(19)	13	(5)	13	(7)	14	(4)
Logins	8.6	(1)	6.4	(0.7)	7.7	(1.2)	5.6	(0.4)
Premium Currency	13	(2)	10	(2)	13	(2)	10	(2)
Coin Events	78	(22)	43	(9)	43	(9)	31	(5)
Quests	4.9	(0.8)	4.5	(0.7)	5.4	(0.9)	5.4	(0.6)
Achievements	0.5	(0.1)	0.5	(0.1)	0.7	(0.1)	0.6	(0.1)
Contraptions	47	(8)	32	(8)	19	(5)	28	(4)

To summarize, our analysis indicates that the moderating influence of player traits on how need satisfaction predicts motivational factors in game play (i.e., enjoyment and effort) can translate directly into in-game behavior of real-world players of a social farming game. In the previous section, we found a moderating effect between achievers, relatedness and enjoyment, showing that there is no increase in enjoyment for low achievers, even when their need for relatedness was satisfied. This lack of difference was also detected by our analysis of the game data (*H2*). Similarly, the moderating effect predicts that for high achievers there is an increase in enjoyment as relatedness is satisfied, and our analysis of game actions allows us to link this increase to differences in specific game actions (*H1*). In particular, we see an increase in social claims for high achievers when relatedness is satisfied. Social claims are of particular interest in this case, because unlike other game events, the underlying mechanism is tied to reciprocal social behavior – it requires having relationships to other players and is comprised of quick social interactions. Achievers are goal-oriented and may use social claims as a means of advancing in the game – however, doing so increases the number of social interactions, potentially increasing the satisfaction of relatedness and ultimately in-game motivation. Our model shows that high achievers with low satisfaction of relatedness also do not have many social claims, perhaps helping to explain their lower in-game enjoyment. As with other Facebook behaviors, social claims are a very lightweight activity that can be considered comparable to an interaction with a loose tie [8], i.e., a quick interaction that still provides value to a relationship between friends. Low achievers, however, have low social claims regardless of their satisfaction of relatedness; it is likely that they draw their enjoyment from other aspects of the game that allow them to satisfy other needs through in-game actions.

Adaptation strategies can be devised based on these results. For example, for high achievers, if few social claims are observed, then additional in-game prompts or quests could be offered to the player to encourage more neighbour visits, which would aid in satisfying their relatedness, thus improving motivation to play the game. Because neighbour visits are not related to enjoyment for low achievers, encouraging this behavior to these players could be intrusive, leading to decreased motivation.

6 Discussion and Conclusions

In this paper, we make a theoretical contribution by clarifying the relationship between personality and player-centric traits, and their relevance in explaining how need satisfaction and motivation during game play are facilitated and expressed in an ecologically-valid video game context. In particular, we uncovered differentiations based on player traits in the established link between need satisfaction and motivation.

An ecologically-valid setting has several advantages when investigating the moderating effects of personality types and player centric traits on the play experience: 1) The relation between need satisfaction and motivation is not investigated under experimental situations, which limits experienced autonomy because of an external source of motivation, e.g. financial compensation; 2) We do not have to extrapolate on how our findings might generalize to real-world in-game behavior because we have access to that data directly; and 3) In-game behavior is not influenced by time pressure, as is often introduced in experiment-based play sessions.

Our results also shed light on how differences in experience are reflected in different in-game behaviors. This is especially important in cases of moderation because we must consider motivation and traits in combination to understand player behavior, and cannot rely on the predictive ability of each construct in isolation.

Our results can give designers concrete insights on how to improve player experience for specific player personas, for instance which need factors are most important to satisfy for players with certain traits. In the long term, we envision a game platform that customizes the game experience for each player by knowing his or her traits. For example, if a player is a high achiever, then the game should foster a sense of relatedness, and this can be achieved by monitoring and triggering specific actions (e.g. social claims). However, if the player is not a high achiever, then there is no need to focus on satisfying relatedness, and the game may need to focus on satisfying other needs by considering a different trait. It is future work to determine how and when to adapt, but we have initiated this effort by building the knowledge of who to adapt for.

Although our findings are limited to Pot Farm, the approach is general and can be extended to other genres. Specific studies are needed in order to uncover how different games, e.g. a first-person shooter, might satisfy needs differently. Future work is also needed to find innovative ways to assess player-centric and personality traits without actually surveying players; e.g. personality predictions based on in-game behavior, or social network profile (i.e., [1,30]).

References

1. Adali, S., Golbeck, J.: Predicting Personality with Social Behavior. In: Proc. ASONAM 2012, pp. 302–309 (2012)
2. Bartle, R.: Hearts, clubs, diamonds, spades: Players who suit MUDs. Journal of MUD Research **1**(1), 19 (1996)
3. Bateman, C., Lowenhaupt, R., Nacke, L.E.: Player typology in theory and practice. In: Proc. of DiGRA 2011 (2011)

4. Bateman, C., Nacke, L.E.: The neurobiology of play. In: Proc. of FuturePlay 2010, pp. 1–8 (2010)
5. Birk, M., Mandryk, R.L.: Control your game-self: effects of controller type on enjoyment, motivation, and personality in game. In: Proc. of CHI 2013, pp. 685–694 (2013)
6. Canossa, A., Drachen, A.: Patterns of play: Play-personas in user-centred game development. In: Proc. of DiGRA 2009 (2009)
7. Cooper, A.: The inmates are running the asylum: Why high-tech products drive us crazy and how to restore the sanity. Sams, Indianapolis (1999)
8. Ellison, N.B., Steinfield, C., Lampe, C.: The benefits of Facebook "friends:" Social capital and college students' use of online social network sites. Journal of Computer Mediated Communication **12**(4), 1143–1168 (2007)
9. Field, A.: Discovering statistics using IBM SPSS statistics, 4th edn. Sage, London (2013)
10. Gosling, S.D., Rentfrow, P.J., Swann Jr., W.B.: A very brief measure of the Big-Five personality domains. Journal of Research in Personality **37**(6), 504–528 (2003)
11. Hayes, A.F.: Introduction to mediation, moderation, and conditional process analysis: A regression-based approach. Guilford Press, New York (2008)
12. Johnson, D., Gardner, J.: Personality, motivation and video games. In: Proc. OZCHI, pp. 276–279 (2010)
13. Johnson, D., Wyeth, P., Sweetser, P., Gardner, J.: Personality, genre and videogame play experience. In: Proc. of FuGa 2012, pp. 117–120 (2012)
14. McCrae, R.R., Costa, P.T.: Validation of the five-factor model of personality across instruments and observers. Journal of Personality and Social Psychology **52**(1), 81 (1987)
15. McAuley, E., Duncan, T., Tammen, V.V.: Psychometric properties of the Intrinsic Motivation Inventory in a competitive sport setting: A confirmatory factor analysis. Research Quarterly for Exercise and Sport **60**, 48–58 (1989)
16. McMahon, N., Wyeth, P., Johnson, D.: Personality and player types in Fallout New Vegas. In: Proc. of FuGa 2012, pp. 113–116 (2012)
17. Nacke, L.E., Bateman, C., Mandryk, R.L.: BrainHex: A neurobiological gamer typology survey. Entertainment Computing **5**(1), 55–62 (2013)
18. Orji, R., Mandryk, R. L., Vassileva, J., Gerling, K.M.: Tailoring persuasive health games to gamer type. In: Proc. of CHI 2013, pp. 2467–2476 (2013)
19. Paavilainen, J., Hamari, J., Stenros, J., Kinnunen, J.: Social Network Games: Players' Perspectives. Simulation & Gaming **44**(6), 761–881 (2013)
20. Park, J., Song, Y., Teng, C.: Exploring the Links Between Personality Traits and Motivations to Play Online Games. Cyberpsychology, Behavior, & Social Networking **14**(12), 747–751 (2011)
21. Peever, N., Johnson, D., Gardner, J.: Personality and Video Game Genre Preferences. In: Proc. of IE 20 (2012)
22. Przybylski, A.K., Weinstein, N., Murayama, K., Lynch, M.F., Ryan, R.M.: The Ideal Self at Play The Appeal of Video Games That Let You Be All You Can Be. Psychological Science **23**(1), 69–76 (2012)
23. Quick, J.M., Atkinson, R.K., Lin, L.: Empirical Taxonomies of Gameplay Enjoyment: Personality and Video Game Pref. Int. J. Game-Based Learning **2**(3), 11–31 (2012)
24. Ryan, R.M., Rigby, C.S., Przybylski, A.: The motivational pull of video games: A self-determination theory approach. Motivation and Emotion **30**(4), 344–360 (2006)
25. Sung, J., Bjornrud, T., Lee, Y.H., Wohn, D.: Social network games: exploring audience traits. In: CHI 2010 Extended Abstracts, pp. 3649–3654 (2010)
26. Tyni, H., Sotamaa, O., Toivonen, S.: Howdy partner! on free-to-play, sociability and rhythm design in FrontierVille. In: Proc. of Academic MindTrek 2011, pp. 22–29 (2011)

27. Teng, C.I.: Online game player personality and real-life need fulfillment. International Journal of Cyber Society and Education **2**(2), 39–49 (2009)
28. Vorderer, P., Klimmt, C., Ritterfeld, U.: Enjoyment: At the heart of media entertainment. Communication Theory **14**(4), 388–408 (2004)
29. Zajonc, R.B.: Feeling and thinking: Preferences need no inferences. American Psychologist **35**(2), 151 (1980)
30. Toker D., Steichen B., Birk M.: Predicting Player Type in Social Network Games. In: Proc. of UMAP 2014 (2014); Posters, demonstrations, and late-breaking results
31. Yee, N.: Motivations for play in online games. CyberPsychology & Behavior **9**(6), 772–775 (2006)

Automatic Gaze-Based Detection of Mind Wandering with Metacognitive Awareness

Robert Bixler(✉) and Sidney D'Mello

Department of Computer Science, University of Notre Dame, Notre Dame, IN 46556, USA
{rbixler,sdmello}@nd.edu

Abstract. Mind wandering (MW) is a ubiquitous phenomenon where attention involuntarily shifts from task-related processing to task-unrelated thoughts. There is a need for adaptive systems that can reorient attention when MW is detected due to its detrimental effects on performance and productivity. This paper proposes an automated gaze-based detector of self-caught MW (i.e., when users become consciously aware that they are MW). Eye gaze data and self-reports of MW were collected as 178 users read four instructional texts from a computer interface. Supervised machine learning models trained on features extracted from users' gaze fixations were used to detect pages where users caught themselves MW. The best performing model achieved a user-independent kappa of .45 (accuracy of 74% compared to a chance accuracy of 52%); the first ever demonstration of a self-caught MW detector. An analysis of the features revealed that during MW, users made more regression fixations, had longer saccades that crossed lines more often, and had more uniform fixation durations, indicating a violation from normal reading patterns. Applications of the MW detector are discussed.

Keywords: Gaze tracking · Mind wandering · Affect detection · User modeling

1 Introduction

A promising strategy to improve the effectiveness of adaptive systems is to take aspects of the user's mental state into account - commonly referred to as user state estimation. Monitoring a user's mental state allows for dynamic strategies such as reorienting their attention to the interface when they become distracted [6] or detecting and responding to affective states such as confusion or boredom [3]. One user state that has received little attention until recently is mind wandering (MW). MW is a pervasive phenomenon that involves thinking about one thing while doing another. For instance, while reading a book or listening to a lecture, it is possible for an individual's thoughts to involuntarily drift toward unrelated thoughts such as unfulfilled plans and anxieties. The frequency of MW depends on the individual and environmental context, but a large-scale experience-sampling study on about 5,000 individuals estimated that MW occurs roughly 40% of the time [13].

Not only is MW frequent, it is also disruptive and detrimental to performance. This is because MW entails a shift in attention from the external environment to internal

F. Ricci et al. (Eds.): UMAP 2015, LNCS 9146, pp. 31–43, 2015.
DOI: 10.1007/978-3-319-20267-9_3

thoughts. Tasks requiring conscious focus are compromised when attention is directed toward task-unrelated thoughts. Hence, research has indicated that MW leads to performance failures on a number of tasks, such as increased error rates during signal detection tasks [20], lower recall during memory tasks [22], and poor comprehension during reading tasks [9], even when users were able to catch themselves mind wandering [18]. There are some potential benefits to MW, in that it boosts creativity and facilitates the planning of future events [14]. However, these benefits are not the norm as a recent meta-analysis on 49 independent samples found that MW was consistently negatively correlated with performance across a range of tasks [17].

The high incidence and negative influence of MW on performance suggests that there might be advantages for adaptive interfaces that reorient attention to the task at hand when MW occurs. This requires MW detection, which is a challenging proposition because MW has more covert cues than some other user states (e.g., facial expressions conveying emotions). This raises the pertinent question of how one collects labeled data (MW reports) to train supervised classifiers for MW detection. Two common methods have emerged in the literature. The first is to ask users to provide MW reports in response to thought probes (probe-caught) [22]. Users are asked to indicate if they are MW (positive instances) or not (negative instances) at the moment the probe is triggered. The second is to ask users to provide MW reports whenever they catch themselves MW (self-caught) [20]. There is a distinct difference between probe-caught and self-caught reports of MW, so it is possible that a detector built from probe-caught MW would not be useful for detecting self-caught MW. First, detection of self-caught episodes of MW does not require the use of potentially disruptive thought-probes. Second, self-caught reports rely on a user's ability to monitor their own thoughts and realize that they are MW. Therefore, they reflect a form of MW that occurs with metacognitive awareness. As discussed in the related works below, all of the previous work on MW detection has focused on probe-caught reports. In this paper we introduce the first automatic user-independent detector of MW with metacognitive awareness. As elaborated below, this raised a number of technical challenges that needed to be addressed.

Related Work. A large amount of research has been done in the field of attentional state estimation, which is a subfield of user state estimation. Attentional state estimation has been explored in a variety of domains and with a variety of end-goals. For example, attention has been used to evaluate adaptive hints in an educational game [15] and to optimize the position of news items on a screen [16]. Attentional state estimators have been developed for several tasks such as identifying object saliency during video viewing [25], and for monitoring driver fatigue and distraction [7]. Although both attentional state estimation and MW detection entail identifying aspects of a user's attention, MW detection is concerned with detecting more covert forms of involuntary attentional lapses as opposed to determining which aspects of the stimulus were being attended to.

In recent years, there have been five studies that have explicitly investigated detection of MW [1, 2, 5, 8, 10]. MW was tracked in each study with online self-reports and with behavioral measures derived from eye gaze, speech, physiology, or reading times. Supervised machine learning was then used to predict the occurrence of each self-report from the behavioral measures.

The first study, by Drummond and Litman [8], entailed detecting MW using acoustic-prosodic information while users read a biology paragraph aloud and then provided a verbal summary. MW was tracked at set intervals where users indicated their degree of "zoning out" on a 7 point Likert scale. Their model discriminated between "high" versus "low" zone outs with an accuracy of 64%, which reflects a 22% improvement over chance. However, it is unclear if their model will generalize to new users.

The second study, by D'Mello et. al [5], used eye gaze data to detect MW during reading with reports of MW obtained in response to auditory probes that were triggered at random points during the reading session. Their best performing model yielded a detection accuracy of 60% on a down-sampled corpus containing 50% "yes" and 50% "no" responses (20% improvement over chance). This study did ensure generalizability to new users, but both the training and testing set were down-sampled prior to classification, so it is unclear if a similar level of fidelity will be observed with the authentic MW distribution.

The third study, by Franklin et. al [10], used reading times to detect MW. Users read 5000 words one at a time, using the space bar to advance to the next word. MW probes were triggered if a user spent too much or too little time on a group of ten words. They were able to classify mind wandering with an accuracy of 72% compared to an expected accuracy of 49%. However, the word-by-word reading paradigm is not necessarily representative of normal reading, and it is unclear if their method will generalize due to the method used to set parameters (parameter values were fixed rather than learned).

The fourth study, by Blanchard et. al [2], detected MW during reading using galvanic skin response and skin temperature obtained with the Affectiva Q sensor. They were able to achieve an above-chance classification accuracy of 22% in a manner that generalized to new users.

The fifth study by, Bixler et. al [1], extended the work of D'Mello et. al [5] and attempted to improve on the results of the Blanchard et. al study [2]. Using an expanded version of the data set from the Blanchard et. al study, we included additional eye-gaze features and performed a more comprehensive analysis of the models developed by D'Mello et al. [5]. Out best models attained an above chance improvement of 28% in a user-independent fashion.

Current Work. Our work entails two major contributions over previous MW detectors: (1) we use a refined and extended feature set, and (2) we focus on building models of MW with metacognitive awareness. We refined our feature set by removing features derived from the task context, as these did not contribute to the performance of previous models and are not generalizable to other tasks. We then added several new features, including those derived from blinks [11], pupil diameters [23], and saccade angles.

Our second contribution is that we focused on detecting self-caught MW (MW with metacognitive awareness). Previous work focused on probe-caught MW, which makes our work the first self-caught MW detector. The lack of a self-caught MW detector represents a gap in the MW detection literature because self-caught MW is distinct from probe-caught MW. Probes have the potential to disrupt the MW experience, while, in reality, MW fades naturally as users realize they are MW. There is also a limit to the number of probes that can be given. Probing too often may be perceived as irritating and may be disruptive to the primary task. Self-caught reports, on the other hand, are provided whenever a user catches themselves MW, which allows reports of MW to be collected whenever it occurs, provided the user is sufficiently capable at monitoring their thoughts. Self-caught MW detectors also have unique applications as listed in the General Discussion.

In line with this, the present study focuses on the use of eye-gaze for detection of self-caught MW during reading. The dataset used is the same as in our previous study [1], but in this study we use the self-caught reports, which have not been analyzed before. As discussed above, self-caught MW is different from probe-caught MW, so it is an entirely open question as to whether it is possible to detect self-caught MW from eye gaze. Furthermore, building a model from self-caught reports has its own set of complications that need to be addressed. For one thing, there is no explicit indication of when MW does *not* occur (called negative instances). Each self-caught report is a positive instance of MW, and each instance without a self-caught report has no data on whether MW occurred or not. A user could have been MW without realizing that they were MW (i.e., MW without meta self-awareness) and thus did not report it. Deciding what constitutes a negative instance of MW is a hurdle that is not encountered when building a model based on probe-caught reports of MW, as each probe response can be explicitly labeled as either a negative or positive instance of MW. There is also the issue of how to select an appropriate window of data to consider for each MW instance. There is a simple solution when using probe-caught MW – simply consider windows that backtrack from the time of the probe. However, the same method cannot be used for negative instances of self-caught MW because they do not include an explicit probe from which to backtrack. The present paper considers multiple approaches to obtain negative instances of MW as well as multiple methods for window selection.

The present work studies MW in the context of reading - an every-day activity that is supported by a number of systems. There is also ample data to suggest that reading comprehension is impaired by MW [9, 22], so there could be considerable benefits from embedding MW detectors in systems that support large amounts of reading (e.g., educational materials, legal texts, news articles, and many others). Further, in addition to demonstrating the first detector of self-caught MW in the context of reading, the results of our systematic experimentation to address the technical challenges discussed above should be useful for researchers interested in building self-caught MW detectors for their own application domains.

2 Data Collection

Users. The users in this study were 178 undergraduate students that participated for course credit. Of these, 93 users were from a medium-sized private Midwestern university while 85 were from a large public university in the mid-South. The average

age of users was 20 years (SD = 3.6). Demographics included 62.7% female, 49% Caucasian, 34% African American, 6% Hispanic, and 4% "Other". Thus, there was considerable gender- and ethnic- diversity in our sample.

Procedure. Users read four different texts on research methods topics (i.e., experimenter bias, replication, causality, and dependent variables). Each text contained 1500 words on average (SD = 10) split into 30-36 pages with approximately 60 words per page. Texts were presented on a computer screen with 36pt Courier New font. The typeface and size were chosen to make text layout simpler and to make it easier to determine when a word was being gazed upon.

Users were given standard instructions [21] on reporting MW. MW was defined as having "no idea what you just read" and realizing that "you were thinking about something else altogether." Both self- and probe-caught MW reports were collected. Probe-caught reports were collected in response to 9 auditory probes triggered on different pages at a randomly chosen point between 4 and 12 seconds from the appearance of the page. Users were also required to supply a report if they tried to advance to the next page before the probe was triggered. Alternatively, the self-caught method entailed users reporting MW whenever they found themselves MW.

Instances of Mind Wandering. Overall, users read 33,595 pages of text. About a third of these were discarded for the present study due to failure to register eye gaze. Of the remaining pages, 30% (6,718 pages) contained a mind wandering report. 6,237 of these reports were probe-caught reports, while 481 were self-caught reports. Of the probe-caught reports, 32% were positive instances of mind wandering. Only a subset of all users (78) provided self-caught reports of mind wandering, but all 178 users were included in the analysis when selecting negative instances of MW.

3 Model Building

Both negative and positive instances of MW are tracked when using probe-caught reports, so it is readily apparent that the classification task involves distinguishing negative probe-caught reports from positive probe-caught reports. When building models using only self-caught reports, however, there are no negative reports of MW. This raises the question: what should be used as a negative instance of MW?

There were three considerations taken when selecting negative instances of MW in our study. The first consideration regarded the types of pages that should be used as negative instances of MW. Pages fell into four categories; *self-caught pages, positive probe-caught pages, negative probe-caught pages*, and *non-report pages* (pages with no report). Positive probe-caught pages were not considered further since the goal was to detect self-caught MW. Pages that included reports of both types were considered to be a self-caught page if the self-caught report occurred first, and vice versa. All self-caught pages were included in the models as positive instances of MW. Negative instances were taken to be (a) only negative probe-caught pages (PC No), (b) only non-report pages (NR), or (c) both negative probe-caught pages and non-report pages (PC No + NR).

The second consideration was how to select the number of negative instances. We chose to randomly select from all available negative instances of MW to achieve a 0.3 proportion of positive instances of MW. This proportion corresponds to the proportion of positive probe-caught reports in our data and is similar to proportions of MW reported in previous studies on MW during reading [11, 23].

The third pertinent issue was to identify a point at which to analyze gaze data for the negative instances for non-report pages. For self-caught report pages we use a window that ended two seconds prior to the self-caught report in order to avoid any confounds associated with the user pressing the report key (e.g., movement, looking at the keyboard). The length of the window was a parameter that varied as noted below. For negative probe-caught pages, the window also ended two seconds before the probe response. One of three methods was used to select comparable windows of data within non-report pages (Figure 1).

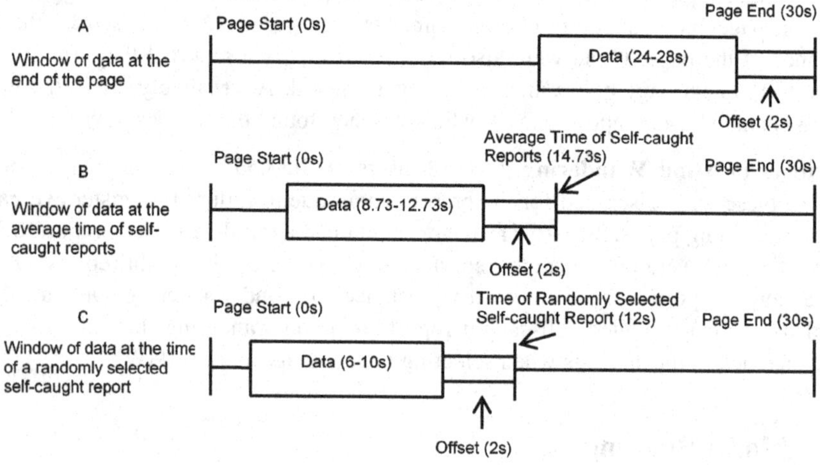

Fig. 1. Three different methods of selecting a window of data within a hypothetical 30s non-report page. The first method (A) is to use a window of data at the end of the page. The second method (B) is to use a window of data at the average time of the report for self-caught pages. The third method (C) is to use a window of data at the same time as the report within a randomly selected self-caught page. A two second offset is used to avoid confounds associated with the button press (to either advance to the next page (A) or provide a self-caught report (B, C)).

The first method was to simply use data from the *end of the page* (EoP) after including a 2-second offset to account for the key press to advance pages. For example, when selecting a four second window from a 30 second non-report page, gaze data from 24 seconds to 28 seconds within the page would be used. The second method is to select the window on the basis of the *average* time a report occurred within self-caught pages (Avg. SC). For our dataset this is 14.73 seconds. Thus, when selecting a four-second window from a 30 second non-report page, gaze data from 8.73 seconds to 12.73 seconds within the page would be used for feature calculation. The third method is to select the window based on a *randomly* selected self-caught page (Rand. SC). For example, when selecting a four second window from a 30 second non-report page, a self-caught page would be randomly selected. If the self-caught report occurred 12 seconds into the page, then gaze data from 6 seconds to 10 seconds within the page would be used for feature calculation (last 2-seconds are considered to be the offset).

Feature Engineering. Raw data was processed into gaze fixations (points where gaze is maintained on the same location) and saccades (movements between subsequent fixations) using a fixation filter from the OpenGazeAndMouseAnalyzer (OGAMA), an open source gaze analyzer [24]. The series of gaze fixations and saccades were segmented into windows of varying length (4, 6, 8, 10, or 12 seconds), each ending at a certain point on the page as noted in the previous section. Windows that contained fewer than five fixations or windows that were shorter than four seconds were eliminated because these windows did not contain sufficient data to compute gaze features. The features used were similar to those used in our previous work [1]. Two sets of features were computed: 46 global gaze features and 20 local gaze features, yielding 66 features overall. A third set of features that relied on the context of the reading task (*context features*) were tested, but will not be discussed further because they did not improve classification accuracy and are not generalizable to different contexts.

Global gaze features were independent of the actual words being read. These included properties of eye movements such as *fixation duration* (ms), *saccade duration* (ms), *saccade length* (pixels), *saccade angle* (degrees between two saccade vectors), and *pupil diameter* (standardized using a within-subject z-score). For these five measurement distributions, the min, max, mean, median, standard deviation, skew, kurtosis, and range were computed, totaling 40 features. Additional features included a measure of *fixation dispersion,* the *fixation duration/saccade duration ratio*, and the *number of saccades*. Three new features were the *number of blinks*, the *proportion of time spent blinking,* and the proportion of *horizontal saccades*, which were saccades with angles less than 30 degrees above or below the horizontal axis.

In contrast to global features, *local features* were sensitive to the words being read. These included measures of the number of specific fixation types as well as the mean and standard deviations their durations. These features were calculated from *first pass fixations* (first fixation on a word during the first pass through a text), *regression fixations* (fixations back onto words already passed), *single fixations* (fixations on words that were only fixated on once), *gaze fixations* (consecutive fixations on the same word), and *non-word fixations*, totaling 15 features. Additional local features captured known relationships between fixation durations and the semantic properties of words, such as their *length, frequency* of use, number of *synonyms*, and *semantic specificity* (e.g. "blue" is more specific than "color"). The final local feature was the *ratio of reading time* to expected reading time, calculated as 200ms times the number of words read.

Tolerance analysis and feature selection were applied to each model. Tolerance analysis consisted of removing highly multicollinear features, as redundant information invites bias towards that information. Similarly, feature selection consisted of using correlation based feature selection (CFS) as implemented in Weka [12], an open source machine learning workbench, to remove features that were strongly correlated with other features and weakly correlated with the class label. Feature selection was performed using just the training set to avoid overfitting.

Model Building. We explored five different parameters at the model building stage in order to ascertain which parameter combination resulted in the most accurate models. First, we varied which features were included in our models. Possibilities were (1) global, (2) local, and (3) global and local. This allowed us to narrow down which set of features was best able to detect MW. Second, we varied the *window sizes* used in the model. Window sizes of 4, 6, 8, 10, and 12 seconds were used in order to determine the ideal amount of data for detecting MW. Third, we used three different sampling methods for our *training set* (testing set was never sampled). We either used the entire data set, downsampled the training set, or synthetically oversampled the training set using SMOTE (Synthetic Minority Over-sampling Technique [4]). Each sampling method was applied to the same training set five separate times, and the average values of all five runs were taken. Fourth, we used three different types of outlier treatment. Outliers were either left in the dataset, trimmed, or Winsorized. Trimming consisted of removing values greater/lower than 3 standard deviations above/below the mean, while Winsorization consisted of replacing those values with the corresponding value +3 or -3 standard deviations above/below the mean.

We used 10 classifiers implemented in Weka, including Bayes net, naïve Bayes, logistic regression, SVM, and decision trees. We considered a wide array of classifiers at this early stage of the research as it is unclear which classifier is the best in this domain.

Our results were evaluated with a leave-several-user-out validation method. Data from a random 66% of the users were included in the training set, while the data from the remaining 34% were included in the training set. This process was repeated 20 times for each model and performance metrics were averaged across these iterations.

Cohen's kappa was used to evaluate model performance because it corrects for random guessing when there are uneven class distributions, as is the case in the current dataset. The kappa value is calculated using the formula K = (observed accuracy - expected accuracy) / (1 - expected accuracy), where *observed accuracy* is equivalent to recognition rate and *expected accuracy* is computed from the confusion matrix to account for the pattern of misclassifications. A kappa value of 0 indicates chance agreement while a kappa value of 1 indicates perfect agreement.

4 Results

We built seven types of models that detected self-caught (SC) MW. Models varied on the type of pages that were included for negative instances of MW (negative probe-caught, non-report pages, or both) and the method to select the window of data for non-probe report pages (end-of-page, average SC, or random SC). Results for the best model of each type are shown in Table 1. Window selection was only necessary for models with non-report pages as there was no explicit point at which MW occurred.

Table 1. Best performing models for each type of negative instance

Negative Instances	Window Selection	Instances	Classifier	Window Size (s)	Feature Types	Feature Count	Kappa
PC No	-	540	Logistic	10	G	10	.33 (.07)
NR	EoP	523	Logistic	12	G	10	.39 (.07)
NR	**Avg. SC**	**410**	**SVM**	**12**	**GL**	**18**	**.45 (.06)**
NR	Rand. SC	400	SVM	12	GL	22	.39 (.07)
PC No + NR	EoP	681	Logistic	12	G	10	.36 (.05)
PC No + NR	Avg. SC	415	SVM	12	GL	21	.43 (.07)
PC No + NR	Rand. SC	361	SVM	12	GL	21	.35 (.09)

Note. **Bolding** indicates the model with the highest kappa value. Standard deviations are in *parentheses*. PC No = Probe-caught negative instances; NR = Non-report; EoP = End of page; Avg. SC = Average self-caught; Rand SC = Random self-caught; Acc. = Accuracy; G = Global; L = Local; GL = Global + Local

The best performing model used only non-report pages as negative instances of MW, with a 12 second window located at the same point as the average time of self-caught reports. This model achieved a kappa value of 0.45, with an accuracy of 74% compared to an expected accuracy of 52%. The confusion matrix for this best model highlights the model's accuracy in classifying positive instances correctly, with a hit rate of .82 compared to a prior probability of .32. The false-alarm rate of 0.30 is not high enough to be of concern depending on the MW intervention (see Discussion).

Parameter Analysis. It is ideal to perform the least number of operations on the data in order to decrease complexity in real time systems. With that in mind, we analyzed the parameters to determine which resulted in the best models. We analyzed each of the parameters across all 108 individual models (3 sampling methods * 3 outlier treatments * 3 window sizes * 4 feature types). For each parameter, the model with the best kappa value (across the 10 classifiers) was selected for further analysis.

Window size and feature type displayed clear trends, but there was no clear trend for either sampling method or outlier treatment. In particular, kappas were higher for larger window sizes as seen in Figure 2. When analyzing feature type, it is apparent that global features were the most useful for detecting MW. The best model using both global and local features resulted in the best performance (kappa = .45), but performance of the best local feature model was quite poor (kappa = .24) compared to the best global feature model (kappa = .43). This suggests that global features were responsible for much of the performance of the combined model. This could be due to the level of precision needed for local features. When using a desk mounted eye tracker, gaze data can be affected by a user's head movements.

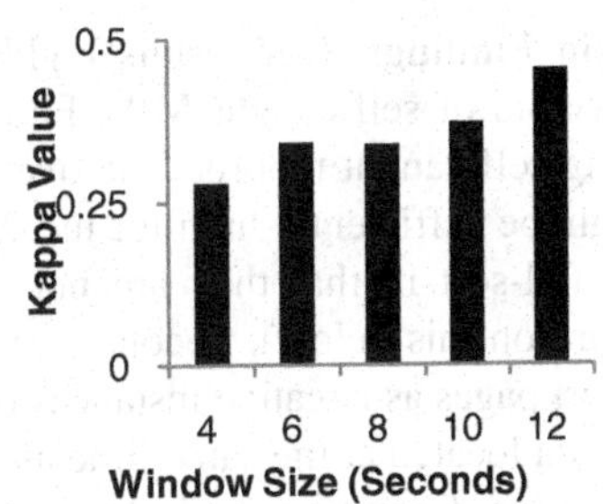

Fig. 2. The effect of window size on kappa value

Head movements have a drastic effect on local features because they require precise information on which words are being gazed upon. Global features, however, are independent of the information being displayed.

Feature Analysis. We performed a deeper analysis of how the features varied between positive and negative instances of MW in order to obtain a better understanding of a user's eye gaze during MW. We analyzed the dataset belonging to the best performing model shown in Table 1 above. Each feature was analyzed with a paired samples t-test of the difference in the mean value of the feature between positive and negative instances of MW. We analyzed data from the 31 participants for which there were both positive (self-report) and negative (non-report pages) instances of MW. There were five features that were significantly different between positive and negative instances of MW below the 0.05 level: (1) proportion of line cross saccades (Mean MW = .125 (standard deviation = .100), Mean not MW = .078 (.101)); (2) proportion of regression fixations (MW = .162 (.062), not MW = .130 (.057)); (3) minimum saccade duration (MW = 7.29 (6.74), not MW = 6.38 (5.89)); (4) fixation duration kurtosis (MW = 3.99 (4.52), not MW = 7.01 (5.75)); and (5) fixation duration skew (MW = 1.66 (.81), not MW = 2.13 (.95)). These features were indicative of a break in normal reading patterns. First of all, there was a greater proportion of regression fixations and line cross saccades during MW, and saccades had a greater duration. Furthermore, the skew and kurtosis of the fixation durations indicate that they were more uniform during MW, whereas fixation durations during normal reading would vary with word difficulty.

5 General Discussion

Our major contribution consists of building the first eye-gaze detector of self-caught MW, studying its accuracy, its parameters, and the features that were most diagnostic of MW. In the remainder of this section, we highlight our main findings, consider applications of the MW detector, and discuss limitations and avenues for future work.

Main Findings. Our results highlight a number of important findings for building detectors of self-caught MW. First, we have developed the first MW detector built using self-caught reports. The overall classification accuracy of 74% is moderate but might be sufficiently high for meaningful interventions, especially if the interventions are fail-soft in that they are not harmful if delivered when detection errors occur (more on this below). Second, we found that the best performing models used non-report pages as negative instances of MW, and had features calculated from a window of data located at the same time as the average time of reports within self-caught pages. This information might be useful to other researchers interested in building self-caught MW detectors in similar contexts. Third, similar to our previous study using probe-caught reports [1], global features were shown to be particularly useful in classifying MW for self-caught reports. This is a significant finding because global features are easier to compute, do not require very high-precision eye tracking, and are more likely to generalize to different tasks beyond reading. Fourth, we found that larger window sizes were associated with more accurate MW detection rates. This shows that a greater amount of information at the page level is important for more accurate MW detection. Finally, an analysis of the features revealed that normal reading patterns were disrupted during MW, such that users made more regression fixations, had a larger proportion of line cross saccades, and saccades were of greater duration. Furthermore, the distribution of fixation durations was more uniform during MW, which may indicate that they were not as affected by word difficulty as they would be during normal reading.

Applications. A self-caught MW detector has a number of applications. For example, it would allow for measurement of MW without interrupting the user. It could be used to advance basic scientific research on MW itself, or to study user strategies for regaining focus. Finally, it could be embedded in any adaptive system that includes a text comprehension component. MW has been shown to negatively affect text comprehension, so any interface that includes text comprehension could be improved by dynamically responding to MW. One example of an intervention would be to recommend that a user re-read or self-explain a passage when the system detects MW. Other possibilities include presenting the information in a different format, such as showing a short animation or film; offering positive encouragement; or suggesting that the user switches topics. It is important to note that interventions should not disrupt the user if MW is detected incorrectly and should be used sparingly so users are not overwhelmed.

Limitations and Future Work. There are several limitations to the current study. First, the data was collected in a lab environment and users were limited to undergraduates from two universities located in the United States. This limits our claims of generalizability to individuals from different populations. Quantifying our method with a more diverse population and setting would boost our claims of generalizability. Second, the font size was larger than what would normally be read, an intentional decision in order to improve eye tracking precision for computing local features. Given that global features did most of the work, future studies could consider smaller font sizes. Third, an expensive, high quality eye tracker was used for data collection, which limits the scalability of using eye gaze as a modality for MW detection. However, this could eventually be addressed by the decreasing cost of consumer-grade eye tracking technology, such as Eye Tribe ($99) and Tobii EyeX ($195), or with promising alternatives that use webcams for gaze tracking [19]. Fourth, it is possible that users did not provide accurate or honest self-caught reports. However, both the probe-caught and self-caught methods have been validated in a number of studies [20, 21], and there is no clear alternative for tracking a highly internal state like MW.

Concluding Remarks. In summary, the present study demonstrated that global eye movements could be used to build a moderately accurate user-independent detector of self-caught MW, or MW with metacognitive awareness. Importantly, our approach used a relatively unobtrusive remote eye tracker that allowed for unrestricted head and body movement and involved an ecologically-valid reading activity. The next step involves integrating the detector into an adaptive system in order to trigger interventions that attempt to reorient attentional focus when MW is detected.

Acknowledgment. This research was supported by the National Science Foundation (DRL 1235958). Any opinions, findings and conclusions, or recommendations expressed are those of the authors and do not necessarily reflect the views of NSF.

References

1. Bixler, R., D'Mello, S.: Toward Fully Automated Person-Independent Detection of Mind Wandering. In: Dimitrova, V., Kuflik, T., Chin, D., Ricci, F., Dolog, P., Houben, G.-J. (eds.) UMAP 2014. LNCS, vol. 8538, pp. 37–48. Springer, Heidelberg (2014)
2. Blanchard, N., Bixler, R., Joyce, T., D'Mello, S.: Automated Physiological-Based Detection of Mind Wandering during Learning. In: Trausan-Matu, S., Boyer, K.E., Crosby, M., Panourgia, K. (eds.) ITS 2014. LNCS, vol. 8474, pp. 55–60. Springer, Heidelberg (2014)
3. Calvo, R.A., D'Mello, S.: Affect Detection: An Interdisciplinary Review of Models, Methods, and Their Applications. IEEE Transactions on Affective Computing **1**(1), 18–37 (2010)
4. Chawla, N.V., et al.: SMOTE: Synthetic Minority Over-Sampling Technique. Journal of Artificial Intelligence Research **16**(1), 321–357 (2002)
5. D'Mello, S., et al.: Automatic Gaze-Based Detection of Mind Wandering during Reading. Educational Data Mining (2013)
6. D'Mello, S., et al.: Gaze tutor: A Gaze-Reactive Intelligent Tutoring System. International Journal of Human-Computer Studies **70**(5), 377–398 (2012)
7. Dong, Y., et al.: Driver Inattention Monitoring System for Intelligent Vehicles: A Review. IEEE Transactions on Intelligent Transportation Systems **12**(2), 596–614 (2011)
8. Drummond, J., Litman, D.: In the Zone: Towards Detecting Student Zoning Out Using Supervised Machine Learning. In: Aleven, V., Kay, J., Mostow, J. (eds.) ITS 2010, Part II. LNCS, vol. 6095, pp. 306–308. Springer, Heidelberg (2010)
9. Feng, S., et al.: Mind Wandering While Reading Easy and Difficult Texts. Psychon Bull Rev. **20**(3), 586–592 (2013)
10. Franklin, M.S., et al.: Catching The Mind in Flight: Using Behavioral Indices to Detect Mindless Reading in Real Time. Psychonomic Bulletin & Review **18**(5), 992–997 (2011)
11. Franklin, M.S., et al.: Window to the Wandering Mind: Pupillometry of Spontaneous Thought While Reading. The Quarterly Journal of Experimental Psychology **66**(12), 2289–2294 (2013)
12. Hall, M., et al.: The WEKA Data Mining Software: an Update. ACM SIGKDD Explorations Newsletter **11**(1), 10–18 (2009)
13. Killingsworth, M.A., Gilbert, D.T.: A Wandering Mind is an Unhappy Mind. Science **330**(6006), 932–932 (2010)
14. Mooneyham, B.W., Schooler, J.W.: The Costs and Benefits of Mind-Wandering: A Review. Canadian Journal of Experimental Psychology/Revue Canadienne de Psychologie Expérimentale **67**(1), 11–18 (2013)
15. Muir, M., Conati, C.: An Analysis of Attention to Student – Adaptive Hints in an Educational Game. In: Cerri, S.A., Clancey, W.J., Papadourakis, G., Panourgia, K. (eds.) ITS 2012. LNCS, vol. 7315, pp. 112–122. Springer, Heidelberg (2012)
16. Navalpakkam, V., Kumar, R., Li, L., Sivakumar, D.: Attention and Selection in Online Choice Tasks. In: Masthoff, J., Mobasher, B., Desmarais, M.C., Nkambou, R. (eds.) UMAP 2012. LNCS, vol. 7379, pp. 200–211. Springer, Heidelberg (2012)
17. Randall, J.G., et al.: Mind-Wandering, Cognition, and Performance: A Theory-Driven Meta-Analysis of Attention Regulation. Psychological Bulletin (2014)

18. Schooler, J.W., et al.: Zoning Out While Reading: Evidence for Dissociations Between Experience and Metaconsciousness. In: Levin, D.T. (ed.) Thinking and Seeing: Visual Metacognition in Adults and Children, pp. 203–226. MIT Press, Cambridge (2004)
19. Sewell, W., Komogortsev, O.: Real-Time Eye Gaze Tracking with an Unmodified Commodity Webcam Employing a Neural Network. In: CHI 2010 Extended Abstracts on Human Factors in Computing Systems, pp. 3739–3744 ACM (2010)
20. Smallwood, J., et al.: Subjective Experience and the Attentional Lapse: Task Engagement and Disengagement During Sustained Attention. Consciousness and Cognition **13**(4), 657–690 (2004)
21. Smallwood, J., et al.: When Attention Matters: The Curious Incident of the Wandering Mind. Memory & Cognition **36**(6), 1144–1150 (2008)
22. Smallwood, J., Schooler, J.W.: The Restless Mind. Psychological Bulletin **132**(6), 946–958 (2006)
23. Smilek, D., et al.: Out of Mind, Out of Sight: Eye Blinking as Indicator and Embodiment of Mind Wandering. Psychological Science **21**(6), 786–789 (2010)
24. Voßkühler, A., et al.: OGAMA (Open Gaze and Mouse Analyzer): Open-Source Software Designed to Analyze Eye and Mouse Movements in Slideshow Study Designs. Behavior Research Methods **40**(4), 1150–1162 (2008)
25. Yonetani, R. et al.: Multi-Mode Saliency Dynamics Model for Analyzing Gaze and Attention. In: Proceedings of the Symposium on Eye Tracking Research and Applications, pp. 115–122. ACM, New York (2012)

The Value of Social: Comparing Open Student Modeling and Open Social Student Modeling

Peter Brusilovsky[1(✉)], Sibel Somyürek[2], Julio Guerra[1], Roya Hosseini[1], and Vladimir Zadorozhny[1]

[1] School of Information Sciences, University of Pittsburgh, Pittsburgh, USA
{peterb,jdg60,roh38}@pitt.edu, vladimir@sis.pitt.edu
[2] Department of Computer Education and Instructional Technologies, Gazi University, Ankara, Turkey
ssomyurek@gazi.edu.tr

Abstract. Open Student Modeling (OSM) is a popular technology that makes traditionally hidden student models available to the learners for exploration. OSM is known for its ability to increase student engagement, motivation, and knowledge reflection. A recent extension of OSM known as Open Social Student Modeling (OSSM) attempts to enhance cognitive aspects of OSM with social aspects by allowing students to explore models of peer students or the whole class. In this paper, we introduce MasteryGrids, a scalable OSSM interface and report the results of a large-scale classroom study that explored the value of adding social dimension to OSM. The results of the study reveal a remarkable engaging potential of OSSM as well as its impact on learning effectiveness and user attitude.

Keywords: Open student modeling · Open social student modeling · Social visualization

1 Introduction

Open student modeling (known also as open *learner* modeling) is a popular technology in the field of adaptive educational systems. In the majority of adaptive educational systems, student models, which represent the current state of student domain knowledge, are hidden and used exclusively to support various kinds of learning personalization. In contrast, systems with open student modeling (OSM) provide an interface for the user to view (and even edit) the content of their models [4]. More than a decade of research on OSM demonstrated a number of valuable features of this technology such as support of self-reflection and self-regulated learning, better personalization transparency, and increased user motivation [4; 5; 8; 11].

Much less explored is a recent extension of OSM known as open *social* student modeling (OSSM). The idea of OSSM is to enhance the cognitive aspects of OSM with social aspects by allowing students to explore each other models or cumulative model of the class. While several pioneer project demonstrated the feasibility of this

F. Ricci et al. (Eds.): UMAP 2015, LNCS 9146, pp. 44–55, 2015.
DOI: 10.1007/978-3-319-20267-9_4

approach and reported first positive results [3; 7], the value of adding social dimension to the classic OSM is still not demonstrated reliably. In this paper we present our most recent attempts to explore the added value of OSSM. We present an implementation of OSSM in an open source system MasteryGrids and report the results of a larger-scale classroom study comparing an OSSM version of MasteryGrids with a baseline OSM version. The results of the study indicate a number of benefits that could be offered by OSSM.

2 Background: Open Student Models

An open student model was originally suggested an innovation in the area of personalized learning systems. While in traditional personalized systems, student models were hidden "under the hood" and used to make education process personalized, the pioneers of open student modeling argued that the ability to view and modify the state of their knowledge could be beneficial for the students. A typical OSM displays the modeled state of student knowledge, although the examples of models displaying interests [1] or learning styles [12] are also known. A common way to display a state of knowledge is a set of skillometers that show the mastered subset of expert knowledge [11; 15; 16] or the probability that a learner knows a concept [6]. More complex OSM could display misconceptions, the size of topics, and other factors [4].

The idea to make open student modeling social has been originally suggested and explored by Bull [3; 4]. The idea of OSSM is to enhance its cognitive aspects with social aspects by allowing students to explore each other models or cumulative model of the class. In our earlier work, we explored several approaches to combine open social student modeling with adaptive navigation support in an adaptive system for Java programming. Our preliminary single-classroom studies demonstrated that open social student modeling increase learner motivation to learn and enhance the impact of adaptive navigation support [7; 9]. The study presented in this paper makes a closer look of the effects of the open student model with and without social comparison features and differs from earlier studies by its more formal nature, larger scale and different domain (SQL).

3 MasteryGrids, an Open Social Student Modeling Interface

To evaluate the effectiveness of OSSM we used MasteryGrids, an open source OSSM interface developed by our group [10]. MasteryGrids uses parallel social visualization approach pioneered in an earlier system Progressor+ [7]. The idea of MasteryGrids is to show progress of student knowledge over multiple kinds of educational content organized by topics, allow to compare personal progress with the progress of the class, and provide direct access to the content. Figure 1 shows MasteryGrids interface displaying a sequence of topics of a Database Management course. The first row of the grid presents the topic-by-topic knowledge progress of the current student using green colors of different density (the darker is the color, the higher is the progress). The third row shows the aggregated topic-by-topic progress of the whole class using blue colors of different density. The second row presents a color-difference comparison between the student progress and the class progress. Green color shows topics where the student estimated knowledge is higher than the class, blue color show the topics where the class is ahead, and the color density shows the magnitude of the difference. By clicking on any topic cell, the student can access learning content associated with the topic. For example, in Figure 1, the student has clicked the topic SELECT-FROM-WHERE and the system displays a bubble with showing content of two kinds: problems (called quizzes) and examples. Depending on the row clicked, the colors of the content items can represent individual progress, class progress, or difference using the color schemas explained before. In Figure 1, comparison colors are displayed since the student accessed content bubble by clicking on the middle comparison row. In addition to displaying the overall class progress, MasteryGrids can display anonymized ranked list of individual student models as shown in Figure 2. To save time and space, this list has to be requested by clicking "Load the rest of learners" button. The position of the current student in the list is shown in green.

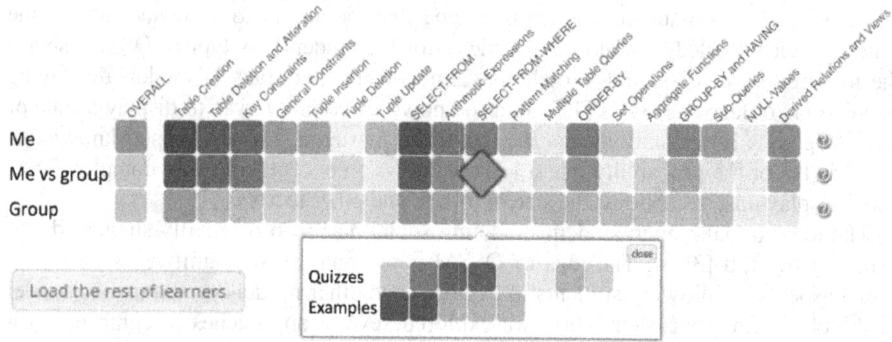

Fig. 1. MasteryGrid interface with social features activated

4 The Study

To assess the added impact of social features in OSM context and its implementation in Mastery Grids system, we focused on the following **research questions**:

1. How the addition of social dimension to OSM impacts system usage?
2. How the addition of social dimension to OSM impacts educational effectiveness?
3. How the addition of social dimension to OSM impacts learning outcomes?
4. How do students evaluate systems with and without social component?

4.1 Study Design

To answer these research questions we ran a classroom study where we compared two different versions of MasteryGrids, one nicknamed *OSM+Social* contains both the OSM and OSSM features (as shown in Figures 1 and 2), and another, nicknamed *OSM* with OSM features only, i.e. only showing first row of the grid in Figure 1 and no access to peer list. The study was performed in a master-level Database Management course at the School of Information Sciences, University of Pittsburgh, during the term of Fall 2014. The class was divided into two comparable sections taught by the same instructor using the same lecture material. Sections had different class meeting times. One section was assigned to work with the OSM version of the system and another section with the OSM+Social version. Both versions provided access to the same educational content. Progress visualization in the OSM+Social group was based on the progress of this group alone.

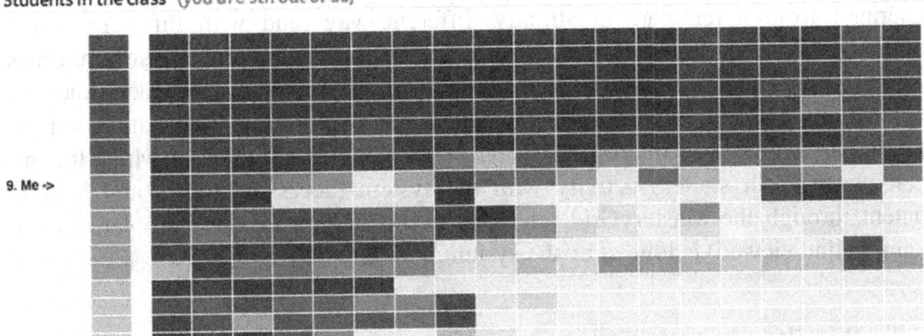

Fig. 2. Sorted list of peers. The current student can find herself, but no names are shown.

MasteryGrids was introduced to both sections in the 3rd week of the course right before the start of SQL part supported by the system. The students were informed about the study and received a quick introduction to the MasteryGrids interface used in the group and the learning content available in the system. Then students were also administered a pretest to check their SQL knowledge. Pretest included ten questions that require writing SQL statements. After the introduction, each student received e-mails with a link to access the system, individual login and password. The use of the system was not mandatory in the course, however, to motivate students to try the system, one extra credit point was offered to students who solve at least 10 problems in the system. All user interaction with the system was logged. At the end of 11th week of the course, the participants took a posttest and filled in a questionnaire about usefulness and usability of the system.

4.2 Participants

The total number of students in two course section was 103, however, 14 students never logged in and were excluded from the study. Out of remaining 89 students, 47 (52.8%) worked with OSM interface and 42 (47.2%) full OSSM (OSM+Social) interface. The descriptive statistics of experiment groups and students' gender are given in Table 1.

Table 1. The descriptive statistics of OSM+Social/OSM groups and students' gender

Systems/ Gender	OSM+Social		OSM	
	f	%	f	%
Female	26	55.3	21	50
Male	21	44.7	21	50
Total	47	100	42	100

4.3 Log Data Collection

MasteryGrids allows students to access 2 types of content: parameterized problems (referred for now on as problems) and examples. We used a set of SQL problems and examples developed for an earlier system Database Exploratorium [2]. Each problem asks the student to write a SQL statement to retrieve a subset of data from a predefined database. Problems are parameterized, which means that they are generated from a template in slightly different way (and with different correct answers) each time. As a result, students can attempt the same problem several times. Examples present various SQL statements with explanations for each line. All explanations are originally hidden; the student can explore line explanations one by one by clicking lines of interest, allowing the system to keep track of which line has been viewed. All student activity with the system (accessing topics and learning content through the MasteryGrid interface, every attempt to solve problems, every example line viewed) is logged by the system.

5 Results

In accordance with the research questions introduced above, the independent variable of the study is the type of interface used by the group (OSM or OSM+Social) and the dependent variables of the study are system usage, instructional effectiveness, educational impact, and students' opinions about systems usability and usefulness. We analyze these aspects in the following sections.

5.1 Student Engagement

In our past work, we observed that the use of open student models increases the number of students who was motivated to work with non-mandatory learning content [8]. To investigate whether OSSM is better or worse than OSM in this respect, we compared the fraction of students engaged to work with OSM and OSM+Social group at six different levels. In total there were 42 students in the OSM group and 47 in the OSM+Social group who logged in the system at least once, i.e. had a chance to see the system and to make an informed decision whether to use the system or not. In Figure 3(a) we use this starting number as 100% to compare the percentage of students in each group who had at least one, more than 10, 20, 30, 40, and 50 attempts on problems. As we can see, the OSM+Social group has much higher student engagement on all levels. The most remarkable difference is observed at the early engagement stages. The social version was apparently looking much more interesting to the students: almost 70% decided to explore the system further attempting at least one question. In contrast, traditional OSM lost more than 70% of its users right after their first login – less than 30% of them decided to move on by at least trying one question. At the level of 30+ questions that we could consider as a serious engagement with the system, the OSM+Social group still retained more than 50% of its original users while OSM engagement was below 20%.

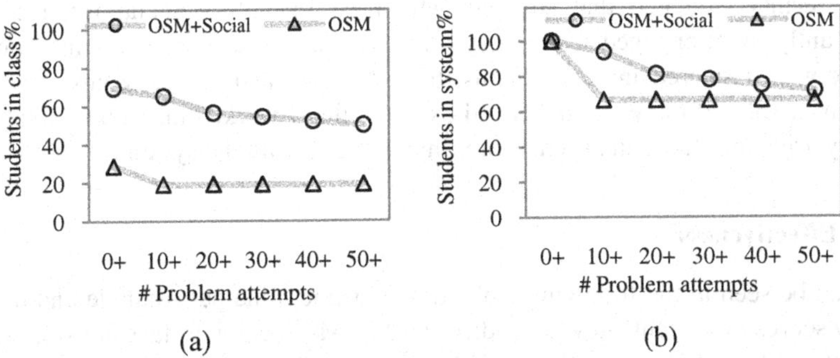

Fig. 3. Percentage of active students with different number of problem attempts in the OSM and OSM+Social group. The levels in the x-axis represent having at least one attempt, more than 10, 20, 30, 40, and 50 attempts.

It could be argued that students were not able to understand the value of the system until they tried at least one problem, so using the number of students who logged in as 100% is unfair. Figure 3(b) provides an alternative look at the student engagement treating the number of students who attempted at least one problem as 100% in each group. Still, we see that OSM group is loosing students at a higher rate than the OSM+Social group even with this adjustment. These observations demonstrate that the OSM+Social group was much more successful than the OSM group in engaging and retaining students.

5.2 System Usage

To further compare the ability of two system versions to engage students, we examined the variables in Table 2. Since the data could not be assumed to be normally distributed, Mann Whitney U, a nonparametric statistical test was used to compare system usage between OSM (N=42) and OSM+Social (N=47) interface groups. The Table 2 shows the results of Mann Whitney U test.

Table 2. The results of Mann Whitney U test about system usage. * Significant result ($p<0.05$) ** Significant result ($p<0.01$).

Variable	OSM	OSM+Social	U
	Mean	Mean	
Sessions	3.93	6.26	685.500*
Topics coverage	19.0%	56.4%	567.500**
Total attempts to problems	25.86	97.62	548.500**
Correct attempts to problems	14.62	60.28	548.000**
Distinct problems attempted	7.71	23.51	549.000**
Distinct problems attempted correctly	7.52	23.11	545.000**
Distinct examples viewed	18.19	38.55	611.500**
Views to example lines	91.60	209.40	609.000**
MG loads	5.05	9.83	618.500**
MG clicks on topic cells	24.17	61.36	638.500**
MG click on content cells	46.17	119.19	577.500**
MG difficulty feedback answers	6.83	14.68	599.500**
Total time in the system	5145.34	9276.58	667.000**
Time in problems	911.86	2727.38	582.000**
Time in MG (navigation)	2260.10	4085.31	625.000**

The results indicated that students who used the OSM+Social interface were significantly more engaged with the system, i.e., logged in more frequently, covered more topics, answered more problems, tried to solve and correctly answered more problems, explored more examples and example lines, worked more extensively with MasteryGrids interface, and spent more time working with the system.

5.3 Effectiveness

As it can be seen in the following table, time per line, time per example and time per activity scores of students in who studied with OSM+Social interface are significantly lower than the other group. To avoid impact of users on early stage of system experience who might work less efficiently, we excluded from calculations users who explored less than 5 example (first two lines), solved less than 5 problems (3rd line) and those explored less than 5 examples or solved less than 5 problems (4th line).

Table 3. The results of Mann Whitney U test about productivity scores. * Significant result ($p<0.05$) ** Significant result ($p<0.01$).

Variable	OSM	OSM+Social	U
	Mean	Mean	
Time per line	22.93	11.61	570.000**
Time per example	97.74	58.54	508.000*
Time per problem	37.96	29.72	242.000
Time per activity	47.92	34.33	277.000*

This result shows students who used OSM+Social interface worked more efficiently than OSM group. This might be the result of social navigation support provided by OSSM interface that brought students to the right content at the right time. It might be also caused by students' attempts to move ahead of their classmates in the visualization. Further research is needed to investigate the nature of this effect.

Instructional effectiveness could be measured more reliably using an approach that takes into account both time and success such as the computational procedure developed by Paas and Van Merrienboer's [13; 14]. To find out instructional effectiveness following this approach, the performance (correctly answered SQL problems) was combined with time (total time that spend to answer SQL problems). The raw scores of performance and time were firstly translated to Z scores and were plotted in a Cartesian Plane. Then relative instructional effectiveness is computed as the distance between the point (z(P), z(t)) to the line of zero effectiveness (E=0).

To compare instructional effectiveness of students, only the data belong to students who solved at least 5 distinct problems in both two groups are used (N=44). According to results of Mann Whitney U test, instructional effectiveness scores of students who studied with OSM+Social interface are significantly higher (N=32, mean=0.22, mean rank=24.88) than the scores of students who studied with the OSM interface (N=12, mean=0.03, mean rank=16.17).

5.4 Learning Impact

To see the effect of social interface on students' learning, we measured the normalized learning gain of students using their scores on the pretest and posttest (ngain=(posttest-pretest)/(maxscore-pretest)). For this analysis, we considered students with at least 5 attempts on problems who answered both pretest and posttest. After this filtering, there were 12 students in the OSM group and 30 students in the OSM+Social group. While the mean learning gain of students in OSM+Social group (M=0.47, SD=0.11) was higher than in the OSM grop (M=0.41, SD=0.17) the different was not significant (p=.173). It is, however, quite common than innovative technology most significantly affect weaker students. To check whether it is true in our case, we measured the learning gain for weak and strong students separately. If a student achieved less than 25% of the score in the pretest (is was ½ of the top pretest score or 50% achieved by our students), we classified the student into the weak group, otherwise strong group[1]. Table 4 reports summary of learning gain for weak and strong students inside each group. As we found, the mean learning gain was higher for both weak and strong students in the OSM+Social group compared to the OSM group and the difference was significant for weak students (p=.033).

Table 4. Mean±SD of normalized learning gain of weak and strong students in the OSM and OSM+Social group

	Weak (n=35)			Strong (n=7)		
	OSM (n=9)	OSM+Social (n=26)	p-value	OSM(n=3)	OSM+Social(n=4)	p-value
ngain	0.35±0.15	0.45±0.1	.033	0.57±0.14	0.6±0.13	.824

We also examined the association between number of activity attempts in each group and the final grades of the students in the class. We fitted a mixed model with group (G), number of attempts on problems (NP), examples (NE), and example lines (NL) as the fixed effects and the final grade as the response variable. We found that the group (G), number of examples (NE), and lines (NL) are not significant predictor of the final grade, while number of attempted problems (NP) significantly predicts the final grade. We obtained the coefficient of 0.09 for NP meaning that attempting 1 problem in the system was associated with an increase of 0.09 in the final grade ranging from 0 to 100 (SE=0.04,p=.017). In other words, attempting 100 problems will increase the final grade by 9. This implies that in both groups, more attempts on problems may help gaining better grade in the final exam. This shows that better ability of OSSM interface to engage students in problem solving is important.

5.5 Questionnaire Analysis

A total of 81 students (42 in OSM+Social group, 39 in OSM group) answered the questionnaire about usability and usefulness of MasteryGrids. To focus on more informed feedback, we discarded all students who have used the system less than

---

1 Using other thresholds such as 10%(median) and 20% did not change the results substantially.

300 seconds, keeping 53 students' responses for further analysis: 32 in OSM+Social group (18 females, 14 males), and 21 in OSM group (10 females, 11 males).

Table 5 presents the questions in each part of the questionnaire with Mean and Standard Error of the Mean for each group. Values range from 1 (strongly disagree) to 5 (strongly agree). Part 1 was answered by all 53 students; part 2 was answered only by students in OSM group; part 3 was answered by students in OSM+Social group, from which we discarded all answers which value (3) was tagged as "Did not notice", keeping 17 to 26 responses (some students did not answer all of the questions). In the next paragraphs we refer to the questions in Table 5 as PXQY where X represents the part (1,2,3) and Y the question number.

The general usability and usefulness of the system in Part 1 are evaluated positively, with values generally above 3.5 and many of them above 4 in OSM+Social. There is a clear tendency of more positive answers in OSM+Social group, although the only significant difference observed between groups is in P1Q3: students in OSM+Social group (N=31) stated to be more motivated than students on the OSM group (N=21) by the self-progress features in MasteryGrids, Mann-Whitney U=225, p=.026 two-tailed. We followed this analysis contrasting the response of OSM+Social group in P1Q3 with the similar question about OSSM features, P3Q10, and we found a significant difference p=.031 (using Wilcoxon Signed Rank test): while log data shows that students in the OSM+Social group used the system much more than the students in OSM group, they were also more eager to trace it to the ability of seeing their own progress.

To examine the impact of in-system experience, we cluster students into *usage* groups, low (N=26) and high (N=27) using a two steps clustering over standardize values of the system usage variables *number of distinct problems attempted*, *number of distinct examples viewed*, *number of clicks in topics cells* and *number of clicks in content cells* (problems and examples). We expected that students who used the system more will evaluate it higher, as it frequently happens with complicated systems, but we did not find any significant difference here. We hypothesized that the system was sufficiently simple and usable to be mastered even the low group.

Part 2, answered by OSM group, presents questions about perceived value of social features. We compared these questions with similar questions in Part 3, answered by the other group (OSM+Social) wondering if, in general, students value more the social features when they experience them or vice versa. P2Q1 was compared to an average score in questions P3Q2, P3Q3, and P3Q5 and the difference was significant, i.e., the real value of the social features was even higher that the perceived value (OSM N=19, OSM+Social N = 15, Mann-Whitney U=80, p=.0396 two-tailed). P2Q2 was compared to P3Q10, but the difference was not significant.

Part 3, answered by the OSM+Social group, was analyzed in different forms. First we look at differences across usage clusters (as defined previously) and gender, and no significant difference was found neither in usefulness questions, nor usability questions. Then we look at possible differences between questions referring to different system features. P3Q2, P3Q3 and P3Q5 refer to group comparison feature (see Fig. 1), and P3Q6 and P3Q8 refer to peer list feature. We compare these two groups of questions to see if students find more useful one or the other features. The difference was not significant.

On usability side, students agree that the colors of the system used for comparing with others are easy to understand (P3Q4, P3Q9). This is a good result, since we had concerns about the use of colors and the difficulties to understand the comparison.

It is also interesting to contrast slightly negative score of P3Q12 and the slightly positive score of P3Q14: in general students disagree with the negative effect of social comparison, although they tend to admit that sometimes it pushes them to work just for the sake of competition. Another interesting finding is the lower scores students gave to the perspective of showing names (P3Q11). Apparently, the effect of comparison does not need to be individualized to be beneficial. We further analyze the relation between P3Q11 and P3Q13 by reversing P3Q13 and classifying answers as positive (above 3) or negative (below 3), discarding answers with value 3. We find a significant difference (using Wilcoxon Signed-Rank test) p=.034: 7 out of 20 students who answer both questions think that they would like to see other names, but would not like to show their names, only 1 student would show her name but think it is not useful to see other names, and 12 students match their opinion.

Table 5. Subjective evaluation questions by part. Part 1 was answered by all students. Part 2 was answered only by students in OSM group, and Part 3 by students in OSM+Social group. Some of the questions refer to figures originally included in the questionnaire (and not reproduced here), and the references were changed to [*reference*], e.g. [in peer list] in question 6 and 8 in Part 3.

		OSM		OSM+Social	
Part 1		M	SE	M	SE
1	In general, it was useful to see my progress in Mastery Grids (MG)	3.76	.228	4.03	.145
2	In general, I liked the interface of MG	3.86	.221	3.84	.163
3	Seeing my progress in the tool motivated me to work on quizzes and examples	3.52	.214	4.09	.130
4	The interface helped me to understand how the class content is organized	3.62	.223	3.81	.176
5	The interface helped me to identify my weak points	3.52	.190	3.84	.186
6	The interface helped me to plan my class work	3.33	.211	3.22	.160
7	It was clear how to access questions and examples	3.81	.264	3.56	.190
8	It was useful to see my knowledge progress for each topic [in MG]	3.71	.171	4.03	.135
9	It was useful to see how I am doing with individual quizzes and examples	3.71	.197	4.16	.128
10	Using green colors in different intensity to show my progress was easy to understand	3.90	.217	4.09	.151

Part 2 (only OSM)		M	SE
1	The ability to see the progress of the rest of the group will make MG more valuable for me	3.53	.246
2	The ability to see the progress of the rest of the group will motivate me to use MG more frequently	3.74	.227

Table 5. (*Continued*)

Part 3 (Only OSM+Social)		M	SE
1	It is important for me to see the progress of the rest of the class	3.87	.220
2	It was useful to see the progress of the whole class as it is represented in the Group row [in MG]	3.96	.183
3	It was useful to see the progress of the top students as it is represented in the Group row [in MG]	4.11	.212
4	The comparison between the group and myself [figure] is easy to understand	4.21	.147
5	It was useful to see the comparison between the selected group and myself [figure]	4.14	.151
6	It is important for me to see the progress of individual classmates [in peer list]	3.71	.322
7	In general, it is useful for me to be able to compare my progress with the progress of others	3.88	.185
8	It is important for me to see my position in the class [in peer list]	3.96	.213
9	Visualizing the progress of others using blue colors of different intensities was easy to understand	4.04	.141
10	Viewing my classmates' progress motivated me to work more in quizzes and examples	3.88	.193
11	I think it would be useful for me to know the names of individual classmates in [peer list]	2.68	.230
12	Viewing that others were more advance than me made me want to quit using MG	2.71	.229
13	If names are shown, I will not like to show my name in the list to others	4.15	.120
14	Sometimes I just checked quizzes and examples to catch up with others rather than to learn more	3.35	.264

6 Discussion and Conclusion

In this paper we presented a visual implementation of open social student modeling approach and compared it to the traditional open student model without social component in a semester-long classroom study. The results confirmed a remarkable engagement power of the OSSM: a much higher ability to engage and retain students. It also motivated students to perform significantly more work with non-mandatory learning content. These features of OSSM make it very attractive for context where motivation and retention are critical, such as modern MOOCs. In addition, social visualization enabled students in OSSM group to work more efficiently, which could be attributed to the navigation support aspect of our OSSM implementation. In our future work we plan to investigate the nature of this impact using detailed student interaction traces. The work with OSSM also positively impacted student learning significantly improving learning gain of weaker students. While this could be attributed to the increased work with the content (as shown also by the correlation between the amount of work and exam grade), it is still valuable in the case of non-mandatory educational content, which the students explore at their own will. Student answers to the administered questionnaire indicated positive attitude to both, traditional OSM features and new OSSM various features. Yet, we should acknowledge that the study confirmed the value of OSSM in one specific context – a graduate class in a large US university. The impact of the same interface might be different for other groups of students and in different countries. For example, it is not clear that the effect of OSSM will be same for considerably larger or smaller groups. We plan to investigate the impact of these factors in the future work.

References

1. Ahn, J.-w., Brusilovsky, P., Grady, J., He, D., Syn, S.Y.: Open user profiles for adaptive news systems: help or harm? In: Proc. of the 16th international conference on World Wide Web, WWW 2007. ACM, pp. 11–20 (2007)
2. Brusilovsky, P., Sosnovsky, S., Lee, D., Yudelson, M., Zadorozhny, V., Zhou, X.: Learning SQL programming with interactive tools: from integration to personalization. ACM Transactions on Computing Education **9**(4), 1–15 (2010). Article No. 19
3. Bull, S.: UMPTEEN: Named and Anonymous Learner Model Access for Instructors and Peers. International Journal of Artificial Intelligence in Education **17**(3), 227–253 (2007)
4. Bull, S., Kay, J.: Student Models That Invite the Learner The SMILI:() Open Learner Modelling Framework. International Journal of AI in Education **17**(2), 89–120 (2007)
5. Bull, S., Kay, J.: Open Learner Models as Drivers for Metacognitive Processes. In: Azevedo, R., Aleven, V. (eds.) International Handbook of Metacognition and Learning Technologies, pp. 349–365. Springer, Berlin (2013)
6. Corbett, A.T., Anderson, J.R.: Knowledge tracing: Modelling the acquisition of procedural knowledge. User Modeling and User-Adapted Interaction **4**(4), 253–278 (1995)
7. Hsiao, I.-H., Brusilovsky, P.: Motivational Social Visualizations for Personalized E-Learning. In: Ravenscroft, A., Lindstaedt, S., Kloos, C.D., Hernández-Leo, D. (eds.) EC-TEL 2012. LNCS, vol. 7563, pp. 153–165. Springer, Heidelberg (2012)
8. Hsiao, I.-H., Sosnovsky, S., Brusilovsky, P.: Guiding students to the right questions: adaptive navigation support in an E-Learning system for Java programming. Journal of Computer Assisted Learning **26**(4), 270–283 (2010)
9. Hsiao, I.H., Bakalov, F., Brusilovsky, P., König-Ries, B.: Progressor: social navigation support through open social student modeling. New Review of Hypermedia and Multimedia **19**(2), 112–131 (2013)
10. Loboda, T.D., Guerra, J., Hosseini, R., Brusilovsky, P.: Mastery Grids: An Open Source Social Educational Progress Visualization. In: de Freitas, S., Rensing, C., Ley, T., Muñoz-Merino, P.J. (eds.) EC-TEL 2014. LNCS, vol. 8719, pp. 235–248. Springer, Heidelberg (2014)
11. Mitrovic, A., Martin, B.: Evaluating the Effect of Open Student Models on Self-Assessment. International Journal of AI in Education **17**(2), 121–144 (2007)
12. O'Keeffe, I., Brady, A., Conlan, O., Wade, V.: Just-in-time Generation of Pedagogically Sound, Context Sensitive Personalized Learning Experiences. International Journal on E-Learning **5**(1), 113–127 (2006)
13. Paas, F., van Merriënboer, J.J.G.: The efficiency of instructional conditions: An approach to combine mental effort and performance measures. Human Factors **35**, 737–743 (1993)
14. Paas, F., van Merriënboer, J.J.G.: Instructional control of cognitive load in the training of complex cognitive tasks. Educational Psychology Review **35**(6), 51–71 (1994)
15. Papanikolaou, K.A., Grigoriadou, M., Kornilakis, H., Magoulas, G.D.: Personalising the interaction in a Web-based Educational Hypermedia System: the case of INSPIRE. User Modeling and User Adapted Interaction **13**(3), 213–267 (2003)
16. Weber, G., Brusilovsky, P.: ELM-ART: An adaptive versatile system for Web-based instruction. International Journal of Artificial Intelligence in Education **12**(4), 351–384 (2001)

MENTOR: A Physiologically Controlled Tutoring System

Maher Chaouachi(✉), Imène Jraidi, and Claude Frasson

Department of Computer Science and Operations, University of Montreal, Montreal, Canada
{chaouacm,jraidiim,frasson}@iro.umontreal.ca

Abstract. In this paper we present a tutoring system that automatically sequences the learning content according to the learners' mental states. The system draws on techniques from Brain Computer Interface and educational psychology to automatically adapt to changes in the learners' mental states such as attention and workload using electroencephalogram (EEG) signals. The objective of this system is to maintain the learner in a positive mental state throughout the tutoring session by selecting the next pedagogical activity that fits the best to his current state. An experimental evaluation of our approach involving two groups of learners showed that the group who interacted with the mental state-based adaptive version of the system obtained higher learning outcomes and had a better learning experience than the group who interacted with a non-adaptive version.

Keywords: Intelligent tutoring system · Engagement · Workload · Real-time adaptive system · EEG · Machine learning · Experience and affect

1 Introduction

The use of physio-cognitive sensing technologies in computer-based learning environments has grown continuously through these last years. More precisely, the emergence of the affective computing domain has made a huge change in the design of such environments by enhancing their capabilities to understand the learners' needs and behaviors [1-5]. Research in the Intelligent Tutoring Systems (ITS) field is increasingly directed towards the integration of new techniques that can provide relevant indicators about the learners' internal and affective states. In fact, one of the main objectives of ITS is to provide an adapted and individualized learning environment to the learner. This adaptation can be operated with regards to several considerations (cognitive, educational, emotional, social, etc.), and can be related to different aspects of the system's interaction strategy (selection of the next learning step, providing an individualized feedback, or help, etc.). The integration of physiological data sources can represent a genuine opportunity for such a system to extract valuable information about the user's state and to proactively adapt to this state.

In this paper, we present a new ITS called MENTOR (MENtal tuTOR), which is entirely based on the analysis of the learner's engagement and workload, extracted from the EEG data, in order to sequence the learning activities. More precisely, the system relies on an adaptive logic that selects the next pedagogical activity which fits

F. Ricci et al. (Eds.): UMAP 2015, LNCS 9146, pp. 56–67, 2015.
DOI: 10.1007/978-3-319-20267-9_5

the best to his current state; this activity can be either a problem solving or a worked example.

This choice between worked examples and problems has often been discussed in educational psychology. On one hand, worked examples tend to have a lower mental load impact compared to problems as all the required steps of the problem resolution are already provided to the learner [6]. On the other hand, the problems are more demanding in terms of mental efforts as the learner has to resolve the problem and in case of a wrong answer, he must also understand the solution. However, providing only worked examples to the learners can have a negative impact. The learner may not identify the relevant information pertaining to the worked example, and focuses rather on useless or secondary information [7]. In this paper, we present a set of rules that we have implanted in our system to adaptively select the best activity for the learner. An experimental study was conducted to evaluate our system. The goal was to verify the following two hypotheses:

(1) The integration of the engagement and the workload brain indexes in an ITS can have a real impact on the learners' outcomes. Our assumption is that if the system controls the learning dynamics according to these mental indicators, then the system's interventions can help the learner understand the tutoring content.
(2) Using a mental state-based strategy in this type of adaptation can improve the learner's experience regarding their tutoring session. In other words, we assume that if the system is aware of the mental challenges the learner is facing, this can be reflected positively on the learner's satisfaction regarding the system.

2 Related Work

Mental workload and engagement are among the most commonly used indicators to dynamically assess changes in the users' states [8-11]. Several physiological sensors such as heart rate variability, oculomotor activity, pupilometry, body temperature, respiration and galvanic skin responses have been employed to detect mental state changes [13-15]. However, the electroencephalography (EEG) is considered as the only physiological signal that can reliably and precisely track restrained changes in mental attention (or engagement) and workload, and that can be identified and quantified on a millisecond time-frame [12].

Developing EEG indexes for workload and engagement assessment is a well-developed research domain. Several linear and non-linear classification and regression methods were used to measure these indexes in different kinds of cognitive tasks such as memorization, language processing, visual, or auditory tasks. These methods rely mainly on a frequency processing approach using either the Power Spectral Density (PSD) or Event Related Potential (ERP) techniques to extract relevant EEG features [12].

In the educational context, the index developed by Berka and his colleague was used within a learning environment to analyze the students' behaviors while acquiring skills during a problem solving session [11]. Recently a workshop was hold to promote the use of EEG input in ITS [16]. This paper represents a straight continuation of these approaches by presenting a tutoring system whose adaptive strategy is entirely based on the values of the engagement and the workload indexes.

3 System Design

MENTOR is a tutoring system that uses indicators extracted from the EEG physiological data to adjust the learning activities according to the learner's mental state. The system uses the Emotiv EEG headset (www.emotiv.com) to collect EEG raw signals. The reasons of choosing this EEG device is that it can be connected wireless to any machine through the receiving USB. The Emotiv device is also light, easy to use and does not require any particular material configuration. The Emotiv headset contains 16 electrodes located according to the 10-20 international standard [28]. It allows recording simultaneously 14 regions (O1, O2, P7, P8, T7, T8, FC5, FC6, F3, F4, F7, F8, AF3 and AF4). Two additional electrodes are used as references, which correspond respectively to the P3 region (called DRL for Driven Right Leg) and the P4 region (called CMS for Common Mode sense). The system's sampling rate is 128 Hz.

Two brain indexes are derived in real-time by MENTOR, namely mental engagement and workload.

3.1 Mental Engagement

The engagement index used comes from the work of Pope and colleagues [17] at the National Aeronautics and Space Administration (NASA). This work is based on neuroscientific research on attention and vigilance [18]. It was found that the user's performance improved when this index is used as a criterion for switching between manual and automated piloting mode. This index is computed from three EEG frequency bands: θ (4-8 Hz), α (8-13 Hz) and β (13-22 Hz) as follows: $\beta / \theta + \alpha$

The engagement index is computed each second from the EEG signal. In order to reduce the fluctuation of this index, we use a moving average on a 40-second mobile window. Thus, the value of the index as the time *t* corresponds to the total average of the ratios calculated on a period of 40 seconds preceding *t*. The extraction of the θ, α and β frequency bands is performed by multiplying one second of the EEG signal by a Hamming window (in order to reduce the spectral leakage) and applying a Fast Fourier Transform (FFT). As the Emotiv headset measures 14 regions at the same time, we used a combined value of the θ, α and β frequency bands by summing their values over all the measured regions.

3.2 Mental Workload and MENTOR's Training Mode

Unlike the engagement index, there is no a common established method to directly assess mental workload from the EEG data. Therefore, we propose to build an individual mental workload predictive model for each learner. This model is trained using data collected from a training phase during which the learner performs a set of brain training exercises. This training phase involves three different types of cognitive exercises, namely: digit span, reverse digit span and mental computation.

The objective of theses training exercises is to induce different levels of mental workload while collecting the learner's EEG data. The manipulation of the induced workload level is done by varying the difficulty level of the exercises: by increasing the number of the digits in the sequence to be recalled for digit span and reverse digit span, and the number of digits to be added or subtracted for the mental computation exercises (see [12,19] for more details about this procedure). After performing each difficulty level, the learner is asked to report his workload level using the subjective scale of NASA Task load index (NASA_TLX) [20].

Once this training phase completed, the collected EEG raw data are cut into 1-second segments and multiplied by a Hamming window. A FFT is applied to transform each EEG segment into a spectral frequency and generate a set of 40 bins of 1 Hz ranging from 4 to 43 Hz (EEG pretreated vectors). These data are then reduced using a Principal Component Analysis (PCA) to 25 components (the score vectors). Next, a Gaussian Process Regression (GPR) algorithm with an exponential squared kernel and a Gaussian noise [21] is run in order to train a mental workload predictive model (the EEG workload index) from the normalized score vectors. Normalization is done by subtracting the mean and dividing by the standard deviation of the all vectors. In order to reduce the training time of the predictive model, we used the local Gaussian Process Regression algorithm, which is a faster version of the GPR [22].

3.3 Analysis of the Computed Indexes

In order to evaluate the learner's mental state, the system analyses the behavior of the engagement and workload indexes throughout the current learning activity. A slope of each index is computed using the least squared error function of the index's values from the beginning of the activity. For the engagement index, if the slope value is postive, then learner is considered as mentally engaged. Otherwise, the learner is considered as mentally disengaged. For the workload index, if the slope value is between - 0.03 and + 0.03, than the workload is considered as positive. Otherwise, if the slope value is above 0.03, the learner is considered as overloaded, and if the slope is below -0.03 the learner is considerd as underloaded. Thus, the learner's mental state is considered positive, if he is mentally engaged and neither overloaded nor underloaded; otherwise, it is considered negative.

3.4 Learning Mode

The MENTOR tutoring system has been designed to help learners understand the Reverse Polish Notation (RPN), which is also known as the postfix notation. The lesson presented by the system includes four successive parts. After the learner finishes each part of the lesson, the system presents four pedacogical activities so that the learner puts into practice the concepts seen in the previous part of the lesson and enhance his understanding. Each activity uses one of the two following pedagogical resources:

Questions: each question presents a problem that the learner has to resolve. Hints are provided with each problem in order to help the learner find the solution and improve his knowledge acquisition. At the end of each question, the system informs the learner whether his answer was correct or not. In case of a wrong answer, the solution of the problem is given without presenting any explanation of the resolution process.

Worked examples: a worked example describes a problem statement with the detailed steps and explanations leading to the solution. The learner is simply asked to read and understand these examples.

3.5 MENTOR's Adaptive Rules

MENTOR's decisional process lies mainly in the selection of the type of the pedagogical resource (a question or a worked example) to be provided as a next activity. In summary, 16 decisions (4 parts × 4 activities) has to be made by the system according to the learner's mental state. The decision of presenting a worked example or a problem within MENTOR is based on a continuous analysis of the learner's mental engagement and workload. The goal is to select the pedagogical resource that maintain the learner in a positive mental state. More precisely, the system has to keep the learner mentally engaged and avoid overload and underload. If the system detects a negative mental state caused by an engaegement drop, an overload or an underload, it will then try to correct this state by switching the type of the next pedagogical activity.

A total of seven adaptive rules are used by MENTOR as shown in Figure1:

(R1) If the learner's mental state is positive (mentally engaged and neither overloaded nor underloaded), then the system selects a question for the next activity. This rule is applied whatever the current activity is (question, worked example or reading a part of the lesson).

(R2) At the end of a question, if the learner's mental state is negative (disengaged, overloaded or underloaded), then the system provides a worked example in the next activity.

(R3) At the end of a worked example, if the system detects a negative mental state due to disengagement or underload, then it provides a question as a next activity.

(R4) At the end of a worked example, if the system detects a negative mental state due to overload, then it provides a worked example in the next activity.

(R5) After reading a part of the lesson, if the system detects a negative mental state due to disengagement or underload, then it provides a question as a next activity.

(R6) After reading a part of the lesson, if the system detects a negative mental state due to overload, then it provides a worked example for the next activity.

(R7) Whatever the learners' mental state is, if he answers a question incorrectly, then the system provides a worked example in the next activity.

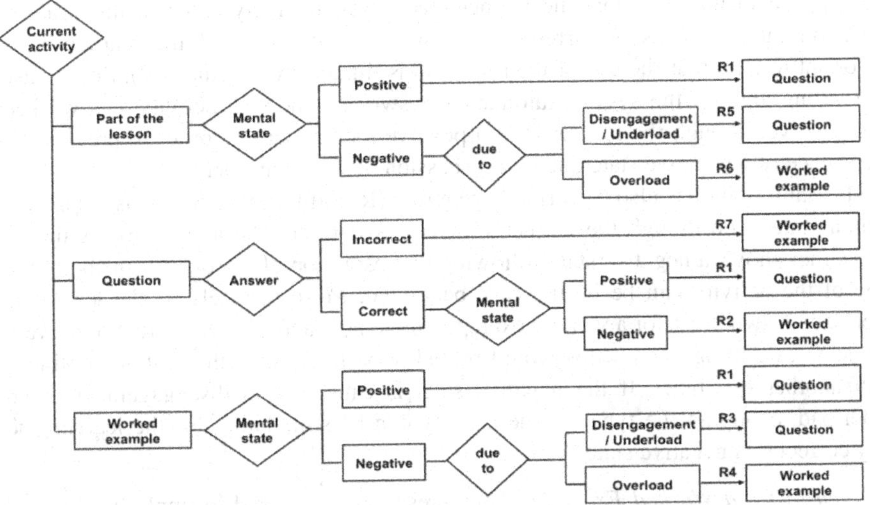

Fig. 1. MENTOR's adaptive logic for selecting the next pedagogical resource

The idea behind the use of these rules is given hereafter.

Decision After Reading a Part of the Lesson. The system uses the questions as a main pedagogical approach to help the learner understand the presented concepts. The rule (R1) makes that the system automatically provide a question if the learner's state is positive. The hypothesis behind this rule is that if the learner reads a lesson while maintaining a positive state, then he likely did not have too much difficulties to understand the presented concepts. So, by choosing a question as a subsequent activity, the system checks the learner's knowledge. However if the learner's mental state is negative, the system analyzes the cause of this state. If this negative state is due to a mental overload, then the rule (R6) makes the system choose a worked example in the next activity. The hypothesis behind this rule is that a mental overload signals generally a cognitive difficulty with regards to the presented concepts. The learner produces then a high level of mental effort to understand what he was reading. So the decision of presenting a worked example after this activity can help the learner to better understand the presented part without producing further mental effort. In this case, we think that giving a problem to solve while the learner is overloaded can worsen his workload level and disturb his learning process. However, if the learner's negative state is due to a disengagement or a mental underload, the system selects a question using the rule (R5). In this case, we assume that this lack of mental investment is either due to the fact that the learner was perfectly mastering what he was reading, or he was rather uninterested and neglecting the lesson. In both cases, a question can be a more stimulating and challenging activity for the learner and can probably enhance his mental investment.

Decision After a Question. At the end of a question, if the system does not detect a negative state, it chooses another question as a next activity using the rule (R1).

We suppose in this case that the learner reacts well mentally and that the strategy based on the questions is currently well suited to the state of the learner. It is important to note that the use of the rule (R1) is limited by the rule (R7). So, in case of a wrong answer, the system automatically switches the next activity to a worked example even though the learner is in a positive mental state in order to prevent the occurrence of a negative state due to a succession of wrong answers.

This same switch is also performed using rule (R2), if the system detects a negative mental state even though the learner's answer is correct. The assumption is that if the learner shows a negative state following the resolution of a problem, changing the type of the activity can be in any case beneficial. More precisely, if the learner is overloaded, switching for a worked example in the next activity can correct or prevent this state of getting worse (this would probably be the case if the system continues with another question). If the negative state is caused by a disengagement or an underload, changing the type of the activity can be stimulating for the learner and may correct this negative state.

Decision After a Worked Example. After presenting a worked example, the system opts for a question as a next activity if the learner's mental state is positive using the rule (R1). The reason of using this strategy is to target an effect known as *the problem completion effect* [6], which is generally obtained by providing a worked example followed immediately by a problem. This type of strategy is used to increase the learning performances and enhance the learner's motivation [23]. For this reason, we decided to choose a question as a subsequent activity to the worked example even if the learner's state is positive, rather than pursuing with another worked example.

Finally, if the system detects a negative mental state caused by an overload, the system continues to present a worked example in the next activity using rule (R4). The assumption behind this rule is that if a learner has some cognitive difficulties to understand the example, or if he is simply tired, it would not be suitable to provide him a problem to solve since that this can worsen his overload. Therefore, another worked example can support his knowledge without beeing mentally much demanding.

4 Experimental Study

In order to highlight the impact of using the learners' mental indicators as an adaptive criterion to manage the system's pedagogical resources, our experimental study relied on two different versions of MENTOR. The difference between these versions lied only in the adaptive logic of the decisional module. The first version left intact the adaptive logic with the seven basic intervention rules described previously. The selection of the resource to be provided was done according to the evolution of the learner's mental state. In particular, the system tends to privilege the questions in case of a positive mental state. In the opposite case, the selection of the type of the resource was made following heuristics that aim to correct the learner's mental state.

The second version of the system did not take into account the mental indexes of engagement and workload in selecting the type of the resource to be provided.

Only the rule (R7) was preserved in the adaptive logic of MENTOR, and the six other rules were ignored. The principle of this version was quite simple: after reading each part of the lesson, the system selected a question for the learner. As long as the learner answered correctly, the system continued to adopt the same strategy: asking questions. However, if an incorrect answer was given, the system selected immediately a worked example as a next activity in order to fix the learner's reasoning. Once the learner finished reading the example, the system automatically followed up with a question in order to increase his motivation and elicit a *problem completion effect*. So the unique parameter that triggered an adaptive action in this version was an incorrect response given by the learner.

The two used versions shared a common point in their operation: if the adaptation parameters are positive, the two versions opt for a question as a next step. The mental state-based adaptive version of the system (the first) represents then an augmented version of the second, insofar as in addition to considering the accuracy of the response (through the 7th rule), it also applies other adaptive actions based on mental parameters.

In summary, we compared two versions of the system, the first used in its adaptive logic an analysis of the mental indexes in addition to the response of the learner, and the second was based solely on the response of the learner. Both versions used, in the same order, exactly the same pedagogical resources.

4.1 Participants and Experimental Protocol

14 participants took part in our study. All were students in the University of Montreal in the same certification program in applied computer science. Upon their arrival, participants were briefed about the experimental procedure and signed a consent form. Each participant was randomly assigned to one of the two following groups. (1) The experimental group (N = 7) used the adaptive version of MENTOR: the learning activities are actively adapted to both the learners' brain indexes and answers. (2) The control group (N=7) used the second version of MENTOR that considers only the learners' answers.

For each participant, the experiment was conducted on two successive days. On the first day, the participant uses the training mode of MENTOR in order to create his individual workload model. In this phase, which lasts about an hour, the participant performs a set of 40 brain training exercices including digit span, reverse digit span and mental computation as described earlier.

On the second day of the experiment, the participant uses the learning mode of MENTOR. The duration of this phase is approximately one hour, including 20 to 30 minutes to learn the four parts of the Reverse Polish Notation lesson. The session starts with a pre-test followed by the lesson, then a post-test, and ends with a debriefing phase. Two 5-minute breaks were taken between the pre-test, the lesson and the post-test.

Pre-Test and Post-Test. These tests use a set of 16 questions relative to the concepts of the lesson. Each of the four parts of the lesson is concerned with four different questions, and the same questions are asked in the pre-test and the post-test. For each question, the learner can answer true or false, or may choose not to respond. A typical example of a question is to check whether two postfix expressions are equivalent. The score in each test is calculated as follows: a correct answer is worth 1 point, while a wrong answer (or a non-response) worths 0.

Debriefing. During this phase, the learner is first asked to report his appreciation of his interaction with the learning environment by rating his *satisfaction level* regarding the lesson, using a scale of seven grades ranging from 1 (strongly disagree) to 7 (strongly agree) on how much he agrees with the following statement: "*Overall, I am satisfied with of my learning experience with the system*".

Then, the learner evaluates the quality of the tutoring provided by the system by reporting his perceived level of *relevance* of the system's proposed activities, using another scale of seven grades ranging from 1 (strongly disagree) to 7 (strongly agree), on how much he agrees with the following statement: "*Overall, I am satisfied with the learning activities selected by the system. The examples and questions are presented at the right time and helped me to understand the lesson. The choice made between asking a question or presenting an example fits my level of understanding*". This scale is therefore an evaluation of the relevance (or the perspicacity) of the tutor's decisions.

5 Results and Discussion

The experimental results are presented in the following subsections. First, we analyze the impact of using the EEG indexes as an adaptive criterion on learning; we compare the learners' outcomes and progression in the two considered groups (experimental group vs. control group) between the pre-test and the post-test. Then, we analyze the impact of using the two versions of the system on the learners' satisfaction level.

5.1 Learning Performance

A 2 (group: experimental vs. control) × 2 (time: pre-test vs. post-test) mixed-model analysis of variance (ANOVA) was conducted to compare the learners' outcomes of the two groups in terms of scores achieved in both tests. The group variable is a between-subject factor that compares the scores between the two experimental conditions, whereas the time variable is a within-subject factor that analyzes, for each participant individually, the score variation (changes) between the pre-test and the post-test. First, the analysis yielded a main effect of the time variable, showing a significant difference of the learners' scores in both groups between the pre-test and the post-test: $F(1, 12) = 2253.353$ $p < 0.001$. Thus, there was significant a learning gain regardless of the group, and hence regardless of the version of the system which was used by the participants.

Second the analysis yielded a significant interaction effect of both factors (group × time) on the learners' outcomes: $F(1, 12) = 29.824$, $p < 0.001$. The results revealed that over time, that is between the pre-test and the post-test, the learners of the experimental group got significantly better learning performances compared to the control group. The means of scores obtained in the pre-test and the post-test for the both groups are listed in Table 1.

The comparison of the learners' scores between the experimental group and the control group revealed that there was no statistically significant differences between the two groups in the pre-test: $F(1, 12) = 4.190$, p = n.s. The overall mean score in the pre-test was $M = 4.21$ ($SD = 1.31$). In contrast, the comparison of the learners' scores in the post-test showed that the scores achieved in the experimental group were significantly higher than the control group: $F(1, 12) = 50.069$, $p < 0.001$. The mean score of the experimental group was $M = 13.86$ ($SD = 0.67$) against $M = 10.71$ ($SD = 0.95$) for the control group.

Table 1. Learners' outcomes in both groups before and after the tutoring session

	Pre-test	Post-test
Experimental group		
M	4.86_a	13.86_b
SD	1.07	0.70
Control group		
M	3.57_a	10.71_c
SD	1.27	0.95

Values with different subscripts differ significantly.

These results confirm our first hypothesis, that is using the workload and the engagement indexes as a main criterion to control the user's activities can have a positive impact on his learning performances. The learners' whose pedagogical resources were selected according to their mental states were able to provide an average of 86,6 % correct answers after the tutoring session. An increase of 22.7 % in terms of learning outcomes was achieved using this adaptive strategy.

5.2 Subjective Measures

An ANOVA was conducted in order to compare the learners' satisfaction levels between the experimental group and the control group. This ANOVA showed an almost significant difference between the two groups: $F(1, 12) = 4.545$, $p = 0.054$. The learners of the experimental group reported higher satisfaction ($M = 5.71$, $SD = 1.604$) in comparison to the control group ($M = 4.29$, $SD = 0.756$).

A second ANOVA was performed to compare the learners' ratings of the relevance of the activities proposed by the tutoring system in both groups. These ratings were significantly higher in the experimental group ($M = 5$, $SD = 1.414$) versus ($M = 2.43$, $SD = 0.787$) in the control group, $F(1, 12) = 17.673$, $p < 0.05$.

These results confirm thus that incresing the system's adaptive logic with the EEG engagement and workload indexes has a positive effect on the users' satisfaction regarding their learning experience in general, and their appreciation regarding the relevance of the decisions taken by the system in the selection of the pedagogical resources more specifically.

6 Conclusion

In this paper we have presented an intelligent tutoring system called MENTOR (MENtal tuTOR) that adapts its tutoring content according to the user's brain activity. The goal was to show that enhancing the ITS adaptive logic with two physiological mental indicators, namely the engagement and the workload indexes, can improve the learners' outcomes and interaction experience.

MENTOR collects the user's EEG data. The training mode of the system uses different types of brain training exercises to build a workload model for a new user. This model is used to derive in real-time the user's workload index from his EEG signals. The learning mode of MENTOR provides a tutoring environment that adapts its content actively to the learner's brain indexes. The system evaluates the learner's mental state, and selects the pedagogical activity that best suits to his state.

Acknowledgements. We acknowledge SSHRC (Social Science and Human Research Council) through the LEADS project and NSERC (National Science and Engineering Research Council) for funding this research.

References

1. Pour, P.A., Hussain, M., AlZoubi, O., D'Mello, S., Calvo, R.A.: The impact of system feedback on learners' affective and physiological states. In: Aleven, V., Kay, J., Mostow, J. (eds.) ITS 2010, Part I. LNCS, vol. 6094, pp. 264–273. Springer, Heidelberg (2010)
2. Banda, N., Robinson, P.: Multimodal affect recognition in intelligent tutoring systems. In: D'Mello, S., Graesser, A., Schuller, B., Martin, J.-C. (eds.) ACII 2011, Part II. LNCS, vol. 6975, pp. 200–207. Springer, Heidelberg (2011)
3. Jraidi, I., Chaouachi, M., Frasson, C.: A hierarchical probabilistic framework for recognizing learners' interaction experience trends and emotions. Advances in Human-Computer Interaction (2013)
4. D'Mello, S.K., Craig, S.D., Gholson, B., Franklin, S., Picard, R.W., Graesser, A.C.: Integrating affect sensors in an intelligent tutoring system. In: Proc of Affective Interactions: The Computer in the Affective Loop Workshop at International Conference on IUI, pp. 7-13 (2005)
5. Jraidi, I., Chaouachi, M., Frasson, C.: A dynamic multimodal approach for assessing learners' interaction experience. In: Proc of ACM International Conference on Multimodal Interaction (2013)
6. Paas, F.G.: Training strategies for attaining transfer of problem-solving skill in statistics: A cognitive-load approach. Journal of educational psychology **84**(4), 429 (1992)

7. Kalyuga, S., Chandler, P., Tuovinen, J., Sweller, J.: When problem solving is superior to studying worked examples. Journal of educational psychology **93**(3), 579 (2001)
8. Berka, C., Levendowski, D.J., Ramsey, C.K., Davis, G., Lumicao, M.N., Stanney, K., Reeves, L., Regli, S.H., Tremoulet, P.D., Stibler, K.: Evaluation of an EEG workload model in an aegis simulation environment. In: Defense and Security Int. Soc. Optics and Photonics, pp.90-99 (2005)
9. Stevens, R., Galloway, T., Berka, C.: Integrating EEG models of cognitive load with machine learning models of scientific problem solving. In: Augmented Cognition: Past, Present and Future. Strategic Analysis, Inc., Arlington, pp. 55-65 (2006)
10. Sterman, M.B., Mann, C.A.: Concepts and applications of EEG analysis in aviation performance evaluation. Biological Psychology **40**(1–2), 115–130 (1995)
11. Stevens, R.H., Galloway, T., Berka, C.: EEG-related changes in cognitive workload, engagement and distraction as students acquire problem solving skills. In: Conati, C., McCoy, K., Paliouras, G. (eds.) UM 2007. LNCS (LNAI), vol. 4511, pp. 187–196. Springer, Heidelberg (2007)
12. Berka, C., Levendowski, D.J., Cvetinovic, M.M., Petrovic, M.M., Davis, G., Lumicao, M.N., Zivkovic, V.T., Popovic, M.V., Olmstead, R.: Real-time analysis of EEG indexes of alertness, cognition, and memory acquired with a wireless EEG headset. International Journal of Human-Computer Interaction **17**(2), 151–170 (2004)
13. Van Orden, K.F., Limbert, W., Makeig, S., Jung, T.-P.: Eye activity correlates of workload during a visuospatial memory task. Human Factors: The Journal of the Human Factors and Ergonomics Society **43**(1), 111–121 (2001)
14. Wilson, G.F.: An analysis of mental workload in pilots during flight using multiple sychophysiological measures. Int. J. Aviat. Psychol. **12**, 3–18 (2002)
15. Gevins, A., Smith, M.E.: Neurophysiological measures of cognitive workload during human-computer interaction. Theoretical Issues in Ergonomics Science **4**(1–2), 113–131 (2003)
16. https://sites.google.com/site/its2014wseeg/
17. Pope, A.T., Bogart, E.H., Bartolome, D.S.: Biocybernetic system evaluates indices of operator engagement in automated task. Biological psychology **40**(1), 187–195 (1995)
18. Lubar, J.F.: Discourse on the development of EEG diagnostics and biofeedback for attention-deficit/hyperactivity disorders. Biofeedback and Self-regulation **16**(3), 201–225 (1991)
19. Chaouachi, M., Jraidi, I., Frasson, C.: Modeling mental workload using EEG features for intelligent systems. In: Konstan, J.A., Conejo, R., Marzo, J.L., Oliver, N. (eds.) UMAP 2011. LNCS, vol. 6787, pp. 50–61. Springer, Heidelberg (2011)
20. Hart, S.G., Staveland, L.E.: Development Of NASA-TLX (Task Load Index): Results of empirical and theoretical research. Human Mental Workload **1**(3), 139–183 (1988)
21. Rasmussen, C.E.: Gaussian processes for machine learning (2006)
22. Nguyen-Tuong, D., Peters, J.R., Seeger, M.: Local gaussian process regression for real time online model learning. In: Advances in Neural Information Processing Systems, pp.1193-1200 (2008)
23. Sweller, J.: Evolution of human cognitive architecture. Psychology of Learning and Motivation, 215-266 (2003)

Context-Aware User Modeling Strategies for Journey Plan Recommendation

Victor Codina[1](✉), Jose Mena[1], and Luis Oliva[2]

[1] Barcelona Digital Technology Center, Barcelona, Spain
{vcodina,jmena}@bdigital.org
http://www.bdigital.org

[2] Technical University of Catalonia, Barcelona, Spain
loliva@lsi.upc.edu
http://www.lsi.upc.edu

Abstract. Popular journey planning systems, like Google Maps or Yahoo! Maps, usually ignore user's preferences and context. This paper shows how we applied context-aware recommendation technologies in an existing journey planning mobile application to provide personalized and context-dependent recommendations to users. We describe two different strategies for context-aware user modeling in the journey planning domain. We present an extensive performance comparison of the proposed strategies by conducting a user-centric study in addition to a traditional offline evaluation method.

Keywords: Recommender systems · Context-awareness · Personalized journey planning · User-centric evaluation

1 Introduction

Nowadays, people commonly plan their holidays by making use of online tools that have access to a huge amount of tourist-related services and products, such as destinations, routes, attractions and hotels. This choice overload problem usually leads tourists to make poor decisions about what products are more appropriate to them.

Recommender Systems (RSs) [14][15] are known to be effective tools to overcome this problem, helping users to separate the wheat from the chaff. Previous approaches to journey plan recommendation are mostly designed for closed domains, that is, domains where the set of potential journey plans is already defined and based on a set of previously recommended Points of Interest (POIs) (*e.g.*, touristic itineraries) [10]; and those able to dynamically generate journey plans usually do not incorporate users preferences and context into the planning process. An exception is PECITAS [17], a mobile recommender that offers users personalized journey plans combining walking and public transportation in the city of Bolzano. However, in PECITAS only a small set of generic preferences are considered (*e.g.*, departure time and cost), which considerably limits its personalization capabilities.

F. Ricci et al. (Eds.): UMAP 2015, LNCS 9146, pp. 68–79, 2015.
DOI: 10.1007/978-3-319-20267-9_6

Context-Aware Recommender Systems (CARSs) [1] differ from traditional recommendation strategies because they predict how a given user will rate an item not only based on past user ratings, but also exploiting the context in which those ratings were produced, and the user's context at request time (*i.e.*, the target context). Previous research on CARSs in the tourism and travel domain has mainly focused on the task of POIs recommendation [2], not considering the journey planning itself as a recommending task.

Unlike previous works, we have investigated the effectiveness of applying state-of-the-art CARS techniques in an existing multi-modal journey planning system in order to provide users with personalized and context-dependent suggestions of dynamically generated journey plans. The main contributions of the paper are:

1. The definition of two different context-aware recommendation strategies for journey plan recommendation, one based on the adaptation of the contextual pre-filtering method presented in [5], and the other one a contextual modeling strategy inspired on the time-aware Matrix Factorization (MF) model presented in [8].
2. An extensive performance comparison of the proposed context-aware strategies combining offline and user-centric experiments. In the offline setting we used a contextually-tagged journey plan rating data set, collected by means of a novel in-context rating acquisition method, and for the user-centric evaluation we conducted a controlled experiment with real users of an existing journey planning mobile application.

The remainder of this paper is organized as follows. Section 2 positions our work with respect to the state of the art. Section 3 presents in detail the CARS strategies for journey plan recommendation evaluated in this work. Section 4 describes the offline evaluation, including the in-context rating acquisition method used to collect the training data. Section 5 presents the method and results of the user-centric experiment. Finally, Section 6 draws the main conclusions and presents some future work.

2 Related Work

CARSs are commonly classified into three paradigms [1]: (1) pre-filtering, where context is used for selecting the relevant ratings before computing predictions with a traditional context-free model; (2) contextual post-filtering, where context is used to adjust predictions generated by a context-free model; and (3) contextual modeling, in which contextual information is directly incorporated in a context-free model as additional parameters.

Most of the research on CARSs have focused on extending Collaborative Filtering approaches with context-awareness (CACF). Currently, pre-filtering and contextual modeling CACF methods extending MF prediction models are the most popular ones because of their superior prediction accuracy in many domains [8]. For example, *Distributional Semantic Pre-filtering* (DSPF) [5] is a recent reduction-based pre-filtering method that, given a target context, builds a local MF prediction model using the ratings tagged with contexts semantically similar to the target one, which is then used for making predictions in that context. A key component of DSPF is the method used to compute the similarity between contextual situations based on the distributional semantics of their composing conditions. Another popular example following the contextual modeling paradigm is *Context-Aware Matrix Factorization* (CAMF) [2]. This method can be seen as a generalization of the standard bias MF model where context dimensions are included as part of the prediction function. Particularly, it incorporates context as additional biases capturing the global influence of contextual conditions on the ratings given to the items.

Pre-filtering and contextual modeling strategies have their own advantages and drawbacks, and it is difficult to know at design stage which algorithm would perform better in a specific recommendation domain [3][13]. A recent empirical analysis presented in [5] indicates that sophisticated pre-filtering methods can perform better in domains with high context granularity, but in contrast, contextual modeling strategies are less affected by data sparsity, since they use all the available training data to build the context-aware model. This uncertainty motivated us to carry out a more in-depth performance comparison of both context-aware strategies in the particular domain of journey planning.

Some authors have also investigated the effectiveness of extending Content-Based (CB) approaches with context-awareness (CACB). For instance, in [11] a contextual modeling method is proposed that learns attribute-based representations of both contextual information and user's interests based on a vector space model enhanced by exploiting the attributes' distributional semantics, which are then aggregated during the calculation of the user-item matching. However, a limitation of this approach is that it is designed to work with textual content data and, therefore, it cannot be applied in domains where only a limited set of categorical attributes are available like in this case. For this reason, differently from [11], in this work we adapted the previously mentioned CACF approaches, *DSPF* and *CAMF*, to be used in combination with a linear CB prediction model.

3 Context-Aware User Modeling Strategies

This section describes the context-aware recommendation strategies implemented to estimate the suitability of a candidate journey plan for a user, based on her past ratings and current context. We begin by describing the context-free recommendation model, which is the basis of the proposed CACB methods. Then, we present in detail the proposed context-aware strategies: the contextual pre-filtering method and the contextual modeling one.

3.1 Context-Free Recommendation Model

Collaborative Filtering (CF) approaches require several ratings of different users on the same items to extract meaningful interest patterns, which implies they are not appropriate for recommending journey plans dynamically generated. In this scenario only CB approaches can produce meaningful recommendations, since they are capable to exploit the knowledge about the items besides the past ratings given by the target user.

To apply a CB approach we first need an attribute-based representation of the items to recommend (*i.e.*, journey plans). Based on the knowledge of mobility experts we identified as relevant the following set of attributes for the journey planning recommendation task:

- Global *time* required to complete the journey plan with respect to an estimated ideal time. In the case of multi-modal journey plans the time required for each transport mode (walk, bike, public and private transport) is also captured;
- *Cost* of the journey plan normalized with respect to the ideal cost. We also modeled the cost per mode of transport in multi-modal journey plans;
- *Physical effort* required (only available in plans including walking or biking as transport mode);
- *Time percentage* of each transport mode with respect to the global time;
- *Number of public interchanges* needed to complete the journey.

CB prediction models are typically designed to function with categorical data. Therefore, we first had to discretize the numeric attributes described above. To do this, we employed a fuzzy-set method [12] that assigns each possible value to one or two predefined categories. In particular, we divided each attribute into 5 equal intervals: *very low*, *low*, *normal*, *high* and *very high*. This method allows for a more accurate discretization by assigning a weight to the categories that are close to the boundaries separating two intervals.

Based on this weighted attribute-based representation, we defined a linear CB prediction model that estimates the utility of a given item i for a user u as the normalized dot product of the attribute-based user vector (p_u) and item vector (q_i):

$$\hat{r}_{ui} = |M_{ui}|^{\alpha} q_i^{\top} p_u \tag{1}$$

where: α is a normalization factor (hyper-parameter) that modifies the dot product score based on the total number of non-zero partial products, and whose value must be fine-tuned to the training data; p_u is the real vector representing the interest scores of user u in each possible attribute value (the model parameters to be learnt); and q_i is the real vector representing the attributes of item i (the vector dimensionality is equal to the number of possible attribute values).

Several methods can be applied to do this user profile learning process. After evaluating several strategies [4], in this work we decided to employ the stochastic gradient descent (SGD) method, widely used for learning the parameters of MF models [8], estimating the optimal values of the model parameters (p^*) by solving the regularized least squares optimization problem.

3.2 Contextual Pre-Filtering Strategy

Here we briefly describe the proposed contextual pre-filtering approach, which is an adaptation of DSPF, the reduction-based method presented in [5]. Given a set of training ratings and a target context, our adaptation of DSPF builds a local CB prediction model using the following two-step process:

1. **Ratings filtering.** Firstly, we select the relevant subset of ratings to make predictions in the given context. This subset contains the ratings tagged with exactly the target context and those whose context is similar enough to the target one. As in the original method, we consider as similar all the candidate contextual situations whose similarity to the target one is larger than a pre-defined threshold.
2. **Local model learning.** Then, a local recommendation model is learned using the relevant subset of in-context ratings selected in the previous step. Differently from the original DSPF method, where local MF models are built, here we learn the linear CB prediction model defined in Equation 1 instead.

To measure the similarity between contexts, we employed the same definition proposed by [5], which is based on the distributional semantics of their composing conditions, assuming that two contexts are similar if they influence ratings in a similar way. Particularly, we measured the influence of contextual conditions as the average rating deviation over the user's ratings produced when the condition holds (i.e., the *per-user* perspective). For the same reason that CF approaches are not applicable in this domain the *per-item* perspective is also not useful in this application.

3.3 Contextual Modeling Strategy

The proposed contextual modeling strategy is inspired on CAMF [2] and the time-aware MF model presented in [8], which extends the bias MF with additional parameters capturing the temporal dynamics as well as periodic effects. Our approach consists in extending the linear CB prediction model defined in Equation 1 by capturing the influence of context at two different granularities:

- As global biases, which capture the global context-specific variability of users' preferences with respect to the attributes of the target journey plan. Denoting as b_{i_a,c_j} the rating bias associated to the item value of the attribute i_a when condition c_j holds, the global bias of a target contextual situation $s = [c_1, c_2, ..., c_k]$ (k represents here the k-th contextual factor captured by the system, and c_k is the specific condition of this k-th factor in the target context) is calculated as the bias summation of s composing conditions:

$$\hat{b}_{ui,c_1 \ldots c_k} = \sum_{j=1}^{k} b_{i_a,c_j} \tag{2}$$

– As preference-specific biases, which capture the context-dependent variability of the target user's interests. More formally, we estimate the user's preference vector p_u as a function of the target context, as follows:

$$\hat{p}_{u,c_1 \ldots c_k} = p_u + \sum_{j=1}^{k} \sum_{l=1}^{o} p_{u,c_l} \cdot S_{c_j,c_l} \tag{3}$$

Where: $S_{c_1,c_2} \in [0,1]$ stands for the similarity value between a candidate condition c_1 and the target condition c_2, and o represents the total number of contextual conditions captured by the system. This semantic aggregation of context-specific user's preferences is aimed to enhance the contextual user modeling process under new-user cold-start scenarios. In this case we used the same context similarity definition as in DSPF (see Section 3.2).

Based on the previous definitions, the implemented contextual modeling strategy, called here *Distributional-Semantics Contextual Modeling* (DSCM), predicts the rating that a target user u and item i under context s by summing the estimations of Equations 2 and 3, resulting with the following estimation function:

$$\hat{r}_{ui,c_1 \ldots c_k} = \hat{b}_{ui,c_1 \ldots c_k} + |M_{ui}|^{\alpha} q_i^{\top} \hat{p}_{u,c_1 \ldots c_k} \tag{4}$$

As in the context-free recommendation model (Section 3.1), we employed the SGD method to learn the DSCM's model parameters (b^* and p^*). However, as suggested by [7], given the higher complexity of DSCM's model here we split the learning process in two sequential phases: firstly, we learn the global contextual biases and static user's preferences independently, and then, we learn the preference-specific contextual biases fixing the global ones. An extended discussion of the implemented user profile learning process can be found in [4].

4 Offline Evaluation

4.1 In-Context Rating Data Collection

To evaluate the effectiveness of the proposed context-aware recommendation approaches in the journey planning domain from a system-centric perspective, we first had to collect a data set of in-context user ratings for a variety of journey plans. To this aim, and based on the methodology presented in [2], we designed a web-based application in which users could make journey plan requests under imaginary contexts and rate them. Figure 1 shows the user interface design of this application. On the top-left corner there are the fields to specify the origin and destination locations, and at the bottom there is the context selection panel where users can specify the current contextual situation.

Based on the knowledge of mobility experts we identified 10 contextual factors as relevant in this domain: 2 user-specific factors, *companionship* and *purpose of journey*, and 8 environmental-based factors (*time of day*, *weather*, *temperature*, *crowdedness*, *illumination*, *moisture*, *pollution* and *pollen* concentrations). The selected conditions are shown by an icon that represents it and, disabled or *unknown* factors are represented by a question mark icon. For example, in Figure 1 there are 5 enabled factors, which describe the following contextual situation: traveling alone, sunny day, high pollution, and high pollen concentration. By default, a set of contextual conditions was randomly picked. Initially, 2 factors at most were enabled to simplify the process. This constraint was gradually relaxed after some provided ratings. Once selected the context and the destination point, the user could request a plan by clicking the *Plan Journey* button. In response, the journey planner generated a non-personalized list of journey plans each of them using a different transport mode combination. Users were asked to analyze and evaluate all the suggested plans. Each suggestion was accompanied by a detailed explanation of the proposed journey plan, and users were able to vote them using a 5-star scale. We also remarked users to rate the journey plans taking into consideration the "active" contextual situation.

Fig. 1. In-context rating acquisition user interface

This experiment lasted one week, and we collected a total of 3256 ratings given by 68 users to 1628 journey plans in 736 different in-context journey plan queries. The set of participants was composed by 40% women and 60% men living in Barcelona (Spain) at the time of the experiment. Each user provided 48 ratings on average.

4.2 Experimental Results

We measured the accuracy of the recommendation models in terms of rating prediction accuracy calculating the Root Mean Square Error (RMSE) on a test set built from the collected journey plan rating data set. To build the training and test sets we used a variant of the *all-but-n* [16] splitting method, where for each user we randomly selected a small portion of her ratings for testing. Based on the design of our in-context rating acquisition application (see previous section), we did not select the ratings individually but in terms of requests (*i.e.*, considering all the ratings given under a particular request and context). For each user we selected the ratings of 2 requests at most, equivalent to 10 test ratings on average. We calculated the statistical significance of RMSE differences by means of the Wilcoxon sign rank test.

The experimental results demonstrate that both context-aware strategies, *DSPF* and *DSCM*, clearly outperform the context-free baseline, whose absolute error is 1.27. Particularly, *DSCM*'s RMSE is 1.09 (reducing by 14% the error with p-value=.002) and *DSPF*'s RMSE is 1.15 (9% reduction with p-value=.008). Based on these results it seems that *DSCM* outperforms *DSPF*; however, their per-user RMSE differences are not statistically significant at the 95% confidence level (p-value=.25). Therefore, we were not able to validate that *DSCM* is the best performing strategy just with this offline study.

5 User-Centric Evaluation

5.1 Experiment Methodology

In order to validate the apparent superiority of DSCM shown in the offline study, we conducted a controlled experiment with a different set of users. They were asked to evaluate the quality of the context-dependent journey plan recommendations in real scenarios, that is, under real contexts while travelling around the city. To this aim, we integrated the proposed recommendation strategies into an existing journey planning mobile application, which implemented a sophisticated multi-modal planner based on modified Dijkstras and A* search algorithms on top of generalized time-dependent graphs [9].

Figure 2 illustrates some screenshots of the application's user interface, which allowed users to set the origin and destination points as well as the user-specific contextual factors; the environmental factors were captured from the available city sensors (Section 4.1 shows the complete list of contextual factors). Finally, the best journey plan candidates were presented to the mobile users as a ranking sorted by predicted user's rating.

The experiment was based on A/B testing, in which users are randomly split in groups using different configurations of the functionality being evaluated. Particularly, we divided participants in 3 groups, each using one of the approaches evaluated in the offline experiment: the context-free baseline, *DSPF* and *DSCM*. The experiment was divided in two phases of 1 week long each:

- **Phase 1**. The goal of this phase was two-fold: (1) to bootstrap the recommendation model by collecting an initial set of users' ratings; (2) to let users experiment with a version of the system with limited personalization capabilities. During this phase all the users received recommendations based only on their user transport preferences (explicitly provided during user's registration). In particular, given a candidate journey plan, a rating estimation was generated as the summation of interest scores in each journey's

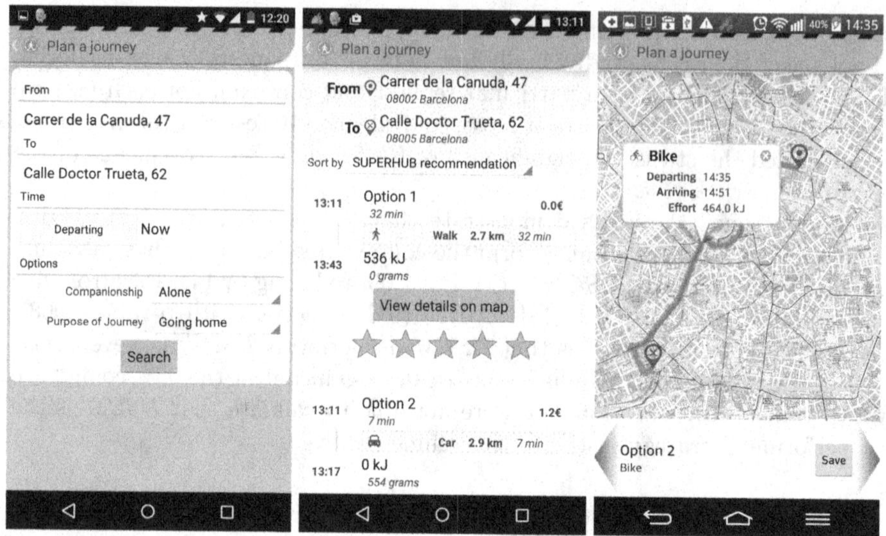

Fig. 2. In-context journey plan request (left), recommendation list (center) and map view (right) of the mobile app user interface

transport mode weighted according to the mode's time percentage. Users were asked to rate the recommended rankings.

– **Phase 2.** We used the collected ratings during the first week for building the context-free and context-aware recommendation models as well as for hyper-parameter fine-tuning. At the beginning of this phase we communicated to the users that a new version of the mobile app, with more sophisticated context-aware recommendation functionality, was available. We also asked them to use the app again under at least six different contextual situations so users could fairly evaluate the effect of context-dependent recommendations. In this phase each user received recommendations generated by the prediction model corresponding to her group. Once the task was completed, users were asked to fill out a questionnaire to evaluate the quality of recommendations across 4 different aspects, as shown in Table 1.

Table 1. User study questionnaire across 4 different quality aspects

Top-n accuracy (TA)	The suggested routes fitted my preferences
Ranking accuracy (RA)	The suggested routes were ranked according to my preferences
Context-awareness (CA)	The suggested routes were adapted to my travel context
Overall satisfaction (OS)	The new recommendation service helped me to find better routes

5.2 Results and Discussion

Figure 3 shows the evaluation scores given by the 67 users that completed the experiment. Users were able to express agreement or disagreement with

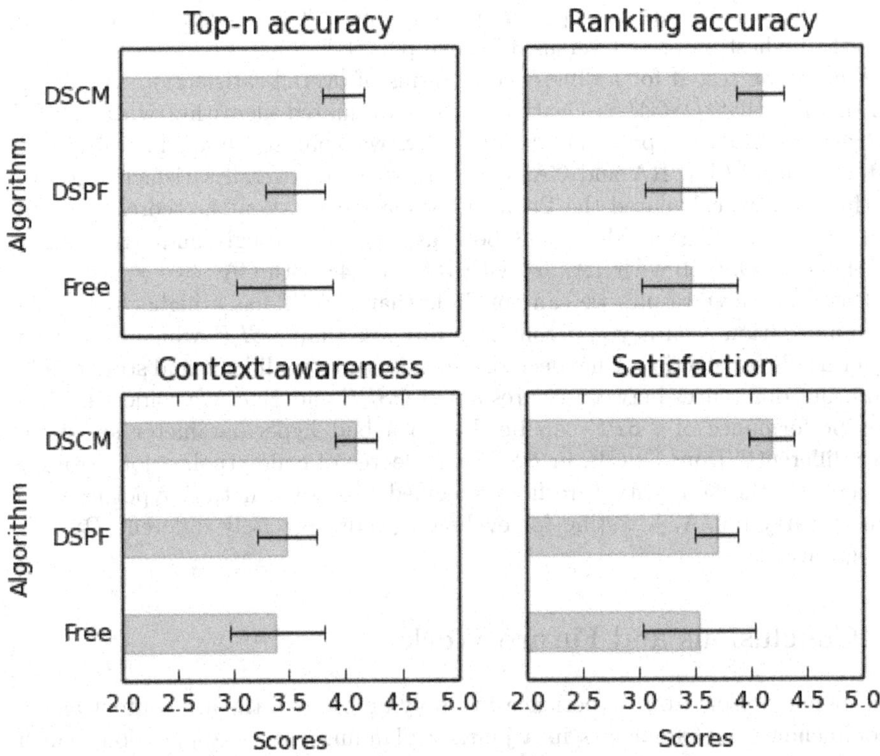

Fig. 3. User study results

the 4 statements on a five-point scale (where 1=*strongly disagree*, 2=*disagree*, 3=*neigher agree nor disagree*, 4=*agree*, and 5=*strongly agree*). Bar charts show the mean score value given by each users' group: *Free* (the context-free baseline), *DSPF*, and *DSCM*, to the four analyzed aspects. The error bar represents the 95% confidence interval. As significance test here we used the Welch's t-test, which is more appropriate for *between-user* studies.

Due to the limited amount of data in our study we followed the pragmatic user-centric evaluation framework presented in [6], where t-tests and simple correlations between the evaluated aspects are used to evaluate the effect of the proposed context-aware strategies on the user experience.

We firstly tested whether users of the three algorithms judge the recommendation accuracy differently. The results showed that the algorithm with the highest mean response for the accuracy statements is *DSCM*. For example, in terms of RA, *DSCM* obtained a 4.1 mean score compared to the 3.4 and 3.5 scores of *DSPF* and *Free*, respectively. The t-tests showed that this superiority is statistically significant (p=.005 w.r.t. *DSPF* and p=.05 w.r.t. *Free*).

Then we tested whether users perceive algorithm's CA differently. Comparing the context-aware strategies, one can observe that *DSCM* is again the algorithm with the highest score (4.1 versus 3.5, with p=.004).

Finally, we tested for a difference in terms of overall satisfaction. Again we can observe that *DSCM* is clearly the best evaluated algorithm w.r.t. *DSPF* (4.2 versus 3.7, with p=.007). Additionally, we analyzed how the subjective system aspects (TA, RA and CA) correlate with the overall satisfaction (OS). To this aim, we calculated the Pearson correlation between the scores given to each aspect. The results show that both aspects are strongly and significantly correlated to OS: .50 with TA, .51 with RA and .48 with CA.

Based on these results we can conclude that *DSCM* has a higher perceived recommendation accuracy and context-awareness than *DSPF*, which leads to a higher user's satisfaction. Unexpectedly, in this study we did not find statistically significant differences between the results of *DSPF* and *Free*. We conjecture this poor performance of *DSPF* can be due to a bad hyper-parameter selection, since differently from *DSCM*, in *DSPF* the degree of contextualization strongly depends on the similarity threshold specified. To confirm this hypothesis we plan to carry out A/A testing for evaluating more precisely different *DSPF*'s configurations.

6 Conclusions and Future Work

This paper presents our experience in applying state-of-the-art context-aware recommendation technologies in a journey planning mobile application, which dynamically generates multi-modal journey plans when requested, in order to provide users with personalized and context-dependent journey plan suggestions. To this aim, we have developed and evaluated two different context-aware recommendation strategies: (1) a sophisticated reduction-based pre-filtering method that exploits finer-grained situation-to-situation similarities to build local content-based prediction models optimized for the target context; and (2) a contextual modeling method that extends a linear content-based model with additional parameters able to capture the context-variability of user's preferences as well as global periodic effects. We have presented an extensive performance comparison of the proposed strategies combining offline with user-centric experiments, showing that the contextual modeling strategy is the best performing strategy.

In the current journey planning prototype, the context-aware recommendation strategies are applied at the end of the plan generation process for ranking. In future versions we want to investigate the effectiveness of the proposed strategies when applied during the construction of the plans. We conjecture that in this way the recommender can have a major impact and also help to speed up the plan generation process by incrementally reducing the search space.

Acknowledgments. This work has been supported by the FP7 IP Project SUPERHUB, funded by the European Comission (FP7-ICT-2011-7 ICT-2011.6.6, no.

289067).The authors want to specially acknowledge the Catalan Agency of Innovation and Internationalization (ACCIÓ) for their research support.

References

1. Adomavicius, G., Mobasher, B., Ricci, F., Tuzhilin, A.: Context-aware recommender systems. AI Magazine **32**(3), 67–80 (2011)
2. Baltrunas, L., Ludwig, B., Peer, S., Ricci, F.: Context relevance assessment and exploitation in mobile recommender systems. Personal and Ubiquitous Computing **16**(5), 507–526 (2012)
3. Campos, P.G., Fernández-Tobías, I., Cantador, I., Díez, F.: Context-aware movie recommendations: an empirical comparison of pre-filtering, post-filtering and contextual modeling approaches. In: Huemer, C., Lops, P. (eds.) EC-Web 2013. LNBIP, vol. 152, pp. 137–149. Springer, Heidelberg (2013)
4. Codina, V., Oliva, L.: Contextual modeling content-based approaches for new-item recommendation. In: IIiX 2014, pp. 259–262. ACM (2014)
5. Codina, V., Ricci, F., Ceccaroni, L.: Distributional semantic pre-filtering in context-aware recommender systems. User Model User-Adapt. Interact. Springer (2015). doi:10.1145/2542668
6. Knijnenburg, B.P., Willemsen, M.C., Kobsa, A.: A pragmatic procedure to support the user-centric evaluation of recommender systems. In: RecSys 2011, pp. 321–324 (2011)
7. Koenigstein, N., Dror, G., Koren, Y.: Yahoo! music recommendations: modeling music ratings with temporal dynamics and item taxonomy. In: RecSys 2011, pp. 165–172. ACM (2011)
8. Koren, Y., Bell, R.: Advances in collaborative filtering. In: Recommender Systems Handbook, pp. 145–186. Springer (2011)
9. Hrncir, J., Jakob, M.: Generalised time-dependent graphs for fully multimodal journey planning. In: Proceedings of IEEE Intelligent Transportation Systems Conference (ITSC), pp. 2138–2145 (2013)
10. Hsieh, H.-P., Li, C.-T., Lin, S.-D.: Measuring and Recommending Time-Sensitive Routes from Location-Based Data. ACM Transactions on Intelligent Systems and Technology **5**(3), 1–27 (2014)
11. Musto, C., Semeraro, G., Lops, P., de Gemmis, M.: Combining distributional semantics and entity linking for context-aware content-based recommendation. In: Dimitrova, V., Kuflik, T., Chin, D., Ricci, F., Dolog, P., Houben, G.-J. (eds.) UMAP 2014. LNCS, vol. 8538, pp. 381–392. Springer, Heidelberg (2014)
12. Nguyen, T., Wu, B.: Random and Fuzzy Sets in Coarse Data Analysis. Comput. Stat. Data Anal. **51**(1), 70–85 (2006). Elsevier Science Publishers B.V
13. Panniello, U., Tuzhilin, A., Gorgoglione, M., Palmisano, C., Pedone, A.: Comparing context-aware recommender systems in terms of accuracy and diversity. User Model User-Adapt. Interact. **24**(1–2), 35–65 (2014)
14. Ricci, F.: Travel recommender systems. IEEE Intelligent Systems **17**(6), 55–57 (2002)
15. Ricci, F., Rokach, L., Shapira, B.: Introduction to recommender systems. In: Recommender Systems Handbook, pp. 1–35. Springer (2011)
16. Shani, G., Gunawardana, A.: Evaluating recommendation systems. Recommender Systems Handbook, pp. 257–297. Springer (2011)
17. Tumas, G., Ricci, F.: Personalized mobile city transport advisory system. In: Information and Communication Technologies in Tourism, pp. 173–183. Springer (2009)

MOOClm: User Modelling for MOOCs

Ronny Cook[(✉)], Judy Kay, and Bob Kummerfeld

School of Information Technology, University of Sydney,
Sydney, NSW 2006, Australia
{ronald.cook,judy.kay,bob.kummerfeld}@sydney.edu.au
http://chai.it.usyd.edu.au/

Abstract. Emerging MOOC platforms capture huge amounts of learner data. This paper presents our MOOClm platform, for transforming data from MOOCs into independent learner models that can drive personalisation and support reuse of the learner model, for example in an Open Learner Model (OLM). We describe the MOOClm architecture and demonstrate how we have used it to build OLMs.

Keywords: MOOCs · Learner modelling · Open Learner Modelling (OLM) · Learner model server

1 Introduction and Background

MOOCs (Massively Open Online Courses) are based on platforms designed for teaching on a massive scale. These can support SPOCs, Small Private Online Courses [Fox, 2013] and MOOClets [Williams, 2014] which teach one topic. These platforms log learner activity extensively. Our MOOClm platform has been designed to harness this data by transforming it into an independent learner model. This means that the model can be reused in other learning systems. We illustrate one such use, in an Open Learner Model (OLM) interface [Bull and Kay, 2010]. This offers promise of the demonstrated benefits of OLMs [Bull and Kay, 2013; Mitrović and Martin, 2002]. It may also help address the problem of high dropout rates in MOOCs [Kizilcec et al., 2013]. Drawing on studies of learner preferences for OLMs [Bull, 2012] and the potential to support metacognitive processes [Bull and Kay, 2013], we designed the learner model and OLM to enable a learner (or other stakeholder, such as a mentor or teacher) answer the following questions:

1. **Overview:** What is the overall progress of this student on the learning activities?
2. **On-track:** In which learning objectives has the learner met the teacher expectations?
3. **Behind:** In which learning objectives are they lagging behind expectations?
4. **Activity-Type-Progress:** What are the answers to Q2-3 for a particular class of activity (video, exercise, discussions....)
5. **Act:** How can the student find learning resources associated with any given learning outcome?

F. Ricci et al. (Eds.): UMAP 2015, LNCS 9146, pp. 80–91, 2015.
DOI: 10.1007/978-3-319-20267-9_7

Current MOOCs store detailed logs for use of learning resources and performance on assessment tasks. There has been work towards standards for such data, for example MOOCdb [Veeramachaneni et al., 2013] and the eXperience API (aka Tin Can) [Mueller et al., 2014]. A recent review of analytics for major MOOC platforms [Muñoz-Merino et al., 2015] concludes they are rudimentary and they do not address our questions. Some MOOCs have analytics that partially answer Q1 and 4; for example Khan Academy's math course has a skillometer for fine-grained skills and badges for coarse grained ones. MOOClm moves beyond these to create a learner model of the course *learning objectives.* This is an independent learner model server [Brusilovsky et al., 2005; Kay et al., 2002].

2 Related Work

MOOCs (Massively Open Online Courses) are defined by the goal to deliver high quality tertiary level courses to thousands of students, at low per-student cost. They are characterised by online video lectures for delivery of content and support for low cost formative assessment based on self-assessment exercises, online discussion forums and peer review tools [Breslow et al., 2013; Kay et al., 2013]. MOOC platforms have also been used for SPOCs (Small Private Online Courses) [Fox, 2013] where they have been used very effectively for blended learning [Waldrop, 2014].

High budget MOOCs draw upon considerable expertise in learning design. This makes use of careful curriculum design, including careful definition of the learning objectives. Some MOOCs, notably some Khan Academy courses, make the learning objectives and individual progress in them available to the learner, in forms of skill-meter like displays and badges [Thompson, 2011]. However, there has been no report of a systematic approach to curriculum mapping to define MOOC curricula and inform the design of the MOOC. This is in stark contrast to the widespread practice in K-12 education [Jacobs, 1997, 2004] where the curriculum as seen as a work-in-progress, with the curriculum designer refining it to ensure that the actual learning materials match the intended learning goals.

For the purposes of this mapping, we define *learning objectives* as what the curriculum is intended to teach and we link these to the *learning objects.* Curriculum mapping distinguishes those learning objectives that are *taught* (as in video lectures) and those that are *assessed.* The latter are critical for evaluating the effectiveness of the curriculum as they can provide evidence of the learning outcomes actually achieved by learners. Gluga's ProGoSs [Gluga et al., 2012, 2013] provided a platform for systematic curriculum mapping, and it completes the loop by linking summative assessment data into the system.

Open Learner Models (OLMs) make the system's model of the learner knowledge and characteristics available to the student [Bull and Kay, 2010]. They vary markedly, with their design driven by the particular purposes of the OLM [Bull and Kay, 2007]. They have been primarily designed for use by learners, to support reflection, planning and seeing progress. A key challenge for the design of an OLM is to create a suitable interface. Some key examples are INGRID

[Conejo et al., 2012] a public tool for visualising learner models and the extensive work of Susan Bull and colleagues, such as their "OLMlets" [Bull et al., 2008]. Our work aims to create a OLM, and associated underlying learner model, that is for use by the MOOC curriculum designer.

3 MOOClm Architecture for the Open edX Platform

Figure 1 gives an overview of the MOOClm architecture. At the left is the MOOC platform, the Open edX platform. This is widely used and open source. This was the reason it was chosen for our SPOC on *C and Unix*. The right of the figure shows the MOOClm server. We now explain its design, in terms of the underlying ontology and the approach to representing the elements needed for a OLM that could enable learners to answer the questions described above.

A key first step in designing the learner model was to create the ontology, or namespace, for the model. To make this systematic, we build upon the standard learning design practice which defines the *intended learning outcomes* for a course. These form a hierarchy, with more general learning objectives being refined as a set of detailed learning objectives.

As our SPOC was a core area of computer science, we started the process of defining the learning objectives by drawing upon those defined in the ACM CS2013 curriculum [ACM Joint Task Force, 2013]. Our approach is similar to ProGoSs [Gluga et al., 2012] with its interface for teachers to define their course in terms of its intended learning objectives, taking foundations from a standard curriculum. This also similar to the approach in [Apted et al., 2004] where an authoritative resource, such as an online dictionary, can be mined to create a base set of key terms that can be used as learning objectives. It is desirable to build from a standard set of learning objectives since that facilitates learner model reuse, across MOOCs and other learning platforms and towards a lifelong learner model [Kay, 2008].

In addition to the standard learning objectives, we found that additional objectives were needed if we were to provide useful answers to our core OLM questions. This happened also in the work of Apted et al. [Apted et al., 2004] where the teacher needed to add local specialised terms, where there were multiple synonyms in wide use, and there the course structure made use of additional concepts. In the case of MOOClm , we needed to augment the ACM CS2013 curriculum because it is lacks the fine grained detail that is relevant for a learner who needs to track their progress in the important MOOC concepts. For example, the ACM CS2013 curriculum has a single learning objective for a collection of several data structures; but the focus of key lectures and exercises in our SPOC were specifically about C linked lists. In addition, the ACM CS2013 curriculum is language agnostic but our students see the subject in terms of the language used in the teaching. To make the OLM ontology meaningful, we need to augment the ACM CS2013 curriculum with these concepts. While this compromises the potential reuse of the learner model across MOOCs/SPOCs, it is essential.

Figure 1 shows how MOOClm augments the MOOC. We will illustrate this with an example of a student 'Alice" tackling a set of learning objectives on C pointers. facilitate re-use of the model in other contexts. [Kay, 2008] She views a video and then does the first three self-test exercises in a set.

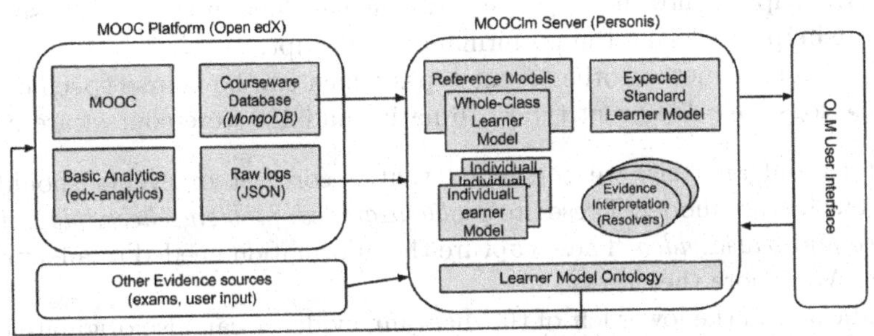

Fig. 1. MOOClm Architecture

First, consider the MOOC platform on the left of the figure. The top left box represents the MOOC interface the users see. Below this is the basic analytics tools. At the upper right, we show the MongoDB "Courseware" database of all learning resources and references, including text for exercises and YouTube references for videos. At the lower right is the raw logs of date-stamped events stored in JSON format. The most recent response for each problem is in the analytics database; the JSON logs have the full history.

The logs are comprehensive but need care to transform into a learner model. For example, when Alice views the video, this is logged as a *load_video* event when the page is opened, then several *play_video* events at two minute intervals until the video finishes. When Alice does an exercise, edX logs a *problem_check* event from browser to server, a *problem_check* event internal to the server, then a *problem_graded* request from server to browser which gives the result. Only the *problem_graded* event indicates if the submission was correct.

We illustrate some event types to indicate challenge in designing MOOClm :

play_video : occurs at a timestamped start of play, then every two minutes.

seek_video : is when the student skips back or forward while playing the video. This indicates more active interaction than *play_video.*

load_video : indicates that the static opening frame video is being shown on a page. Of negligible interest.

pause_video : indicates that the video has been paused. When play is resumed, a *play_video* event is logged.

problem_check : occurs when the learner submits a short-answer question. This event is always followed by *problem_graded.* A *problem_check* event may or may not also include whether the submitted answer is correct.

problem_graded : is an internal entry, logged when edX checks a submitted problem. Unfortunately the result is not clearly logged as correct or incorrect - instead the HTML for the generated result is logged and this must be parsed to determine the result.

load_document : is for document download - e.g. PDF the slides used in a video.

show_transcript : Show how well the student has done in the MOOC so far.

hide_transcript : Closing the performance transcript.

Others : covers numerous other event types which can be course specific. Our system logs have 474 event types, 16 native and 458 were courseware links.

After careful analysis, we concluded that a core set of events should be used for our learner model. These are *problem_graded*, *problem_check*, *play_video*, *seek_video* and *pause_video*. These capture the information needed to answer our questions. We ignore the others.

As indicated in the lower left of the diagram, evidence can also originate from external sources, such as examinations or other MOOCs. Any such evidence must also be interpreted in light of relevant learning objectives.

We now explain how the log data is treated as evidence in the learner model, on the right of the diagram. This transformation required several design decisions. This process unifies our learner model ontology of *learning objectives* with the raw MOOC data. The log entries use edX's internal courseware ID for learning materials such as video and exercises. To process the JSON log files, this ID is checked against the courseware database, mapping it to a human-readable form, for example:

```
2014-05-19T09:58:46.369909+00:00 COMP2129 RonnyCook2 problem_check Operating Systems and Machine Principles/Week 2/C Aggregates and Pointers/Scope quiz/Multiple Choice #2 (correct);
```

The source line from the log here is about half a page; we omit it for brevity. Pardos et al [Pardos and Kao, 2015] have more recently done useful work in standardising the edX logs as part of a larger work.

Alice's events show that she viewed the Week 2 "Pointers" video and answered the first three exercises. These events are then cross-checked against our MOOClm mapping of *learning objectives* for each learning object. Video events are recorded as evidence if part of the individual event occurs within the time interval when that learning objective was taught.

In our example, as Alice watched the introductory material explaining pointers, we transform the associated log data to a series of *play_video* evidence items in part of the learner model for C and the learning objective: *"Understands how to use the $*$, & and $->$ C operators to reference and dereference pointers"* in the C language portion of the model. The exercises *problem_graded* events also contribute to the same learning objective. A single MOOC resource may be associated with multiple learning outcomes; in this instance, the same material is associated with the learning objective: *Understands the nature and use of C pointers.*

The end result of this process is a collection of evidence events for each learning objective. The next step is to draw conclusions from this evidence about what the student knows. For this, Personis supports creation of interpretive elements called "*Resolvers*". MOOClm provides several of these. Each Resolver examines the evidence for and against for each learning outcome and draws a conclusion about the "knowledge level" of a learning objective. One very simple resolver, "Optimistic" treats a learning objective as known if there is any positive evidence for it. A more useful resolver compares the evidence for this learner against the model shown in the figure as the "expected standard". This indicates the expected evidence available for a learner who has completed all the materials that the teacher had expected for this time in the course.

In this fashion we create a set of "reference models" against which the student can compare their own performance. This set can include models belonging to other students. The specific reference models we build included:

- A complete reference model, as outlined above, populated with evidence for all recorded learner outcomes.
- A model covering all learning objectives covered by the MOOC, as an overview of the student's use of the MOOC.
- Three models covering: just the material taught in videos; just the material tested in exercises; and just the material tested in the exam. These facilitate seeing in which parts of the course the student participated, and in seeing how coverage by the different teaching and assessment mechanisms overlap.
- A model showing the material taught by the MOOC up until week 4, to check whether students had progressed beyond this point in the MOOC.
- A model covering all learning objectives in the ACM CS2013 curriculum, as a guide to the level of overlap between MOOC materials and the ACM curriculum
- a model showing all learning objectives *not* in the ACM curriculum, to check how much of students are learning is additive to ACM learner outcomes.

In service of interpreting the OLM, we built a simple interface based on the "pack" visualisation in the Javascript D3 library. This interface permits comparing different OLMs, applying a structure/visibility filter, and selection of the preferred resolver and timestamp.

The MOOC's use of the OLM is subject to some restrictions due to cross-site scripting protections in many browsers. This limits embedding of javascript into HTML sources which may wish to connect to the OLM API directly. Instead, we use a CGI script which consults the OLM before selecting appropriate text. Use of a web service is another possible approach.

The approach used here has some marked similarities to CUMULATE [Brusilovsky et al., 2005] but also several important differences. Where CUMULATE breaks down material by topic, MOOClm attempts to approach atomicity in its learning objectives, so that differently structured courses covering similar material can be compared. MOOClm integrates the evidence store with its user models rather than using a separate store, making migration easier. The Personis resolvers used by MOOClm are very similar in function to the inference agents used by CUMULATE, but there is a greater emphasis on student feedback for the model to ensure accuracy rather than a strict reliance on observed student activities.

Some elements of our visualisation interface, particularly the overlay and filtering facilities, provide insights that can be obscured with the CUMULATE framework.

4 Validation

To validate the MOOClm framework, we implemented a learner model for a SPOC being run for a computer science course at the University of Sydney. Participation in the SPOC was voluntary; although students were expected to view all videos, access to the videos was not exclusively through the SPOC.

The SPOC consisted of 37 videos, which in turn were broken down into a total of 187 topic-specific segments, with 156 multiple-choice and short-answer self-assessment questions. We added evidence from the students' final exam, with 38 questions of which 32 were multiple-choice.

We identified 514 ties to our learning objectives in this material, with 170 distinct learning objectives assessed. The model as a whole consisted of 1105 learning objectives extracted from the ACM CS2013 curriculum, plus 171 supplementary objectives not addressed by the ACM curriculum but covered, directly or indirectly, in the SPOC course materials. Only 19 of the ACM course objectives were addressed in the course, as the ACM curriculum is largely language- and platform-agnostic whereas the material in the SPOC is specific to C and UNIX.

The SPOC had 345 participants, with 1753506 lines of edX logs collected, of which 814035 were classified as useful evidence by the criteria discussed earlier.

All examples here use the Optimistic ("any evidence is good evidence") resolver to interpret Alice's model.

Figure 2 shows a simple view of "Alice's" knowledge as represented in our OLM. This answers the first of our representative questions, giving a broad overview of the student's knowledge. Black dots represent "known" items; white dots are "unknown". The full (complete reference) ontology has been narrowed by a software filter in our viewer to show only those learner outcomes present in the MOOC; that is, it incorporates both ACM and "augmented" outcomes, but omits any outcome which is not present in the videos or self-assessment questions from the MOOC.

When Alice clicks on the circle at bottom right, she sees the *zoomed* view of the UNIX subtopic represented in figure 3. She can zoom in or out of the model freely, down to the level of individual learning objectives.

Figure 4 attempts to address our second and third questions by comparing Alice's performance against a sample benchmark for an "expected standard" student who has completed all MOOC material through to week 4. With this colour scheme, black shows items that are known and expected to be known, yellow shows outcomes that are expected to be known but which she does *not* know,

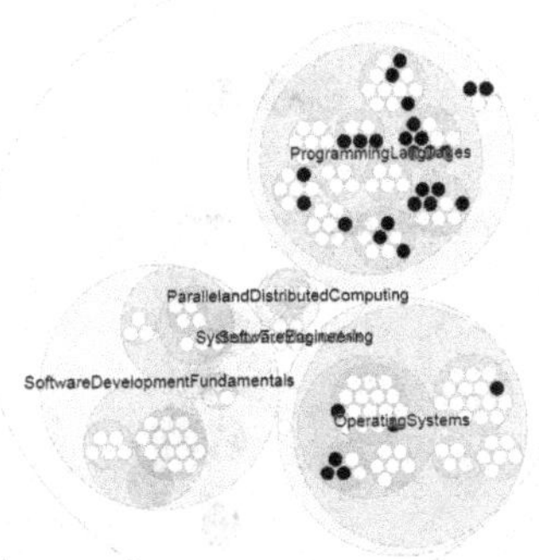

Fig. 2. Alice's OLM

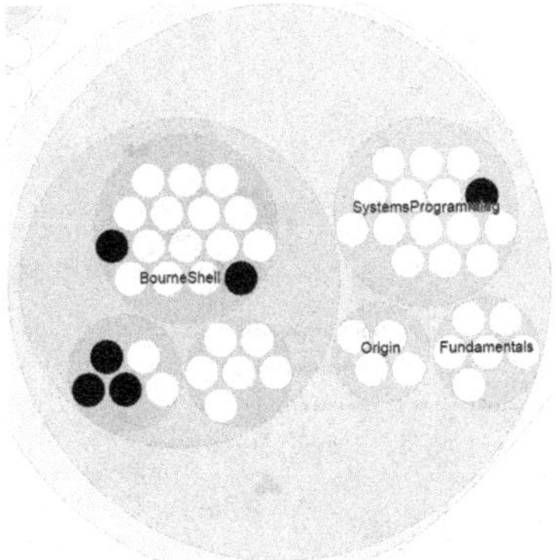

Fig. 3. Alice's OLM - Zoomed View

and the sole green dot, between the cluster of three black dots and the singleton at the bottom of the "ProgrammingLanguages" bubble, is where Alice knows something beyond the Week 4 material. Unfortunately the colour scheme does not show up well in black and white; green shows up as dark grey and yellow as very light grey.

Essentially, the yellow dots tell us where Alice is failing to meet expected performance as of week 4. The green dot tells us where she is exceeding expectations.

A similar view can be used to compare student performance against any of the reference models mentioned in section 2. Several colour schemes are available, to address colour-blindness issues and to lend emphasis to particular types of comparison.

Figure 5 answers an interesting compound question related to our earlier question 4: Of the learning objectives tested in the exam, how many have been taught by week 4 of the course? Of this set of exam-tested objectives, how well is Alice doing?

This is done by specifying a filter that only displays exam-tested results, then applying an overlay to compare our student against the set of outcomes tested by week 4 (the "week 4 curriculum").

The set involved is much smaller, since the exam can only test a small portion of the course. We see that the exam mostly tests objectives categorised under "ProgrammingLanguages", with remaining outcomes spread across "OperatingSystems" and "ParallelandDistributedComputing". The MOOC has by this time taught the material corresponding to learning outcomes for the yellow and black bubbles. Alice has learned one additional exam-related topic not covered by week 4.

In fact, comparing with figure 4 we can see that Alice has been very lucky. The former figure shows that there is a great deal of MOOC material up to week 4 of which Alice has not demonstrated knowledge. Figure 5 tells us that most of the material that Alice missed was not covered in the exam.

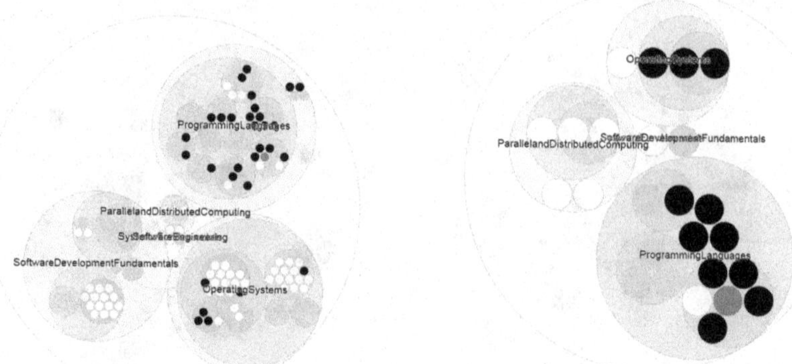

Fig. 4. Student performance against Week 4 complete reference model

Fig. 5. Student performance against Week 4 benchmark for exam-tested learning outcomes

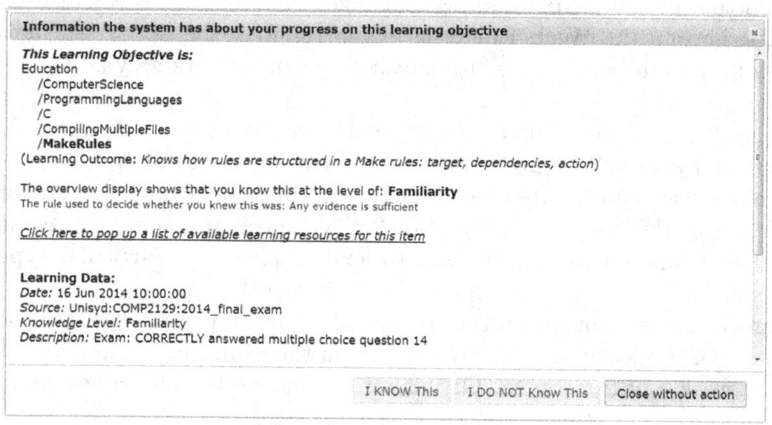

Fig. 6. Sample Evidence Snapshot

If we want to look at Alice's exam results in particular, ignoring MOOC evidence, we select a resolver that ignores MOOC evidence and only uses exam evidence. (As Alice did not participate in the final exam, the diagram showing this is quite boring.)

This viewpoint is also useful as a quick-and-dirty check that no particular part of the course was favoured in the exam. Figure 5 suggests that the UNIX-specific material may have been covered inadequately. On the other hand, it may be that the UNIX learning objectives are much more complex, so fewer individual objectives could be tested.

Figure 6 shows a snapshot of the detail for one particular learning outcome. The component's path in the model is shown, as well as a description, the resolved outcome, and a scrollable list of the evidence used to conclude this outcome. A link is also included to a list of reference resources that the student may follow for further learning on a specified topic, directly addressing our fifth foundational question.

The interface also offers the viewer an option to override or force a value for the component, inserting an evidence item specifying the value to be resolved. This allows the student to override the value for any learning outcome that they believe to be incorrect, in principle enhancing the reliability of the model. If there is a need to exclude such explicit changes, a suitable Resolver may be used.

The same view, used against the "expected standard" model, can be used to address our fifth question. Students can view the "expected standard" model to examine evidence stored for a particular learning objective and see which learning resources will assist them with any particular learning outcome.

The interface blocks any attempt to make changes to reference models.

5 Conclusion

We have demonstrated MOOClm as a uniform framework tying together MOOCs and Open Learner models to facilitate lifelong learner models.

Integration of target models for typical and "plausibly ideal" usage gives the student a guide to their present progress, while opening the model ensures that it remains accurate. By opening the aspirational models, complete with sample evidence, we also give the learner a guide to where they should target additional learning. The MOOC may also adapt its presentation to data in the OLM, ensuring a two-way data flow.

Our contribution is the end-to-end integration of curriculum design, MOOC course construction and OLM in an integrated, open framework which facilitates re-use and lifelong learning.

In future work, we intend to adapt the framework for easier use across multiple MOOCS. The model was designed with a standardised curriculum for this reason. Use as an integrating agent across multiple MOOCs and MOOClets [Williams, 2014] will allow students to take advantage of the best parts of each platform towards lifelong learning goals. Currently, Open edX has no facility to integrate specification of learning objectives against learning objects. A critical next step is to add this capability to edX. Importantly, we need to conduct user studies to evaluate and refine the interfaces and to gain insights into the ways that learners make use of the OLM.

Acknowledgments. This research was supported by funding from the Faculty of Engineering and Information Technologies, The University of Sydney, under the Faculty Research Cluster Program. The views expressed herein are those of the authors and are not necessarily those of the Faculty.

References

ACM Joint Task Force. Computer science curricula 2013: Curriculum guidelines for undergraduate degree programs in computer science. Technical report, Association for Computing Machinery (ACM) IEEE Computer Society (2013)

Apted, T., Kay, J., Lum, A.: Supporting metadata creation with an ontology built from an extensible dictionary. In: De Bra, P.M.E., Nejdl, W. (eds.) AH 2004. LNCS, vol. 3137, pp. 4–13. Springer, Heidelberg (2004)

Breslow, L., Pritchard, D.E., DeBoer, J., Stump, G.S., Ho, A.D., Seaton, D.: Studying learning in the worldwide classroom: Research into edX's first MOOC. Research & Practice in Assessment **8**, 13–25 (2013)

Brusilovsky, P., Sosnovsky, S., Shcherbinina, O.: User modeling in a distributed E-learning architecture. In: Ardissono, L., Brna, P., Mitrović, A. (eds.) UM 2005. LNCS (LNAI), vol. 3538, pp. 387–391. Springer, Heidelberg (2005)

Bull, S.: Preferred Features of Open Learner Models for University Students. In: Cerri, S.A., Clancey, W.J., Papadourakis, G., Panourgia, K. (eds.) ITS 2012. LNCS, vol. 7315, pp. 411–421. Springer, Heidelberg (2012)

Bull, S., Kay, J.: Student models that invite the learner in: The smili:() open learner modelling framework. Intl Journal of Artificial Intelligence in Education **17**(2), 89–120 (2007)

Bull, S., Kay, J.: Advances in Intelligent Tutoring Systems, chapter 15: Open learner models, pp. 301–322. Springer (2010)

Bull, S., Kay, J.: Open learner models as drivers for metacognitive processes. In: Intl Handbook of Metacognition and Learning Technologies, pp. 349–365. Springer (2013)

Bull, S., Mabbott, A., Gardner, P.H., Jackson, T., Lancaster, M.J., Quigley, S.F., Childs, P.A.: Supporting interaction preferences and recognition of misconceptions with independent open learner models. In: Nejdl, W., Kay, J., Pu, P., Herder, E. (eds.) AH 2008. LNCS, vol. 5149, pp. 62–72. Springer, Heidelberg (2008)

Conejo, R., Trella, M., Cruces, I., Garcia, R.: INGRID: a web service tool for hierarchical open learner model visualization. In: Ardissono, L., Kuflik, T. (eds.) UMAP Workshops 2011. LNCS, vol. 7138, pp. 406–409. Springer, Heidelberg (2012)

Fox, A.: From MOOCs to SPOCs. Commun. ACM **56**(12), 38–40 (2013)

Gluga, R., Kay, J., Lister, R.: Progoss: mastering the curriculum. In: Proceedings of The Australian Conference on Science and Mathematics Education (formerly UniServe Science Conference) (2012)

Gluga, R., Kay, J., Lister, R., Kleitman, S.: Mastering cognitive development theory in computer science education. Comput. Sci. Educ. **23**(1), 24–57 (2013)

Jacobs, H.H.: Mapping the Big Picture. Integrating Curriculum & Assessment K-12. ERIC (1997)

Jacobs, H.H.: Getting Results with Curriculum Mapping. ERIC (2004)

Kay, J.: Lifelong learner modeling for lifelong personalized pervasive learning. IEEE Transactions on Learning Technologies **1**(4), 215–228 (2008)

Kay, J., Kummerfeld, B., Lauder, P.: Personis: a server for user models. In: De Bra, P., Brusilovsky, P., Conejo, R. (eds.) AH 2002. LNCS, vol. 2347, pp. 203–212. Springer, Heidelberg (2002)

Kay, J., Reimann, P., Diebold, E., Kummerfeld, B.: MOOCs: So many learners, so much potential. IEEE Intell. Syst. **28**(3), 70–77 (2013)

Kizilcec, R.F., Piech, C., Schneider, E.: Deconstructing disengagement: analyzing learner subpopulations in massive open online courses. In: Proceedings of the 3rd Intl Conference on LAK, pp. 170–179 (2013)

Mitrović, A., Martin, B.: Evaluating the effects of open student models on learning. In: De Bra, P., Brusilovsky, P., Conejo, R. (eds.) AH 2002. LNCS, vol. 2347, pp. 296–305. Springer, Heidelberg (2002)

Mueller, N., Dikke, D., Dahrendorf, D.: Experience API vs SCORM-how xAPI benefits technology-enhanced learning. In: EDULEARN14 Proc., pp. 1276–1284 (2014)

Muñoz-Merino, P.J., Ruipérez, J.A., Sanz Moreno, J.L., Delgado Kloos, C.: Assessment activities in MOOCs (2015)

Pardos, Z.A., Kao, K.: moocrp: An open-source analytics platform. In: Proceedings of the Second (2015) ACM Conference on Learning @ Scale, L@S 2015, pp. 103–110. ACM, New York (2015)

Thompson, C.: How khan academy is changing the rules of education. Wired Magazine, vol. 126 (2011)

Veeramachaneni, K., Dernoncourt, F., Taylor, C., Pardos, Z., O'Reilly, U.-M.: MOOCdb: developing data standards for MOOC data science. In: Proceedings of the 1st Workshop on MOOCs at the 16th Annual Conference on AIED (2013)

Waldrop, M.M.: Massive open online courses, aka MOOCs, transform higher education and science (2014)

Williams, J.J., Li, N., Kim, J., Whitehill, J., Maldonado, S., Pechenizkiy, M., Chu, L., Heffernan, N.: The MOOClet framework: Improving online education through experimentation and personalization of modules. Social Science Research Network, November 12, 2014

Dynamic Approaches to Modeling Student Affect and Its Changing Role in Learning and Performance

Seth Corrigan[1(✉)], Tiffany Barkley[2], and Zachary Pardos [1,2]

[1] Graduate School of Education, University of California, Berkeley, CA 94720, USA
{sethcorrigan,pardos}@berkeley.edu
[2] School of Information, University of California, Berkeley, CA 94720, USA
tbarkley@ischool.berkeley.edu

Abstract. We investigate the relation between students' affect, learning and performance in the context of the ASSISTments online math tutoring system. Moment-by-moment estimates of students' affective states derived from a series of affect detectors accompany each student response within the tutoring system. By applying a series modified factorial hidden Markov models that account for students' affective state at the time of the given response and comparing the models' performance to the standard Bayesian Knowledge Tracing (BKT) approach, we evaluate the impact of affect on estimates of students' guess and slip behavior. The investigation suggests a model based approach to improving student models in the context of online tutoring systems.

Keywords: Knowledge tracing · Emotion · Affect · Learning · Performance · Hidden markov models · Factorial hidden markov models · Automated tutoring systems

1 Introduction

Major theories of emotion hypothesize a variety of relations between affect and cognition (D'Mello, 2011; Barrett, 2009; Frijda, 2009; Russell, 2003; Scherer, 2009). There have been promising efforts to investigate the proposed relations between affect, learning and performance. Notably, clear accounts have emerged in the fields of psychology, cognitive science and education (D'Mello, 2011; Picard, et. al., 2004). Where awareness of students' affective states impact learning and performance, developing a detailed understanding of the relationship will be important for advancing the design of responsive digital systems such as online tutoring systems (D'Mello, Craig, Gholsom, Franklin, Picard and Graesser, 2005; D'Mello, Craig, Witherspoon, McDaniel and Graesser, 2005; San Pedro, Baker, Gowda, and Hefferman, 2013). Making systems that are capable of accounting for users' affective states in their interactions stands to improve their ease-of-use and efficacy.

Several groups have had success in specifying and gathering empirical evidence for the relationship between affect, learning and performance. In each case, the focus has been on *academic emotions* (Pekrun, 2010; D'Mello, 2011; Pekrun and Linnenbrink-Garcia, 2012). Academic emotions are hypothesized to arise as a result of

F. Ricci et al. (Eds.): UMAP 2015, LNCS 9146, pp. 92–103, 2015.
DOI: 10.1007/978-3-319-20267-9_8

students' perception of their ability with regard to the demands of the given task and their evaluation of its utility. They can be divided into four types; achievement emotions, topic emotions, social emotions and epistemic emotions (Pekrun, 2010; D'Mello, 2011).

Achievement emotions and epistemic emotions are relevant for the current effort. Examples of achievement emotions include contentment, anxiety, boredom and frustration. Epistemic emotions result from processes associated with information processing. Examples of epistemic emotions include surprise and confusion. In general, academic emotions are hypothesized to impact problem solving strategies and engagement - the active, energetic, and approach-oriented involvement with academic tasks (Pekrun and Linnenbrink-Garcia, 2012). As a result they are also hypothesized to have an indirect, or mediating, effect on performance and learning. Concentration, frustration, boredom and confusion are the focus of the current study.

2 Previous Work

Full investigation of affect, learning and performance requires a modeling approach that is dynamic along three dimensions: dynamic with regard to students' changing affective states, changes in performance and changes in students' knowledge. Given these requirements, there exist several candidates for modeling relationships between student affect, learning, and performance.

2.1 Item Response Theory (IRT)

$$P(Y_i = Correct|\theta) = \frac{\exp(\theta - b_i)}{1 + \exp(\theta - b_i)}$$

Item response theory has a long tradition in educational assessment. The one-parameter, two-parameter, and three-parameter logistic versions of the item response model are most common. They each assume a single underlying ability. The simplest item response model estimates two parameters: the difficulty (b_i) parameter, an estimate of the difficulty of a given task in logits; and the person parameter (θ), an estimate of the given student's ability. What is required is a way to account for student affect when estimating person ability. The latent regression Rasch model (De Boeck and Wilson, 2004) supports such a decomposition of the person parameter and allows for a series of associated fixed effects, permitting investigation of properties.

Use of item response models poses a trade-off, however. Standard IRT approaches yield a single estimate of a student's static ability. While a dynamic item response has been specified (Verhelst and Glas, 1993), it is not widely used. And, to the authors' knowledge it does not yet have a form that would allow for changing covariates.

2.2 Dynamic Mixture-Item Response Model (DMM-IRM)

Dynamic mixture models pose an interesting alternative to more standard applications of IRT. Importantly, Johns and Woolf (2006) have specified a dynamic mixture model (DMM) that is based on item response theory and the hidden Markov model. Conveniently, it allows for person characteristics such as affect to change over time. As originally conceived, the latent variables in the model represent person ability (θ) and a single person characteristic (originally motivation (M_t)) that can also change over time. The DMM-IRM also has two observed variables for each time point. the student's initial response (Ui), or performance; and (Hi), which carries information about student behaviors indicative of their motivation (John and Woolf, 2006). A link between students' motivation (Mi) and their initial responses (Ui) allows one to model the impact of person characteristics on performance. The DMM-IRM has clear application in the current investigation but also treats student ability as static.

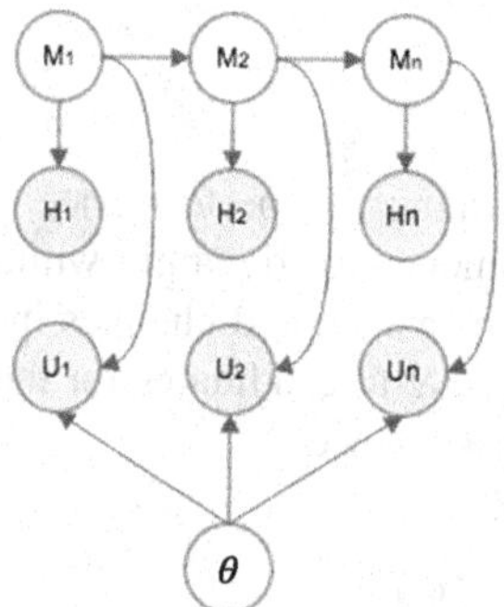

Fig. 1. A dynamic mixture model based on IRT (Johns and Wolf, 2006)

2.3 Bayesian Knowledge Tracing

The Bayesian Knowledge Tracing (BKT) approach poses an alternative. Knowledge tracing is based on work initially carried out by Atkinson (1972) and was made popular by Corbett and Anderson (1995) as an approach to modeling learning in the context of intelligent tutoring systems (Pardos and Heffernan, 2010). Knowledge tracing makes use of dynamic Bayesian networks. It is also appropriately identified as a Hidden Markov Model (Reye, 2004). In the education related literature, the model is used to estimate the probability a given student has the targeted knowledge, skill or ability at each time point of interest.

Knowledge tracing typically uses four parameters. Two parameters describe probabilities associated with student knowledge: Pr(Lo), the probability of already having the requisite knowledge before interaction with the tutor, and Pr(T), the probability of gaining the knowledge between responses. The probability of guessing (Pr(g)) is an estimate for the probability of succeeding on a task without having the requisite knowledge. Slip (Pr(s)) describes the probability of failing a task in spite of having the requisite knowledge.

3 Approach

For the current effort, we investigate the hypotheses that students' affective states impact performance in a univariate fashion. We accomplish this by designing and running a model for each affective state observed in the context of the ASSISTments online tutoring system using a modified factorial Hidden Markov Model, shown in figure 2 in comparison with the BKT standard HMM model form. We term this model 'modified' because while it is similar to the Factorial HMM it is not identical to it. In particular, the model does not condition affect at time t on the affect at an earlier point in time. What we are calling the modified factorial model can treat person properties and ability in a dynamic fashion while also allowing for relations between affect and student performance. The model has two observed nodes - one for student affect (Ai) and another for performance for each task, or question (Qi). Both are indexed by time (i). The model also has the typical guess and slip parameters associated with BKT.

Affect can be entered into the model as a dichotomous level variable where, 1 = present and 0 = absent for each of the target affective states. This is the simplest form of the model that would allow for investigation of the relationship between student affect and performance.

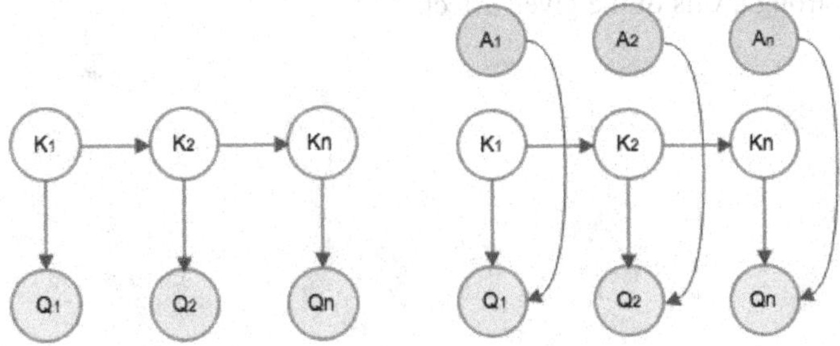

Fig. 2. HMM (left), and Modified Factorial HMM with Affect (right)

4 Data and Design

4.1 ASSISTments Tutor and Content

The ASSISTments platform (Pardos et al., 2013; San Pedro et. al. 2013) is a web-based tutoring system for mathematics instruction and assessment developed at Worcester Polytechnic Institute. It is targeted for use in grades seven through twelve. Students using the system complete a series of mathematics problems across subdomains that span the standards defined in the Massachusetts Comprehensive Assessment Systems and now the Common Core. The ASSISTments platform scores student responses and delivers feedback, hints and scaffolding in real time and provides detailed reporting about their performance to the student and their teacher. ASSISTments data used for the current work was generated during student use of the tutoring system.

4.2 ASSISTments Affect Data Collection Process

The affect data used for the current work was derived in three phases (Baker, D'Mello, Rodrigo, and Graesser, 2010). In Phase 1, students from two randomly chosen rural and urban classrooms were observed by trained researchers for relevant displays of affect and associated behavior. The aim was to record direct observations of student behavior and student-system interactions indicative of the four target states. There were a total of 3,075 field observations of 229 students by two observers. These observations served as a source of 'ground truth' for subsequent efforts to automate detection of student affect.

In Phase 2 the direct observations were used to generate and test a series of engineered features that now serve as evidence for claims about the affective state of subsequent ASSISTment users. Using the engineered features in Phase 3, a series of automated detectors were trained in ASSISTments in order to detect student affect at scale using patterns in student interactions with the ASSISTment system. This step allowed the researchers to make inferences about student affect that were not based directly on observations of students, but were instead based on the telemetry generated by students' interactions with the tutoring system. Use of the automated detectors results in an estimate ranging from zero to one for each affective state. Values of zero suggest exhibitions of very low levels of that particular affect, with values of one suggesting strong levels of the given affect.

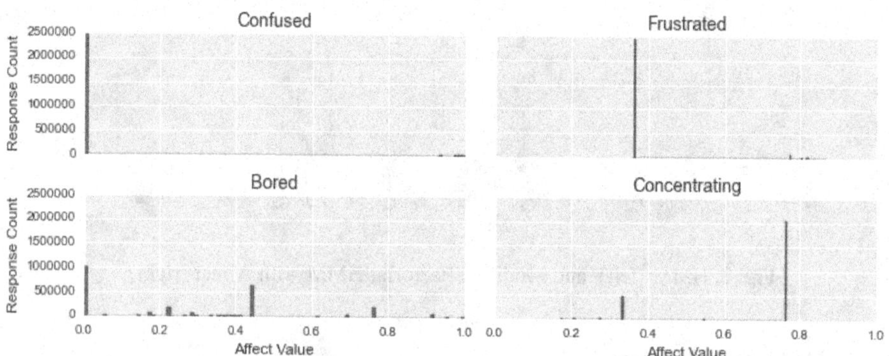

Fig. 3. Distribution of affect values on ASSISTments questions showing very low levels of confusion and frustration and higher levels of boredom and concentration

4.3 The Dataset

The ASSISTments dataset consists of 6.14 million rows from the 2012-2013 school year, each containing a record of a student's first response to a given question (1 for correct, 0 for incorrect), estimated boredom, frustration, concentration, and confusion probabilities for the student at the time of the question, the question start time, the question skill, and other associated metadata. The data includes responses from 48,730 unique students, each identified with a user id. Not all students completed all problems in the item bank. The distribution of affect values - measured from 0 to 1 - with 0 suggesting no experience of the particular affect, to a 1 in which there was a great amount of the affect) across student responses is shown in Figure 3.

4.4 Data Processing

Student responses were subdivided by skill (example skills include order of operations, using the Pythagorean theorem to find distances, and calculating the area of a surface or volume of a cube). At least 500 unique students had to have responded to at least one question of a particular skill type for that skill to be used in our analysis. Ultimately, the BKT and Modified-Factorial BKT models were applied to 145 out of 197 total skills. Only responses and affect values from within a 24-hour window of the student's first attempt at a problem of that skill type were included in the modeling, to avoid potential impacts of forgetting.

To simplify application of the project's models, each of the four student states (boredom, frustration, confusion, and concentration) was dichotomized to distinguish between students who did and did not exhibit the state during the given time point. For each affective state, the threshold of exhibiting an affective state was set at 0.7, which provided a clear dividing line in the data between students in the confused, frustrated, and concentrating categories, and a reasonable threshold for distinguishing bored students from not-bored students. Figure 4 shows for each skill, the percentage of responses in the sample dataset during which students exhibited that affect. The percentage of responses exhibiting confusion or frustration are very low and vary little by skill. A higher percentage of responses come from students exhibiting boredom, but there is little variation in the percentage of bored responses from skill to skill. The most variation across skills occurs with concentration where, in some skills, students are concentrating during nearly all responses, whereas in other skills, less than 40% of responses were made during concentration.

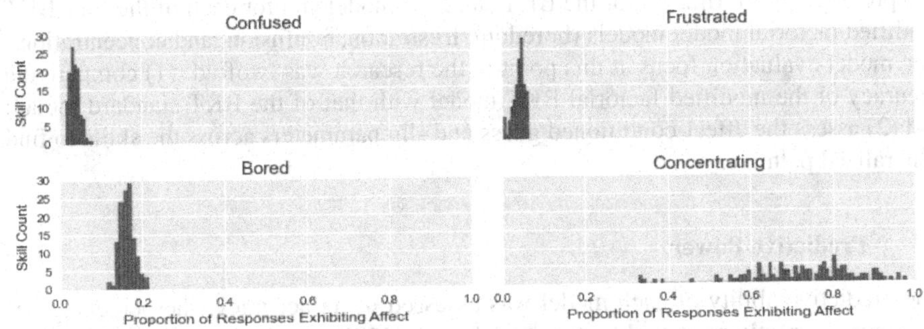

Fig. 4. Count of skills by the proportion of student responses exhibiting each affect

5 Methods

The target BKT models were applied using the Bayes Net Toolbox (BNT), an open-source MATLAB library developed by Kevin Murphy to perform Bayesian inference (Murphy, K. 2001). Specifically, the models were implemented using the Dynamic Bayesian Network (DBN) functionalities within the BNT toolbox. The DBN framework requires the specification of nodes and dependencies for the first and second time slices within a model, then allows for the dynamic extension of the model to additional time slices. In the case of the ASSISTments system, a time slice is dedicated to each student submission or response within the tutoring system. Observables included with each time slice includes the score for that response (correct or incorrect) in the case of the standard model. Observables included with each time slice of the augmented model include the estimated student affect at the given time point as well as the accuracy of the response for that same given time point.

The overall goal of the analysis was to compare the parameters and predictive accuracy of the standard BKT with those of an augmented version of the model that accounts for students' affective states - the modified factorial model discussed above. For each skill, one BKT standard model and four modified factorial models (one for each affective state) were parameterized and used to predict student responses. Five-fold cross validation was used to train and test each model.

For the modified factorial model, we had to decide whether to use the affect associated with a student's response to predict that same response, or whether to only use affect to predict the next and subsequent responses. Observations of affect and concentration used in this study were estimated in 20-second increments based on student interactions with the tutoring system, and then associated with particular questions. Given that affect may have been measured during a window primarily consisting of time immediately after a question response, the more conservative approach would be to use affect only to predict subsequent question responses. Results using both approaches are presented here.

6 Results

For each of the 145 evaluated skills, this effort yielded five sets of results: parameters and prediction performance for the BKT standard model and for each of the four BKT modified factorial model models (boredom, frustration, confusion, and concentration). The model evaluation focus at this point in the research was twofold: (1) compare the accuracy of the modified factorial BKT model with that of the BKT standard model; and (2) assess the affect-conditioned guess and slip parameters across the skills to find generalized patterns.

6.1 Predictive Power

The predictive ability of each model was assessed using accuracy (the percentage of responses correctly predicted by the model) and RMSE (where the error is the difference between the model's estimated probability of the actual response and the actual response). The measures for each model (BKT standard, BKT modified factorial using affect to predict the response at the subsequent timeslice, and BKT modified factorial using affect to predict the response at the current timeslice) are shown in Table 1. Results indicate that the modified factorial models do not offer any additional predictive power beyond BKT standard. One reason for this may be the lack of variability in the binary affective state measured across student responses.

A large number of skills have baseline accuracies exceeding 70%- in all cases, this meant that more than 70% of student responses were correct. Not only did many skills have more correct than incorrect responses; they also had a very high percentage of correct responses on a student's first attempt. This yielded a prior probability of knowledge (P(L0)) exceeding 50% for the majority of skills. The high priors for most skills explain the high correlation between modified factorial model accuracy and baseline accuracy when baseline accuracy exceeds 60%; in these cases, the high prior probability of knowledge causes the BKT model to predict a correct response for all or nearly all questions, making its predictions equivalent to the baseline case. The highlighted region in Figure 5 does suggest that the modified factorial models have some predictive power for skills that have a more even mix of correct and incorrect responses in the tutoring system, i.e. skills in which the majority of students do not begin the tutorial having already mastered the skill.

Table 1. Prediction Results

	Affect	Standard	Affect 1*	Affect 2*
Accuracy (%)	Bored	70.16	70.16	70.16
	Concentrating	70.16	70.14	70.14
	Confused	70.16	70.13	70.13
	Frustrated	70.16	70.17	70.17
RMSE	Bored	0.4473	0.4472	0.4471
	Concentrating	0.4473	0.4477	0.4390
	Confused	0.4473	0.4475	0.4459
	Frustrated	0.4473	0.4472	0.4461

Note: Affect 1 does not use affect measured during the response to predict that response. Affect 2 uses the affect measured during the response to predict that response.

The next question is whether the modified factorial models outperform standard BKT. For the ASSISTments data, in which our operationalized binary affective state values vary little by skill or student, it appears that incorporating affect does not improve prediction over standard BKT. Results from each of the four models are combined into the accuracy plot in Figure 5. For some skills, the modified factorial models provide better predictions over BKT standard, but there is no evidence to suggest that the modified factorial models systematically outperform the standard models.

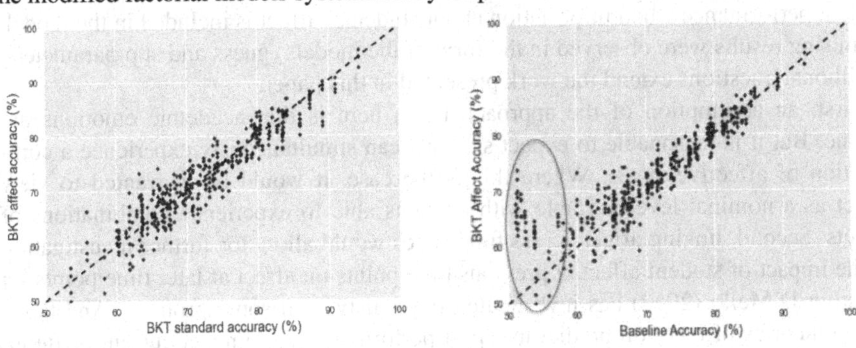

Fig. 5. Accuracy, modified factorial BKT vs. BKT standard (left) and vs. modified factorial BKT baseline (right); highlighted region where modified factorial BKT appears to outperform baseline accuracy

6.2 Affect Parameters

The BKT standard model emits four parameters: prior probability of knowledge $P(L_0)$, probability of learning P(T), probability of guess P(G), and probability of slip P(S). In the modified factorial model, learning, guess and slip are conditioned on the affective state, which generates six learn, guess and slip parameters: probability of learn given affect (eg, boredom), probability of learn given no affect (eg, no boredom), probability of guess given affect, probability of guess given no affect, probability of slip given affect, and probability of slip given no affect. Figure 6 shows, for learn, guess and slip (columns) and affect (rows), the comparison between the parameters when a given affect is observed versus not observed in a student.

As we would expect, the relationship between guess and slip given presence or absence of a given affect varies depending on the specific academic emotion (boredom, confusion, frustration, etc.) students are experiencing at the moment. Across skills, BKT model parameters suggest that bored students exhibit a higher probability of guessing than those who are not bored. For some skills, not concentrating leads to a much higher probability of guess than does concentrating. For frustration and confusion, there is a large amount of scatter in the guess given affect across the skills, possibly due to the infrequency of these affective states in the dataset. Among slip, the most marked relationship across skills is for concentration; not concentrating exhibits a much higher slip parameter than does concentrating.

7 Next Steps

Several forms of the Hidden Markov model utilize information about student affect in estimates of student knowledge, guess and slip behavior. Incorporating contextual features and person characteristics stands to improve the efficacy and realism of interactions with automated systems such as the ASSISSTments system. While the current investigation shows no overall difference in the accuracy of predictions of student performance when information about students' affect is included in the model, promising results were observed in the form of the models' guess and slip parameters. Additional questions extend the work presented in this paper.

First, an assumption of the approach taken here is that academic emotions are atomic. But it is reasonable to expect students can simultaneously experience a combination of affective states. Where this is the case, it would be warranted to view affect as a nominal level variable with students able to experience combinations of affects. Second, linking affect across time slices would allow for further investigation of the impact of student affect at previous time points on affect at later time points - a question D'Mello (2012) has investigated previously with some promise. And third, where theories of emotion predict that past performance can impact current or future affect, the models we use should reflect or at least support investigation of that possibility. This possibility can be investigated by using a modified HMM with cross linkages running from the performance node (Q) at time t to the affect node at time $(t+1)$. Treating affect as latent and using the model to predict affect given students' performance would allow investigation of how information about performance impacts students responding to the next task. More complex cross linkages would support a better understanding of how previous performances may shape or impact students' affective experiences.

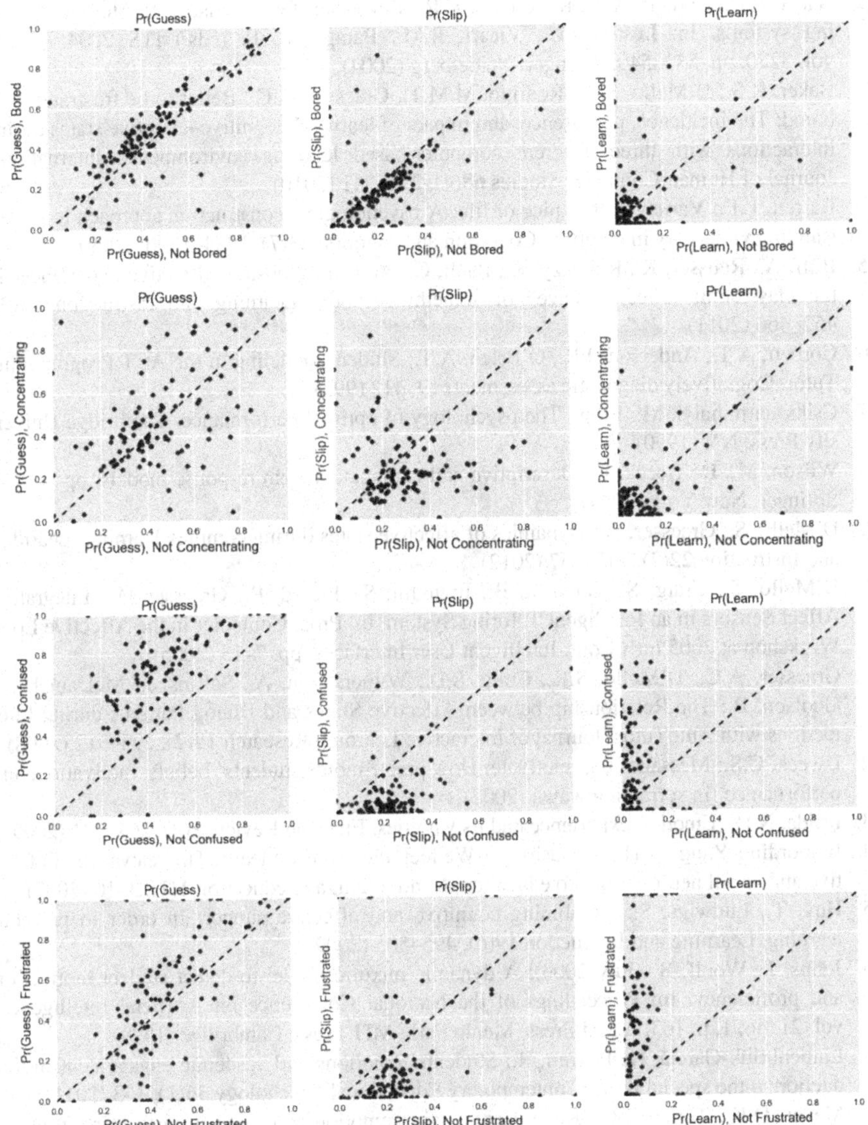

Fig. 6. Probability of guess and slip conditioned on affective state

References

1. Atkinson, R.C.: Ingredients for a theory of instruction. American Psychologist **27**(10), 921 (1972)
2. Baker, R.S., Corbett, A.T., Koedinger, K.R.: Detecting student misuse of intelligent tutoring systems. In: Lester, J.C., Vicari, R.M., Paraguaçu, F. (eds.) ITS 2004. LNCS, vol. 3220, pp. 531–540. Springer, Heidelberg (2004)
3. Baker, R.S., D'Mello, S.K., Rodrigo, M.M.T., Graesser, A.C.: Better to be frustrated than bored: The incidence, persistence, and impact of learners' cognitive–affective states during interactions with three different computer-based learning environments. International Journal of Human-Computer Studies **68**(4), 223–241 (2010)
4. Barrett, L.F.: Variety is the spice of life: A psychological construction approach to understanding variability in emotion. Cognition and Emotion **23**(7), 1284–1306 (2009)
5. Buff, A., Reusser, K., Rakoczy, K., Pauli, C.: Activating positive affective experiences in the classroom: "Nice to have" or something more? Learning and Instruction **21**(3), 452–466 (2011)
6. Corbett, A.T., Anderson, J.R., O'Brien, A.T.: Student modeling in the ACT Programming Tutor. Cognitively diagnostic assessment, 19–41 (1995)
7. Csikszentmihalyi, M.: Flow: The psychology of optimal performance. Cambridge University Press, NY (1990)
8. Wilson, M., De Boeck, P.: Descriptive and explanatory item response models, pp. 43–74. Springer, New York (2004)
9. D'Mello, S., Graesser, A.: Dynamics of affective states during complex learning. Learning and Instruction **22**(2), 145–157 (2012)
10. D'Mello, S., Craig, S., Gholson, B., Franklin, S., Picard, R., Graesser, A.: Integrating Affect Sensors in an Intelligent Tutoring System. In: Proc. Computer in the Affective Loop Workshop at 2005 Int'l Conf. Intelligent User Interfaces, pp. 7–13 (2005)
11. Graesser, A.C., D'Mello, S.K., Craig, S.D., Witherspoon, A., Sullins, J., McDaniel, B., Gholson, B.: The Relationship between Affective States and Dialog Patterns during Interactions with AutoTutor. Journal of Interactive Learning Research **19**(2), 293–312 (2008)
12. Dweck, C.S.: Messages that motivate: How praise molds students' beliefs, motivation, and performance (in surprising ways) (2002)
13. Frijda, N.H.: Emotion experience and its varieties. Emotion Review **1**(3), 264–271 (2009)
14. Immordino-Yang, M.H., Damasio, A.: We feel, therefore we learn: The relevance of affective and social neuroscience to education. Mind, brain, and education **1**(1), 3–10 (2007)
15. Huk, T., Ludwigs, S.: Combining cognitive and affective support in order to promote learning. Learning and Instruction **19**(6), 495–505 (2009)
16. Johns, J., Woolf, B. (July 2006): A dynamic mixture model to detect student motivation and proficiency. In: Proceedings of the National Conference on Artificial Intelligence, vol. 21, no. 1, p. 163. AAAI Press, Menlo Park. MIT Press, Cambridge (1999)
17. Linnenbrink-Garcia, L., Pekrun, R.: Students' emotions and academic engagement: Introduction to the special issue. Contemporary Educational Psychology **36**(1), 1–3 (2011)
18. Meyer, D.K., Turner, J.C.: Re-conceptualizing emotion and motivation to learn in classroom contexts. Educational Psychology Review **18**(4), 377–390 (2006)
19. Murphy, K.: The Bayes Net Toolbox for Matlab. Computing Science and Statistics **33**(2), 1024–1034 (2001). Chicago
20. Pardos, Z.A., Heffernan, N.T.: Modeling individualization in a bayesian networks implementation of knowledge tracing. In: De Bra, P., Kobsa, A., Chin, D. (eds.) UMAP 2010. LNCS, vol. 6075, pp. 255–266. Springer, Heidelberg (2010)

21. Pekrun, R., Stephens, E.J.: Achievement Emotions: A Control-Value Approach. Social and Personality Psychology Compass **4**(4), 238–255 (2010)
22. Pekrun, R., Linnenbrink-Garcia, L.: Academic emotions and student engagement. In: Handbook of research on student engagement, pp. 259–282. Springer US (2012)
23. Reye, J.: Student modelling based on belief networks. International Journal of Artificial Intelligence in Education: **14**(63), 96 (2004)
24. Russell, J.A.: Core affect and the psychological construction of emotion. Psychological review **110**(1), 145 (2003)
25. San Pedro, M.O.Z., Baker, R.S., Gowda, S.M., Heffernan, N.T.: Towards an understanding of affect and knowledge from student interaction with an intelligent tutoring system. In: Lane, H., Yacef, K., Mostow, J., Pavlik, P. (eds.) AIED 2013. LNCS, vol. 7926, pp. 41–50. Springer, Heidelberg (2013)
26. Scherer, K.R.: The dynamic architecture of emotion: Evidence for the component process model. Cognition and emotion **23**(7), 1307–1351 (2009)
27. Schutz, P.A., Pekrun, R.: Introduction to emotion in education. Emotion in education, 3–10 (2007)
28. Verhelst, N.D., Glas, C.A.: A dynamic generalization of the Rasch model. Psychometrika **58**(3), 395–415 (1993)

Analyzing and Predicting Privacy Settings in the Social Web

Kaweh Djafari Naini[1(✉)], Ismail Sengor Altingovde[2], Ricardo Kawase[1], Eelco Herder[1], and Claudia Niederée[1]

[1] L3S Research Center, Hannover, Germany
{naini,kawase,herder,niederee}@L3S.de
[2] Middle East Technical University, Ankara, Turkey
altingovde@ceng.metu.edu.tr

Abstract. Social networks provide a platform for people to connect and share information and moments of their lives. With the increasing engagement of users in such platforms, the volume of personal information that is exposed online grows accordingly. Due to carelessness, unawareness or difficulties in defining adequate privacy settings, private or sensitive information may be exposed to a wider audience than intended or advisable, potentially with serious problems in the private and professional life of a user. Although these causes usually receive public attention when it involves companies' higher managing staff, athletes, politicians or artists, the general public is also subject to these issues. To address this problem, we envision a mechanism that can suggest users the appropriate privacy setting for their posts taking into account their profiles. In this paper, we present a thorough analysis of privacy settings in Facebook posts and evaluate prediction models that can anticipate the desired privacy settings with high accuracy, making use of the users' previous posts and preferences.

Keywords: Facebook · Privacy · Social networks

1 Introduction

Social networking sites such as Google+, Twitter and Facebook allow their users to post updates, tweets, pictures, links and videos to their circles of friends, their followers or to the whole world. By doing so, users generate a digital footprint that defines their 'online presence'.

Similar to the 'offline world', the various digital platforms provide means to define and structure a user's social network. Most of the services support a way to define different groups for information sharing within a user's social network, although each service provides its own implementation and terminology for this. Earlier social networks like Orkut had communities, for example. A member of a community could share posts, pictures and different sorts of information that were only visible to the members. In a similar fashion, current social network

F. Ricci et al. (Eds.): UMAP 2015, LNCS 9146, pp. 104–117, 2015.
DOI: 10.1007/978-3-319-20267-9_9

platforms such as Facebook and Google+ provide analogous features with Facebook Groups and Google+ Circles. The common goal is to facilitate the social network users to manage the audience of their interactions and shared content.

The use of such structuring facilities becomes a necessity, because we increasingly share the same social networking sites with persons from different spheres of our real world social networks, such as colleagues, acquaintances, friends and family members. Since each of these groups represent different aspects of our lives, it is often desirable to also be able to maintain this separation in the digital world. For example, certain family affairs might better not be shared with colleagues or acquaintances. Maintaining the right balance of interaction and involvement within those social groups helps us to manage our different roles in life. For this purpose, social networks support their users to manage their groups and to keep control of their privacy settings. Unfortunately, in many cases, these settings are buried in menus, tabs and configurations that are notoriously hard to understand for the regular user [22]. Contributing to this discussion, Facebook founder Mark Zuckerberg claimed that the rise of social networking online means that people no longer have an expectation of privacy, adding 'we decided that these would be the social norms now and we just went for it' [13].

As a consequence, in the past years, there have been several cases of people who involuntarily, unknowingly 'leaked' information to the wrong audience. Common cases include public messages that were supposed to be privately sent to one particular recipient, and posts that are targeting a specific audience and are in fact publicly available (a recurrent issue on Twitter). The presence of inadequate or inappropriate information about a person in the public sphere can have serious impact, for example on employment opportunities. Exemplary cases are reported in [24]. An indication for the increasing awareness for this topic is the current legal discussion about the *right to be forgotten* now called the *right to erasure* in the European community. This discussion addresses the right of individuals not to be stigmatized as a consequence of a specific action performed in the past [23]. Although there is a distinction between the right to be forgotten and the right for privacy - the right for privacy constitutes information that is not publicly known, whereas the right to be forgotten involves removing information that was publicly known - there is a clear link: if people unintentionally share information to wrong audiences, they might later regret it and want the information to be 'forgotten'. Ideally, it should be prevented that such information would be unintentionally publicly shared in the first place.

This implies that there is a need for better support for selecting adequate privacy settings in social networks. With that in mind, in this work, we investigate to what extent it is possible to predict the privacy setting of posts. We build our work on top of Facebook's privacy settings. Facebook is arguably the most popular social network and it provides its users a range of privacy options. In order to understand the users' privacy behavior, we first provide an analysis of privacy settings for Facebook posts. Subsequently, we present a method for predicting privacy settings by employing classification based on a small but effective set of features that are available at post creation time. Evaluations show that privacy settings can be predicted with high accuracy, which may allow automatic privacy-setting assistance for the end users and third party apps.

The remainder of this paper is structured as follows. In Section 2, we summarize the relevant related work. In Section 3, we describe our efforts to collect the sensitive data, followed by a data analysis in Section 3.1. In Section 4, we describe the experiments and results towards a privacy prediction method. We finally discuss and conclude our work in Section 5.

2 Related Work

Social media sites, such as Twitter, Facebook and Google+, are designed to share information - and other content, such as pictures, videos and links - with other users. Studies on the usage of social media platforms focus, among others, on usage motivations [14], user behavior [16], and relations and social capital [4,5]. A recent study on Facebook [33] shows that the dynamic and temporal changes of the relationships between users lead to conflicting privacy needs of the user.

Apart from relatively harmless updates, such as sharing a link or other types of public content, messages on Twitter and Facebook may contain highly personal information such as the user's location or email address. For this reason, social media sites typically offer their users several ways for indicating the intended audience of shared messages. First of all, there are *default* settings, which can be adapted by the user. Second, users can overrule these default settings for specific messages. Third, in many cases it is possible to delete, hide or edit a message post hoc.

However, as indicated by several studies (e.g. [20]), users often do not inspect or adapt the default settings offered by the system; thus, most messages are sent with the default settings. Due to this behavior, messages often have a wider audience than intended or expected by the user. According to a recent report from the Pew Internet & American Life Project [21], particularly males and young adults have posted content that they regret. Not surprisingly, these are also the users with the least restricted privacy settings. However, due to the raising awareness of privacy issues and their implications, more and more users actively manage their privacy settings and prune their profiles.

Other studies on Facebook privacy analyze user concerns regarding sharing personal content with a public audience or with third-party applications [9,11]. Similarly, in YouTube it has been observed [17] that users follow different strategies for balancing the pros and cons of sharing with privacy. As an example, users do share videos with private content, but can ensure that their faces are not displayed and their identities are not disclosed. In the context of mobile apps, it is again reported that users' privacy settings are diverse, yet can be represented via a relatively small number of privacy profiles [18,19].

Still, research has shown that users typically disclose more personal information online than they would do in face-to-face situations. There are many risks associated with content that is unknowingly disclosed to the public. Some of these risks - including mobbing, loss of reputation, family problems and lost career opportunities - are summarized in [25,29]. A remarkable initiative to raise attention for these issues is the site PleaseRobMe[1], which aggregates and shows tweets of users who report to be away from home. In addition, the user is informed via a (public) tweet.

With the goal of raising awareness for the problems related to sensitive information leaks and privacy settings, Kawase et al. [15] introduced FireMe!, a website that contains live streams of people who publicly tweet offensive comments towards their working environment, bosses and coworkers. In their work, they built a system that, once an offensive message was detected in the twittersphere, the author of the offending tweet was sent an alert message. Their results show that only 5% of the users who were alerted by the system later on deleted the compromising tweet. The authors called for the deployment of an alert system that prompts users before a compromising tweet is sent. In fact, our work goes into this direction. By understanding and predicting privacy settings, we might be able to advise (suggest) users the appropriate privacy settings for a given post, before it is effectively out there.

There are other works in the literature that aim to recommend privacy settings. Fang et al. suggest building models that can predict whether a user's friends should be allowed to see certain attributes (such as the birth date or relationship status) in the Facebook profile of the user [7,8]. Similarly, Ghazinour et al. build a classifier to predict the privacy-preference category of a user (such as "pragmatic" or "unconcerned"). Furthermore, they employ a simple kNN approach to determine the similar users to a given user, and based on the preferences of these similar users, they suggest privacy settings, again, for the attributes in the user's Facebook profile [10]. Our work differs from those in that we do not address such general attributes but we aim to recommend a privacy setting for every post (be it a status update, a video link or a photo) made by the user. Machine learning and/or collaborative filtering methods are further employed to recommend privacy settings for the location-sharing services [28,31] and mobile apps [18]. The latter domains involve different dynamics and/or features for setting privacy options than those in Facebook; the social network addressed in our study.

In our approach, we aim to directly support users in choosing privacy settings at the moment that they submit a post. This goal is similar to the work presented in [32], although addressing a different media type. In their work, Zerr et al. propose a method for detecting private photos in Flickr that are posted publicly by extracting a set of visual features. Their results show that a combination of visual and textual features achieves a considerable performance for classifying and ranking private photos. While following a similar goal, we operate in a different setting: we use social network specific features and we aim to predict more fine-granular privacy settings. In our previous work [3], we have also used different types of social network features, but for different prediction tasks, namely for suggesting Facebook posts for content retention and summarization.

[1] http://pleaserobme.com/

3 Dataset

In this section we present the two datasets that we used for our experiments. Both datasets have been collected using an experimental Facebook App[2]. This app has been developed in the context of a different work [3], where all the participants authorized us to use their Facebook data (i.e., the content and privacy settings of the posts as well as the basic user profile) for research purposes. Further, to comply with Facebook's Platform Policies[3], we took extra care regarding the participants' privacy. Most importantly, the data will not be disclosed to third parties and the data collected represent the minimal amount of information needed in order to perform the experiments.

Dataset 1. The first dataset contains 45 users from 10 different countries. The users are all researchers and/or students in the field of computer science from the first authors' institution. We expect the data from these users to be trustworthy; the users are presumably more knowledgeable in using such digital platforms. From these 45 users, we collected all their posts, summing up to 26,528 posts (posts per user varies from 13 up to 3,176 posts). This dataset has been collected during February and March 2014.

Table 1. Datasets

	Dataset 1	Dataset 2
No. of users	45	649
No. of posts	26,528	769,205
Avg. no. of posts per user	602.431	1,185.215
Variance no. of posts per user	545,343	5,484,176
Min no. of posts per user	13	100
Max no. of posts per user	3,176	30,715

Dataset 2. The second dataset has been collected using the CrowdFlower crowdsourcing platform, where the workers were asked to use the same Facebook app mentioned above. In this case, the authors are not personally familiar with the participants and therefore we have no a priori information on their knowledge of using social networking sites. Especially the former issue raised the concern of reliability, as there could be some workers who use fake profiles to finish the task and get paid. As a remedy, we considered only the data from workers who have a Facebook account that exists for at least 4 years and who have posted at least 25 posts each year. Using the CrowdFlower platform, we ended up with a much larger dataset, including 649 users and 769,205 posts in total. The crowdsourcing task has been running only for one day on November 27, 2014. In Table 1, we summarize the characteristics of both datasets.

[2] http://www.l3s.de/~kawase/forgetit/evaluation2015/

[3] https://developers.facebook.com/policy/

3.1 Data Analysis

The privacy settings in Facebook regarding the audience of a post can be one of the following five main alternatives:

- **EVERYONE**: This setting means that the post is public. Even non-Facebook users are able to see these posts.
- **SELF**: Only the user who created the post can see it.
- **ALL_FRIENDS**: Posts with this setting are visible to users who are friends with the post creator, and to the friends of those tagged in the post.
- **FRIENDS_OF_FRIENDS**: In addition to the friends, posts with this setting are also visible to friends of the poster's friends, and to friends of friends of those tagged in the post.
- **CUSTOM**: In this setting the user deliberately specifies a customized privacy setting that includes or excludes specific users or groups from the audience. This option is usually accompanied by the fields *privacy_allow* and/or *privacy_deny*. These fields list users or group ids. CUSTOM includes three sub-values:

  - **ALL_FRIENDS**: Posts with this setting are visible to all friends of the post creator, except to some users or groups that are manually chosen by the creator.
  - **FRIENDS_OF_FRIENDS**: Posts with this setting are visible to all friends of friends of the post creator, except to some users or groups that are manually chosen by the creator.
  - **SOME_FRIENDS**: Posts with this setting are only to specific users or groups that were manually chosen by the post creator.

In Figure 1, we present the distribution of the alternative privacy settings for the posts in Datasets 1 and 2. We can observe some interesting patterns regarding the usage of Facebook privacy settings. First of all, for both datasets, we see a clear dominance of posts that are visible to all of the users' friends (45 to 50%) and of public posts (around 30%). We also observe a rather high demand for the option that denies access to specific users or groups (around 10%

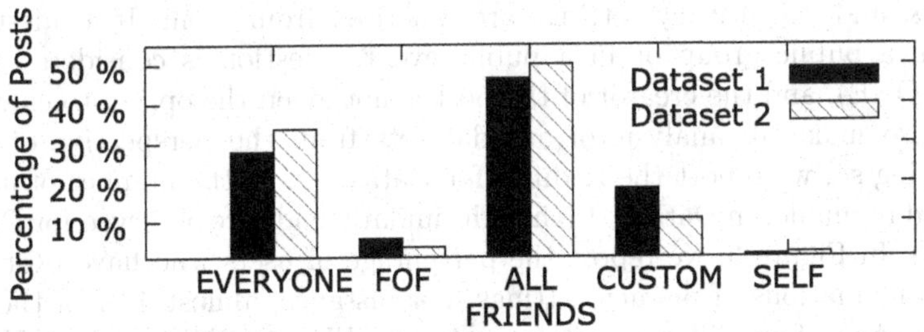

Fig. 1. Distribution of the privacy settings for Datasets 1 and 2

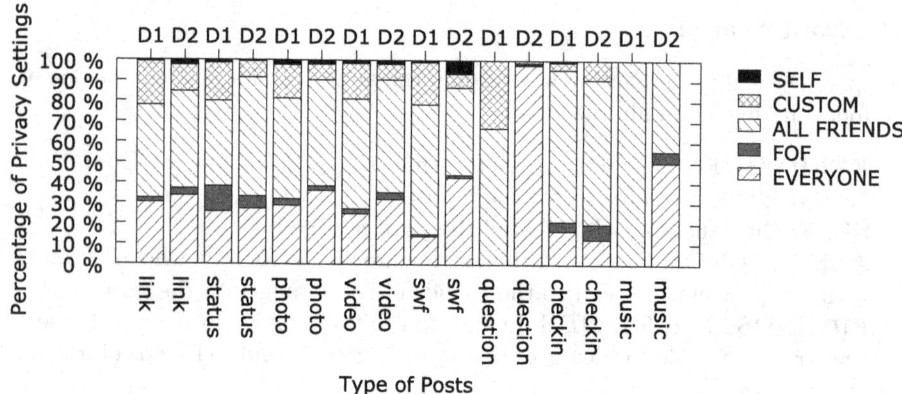

Fig. 2. Distribution of posts normalized by post type for Dataset 1 (D1) and Dataset 2 (D1)

for Dataset 1 and 20% for Datasets 2), which is in line with our expectations from Section 1. This shows that quite often, users carefully 'hide' posts from particular users in their social networks.

Next, we provide a more detailed analysis taking into account the types of the posts. In total, there are eight different types that we identified in our datasets. Each type has unique characteristics that may influence the users in choosing the appropriate privacy setting. In Figure 2, we plot the distribution of privacy setting over post types. We see that especially post types of *music* and *Flash content* (shown as *swf*) are the ones that are shared with more general audiences (i.e., EVERYONE and FRIENDS_OF_FRIENDS), whereas post types like *link*, *status*, *video* and *photo* are more likely to be visible to restricted audiences (e.g., with privacy setting CUSTOM). As another interesting observation, almost all the posts of type the *question* (97.79%) are public in Dataset 2 (note that, while the situation is different for Dataset 1, we notice that there are only two posts of type *question* in this dataset, and hence findings are not representative). This is because of the fact that the privacy settings for *Questions* are not directly chosen by the user. In Facebook, *Questions* can only be posted in *Groups* or in *Events*, and the privacy settings are inherited from them. If a question is posted in a public group or in a public event, question is considered public (EVERYONE), and the creator of the post is not given the option to change it.

We also make an analysis of our datasets from the perspective of users. While doing so, we report the findings for Dataset 2, as the number of users is considerably smaller in Dataset 1 (though similar trends are observed for Dataset 1 as well). In Figure 3, we report the percentage of users who have posts with certain combinations of privacy settings. For instance, almost 43% of the users have posts from four different privacy settings, EVERYONE, ALL_FRIENDS, CUSTOM and SELF. Similarly, another 34% of users have posts from all the privacy settings. In general, the distribution in Figure 3 implies that these users

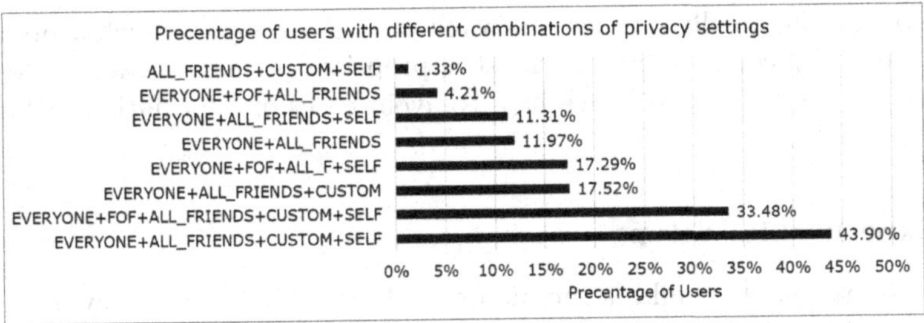

Fig. 3. Distribution of users by their privacy settings combination (for Dataset 2)

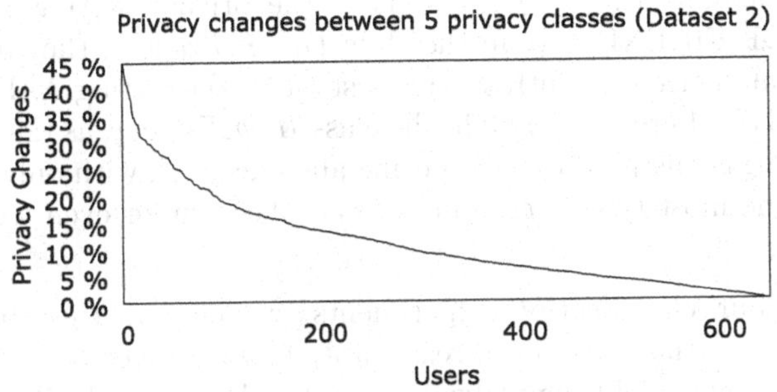

Fig. 4. Distribution of the privacy changes by each user (for Dataset 2)

are not unaware of the privacy setting, and indeed they intentionally use different privacy settings for their different posts.

For a deeper insight, we investigate how often users change their privacy settings in different posts. We performed a temporal analysis on the posts of each user to compute how many times she changed her settings; i.e., the number of times a user selects a different privacy setting for her post than that of the preceding post in chronological order. Figure 4 depicts the percentages of such changes for each user as shown on the x-axis. On the average, the users choose different privacy settings in 10.8% of the posts. This further supports our previous finding showing that at least some users deliberately choose different privacy settings. Given the fact that choosing the privacy settings is a task that is frequently triggered, and that the decision is quite often varying, we believe that users could benefit from tools that suggest the appropriate settings. Therefore, in the next section, we present a first step in the direction of predicting privacy settings.

4 Privacy Prediction Experiments

The data analysis in the previous section suggests that there might be dependencies between the privacy settings of a post and some characteristics of the the post or the user who wrote the post. In this section, we investigate whether it is possible to automatically predict a privacy setting for a post. Such a predictor can be used for recommending the most appropriate privacy setting to the user at the time of posting, and hence help to avoid cases of information leaking as exemplified before.

4.1 Experimental Setup

Target Classes. To build a predictor with reasonable accuracy that can be employed in a practical setting, we opt for building a binary classifier and predicting whether a post has low or high privacy at an abstract level, rather than assigning each post to one of the privacy levels described in Section 3. We assume that posts that have the privacy setting EVERYONE or FRIENDS_OF_FRIENDS are in the class *Low_Privacy*, as they are visible to a very general audience. In contrast, the posts with the setting ALL_FRIENDS, SELF and CUSTOM are said to be in the class *High_Privacy*, as the user has the intention of sharing the post with a specific audience, i.e.; with only her friends, which can be the most typical case in a social platform, or even with a certain subset of them.

Dataset. For our classification experiments, we employ the crowd-sourced dataset (Dataset 2) that includes a reasonably large number of users and postings and, hence, can yield generalizable results. From the latter dataset, we discard all non-English posts using the language detector tool provided by [26], as we aim to construct features based on the post content. Furthermore, for each user, we label the posts as Low and High Privacy; and get all the posts in the class with smaller number of instances, and undersample the posts from the other class. This is to obtain a balanced dataset (as the dataset is otherwise skewed in various ways; some users have a large number of posts, and furthermore, they are biased for a certain privacy class only). At the end, our dataset includes a total of 93,460 posts from 469 users; with an average of approximately 100 posts from each class, per user.

Features. In our experiments, we use features from six different categories (see Table 2). First, we have *metadata* features obtained from a post, such as the type of the post (e.g., link, photo, status, video, etc.), whether the post includes one or more of the predefined Facebook fields (such as message, story or decription) and its length, and number of tagged users in the post. The *context* features capture the platform and time related information. From the post content, we first extract *sentiment* features, i.e., the positivity, negativity and objectivity scores computed using a vocabulary based sentiment analysis tool, namely, SentiWordNet [6]. The *keyword* feature category captures whether a post includes a keyword that might be related to a certain concept like family, friends, work, travel, etc. Note that, for each of the latter concepts, we manually compiled a small list (up to 20 words) of representative words. Another feature category is the *word vector*, i.e., the entire content of the post as a bag of words, as typical in text classification. We keep top-1000 most words with the highest tf-idf scores in the word vector. Finally, we have the *user* features, such as the number of posts

Table 2. The list of features used for the privacy prediction task

Feature	Description	Feature	Description
Post metadata		**Context**	
has(message)	post has a message	sendFromMobile	post sent from an mobile application
length(message)	length of the message	dayTimes	(morning, afternoon, evening, night)
norm(length(message))	length normalized per user	sendAtWeekend	post sent during weekend
has(story)	has a story	**Sentiment**	
length(story)	length of the story	negative	the negativity score of a post
norm(length(story))	length normalized per user	positive	the positivity score of a post
has(description)	has a description	objective	the objectivity score of a post
length(description)	length of the description	**Users**	
norm(length(description))	length normalized per user	no_posts	total number of posts of a user
has(link)	post includes a link	no_friends	total number of friends of a user
has(icon)	post has an icon	gender	gender of the user
has(caption)	post has an caption	age	age of the user
type	type of post	country	country of the user
status_type	status_type of a post	education	the education level of the user
icons	describes user activity	**Keywords**	
tagged users	users tagged in a post	words_family	contains word from the list
Word vector		words_friends	contains word from the list
bag of words	top-1000 words using tf/Idf	words_work	contains word from the list
		words_holiday	contains word from the list
		words_travel	contains word from the list

and friends, gender, age, country and education (the latter is obtained from the crowdsourcing platform). All the features in these categories are concatenated to obtain a single instance vector, i.e., applying the early fusion approach for different types of features (e.g., see [27]). Note that since our predictor is to be employed during the post creation time, it is not possible to use typical social network features based on community feedback (e.g no. of likes, no. of comments etc.) employed in other contexts [2].

Classifiers and Evaluation Metrics. We apply the well-known classification algorithms NaiveBayes[12] as well as a fast decision tree learner, REPTree [30][1]. For both algorithms, we use the implementation provided by the WEKA library[4]. For the evaluation, we use well-known measures from the literature: the true positive rate (TPR), false positive rate (FPR), precision, recall, F-Measure, and area under the ROC curve (AUC). All the reported results are obtained via 5-fold cross-validation. Remarkably, this implies that the posts of a particular user are distributed to training and test sets at each fold; and hence, the model will learn to predict the privacy based on not only other users previous decisions, but the user's own decisions, as well.

Results and Discussions. In Table 3, we compare the prediction performance for NaiveBayes and RepTree classifiers. The average TPR (i.e., accuracy) of the NaiveBayes predictor is 0.692, which is better than the random baseline with 0.5 accuracy (as we have a balanced dataset). Moreover, when predicting the High Privacy class, the classifier has a higher TPR (i.e., 0.745). This is useful in practice, as predicting a highly private post as public is more dangerous (as these are the cases where the information is exposed to a larger audience

[4] http://www.cs.waikato.ac.nz/ml/weka/

Table 3. Classification results using all the features

Naive Bayes						
TP Rate	FP Rate	Precision	Recall	F-Measure	AUC	Class
0.640	0.255	0.715	0.640	0.675	0.780	LOW_PRIVACY
0.745	0.360	0.674	0.745	0.708	0.780	HIGH_PRIVACY
0.692	0.308	0.694	0.692	0.691	0.780	Avg.
REPTree						
TP Rate	FP Rate	Precision	Recall	F-Measure	AUC	Class
0.810	0.191	0.809	0.810	0.810	0.887	LOW_PRIVACY
0.809	0.190	0.810	0.809	0.809	0.887	HIGH_PRIVACY
0.809	0.191	0.809	0.809	0.809	0.887	Avg.

Table 4. Classification results for each category of features

REPTree						
Feature category	TP Rate	FP Rate	Precision	Recall	F-Measure	AUC
Word vector	0.715	0.285	0.719	0.715	0.714	0.793
Post	0.641	0.358	0.642	0.641	0.640	0.709
Users	0.600	0.400	0.601	0.600	0.598	0.673
Sentiment	0.591	0.408	0.593	0.591	0.588	0.652
Context	0.583	0.417	0.588	0.583	0.577	0.634
Keywords	0.553	0.446	0.553	0.553	0.553	0.592

than intended) than vice versa. The overall performance of the RepTree classifier is even more impressive, as it yields an accuracy of 0.809 for both classes (and, on the average). For this classifier, average F-measure and AUC metrics are also over 0.80. These findings reveal that it is possible to predict the privacy class of a post with good accuracy, and such a predictor can serve in suggesting the privacy setting of a post when it is first created.

Note that, since our dataset includes different numbers of posts from each user (but with the same number of instances from each class), it is also interesting to investigate whether classification performance is biased for the users who have more posts than the average. To this end, we filtered the dataset used in previous experiments, so that each user remaining in the dataset now has exactly 100 posts (50 from each class). In this new setup, the accuracy of the RepTree classifier is still 0.788, which implies that the accuracy can improve with more training instances from a particular user. Nevertheless, even for the case of 100 posts per user, the prediction accuracy is high (note that the scores for the other evaluation metrics are also similar and not reported here for brevity).

Finally, for the RepTree classifier reported in Table 3, we further investigate the performance of each feature category in isolation. Table 4 reveals that keyword features and word vectors are the least and most useful features, respectively. It is further remarkable that the classifier that use all features in combination perform considerably better than those based on a single feature category.

5 Conclusion

In this paper, we presented an approach for supporting users in selecting adequate privacy settings for their posts. This work is based on a thorough analysis on privacy settings on social networks, particularly in Facebook. Our analysis shows that users customize their privacy settings quite often: for roughly one out of ten posts, a new privacy setting is chosen over time. The data also has shown that the type of post has a significant impact on the the choice of privacy settings. While posts of the type 'music' and 'question' tend to have a larger (less restricted) audience, 'status', 'photo' and 'video' are more often restricted to a smaller audience.

Targeting a supporting tool that could suggest users preferable privacy settings, we performed experiments for the privacy settings prediction task. By relying on different categories of features that can already be identified at the time of post composition, we were able to achieve a very good prediction performance with a recall and precision of more than 80% on average.

Additionally, our analysis demonstrated clear differences in users' behavior with respect to privacy settings. We observed that there are some users who are very sloppy regarding privacy settings, having most of their posts publicly available and not changing the settings. We also observed users who very often customized their settings, and users who prefer sharing data mostly with their friends. This difference in behavior indicates that a personalized model for privacy prediction might improve the already good results of the experiments presented in this paper. This is part of our future work, where we plan to collect more contributors (users) willing to collaborate with our research, and on top of a bigger user base, we plan to explore the best personalized methods for privacy settings prediction.

Acknowledgments. This work was partially supported by the K3 project funded by the German Federal Ministry of Education and the European Commission Seventh Framework Program under grant agreement No.600826 for the ForgetIT project.

References

1. Breiman, L.: Bagging predictors. Machine Learning **24**(2), 123–140 (1996)
2. Chelaru, S., Orellana-Rodriguez, C., Altingovde, I.S.: How useful is social feedback for learning to rank youtube videos? World Wide Web **17**(5), 997–1025 (2014)
3. Djafari Naini, K., Kawase, R., Kanhabua, N., Niederée, C.: Characterizing high-impact features for content retention in social web applications. In: Proc. of WWW 2014, pp. 559–560 (2014)

4. Ellison, N.B., Gray, R., Vitak, J., Lampe, C., Fiore, A.T.: Calling all facebook friends: exploring requests for help on facebook. In: Proc. of ICWSM 2013 (2013)
5. Ellison, N.B., Steinfield, C., Lampe, C.: Connection strategies: Social capital implications of facebook-enabled communication practices. New Media & Society **13**(6), 873–892 (2011)
6. A. Esuli and F. Sebastiani. Sentiwordnet: a publicly available lexical resource for opinion mining. In: Proc. of LREC 2006, pp. 417–422 (2006)
7. Fang, L., Kim, H., LeFevre, K., Tami, A.: A privacy recommendation wizard for users of social networking sites. In: Proc. of the 17th ACM Conference on Computer and Communications Security, CCS 2010, pp. 630–632 (2010)
8. Fang, L., LeFevre, K.: Privacy wizards for social networking sites. In: Proc. of WWW 2010, pp. 351–360 (2010)
9. Felt, A., Evans, D.: Privacy protection for social networking platforms. In: Proc. of Web 2.0 Security and Privacy (2008)
10. Ghazinour, K., Matwin, S., Sokolova, M.: Monitoring and recommending privacy settings in social networks. In: Proc. of the Joint EDBT/ICDT Workshops, pp. 164–168 (2013)
11. R. Gross and A. Acquisti. Information revelation and privacy in online social networks. In: Proc. of the ACM Workshop on Privacy in the Electronic Society, pp. 71–80 (2005)
12. John, G.H., Langley, P.: Estimating continuous distributions in bayesian classifiers. In: Proc. of the 11th Annual Conference on Uncertainty in Artificial Intelligence (UAI), pp. 338–345. Morgan Kaufmann (1995)
13. Johnson, B.: Privacy no longer a social norm, says facebook founder (2010). http://www.theguardian.com/technology/2010/jan/11/facebook-privacy/
14. Joinson, A.N.: Looking at, looking up or keeping up with people?: motives and use of facebook. In: Proc. of CHI 2008 (2008)
15. Kawase, R., Nunes, B.P., Herder, E., Nejdl, W., Casanova, M.A.: Who wants to get fired? In: Proc. of WebSci 2013, pp. 191–194 (2013)
16. Lampe, C., Ellison, N.B., Steinfield, C.: Changes in use and perception of facebook. In: Proc. of CSCW 2008 (2008)
17. Lange, P.G.: Publicly private and privately public: Social networking on youtube. Journal of Computer-Mediated Communication **13**(1), 361–380 (2007)
18. Lin, J., Liu, B., Sadeh, N.M., Hong, J.I.: Modeling users' mobile app privacy preferences: restoring usability in a sea of permission settings. In: Proc. of the 10th Symposium on Usable Privacy and Security (SOUPS 2014), pp. 199–212 (2014)
19. B. Liu, J. Lin, and N. M. Sadeh. Reconciling mobile app privacy and usability on smartphones: could user privacy profiles help? In: Proc. of WWW 2014, pp. 201–212 (2014)
20. Liu, Y., Gummadi, K.P., Krishnamurthy, B., Mislove, A.: Analyzing facebook privacy settings: user expectations vs. reality. In: Proc. of the 11th ACM SIGCOMM Conference on Internet Measurement (IMC 2011), pp. 61–70 (2011)
21. Madden, M.: Privacy management on social media sites. Technical report, Pew Internet and American Life Project (2012)
22. Madejski, M., Johnson, M., Bellovin, S.M.: A study of privacy settings errors in an online social network. In: Proc. of PerCom 2012 Workshops, pp. 340–345 (2012)
23. Mantelero, A.: The eu proposal for a general data protection regulation and the roots of the 'right to be forgotten'. Computer Law & Security Review **29**, 229–235 (2013)
24. Mayer-Schönberger, V.: Delete - The Virtue of Forgetting in the Digital Age. Morgan Kaufmann Publishers (2009)

25. Rose, C.: The security implications of ubiquitous social media. International Journal of Management and Information Systems **15**(1) (2011)
26. Shuyo, N.: Language detection library for java (2010)
27. Snoek, C., Worring, M., Smeulders, A.W.M.: Early versus late fusion in semantic video analysis. In Proc. of the 13th ACM Int'l Conference on Multimedia, pp. 399–402 (2005)
28. Toch, E., Sadeh, N.M., Hong, J.I.: Generating default privacy policies for online social networks. In: Proc. of CHI 2010 (Extended Abstracts Volume), pp. 4243–4248 (2010)
29. Toch, E., Wang, Y., Cranor, L.: Personalization and privacy: a survey of privacy risks and remedies in personalization-based systems. User Modeling and User-Adapted Interaction **22**, 203–220 (2012)
30. Witten, I.H., Frank, E.: Data Mining: Practical Machine Learning Tools and Techniques, 2nd edn. Morgan Kaufmann Publishers Inc., San Francisco (2005)
31. Xie, J., Knijnenburg, B.P., Jin, H.: Location sharing privacy preference: analysis and personalized recommendation. In: Proc. of the 19th Int'l Conference on Intelligent User Interfaces, pp. 189–198 (2014)
32. Zerr, S., Siersdorfer, S., Hare, J., Demidova, E.: Privacy-aware image classification and search. In: Proc. of SIGIR 2012, pp. 35–44 (2012)
33. Zhao, X., Salehi, N., Naranjit, S., Alwaalan, S., Voida, S., Cosley, D.: The many faces of facebook: experiencing social media as performance, exhibition, and personal archive. In: Proc. of CHI 2013 (2013)

Counteracting Anchoring Effects in Group Decision Making

Martin Stettinger[1], Alexander Felfernig[1](✉), Gerhard Leitner[2], and Stefan Reiterer[1]

[1] Institute for Software Technology, Inffeldgasse 16b, 8010 Graz, Austria
{stettinger,felfernig,reiterer}@ist.tugraz.at
[2] Institute for Informatics Systems, UniversitätsstraßE 65–67, 9020 Klagenfurt, Austria
gerhard.leitner@aau.at

Abstract. Similar to single user decisions, group decisions can be affected by decision biases. In this paper we analyze anchoring effects as a specific type of decision bias in the context of group decision scenarios. On the basis of the results of a user study in the domain of software requirements prioritization we discuss results regarding the optimal time when preference information of other users should be disclosed to the current user. Furthermore, we show that explanations can increase the satisfaction of group members with various aspects of a group decision process (e.g., satisfaction with the decision and decision support quality).

Keywords: Group decision making · Recommender systems · Decision biases · Anchoring effects

1 Introduction

Many decisions in everyday life occur in the context of groups, for example, a decision regarding the restaurant to choose for a dinner with friends or a decision regarding the next years' conference or workshop location. A major objective of the CHOICLA[1] group decision support environment is to support different types of group decision scenarios in an efficient fashion. CHOICLA includes functionalities that determine recommendations on the basis of individual preferences of group members. When dealing with group decisions, one has to cope with different types of *decision biases* which can deteriorate decision quality. We will first provide a short overview of such biases and then focus on the aspect of how to counteract anchoring effects in group decision making. For a more detailed overview of such biases we refer to [4].

Serial position effects occur in situations where items at the beginning and the end of a list are evaluated more often (behavioural aspect) and also recalled (cognitive aspect) more often [5,15] than items in the middle of a list.

[1] www.choicla.com.

F. Ricci et al. (Eds.): UMAP 2015, LNCS 9146, pp. 118–130, 2015.
DOI: 10.1007/978-3-319-20267-9_10

Such items can be argumentations in product descriptions [18], products and their attributes [5], and lists of links [15]. Such effects can occur independent of the popularity of an attribute or item, for example, item properties presented at the beginning and the end of a recommendation dialog are recalled more often independent of their popularity [5]. A possibility to counteract serial position effects in group-based recommendation is to change the preference acquisition interface, for example, from a star-based rating to a utility-based rating (items are evaluated with regard to a predefined set of interest dimensions) which encourages users to analyse item descriptions in more detail [18].

Decoy effects cause shifts in preference construction since decisions are taken depending on the context in which alternatives are presented to the user [22]. For example, including a completely inferior alternative (e.g., with the lowest overall utility compared to all other alternatives in a list of recommended items) can change a user's evaluation of the remaining items in the list. In the context of recommenders, such effects have been analyzed by Teppan et al. [20] who showed the existence of decoy effects on the basis of real-world financial services datasets. Counteracting decoy effects can be based on predictive models that predict decoy items which could be eliminated from a result set [20].

Explanations can have a significant impact on the way that items are perceived/evaluated and – as a consequence – on the corresponding decision. Thus, explanations play an important role in recommender systems [8,21], for example, a digital camera will be purchased or not, a movie will be watched or not, a car feature will we included or not, a project proposal will be accepted or not, and a software requirement will be regarded as important or not. Stettinger et al. [18] analyze the impact of argument orderings of item explanations on the decision outcome, Felfernig et al. [6] and Pu et al. [16] show the (positive) influence of explanations on a user's trust in recommender systems, and Herlocker et al. [10] discuss different explanation-relevant dimensions in recommender systems where beside *justification*, *user involvement*, and *education*, *acceptance* is mentioned as a major relevant factor.

Anchoring effects cause decisions which are influenced by the group member who first articulated his/her preferences [1,11] – these results in the context of decision support environments are confirmed by social-psychological studies that point out the relationship between decision quality and the visibility of individual preferences for other group members [9,14]. Interestingly, hidden preferences in early phases of group decision scenarios can increase the overall amount of information exchange between group members and the higher the amount of information exchange the higher the quality of the decision outcome. In collaborative filtering scenarios, anchoring effects can be triggered by disclosing, for example, the average rating of other (similar) users. An adaptation of the preference acquisition interface (e.g., a rating scale adapted from a 5-star to a binary one) can help to counteract such biases in collaborative filtering [1,2].

The existence of anchoring effects in group decision scenarios has also been shown in Felfernig et al. [7] who analyzed bias-induced preference shifts in the context of requirements engineering. In this scenario, the task of the project team was to make decisions regarding different technical and organizational aspects of their software project. Examples of such decisions are the way in which their software project should be evaluated and the type of technology that should be used for implementing the requirements. Masthoff and Gatt [13] discuss algorithmic approaches to satisfaction prediction in group decision scenarios where *conformity* (judgments are influenced by the judgements already articulated by other group members) and *emotional contagion* (influence of an individual's affective state on that of other group members) are mentioned as influence factors. Compared to Masthoff and Gatt [13], we did not analyze emotional states of group members and focused on the impacts of different degrees of judgement visibility. An analysis of intra-group dynamics in CHOICLA decision scenarios is within the scope of future work. Our major focus in this paper is to show in which way anchoring effects can be counteracted in the context of group decision making. In this context, we focus on a *requirements prioritization scenario* where groups of students (teams) had to agree on the set of additional requirements (and their priority) they are willing to implement in their software project. In addition, we investigated the impact of explanations in group decision scenarios (explanations textually entered after a final decision has been taken). In this context we were interested on the impact that explanations can have on the overall acceptance of a group decision by individual group members.

As a basis for completing the requirements prioritization task the teams of our study used the CHOICLA group decision support environment. Example CHOICLA scenarios for industrial settings are the selection of new employees, the selection of conference locations, and the evaluation of project proposals. In the private context, CHOICLA can, for example, support the selection of a restaurant for a dinner with friends, the selection of a hotel for a holiday trip, and the selection of a cinema movie to watch with friends. In addition to CHOICLA, there exist many other group decision support environments. DOODLE[2] focuses primarily on the aspect of coordinating meetings and does not include additional mechanisms to determine recommendations for groups of users. Similarly, VERN [23] is a tool that supports the identification of meeting times based on the idea of unconstrained democracy where individuals are enabled to freely propose alternative dates themselves. SMARTOCRACY provides support for voting scenarios in social network contexts where information from the social network is applied to rank recommendations [17]. DOTMOCRACY[3] deals with larger groups of users and provides a method for collecting and visualizing group preferences. The system is based on the idea of participatory decision making – it's major outcome is a graph type visualization of the group-immanent preferences. Compared to CHOICLA, these tools focus on specific domains and do not offer the possibility for a flexible definition of domain-independent decision scenarios.

The contributions of this paper are the following: (1) we provide a short overview of the CHOICLA group decision support environment on the basis of a working example from the area of software requirements prioritization, (2) we

[2] doodle.com.

[3] dotmocracy.org.

show (a) the existence of anchoring effects and (b) possibilities of counteracting these effects in the context of group decision making, and (3) we show that explanations in group decision scenarios can have a positive impact on the overall acceptance of group decisions. The remainder of this paper is organized as follows. In Section 2 we provide an overview of the CHOICLA decision support environment. In Section 3 we report the results of an empirical study which focused on (a) anchoring effects within group decision scenarios and (b) the impact of explanations. The paper is concluded with Section 4.

2 The Choicla Environment

Decision tasks often differ in their basic properties, for example, *decision heuristics* [12] such as *majority voting* or *least misery* should be preselected or not, *alternatives* can only be defined by the administrator (also denoted as *creator*) of a decision task (app), *preferences of other group members* should be visible (or not), and decisions should be *explained* or not (by the creator of a decision task). Due to the many existing options, decision tasks must be configured before being provided to a group of users – for details see Stettinger et al. [19]. An example of a definition (configuration) of a CHOICLA decision app is depicted in Figure 1. In this example, a group of users (stakeholders) should *decide about the priority of requirements that should be additionally implemented in a software project.* In this context, all group members are allowed to add their own alternatives (software requirements), to add additional material (links and files), and to see the preferences of other users (regarding the prioritization of requirements). Making the process design of decision tasks configurable introduces the flexibility that is needed due to the heterogeneity of decision problems. The achieved flexibility provides the basis for organizing the CHOICLA components in a kind of a software product line that is open in terms of the generation (implementation) of problem-specific decision applications.

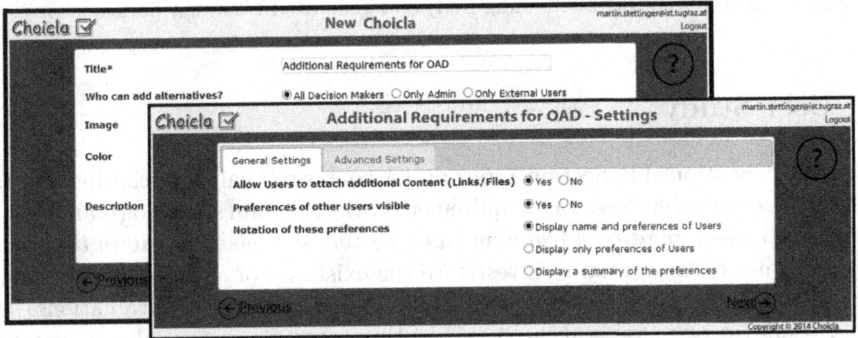

Fig. 1. Interface for configuring CHOICLA decision apps

After a CHOICLA *decision app configuration* has been completed, the corresponding *decision app* is automatically generated and installed on the home screen of the decision app creator. The creator can now invite relevant users (in our case stakeholders) to participate in the decision process – this is currently possible via email. Figure 2 depicts examples of already configured and generated CHOICLA decision apps: *requirements prioritization* (our working example), *appointment scheduling*, *hardware procurement*, and *personnel decision*[4].

Figure 2 includes two more tabs which are denoted as *DecisionApp Store* and *Create DecisionApp*. The former can be used for searching and installing new decision apps (this is only possible if a decision app has been defined as *public* and therefore been made *reusable* by the app creator), the latter can be used for creating (configuring) your own decision app (for details see Stettinger et al. [19]). CHOICLA decision apps can entail an arbitrary number of decision *instances*, for example, if a requirements prioritization decision has to be taken for a new project or a new set of requirements, the same decision app can be used by simply creating a new instance inside the given decision app. Also after completion of the decision process, each individual instance of the decision app is accessible in a *decision history* (documentation).

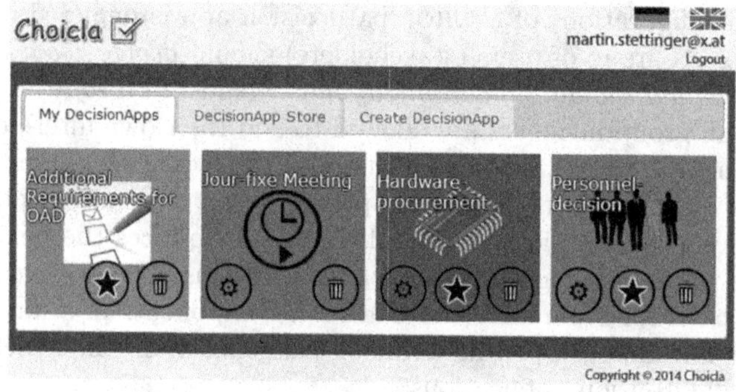

Fig. 2. Examples of defined (configured) and generated CHOICLA decision apps

3 User Study

As already mentioned in Section 1, our major goal is to analyze anchoring effects in group decision scenarios. In a requirements prioritization scenario (team members had to select *additional requirements they had to implement within the scope of their project*) we wanted to investigate the existence of anchoring effects and also to figure out when to best disclose individual preferences (evaluations) to other users (in our case stakeholders). In this context we were also interested in the impact of preference invisibility on the degree of information exchange between individual stakeholders. Finally, we wanted to investigate factors such as the impact of the existence of explanations for group decisions on the degree

[4] The CHOICLA *personnel decision app* is already applied by an Austrian university.

of satisfaction with the decision support and the perceived understandability of the group decision. In the remainder of this paper we will first present the CHOICLA decision app generated for the purposes of requirements prioritization (software requirements for an online game) and then discuss the design of our user study and the corresponding study results in detail.

The generated requirements prioritization decision app supports the prioritization of requirements on the basis of a multi-utility based evaluation scheme [3]. Team members (subjects of the study) were enabled to evaluate each requirement with regard to the dimensions *Risk*, *Effort*, and *Profit*. Note that such dimensions are freely definable in CHOICLA if a MAUT-based aggregation function (group recommendation heuristic) has been selected. An example of the evaluation of the requirement *Change Background* is depicted in Figure 3.

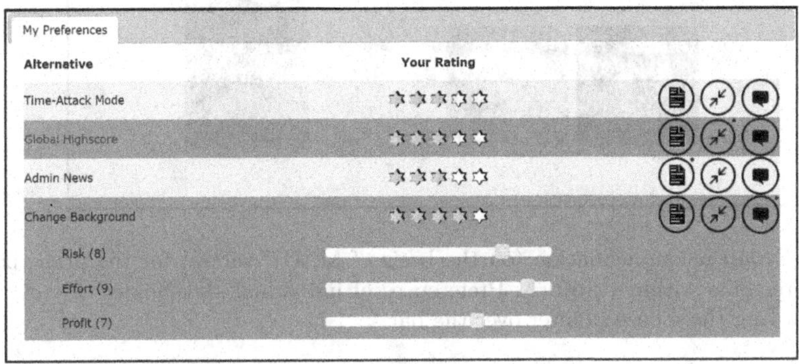

Fig. 3. Evaluation interface of the requirements in CHOICLA. Participants can enter their ratings by selecting a value for the dimensions *Risk*, *Effort*, and *Profit*.

This requirement is linked to a detailed textual description – in our case, the background style should be changeable in an online game. Note that in utility-based scenarios CHOICLA supports a group-based MAUT approach, where individual ratings defined for interest dimensions are aggregated using arithmetic mean and then added up (for details see Stettinger et al. [18]). The utility of each individual alternative (*requirement*) is then transposed to a five-star rating scale as depicted in Figure 3. Since the goal of our study was to investigate anchoring effects in the context of group decision scenarios, the *visibility of the preferences of other group members* was one of the major variation points in the user study.

Figure 3 includes a CHOICLA user interface version where the preferences of other users are not disclosed to the current user. In contrast, Figure 4 depicts an interface version were the preferences (priorities) of the individual stakeholders are visible (the height of each bar corresponds to the corresponding MAUT value [3,18] of a requirement, individual preferences are visible when moving the mouse pointer over the corresponding bar). If all stakeholders have articulated their requirements, the creator of a decision app can close the decision process, i.e., no further changes/adaptations of the individual user preferences are possible from that time on. Closing the decision process means that one or more options are selected by the administrator and these alternatives altogether then represent the final decision. The selected alternatives may not correspond with the alternatives proposed by the aggregation heuristic (in our case MAUT).

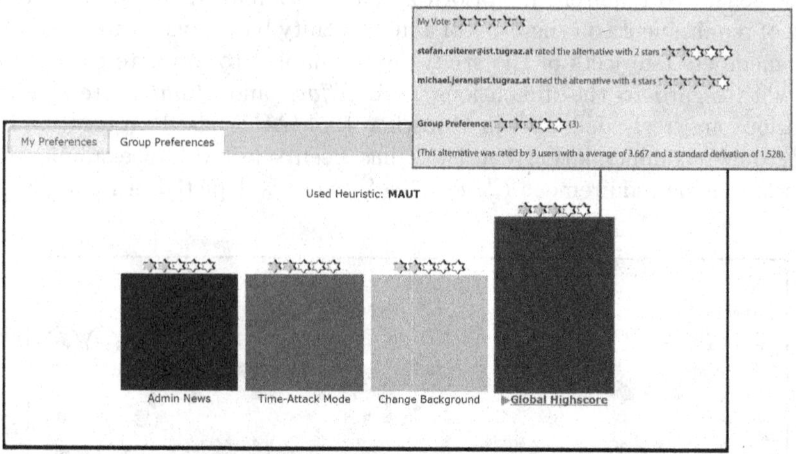

Fig. 4. Group recommendation (on the basis of MAUT values) for the prioritization of requirements within CHOICLA. Preferences of individual stakeholders are disclosed when moving the mouse pointer over the bar.

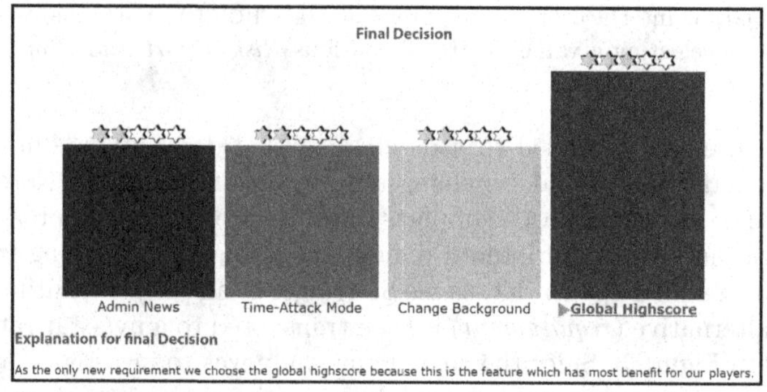

Fig. 5. Representation of a final decision in CHOICLA in terms of a bar chart

In our working example, the creator of the decision app selected only one requirement (*Global Highscore*) as an additional requirement to be implemented in the project (see Figure 5). In this case, the creator follows the group recommendation and also explains the reason for the final decision. Note that the possibility of explaining final decisions is another major variation point in the user study, i.e., some versions included this option, some versions not.

We conducted a user study with computer science students at the Graz University of Technology (N=229 participants, 16% female, and 84% male) who took a course on *object oriented analysis and design*. Students formed software teams with 5–6 participants (in total 45 teams) who had then to implement an online game environment. Each team had to develop the same set of basic requirements but could choose 5 out of a set of 10 additional requirements using CHOICLA as the sole decision and communication platform.[5] The 45 software teams (groups) were assigned to different categories as follows (see also Table 1). First, 23 groups were confronted with a CHOICLA user interface which enforced the explanation of final decisions, the remaining 22 groups had the option to explain their decisions but this was not mandatory. Second, the individual CHOICLA versions differed in terms as of when individual preferences are made public to all group members (after one, two, three, or all group member(s) has(have) articulated his/her(their) preferences).

Table 1. Assignment of versions to groups in the user study, for example, *"explanation mandatory+after 1."* denotes a CHOICLA version with *mandatory explanations* and *individual preferences were disclosed* after one group member defined his/her preferences.

explanation mandatory				explanation not mandatory			
after 1.	after 2.	after 3.	after all	after 1.	after 2.	after 3.	after all
6 groups	6 groups	5 groups	6 groups	6 groups	6 groups	5 groups	5 groups

The hypotheses as input for our user study were the following. First, we assumed that anchoring effects occur especially in cases were preference information of individual users is disclosed although this information has not been provided by all group members, i.e., the lower the number of completed preference definitions the higher the probability of anchoring effects (H1).

Second, we assumed that the best time to disclose individual preferences is a situation where each group member has already articulated his/her requirements (H2). This strategy should lead to the best results regarding (a) *the satisfaction with the final group decision* as well as (b) *the perceived degree of decision support*, (c) *perceived understandability of the final group decision*, and (d) *consideration of one's personal preferences*. In our study, data to answer (a)–(d) were collected in a post-decision questionnaire. The rating scale for questions (a)–(b) was [very satisfied (5) .. very unsatisfied (1)], for question (c) it was [understood immediately (5) .. no chance to understand without asking a couple of times (1)], and for (d) it was [excellent (5) .. very bad (1)].

In the line of decision psychological experiments [9,14] we assume that the later individual preferences are disclosed the higher will be the number of comments in the CHOICLA forum (H3). A higher degree of information exchange also has a direct positive impact on decision quality – see also [9,14]. Hypothesis H3 is related to the fact that groups tend to focus on the preferences of other

[5] Due to space limitations we limited our example set to 3 requirements.

group members if this information is available but otherwise focus on information exchange to gain a better understanding of the problem setting [9,14].

With hypothesis H4 we want to express the assumption that the explanation of a final decision can increase (a) *the satisfaction with the final group decision* as well as (b) *the perceived degree of decision support*, (c) *perceived understandability of the final group decision*, and (d) *consideration of one's personal preferences.*

The results of our user study were the following. We can confirm hypothesis H1, i.e., anchoring effects are triggered by an earlier disclosure of preference information to other group members. In this context, we analyzed the standard deviations of the individual user ratings (i.e., we used the standard deviation of ratings as an indicator of anchoring effects) depending on the time of the disclosure of the ratings (preferences) of individual group members. Figure 6 depicts the standard deviations of user ratings depending on the time of preference disclosure; standard deviations increase monotonously in the number of anonymously articulated preferences. The series of standard deviations related to versions *after 1.* and *after 2.* (and above) significantly differ in terms of their mean values ($p < 0.05$, t-test).

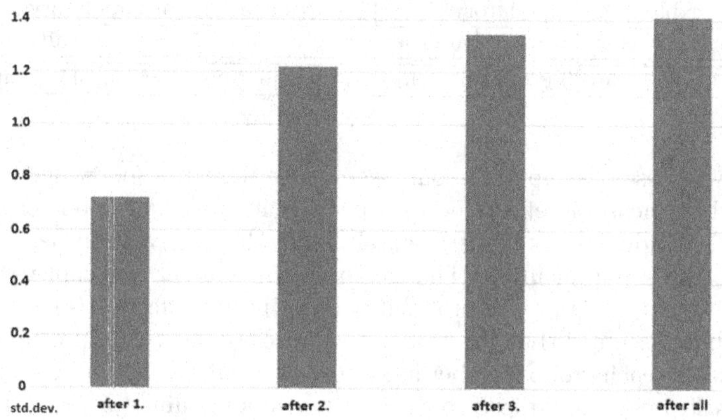

Fig. 6. Standard deviations of user ratings of alternatives (requirements) depending on preference disclosure time (after 1..3, or all users articulated preferences)

We can also confirm hypothesis H2. The later the time of preference disclosure (the more group members have articulated their preferences without viewing the preferences of other users), the higher the evaluation with regard to the dimensions (a) satisfaction with the final group decision, (b) perceived degree of decision support, (c) perceived understandability of the final group decision, and (d) consideration of one's personal preferences. Figure 7 depicts, for example, the user evaluations with regard to (a) satisfaction with final group decision and (b) perceived degree of decision support. The average evaluations of all dimensions, i.e., (a) .. (d), are depicted in Table 2.

T-tests also confirm significant user evaluation improvements with an increasing number of defined but undisclosed preferences. The average user evaluations regarding (a) and (b) related to versions *after 1.* and *after 3.* (and above) differ in terms of their mean value ($p < 0.05$, t-test, see also Figure 7). Significant results ($p < 0.05$, t-test) could also be observed for average user evaluations regarding (c) and (d) related to versions *after 1.* and *after all.*

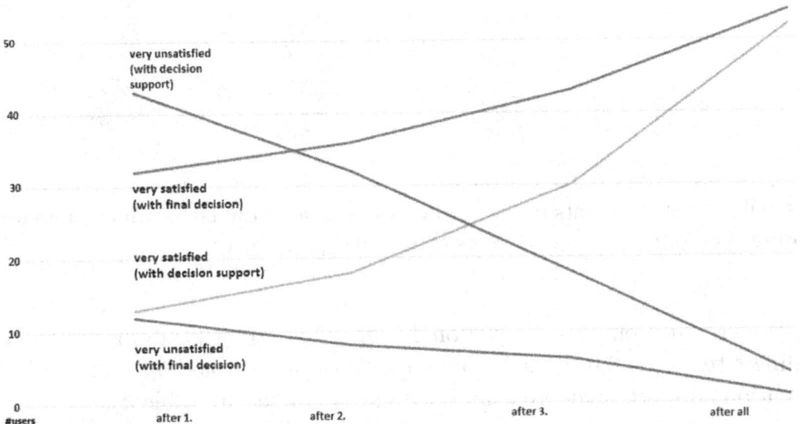

Fig. 7. *Satisfaction with final group decision* and *perceived degree of decision support* depending on preference disclosure time (after 1..3, or all users articulated preferences)

Table 2. Avg. evaluations and std.dev. regarding (a) satisfaction with the final group decision, (b) perceived degree of decision support, (c) perceived understandability of the final group decision, and (d) consideration of one's personal preferences

	All			
	after 1.	after 2.	after 3.	after all
a	2.87(1.67)	3.01(1.5)	3.31(1.19)	3.73(0.73)
b	1.75(1.77)	2.2(1.62)	2.83(1.59)	3.72(1.02)
c	3.44(1.65)	3.54(1.54)	3.79(1.22)	4.04(0.81)
d	3.02(1.77)	3.55(1.75)	3.91(1.46)	4.16(1.04)

We can confirm hypothesis H3: the later individual preferences are disclosed to other users, the higher the amount of comments/discussions in the CHOICLA forum. The number of comments depending on the degree of already available preference definitions not disclosed to other users is shown in Figure 8.

Finally, we can also confirm hypothesis H4: groups with (enforced) explanation support for group decisions have significantly higher evaluations in terms of the dimensions (a) satisfaction with the final group decision, (b) perceived degree of decision support, (c) perceived understandability of the final group decision,

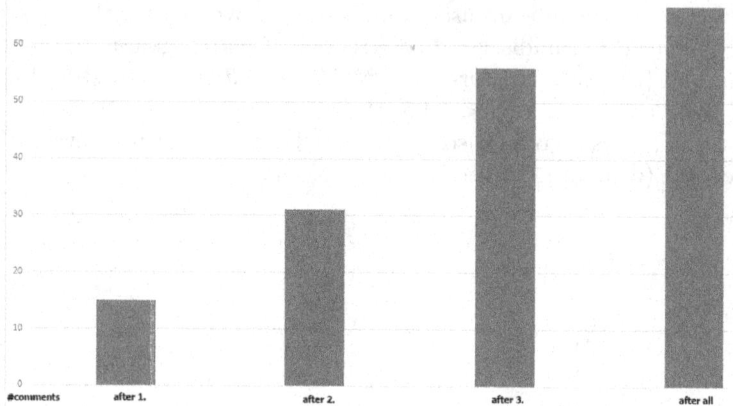

Fig. 8. Number of comments in the CHOICLA discussion forum depending on preference disclosure time (after 1..3, or all users articulated preferences)

and (d) consideration of one's personal preferences. This is confirmed by corresponding t-tests ($p<0.05$) when comparing groups with and without (enforced) explanation support (average evaluations are depicted in Table 3).

Table 3. Avg. evaluations and std.dev. regarding (a) satisfaction with the final group decision, (b) perceived degree of decision support, (c) perceived understandability of the final group decision, and (d) consideration of one's personal preferences

	Explanations Enforced				Explanations Not Enforced			
	after 1.	after 2.	after 3.	after all	after 1.	after 2.	after 3.	after all
a	3.67(1.27)	4.01(1.15)	4.31(0.89)	4.93(0.23)	2.4(1.76)	2.87(1.66)	3.17(1.47)	3.22(1.33)
b	1.95(1.66)	2.5(1.51)	3.45(1.19)	4.69(0.82)	1.63(1.94)	2.02(1.82)	2.67(1.63)	3.18(1.47)
c	3.84(1.35)	3.94(1.24)	4.29(0.92)	4.87(0.41)	3.12(1.72)	3.25(1.78)	3.57(1.58)	3.73(1.22)
d	3.62(1.37)	3.95(1.15)	4.41(0.66)	4.86(0.31)	2.88(1.96)	3.17(1.81)	3.29(1.73)	3.87(1.4)

4 Conclusions and Future Work

With the work presented in this paper we have shown the existence of anchoring effects in group decision scenarios: the earlier individual user preferences are disclosed to other group members, the higher the probability of the occurrence of anchoring effects. The time of preference disclosure also has a direct impact on the perceived quality of the decision outcome and the perceived decision support. Furthermore, late preference disclosure can lead to a higher discussion intensity inside a group which can have a direct positive impact on the quality of the decision outcome. It is important to take into account these aspects in application development; especially one has to analyze the need of preference disclosure since non-disclosed preferences can help to significantly improve decision quality. The analysis of further decision biases and their impact on group decision making is within the major focus of our future work since this will help to further advance the quality of group decision support in the CHOICLA environment. With regard to anchoring effects we want to analyze in further detail the impact of different representation types of user preferences (e.g. aggregated representations vs. user-specific representations) on evaluation dimensions such as perceived decision quality and quality of decision support. Finally, we are also interested in a deeper understanding of intra-group dynamics that can potentially help to further improve the quality of group decisions.

References

1. Adomavicius, G., Bockstedt, J., Curley, S., Zhang, J.: Recommender systems, consumer preferences, and anchoring effects. In: Decisions@RecSys 2011, Chicago, IL, USA, pp. 35–42 (2011)
2. Adomavicius, G., Bockstedt, J., Curley, S., Zhang, J.: De-biasing user preference ratings in recommender systems. In: RecSys 2014 Workshop on Interfaces and Human Decision Making for Recommender Systems (IntRS 2014), Foster City, CA, USA, pp. 2–9 (2014)
3. Dyer, J.: MAUT - multi attribute utility theory. In: Multiple Criteria Decision Analysis: State of the Art Surveys of Intl. Series in Operations Research & Management Science, vol. 78, pp. 265–292. Springer, New York (2005)
4. Felfernig, A.: Biases in decision making. In: Intl. Worksh. on Decision Making and Recommender Systems, vol. 1278, pp. 32–37. CEUR Proceedings (2014)
5. Felfernig, A., Friedrich, G., Gula, B., Hitz, M., Kruggel, T., Leitner, G., Melcher, R., Riepan, D., Strauss, S., Teppan, E., Vitouch, O.: Persuasive recommendation: serial position effects in knowledge-based recommender systems. In: de Kort, Y.A.W., IJsselsteijn, W.A., Midden, C., Eggen, B., Fogg, B.J. (eds.) PERSUASIVE 2007. LNCS, vol. 4744, pp. 283–294. Springer, Heidelberg (2007)
6. Felfernig, A., Gula, B., Teppan, E.: Knowledge-based Recommender Technologies for Marketing and Sales. Intl. Journal of Pattern Recognition and Artificial Intelligence (IJPRAI) **21**(2), 1–22 (2006)
7. Felfernig, A., Zehentner, C., Ninaus, G., Grabner, H., Maalej, W., Pagano, D., Weninger, L., Reinfrank, F.: Group decision support for requirements negotiation. In: Ardissono, L., Kuflik, T. (eds.) UMAP Workshops 2011. LNCS, vol. 7138, pp. 105–116. Springer, Heidelberg (2012)
8. Gkika, S., Lekakos, G.: The persuasive role of explanations in recommender systems. In: 2nd Intl. Workshop on Behavior Change Support Systems (BCSS 2014), vol. 1153, pp. 59–68. CEUR Proceedings, Padua (2014)
9. Greitemeyer, T., Schulz-Hardt, S.: Preference-consistent evaluation of information in the hidden profile paradigm: Beyond group-level explanations for the dominance of shared information in group decisions. Journal of Personality & Social Psychology **84**(2), 332–339 (2003)
10. Herlocker, J., Konstan, J., Riedl, J.: Explaining collaborative filtering recommendations. In: CSCW 2000, pp. 241–250. ACM, Philadelphia (2000)
11. Jacowitz, K., Kahneman, D.: Measures of Anchoring in Estimation Tasks. Personality and Social Psychology Bulletin **21**(1), 1161–1166 (1995)

12. Masthoff, J.: Group recommender systems: combining individual models. In: Recommender Systems Handbook, pp. 677–702 (2011)
13. Masthoff, J., Gatt, A.: In Pursuit of Satisfaction and the Prevention of Embarrassment: Affective State in Group Recommender Systems. User Modeling and User-Adapted Interaction **16**(3–4), 281–319 (2006)
14. Mojzisch, A., Schulz-Hardt, S.: Knowing other's preferences degrades the quality of group decisions. Jrnl. of Personality & Social Psy. **98**(5), 794–808 (2010)
15. Murphy, J., Hofacker, C., Mizerski, R.: Primacy and Recency Effects on Clicking Behavior. Computer-Mediated Communication **11**, 522–535 (2012)
16. Pu, P., Chen, L.: Trust-inspiring Explanation Interfaces for Recommender Systems. Knowledge-Based Systems, 542–556 (2007)
17. Rodriguez, M., Steinbock, D., Watkins, J., Gershenson, C., Bollen, J., Grey, V., deGraf B.: Smartocracy: social networks for collective cecision making. In: HICSS 2007, pp. 90. IEEE, Big Island (2007)
18. Stettinger, M., Felfernig, A., Leitner, G., Reiterer, S., Jeran, M.: Counteracting serial position effects in the CHOICLA group decision support environment. In: 20th ACM Conference on Intelligent User Interfaces (IUI2015), pp. 148–157. ACM, Atlanta (2015)
19. Stettinger, M., Felfernig, A., Ninaus, G., Jeran, M., Reiterer, S., Leitner, G.: Configuring decision tasks. In: Configuration Workshop, Novi Sad, pp. 17–21 (2014)
20. Teppan, E., Felfernig, A.: Minimization of Decoy Effects in Recommender Result Sets. Web Intelligence and Agent Systems **10**(4), 385–395 (2012)
21. Tintarev, N., Masthoff, J.: Explanations of recommendations. In: ACM Conf. on Recommender Systems 2007, pp. 203–206. ACM, Minneapolis (2007)
22. Tversky, A., Simonson, I.: Context-dependent Preferences. Management Science **39**(10), 1179–1189 (1993)
23. Yardi, S., Hill, B., Chan, S.: VERN: facilitating democratic group decision making online. In: Intl. ACM SIGGROUP Conference on Supporting Group Work (GROUP 2005), pp. 116–119. ACM, Sanibel (2005)

Gifting as a Novel Mechanism for Personalized Museum and Gallery Interpretation

Lesley Fosh[1,2(✉)], Steve Benford[1,2], Boriana Koleva[1,2], and Katharina Lorenz[1,2]

[1] School of Computer Science, University of Nottingham, Jubilee Campus, Wollaton Road, Nottingham NG8 1BB, UK
{lesley.fosh,steve.benford,boriana.koleva, katharina.lorenz}@nottingham.ac.uk
[2] School of Humanities, University of Nottingham, University Park, Nottingham NG7 2RD, UK

Abstract. The designers of mobile guides for museums and galleries are increasingly concerned with delivering rich interpretation that can be personalized to meet the diverse needs of individual visitors. However, increased personalization can mean that the sociality of museum visits is overlooked. We present a new approach to resolving the tension between the personal and the social that invites visitors themselves to personalize and gift interpretations to others in their social groups. We tested the approach in two different museum settings and with different types of small group, to investigate how visitors personalized experiences for one another, how the personalized experiences were received by visitors, and how they worked as part of a social visit. We reveal how visitors designed highly personal interpretations for one another by drawing inspiration from both the exhibits themselves and their interpersonal knowledge of one another. Our findings suggest that the deep level of personalization generated by our approach can create rich, engaging and socially coherent visits that allow visitors to achieve a balance of goals. We conclude by discussing the broader implications of our findings for personalization.

Keywords: Museums · Galleries · Personalization · Interpretation · Collaboration

1 Introduction

Each and every visitor to a museum or art gallery brings their own unique set of characteristics, motivations, preferences and understandings. The growing use of modern technology to support the visit gives visitors access to large volumes of online content and the ability to look up diverse information about exhibits. This runs the risk, however, of overwhelming visitors with more information than they can process while visiting, which is why it is increasingly common to turn to automated personalization, where the vast amounts of content available are filtered or adapted to meet the needs of individual visitors.

A wider trend in museums and galleries has seen curators and exhibition designers move away from providing a single interpretation of exhibits, intended to support as wide a range of visitors as possible, towards helping visitors to engage with multiple,

F. Ricci et al. (Eds.): UMAP 2015, LNCS 9146, pp. 131–142, 2015.
DOI: 10.1007/978-3-319-20267-9_11

and possibly contrasting, interpretations and narratives, and even providing material that supports visitors in making their own interpretations.

Personalizing the museum experience can be a uniquely challenging task that can work on two levels: first, a system might provide personalized exhibit recommendations, filtering large collections to support the visitor in engaging only with exhibits that are of interest or relevance. A second opportunity for personalization is the interpretation of exhibits: information or resources that help visitors make meaning. There are many ways of tailoring interpretation to the visitor, from a simple change of language to a focus on the visitor's goals, which might be to learn about a particular topic or to have a good day out with friends.

A further complicating factor is that most people visit museums not alone, but with small groups of friends or family [10] and the social context of a visit can shape how artifacts are experienced. Audio guides can inhibit group interaction even when shared [1], and studies of groups visiting museums has revealed the challenges arising from splitting attention between the museum content and the needs of fellow visitors, which can see visitors being 'dragged away' from their interactions with exhibits in order to maintain group coherence [21]. Attempts to personalize content to individual visitors need to respect the complex social nature of visiting. For example, might tailoring information to individuals heighten existing tensions around group cohesion? Alternatively, might we find ways of using personalization to actually enhance the social nature of the experience?

Motivated by these observations, we explore a new approach to personalization that aims to support rich individual interpretations while at the same time enhancing the social experience of visiting. In this paper, we propose an approach that harnesses the interpersonal knowledge contained within groups of visitors to generate experiences that are at once personal and social. We realized this by inviting visitors who knew each other well to design personalized experiences as gifts for each other, drawing upon their knowledge of one another's interests and backgrounds to tailor interpretations. We draw upon two studies in which we tested this approach with different types of small group, before discussing what our findings mean for personalization in group visiting.

2 Related Work

There is already an extensive body of literature related to personalization in museums spanning the building of user models, matching content to users, and supporting groups.

Visits to individual museums are often one-off and relatively short-term activities, which makes it difficult for systems to build up knowledge about a visitor. Methods of obtaining information on visitors' interests and behaviors include asking the visitor to fill in a questionnaire [6] and assign themselves an avatar [20] or category [11]. Context-aware systems typically gather information without the visitor's input, by monitoring the user's behavior [16] or location [17].

Once the system has gathered information about the user, its next task is to deliver content that best matches this model. Collaborative filtering techniques have been used to recommend exhibits based on comparing paths and visit times to those of other visitors [4], while content-based approaches have been used to match user-generated tags to official curatorial descriptions, to deliver personalized content [9]. Semantic web technologies have also been used to advance these methods, for example by increasing the range of recommendation to include semantically linked artifacts and objects [22].

The relationships between visitors have been exploited in social recommender systems by employing user tags as a basis for recommending content [5], however personalized systems have yet to sufficiently address the challenges arising from group visiting. One visiting guide for tourists combined preferences from multiple group members to recommend city attractions for the whole group to visit [3]. The recommendations were based on the group members' general interests and practical requirements, but did not need to address the additional complexity involved in delivering tailored interpretations for groups or advancing social coherence during the visit. Support for groups visiting museums has included allowing visitors to make connections with others around exhibits [7], sending messages to one another [13] and sharing expressive responses [14].

We sought to build upon previous research to address the combined problem of delivering personalized interpretations in a way that accommodates group visiting. In this paper, we present a novel mechanism for personalizing interpretations that invites visitors to design and gift personalized experiences to other members of their small groups. We report on two studies testing this approach, detailing how visitors personalize museum experiences to one another, before discussing the implications of our results for personalization in museums and galleries.

3 Our Approach

3.1 Motivation

Our approach is motivated by the age-old practice of gift-giving. Gifts are exchanged between people for reasons of obligation and reciprocity, but the practice is also important in building relationships and human solidarity [15]. To buy or make a gift for somebody involves reflecting upon the person's interests, personal characteristics and the relationship between gift-giver and recipient. Choosing a gift in this way imbues the gift with emotional and instrumental meaning for the giver and recipient [19] which may be explained or alluded to in the exchange. The gift exchange is a strongly social occasion that involves a gift-giver, a gift-recipient and possibly onlookers, and involves the recipient carefully managing assessments to decode the gifter's intent and give an appropriate response [18].

It's not uncommon for people to visit attractions such as museums as part of a gift experience, treat or holiday, and the literature tells us that gifting is a powerful mechanism that involves deep personalization and is embedded into a social occasion. We therefore hoped that by bringing the two together as a novel mechanism for personalizing museum experiences within groups, we could create deeply personal experiences that are also inherently social.

Our approach involved inviting visitors to choose exhibits for another and then design interpretations of those exhibits that were specifically tailored for others they were visiting with, to be delivered as part of a mobile guide. We anticipated that visitors could use this method of personalizing gift experiences from one person to another to communicate interpretations that were tailored to visitors by drawing upon interpersonal knowledge of one another, facilitating experiences that are at once personal and social.

3.2 Design of the Experience Template

Instead of asking visitors to design an interpretation from scratch, we provided a template to use as a basis for their gifts. Our template was based on a previously designed experience for pairs of visitors at a sculpture garden [12]. The experience consists of a tour of a set of sculptures with, for each sculpture, a curated music track, an instruction for how to engage with the sculpture, and a portion of text to read after engaging. The delivery of the different components of the experience was structured to support social interaction between pairs of visitors using mobile audio guides. This provided a template that required visitors to choose a set of objects to visit, and for each object, a piece of music, an instruction for how to engage and a portion of text. It was then our job to take the visitors' designs and produce a mobile guide that delivers the content.

3.3 Study Design

We explored the opportunities and challenges associated with this approach through two formative studies, following an 'in the wild' approach [8]. The first study investigated pairs of visitors, while the second looked at scaling the approach to larger groups of friends and family. Our studies involved two stages of participation: an initial design workshop and a second visit where participants were able to use the experiences that we produced from their designs.

Participants and Design Configurations

Study one: Pairs of visitors at Nottingham Contemporary art gallery

Our first study looked at pairs of visitors. We recruited eight pairs to take part, six of whom were romantic partners and two of which were close friends. Of the 16 participants, ten were aged 20-29, four were aged 30-39 and two were over 50. One member of each pair was invited to design a personal tour for their partner, who came along to use the experience once it was designed.

Study two: Groups of three or more visitors at Nottingham Castle Museum

Our second study was designed to extend the approach to larger groups of friends and family. We recruited twelve groups of 3-4 people: six groups of 3-4 friends who knew each other from University, art appreciation groups or were old friends, and six families that included one or two adults and one or two children. Of the 20 participants that made up the adult groups, 13 were aged 20-29, three were aged 30-39 and four were aged over 50. In the family groups, all of the parents were aged 30-49 and the children were aged between three and ten. This time, we invited all group members to design part of a tour. Each member chose one object for each other member of their group, designing the interpretation resources with that person in mind. The designs were collected together and delivered together in a mobile tour for the whole group to use. Four of the six family groups decided to pair up so that children and adults could help each other with the design task.

Design Workshops

Both of our studies began with an initial design workshop held at the museum or gallery, where a workshop facilitator guided the visitors through the design process. The workshops were audio-recorded and we also collected participants' written responses to a set of worksheets used to help generate and structure ideas. The participants were first asked to identify one or more broad aims for the experience they were designing, thinking about the person they were designing for, before browsing the exhibition to select objects they thought would meet these aims.

The participants were then able to design the resources that would make up the personalized interpretation to support the objects: a piece of music, an instruction for how to engage and a portion of text. For each of these, the design work was structured by first asking the participant to think broadly about the type or style of that resource, before considering different possibilities and settling on a final selection. So, for music, participants were encouraged to think about what style or genre might be most effective in suggesting the theme or overall idea they wanted to communicate, then narrowing down to a specific track by listening to tracks online. To choose an instruction, participants were encouraged to think about what style of interaction would be appropriate for their design, for example a physical action or a thought exercise, before deciding on a specific interaction and phrasing for the voice instruction. Finally, they were prompted to consider what style of text to include at each object. This might be a portion of factual information or a more personal message. They then found or wrote the portion of text that would be used in the experience.

Implementation

The participants' designs were implemented into individual smartphone applications using the AppFurnace prototyping tool [2]. We recruited a voice artist to record the instructions that were designed, and mixed these into the introduction of each music track. Given that visitors were finding their way around a constrained gallery space, we chose to present them with a list of exhibits to visit, with a suggestion of where they were, and assumed they would be able to find them for themselves rather than requiring the support of an automated navigation service.

Visits

The participants were invited back to the museum or gallery to use their experiences together in their pairs or groups. We briefly showed them how to use the guide before leaving them to explore the exhibition at their own pace while we video-recorded them from a distance. Once they had completed their visit they were invited to take part in an interview in their groups, asking each of them to reflect on the episodes of their visit.

Analysis

We captured a rich set of data for each group of participants, beginning with audio recordings of the design workshops and the worksheets that participants used to plan their designs. These provided a record of how participants designed interpretations for each other, tracking their motivations, ideas and final designs. We captured video recordings of the participants using their experiences, which were analyzed ethnographically to review how each group interacted with each other and the objects they visited. Over a number of data sessions we were able to summarize what happened over each visit, based on our analysis of participants' interactions, gaze, gesture and utterances. The interview data was used in conjunction to expand on what we saw, collecting visitors' own accounts of their experience at each stage of the visit, and their reflections on the personalized content.

4 Findings

Over the two studies, 49 participants took part in the design of 122 interpretations. Of these, 111 were tried out by the intended recipient (one group of participants in each study was unable to return to use the designed experience), and 110 were completed to the point where the music track faded out and the text was read (in one case the recipient prematurely disengaged with the experience by removing his headphones). In all but one case, the groups reported enjoying using the experience - one pair in our first study found the experience too restrictive. We now present our findings to explore three key areas of interest: how visitors personalized to one another, what it was like to receive a personalized gift, and what it was like to use the experience in a group visit.

4.1 How did Visitors Personalize Experiences for Each Other?

Visitors were able to personalize experiences for one another on a number of levels. Participants in study one, who designed a tour of five objects for their partner, first identified an overarching type of experience they wanted their partner to have. Three main types of experience were cited: *personal* experiences that delivered a personal message; *educational* experiences that were crafted to give information; and *emotional* experiences, designed to suggest an emotion such as enjoyment. Most participants, in describing the type of experience they wanted to design, used a combination of these types, for example a "personal emotional journey" or "a fun experience that might teach him something new".

Participants in both studies then chose objects from the exhibition to form an experience for their friend, family member or partner. Their reasons for choosing particular objects were varied. For participants in study one, the objects were often related to the overall theme or type of experience they had chosen, but in both studies the choice was also guided by the participants' knowledge of the person they were choosing for. This knowledge could relate to the person's interests, their personality, their background, or their beliefs and values. It was often also necessary to draw on their own knowledge and the way they interpreted the objects themselves, choosing something that they found interesting or knew something about, and so were able to offer a useful insight. The selection process therefore involved browsing the exhibition, engaging with objects to draw inspiration, until the participant found a suitable match between their knowledge of the person they were choosing for, their own ideas for a particular theme, the properties of the object itself and how they interpreted the object. Figure 1 shows how the choice of object, and resources, was influenced.

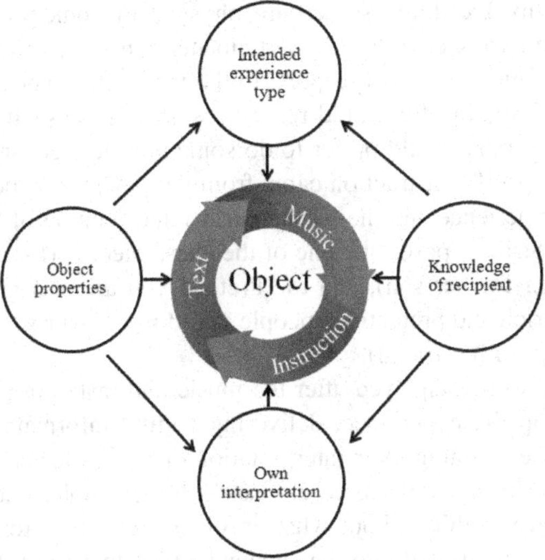

Fig. 1. Factors influencing a participant's design of a personalized experience including choosing an object and a piece of music, an instruction and a portion of text

Next, the participants chose the resources that would accompany the object in the experience to provide an interpretation: a piece of music, an instruction for how to engage and a portion of text. The key influences on the participants' choices for these resources were the objects themselves and their knowledge of the person they were designing for, but the resources were also chosen to support one another, for example a participant might choose a piece of music and an instruction to complement each other to suggest a particular theme or idea, and then a portion of text that expanded on the theme suggested in the music and instruction. The particular reasons for choosing resources were not straightforward, and we now consider each resource separately to understand more about participants' choices.

Music was often used to reflect themes brought up by the object or to set a particular mood or emotional tone. These themes or moods were set by the participants' own interpretations of the object, which in turn were influenced by the participant's knowledge of the recipient – since they were interpreting the objects in relation to the person they were designing for – and their overarching ideas for the theme or type of experience. The music choice tended to be a piece that was known and liked by both the designer and recipient, and matched the interpretation the designer wanted to get across. For example, in study two, participant C chose *Homeward Bound* by Simon and Garfunkel to accompany a decorative tea pot chosen for her friend D, stating that she thought it was about "home and comfort". Other times participants drew inspiration directly from the object itself, choosing, for example, a traditional piece of music from the era or culture the object belonged to, which was the case for participant E who chose to set a Japanese arrow quiver to a piece of traditional Japanese music.

The choice of instruction was also used to set an emotional tone for how the object would be experienced. Participants were given a free choice, but were told that their instruction might involve doing something physical or something thoughtful, or a combination of the two. Generally the participants considered the person they were designing for and how they would respond to the instruction type – some thought the person they were designing for would respond well to a physical engagement while others thought the person would prefer to do something less conspicuous. Again, the inspiration for the specific instruction came from the object's properties, the intended theme or type of experience and the participant's interpretation of the object. Instructions included to "Strike a pose, like one of the chess pieces" (for a Chinese chess set chosen for a mother for her son), and to "Pretend you are at a grand tea party, and think about all the rich and pretentious people you'd meet" (for a tea caddy chosen by a female participant for her friend).

Finally, the text, to be displayed after the music and instruction, was used by participants to wrap up the experience, delivering factual information they had found about the object or explaining their interpretation or reason for choosing it. It tended to follow on from the other resource choices – for example, one participant, after instructing his father to think about what an object was used for, chose to explain "This curved spike was twisted into the elephant's hide to make it behave in a certain way. I thought that you would put a piece of fruit on the spike to tempt the elephant to go in different directions as the elephant would respect you more." Text was also used to deliver personal messages, for example, "I feel this sums up a part of your character and is a nice object to link our friendship…"

Design Example

We now turn to an example from our first study to illustrate the process of designing an experience for somebody. Here, participant A designed an experience for her boyfriend, B. She wanted it to be "a fun experience that lets him see himself through my eyes", and also that would teach him something new. She chose a working version of a Wurlitzer SideMan drum machine, because she thought that being an engineer, B would "like seeing all the inner workings of the machine" and might find its movement "therapeutic". Her interpretation of the object was that it was "calming" and made her aware of the passing of time because of its rhythmic drum beat. Although A perceived the drum machine as slow and steady, she chose a more briskly upbeat song that she felt could convey the potential of the drum machine, and was also a direct reference to the object: *Wurlitzer Jukebox* by Young Marble Giants. When designing the instruction, A said, "I'm thinking about the person I'm doing this for and I know he will not want to do anything that draws attention to himself." She therefore instructed him to "look closely at all the wires and watch the movements. Take off your headphones and listen to the drum machine," which she thought would engage him with the object and set a therapeutic tone. She chose to then give information about the drum machine which she thought B would find interesting: "This is the first drum machine ever made. A knob selects one of 10 preset combinations of sound to create patterns such as Tango, Fox Trot, Waltz, and so on. One setting just produces a metronome click. Shall we dance?" The references to dancing, A said, related to their recent commencement of a series of ballroom dancing classes.

4.2 What was the Effect of Receiving a Personalized Experience?

Our findings show that visitors were generally able to design experiences for one another by drawing inspiration from the exhibits themselves and their knowledge and feelings towards the person they designed for. One of the goals of personalization is to match content onto a model of the user, so we were interested in how well the designs that visitors came up with met the tastes and requirements of the visitors they were designed for. In the interviews that followed the visits, we asked the recipient of each exhibit experience to comment generally on how they found it, and particularly whether they felt the personalization towards them was successful.

On some occasions, visitors noted how the object chosen for them was particularly in line with their tastes or interests, for example because "the colors were right, the patterns were right and everything fitted with things that I do like". Our approach also generated objects that were not to the recipients' tastes, and this came about for a number of reasons. First, it was often the designer's own knowledge and tastes that guided their choice of object, rather than just the recipient's (e.g. one participant had recently read about the history of an artwork and wanted to share the story with her partner). Recipients were generally able to pick up on when this had happened, and find value in these objects for that reason, for example one commented: "It was nice to sort of have an insight into how somebody else has viewed a thing, what they've thought about." Other times, the choice of object was intended to raise a personal issue rather than simply satisfy the recipient's tastes, and recipients were often surprised to find out the reasons they were chosen. For example, a seven year old boy chose a sword in response to a memory he had of his father's time in the military. The father commented that upon finding out the reason: "I felt special that it was chosen for me, and that it wasn't just chosen at random. It was a thought through choice and it had a link to his understanding about my interests". These objects tended to provoke recipients to reflect on the deep interpretations gifted to them in light of their relationships with those who had designed them.

4.3 How did It Work as a Group Experience?

In both studies, all of the group members were given a mobile guide with the same set of gifts, regardless of who designed for whom. The interface presented the set of objects in a list, however the order in which they were chosen was not enforced, so each participant could choose to follow the order presented or choose their own order.

Our studies saw the groups of participants organize themselves in various different ways. Six of the seven pairs who used their experience in our first study negotiated the experience together – visiting the same objects at the same time - while one split up as was their usual visiting pattern. In our second study, the groups of 3-4 people organized themselves much more fluidly. Some groups, including two of the groups of friends and all but one of the families, stayed together for the entire duration, but we also saw groups splitting up for the whole visit or separating and coming together more flexibly, or splitting into subgroups.

Unsurprisingly, we saw the highest levels of social interaction between the groups that stayed together for the visit, who worked together to navigate between objects, coordinate starting each experience, share reactions and reflect on the interpretation. We also observed social contact between the visitors who visited separately, either when coming into contact by chance or expressly seeking one another out to share reactions to each others' designs, ask questions and offer additional explanations.

Our analysis of the video observations suggests that by giving visitors a semi-flexible framework in the form of the mobile guide, they were able to generally organize their own structure for the group visit, thus accommodating a range of changeable visiting styles. Giving each group member control over their own experience – rather than enforcing a coordinated visit – reflects previous findings that highlight the tensions that arise when managing group coherence [21], not by getting people to stick together, but by allowing them to flexibly order when and how things are done and by whom for themselves. The unveiling of personalized gifts throughout the experience added richness to social interactions across the different visiting styles.

5 Discussion

Our research aims to address how museum and gallery interpretation can be personalized in a way that supports group visiting. In this paper, we have explored the novel mechanism of gifting between those who visit together, and our two studies have provided evidence that this is a powerful approach for generating personalized experiences within groups. By drawing on not just the visitor's general interests, but their personal characteristics, shared memories, relationships and issues, we saw many examples of a 'deep' personalization that connected the museum experience with these aspects of visitors' lives.

Our approach generated a uniquely different kind of personalized experience than has been seen in previous research. We saw instances where the personalized gifts markedly did not match with the recipient's interests or tastes, but, through provoking interest or revealing the careful thought that had gone into choosing it, were valued nonetheless. We also found the approach generated gifts that were matched to the person giving, or, in particular, the relationship between the giver and recipient. This allowed visitors to find personal meaning in their interpretations of exhibits, and also to use the museum experience to comment on wider issues in their lives. This is not to say that the focus was shifted entirely from learning about the exhibition content; our studies provide evidence that visitors were able to embed educational content within engaging experiences.

Our observations of how groups used their experiences suggest that personalization systems need to respect the complex and fluid dynamics of group visiting. We suggest that flexibility was key to the success of our approach. By avoiding trying to impose a linear order on visitors' experiences, visitors were able to configure themselves as desired. Future work wishing to automate the selection and ordering of the visit may need a deeper understanding of the social organization of a group visit, as previous work on individual visiting styles may not extend to groups [16].

Finally, our current approach relies entirely on visitors who are willing to design their own content, and it is both the effort involved and the 'human touch' that gives our experiences their unusually deep personalization and shared value. That said, it is interesting to consider ways in which the approach could be streamlined by integrating with recommender systems. Could, perhaps, an online tool show other groups' designs as inspiration for those designing experiences? Could visitors' designs be collected together and tagged by the intended experience type, emotional tone, genre of music, and so on, in order for future users to seek out ideas? It's also important to consider the types of collections our approach would work with, and the level of input that might be required from curators in providing resources for exhibits that are less easy to visitors to design interpretations around. Future research might consider how designs could be re-used, and whether the same levels of deep personalization can be achieved with a partially automated system.

6 Conclusions

Our findings suggest that a human-centered, gifting approach to personalization has the potential to generate deeply personal experiences that add value to shared visiting experiences. Visitors are able to draw on interpersonal knowledge of one another to design engaging experiences that can be enjoyed together in a shared visit. Rather than seeing this as an alternative to automated personalization, what is needed are tools and methods that on the one hand make designing content easier for visitors to do, and on the other, integrate deep personalization into experiences generated by conventional recommender systems.

Acknowledgements. Lesley Fosh is supported by the Horizon Centre for Doctoral Training at the University of Nottingham (RCUK Grant No. EP/G037574/1). This work was supported by the CHESS project, co-funded by the European Commission (Grant No. 270198), EPSRC Dream Fellowship award EP/J005215/1 and Platform Grant award EP/FO3038X/1.

References

1. Aoki, P., et al.: Sotto voce: exploring the interplay of conversation and mobile audio spaces. In: CHI 2002, pp. 431–438. ACM (2002)
2. AppFurnace (2015). http://appfurnace.com. (accessed 24 January 2015)
3. Ardissono, L., et al.: INTRIGUE: Personalized recommendation of tourist attractions for desktop and handset devices. Applied Artificial Intelligence **17**(8–9), 687–714 (2003)
4. Bohnert, F., et al.: Using interest and transition models to predict visitor locations in museums. AI Commun. **21**(2–3), 195–202 (2008)
5. Carmagnola, F., et al.: Tag-based user modeling for social multi-device adaptive guides. User Model. User Adapt. Interact. **18**(5), 497–538 (2008)
6. Cheverst, K., Mitchell, K., Smith, P.: Providing tailored (context-aware) information to city visitors. In: Brusilovsky, P., Stock, O., Strapparava, C. (eds.) AH 2000. LNCS, vol. 1892, pp. 73–85. Springer, Heidelberg (2000)
7. Cosley, D., et al.: ArtLinks: fostering social awareness and reflection in museums. In: CHI 2008, pp. 403–412. ACM (2008)
8. Crabtree, A., et al.: Intro to "The Turn to The Wild". ACM TOCHI **20**(3), 4 (2013)
9. de Gemmis, et al.: Integrating tags in a semantic content-based recommender. In: Pu, P., Bridge, D., Mobasher, B., Ricci, F. (eds.) Proceedings of the 2008 ACM Conference on Recommender Systems, pp. 163–170. Lausanne, Switzerland (2008)
10. Falk, J.H.: Identity and the museum visitor experience. Left Coast Press Inc., Walnut Creek (2009)
11. Filippini Fantoni, S.: Personalization through IT in Museums. Does it really work? The case of the marble Museum website. In: Proceedings of ICHIM 2003 (2003)
12. Fosh, L., et al.: See me, feel me, touch me, hear me: trajectories and interpretation in a sculpture garden. In: CHI 2013, pp. 149–158. ACM (2013)
13. Kuflik, T., et al.: A visitor's guide in an "Active museum": presentations, communications, and reflection. ACM J. Comput. Cult. Herit. **3**(3) (2011)
14. Laaksolahti, J., et al.: The LEGA: a device for leaving and finding tactile traces. In: TEEI 2011, pp. 193–196. ACM (2011)
15. Mauss, M.: The gift: the form and reason for exchange in archaic societies. Routledge Classics, London (1990)
16. Oppermann, R., Specht, M.: A context-sensitive nomadic exhibition guide. In: Thomas, P., Gellersen, H.-.-W. (eds.) HUC 2000. LNCS, vol. 1927, pp. 127–142. Springer, Heidelberg (2000)
17. Rocchi, C., et al.: Fostering conversation after the museum visit: a WOZ study for a shared interface. In: Proceedings of the Working Conference on Advanced Visual Interfaces (AVI 2008), pp. 335–338 (2008)
18. Robles, J.S.: Troubles with assessments in gifting occasions. Discourse Studies **14**(6), 753–777 (2012)
19. Sherry Jr., J.F.: Gift giving in anthropological perspective. Journal of Consumer Research **10**(2), 157–168 (1983)
20. Stock, O., et al.: Adaptive, intelligent presentation of information for the museum visitor in PEACH. User Model. User Adapt. Interact. **17**(3), 257–304 (2007)
21. Tolmie, P., et al.: Supporting group interactions in museum visiting. In: CSCW 2013, pp. 1049–1059. ACM (2013)
22. Wang, Y., et al.: Semantic relations in content-based recommender systems. In: Gil Y., Fridman Noy, N. (eds.) Proceedings of the Fifth International Conference on Knowledge Capture, pp. 209–210 (2009)

Supporting Cross-Device Web Search with Social Navigation-Based Mobile Touch Interactions

Shuguang Han[1](✉), Daqing He[1], Zhen Yue[2], and Peter Brusilovsky[1]

[1] University of Pittsburgh, Pittsburgh, PA 15213, USA
{shh69,dah44,peterb}@pitt.edu
[2] Yahoo! Labs, 701 First Ave., Sunnyvale, CA 94089, USA
zhenyue@yahoo-inc.com

Abstract. The wide adoption of smartphones eliminates the time and location barriers for people's daily information access, but also limits users' information exploration activities due to the small mobile screen size. Thus, cross-device web search, where people initialize information needs on one device but complete them on another device, is frequently observed in modern search engines, especially for exploratory information needs. This paper aims to support the cross-device web search, on top of the commonly used context-sensitive retrieval framework, for exploratory tasks. To better model users' search context, our method not only utilizes the search history (query history and click-through) but also employs the mobile touch interactions (MTI) on mobile devices. To be more specific, we combine MTI's ability of locating relevant subdocument content [10] with the idea of social navigation that aggregates MTIs from other users who visit the same page. To demonstrate the effectiveness of our proposed approach, we designed a user study to collect cross-device web search logs on three different types of tasks from 24 participants and then compared our approach with two baselines: a traditional full text based relevance feedback approach and a self-MTI based subdocument relevance feedback approach. Our results show that the social navigation-based MTIs outperformed both baselines. A further analysis shows that the performance improvements are related to several factors, including the quality and quantity of click-through documents, task types and users' search conditions.

Keywords: Mobile touch interaction · Cross-device web search · Social navigation

1 Introduction

The wide adoption of mobile phones facilitates people's information seeking process so that they can search for information at any time/place when their information needs are triggered. Although bringing the convenience, it is also observed that mobile users sometimes cannot complete a whole search task at one time and on one device. This is particularly common when users were handling complex search tasks [16]. Therefore, users may sometimes halt a search task on

F. Ricci et al. (Eds.): UMAP 2015, LNCS 9146, pp. 143–155, 2015.
DOI: 10.1007/978-3-319-20267-9_12

mobile and resume it on desktop. This is called the cross-device web search in literature [16,22]. Existing studies of cross-device search mainly focused on providing simple descriptive statistics for cross-device web searches and predicting device transition. In contrast, this paper explores automatic support of cross-device search queries (e.g., better ranking of relevant documents). Since simple tasks that can be fulfilled by one or two queries are less common in cross-device web search, we focus specifically on the exploratory search tasks. Furthermore, considering the difficulty of inferring search contexts for the search queries in late stage of a search process [7,15], we set our target to support these queries.

A common approach for modeling search context is to utilize search history [12,18]. The history from mobile devices may be sparse – given the same time, users may produce fewer histories because of the input difficulty on mobile [13]. One solution is to use search and interaction histories from other users who undertook similar tasks. This method, known as social search or social navigation [5,6], has been explored by Farzan [8], Smyth et al. [19] and White et al. [23]. For example, Farzan [8] found that providing social cues (e.g. highlighted content) from other users helped the current user quickly identify relevant information. Our study is closer to [23] because our goal is to provide better document ranking for search queries rather than visualizing social cues to end users. However, we still name our method as social navigation because it is based on user exploration data that are traditionally used by social navigation. Including additional information increases the risk of having noise. Previous studies found that applying subdocument relevant information can help to reduce noise [4,10]. Such information can be inferred either from gaze attention [4] or from mobile touch interactions (MTI) [10]. The latter does not require additional resources to obtain eye-gaze information, and thus is easier to scale up in live systems.

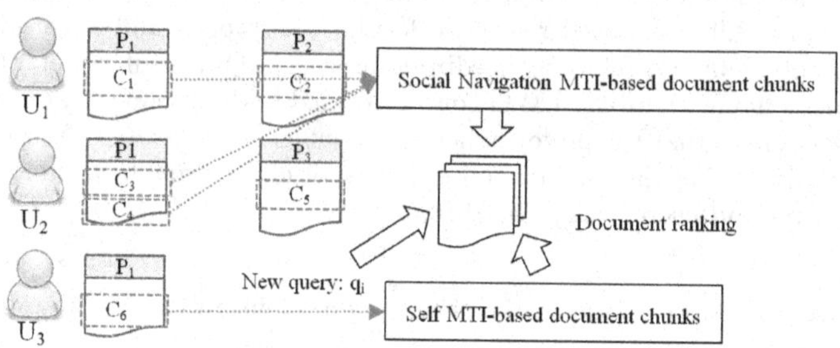

Fig. 1. Self MTI-based and social navigation MTI-based document chunks

Our method combines MTI's ability of pinpointing relevant subdocument content with social navigation's ability of aggregating relevant information. The aggregated content is then used as relevance feedback to support queries in cross-device web searches. To be more specific, a user can have two types of MTI: self MTI and social navigation MTI. The former refers to the MTIs performed by the user herself while the latter refers to the MTIs performed by other users on the web pages visited by the given user. This can be illustrated by Figure 1. Suppose that we have three users (U_1, U_2 and U_3) working on the same task. They visited three web pages (P_1, P_2 and P_3). Based on the logged MTIs, we can infer six relevant document chunks (C_1, C_2, ..., C_6) using the method described in Section 3.2. To support a new query q_i for U_3, besides using q_i itself, we can also incorporate U_3's search history (i.e., P_1). Instead of using the full text of P_1, we may only use C_6 because we have identified that U_3 is only interested in C_6. We name it as the self MTI based method. When applying social navigation MTIs, we use C_1, C_3 and C_4 (C_6 is not included because it is self MTI) as relevant document chunks because other users (i.e., U_1 and U_2) who conducted the same task have shown interests in those document chunks. Note that, we do not include C_2 and C_5 because U_3 didn't click on P_2 or P_3.

Social navigation information can only be applied when users performed the same or similar tasks. White et al. [23] computed the similarity of two tasks by their query similarity. This approach requires a large-scale search log, which is difficult to acquire. Thus, we followed the approach used in Farzan [8] that performed lab-based user studies and preset the same task goals for all participants. To make our search tasks resemble real-world cross-device web searches, our tasks were directly adopted from Han et al. [10], where tasks were designed based on the results of an online survey. Among the collected information needs, we selected the ones that seek for multi-facet answers to simulate the intrinsic diversity (ID) tasks, which was identified as a popular type of information need in modern search engines [17].

Overall, we are interested in the following two research questions. First, can social navigation MTIs be used to improve the cross-device web search (we only study mobile-to-desktop web search in this paper) performance? Second, can social navigation-based MTIs also be used to improve the same-device cross-session web search (we only study the desktop-to-desktop web search in this paper) performance when MTIs are unavailable?

2 Related Work

Despite the popularity of cross-device web search in modern search engines [16], related studies on this topic, particularly the automatic support of such search scenario, are still rare. Existing work mainly focused on providing simple descriptive statistics and predicting device continuation [16,22]. For example, Wang et al. [22] studied the task resumption in cross-device web search tasks and identified several interesting patterns that are associated with device transition. The support of mobile web search was explored in Song et al. [20]. They studied the search process on different devices (desktop, tablet and smartphones) and found that mobile search performance could be improved by transferring user behaviors from desktop. However, their focus is not on cross-device web search.

To support cross-device web searches, the techniques from context-sensitive information retrieval [18] and search personalization [1] can be used. A common approach is to treat users' search history as relevance feedback to re-rank relevant documents. Shen et al. [18] found that both query history and click-through are useful feedback resources but the latter is more effective. When applying the click-through, previous studies either incorporated the full text [12] or subdocument chunks within a document [4]. It is reported that using subdocument content is more effective [4,14]. However, obtaining subdocument chunks is a non-trivial task. Liu and Croft [14] treated the best-matched passages in a document for the given query as relevant subdocument chunks. Buscher et al. [4] obtained subdocument chunks through eye-tracking, where the content with more gaze attentions are chosen as relevant subdocument chunks. Han et al. [11] located subdocument chunks through touch-based interactions. The study presented in this paper takes a similar approach as Han et al. [11], but also differs from their study. In addition to the touch position and touch speed used in Han et al.[11], the inactive time is also adopted in our work based on a recent study [9], finding that the inactive time is a strong indicator for content relevance. Besides, we study both self MTIs and social navigation-based MTIs, which were not considered in Han et al. [11].

One challenge of utilizing search history is to handle the data sparseness. White et al. [23] found that it is possible to include the feedback information from other users who conducted similar search tasks. Similar idea were also explored as social navigation in literature [6], where social cues generated from other users are used to assist the current user on navigating the complex information space. Previous studies showed that applying social navigation in web search [8] and e-learning systems [3] enables people to access and utilize relevant information more effectively. However, social navigation has the risk of introducing noise because different users may have different search intentions, even when visiting the same page. A possible remedy is to differentiate user?s intentions and utilize the social cues only from people within the same user cohorts [23] or search community [19]. These approaches require acquiring user information which may be hard to obtain. Other information such as users' MTI behaviors can also help to identify a fine-grained user interest, and thus can be used to filter out the noise [10]. In this paper, we try to combine the advantages of social navigation and MTIs, and expect further improvement on search performance.

3 Experiment Setup

We built a cross-device web search dataset through a controlled lab study. In this paper, the cross-device search referred to mobile-to-desktop (M-D) web search. A desktop-to-desktop (D-D) search was also included for two reasons. First, one of our research questions is to apply social navigation based MTIs in D-D. Second, users can explore information more conveniently and thoroughly on desktop, which help us build a more reliable ground truth. After obtaining such dataset, we applied the context-sensitive retrieval model [18] to re-rank search results for the queries from the second session, as stated in the Introduction.

3.1 Data Collection

Obtaining our experimental data requires: (1) a cross-device web search system to record user behaviors; (2) properly designed cross-device web search tasks; (3) a well-designed experiment procedure; and (4) a ground-truth.

CrossSearch. Recording user behaviors, particularly the MTIs, is the most important component in our study. Such information was logged in CrossSearch, our self-developed system. When receiving a query, CrossSearch triggers Google API and displays search results returned by Google. Besides, CrossSearch also logs users? queries and clicked documents.

Search Tasks. As stated, the cross-device search tasks we used are directly adopted from Han et al. [10], which included six tasks from three categories: news search (NE), product search (PD) and people search (PE). Each category had two tasks, each task was designed on top of the results from an online survey.

User Study Design. Our study included both M-D and D-D. We employed a within subject design so that each participant searched for all six tasks with three under M-D and the other three under D-D. The combination of tasks, search conditions (M-D or D-D) and task sequence were rotated based on Latin square to minimize fatigue and learning effects. Each task was divided into two sessions, 7 minutes for each. In the first session, the participants performed three tasks on mobile and the other three on desktop and all the six tasks were resumed on desktop in the second session. Whenever they found relevant documents, the participants can save the documents. At the end of each task, the participants were asked to rate the relevance of each saved webpage on a 5-point Likert scale with 1 denoting not relevant and 5 being highly relevant.

Data Collection. We recruited 24 participants (15 females and 9 males, 16 undergraduates and 8 graduates) from University of Pittsburgh and Carnegie Mellon University during October to November in 2013. All participants were self-rated experienced searchers. The participants issued 961 unique search queries, visited 1,790 unique webpages and saved 1,125 of them. In total, we logged 3,286 MTIs on the clicked web pages, where the dragdown (53.1%), dragup (17.5%) and tap (12.7%) were three dominating behavior types. Pinch-in and pinch-out were ignored because of the number was too few (less than 1%).

Ground Truth. The ground-truth relevance of each document was computed based on users' post-task self-rated document relevance. Since a document can be saved by different users with different relevance scores, the simplest way for aggregation is to compute average. However, it may be biased for the documents saved only by few users. Thus, a Bayesian smoothing method was adopted to remove this bias [10,21]. When generating ground truth for the search queries on M-D, we aggregated the saved documents from D-D because the information from M-D was used for producing the relevance feedback. When generating ground truth for D-D, we excluded information from a given participant but included that from all other participants.

3.2 Applying Context-Sensitive Retrieval Model

Our next step is to re-rank search results based on the context-sensitive retrieval model [18]. In this paper, we only used the click-through information. First, previous studies [10,12,18] identified that the click-through is superior to query history. Second, the focus of our later studies is to recognize relevant subdocument content chunks from click-through documents. Using click-through makes our results more consistent in comparing to different click-through models. Following the majority of previous studies [10,12,18], we employed language modeling approach to represent different click-through models.

Unigram Click-Through Language Model was inferred by the method proposed in Shen et al. [18]. Their approach estimated the click-through language model through averaging all unigram word distributions inferred from the full text of click-through documents.

MTI-Based Click-Through Language Model. Biedert et al. [2] found that users' touch positions usually lie within their reading zones. Thus, we assumed that if a user touched on position P (string index of the touched content in the whole document), she can read at most M characters before and after P, which means that the reading zone is [P-M, P+M]. We further measured the relevance of a reading zone based on inactive time and gesture speed [9,11] because they are two strongest indicators for content relevance. We used two rules to define a relevant reading zone: (1) the reading speed that is slower than S and had an inactive time longer than I; (2) top M characters of a clicked document are used as relevant content if there are no MTIs. In this paper, we set S=500(pixels/second), I=1(second) and M=85(characters, ~14-15 words) because of their best performance in training datasets. The employed MTIs were dragup and dragdown because they took high proportion in MTIs. Tap was not used because it is the same as click in desktop. Finally, depending on the MTIs we used, we can either build a self-MTI or social navigation-MTI based click-through language model.

Utilizing Estimated Language Model for Document Re-Ranking. We applied the following procedure to re-rank relevant documents for each query in the second session: for each to-be-ranked candidate document, we estimated its document language model. The matching between a candidate document and the click-through was measured by the KL divergence between their language models. The matching between a candidate document and the given query was measured by Google rank position. The two scores were combined for a final document ranking. Instead of using linear interpolation as [18], we used LambaMART in RankLib (http://sourceforge.net/p/lemur/wiki/RankLib/) because of its better performance and easy parameter tuning. Therefore, for each query-document pair, we applied two ranking features: the Google rank position, and the KL-divergence between the click-through language model and candidate document language model. Depending on the methods we used for estimating the click-through language model, we had different variants of KL divergence.

Evaluation. The dataset was divided into the training and testing parts. The training part was used to estimate model parameters and the testing part was used to test the effectiveness of each method. Training-testing division was based on task type. Then, we can obtain three datasets: PD (PD for testing and the rest for training), PE (PE for testing and the rest for training) and NE (NE for testing and the rest for training). We chose nDCG@20 as an evaluation metric because our study is to support exploratory search tasks, where users usually explored the result space in depth and saved many relevant web pages. In our study, the participants saved 13.00($\pm$6.65) documents on M-D and 15.88($\pm$9.77) documents on D-D. This is different from studying the navigational information needs, where nDCG at lower cutoffs were often used. Besides, in another study [10] with similar experiment setting, we found that using nDCG at different cutoffs produced consistent results. Therefore, we only reported nDCG@20 results.

4 Results Analysis and Discussions

This section begins with testing the utility of applying social navigation-based MTIs in M-D. Then, a similar approach is applied for D-D, in which the MTIs from M-D are adopted. The compared baselines and context-sensitive retrieval models include: (1) pure Google search results (G); (2) Google ranks with click-through language model estimated from the full-text of click-through documents (G+H_F); (3) Google ranks with click-through language model estimated from the self MTI-based document chunks (G+H_{MTI-S}); and (4) Google ranking position with social navigation MTI-based document chunks (G+H_{MTI-SN}).

4.1 Applying Social Navigation-Based MTIs in M-D

Overall results. As the results shown in Table 1, G+H_{MTI-SN} achieves the best performance, which demonstrates the usefulness of social navigation MTIs. Comparing to the use of full text, MTIs indeed help locate more relevant content: both G+H_{MTI-S} and G+H_{MTI-SN} are significantly better than G+H_F. The social navigation MTIs (G+H_{MTI-SN}) further improve the search performance over the self-MTIs. The reasons might be that the social navigation MTIs are less likely to encounter the data sparseness problem and the document chunks identified by social navigation MTIs can also vote for the most relevant information.

Table 1. nDCG of different runs on M-D. ↑/↓ mean the increase/decrease; ∼Hx means a significance test comparing to Hx. p-values are based on Wilcoxon signed-rank test.

	nDCG@20	**Sig.(∼H_F)**	**Sig.(∼H_{MTI-S})**
G	0.3974	↓,p<0.001	↓,p<0.001
G+H_F	0.4298	-	↓,p=0.004
G+H_{MTI-S}	0.4421	↑,p=0.004	-
G+H_{MTI-SN}	0.4497	↑,p<0.001	↑,p<0.003

Task Effects. We separate the search performance by task to understand the task effect. The results are provided in Table 2. We find that PE and NE tasks show the same trends as the overall nDCG changes while PD presents fewer significant differences. We think it may be related to the task nature: some tasks may need to explore diverse topics while the others tend to find more similar results. If PD belongs to the former task type, simply applying relevant information from search history may not work. To test this hypothesis, we compute the overall query similarity between the first and second search session. If our hypothesis is correct, the query similarity of PD should be smaller.

Query similarity is measured by the cosine similarity (with tf-idf weights) of their corresponding Google search result pages. We did not use the query keyword matching due to the word mismatching problem. The final query similarity is averaged over all of the possible query pairs between the first and the second session. We find that the average query similarity for PD is 0.0146, which is statistically significantly lower than 0.0199 for NE (p-value=0.041) and 0.0194 for PE (p-value=0.039). This indicates that users are more likely to explore different information in PD. This result suggests the importance of considering task nature when utilizing MTI-based relevant content.

Table 2. nDCG of different runs on M-D. Numbers in bold (italics) indicates $p<0.05$ compare with H_F (H_{MTI-S}) using Wilcoxon signed-rank test.

	PD	PE	NE
G	**0.4012**↓	**0.4648**↓	**0.3286**↓
G+H_F	0.4300	0.4835	0.3773
G+H_{MTI-S}	0.4276	**0.5077**↑	0.3902
G+H_{MTI-SN}	0.4249	***0.5197***↑	**0.4019**↑

Impacts of Click-Through. We also examine the impacts of the quantity and quality of click-through documents to the search performance. First, we categorize the to-be-supported queries into three groups based on the number of corresponding click-through documents: "1-7", "8-10" and "11+". Each group has about equal number (~110) of queries. To achieve a better understanding of how different feedback information performs in each click-through group, we compute nDCG changes, ΔnDCG=nDCG(G+H_X)–nDCG(G), before (G) and after (G+H_X) applying the click-through in each group and then plot them in Figure 2. A positive value means that applying the click-through is better than pure Google results. Here, H_X refers to different types of feedback information, which can either be H_F, H_{MTI-S} or H_{MTI-SN}. We name the corresponding nDCG changes as ΔNDCG_HF, ΔNDCG_HMTI_S and ΔNDCG_HMTI_SN.

All three curves in Fig. 2 are above zero, which shows the effectiveness of applying click-through information. In the ideal case, increasing the click-through quantity can result in a better performance because of having more information. However, although nDCG of G+H_F is positive in "11+", it is smaller than that in "8-10". We think the quality of click-through may also

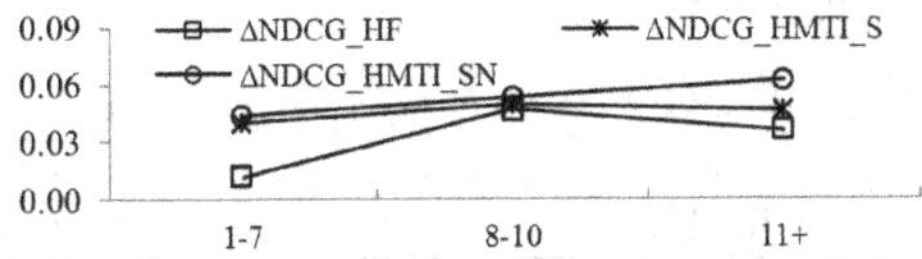

Fig. 2. ΔNDCG (Y axis) against the quantity of click-through (X axis) on M-D

play important role here. Indeed, the average relevance for the click-through documents in "11+" is 2.11, while it is 2.40 in "8-10". The two values have significant difference (p=0.01).

One way to improve search performance is to employ the relevant subdocument content instead of the full text. In the group "11+", we indeed observe that the nDCG of $G+H_{MTI-S}$ (p-value=0.034) and $G+H_{MTI-SN}$ (p-value<0.001) are statistically significantly higher than the nDCG of $G+H_F$. The same trend is also observed in the group "1-7". This shows the robustness of MTI-based approaches. However, we do not observe significant differences in the group "8-10", probably because they have already achieved very good performance. Furthermore, the performance of the self-MTI method does not always increase as the click-through quantity increases while that of the social navigation-based method keeps increasing. This also shows the robustness of social navigation-based MTIs in comparison with self-MTIs.

4.2 Applying Social Navigation-Based MTIs in D-D

Overall results. Social navigation MTI-based method does not use information from the current querying user, which enables us to employ MTIs from mobile devices (there are no MTIs on desktop) to support the search queries in D-D. Suppose that we know a user U_i's click-through $C(c_1, c_2, ..., c_n)$ in the first session of D-D. For each to-be-supported query q_m of user U_i, when applying the click-through C, we can use MTIs from M-D on c_i to infer the relevant subdocument chunks and then apply them to estimate the click-through language models for document ranking. Given the best performance of social navigation MTI-based approach on M-D, we expect the same effects on D-D.

Yet, applying the same method as we did on M-D does not result in performance improvement as we expected (see Table 3). There are no significant difference between $G+H_{MTI-SN}$ and $G+H_F$. Further studies on the impact of click-through quantity/quality and task effect (see later sections) also do not reveal any difference. We think this is due to the device difference between M-D and D-D in the first session. Since there are more click-through documents in D-D, the social navigation based method may potentially introduce more noise, particularly when considering that users who visited the same documents may not have the same purposes. Therefore, we conduct further studies to understand whether it is possible to identify and differentiate users' search purposes.

Table 3. nDCG of different runs on D-D. Notations are the same as Table 1.

	nDCG@20	**Sig.(~$\mathbf{H_F}$)**	**Sig.(~$\mathbf{H_{MTI-SN}}$)**
G	0.4068	↓,$p<0.001$	↓,$p<0.001$
G+H_F	0.4452	-	↓,$p=0.610$
G+H_{MTI-SN}	0.4491	↑,$p=0.610$	-
G+$H_{MTI-SN-Q}$	0.4549	↑,$p=0.021$	↑,$p=0.006$

Utilizing MTIs from Similar Search Queries. To find relevant documents, users need to issue queries, click webpages and interact with these webpages. Thus, each webpage and each interaction are associated with at least one query. We hypothesize that the same webpage under the same/similar queries may better reveal users' similar search purposes. In this case, when applying the social navigation MTI-based approach, we can use MTIs that are not only from the same webpage but also associated with similar queries. Query similarity is computed using cosine similarity (with tf-idf weights) of their corresponding Google search result pages. If cosine similarity is higher than 0.125, we define the two queries as similar. Based on this, we can build a new MTI-based click-through language model, where we still use social navigation MTI-based document chunks but filter out the MTIs that are not associated with similar queries. We named this feedback information as $H_{MTI-SN-Q}$. Results in Table 3 show that G+$H_{MTI-SN-Q}$ does improve the search performance: it is significantly better than both G+H_F, and G+H_{MTI-SN}. This indicates the importance of differentiating the MTIs under similar search queries when applying the social navigation based approach.

Task Effects. Table 4 presents the performance for each task, which shows that the effectiveness of social navigation approach is different for different tasks. Applying the query-based differentiation on MTIs (G+$H_{MTI-SN-Q}$) does improve nDCG, but its effect is task-dependent. It improves nDCG on NE, and has a trend on PE. However, it still has no impact on PD. The explanation may be the same as we hypothesized for M-D (see Table 2). This, again, illustrates the importance of considering task effects when applying such method.

Table 4. nDCG on the use of different runs on D-D. Numbers in bold (italics) indicates $p<0.05$ compare with H_F(H_{MTI-SN}) using Wilcoxon signed-rank Test.

	PD	**PE**	**NE**
G+H_F	0.3612	0.5420	0.4308
G+H_{MTI-SN}	0.3575	0.5462	0.4498
G+$H_{MTI-SN-Q}$	0.3608	0.5529↑($p=0.06$)	***0.4576***↑

Impacts of Click-Through. We also analyze the impact of click-through to the search performance. Similar to our M-D analysis, we divide the to-be-supported queries into three groups (each has ~100 queries): "4-10", "11-17" and "18+". In each group, we compute ΔNDCG: the nDCG of each approach minus the nDCG of pure Google search (G). The results are plotted in Figure 3. G+H_F shows the same trend as that on M-D: ΔNDCG is growing from the "smallest" group to the "medium" group but is decreasing from the "medium" to the "largest". However, it is different from the trend on M-D for G+H_{MTI-SN}: the performance does not grow from the "medium" group to the "largest" group. Thus, we analyze the change of relevance for the click-through documents from the "medium" group to the "largest" one on both M-D and D-D. The value is calculated using the "largest" group minus the "medium". We find that the change is -0.48 for D-D and -0.29 for M-D. The drop of click-through document quality may account for decreasing of ΔNDCG from the "medium" group to the "largest" group in D-D.

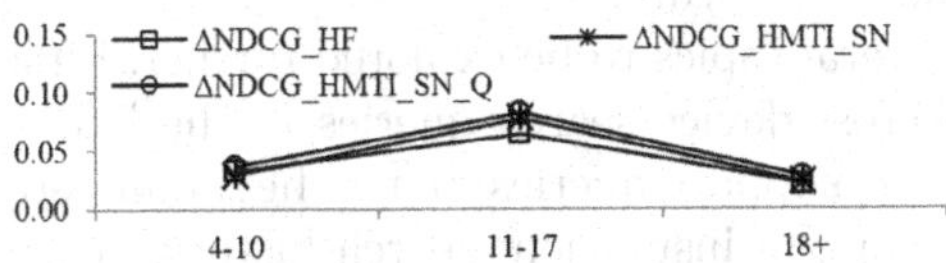

Fig. 3. ΔNDCG (Y axis) against the quantity of click-through (X axis) on D-D

4.3 Summarizations, Discussions and Implications

Consistent with our previous study [10], we observed that the self MTI-based subdocument relevance feedback outperformed both the initial Google ranking and the full text-based relevance feedback. This study went further by proving that the social navigation-based relevance feedback could achieve even better results than self MTI-based relevance feedback. The effectiveness of social navigation-based approach may come from two aspects: (1) it relieves the data sparseness problem when users' own behaviors provide too little information; and (2) MTIs from different users can vote for the most relevant subdocument chunks. More importantly, we demonstrated that the social navigation-based MTI can be applied to both D-D and M-D conditions. This would be a very exciting finding for modern search engines since they have search logs about users from both their mobile and desktop search activites. Rich and fine-grained interactions obtained from MTIs enable search engines to accurately infer user interests, which in turn could better support both mobile and desktop searches.

A critical prerequisite for applying social navigation is that users share common task goals. Our study showed that this might not be enough. Different search queries might focus on different aspects even within the same task. Therefore, it is critically needed to have proper search intention discernment mechanisms such as using query similarity to differentiate social navigation information.

5 Conclusion and Future Work

With the wide adoption of smartphones, it is more common for people to conduct cross-device web search. Therefore, more and more users' mobile touch interactions (MTI) are collected when they access information through mobile devices. In this paper, we study whether the social navigation-based MTIs (MTIs collected from other users who visited the same webpages) can be employed to support the current user's cross-device web search. The MTIs used in this paper were collected through a lab study with 24 participants working on six cross-device web search tasks. Using the collected data, we then setup a relevance feedback experiment to evaluate our proposed approach. We find that the social navigation-based MTIs indeed help to improve search performance for cross-device web search over the methods of not using MTIs or only using self-performed MTIs. Further studies show that the effectiveness of social navigational based MTI is relates to many factors such as the quantity/quality of click-through and the task nature.

There could be several topics to be explored further. Firstly, we only considered the support of cross-device search queries in the late search stages, while it is also interesting to support queries at the beginning stage. This would be more challenging because of insufficient search history. Secondly, we found that both self-MTI and social navigation-based MTI can lead to the performance improvements. However, we have not studied whether they could be combined to further improve the search performance. Thirdly, we recruited only 24 participants and performed our study in a lab-controlled environment, which may not trully reflect users' interactions in a live search environment. Thus, a large-scale analysis of our approach from real search engine logs might be needed to confirm some of our findings. Finally, although we focused on cross-device web search in this paper, our approach can be easily adapted to other search scenarios such as pure mobile search or desktop search. Overall, MTI provides us many interesting challenges and opportunities.

References

1. Bennett, P.N., White, R., Chu, W., Dumais, S.T., Bailey, P., Borisyuk, F., Cui, X.: Modeling the impact of short-and long-term behavior on search personalization. In: SIGIR, pp. 185–194 (2012)
2. Biedert, R., Dengel, A., Buscher, G., Vartan, A.: Reading and estimating gaze on smart phones. In: ETRA, pp. 385–388 (2012)
3. Brusilovsky, P., Chavan, G., Farzan, R.: Social adaptive navigation support for open corpus electronic textbooks. In: De Bra, P.M.E., Nejdl, W. (eds.) AH 2004. LNCS, vol. 3137, pp. 24–33. Springer, Heidelberg (2004)
4. Buscher, G., Dengel, A., van Elst, L.: Query expansion using gaze-based feedback on the subdocument level. In: SIGIR, pp. 387–394 (2008)
5. De Bra, P., Brusilovsky, P., Houben, G.: Adaptive hypermedia: from systems to framework. ACM Computing Surveys (CSUR) **31**(4es), 12 (1999)
6. Dourish, P., Chalmers, M.: Running out of space: models of information navigation. In: Short Paper Presented at HCI, vol. 94, pp. 23–26 (1994)
7. Evans, B.M., Chi, E.H.: An elaborated model of social search. Information Processing & Management **46**(6), 656–678 (2010)
8. Farzan, R.: A study of social navigation support under different situational and personal factors. Doctoral Thesis of University of Pittsburgh (2009)

9. Guo, Q., Jin, H., Lagun, D., Yuan, S., Agichtein, E.: Mining touch interaction data on mobile devices to predict web search result relevance. In: SIGIR, pp. 153–162 (2013)
10. Han, S., He, D., Yue, Z.: Understanding and Supporting Cross-Device Web Search for Exploratory Tasks with Mobile Touch Interactions. TOIS (2015)
11. Han, S., Hsiao, I.-H., Parra, D.: A study of mobile information exploration with multi-touch interactions. In: Kennedy, W.G., Agarwal, N., Yang, S.J. (eds.) SBP 2014. LNCS, vol. 8393, pp. 269–276. Springer, Heidelberg (2014)
12. Jiang, J., Han, S., Wu, J., He, D.: PITT at TREC 2011 Session Track (2011)
13. Kamvar, M., Baluja, S.: Deciphering trends in mobile search. IEEE Computer **8**, 58–62 (2007)
14. Liu, X., Croft, W.B.: Passage retrieval based on language models. In: CIKM, pp. 375–382 (2002)
15. Marchionini, G.: Exploratory search: from finding to understanding. Communications of the ACM **49**(4), 41–46 (2006)
16. Montañez, G.D., White, R.W., Huang, X.: Cross-device search. In: CIKM, pp. 1669–1678 (2014)
17. Raman, K., Bennett, P.N., Collins-Thompson, K.: Toward whole-session relevance: exploring intrinsic diversity in web search. In: SIGIR, pp. 463–472 (2013)
18. Shen, X., Tan, B., Zhai, C.: Context-sensitive information retrieval using implicit feedback. In: SIGIR, pp. 43–50 (2005)
19. Smyth, B.: A community-based approach to personalizing web search. IEEE Computer **40**(8), 42–50 (2007)
20. Song, Y., Ma, H., Wang, H., Wang, K.: Exploring and exploiting user search behavior on mobile and tablet devices to improve search relevance. In: WWW, pp. 1201–1212 (2013)
21. Särkkä, S.: Bayesian filtering and smoothing, vol. 3. Cambridge University Press (2013)
22. Wang, Y., Xiao, H., White, R.: Characterizing and supporting cross-device search tasks. In: WSDM, pp. 707–716 (2013)
23. White, R.W., Chu, W., Hassan, A., He, X., Song, Y., Wang, H.: Enhancing personalized search by mining and modeling task behavior. In: WWW, pp. 1411–1420 (2013)

A Utility Model for Tailoring Sensor Networks to Users

Masud Moshtaghi(✉) and Ingrid Zukerman

Faculty of Information Technology, Monash University, Clayton, VIC 3800, Australia
{masud.moshtaghi,ingrid.zukerman}@monash.edu

Abstract. The proportion of people aged over 65 has significantly increased in recent times, with further increases expected. Multiple sensor-based monitoring solutions have been proposed to tackle the main concerns of elderly people and their carers, viz fall detection and safe movement in the house. At the same time, user studies have shown that cost is the most important factor when deciding whether to install a monitoring system. In this paper, we offer a utility-based approach for selecting a sensor configuration for a user on the basis of his/her behaviour patterns and preferences regarding false alerts and delay in the detection of mishaps, while taking into account his/her budget. Our evaluation on two real-life datasets shows that our utility function supports the selection of cost-effective sensor configurations.

Keywords: Older adults · Sensor selection · Monitoring systems · Inactivity detection

1 Introduction

The ageing of the world's population has put a large strain on health services, which is expected to increase in the coming years. This has prompted a plethora of projects investigating *In-Home Monitoring Systems* (*IHMSs*) that rely on sensor networks to support elderly people in their homes, e.g., [1–3].

Our own IHMS [3] detects abnormally long periods of inactivity in a home as a proxy of unsafe events. Our approach to the design of this IHMS is based on requirements of elderly people and their carers, which were canvassed in a formative study [4]. In this study, we found, *inter alia*, that the main reason for installing an IHMS was *fall detection and safe movement in the home*, that *intrusiveness* of the monitoring equipment was a recurring concern, and that *affordability* was considered the most important factor when deciding to install an IHMS. However, selecting the best set of sensors for a home is a challenging problem, which has been studied in the context of IHMSs only in terms of sensor intrusiveness and reliability [5,6].

The *sensor selection* problem has also been studied in a general sense [7], and in specific application areas, such as Wireless Sensor Networks, in order to save energy [8]. Clearly, an exhaustive search of all possible subsets of a sensor network

F. Ricci et al. (Eds.): UMAP 2015, LNCS 9146, pp. 156–168, 2015.
DOI: 10.1007/978-3-319-20267-9_13

is feasible only when the size of the network is very small. Instead, we suggest that, in order to select a useful set of sensors within a set of constraints (e.g., budget, energy consumption), it makes sense to develop application-dependent utility functions that can be optimized by applying a search algorithm. Such an approach was adopted by Schneider [9], who developed an *information utility function* for a plan recognition application in an instrumented environment, and employed search algorithms to improve this function using simulated data. In Schneider's application, the utility of a sensor configuration depends on the extent to which it enables a user to reach higher-valued goals, and helps the user reach his/her goals efficiently. In contrast, in the context of an IHMS, the utility of a sensor configuration depends on the delay in the detection of mishaps, and the number of generated false alerts. These two factors counter-balance each other, i.e., the number of false alerts usually increases as the detection delay decreases, and vice versa [3].

In this paper, we propose a utility-based approach for selecting an optimal sensor configuration for an IHMS in the home of a user. Importantly, the best configuration for one user may differ from the optimal configuration for another user depending on (1) the user's budget, (2) his/her behaviour patterns, and (3) his/her preferences in terms of the balance between false alerts and anomaly-detection delay (e.g., some people prefer a shorter delay at the expense of additional false alerts). Since the number of false alerts is mainly controlled through the parameters of the statistical model for inactivity detection [2,3,6], in this paper we focus on the other factors. Like Schneider [9], we start with an over-sensored environment, and assume that the layout of the sensors in this environment has been pre-determined. During a *training period*, we select the best-performing subset of the available sensors for a particular budget without modifying the layout. This is the sensor configuration that is used for testing. Our approach differs from Schneider's in our utility function, which is designed for the IHMS context, and in our use of dynamic programming, instead of heuristic search algorithms.

This paper is organized as follows. A brief overview of our IHMS and inactivity detection model [3,6] appears in Section 2. Section 3 formalizes the problem statement, and Section 4 describes our utility function. The evaluation of the utility function, and a demonstration of its application to sensor selection, appear in Section 5. Section 6 presents concluding remarks.

2 Background

The components of a typical IHMS for detecting anomalous events are: (1) a network of sensors, (2) a module for data collection, (3) an anomaly-detection module, and (4) a response generation module. The sensors transmit signals about observed events, such as opening a door or moving within a room, to the data-collection module via a base station. The data-collection module logs the data, and prepares it as input to the anomaly-detection module. This module in turn builds a model of a user's normal behaviour from the data collected so far, and determines what constitutes a significant departure from this behaviour.

When such a departure has been detected by the anomaly-detection module, it activates the response generation module, which then generates an appropriate response, e.g., alerting a carer.

In [6], we presented an outlier-based statistical model for inactivity detection which outperforms the state-of-the-art. Like our previous model [3], our new model learns an *alert threshold* for each region in a house and hour of the day. If an inactivity period in a region-hour pair exceeds this threshold, an alert is issued by the system. Ideally, an IHMS should minimize the number of false alerts, while issuing true alerts with the least delay. Intuitively, higher alert thresholds reduce the number of false alerts, while lower thresholds reduce the delay for real alerts.

We employed two main criteria to evaluate the performance of different anomaly-detection models [3,6]. A week was used as a time unit, since people often repeat patterns of behaviour on a weekly basis.

- *Average number of false alerts* – Inactivity detection techniques do not yield false negatives (i.e., activities that didn't take place), but they may incur a delay in detecting true positives.
- *Average delay in detecting abnormally long periods of inactivity* – This measure provides a coarse estimate of the delay in detecting true positives. It is calculated by assuming that a mishap occurred immediately after each observed activity in a house, and averaging the delay in detecting these mishaps.

Due to the trade-off between false alerts and anomaly-detection delay, we proposed the following *Combined Cost Measure* (*CCM*) as the main criterion for comparing different techniques [6]:

$$CCM = RIR \times \text{Average\_\#\_False\_Alerts} + \text{Average\_Detection\_Delay}\,, \qquad (1)$$

where a lower cost implies a better performance, and *RIR* (*Relative Importance Ratio*) indicates the importance of a minute of average delay relative to a false alert. For example, *RIR*=5, means that the annoyance caused to the user by one false alert is equivalent to the damage perceived by the user due to a 5 minute delay in raising a true alert. In Section 5.2, we evaluate our system's performance for the values *RIR*= 5 and *RIR*= 15 — the two ends of a reasonable range suggested in [6]. Since *CCM* is linear with respect to *RIR*, the system's performance in the limits of the range is informative with respect to *RIR* values inside the range.

3 Problem Statement

We start by installing a set of N sensors $S = \{s_i | i = 1, \ldots, N\}$ in a house, where each sensor s_i has a cost c_i. Our model divides the house into L regions $(L \leq N)$ $R = \{r_j | j = 1, \ldots, L\}$ roughly according to the activity performed in each region, e.g., bedroom, kitchen and bathroom. Our objective is to select a subset S^* of S that will provide the best performance in detecting abnormally long inactivity periods within a certain budget B.

This problem can be formulated as the following optimization problem:

$$S^* = \text{argmax}_{S' \subset S}\, U(S') \quad \text{subject to} \sum_{s_i \in S'} c_i \leq B\,, \tag{2}$$

where U is a utility function that measures the informativeness of each sensor for inactivity detection.

In principle, the performance measure defined in Equation 1 may be used as the utility function in a set-up where the performance of each of the 2^N subsets of S is assessed for some training data. However, this is not feasible when N is relatively large, as is the case in realistic IHMSs. Clearly, the search space can be reduced by applying heuristics to guide a search algorithm. However, a more common approach to sensor selection consists of defining a utility function for individual sensors, and using dynamic programming or greedy algorithms to solve the optimization problem [7,9]. This is the approach adopted in this paper: we formulate sensor selection as a 0/1 knapsack problem, which we solve using dynamic programming.

4 Utility-Based Sensor Selection

In this section, we describe our utility function for a sensor, followed by our procedure for selecting a sensor configuration.

4.1 Utility Function

Our utility function for a sensor reflects the informativeness of the sensor in the context of an IHMS. We consider the following four criteria to measure a sensor's utility:

- *Frequency of activation of sensor* s_i $(F(s_i))$ – if a sensor is frequently being triggered, then the sensor is observing a frequent activity in a house.
- *Effect of sensor* s_i *on the mean duration of inactivity periods* $(D(s_i))$ – if the removal of a sensor increases the mean of the inactivity periods detected in a house, then the sensor has a significant effect on the reduction of the length of observed inactivity periods, and hence on the resultant alert thresholds.
- *Importance of sensor* s_i *in a region* r $(R(s_i, r))$ – if the performance of an IHMS when using only one sensor in a region is similar to its performance when using all the sensors in the region, then this is an important sensor in the region.
- *Importance of a region* r $(I(r))$ – conversely, if the performance of an IHMS without the sensors in a region is similar to its performance with the sensors in this region, then the region is unlikely to be important.

The utility U of a sensor s_i in region r is then defined as follows:[1]

$$U(s_i) = \bar{F}(s_i) + \bar{D}(s_i) + \bar{R}(s_i, r) + \bar{I}(r), \quad (3)$$

where $\bar{F}$, $\bar{D}$, $\bar{R}$ and $\bar{I}$ are estimators of the four criteria. These estimators are calculated as follows over a training period of T weeks, and normalized to the [0,1] range using a linear function.

- $\mathbf{\bar{F}(s_i)}$ is defined as the probability of sensor s_i firing in an hour, which is estimated for each hour of the day over the training period T. The probabilities are added over 24 hours, and normalized.
- $\mathbf{\bar{D}(s_i)}$ is calculated by measuring the increase in the mean duration of detected inactivity periods in an hour when sensor s_i is turned off, compared to having all the sensors turned on. This increase is measured for each hour of the day over the training period T, added over 24 hours, and normalized.
- $\mathbf{\bar{R}(s_i, r)}$ is calculated by measuring the difference between the average detection delay when all the sensors in a home are turned on, and when all the sensors in r, except s_i, are turned off. Since lower differences imply a higher importance, we subtract the normalized difference from 1.
  The behaviour of sensors in the same region is generally correlated, in the sense that they may be triggered by similar activities. In order to avoid double-counting the contribution of a sensor, we use the idea of *Maximal Marginal Relevance* (*MMR*) [10], borrowed from discourse summarization, which discounts candidate sentences that resemble sentences that have already been included in a summary, as these candidates add little new information. Similarly, we discount the values of $\bar{R}(s_i, r)$ based on the similarity between the activation patterns of the sensors in region r.
  We define the similarity between sensors s_i and s_j as the probability of s_j being activated within one minute of s_i, i.e., $\Pr(\text{Time}(s_j) - \text{Time}(s_i) \leq 1 \text{ min})$ (the self-similarity of sensor s_i is set to 0). *MMR* is applied by selecting the sensor $s_{\max}$ with the highest value for $\bar{R}$ in region r, and discounting the regional importance of all sensors s_j within region r as follows:

$$\bar{R}(s_j, r) = \bar{R}(s_j, r) \cdot (1 - \Pr([\text{Time}(s_j) - \text{Time}(s_{\max})] \leq 1 \text{ min})). \quad (4)$$

- $\mathbf{\bar{I}(r)}$ is defined as the normalized difference between the average anomaly-detection delay when all the sensors in region r are turned off, and when all the sensors in r are turned on.

The utility function U for sensor selection differs from the IHMS performance measure in Equation 1 in that *CCM* evaluates *an IHMS's overall performance* from a user's perspective by considering both the number of false alerts and the anomaly-detection delay *under test conditions*. In contrast, U estimates the utility of *each sensor* on the basis of its coverage of a user's behaviour ($\bar{F}$ and $\bar{D}$) and its effect on anomaly-detection delay for this user ($\bar{R}$ and $\bar{I}$) *under training conditions*. The idea is that these estimates should be indicative of future

[1] In principle, each term may be associated with a weight that reflects its contribution to the utility of a sensor — learning these weights is the subject of future work.

overall performance (*CCM*), thus providing a sound basis for sensor selection (Section 5.2).[2]

4.2 Selecting the Best Sensor Configuration

To select the best sensor configuration, we calculate the utility function for each sensor, and then solve the optimization problem.

Calculating the Utility Function for Each Sensor. We use data collected over T weeks after setting up the IHMS (our datasets are described in Section 5.1). The values for terms $\bar{F}$ and $\bar{D}$ in Equation 3 are obtained directly from the sensor activations, and the values for $\bar{R}$ and $\bar{I}$ are obtained from the results of our inactivity detection algorithm [6]. This algorithm is trained over T weeks with the appropriate sensor configurations for computing $\bar{R}$ and $\bar{I}$ *for each sensor*, and run over the same T weeks to calculate the average detection delay (required to compute $\bar{R}$ and $\bar{I}$).[3]

Solving the Optimization Problem. We select the best set of sensors for a budget B by applying dynamic programming to solve the 0/1 knapsack problem (the utilities of the sensors are used as the weights). Note that different values of B may yield different sensor configurations, as each value specifies a new knapsack problem. For example, in the *GT5* dataset (Section 5.1), a budget of \$100 led to the selection of sensor 21 (reed sensor in the Entry in Figure 1(a)) and 27 (PIR motion sensor covering the Lounge/Dining/Kitchen areas). When the budget increased to \$200, sensor 27 was retained, but sensors 35 (bed-pressure mat in the Bedroom) and 39 (PIR in the Study) replaced sensor 21. Note that the value of B indicates a maximum cost, hence the total cost of the selected sensors may be slightly less than B.

5 Evaluation

In this section, we first describe the two real-life datasets used in our evaluations, which comprise data collected from two homes. Next, we evaluate the predictive power of our utility function, recommend an optimal sensor configuration for the resident(s) of the house in each dataset, and analyze the selected sensors. The utility function is evaluated and the recommendations are made 6 weeks after setting up the IHMS ($T = 6$ in Section 4.2).

---

[2] The per-sensor utility function omits the number of false alerts, because this number is sensitive to the statistical model, which is designed to achieve a certain level of performance in terms of false alerts (by defining an outlier region [3,6]). In contrast, the detection delay is mainly influenced by the sensor configuration, and hence provides a reliable measure for sensor selection.

[3] This is *not* a classical training/testing protocol. Rather, we use the training data to calculate the parameters of the utility function.

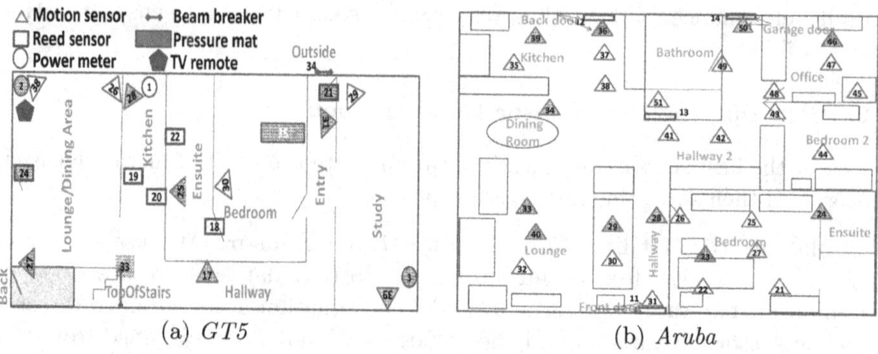

(a) *GT5* (b) *Aruba*

Fig. 1. House layout with sensors and regions: *GT5* and *Aruba* datasets, with highlighted sensors for a budget of $700 for *GT5* and $600 for *Aruba*

Table 1. Details of the *GT5* and *Aruba* datasets

Dataset	# of Residents	Gender & Age	House Size	Trial length	# of sensors						
					PIR	Reed	TV	Beam	Bed	Power	Total
GT5	2	couple late 50s	11 regions	27 weeks	10	6	1	2	1	3	23
Aruba	1	elderly female	13 regions	18 weeks	31	4	0	0	0	0	35

5.1 Datasets and Sensors

We conducted our experiments on two datasets: *GT5*, which extends the dataset described in [3]; and *Aruba*, from the Washington State University CASAS Smart Home project [1] (ailab.wsu.edu/casas/datasets/). We consider both houses to be over-sensored, i.e., we expect that a similar inactivity-detection performance can be obtained with fewer sensors, and hence with a lower budget. Figure 1 shows the layouts of the houses and the regions we identified within them (the highlighted sensors are explained in Section 5.3); details of the datasets appear in Table 1.

As outlined in Table 1, there are six types of sensors in the *GT5* house. Four of them detect instantaneous actions: reed sensors detect the opening and closing of doors, the in-house built IR (infra-red) remote sensor detects pressing buttons on the TV remote control, the beam breaker detects going through an IR beam (e.g., when crossing a threshold), and the bed-pressure mat detects movement in bed. The other two types of sensors detect the duration of an activity: a PIR (passive infra-red) motion sensor detects the duration of a person's movement in the sensor's coverage area, and a power monitor detects the duration of the usage of a device (in *GT5* there are three devices connected to power monitors: an electric tea kettle, a TV and a computer monitor). Since power monitors are associated with devices, rather than people (e.g., a person may fall after

Table 2. Cost and characteristics of sensors (average retail price in AUD)

Sensor type	Cost (AUD)	Monitoring purpose
PIR motion	60	Duration (movement)
Reed	40	Instantaneous action
IR TV remote	55	Instantaneous action
Power	50	Duration (device)
Pressure mat	80	Instantaneous action
Beam breaker	80	Instantaneous action

activating a device), extra care must be taken when interpreting the output of these sensors in the context of inactivity detection. Therefore, in *GT5*, we use device-specific changes in drawn voltage as a sign of activity. In *Aruba*, there are only PIR motion sensors and reeds, with a high level of redundancy for motion sensors. An important difference between the two datasets is that in *GT5* we adjusted the number, type and layout of the sensors based on the initial output of the statistical model and our knowledge of the user's behaviour; whereas in *Aruba* we had no control over the set-up. Table 2 shows the cost of each sensor in Australian dollars and the type of information provided by each sensor.

5.2 Evaluating our Per-Sensor Utility Function

Our evaluation protocol assesses the predictive power of the utility function U in terms of the combined cost measure *CCM* (Equation 1). A good utility function should select sensors such that an IHMS's performance improves as the budget increases. In fact, we expect to observe an exponential decay in *CCM* as the budget increases. This is because a configuration with very few sensors would yield very high detection delays, with every additional sensor having a large impact on reducing this delay. Once a large number of sensors has been installed, the effect of each additional sensor should be relatively small.

We selected a sensor configuration as described in Section 4.2 under a range of budgets. We started at $B = \$100$, increasing B by steps of \$100 until a budget could accommodate all the sensors in a dataset. We then used a traditional training/testing protocol with 6 weeks of training and the rest of the data for testing (21 weeks for *GT5* and 12 weeks for *Aruba*) to evaluate the performance of our inactivity detection algorithm [6] under the sensor configuration obtained for each budget B.

Figure 2 depicts *CCM* over the test period as a function of budget size for the two ends of the reasonable range of *RIR* (Section 2) (the red dots represent the value of *CCM* for the sensor configurations selected in Section 5.3). The figure largely confirms our expectations of exponential decay in *CCM*. The performance graph flattens out later for *GT5* than for *Aruba*, because the *GT5* sensors were carefully set up, hence, each sensor has a relatively high utility. In contrast, due to the high sensor redundancy in *Aruba*, there is a relatively large number of sensors that have a low utility.

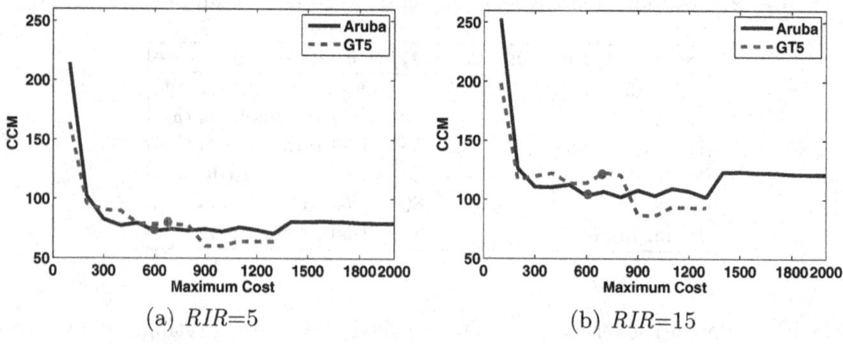

(a) *RIR*=5 (b) *RIR*=15

Fig. 2. *CCM* over the test period as a function of the total budget spent on sensors

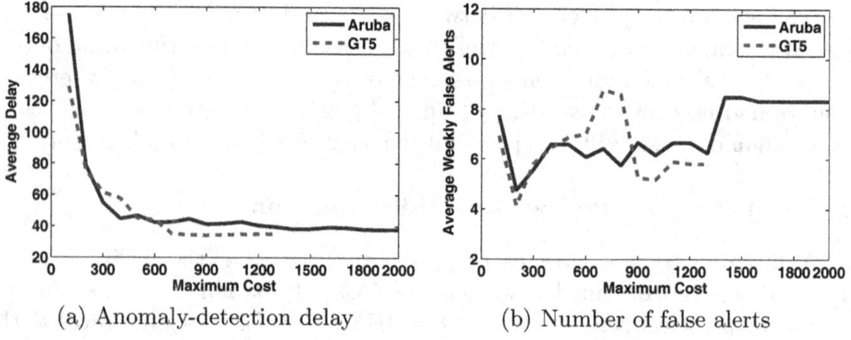

(a) Anomaly-detection delay (b) Number of false alerts

Fig. 3. Average weekly anomaly-detection delay and number of false alerts over the test period as a function of the total budget spent on sensors

Figure 3 shows the two performance criteria that make up *CCM*, i.e., anomaly-detection delay and number of false alerts, as a function of budget size over the test period. In general, increasing the number of sensors reduces the detection delay. Such reductions are associated with an increase in the number of false alerts given a *fixed* number of sensors [3]. However, when detection delays are reduced owing to increases in the number of sensors, we observe fluctuations in the number of false alerts, as seen in Figure 3(b). The effect of these fluctuations on *CCM* can be seen in Figure 2, in particular as the detection delay becomes stable. This effect is more pronounced for $RIR = 15$, which assigns a higher importance to false alerts than $RIR = 5$. Nonetheless, the general trend of the *CCM* graphs is similar for different values of *RIR*.

Overall, even though we used only 6 weeks of data for sensor selection (and model training), the behaviour of the combined cost measure *CCM* during testing validates the predictive power of our utility function.

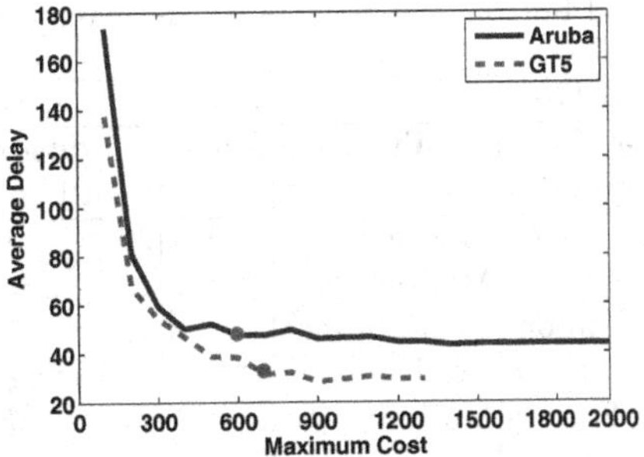

Fig. 4. Average weekly anomaly-detection delay over the training period as a function of the budget for sensor selection

5.3 Recommending a Sensor Configuration for an IHMS

In the previous section, we validated our utility function by using *CCM* over a test period to evaluate the performance of the sensor configurations selected for different budgets. However, in realistic settings, a sensor configuration for an IHMS must be suggested after a relatively short time. Hence, we cannot employ a traditional training/testing protocol. Instead, we determine a sensor configuration for different budgets as described in Section 4.2, and make our recommendations after 6 weeks of training. This course of action is validated by the results described below.

Figure 4 shows the average detection delay for the training period after selecting sensor configurations with different budgets for both datasets. These plots agree with the detection-delay plots for the test data (Figure 3(a)), which in turn are indicative of IHMS performance in terms of *CCM* (Figure 2).

Owing to the fluctuations in the number of false alerts due to changes in sensor configurations, and the dependence of false alerts on the statistical model, we base our recommendations on detection delay. As seen in Figure 4, there is a point where budget increases yield insignificant reductions in detection delay, which means that adding sensors is not productive. This point is highlighted by the red dots in Figure 4, suggesting a budget of around \$700 for *GT5* and \$600 for *Aruba* (the selected sensor configurations are highlighted in the layouts of the two houses in Figure 1). The plot depicting the values of *CCM* on the test data for both datasets (Figure 2) confirms this selection. The selected *GT5* budget is 53% of the \$1300 cost of the over-sensored configuration, while *Aruba*'s budget is 30% of the \$2000 over-sensored cost. These differences are due to our careful initial sensor set-up for *GT5*, compared to the high redundancy of PIR motion sensors in *Aruba* (Section 5.1).

Analysis. Table 3 shows the five sensors with the highest and the lowest utility in each dataset. Eight of the ten high-utility sensors for both datasets are PIR motion sensors, possibly because they detect continuous motion, thereby making other types of sensors (in particular reeds) redundant for inactivity detection.

Table 3. Top and bottom five sensors ranked based on their utility

GT5			*Aruba*		
Rank	**Sensor # and region**	**Type**	**Rank**	**Sensor # and region**	**Type**
1	27 Lounge/Dining	Motion	1	29 Lounge	Motion
2	39 Study	Motion	2	23 Bedroom	Motion
3	35 Bedroom	Pressure mat	3	39 Kitchen	Motion
4	21 Outside	Reed	4	34 Dining Room	Motion
5	25 Ensuite	Motion	5	24 Ensuite	Motion
...	...	...	...	...	...
19	19 Kitchen	Reed	31	45 Office	Motion
20	20 Kitchen	Reed	32	43 Bedroom 2	Motion
21	18 Ensuite	Reed	33	11 Front Door	Reed
22	22 Ensuite	Reed	34	12 Back Door	Reed
23	1 Kitchen	Power	35	13 Bathroom	Reed

In fact, seven of the ten low-utility sensors are reeds. The two high-utility non-PIR motion sensors in *GT5* are the bed-pressure mat, ranked third owing to its impact on the nighttime thresholds; and the reed sensor on the main entrance door to the house (Outside), ranked fourth due to its contribution to detecting departures from the house.

The two low-utility PIR motion sensors in *Aruba* are positioned in the Office, which has three other motion sensors, and in Bedroom 2, which is rarely visited by the elderly resident of the house. In fact, Bedroom 2 is one of the three regions that are not allocated sensors within *Aruba*'s \$600 budget. The other two un-sensored regions are Hallway 2 and Bathroom, which may be explained by the observation that the entrances to these regions are from regions with similar levels of activity, viz Hallway and Garage Door. This reduces the utility of the sensors in Hallway 2 and Bathroom through criteria D and I (Section 4). In general, the utility of the sensors in a region r is significantly reduced when a user's level of activity in that region is similar to that exhibited in *all* its neighbouring regions. However, if at least one of the neighbouring regions has a lower level of activity than region r, the utility of the sensors in r is not affected or can even increase. For example, sensor 24 in *Aruba*'s Ensuite is the fifth most important sensor, as Bedroom, which adjoins the ensuite, is not a high-activity region compared to Ensuite.

The \$700 sensor configuration for *GT5* contains at least one sensor in each region of the house, with each of the Study and the Lounge/Dining area receiving more than one sensor. A noteworthy user-tailored sensor selection is sensor 39 in the Study instead of sensor 29, as sensor 39 is near the resident's desk, and responds to small movements (e.g., typing or writing), which do not trigger sensor 29 in the opposite corner of the room.

The lounge and dining room in both datasets attract more sensors than other regions, owing to the different types of activities performed in these areas, i.e., activities with small movements, such as typing, and activities with gross movements, such as walking around.

6 Conclusions and Future Work

We have proposed a utility function that represents the informativeness of sensors for detecting abnormally long periods of inactivity in a house. We used *CCM* — a measure that balances the number of false alerts and anomaly-detection delays — to evaluate this function on two real-life datasets. Our results show that the utility function has a high predictive power in terms of *CCM*. Further, the recommendations based on the anomaly-detection delay obtained during training yield a cost-effective combination of sensors for a particular user. Specifically, our sensor-selection process resulted in savings of 70% in *Aruba* and 47% in *GT5*, despite its carefully configured initial set-up, without significantly reducing performance in either dataset.

Acknowledgments. This research was supported in part by grant LP100200405 from the Australian Research Council, and endowments from Meticube, Portugal, VicHealth and the Helen McPherson Smith Trust.

References

1. Cook, D.: Learning setting-generalized activity models for smart spaces. IEEE Intelligent Systems **27**(1), 32–38 (2012)
2. Weisenberg, J., Cuddihy, P., Rajiv, V.: Augmenting motion sensing to improve detection of periods of unusual inactivity. In: HealthNet 2008 - Proceedings of the 2nd ACM International Workshop on Systems and Networking Support for Healthcare and Assisted Living Environments, Breckenridge, Colorado, pp. 2:1–2:6 (2008)
3. Moshtaghi, M., Zukerman, I., Albrecht, D., Russell, R.A.: Monitoring personal safety by unobtrusively detecting unusual periods of inactivity. In: Carberry, S., Weibelzahl, S., Micarelli, A., Semeraro, G. (eds.) UMAP 2013. LNCS, vol. 7899, pp. 139–151. Springer, Heidelberg (2013)
4. Larizza, M., Zukerman, I., Bohnert, F., Russell, R.A., Busija, L., Albrecht, D.W., Rees, G.: Studies to determine user requirements regarding in-home monitoring systems. In: Masthoff, J., Mobasher, B., Desmarais, M.C., Nkambou, R. (eds.) UMAP 2012. LNCS, vol. 7379, pp. 139–150. Springer, Heidelberg (2012)
5. Tunca, C., Alemdar, H., Ertan, H., Incel, O., Ersoy, C.: Multimodal wireless sensor network-based ambient assisted living in real homes with multiple residents. Sensors **14**(6), 9692–9719 (2014)
6. Moshtaghi, M., Zukerman, I.: Modeling the tail of a hyperexponential distribution to detect abnormal periods of inactivity in older adults. In: Pham, D.-N., Park, S.-B. (eds.) PRICAI 2014. LNCS, vol. 8862, pp. 985–997. Springer, Heidelberg (2014)
7. Debouk, R., Stéphane Lafortune, D.T.: On an optimization problem in sensor selection. Discrete Event Dynamic Systems **12**(4), 417–445 (2002)

8. Mo, Y., Ambrosino, R., Sinopoli, B.: Sensor selection strategies for state estimation in energy constrained wireless sensor networks. Automatica **47**(7), 1330–1338 (2011)
9. Schneider, M.: Plan recognition in instrumented environments. In: Proceedings of the 5th International Conference on Intelligent Environments, Barcelona, Spain, vol. 2, pp. 295–302 (2009)
10. Carbonell, J., Goldstein, J.: The use of MMR, diversity-based reranking for reordering documents and producing summaries. In: SIGIR 1998 - Proceedings of the 21st Annual International ACM Conference on Research and Development in Information Retrieval, Melbourne, Australia, pp. 335–336 (1998)

Towards a Recommender Engine for Personalized Visualizations

Belgin Mutlu(✉), Eduardo Veas, Christoph Trattner, and Vedran Sabol

Know-Center GmbH, Inffeldgasse 13, 8010 Graz, Austria
{bmutlu,eveas,ctrattner,vsabol}@know-center.at

Abstract. Visualizations have a distinctive advantage when dealing with the information overload problem: since they are grounded in basic visual cognition, many people understand them. However, creating them requires specific expertise of the domain and underlying data to determine the right representation. Although there are rules that help generate them, the results are too broad to account for varying user preferences. To tackle this issue, we propose a novel recommender system that suggests visualizations based on (i) a set of visual cognition rules and (ii) user preferences collected in Amazon-Mechanical Turk. The main contribution of this paper is the introduction and the evaluation of a novel approach called *VizRec* that can suggest an optimal list of top-n visualizations for heterogeneous data sources in a personalized manner.

Keywords: Personalized visualizations · Visualization recommender · Recommender systems · Collaborative filtering · Crowd-sourcing

1 Introduction

Despite recent technical advances in search engines and content provider services, the information overload problem still remains a crucial issue in many application fields. Finding the right piece of information in huge information spaces is a tedious and time consuming task. Recent innovations, such as recommender systems, help to resolve the issue, though with limited success, due to limitations in the way the recommended items are presented, typically as a list in the textual form. Alternatively, visualizations have shown to be an effective way to deal with the overload issue by opportunity to display and explore a huge set of data points simultaneously. However, creating useful visual representations of data typically requires expert knowledge. To date, only a few approaches attempted to automatically generate visual representations given a set of data [14] [9], albeit with certain limitations. Despite their usefulness, these approaches are ineffective in terms of dealing with highly heterogeneous data and ignore the fact that visual representation of data is a matter of the users' taste or preferences. To address this issue, in this paper we present a novel approach – called *VizRec* – which tackles these challenges by: (i) automatically generating a set of visualizations in the context of heterogeneous data and (ii) recommending the most useful

F. Ricci et al. (Eds.): UMAP 2015, LNCS 9146, pp. 169–182, 2015.
DOI: 10.1007/978-3-319-20267-9_14

visualization in a personalized manner, helping the user to explore large amounts of data efficiently.

Problem Statement. The problem we are dealing with in this work is the generation of an optimal list of top-n visualizations for the user given a set of heterogeneous data sources as input. Considering just visual encoding rules proposed in the literature [14] leads to a large set of possibilities, valid in terms of representing the data visually, but without considering which type serves the users' needs best.

VizRec deals with the issue by (1) automatically identifying the set of appropriate visualizations using a rule-based algorithm to analyze the compatibility between the visuals and the input data, and (2) filtering a subset based on user's preferences to be recommended as the list of top-n visualizations that best reflect the user's information needs.

Contributions. The contributions of this work can be summarized as follows:

- A novel visual recommender approach to generate and recommend personalized visualizations.
- An extensive evaluation of visualization types in the context of three data repositories conducted in Amazon Mechanical Turk, providing insights on the usefulness of the approach.

The paper is structured as follows: Section 2 presents the related work in the area. Section 3 introduces *VizRec*. Section 4 presents our methodology for evaluating our approach. Section 5 highlights the results of our evaluation and Section 6 concludes the paper and provides insights into how the current work will be extended.

2 Related Work

Recommending visualizations is a relatively new strand of research and only few efforts have been made in so far to tackle this challenge. The closest approach to our suggestion is a system described by Voigt et al. [4], which uses a knowledge base of numerous ontologies to recommend visualizations. It is essentially a rule-based system that pre-selects visualizations based on the device, data properties and task involved. At a second stage, the system ranks visualizations following the rules concerning visualization facts, domain assignments, and user context. One disadvantage of Voigt et al.'s approach is that both visualizations and data inputs have to be annotated semantically beforehand. Furthermore, the pre-selection and the ranking stages are rule-based. More importantly, a large theoretical part of the work lacks the empirical support. While user preferences, such as graphical representations and visualization literacy, are outlined, the actual collection and validation of user preferences are tasks for future work.

In contrast, we present a complete Collaborative Filtering (CF) approach by collecting user preferences for personalization from a large study involving the general public, validating them in an offline experiment and drawing conclusions based on the empirical evidence. Our approach starts by strictly describing the visual encoding process, i.e., we represent visualizations in terms of their visual components (see [3] for thorough description of the visual components). Instead of pursuing a through specification encompassing all known expert knowledge about visual perception, we concentrate on pragmatic, simple facts that will aid the sensible mapping of data onto visual components (e.g., [6]), extending the description to many types of visualizations. Next, instead of focusing only on specific data format and domain, we obtain and visualize heterogeneous data sources.

Mackinlay et al. propose an influential, albeit conceptually different approach, in the ShowMe [8] system. It integrates a set of user interface commands and functions aimed to automatically generate visualizations for *Tableau*[1]. ShowMe attempts to help the user by searching for graphical presentations that may address their task. Appropriate visualizations are selected based on the data properties, such as datatype (text, date, time, numeric, boolean), data role (measure or dimension) and data interpretation (discrete or continuous). The ranking of visualizations is based on static ratings (scores) globally defined for every supported chart type. We follow a similar approach and select visualizations based on the encoding rules. Rather then using global ratings, our method allows us to personalize the resulting visualizations according to the interests of the individual user using a CF approach.

Nazemi et al.'s system suggests visualizations based on user preferences [9] incrementally gathered during interaction with the visualization system in the form of usage profiles for particular charts. Nazemi et al. follow a bottom-up approach, analyzing user interaction via visualization to describe user behavior. In contrast, we apply a top-down method to elicit user preferences by collecting ratings. These methods are complementary and can be deployed together with user behaviour analytics. Similar to us, Nazemi et al. utilize a personalized approach to suggest visualizations but only target the content from digital libraries (i.e., bibliographical notes, publications).

Ahn et al.'s work on adaptive visualization attempts to provide user-adapted visual representation of their search results [11]. The user context is a collection of user actions accumulated over time, such as the issued search queries, selected documents from the search results and traversed links. The collection captures user interests beyond the query and in turn defines a user model, which is applied to visually highlight the relevance of a particular result set. In contrast, *VizRec* augments user queries with preferences in order to find the best representation of the information behind the queried content instead of only displaying relevant results as clusters.

Despite these notable efforts, the problem of recommending visualizations is still insufficiently explored, especially little research has been performed on generating and suggesting useful visualizations for heterogeneous multidimensional data.Moreover there seems to be a gap in the literature on doing this in a personalized manner, since previous work on recommender systems has shown

[1] Tableau: http://www.tableausoftware.com/

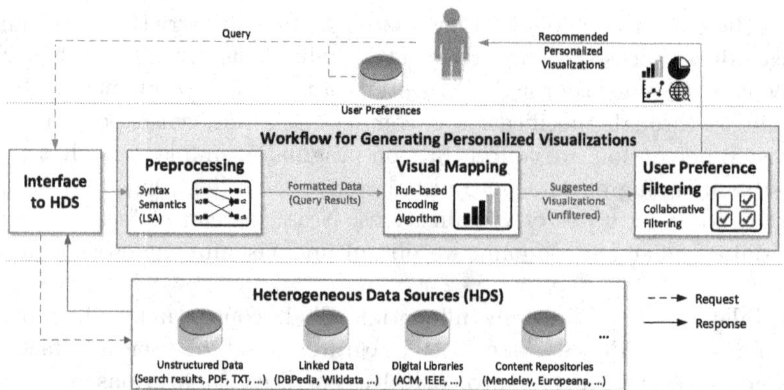

Fig. 1. Schematic representation of the VizRec recommendation pipeline

that the one-size-fits-it-all principle typically does not hold. To contribute to this small body of research we developed and evaluated *VizRec*, a novel visual recommender engine capable of recommending various types of visualizations for heterogeneous datasources in a personalized manner.

3 The VizRec Approach

Figure 1 shows the general workflow of *VizRec* to generate personalized visualizations for heterogeneous data sources (HDS). As highlighted, the system responds to a given search query and a given data source with a set of visualizations that reflect the user's personal preferences in a top-n sorted manner. Before deciding on the appropriate visualizations, the filter pipeline, first, annotates retrieved data and then performs data analysis tasks to categorize them into standard and/or specific datatypes. After that, a mapping operation is performed (based on the visual perception and visual encoding guidelines [14]) that maps the data to the visual components (encoding some attributes of the data, e.g., using axes of a visualization) of the appropriate visualizations.

As the final step, the system includes user preferences via a collaborative filtering [2] approach, which takes into account a set of specific usability preferences that have been collected in the past. In summary, the three steps to generating personalized visual recommendations are: (1) preprocessing, (2) visual mapping and (3) user preference filtering. In the following subsections, we briefly describe each of those units:

Step 1: Preprocessing. The preprocessing unit is responsible for extracting and annotating data attributes appropriate for mapping. Associated data sources, such as Linked Data, ACM digital library and Mendeley, collect and index various kinds of documents, e.g., conference publications, books, journals, lectures and images. Each data source defines and organizes its repositories according to an (often closed) proprietary data model. Many scientific digital

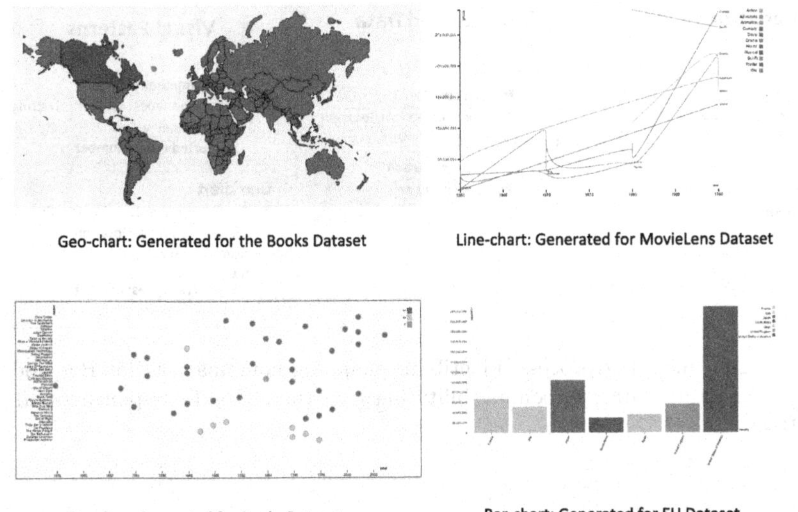

Fig. 2. Four example charts generated via *VizRec*. Note that not all charts are equally useful (see e.g., top-right chart).

libraries, for instance, define the structure of their literature archives in terms of some important attributes, such as title, abstract, author, keywords, etc., following, e.g., the Dublin Core metadata format.

Before the mapping algorithm can begin to establish correspondence with visualizations, the data in these various formats have to be, first, collected in series and then categorized according to datatypes. The data is categorized into standard datatypes, such as categorical, temporal and numerical – represented by primitive data types string, date and number, respectively. This categorization into primitive datatypes is basically performed by analyzing values of the individual attributes. To do so, the analysis employs a top-down approach, i.e., for a given value it is first decided to which of the aforementioned standard datatypes it belongs. Next, by using gazetteer lists more specialized datatypes are derived, e.g., for spatial information.

Step 2: Visual Mapping. A visualization can be broken down in a number k of visual components, each of which encodes a single piece of information visually [3]. If every visual component could encode any kind of data, the possible number of combinations for a visualization type would be given by $\binom{n}{k}$, where n is the number of data attributes in a dataset (i.e., number of fields). For example a dataset with one *date*, two *strings* and two *numbers* to be represented in a barchart with two visual components, the total number of combinations would be $\frac{n!}{(n-k)!} = \frac{5!}{(5-2)!} = 20$. However many of these combinations would be perceptually incorrect, since visual components are often suited to represent only some kinds of data attributes given by the perceptual properties of the channel and the characteristics of the data attribute [3].

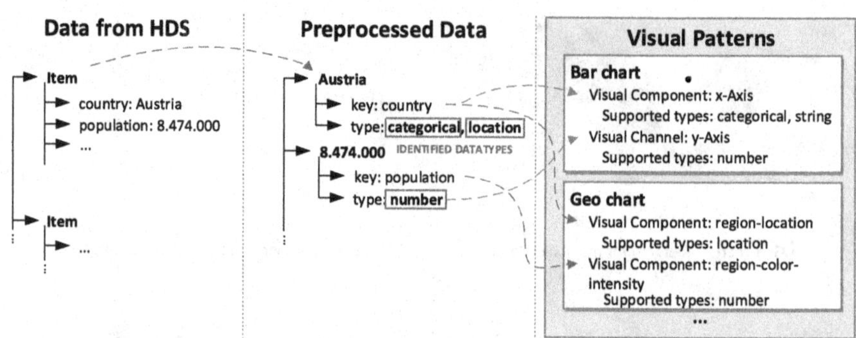

Fig. 3. Visual mapping process: identifying mapping combinations for Bar and Geo charts considering datatype compatibility between their visual components and data form HDS

Visual mapping identifies which attributes of the data can be related to which visual components of a visualization type [7]. The relationship is established based on the datatype similarity between the data attributes and the visual components. To do so we benefit from an ontology of patterns [14] for a type of visualization. Each pattern describes one possible mapping for a concrete visualization in terms of its visual components and supported datatypes. For instance, possible patterns for the bar chart could be (1) $\{x - axis : string,\ y - axis : number\}$, and (2) $\{x - axis : date,\ y - axis : number\}$. The patterns specify the types of data that are required for each visualization to be instantiated. Hence, each pattern i defines for each visual component j which r_j attributes should be selected from n_j data attributes: $\frac{n_j!}{r!(n_j - r_j)!} = \binom{n_J}{r_j} = C^r_{n_i}$. Note that n_j is a subset of n that complies with datatype compatibility for the j visual component r_j. To obtain the total number of combinations M_i, generated for a particular pattern i, we multiply every suitable $\binom{n_j}{r_j}$ visual component of a pattern: $M_i = \prod C^{r_j}_{n_j}$. Thus, the final number of patterns M of a visualization is nothing else then the sum of every M_i. In our working example, for bar chart's pattern (1) one attribute with datatype *string* and one with datatype *number* we obtain $M_i = C^2_1 \times C^2_1 = \binom{2}{1} \times \binom{2}{1} = 4$ possible mappings. And for pattern (2) one attribute with datatype *date* and one with datatype *number*, we obtain $M_i = C^1_1 \times C^2_1 = \binom{1}{1} \times \binom{2}{1} = 2$ possible mapping combinations. Hence, using this particular dataset the total number of combinations for this type of chart would be 6.

Having obtained all the combinations, the mapping operator maps data to the corresponding visual components of a visualization based on the following principles: (i) one data attribute will be instantiated to one visual channel of a visualization, (ii) the datatype of the attributes should be compatible with the datatypes of the channels and (iii) every mandatory visual channel of a visualization should be instantiated. Once the mapping process is completed,

VizRec presents the mapping combinations as a set of appropriate visualization configurations to the user. This process is illustrated in Fig. 3.

Visual patterns together with rule-based mapping algorithm generate all mapping combinations which are plausible for the data. Since not all of them represent what the user needs or prefers, better mechanisms for selecting the visualization are required. To that end, we ask users to validate the mapping results. We benefit from collaborative filtering (CF) [18], which allows us to collect user feedback in form of ratings and to apply them in a way that provides reasonable prediction of the active user's preferences. In our context, we make predictions for the mapping combinations that the user might prefer based on her and similar users' preferences.

Step 3: User Preference Filtering. To finally filter the generated mapping combinations according to the user's preferences, we employ a simple user-based CF approach. For a given dataset, the mapping algorithm provides a set of possible combinations M, each serving as a possible *item* to be recommended to the user. The list of recommendations R for the current user is nothing else but a subset of M. Concretely, given a set of active user's ratings U and a set of predictions P, both of which should contain ratings for the items from M, we denote $R = U \cup P$. Note that the calculation of P involves calculating the k-nearest neighbors (based on *Pearson correlation*) of the active user, who liked the same mapping combinations as the active user in the past and rated mapping combinations $x \in M$ active user has not seen yet.

For the calculation of R, we first take the set U_p containing all ratings of the active user given for various mappings and the set N_p containing all ratings given by other users and develop the set $M_p = U_p \cup N_p$. Based on M_p, we construct the matrix A consisting of user-IDs, item-IDs and the ratings, that generates the predictions for the current user. For this purpose, we applied the memory based CF approach [2] that generates a list of top-n visual recommendations.

4 Evaluation

This section describes the experimental setup, the data sources, the method and metrics used to validate our approach in detail.

Datasets and Mappings. The study used the following three open-source datasets:

Movielens[2] *Dataset (*movies*):* This dataset comprises information about the top-ranked movies for the years 1960, 1970, 1980, and 1990. It has 41 entries, which are selected from items of the respective dataset and are characterized by the attributes (movie) name, budget, gross, creation year, and shooting location. Based on this, the mapping unit produced four types of visualizations (see Fig. 2) with the following mapping frequencies: 32 bar-charts, 9 line-charts, 13 timelines and 1 geo-chart. Hence, a total of 55 mapping combinations were generated.

[2] Movielens: https://movielens.org/

EU Open Linked Data Portal[3] *Dataset (*eu*):* The *eu* dataset collects the percentage of the population looking for educational information online in the years 2009–2011 for 28 EU countries. It has 91 entries characterized by attributes (country) name, year, language, population, constitutional form and value (in percent) of the population looking for educational information. The mapping unit suggested 30 possible chart combinations, concretely 15 bar charts, 6 line charts, 8 timeline and 1 geo chart.

Book-Crossing Dataset[4] *(books):* This dataset contained 41 randomly chosen books published between 1960 and 2003 and characterized by the attributes name, country, publisher, and year. The mapping unit suggested 3 chart types: bar chart with 2 combinations, geo chart with 1 combination and timeline with 3 combinations, the total of 7 mapping combinations.

Procedure. Our experimental approach was to gather user preferences for visualizations obtained from the rule-based system and train a RS to suggest visualizations. A crowdsourced study was designed to obtain personalized scores for each chart suggested by the visual recommender. Before giving a score, a participant had to perform some cognitively demanding task with the chart (i.e., a minimal analysis). Based on the experiments conducted by Kittur et al. [13], this preparatory task should bring participants to accurately study the combination and prevent a random or rash rating. We designed the task as follows: 1) a participant was given a one line description of a dataset originating the chart, 2) looking at the chart she had to write tags (at most five) and a title for it and 3) rate the chart. The score system used a multidimensional scale adapted from a list of usability factors presented in [10] and [12]: (1) cluttered, (2) organized, (3) confusing, (4) easy to understand, (5) boring, (6) exciting, (7) useful, (8) effective and (9) satisfying. Note that dimensions 1–6 are duplicated with opposing sentiment (e.g., cluttered vs. organized). Opposing dimensions were used to ensure meaningful ratings for scales with complex meaning.Dimensions were rated on a 7-point Likert scale (1=not applicable – 7=very applicable).

Since the chart scores were intended for the offline experiment, the participant had to rate more than one chart. We experimented with varying sizes of HITs (Human Intelligent Task), collecting ten (10) and five (5) tasks (chart/combinations and their corresponding ratings). Since in pilot studies these turned out to take overly long (around 15mins), we settled for collecting three (3) chart/combinations per HIT. Suggested combinations were distributed in 32 HITs, each of which contained 3 randomly chosen mapping combinations. Pilot studies also helped to streamline dataset descriptions, task descriptions and instructions across the experiment. After accepting a HIT, the participant (worker or turker) received a tour to complete a task, which showed a chart and corresponding tags, title and ratings in the exact same format as the subsequent experiment. When ready, the worker started the first task in the HIT by pressing a button. Workers were allowed to write *not applicable* or NA for tags

[3] Eu: https://open-data.europa.eu/en/linked-data
[4] Book-Crossing Dataset: http://www2.informatik.uni-freiburg.de/~cziegler/BX/

but were alerted if they failed to write any tags. The rating dimensions were not assigned a score until the worker did it. Workers could only proceed if they had rated all dimensions. A HIT with three chart/combinations was compensated with \$1.00. A worker rated a minimum of three charts, but to ensure a more realistic training set for the CF-RS, workers were allowed to perform more than one HIT. Only expert workers who consistently achieved a high degree of accuracy by completing HITs were allowed to take part in the study.

Evaluation Protocol. A set of studies was carried out to analyze the variability in preference scores. To compute the overall score for a chart for each worker, the scores in opposing dimensions (clutter, confusing, boring) were inverted and then all dimensions were averaged together according to the following formula: $SC = \left(\sum_{i=1}^{k} \rho_k D_k\right)/k$. Where $k = 9$ is the number of dimensions, ρ_k is the coefficient 1 and D_k is k dimension score. The chart score was obtained by averaging the worker scores.

In the second part of our evaluation, we performed an offline experiment to estimate the performance of personal preferences for visualization recommendations. To this end, we used the preferences collected from workers as training data for our recommender. Following the method described in [15], we split the preference model into the two distinct sets: one for training the recommender (training set), and another one for testing (test set). The test set is a reference value that, ideally,can be fully predicted for the given training set. From each of the datasets in the preference model, we randomly selected 20% of user-rated mapping combinations (visualizations) and entered them into the test set. The recommendations produced out of the training set are further used to evaluate the performance of *VizRec*. The performance of *VizRec* generally depends on how well it predicts the test set. We compared the generated recommendations (prediction set) and the test set by applying a variety of well-known evaluation metrics in information retrieval [16]: Recall (R), Precision (P), F-Measure (F), Mean Average Precision (MAP) and the Normalized Discounted Cumulative Gain ($nDCG$). The first three metrics basically express the quantity of relevant recommended results, whereas MAP and $nDCG$ quantify the concrete ordering of the results (i.e., giving penalties if the results are not on the top but are relevant for the user).

5 Results

Participants. Each HIT was completed by ten workers. For 92 visualizations, 8280 scores across 9 dimensions were collected from 70 participants. The participants completed on average 4.7 HITs. The experiment started on November 26,2014 and ended on December 3, 2014. The allotted working time per HIT was 900 sec and the average working time of workers was 570 sec per HIT.

Visual Quality. The heatmap in Fig. 4 shows the mean rating for every dimension for each chart. The results confirm a clear understanding of the opposing

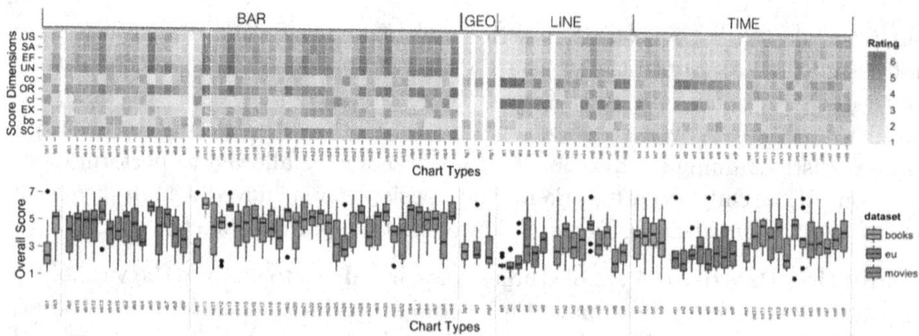

Fig. 4. Mean and variability in scores (1=completely disagree, 7=totally agree). The heatmap illustrates the contribution of 9 dimensions (US=useful, SA=satisfying, EF=efficient, UN=understandable, co=confusing, OR=organized, cl=cluttered, EX=exciting, bo=boring) to the overall score (SC). The boxplot below illustrates the high variability in personal ratings.

dimensions. Negative dimensions in the lower case received opposite scores to corresponding positive ones (UN-co, OR-cl, EX-bo, in Fig. 4 top). The aggregated score for each chart in the bottom row of the heat map (SC) shows that only a handful of charts achieved clearly high scores, whereas in the category there were charts above the midline. More importantly, boxplot at the bottom explains these scores: there is a broad variability in scores for most chart instances. This confirms our assumption that user preferences matter when choosing the right representation. The results confirm that only a very small number of charts achieved high scores and the rest were variable.

From the heat map individual top-scoring charts can be identified. To establish differences in the chart categories and datasets, we performed a factorial ANOVA with the chart type and dataset as factors (chart-type: *bar, line, time, geo* and dataset: *Movies, Books, Eu*). Homogeneity of variance was confirmed by a Levene test. The factorial ANOVA revealed a significant effect of dataset $F(2,908) = 21.19, p < 0.0001$, a significant effect of chart type $F(3,908) = 38.98, p < 0.001$ and significant interaction effect dataset chart type $F(5,908) = 3.81, p < 0.01$. TukeyHSD multiple comparisons revealed a significant difference in scores between *movies* ($M = 4.86$) and *books* ($M = 3.82$) $p < 0.05$, as well as between *movies* and *Eu* data ($M = 3.68$), $p < 0.001$. For the chart type, there was a significant difference in scores between *bar* ($M = 4.60$) and *geo* ($M = 3.06$) $p < 0.001$, *bar* and *line* ($M = 3.29$) $p < 0.001$, *bar* and *time* ($M = 3.72$) $p < 0.001$, as well as between *time* and *line*, $p < 0.02$. The significant effects of multiple comparisons for interaction are shown in Fig. 5.

The main outcomes are the information about user preferences and the clear differences among them. The interaction effects illustrate several differences amongst chart type. For instance, the majority of the users preferred bar chart, probably since it is familiar to most people. Another reason may be that it is easier to compare the values of several numbers at once using bar chart. Yet

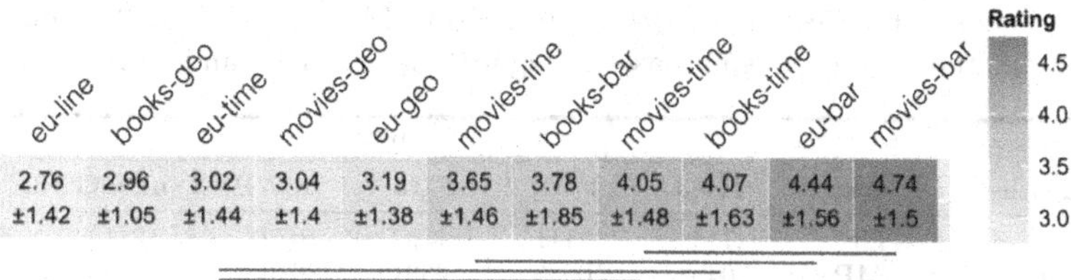

Fig. 5. Significant Interactions Chart Type / Dataset. The heat-map illustrates the mean score and standard deviation for each combination of *dataset-chart type* (1=completely disagree, 7=totally agree). The lines below show where differences begin to be significant. Note that due to its high variability, *books-bar* is not significantly better than *eu-line*, whereas *movies-line* is.

these results merely indicate that there are varied preferences. Looking at each dataset, chart and chart type in the heat map of Fig 4, it is clear that while a small number of charts are generally preferred, in most cases the ratings vary widely and a personalized approach would accommodate those user preferences better.

Recommendation Quality. At a glance, the results of our offline evaluation show significant improvements in the recommendation quality achieved through the use of individual user preferences. To measure the improvements in quality, we compared the *VizRec* CF with the baseline filtering algorithms: Most Popular (MP) [17] and Random (RD). The RD simulates the recommender behavior providing an arbitrary order of visualizations – i.e., it can be compared with having only the first two units in the *VizRec* pipeline from Fig. 1. The MP, in contrast, generates the results sorted according to global ratings, in our case accumulated from ratings of individual users. Considering RD and MP, baseline algorithms should unveil whether the recommender systems can in general help with providing useful visualizations and whether the personalized approach improves the quality of the results, respectively.

For the comparison, we analyzed the top 3 recommendations, since our datasets relatively smaller than some commonly used datasets, such as BibSonomy and CiteULike [15]. The results of the evaluation are summarized in Table 1.

The results show that *VizRec* CF outperforms both baseline algorithms in all three datasets. Concretely for the RD, the first three quality metrics clearly indicate that the results are more accurate using *VizRec* CF than simply generating arbitrary visualizations (cf., $F@3(CF) = .1257$ and $F@3(RD) = .0055$ for Movies). Additionally, *MAP@3* and *nDCG@3* reveal that *VizRec* CF can sort individual visualizations according to their relevance to user significantly better. Note that the difference between individual metrics amongst datasets is to a large extent influenced by the considerable difference in size of the three datasets (e.g., Books has only 7 different visualizations – $F@3(CF) = .4778$, whereas Movies has 55 – $F@3(CF) = .1257$, see Fig. 4).

Table 1. Quality metrics values P@3, R@3, F@3 MAP@3, NDCG@3 estimated for the three different datasets using baseline algorithms MP, RD, and *VizRec* CF

		Metric				
Dataset	**Alg.**	**R@3**	**P@3**	**F@3**	**MAP@3**	**nDCG@3**
Movies	**CF**	.1152	.2111	.1257	.0793	.1271
	MP	.0488	.0926	.0591	.0163	.0419
	RD	.0039	.0093	.0055	.0020	.0048
EU	**CF**	.1526	.2632	.1877	.1263	.1721
	MP	.0263	.0175	.0211	.0088	.0161
	RD	.0132	.0175	.0150	.0044	.0103
Books	**CF**	.5333	.4555	.4778	.4889	.5000
	MP	.1333	.0444	.0667	.0444	.0667
	RD	.0667	.0222	.0333	.0333	.0420

Another interesting finding is that the recommender strategy based on global ratings, MP, generated less accurate results than *VizRec* CF for collected user preferences, both with regard to providing relevant visualizations and their ranking order. This supports our main assumption that in terms of the wide variability in user preference ratings, the personalized approach performs better recommendations.

6 Discussion and Outlook

This work is based on the premise that the preference of a visual representation for a dataset is a personal preference. Empirical evidence collected through a crowd sourced experiment supports the assumption that preferences widely vary for visual representations generated automatically. The second motivation driving our work is that a CF approach to recommending visualizations can account for such variability in personal preferences and significantly improve the recommendations. Our offline experiment supports our assumptions, showing that *VizRec* CF outperformed both the random approach (RD) and the global best approach (MP). A major contribution of our work is that it is based on the empirical evidence collected via a methodical study involving the general public. Our approach to generating and suggesting visualizations, the process of elicitation of users' preferences and the insights described in this paper are to the best of our knowledge, novel.

Several open questions remain that we plan to address in our continuing research. First, our solution suffers the cold start problem of CF-RS: a user who has not rated any chart cannot be recommended anything. To tackle this issue, we will investigate applying the measuring semantic similarity of the data attribute array to establish if a similar structure has been observed before and suggest from global ranking of other users. Furthermore, the investigation associated with our crowdsourced experiment is still ongoing. Although exploration of the relationship between quality of content features (such as textual description) and the valued quality of a visualization is beyond the scope of this paper.

But we are currently investigating the application of content features to the cold start problem and attempting to determine the tasks that a user associates with the preferred visualizations. Furthermore, we will conduct an online evaluation to ascertain whether our recommender performs as expected, compared with the results of the offline experiment.

Acknowledgments. This work is funded by the EC 7th Framework project EEXCESS (grant 600601). The Know-Center GmbH is funded within the Austrian COMET Program - managed by the Austrian Research Promotion Agency (FFG). The study was carried out during the tenure of an ERCIM "Alain Bensoussan" fellowship program by the third author. The authors would like to thank Dominik Kowald for providing very constructive and helpful suggestions with regard to the offline evaluation.

References

1. Deerwester, S., Dumais, S.T., Furnas, G.W., Landauer, T.K., Harshman, R.A.: Indexing by latent semantic analysis. Journal of the American Society for Information Science **41**, 391–407 (1990)
2. Xiaoyuan, S., Khoshgoftaar, T.M.: A Survey of Collaborative Filtering Techniques. Adv. in Artif. Intell. (2009)
3. Bertin, J.: Semiology of graphics. University of Wisconsin Press (1983)
4. Voigt, M., Franke, M., Meissner, K.: Using and empirical knowledge for context-aware recommendation of visualization components. In: Proc. of eKnow 2012 (2012)
5. Schelter, S., Owen, S.: Collaborative filtering with apache mahout. In: RecSysChallenge 2012 (2012)
6. Mackinlay, J.: Automating the design of graphical presentations of relational information. ACM Trans. Graph., 110–141 (1986)
7. Rahm, E., Bernstein, P.A.: A Survey of Approaches to Automatic Schema Matching. The VLDB Journal (2001)
8. Mackinlay, J., Hanrahan, P., Stolte, Ch.: Show Me: Automatic Presentation for Visual Analysis. IEEE Transactions on Visualization and Computer Graphics, 1137–1144 (2007)
9. Nazemi, K., Retz, R., Bernard, J., Kohlhammer, J., Fellner, D.: Adaptive semantic visualization for bibliographic entries. In: Bebis, G. (ed.) ISVC 2013, Part II. LNCS, vol. 8034, pp. 13–24. Springer, Heidelberg (2013)
10. Seffah, A., Donyaee, M., Kline, R., Padda, H.: Usability measurement and metrics: A consolidated model. Software Quality Journal, 159–178 (2006)
11. Ahn, J., Brusilovsky, P.: Adaptive Visualization of Search Results: Bringing User Models to Visual Analytics. Information Visualization, 167–179 (2009)
12. Zheng, X.S., Lin, J.J.W., Zapf, S., Knapheide, C.: Visualizing user experience through "Perceptual Maps": concurrent assessment of perceived usability and subjective appearance in car infotainment systems. In: Duffy, V.G. (ed.) HCII 2007 and DHM 2007. LNCS, vol. 4561, pp. 536–545. Springer, Heidelberg (2007)
13. Kittur, A., Chi, E.H., Suh, B.: Crowdsourcing user studies with mechanical turk. In: Proc. of CHI 2008 (2008)
14. Mutlu, B., Hoefler, P., Tschinkel, G., Sabol, V., Granitzer, M., Stegmaier, F.: Suggesting visualizations for published data. In: Proc. of VISIGRAPP 2014 (2014)

15. Trattner, C., Kowald, D., Lacic, E.: TagRec: Towards a Toolkit for Reproducible Evaluation and Development of Tag-Based Recommender Algorithms. ACM SIGWEB Newsletter (2015)
16. Herlocker, J.L., Konstan, J.A., Terveen, L.G., Riedl, J.T.: Evaluating collaborative filtering recommender systems. ACM Trans. Inf. Syst. **22**(1), 5–53 (2004)
17. Jaeschke, R., Marinho, L., Hotho, A., Schmidt-Thieme, L., Stumme, G.: Tag recommendations in social bookmarking systems. Ai Communications **21**(4), 231–247 (2008)
18. Schafer, J.B., Frankowski, D., Herlocker, J., Sen, S.: Collaborative filtering recommender systems. In: Brusilovsky, P., Kobsa, A., Nejdl, W. (eds.) Adaptive Web 2007. LNCS, vol. 4321, pp. 291–324. Springer, Heidelberg (2007)

Cross-System Transfer of Machine Learned and Knowledge Engineered Models of Gaming the System

Luc Paquette[1(✉)], Ryan S. Baker[1], Adriana de Carvalho[2], and Jaclyn Ocumpaugh[1]

[1] Teachers College, Columbia University, New York, NY, USA
{paquette,jo2424}@tc.columbia.edu,
baker2@exchange.tc.columbia.edu
[2] Google, New York, NY, USA

Abstract. Replicable research on the behavior known as gaming the system, in which students try to succeed by exploiting the functionalities of a learning environment instead of learning the material, has shown it is negatively correlated with learning outcomes. As such, many have developed models that can automatically detect gaming behaviors, towards deploying them in online learning environments. Both machine learning and knowledge engineering approaches have been used to create models for a variety of software systems, but the development of these models is often quite time consuming. In this paper, we investigate how well different kinds of models generalize across learning environments, specifically studying how effectively four gaming models previously created for the Cognitive Tutor Algebra tutoring system function when applied to data from two alternate learning environments: the scatterplot lesson of Cognitive Tutor Middle School and ASSISTments. Our results suggest that the similarity between the systems our model are transferred between and the nature of the approach used to create the model impact transfer to new systems.

Keywords: Gaming the system · Cognitive tutors · ASSISTments · Machine learning · Cognitive modeling · Cross-system transfer

1 Introduction

In intelligent tutoring systems (ITSs) and other learning environment, student disengagement often manifests in a behavior known as gaming the system. This behavior, which is neither clearly off-task nor on-task, is defined as "attempting to succeed in an educational environment by exploiting properties of the system rather than by learning the material and trying to use that knowledge to answer correctly" [1]. Research in multiple learning environments [1, 2, 3, 4, 5, 6, 7] has linked gaming to poor learning outcomes [8, 9, 10, 11], increased boredom [2] and lower long-term levels of academic attainment [12]. Both knowledge engineering [4, 5, 6, 7, 13, 14] and machine learning [1, 3, 7] approaches have been used to create models of gaming the system for specific learning environments. These detectors have been successfully applied (driving interventions) [15, 16] and used in discovery with models analyses [17], but only after a painstaking development process where researchers essentially start from scratch for each new learning environment.

F. Ricci et al. (Eds.): UMAP 2015, LNCS 9146, pp. 183–194, 2015.
DOI: 10.1007/978-3-319-20267-9_15

Little work has focused on the generalizability of gaming detectors. Nearly a decade ago, researchers showed that gaming detectors developed using machine learning could be generalized across different lessons in the same tutoring system [1]. Since that time, others have applied models to multiple learning systems [e.g., 6], but without validating that the model reliably captures gaming behavior across systems. Validating that some gaming detectors can be effectively applied across learning systems would facilitate broader use of gaming detectors. Currently, creating a model of gaming the system is a time consuming process that requires either field observations or the use of text replays, where log files of students interactions with the learning environment are segmented and formatted for presentation to a trained expert human coder who then labels whether each segment includes gaming behavior [18]. After this step, the feature engineering and model development process is time-consuming, complicated, and costly. The development of a model that allows us to skip (or reduce) the time-intensive development process for new learning systems would facilitate greater use of gaming detectors in intervention and analysis.

In this paper, we evaluate the generalizability of four recently published gaming models. Each were initially developed for use within an ITS known as Cognitive Tutor Algebra, but were constructed using different modeling techniques [19]. Specifically, we compare the generalizability of a detector developed with a form of knowledge engineering known as cognitive modeling [20] to that of three detectors that were developed by using machine learning to improve the cognitive model [21]. We assess each model's generalizability by comparing its performance when applied to two other ITSs for mathematics: the scatterplot lesson of Cognitive Tutor Middle School [22] (also called the scatterplot tutor) and ASSISTments [23]. Studying the generalizability of each model to these different systems allows us to investigate the degree to which each captures characteristics of the gaming construct that extend beyond a single system's features. We investigate how the nature of each system and the nature of each model interacts. More broadly, we discuss how the procedures used in this study might facilitate future development of detectors that generalize across learning environments, increasing their applicability and impact.

2 Gaming the System in Cognitive Tutor Algebra

2.1 Data

All four models of gaming behavior discussed in this paper were created using Cognitive Tutor Algebra (CTA) data [1, 21]. Specifically, these models were constructed from data produced by 59 students who used CTA as part of their regular mathematics curriculum throughout an entire school year (Pittsburgh Science of Learning Center DataShop "Algebra I 2005-2006 (Hampton only)" dataset [24]). The Cognitive Tutor environment presents students with complex mathematical problems that have been broken down into component steps, using a cognitive model of the task to assess whether answers correctly map to each step. Struggling students can request help at any time, and the tutor will provide increasingly specific, multi-step hints.

Data from 12 CTA lessons were segmented into short sequences of actions, called *clips*. For this study, clips were defined as sequences of at least 5 actions with a minimum duration of 20 seconds. If a 5-action sequence lasted less than 20 seconds, additional 5-action sequences were added to the clip until the total time duration was greater than 20 seconds. A total of 10,397 clips were randomly selected from this dataset; the chance of a clip being selected was weighted for each lesson based on the total number of clips in that lesson, so that each of the lessons in CTA were equally represented.

These clips were then presented to an expert coder (the 3rd author, henceforth expert #1), who had previously reached an interrater reliability with another expert (Cohen's Kappa > 0.6) through an extensive training process [22]. Cohen's Kappa [26] assesses the degree to which agreement between the expert is better than chance. A Kappa of 0 indicates chance level agreement and a Kappa of 1 indicates perfect agreement.

The clips were presented to expert #1 in the form of *text replays* [25, 18], where each clip is presented in a layout that highlights the relevant information needed to code student behaviors in a contextualized manner. Fig. 1 shows an example of a text replay taken from our CTA data. It displays each action's time (relative to the 1st action in the clip), the step's context, the input entered, the relevant skill (production) and the system's assessment of the action (a right or wrong answer, a help request or a predicted wrong answer, called a "bug"). In this way coders can quickly assess the actions in each clip to determine whether the student's interactions suggest gaming behaviors. In this case, the coder classified 6.81% (708) of clips as involving gaming the system behaviors and 93.19% (9,689) as not gaming.

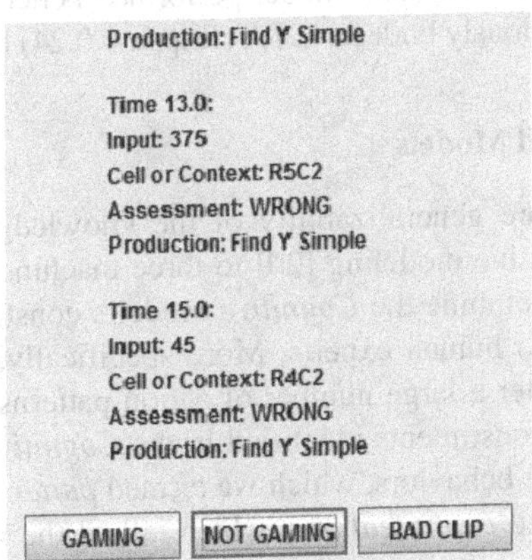

Fig. 1. The last actions of a 5-action text replay clip

2.2 Cognitive Model

The first step toward developing a generalizable model of gaming the system was to achieve a deeper understanding of how experts think about this construct [20]. To this end, we conducted a cognitive task analysis [27, 28] of expert #1's coding task using text replays from CTA. This involved a combination of active participation [28, 29] (in which the person performing the cognitive task analysis actively participated in the coding of text replays), think aloud observations [30] and interviews to explicate the coding process. Results indicated that the expert's coding method could be classified into two cognitive processes: interpreting the student's individual actions and identifying patterns of gaming across those actions. Although the expert executes these in parallel, our resulting cognitive model executes these as consecutive steps without changing the fundamental reasoning process.

In [1], we modeled expert #1's assessment of individual actions by constructing a list of 19 *constituents*—meaningful units of student behavior that the expert regularly relies upon when making gaming judgments, sometimes across more than one action. For example, the expert interprets a *short pause* between actions as a [*guess*], which is likely to indicate gaming behavior. She is similarly suspicious when a student enters a [*similar answer*] in two consecutive actions. (A detailed list of the 19 constituents we identified is available in [1].) Next, we developed a set of 13 *action patterns*, composed of 2-4 actions, each matching a predefined set of gaming constituents [1]. For example, consider a 2-action sequence where a student's 1st answer is incorrect. If they quickly attempt to answer a different problem step using the same response, the expert is likely to interpret the second action as a [*guess*], which she is trained to recognize as typical gaming behavior. This pattern was modeled as the following sequences of actions and constituents: **incorrect** → [*guess*] & [*same answer/diff. context*] & **incorrect**. In our *Cognitive* model of gaming the system, any clip containing actions that matching these 13 patterns was given a gaming label. These patterns were validated (Kappa = 0.330) on a test set, composed of 25% of the data from 2.1, which was held out during the cognitive task analysis [1]. This *Cognitive* model performed better on new data than a machine-learned model previously built for CTA (Kappa = 0.24) [25].

2.3 Machine Learned Models

In this paper we compare generalizability of the knowledge-engineered model we developed through cognitive modeling [20] to three machine-learned models derived from it [21]. The latter combine the *Cognitive* model's constituents into new patterns that were not apparent to human experts. More specifically, we developed an algorithm to generate and filter a large number of action patterns (similar to the one presented above) from the constituents identified in the *Cognitive* model, selecting those that best detected gaming behaviors, which we termed *pattern features.* We combined these with what we called *count features,* which tallied the number of times each of the 25 action types and constituents were present in a given clip.

Naïve Bayes classification was then used to generate three cross-validated, machine-learned models. The first, *CognitiveHybrid-PF*, contained 22 features, including 20 *pattern features* and 2 *count features* (Kappa = 0.477, A' = 0.770). The second, *CognitiveHybrid-C*, was trained using only the *count features*. The resulting model contained 6 features (Kappa = 0.332, A' = 0.875). The performance differences between these models reflect the nature of their features. Pattern features better capture the sequential nature of gaming behaviors, improving that model's Kappa, but their binary nature prevents it from achieving a high A'. Likewise, the gradient nature of the count features improves that modes' A' performance despite its lower Kappa. For this reason, we created a third model, *CognitiveHybrid-E*, that *Ensembled* the predictions from both these models. *CognitiveHybrid-E* achieves a high performance for both Kappa (0.457) and A' (0.901).

3 Evaluation of Cross-System Transfer

Because the four CTA gaming models were constructed from features that closely match the expert's conception of gaming, we hypothesized that they might capture characteristics of gaming that extend beyond system-specific behaviors, thereby allowing them to generalize to new systems. In this section we report on the performance of each model when it was applied, without additional training or modification, to data collected from the scatterplot lesson of Cognitive Tutor Middle School and ASSISTments.

3.1 Transfer to the Scatterplot Lesson of Cognitive Tutor Middle School

The 1st system we attempted to transfer our gaming models to was the scatterplot lesson of Cognitive Tutor Middle School [19]. This system was built using the same platform as CTA, meaning that their hint features, bug messages, and common interfaces (e.g., virtual problem worksheets) are quite similar. The primary differences are in the mathematical domain taught by each, which result in some interface differences. For example, the scatterplot lesson has additional interfaces for creating data representations (e.g., histograms) but lacks some of the complex algebraic equation manipulation seen in CTA. Nonetheless, given their similarities, we assumed transfer would be more successful for this system than ASSISTments (discussed below).

Data. The data for evaluating the transfer of the CTA models to the scatterplot lesson of Cognitive Tutor Middle School system was taken from a study of interrater agreement of experts coding text replays [18]. As such, we had access to gaming labels from 2 coders, neither of whom is expert #1, who provided the labels for CTA. These coders coded the same 600 clips (with some disagreement on which text replays constituted "bad clips," which did not get coded). We used these experts' gaming labels to develop three datasets for the scatterplot tutor. The first dataset (N = 595) was coded by expert #2, who labeled 29 as gaming and 566 as not. The second dataset (N = 592) was coded by expert #3, who labeled 33 as gaming and 559 as not. Finally, a third "Agreement" dataset is composed of all clips that were consistently coded by both experts (N=571), which includes 19 labeled as gaming and 552 labeled as not.

One important difference between the text replays from the scatterplot tutor and CTA is in the definition of a clip. Although clips from both systems have at least 20 seconds of data, the scatterplot tutor clips do not enforce a minimum number of actions (so may contain fewer than 5). Since gaming the system is a systematic pattern of behaviors, this could make it more challenging for experts to identify gaming actions within the scatterplot tutor clip.

Performance. We applied each of the four CTA gaming models to the three datasets from the scatterplot lesson of Cognitive Tutor Middle School. Table 1 summarizes the performance achieved by each on the new datasets, using both the Kappa and the A' [31] metrics. A' is the probability that given a pair of two clips, one coded as gaming and the other coded as not-gaming, the model can accurately detect which clip was coded as gaming. A' is equivalent to the area under the ROC curve in signal detection theory [31]. Note that A' could not be calculated for the *Cognitive* model, which does not produce confidences.

Table 1. Comparison of the models performance across the Cognitive Tutor Algebra (CTA) and the scatterplot lesson of Cognitive Tutor Middle School datasets

Model	*Cognitive Tutor Algebra (CTA)*	*Scatterplot Expert #2*	*Scatterplot Expert #3*	*Scatterplot Agreement*
Cognitive	Kappa = 0.330 A' = N/A	Kappa = 0.459 A' = N/A	Kappa = 0.479 A' = N/A	Kappa = 0.483 A' = N/A
CogHybrid-PF	Kappa = 0.477 A' = 0.770	Kappa = 0.440 A' = 0.819	Kappa = 0.438 A' = 0.795	Kappa = 0.451 A' = 0.877
CogHybrid-C	Kappa = 0.332 A' = 0.875	Kappa = 0.345 A' = 0.894	Kappa = 0.360 A' = 0.889	Kappa = 0.331 A' = 0.949
CogHybrid-E	Kappa = 0.457 A' = 0.901	Kappa = 0.430 A' = 0.917	Kappa = 0.427 A' = 0.905	Kappa = 0.438 A' = 0.973

All four models transfer well to the scatterplot lesson of Cognitive Tutor Middle School despite differences in the mathematical domain, in the definition of a clip, and among the experts who labeled the data. The most notable finding was that, when applied to the scatterplot tutor data, the *Cognitive* model achieved a higher Kappa than the machine-learned models. Surprisingly, the *Cognitive* model achieved considerably higher performance for the scatterplot tutor than for CTA. The machine-learned models also transfer well, achieving performance metrics for the scatterplot tutor datasets that are comparable to those for the CTA data. *CogHybrid-PF* obtains a slightly lower Kappa on each of the three scatterplot datasets, whereas its A' performance actually increased. Performance for *CogHybrid-C* slightly increases for both metrics. The ensemble model, *CogHybrid-E*, achieves slightly lower Kappa for the scatterplot datasets than for CTA, similar A' for both experts, and an increase in A' for the Agreement set.

In general, models transfer best to the Agreement dataset. Kappa performance is slightly higher for three of the four models (*Cognitive*, *CogHybrid-PF* and *CogHybrid-E*), and A' performance is considerably greater. This may suggest that the text replays that showed expert disagreement were contributing significant noise to the datasets.

3.2 Transfer to ASSISTments

We also studied the degree to which these models could generalize to ASSISTments [23], a web-based tutoring system for middle school mathematics. Two models of gaming the system have previously been developed for ASSISTments. The first, published in 2006 [7], achieved a Kappa of 0.181 for new data. The second, published in 2013 [11], achieved a Kappa of 0.370 and A' of 0.802 [11].

Although both ASSISTments and CTA are problem-solving intelligent tutors for mathematics, the structure and presentation of problems in ASSISTments is quite different from either of the Cognitive Tutor platforms. In Cognitive Tutor, problems are partitioned in multiple steps that must be completed to finish each problem. The Cognitive Tutor indicates whether each step is right or wrong, providing assistance as necessary. In ASSISTments, when students are presented with an "original" problem, they only need to provide its final answer. Individual steps are not required of students who solve the problem on the first attempt. However, students who do not provide the correct answer may be required to correctly answer scaffolding questions in order to successfully complete the problem.

At the same time, there are considerable similarities between the two systems. Both provide immediate feedback indicting whether their answer was right or wrong, including detailed feedback for "bugs," where the student's error indicates a known misconception. ASSISTments also offers help functionality similar to that found on the Cognitive Tutor platforms.

Data. ASSISTments data produced by 1,367 students was used to test the generalizability of our CTA gaming models. This data includes a total of 822,233 problem-solving steps, which were segmented into 240,450 clips. A selection of these (discussed below) was presented to expert #1 for coding.

Again the definition of a clip for the new system was different than it was for CTA, this time because of differences in how the systems present problems to students. Whereas Cognitive Tutor platform always requires students to solve multiple steps before completing a main problem, ASSISTments problems can be solved in one step if the student's first attempt is correct. As such, we define a clip in ASSISTments as starting from the first action on an original unscaffolded problem to the last attempt before the next original, unscaffolded problem. This definition means that a clip can be composed of only 1 action or it can contain more than 50.

As such, when selecting clips for coding by expert #1 (who also coded the CTA data), we filtered them with respect to length. Clips containing more than 25 actions were removed from the dataset because it was difficult to present such a large number of actions in a text replay. We also felt that it was unlikely that the constituent behaviors (e.g., [20]) that comprise gaming behaviors would be different in clips containing 40 or 50 actions than they would be in clips containing 20-25. On the other hand, if there were longer action patterns present in these clips, which comprised less than 0.7% of the dataset, it could create a serious bias towards a different gaming pattern that was being identified by the expert.

Shorter clips (fewer than 3 actions) presented a different problem. Because gaming is a systematic pattern of behavior that often occurs among students who do not understand the material, it is unlikely to be seen in clips where students solve the problem correctly in very few attempts [20, 21]. On the other hand, shorter clips comprise 73.0% of the original data, so filtering them entirely could have biased the coding.

As such, we created two datasets for ASSISTments. Sample #1 was comprised of 1,000 clips with 1-25 actions each, so that clip length distribution closely matches the original dataset. Sample #2 was comprised of 1,000 clips with 4-25 actions; this allowance was intended to increase the odds that clips containing gaming behaviors would be presented to the coder.

As in [1], clips were presented to expert #1 in the form of text replays. The order in which the expert coded these replays was randomized, mixing clips from both samples in order to avoid coding biases. A technical glitch kept the expert from completing all 2000 clips (with the replay software hanging after 1063 codes). Randomization ensured that the two samples had balanced numbers ($N_1 = 520$, $N_2 = 543$). The expert identified gaming behaviors in 3.46% of sample #1 and 8.47% of sample #2 ($N_1 = 18$, $N_2 = 46$), in line with the design of the latter, which increased the odds of drawing clips which contain this systematic behavior. Combining samples provided 64 gaming clips (6.02%) 996 non-gaming clips (93.70%) and 3 clips where the replay software or data had an error (0.28%).

Performance. Each of the four models of gaming the system were applied to sample #1, sample #2, and the two samples *combined*. As Table 2 shows, each performed above chance when applied to the ASSISTments datasets, but both Kappa and A' were considerably lower than when these models were applied to either of the Cognitive Tutor platforms.

Performance of the *Cognitive* model was similar across all three ASSISTments datasets (Kappa = 0.228-0.256), and as with the scatterplot lesson of Cognitive Tutor Middle School, it generally outperformed the machine-learned models. This difference seems to be driven primarily by the performance of the detectors on sample #1, which was far more likely to contain shorter clips than sample #2. Although the *Cognitive* model performed slightly worse on sample 1 than it had on the CTA data (Kappa = 0.228 compared to Kappa = 0.330), the Kappa values for the machine-learned models were quite low for this sample (Kappa = 0.075-0.124).

Table 2. Comparison of the models performance across the Cognitive Tutor Algebra (CTA) and ASSISTments datasets

Model	*Cognitive Tutor Algebra (CTA)*	*ASSISTments Sample #1*	*ASSISTments Sample #2*	*ASSISTments Combined*
Cognitive	Kappa = 0.330 A' = N/A	Kappa = 0.228 A' = N/A	Kappa = 0.240 A' = N/A	Kappa = 0.256 A' = N/A
CogHybrid-PF	Kappa = 0.477 A' = 0.770	Kappa = 0.075 A' = 0.565	Kappa = 0.285 A' = 0.694	Kappa = 0.248 A' = 0.665
CogHybrid-C	Kappa = 0.332 A' = 0.875	Kappa = 0.124 A' = 0.890	Kappa = 0.156 A' = 0.763	Kappa = 0.173 A' = 0.810
CogHybrid-E	Kappa = 0.457 A' = 0.901	Kappa = 0.121 A' = 0.892	Kappa = 0.246 A' = 0.803	Kappa = 0.235 A' = 0.829

Among the machine-learned models, Kappa performance was variable. *CogHybrid-PF's* performance was unstable across the three data sets. Performance on sample #2 and the combined dataset was acceptable (Kappa = 0.285, Kappa = 0.248), if lower than its performance on either of the Cognitive Tutor systems. However, performance on sample #1, where the number of actions per clip most closely matches what is typical in ASSISTments, was low (Kappa = 0.075). *CogHybrid-C* achieved relatively poor but more stable performance across the 3 datasets (Kappa = 0.124-0.173). Kappa results for the ensemble model, *CogHybrid-E*, were similar to *CogHybrid-PF*, performing more poorly on sample #1 than on the other 2 datasets. Its A' values were closely aligned to those of *CogHybrid-C*.

The A' performance of these models (which was not calculated for the *Cognitive* model) was more promising. *CogHybrid-PF's* performance, which had been low even on the CTA data, was particularly low for Sample #1, but other A' values were surprisingly high. For instance, *CogHybrid-C*, which was constructed by counting the number of gaming constituents (action sequences) that were present in a clip had an A' for Sample #1 that was higher than for CTA, and *CogHybrid-E*, had an A' for Sample #1 that was nearly as high as the one it achieved for CTA.

Although performance decreased when transferring from CTA to ASSISTments, our models still performed substantially above chance (Kappa = 0.075-0.256 and A' = 0.665-0.829). Their performance is also comparable to previous models of gaming the system developed specifically for the ASSISTments system. For Kappa, performance was moderately worse than the model in [11] (0.370), but, except for *CogHybrid-C*, our models performed better than that in [7] (0.181). Likewise, one of the previously published gaming model for ASSISTments achieved an A' of 0.802 [11], and two of our machine learned models outperform that. (Note that [7] did not report A'.)

4 Discussion and Conclusions

This paper examines the performance of gaming the system models previously developed for Cognitive Tutor Algebra (CTA) to determine the degree to which each can be reliably applied to other systems without additional modifications. To this end, we compared the degree to which these models, which had performed well on the CTA data used to train them, could transfer to two other intelligent tutoring systems that provide similar mathematics instruction: (1) the scatterplot lesson of Cognitive Tutor Middle School, which shares many of the same design features as CTA and (2), ASSISTments, which has more design differences, but covers content that is similar to that provided in CTA.

The first model we tested was developed using a cognitive task analysis to model expert judgments about gaming behaviors [20], while the other 3 models were developed using machine learning techniques to improve the first [21]. That is, machine learning was used to discover patterns in the behavioral constituents that were tacitly used by the expert human coders who provide the training labels for gaming detectors. It was hypothesized that since all four models were developed from features that map to the expert's coding process (rather than the features that were more specific to the learning system), they would be more likely to transfer.

Results from our study indicate, perhaps unsurprisingly, that learning system differences affected how well models were able to generalize. Models performed better when transferred to the scatterplot lesson of Cognitive Tutor Middle School, which shares many design features with CTA than when transferred to ASSISTments, which has a more distinctive interface. It is likely that these interface differences lead students using ASSISTments to adopt different gaming strategies than those used in the Cognitive Tutor platforms.

Other results were less predictable. Our findings suggest that the machine learning techniques used by [21] to improve performance within CTA may not be necessary for the development of generalizable detectors. That is, the knowledge engineering model (the *Cognitive* model), when applied to new systems, performed as well as or outperformed the three machine learned models on the Kappa metric. This suggests that machine-learning, which optimizes a model's performance on the system it was trained for, may overfit to the specific system.

On the other hand, the results for *CognitiveHybrid-E* model suggests that this finding warrants further research. This model—which ensembled the confidence values of the machine learned models produced with pattern features and with count features—showed superior performance on the original CTA data set and performed almost as well as the *Cognitive* model on the new systems. What's more, the strong A' performance of the machine learned models (two of which were comparable to previously published models of gaming that were developed specifically for ASSISTments) also suggests that this method deserves further consideration. That said, the *Cognitive* model's performance shows substantial stability across systems, an important consideration, particularly for models that will be used to trigger interventions.

Although our models transferred reasonably well to two new learning systems, both were designed for the tutoring of mathematics problem. The current study does not present evidences that these gaming detectors will transfer to mathematics tutors with different intervention strategies or to tutors that provide instruction in other domains. Such differences are likely to trigger different gaming strategies, making this an important area for future research.

Acknowledgments. This research was supported by a Fonds de Recherche du Québec - Nature et Technologies (FRQNT) post-doctoral fellowship and by National Science Foundation (NSF) grant #SBE-0836012.

References

1. de Baker, R.S.J., Corbett, A.T., Roll, I., Koedinger, K.R.: Developing a Generalizable Detector of When Students Games the System. User Modeling & User Adapted Interaction **18**, 287–314 (2008)
2. de Baker, R.S.J., D'Mello, S.K., Rodrigo, M.M.T., Graesser, A.C.: Better to be Frustrated than Bored: The Incidence, Persistence, and Impact of Learners' Cognitive-Affective States During Interactions with Three Different Computer-Based Learning Environments. Int'l Journal of Human-Computer Studies **68**, 223–241 (2010)
3. de Baker, R.S.J., Mitrović, A., Mathews, M.: Detecting gaming the system in constraint-based tutors. In: De Bra, P., Kobsa, A., Chin, D. (eds.) UMAP 2010. LNCS, vol. 6075, pp. 267–278. Springer, Heidelberg (2010)

4. Beal, C.R., Qu, L., Lee, H.: Classifying learner engagement through integration of multiple data sources. In: Proc. of the National Conf. on Artificial Intelligence, pp. 151–156 (2006)
5. Johns, J., Woolf, B.: A dynamic mixture model to detect student motivation and proficiency. In: Proc. of the National Conference on Artificial Intelligence, pp. 163–168 (2006)
6. Muldner, K., Burleson, W., Van de Sande, B., VanLehn, K.: An Analysis of Students' Gaming Behaviors in an Intelligent Tutoring System: Predictors and Impact. User Modeling and User Adapted Interaction **21**, 99–135 (2011)
7. Walonoski, J.A., Heffernan, N.T.: Detection and analysis of off-task gaming behavior in intelligent tutoring systems. In: Ikeda, M., Ashley, K.D., Chan, T.-W. (eds.) ITS 2006. LNCS, vol. 4053, pp. 382–391. Springer, Heidelberg (2006)
8. Beck, J., Rodrigo, M.T.: Understanding wheel spinning in the context of affective factors. In: Trausan-Matu, S., Boyer, K.E., Crosby, M., Panourgia, K. (eds.) ITS 2014. LNCS, vol. 8474, pp. 162–167. Springer, Heidelberg (2014)
9. Cocea, M., Hershkovitz, A., de Baker, R.S.J.: The impact of off-task and gaming behaviors on learning: immediate or aggregate? In: Proc. of the 14th Int'l Conference on Artificial Intelligence in Education, pp. 507–514 (2009)
10. Fancsali, S.E.: Data-Driven Causal Modeling of "Gaming the System" and Off-Task Behavior in Cognitive Tutor Algebra. NIPS Workshop on Data Driven Education
11. Pardos, Z.A., Baker, R.S., San Pedro, M.O.C.Z., Gowda, S.M., Gowda, S.M.: Affective States and State Tests: Investigating how Affect and Engagement During the School Year Predict End of Year Learning Outcomes. J. of Learning Analytics **1**(1), 107–128 (2014)
12. San Pedro, M.O.Z., de Baker, R.S.J., Bowers, A.J., Heffernan, N.T.: Predicting college enrolment from student interaction with an intelligent tutoring system in middle school. In: Proc. of the 6th Int'l Conference on Educational Data Mining, pp. 177–184 (2013)
13. Aleven, V., McLaren, B.M., Roll, I., Koedinger, K.R.: Towards Meta-Cognitive Tutoring: A Model of Help Seeking with a Cognitive Tutor. Int'l J. of Artificial Intelligence in Education **16**, 101–130 (2006)
14. Gong, Y., Beck, J.E., Heffernan, N.T., Forbes-Summers, E.: The fine-grained impact of gaming on learning. In: Aleven, V., Kay, J., Mostow, J. (eds.) ITS 2010, Part I. LNCS, vol. 6094, pp. 194–203. Springer, Heidelberg (2010)
15. Arroyo, I., et al.: Repairing disengagement with non-invasive interventions. In: Proc. of the 13th Int'l Conference on Artificial Intelligence in Education, pp. 195–202 (2007)
16. Walonoski, J.A., Heffernan, N.T.: Prevention of off-task gaming behavior in intelligent tutoring systems. In: Ikeda, M., Ashley, K.D., Chan, T.-W. (eds.) ITS 2006. LNCS, vol. 4053, pp. 722–724. Springer, Heidelberg (2006)
17. de Baker, R.S.J., Yacef, K.: The State of Educational Data Mining in 2009: A Review and Future Visions. Journal of Educational Data Mining **1**(1), 3–17 (2009)
18. de Baker, R.S.J., Corbett, A.T., Wagner, A.Z.: Human classification of low-fidelity replays of student actions. In: Proc. of the Educational Data Mining Workshop at Intelligent Tutoring System 2006, pp. 29–36 (2006)
19. Koedinger, K.R., Corbett, A.T.: Cognitive tutors: technology bringing learning sciences to the classroom. In: Sawyer, R.K. (ed.) The Cambridge Handbook of the Learning Sciences, pp. 61–77 (2006)
20. Paquette, L., de Carvalho, A.M.J.A., Ryan, S.B.: Towards understanding export coding of student disengagement in online learning. In: Proc. of the 36th Annual Cognitive Science Conference, pp. 1126–1131 (2014)
21. Paquette, L., de Carvalho, A.M.J.A., Ryan, S.B., Ocumpaugh, J.: Reengineering the feature distillation process: a case study in the detection of gaming the system. In: Proc. of the 7th Int'l Conference on Educational Data Mining, pp. 284–287 (2014)

22. Baker, R.S., Corbett, A.T., Koedinger, K.R.: Learning to distinguish between representations of data: a cognitive tutor that uses contrasting cases. In: Proc. of the International Conference of the Learning Sciences, pp. 58–65 (2004)
23. Razzaq, L., et al.: The assistment project: blending assessment and assisting. In: Proc. of the 12 Annual Conference on Artificial Intelligence in Education, pp. 555–562 (2005)
24. Koedinger, K.R., et al.: A Data Repository for the Community: The PLSC DataShop (2010)
25. de Baker, R.S.J., de Carvalho, A.M.J.A.: Labeling student behavior faster & more precisely with text replays. In: Proc. of the 1st Int'l Conf. on Educational Data Mining 2008, pp. 38–47 (2008)
26. Cohen, J.: A Coefficient of Agreement for Nominal Scales. Educational and Psychological Measurement **20**(1), 37–46 (1960)
27. Clark, R.E., Feldon, D., van Merriënboer, J., Yates, K., Early, S.: Cognitive task analysis. In: Spector, J.M., Merrill, M.D., van Merriënboer, J.J.G., Driscoll, M.P. (eds.) Handbook of Research on Educational Communications and Technology, 3rd edn., pp. 575–593 (2008)
28. Cooke, N.J.: Varieties of Knowledge Elicitation Techniques. Int'l Journal of Human-Computer Studies **41**, 801–849 (1994)
29. Meyer, M.A.: How to Apply the Anthropological Technique of Participant Observation to Knowledge Acquisition for Expert Systems. IEEE Transactions on Systems, Man, & Cybernetics **22**, 983–991 (1992)
30. Van Someren, M.W., Barnard, Y.F., Sandberg, J.A.C.: The Think Aloud Method: A Practical Guide to Modeling Cognitive Processes (1994)
31. Hanley, J., McNeil, B.: The Meaning and Use of the Area Under a Receiver Operating Characteristic (ROC) Curve. Radiology **143**, 29–36 (1982)

MobiScore: Towards Universal Credit Scoring from Mobile Phone Data

Jose San Pedro[1](✉), Davide Proserpio[2], and Nuria Oliver[1]

[1] Telefonica Research, Barcelona, Spain
{jose.sanpedro,nuria.oliver}@telefonica.com
[2] Computer Science Department, Boston University, Boston, MA, USA
dproserp@bu.edu

Abstract. Credit is a widely used tool to finance personal and corporate projects. The risk of default has motivated lenders to use a credit scoring system, which helps them make more efficient decisions about whom to extend credit. Credit scores serve as a financial user model, and have been traditionally computed from the user's past financial history. As a result, people without any prior financial history might be excluded from the credit system. In this paper we present MobiScore, an approach to build a model of the user's financial risk from mobile phone usage data, which previous work has shown to convey information about *e.g.* personality and socioeconomic status. MobiScore could replace traditional credit scores when no financial history is available, providing credit access to currently excluded population sectors, or be used as a complementary source of information to improve traditional finance-based scores. We validate the proposed approach using real data from a telecommunications operator and a financial institution in a Latin American country, resulting in an accurate model of default comparable to traditional credit scoring techniques.

1 Introduction

Credit scores are widely used in the financial sector as a way to control risk when lending to potential credit customers. Credit scores convey information about the ability of customers to pay back their debt or conversely to default. Therefore, they are a key variable to build financial user models. Traditionally, credit scores have been computed by modeling the past financial history of users. Credit bureaus, such as Equifax or Experian, provide these scores to interested parties by aggregating all the available financial information from customers across different financial products and institutions.

Scores generated using the past financial history have shown to be very reliable. Hence, lenders prefer to focus on cross-selling to existing customers or catering to those for whom credit history information is more readily accessible [13]. As a result, financially responsible customers could be excluded from credit because they lack any prior financial history. These customers are referred to as *no-file* or *thin-file*.

F. Ricci et al. (Eds.): UMAP 2015, LNCS 9146, pp. 195–207, 2015.
DOI: 10.1007/978-3-319-20267-9_16

While *no-file* or *thin-file* consumers are prevalent in developing economies – the World Bank estimates that there are 2.5 billion *unbanked* adults who lack access to formal financial services[1] – millions of consumers today don't receive credit scores in developed economies either. New immigrants (only in the U.S. there are 1.1 million working immigrants per year), recent college graduates, people recovering from earlier financial missteps and the *underbanked* – individuals who have a bank account but do not use it on a regular basis, accounting for 20% of the U.S. population in 2013 [2] – are also in the no-file category.

The growing need to access credit has motivated the search of alternative sources of information that could serve as accurate proxies of traditional credit scores to model user proneness to credit default. In this direction, a large body of literature has studied demographic aspects and variables related to personality and socioeconomic status that correlate with unreliable financial behavior and lead to default. Among these characteristics we find impulsiveness, education level or marital status [10,11].

In this paper we propose MobiScore, an approach that leverages data passively captured from the mobile phone network, *i.e.*, patterns of mobile phone usage, to build a user model of propensity to credit default by using supervised machine learning methods. This concept is supported by the results of previous studies that leverage mobile phone usage data for modeling users, such as inferring personality traits or socioeconomic status [5,6,17], which have been shown to correlate with financial behavior [9]. Given the ubiquity of mobile phones both in developing countries and developed economies, MobiScore could help currently excluded users in getting access to financial services such as loans or credit cards.

The main contributions of this paper are twofold. First, we introduce MobiScore, a methodology to build a consumer credit default model using as input data call detail records obtained from telecommunications companies. Second, to asses the feasibility of the model, we conduct a large study with real credit default data for a large population of over 60,000 customers from a Latin American country. This study benchmarks the performance of a traditional credit scoring approach along with our proposed methodology. To the best of our knowledge, this is the first work that reports results on such a large scale population.

2 Related Work

Credit scores have been extensively used in the financial industry during the last two decades to improve customer credit collections [13]. However, research reporting the performance of this tools is scarce due to their proprietary nature. In this work, we focus on the particular problem of customer credit scores, namely to predict individual risk. In this area, credit scoring techniques are based

[1] http://www.worldbank.org/en/results/2013/04/02/financial-inclusion-helping-countries-meet-the-needs-of-the-underbanked-and-underserved

[2] https://www.fdic.gov/householdsurvey/

on statistical models that use different data sources that reflect user behavior, financial or not, to determine their likelihood to default [1,3].

The most widespread way to compute credit scores uses financial and demographic data. Credit bureaus, including Equifax and Experian, or specialized technological companies like Fico, rely on specific financial information, such as credit history, current credit use, or ratio between credit limit and outstanding balance. As previously discussed, these methods need access to the financial history of users, which is not always available. Hence, alternative methods to score users that do not rely on such information have been proposed in the last few years.

There is a vast amount of literature trying to understand the socio-economic and behavioral factors that can be correlated with financial risk and spending behavior, as well as with credit default. Socio-economic factors including education, marital status, net worth, financial knowledge, and household income, as well as several environmental factors (*e.g.* income or home ownership status) and demographic factors (*e.g.* racial background, age, and gender) are all correlated with financial risk [10]. Furthermore, it has been shown that personality affects the predisposition to financial risk. For example in [11] the authors show how impulsiveness is correlated with credit card behavior, while in [12] the authors show that impatient people are more prone to default. Finally [2] shows how user mobility is (inversely) correlated to default rates.

Mobile phone usage logs have been studied for modeling users and community dynamics in a wide range of applications. For example, a framework to discover places-of-interest from multimodal mobile phone data is described in [14], and [7] shows that it is possible to accurately infer friendships based on observational mobile data alone. Socio-economic status has also been inferred from mobile phone activity data [17]. More broadly mobile data has been used to uncover individual and collective human dynamics [4], infer gender [8] and personality [5, 6]. In [16], the authors study the interconnection between social and mobile features and spending behavior. Our work relates with all the above in that we model user behavior from phone usage, and in particular the user's propensity to default on their credit.

The use of mobile data for financial risk assessment has attracted the attention of some entrepenurial efforts, such as Cignifi[3]. However, a comparison is difficult as they use a proprietary technology and the details of their approach are unknown. To the best of our knowledge, this paper is the first to disclose the potential of mobile phone usage data in this problem setting.

3 Dataset

In this section, we describe the dataset used in MobiScore to model the users' financial reliability from their mobile phone usage data. This dataset combines two main sources of information: (1) mobile phone usage logs, which we use as

[3] http://www.cignifi.com/en-us/technology

raw data to find behavioral patterns consistent with unreliable financial behavior; and (2) financial information in the form of credit default reports, which serves as ground truth to train user models of credit default using a supervised learning paradigm. We obtained the data for over 60,000 people from a Latin American country in which both the telecommunications company and the financial institution operate. The data was completely anonymzed and stripped of all personal information, such that it was not possible to identify any individual. The Telco and Financial institution generated a unique user identifier applying a common hash function unknown to us. This enabled us to anonymously merge the two datasets. Moreover, the analysis of the data was in compliance with the terms and confitions of data usage of that particular service.

3.1 Mobile Phone Usage Dataset

Mobile phone networks are built using a set of cell towers (BTS) which connect phone devices within the network. Each BTS is identified by the latitude and longitude of its geographical location. Whenever a phone in the network makes or receives a call or uses a service (*e.g.* SMS, MMS), this communication event is logged into a raw database known as Call Detail Records (CDRs). CDRs include information about all the different aspects of the communication event: phone lines involved in the event, type of event, timestamp, etc. BTS details are also logged, providing a proxy of the geographical position of the user at the time of the call (at the granularity of the area of coverage of the BTS).

From all the information contained in a CDR, MobiScore analyzes the two most common events: calls and text messages (SMS). We extract the following fields from the CDRs: anonymized originating and destination numbers, time and date of the call or SMS, and an identifier of the BTS that the originating phone was connected to when the call was placed. For calls, we also extract their duration in seconds. Note that the dataset neither contains personally identifiable information nor the content of the calls or the SMS.

Our CDR dataset contains three months of data from January to March 2014, consisting of daily cell phone events from pre-paid and contract subscribers in the Latin American country of study. The collected dataset contains over 35 million call events, and over 11 million SMS events, with an average of around 12 million calls and 3.5 million text messages per month.

3.2 Financial Dataset

Lenders normally report payments in arrears to credit bureaus on a monthly basis. Two payments in arrears, *i.e.* 30 days past due, is the first level reported to bureaus, as dictated by the Fair Credit Reporting Act.[4] We collected such records for a credit card offered by a financial institution operating in the considered Latin American country. The dataset of customers in arrears was collected for a period of 15 months, from January 2013 to March 2014. For each customer we

[4] http://www.ftc.gov/os/statutes/fcradoc.pdf

obtained a monthly record stating the amount of pending balance and the days in arrears of payment.

Customers are considered to be in default only when the lender deems their pending balance to be uncollectible; the exact number of days for this condition to hold depends on the financial product, the lending institution and the legal framework of the country where the institution operates. In the context of this paper we consider two definitions of customers in default that are common in the literature: customers who are more than 30 days in arrears (*Default @30*), and customers who are more than 90 days in arrears (*Default @90*). Using the aforementioned reports, we could determine whether each customer was in default for any of the two definitions used.

4 Methodology

We pose the credit scoring problem as a binary classification task, which we model using a supervised learning strategy. For each potential credit customer, we intend to model a score P which can be interpreted as the probability of default. Customers are represented in a feature space that captures different orthogonal aspects of their use of the phone, which we expect to convey behavioral information with discriminative power in this problem setting.

4.1 Feature Extraction

In Sec. 2, we introduced previous research focused on identifying correlations between financial risk and user socioeconomic status, personality and demographic factors among others. We follow this line of work to extract from the CDRs a set of features of mobile phone usage that convey user behavioral information related to financial risk. Furthermore, we take advantage of additional information collected by the telecommunications company about their customers, known as Customer Relationship Management (CRM), to extract demographics and socioeconomic features.

CDR Features. CDRs amass all the communication actions carried out by customers, and therefore has great potential as a source of information for user modeling. We are especially interested in studying traits of personality and specific behaviors of stationary nature, as to discern which of those could lead to credit default with higher probability. Previous literature has found such correlation in subjects with impulsive behavior or with more impatient personalities. In our context, we do not count with such high level information about users, but previous work on analyzing phone logs encourages us to think that we can find such correlations also in features extracted from CDRs. In order to be as comprehensive as possible, we study CDR logs across three complementary dimensions: consumption, mobility and social network. A detailed list of the CDR-based features is shown in Table 1.

Consumption features are related to the amount of use of the communications network, and provide a high level view of the access frequency for different communication methods, both calls and SMS. We compute the above features for different temporal partitions: by day of the week (weekdays *vs* weekends), and by time of the day (office hours, 9am to 6pm, *vs* evenings). This slicing of the temporal dimension in four partitions (or time windows) allows to profile users at different significant moments, helping to generate a more holistic view of their phone usage. Furthermore, since mobile communications are intrinsically directional, some features are subdivided in incoming (received by the user) or outgoing (originated by the user).

?Social network features focus on capturing information about the characteristics of the graph of connections between customers, which could convey information about empathy and other social-related traits of personality. We include in these features the number of unique correspondents in incoming and outgoing calls/SMS (i.e. in and out degrees) and the in/out degree variation between between temporal windows as defined above (delta degrees).

Finally, *mobility features* capture mobility patterns of customers in their everyday life inferred from the position of the BTS the users connected to. Radius of gyration is computed as the minimum radius that encompasses all the locations (BTS) visited by a user daily. Distance traveled adds the distance traveled to visit all the BTS connected every day. Popular antennas is computed as the number of BTS connected to account for 66% of the communications activity, serving also as a proxy of mobility.

We also include the number of events that are reciprocated. An event is marked as reciprocated if the current customer A calls (or texts) another customer B within one hour from an incoming call (text) from customer B. Reciprocated events such as calls or SMSs are used in the mobile data analysis literature as an evidence of the existence of strong ties between users [15]. While a single call between two individuals may not carry much information, reciprocated calls between two users indicate some degree of relationship (work, family, or other), helping us to better characterize the user's social interactions.

Moreover, we extract regularity features by computing Shannon's entropy for variables related to calls, messaging, and mobility. *Communication time entropy* measures the regularity of customers regarding the time window used to contact individual interlocutors. We consider the multinomial distribution of events over the temporal dimension for each customer and unique interlocutor. That is, for every customer i and interlocutor j, their *communications time entropy* is:

$$H_{ij}(X) = -\sum_{x \in V} p(x) log(p(x)) \qquad (1)$$

where X is a discrete random variable taking values from the set V (every one of the four temporal partitions), and $p(x)$ is its probability mass function (the fraction of times user i contacted user j in the given time window x). The final entropy is computed as the mean value $H_{ij}(X)$ for all interlocutors of i.

Communication entropy measures how regular a user is with respect to the interlocutors (s)he has contacted. Using the formulation of Eq 1, V would refer to the complete set of interlocutors of i, and $p(X)$ to the probability that i calls/texts this particular interlocutor x (relative frequency *w.r.t.* the rest of interlocutors). Similarly, *mobility entropy* is computed by considering the fraction of calls made from every BTS in the set of popular antennas.[5]

Customer Relation Management (CRM) Features. In addition to usage logs, telecommunication companies collect additional information related to their customers, typically stored in Customer Relation Management or CRM logs. For instance, demographic information (age, gender) is required for signing the contract of specific products. Socioeconomic information is inferred from the customers home address, required for landlines. Additional data related to socioeconomic status can be extracted from the type and number of products owned by the customer, as well as data related to the devices used (*e.g.* brand of phone). We collected some of this CRM information and use it both as a standalone dataset to predict financial risk and to complement the CDR features. A detailed list of the CRM features used is presented in Table 2.

Table 1. Event log features

Consumption features
By time window and direction
Daily call (SMS) events
Daily duration of call events
Daily time between consecutive call (SMS) events
Daily time between consecutive events (either call or SMS)
Global
Communications time entropy
Communications entropy
Social network features
Number of unique call (SMS) correspondents
Call (SMS) delta degrees
Number of reciprocated call (SMS) events
Fraction of reciprocated call (SMS) events
Median of time between reciprocated call (SMS) events
Mobility features
Radius of gyration
Distance traveled
Popular antennas
Popular antennas entropy

Table 2. CRM Features

Product features
Device brand
Device operating system
Device type
Line type
Line status
Line quantity
Late payments
Month elapsed since activation
Socioeconomic features
Age
Gender
Estimated customer income
High risk ZIP code
Regional area code

4.2 Model Building

We use supervised learning for building user credit score models. To this end, we represent users in the presented feature space, which we extract from the CDRs in the period January 2014 to March 2014. Our financial information for this population predates these CDRs for the most part, as it goes from January 2013 to March 2014. As we are interested in stationary personality traits and behavior, we use the following methodology to generate the ground truth.

[5] SMS were not associated with a BTS in our dataset.

We consider only customers that activated their card during the period January 2013 to March 2014 (our range of financial reports). Given that the probability of default at a time greater than T is $P(t > T) = 1$ for a sufficiently large T, we decided to consider the same period of maturity for all customers. That is, we study the credit default during the first M months since customers activate their card. We use two different values for M depending on the default definition. For the *Default @30* scenario, we assign $M = 7$. That is, we observe the customers' default history up to the beginning of their seventh month of card use, resulting in six full months of observations. For *Default @90*, we assign $M = 9$, which gives users six full months to default so that their debt at 90 days is observable at the beginning of the ninth month. In both scenarios, we label users that defaulted at any point during the first M months as positive samples, disregarding later payments that would have cleared their default status.

To give an example, customers that activated their card during March 2013 (Month 0) are observed during the next six months, April to September, and their default status is obtained from the financial reports in October (Month 7) for the *Default @30* scenario. In the *Default @90*, the same procedure is followed, but the observation period goes from April to November, and the default status is obtained from the financial reports in December (Month 9). Analogously, customers that activated their card during April 2013 will have their default evaluated in November or January, depending on the default definition.

Observing default status after a fixed interval since the credit is granted is a common methodology used by financial institutions to measure the performance of their scores. We fixed the observation interval at 6 months as it provides the best trade-off between the number of subjects and the interval duration given the characteristics of our dataset. Using this setup, we were able to train the model using all the customers that activated their card by August 2013 (*Default @30*) or June 2013 (*Default @90*). Although the CDR data used for part of the population post-dates the used ground truth, we believe that the stationary nature of the behavioral and personality features sought by our method should not experience noticeable variations.

We tried three different classification methods to compare their performance in this specific problem setting: L2-regularized logistic regression (LR), linear Support Vector Machines (SVM), and Gradient Boosted Trees (GBT). We tune the hyper-parameters automatically using a grid-search strategy over a validation set extracted from the training collection. We use fivefold cross validation to predict the customers in default for the whole dataset, where the evaluated fold in each step is not used during the training phase at any point.

5 Experimental Results

In this section we report the experimental results obtained by MobiScore for the credit card default inference task. We considered the following different configurations of the input data and ground truth:

Feature sets. We use three different feature representations of mobile phone behavior: features extracted from **CDR** only, from **CRM** only, and from both (**CDR+CRM**). The goal of this partition is twofold. First we want to determine the financial risk modeling power of the different data sources considered. Second, we want to understand the performance of CDR features, which capture behavioral information, when compared with the higher level socioeconomic and demographic CRM features. To the best of our knowledge, our analysis is the first study to assess the value of CDRs –particularly when compared to CRM information– to build a model of the user's financial risk.

Time dimension. We use three different time windows of CDRs: two weeks, one month and three months. The goal is to study the effect in classification performance of observing mobile data for longer time periods. We consider CRM features to be invariant during the period considered, so this dimension has no effect on them. Two weeks is the minimum amount of data needed to obtain meaningful results given the user activity levels in our CDR data. Conversely, three months is the maximum amount of data that was available in this dataset.

Default definition. We use two default definitions which are common in the financial domain, as described in Sec. 3: *Default @30*, and *Default @90*. Default @30 includes all customers with six or more months of credit card use (only the first six are used to generate their ground truth). This subset had $\simeq 55,000$ users, with a positive sample rate of 19.6%. Default @90 considers customers with nine or more months of credit card use. This subset of the population accounted for $\simeq 30,000$ users, with a lower 12.7% rate of positive samples.

Given the unbalanced nature of the ground truth, we used the following two metrics to evaluate classification performance: *Average Precision*, which refers to the area under the precision-recall curve, and *AUCROC*, which refers to the area under the Receiver Operating Characteristic curve and provides information about the ability of the trained models to rank users according to their probability of default. Ranking customers allows to cluster them in different risk groups (*e.g.* low risk, medium risk, high risk) and make different decisions for each group. For example, lower interest rates could be applied to the low risk group given their increased financial reliability. For this reason, AUCROC is a commonly used performance metric in the credit scoring literature [18].

We also had access to the credit scores provided by a major Credit Bureau agency for our population. Credit Bureaus use proprietary methods and data sources to compute credit scores, which are unknown to us. These scores are commercially available, and were provided to us by the financial partner in this study. We used this information as a baseline to benchmark the performance of the proposed approach given that this is the information used today as the state-of-the-art.

Table 3. Classification performance (AUCROC) as a function of the CDR time window considered

		CDR			**CDR+SMS**		
		2 weeks	1 month	3 months	2 weeks	1 month	3 months
	GBT	63.0	64.5	**67.5**	68.5	69.4	**71.6**
@30	LR	62.2	64.0	66.4	67.6	68.8	70.7
	SVM	62.1	63.9	66.7	67.9	68.8	70.6
	GBT	63.1	64.4	**67.5**	70.2	70.8	**72.5**
@90	LR	62.4	64.5	67.4	68.7	70.5	72.1
	SVM	63.1	64.1	67.2	69.7	70.3	72.1

In Table 3 we present the classification results for the AUCROC metric, focusing on the two CDR-based feature representations. First, we observe that longer observation periods are consistent with better performance. Our dataset contains a monthly average number of $\simeq 200$ calls made/received and $\simeq 65$ SMS messages sent/received per customer. When using longer periods of CDRs we get access to a larger amount of user activity, fostering the discovery of behavioral patterns and hence yielding better performance. Second, the *Default @90* scenario consistently achieves better performance than *Default @30*; the latter corresponds to a riskier financial profile that is expected to be consistent with behavioral traits that would be more prominently captured in the CDRs. Finally, we observe that the GBT classification approach consistently outperforms both logistic regression and SVMs in the given classification task. This is explained by the higher degree of complexity and flexibility of boosted trees ensembles, which produce non-linear models composed of thousands of weak predictors. Ensembles have been shown to outperform single models in many contexts, including financial modeling problems [18].

We also study the inference power of each feature representation. In particular, we compare the performance of the CDR-based feature representations to two static baselines: CRM-features, and Bureau data. For this comparison, we select the best performing configuration of CDR-based models (GBT classifier using 3 months of CDR data). The results of this comparison for the average precision and AUCROC metrics are shown in Fig. 1.

We observe that CDR-based features provide the highest discriminative power. Interestingly, **CDR** (alone) and **CRM** are similarly discriminative. This result suggests that the aspects of human behavior that can be inferred from mobile phone data (*i.e.* mobility, consumption and social variables) serve to model financial risk with similar performance as the socioeconomic and demographic variables included in the CRM. It is also worth mentioning that the combination of CDR and CRM increases performance noticeably for all metrics considered, which suggests that the information conveyed by these two sources of data is complementary. Moreover, all the scoring models built from mobile phone data outperform the Credit Bureau score by a large margin, supporting the validity of MobiScore as an alternative to traditional credit scoring approaches.

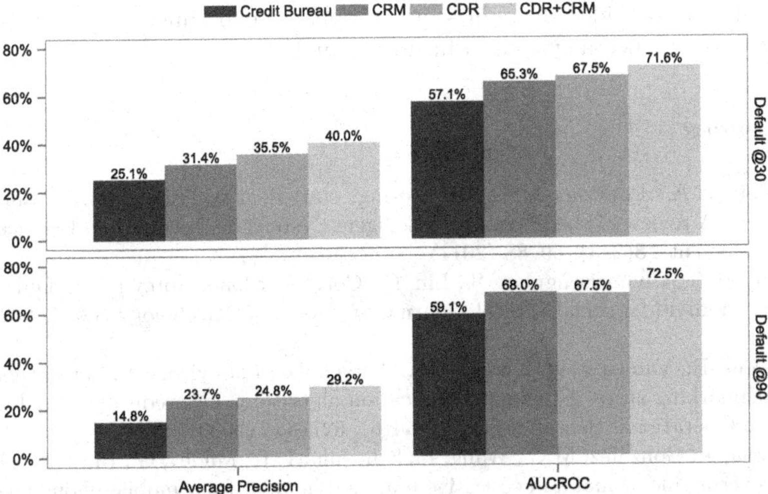

Fig. 1. Classification performance (Average Precision and AUCROC) of CDR-based representations compared to CRM and Credit Bureau baselines

6 Conclusions and Future Work

In this paper we have presented MobiScore, a novel approach to compute credit scores from mobile phone activity data. Standard approaches use prevalently past financial history, and therefore cannot be applied to users with no (or limited) financial history. We carried out experiments with a large-scale population and show that MobiScore achieves better performance when compared to current techniques used by Credit Bureaus. Moreover, even a limited time window of two weeks of mobile phone data can be enough to generate a reliable score. Overall, these results provide strong evidence that mobile phone data is a reliable signal of a person's financial risk.

MobiScore has the main advantage of leveraging passively collected data from the mobile network infrastructure and having wider applicability than traditional credit scores since it only requires the use of mobile phone, which most of the world population has access to. The mobile phone has become such an integral part of our lives that behavioral data captured with it adds informative value to a variety of applications, included the one proposed in this paper. The most important implication of the presented study is the opportunity MobiScore brings to enable access to credits and loans to the millions of *thin-file* individuals.

In the future, we plan to investigate in detail the discriminative power of the different features used in our experiments. Further, we are interested in assessing how our model changes as a function of the geographical areas and financial products analyzed. An additional interesting aspect, common to any project dealing with human behavioral data, is addressing any potential privacy concerns and data protection laws compliance. A straightforward way in which our model can be implemented and provided to users is through an opt-in mechanism, where the user gives to the mobile operator explicit consent to use mobile data to generate and provide the credit score. We plan to experimentally evaluate the attractiveness of such a system in future research.

References

1. Abdou, H.A., Pointon, J.: Credit scoring, statistical techniques and evaluation criteria: A review of the literature. Intelligent Systems in Accounting, Finance and Management **18**(2–3), 59–88 (2011)
2. Agarwal, S., Chomsisengphet, S., Liu, C.: Consumer bankruptcy and default: The role of individual social capital. Journal of Economic Psychology **32**(4), 632–650 (2011)
3. Baesens, B., Van Gestel, T., Viaene, S., Stepanova, M., Suykens, J., Vanthienen, J.: Benchmarking state-of-the-art classification algorithms for credit scoring. Journal of the Operational Research Society **54**(6), 627–635 (2003)
4. Candia, J., González, M.C., Wang, P., Schoenharl, T., Madey, G., Barabási, A.-L.: Uncovering individual and collective human dynamics from mobile phone records. Journal of Physics A: Mathematical and Theoretical **41**(22), 224015 (2008)
5. de Montjoye, Y.-A., Quoidbach, J., Robic, F., Pentland, A.S.: Predicting personality using novel mobile phone-based metrics. In: Greenberg, A.M., Kennedy, W.G., Bos, N.D. (eds.) SBP 2013. LNCS, vol. 7812, pp. 48–55. Springer, Heidelberg (2013)
6. de Oliveira, R., Karatzoglou, A., Concejero Cerezo, P., Armenta Lopez de Vicuña, A., Oliver, N.: Towards a psychographic user model from mobile phone usage. In: CHI 2011 Extended Abstracts on Human Factors in Computing Systems, CHI EA 2011, New York, NY, USA, pp. 2191–2196. ACM (2011)
7. Eagle, N., Pentland, A.S., Lazer, D.: Inferring friendship network structure by using mobile phone data. Proceedings of the National Academy of Sciences **106**(36), 15274–15278 (2009)
8. Frias-Martinez, V., Frias-Martinez, E., Oliver, N.: A gender-centric analysis of calling behavior in a developing economy using call detail records. In: Proceedings of the AAAI Spring Symposium: Artificial Intelligence for Development (2010)
9. Gathergood, J.: Self-control, financial literacy and consumer over-indebtedness. Journal of Economic Psychology **33**(3), 590–602 (2012)
10. Grable, J.E., Joo, S.-H.: Environmental and biophysical factors associated with financial risk tolerance. Journal of Financial Counseling and Planning **15**(1) (2004)
11. Henegar, J.M., Archuleta, K., Grable, J., Britt, S., Anderson, N., Dale, A.: Credit card behavior as a function of impulsivity and mothers socialization factors. Journal of Financial Counseling and Planning **24**(2), 37–49 (2013)
12. Meier, S., Sprenger, C.: Impatience and credit behavior: Evidence from a field experiment. Social Science Research Network Working Paper Series (2007)
13. Mester, L.J.: Whats the point of credit scoring? Business review **3**, 3–16 (1997)
14. Montoliu, R., Gatica-Perez, D.: Discovering human places of interest from multimodal mobile phone data. In: Proceedings of the 9th International Conference on Mobile and Ubiquitous Multimedia, p. 12. ACM (2010)
15. Onnela, J.-P., Saramäki, J., Hyvönen, J., Szabó, G., Lazer, D., Kaski, K., Kertész, J., Barabási, A.-L.: Structure and tie strengths in mobile communication networks. Proceedings of the National Academy of Sciences **104**(18), 7332–7336 (2007)

16. Singh, V.K., Freeman, L., Lepri, B., Pentland, A.S.: Predicting spending behavior using socio-mobile features. In: 2013 International Conference on Social Computing (SocialCom), pp. 174–179. IEEE (2013)
17. Soto, V., Frias-Martinez, V., Virseda, J., Frias-Martinez, E.: Prediction of socioeconomic levels using cell phone records. In: Konstan, J.A., Conejo, R., Marzo, J.L., Oliver, N. (eds.) UMAP 2011. LNCS, vol. 6787, pp. 377–388. Springer, Heidelberg (2011)
18. Wang, G., Hao, J., Ma, J., Jiang, H.: A comparative assessment of ensemble learning for credit scoring. Expert Systems with Applications **38**(1), 223–230 (2011)

Where to Next? A Comparison of Recommendation Strategies for Navigating a Learning Object Repository

Jennifer Sabourin(✉), Lucy Kosturko, and Scott McQuiggan

SAS® Curriculum Pathways®, SAS Institute, Cary, NC, USA
{Jennifer.Sabourin,Lucy.Kosturko,Scott.McQuiggan}@sas.com

Abstract. This paper explores the initial investigation of six recommendation algorithms for deployment in SAS® Curriculum Pathways®, an online repository which houses over 1250 educational resources. The proposed approaches stem from three basic strategies: recommendations based on resource metadata, user behavior, and alignment to academic standards. An evaluation from subject experts suggests that usage-based recommendations are best aligned with teacher needs, though there are interesting domain interactions that suggest the need for continued investigation.

Keywords: Recommender systems · Learning object repository · Technology enhanced learning

1 Introduction

The majority of U.S. states are experiencing shrinking education budgets [1], yet educators are highly encouraged to integrate technology into daily lessons. As a result, many teachers are turning to free or open-source supplements to instruction (e.g., Khan Academy, MIT OpenCourseWare) as a viable solution [2]. The high demand in this area is leading to an increase in the number of open educational resources (OER). While this increase can be a benefit for the community, it brings many challenges for users, such as selecting the most beneficial resources from the many available options. It is difficult for users to read all the information about each resource and then select the appropriate ones for their studies at school. Search engines have been commonly used to search the materials that meet the users' needs. In practice, search engines are not effective for this task, and many new users are not satisfied with the quality of the search results. This situations leads to many issues, such as users spending increased time searching for resources to meet their personal needs and possibly leaving the system if they are unable to find appropriate resources, even though they may exist. Alternatively, if a preferred resource is located, it can be difficult to evaluate effectiveness and quality or find additional, similar resources [3].

Recommender systems provide methods to consider vast amounts of information in order to suggest alternatives to users that better align with their interests. Using resource metadata or historical information from other users with similar interests and backgrounds as a starting point, recommender systems serve to narrow the scope of

F. Ricci et al. (Eds.): UMAP 2015, LNCS 9146, pp. 208–215, 2015.
DOI: 10.1007/978-3-319-20267-9_17

search in many cases. This approach not only saves time, but also ensures educators and students find high-quality resources that might otherwise go undiscovered.

In this paper, we explore six approaches for generating recommendations in the learning object repository, SAS® Curriculum Pathways®. The approaches use three different data sources: expert-generated metadata, state standards alignment, and usage behavior. Domain and product experts evaluated the quality of generated recommendations, and the results of the evaluations point to several directions for future investigation.

2 Background

In recent years, we have seen a surge in the development of learning object repositories [2], [4]. Such repositories aim to provide students around the world access to high-quality educational resources (e.g., videos, interactivities, documents, data sets) regardless of location or socioeconomic status [5]. However, the surge has also made it difficult for educators and students to navigate the sea of resources and evaluate quality at a glance [3]. Manouselis and colleagues [4] identify two primary issues: 1) "the problem of overwhelming numbers of on-topic items (ones which would be all selected by a keyword filter)," and 2) "the problem of filtering non-text items" as interactive learning tools may not have associated documents or scripts. Recommender systems, similar to those widely present in the retail market [6], have proven to be a viable solution to this problem. The most common installments of recommender systems in education, as in most applications, generate recommendations based either on user preferences (collaborative methods), or using only item data (content-based methods) [4].

Usage-based approaches such as collaborative filtering "use the known preferences of a group of users to predict the unknown preferences of a new user; recommendations for the new users are based on these predictions" [7]. User preferences can be explicit using ratings or 'likes', or implicit such as visits or purchases. They offer advantages over content-based approaches by focusing on the real patterns of actual users to make assumptions about future patterns of behavior. In an educational context, this allows us to capitalize on the expertise of a large network of educators who are navigating the repositories. When a trustworthy user population is present [8], usage-based approaches have proven to be a successful and popular model [9, 10, 11]

However, in some cases, user-preference recommendations are not appropriate as they suffer from certain limitations [4]. First, the sparsity problem arises when a data set lacks adequate information about a particular item. For example, a resource might have low usage or no ratings only because it has not been discovered by the user population; however, this should not imply the resource is low-quality or unrelated to other resources. Similar effects are seen when new resources added to a repository or when new users lacking an established preference profile search the system. The reliance on an established user network can also hinder the scalability of the system to other populations [8].

Content-based approaches rely on the similarity between items to generate recommendations. While such algorithms are often a more simplified version of those described above, there are notable advantages in some cases. Instead of building an explicit model, recommendations are based on similarity between two items based on some set of specific attributes (e.g., metadata, academic standards alignment). Content-based systems may rely on human-generated information (e.g. titles, descriptions, keywords) or resource content (e.g. document text, data). Such manifestations compensate for limitations of user-based systems in terms of scalability and real-time performance. These systems may rely on the actual content of learning objects, such as document text or scripts [12], or may use a structured ontology of the underlying domain concepts [13, 14] that is unique to educational contexts.

Given the variety of possible approaches to recommendations of learning objects, the purpose of this work is to examine the performance of several approaches within a specific repository, SAS Curriculum Pathways.

3 SAS Curriculum Pathways

Available at no cost, SAS® Curriculum Pathways® provides interactive, standards-based resources in the core disciplines (English language arts, mathematics, science, social studies, and Spanish). Resources range from simulation-style tools to full-length lessons, so educators can use resources to accommodate a variety of applications. SAS Curriculum Pathways provides learner-centered activities with measurable outcomes and targets higher-order thinking skills. In order to provide educators high-quality resources in an era of budget cuts and minimal funding, SAS Curriculum Pathways has been available at no cost since 2008. At present, more than 275,000 users in more than 50,000 schools are actively using SAS Curriculum Pathways as part of their classroom instruction.

Presently, users can find resources of interest by browsing subject areas (e.g., English language arts, mathematics) or through a search option. Searching matches text from resource metadata (e.g., title, keywords, description) and, when available, will search resource content and lesson guides as well. Both search and browsing results are displayed by grouping resource activity type (e.g., web lesson, interactive tool, inquiry lesson) and new resources are promoted to the top of the list. Specific subject, resource type, and grade level can further filter results. Currently, there is no functionality to surface resources based on personalized interest.

Personalization and recommendations are desired to support the potential of future functionality. First, a new user home page could list recommended resources based on that user's prior interaction within the repository. Second, each resource could provide a list of related and recommended resources that may be of interest to users who are viewing or using that resource. Finally, targeted email campaigns could encourage users to explore unseen resources by suggesting personalized recommendations.

3.1 Data Sources

Three data sources are used for this investigation. The recommendations based on user activity utilized a corpus of teacher interaction data with SAS Curriculum Pathways from the past 5 years (August 2008 - August 2013). After removing data from users who do not identify themselves as teachers, the corpus included data from 67,738 users. In total this corpus represents 4.9 million interactive sessions and observations with over 10.4 million resource hits. This data was transformed into a binary user-item matrix indicating if a user had accessed a particular resource during the 5-year time span.

The recommendations based on resource metadata used the developer provided keywords and descriptions for each of the 1,242 resources in the corpus. Descriptions contained an average of 51.2 words and described the activity and content of the resource. These descriptions are surfaced to the user to aid them in selecting activities. Resources were associated with an average of 9.8 keywords, which are primarily used to facilitate search functionality and are not surfaced to the user.

Finally, the corpus based on state standards alignment[1] is based on expert evaluation of how the content of each resource aligns to specific state standards. In this case we focus on the standards alignments of two states. North Carolina state standards as this is the state with the largest overall usage. Texas state standards were also selected for comparison as this state has the fastest growing usage of Curriculum Pathways. The data was transformed to a binary standards-resource matrix indicating if a resource was aligned to that standard. In total 656 standards were included in the North Carolina dataset and 1408 standards were included in the Texas dataset.

4 Recommendation Approaches

In total, six approaches were explored using the three corpora. Data modeling was done using SAS® Enterprise Miner®. SAS Enterprise Miner streamlines the data mining process to create highly accurate predictive and descriptive models using graphical process flow diagrams. The process flow diagrams serve as self-documenting templates that can be updated easily or applied to new problems without starting over from scratch. In addition to process flow diagrams, Enterprise Miner provides a programming interface for advanced users.

The first two approaches were based on expert-generated metadata of learning object keywords (MD-KEY) and descriptions (MD-DES). This text was first processed using Enterprise Miner Text Analytics to identify text topics. The text topic procedure identifies terms that are strongly associated within the corpus. The procedure requires a maximum of text topic to identify, which was set to 50 for this analysis. The resulting data set is a topic frequency matrix, which indicates how frequently the text fell into one of the identified topics. We then select the most similar resources for recommendation using a nearest neighbor approach from the topics.

Two approaches stem from the binary user-item matrix of resources visited. The first is based on the co-occurrence (UB-CO) of resources visits for a particular user. The value of *co-occur(s→r)* is calculated as the proportion of users of resource *s*, who

---

[1] Standards Database and Alignment System by Academic Benchmarks. Copyright © Academic Benchmarks. Cincinnati, Ohio, USA. All rights reserved.

Table 1. Text Topic Results

	Terms in Topic	Resources Covered	Example Topics
Keyword	M = 46.6 SD = 23.2	M = 73.2 SD = 23.5	**Topic 1** (131 res): algebra, function, graph, polynomial… **Topic 15** (75 res): physics, acceleration, motion, velocity, energy… **Topic 32** (47 res): drama, shakespeare, play, tragedy…
Description	M = 79.7 SD = 29.3	M = 78.8 SD = 37.0	**Topic 1** (175 res): information, resource, historical, history, event… **Topic 18** (83 res): coordinate, graph, line, plane… **Topic 22** (68 res): lab, virtual, simulation, observation…

also used resource *r*. This value (Equation 1) was calculated for all pairs of resources. The recommendations for *s* are the resources that generate the highest value of *co-occur(s→r)*. The next approach (UB-NOR) extends this by normalizing over the base rate of use of each potentially recommended resource *r* (Equation 2). This is important since some resource are significantly more heavily used than others. For example, the top resource Writing Reviser, made up 7% of the total usage across the 5 year collection. The value of *norm(s→r)* was also calculated for all pairs of resources, and the recommendations were chosen based on the highest values.

$$cooccur(s \to r) = \frac{|U_s \cap U_r|}{|U_s|} \quad (1) \qquad norm(s \to r) = \frac{\frac{|U_s \cap U_r|}{|U_s|}}{\frac{|\overline{U_s} \cap U_r|}{|\overline{U_s}|}} \quad (2)$$

The standards-items matrices from North Carolina and Texas were used for the last two recommendation approaches, (ST-NC and ST-TX). Because of the sparse data set principle components analysis was used to reduce the dimensionality of the data. Using Enterprise Miner, a maximum of 20 components was selected. For the North Carolina standards, this accounted for 31% of the variance, while the reduction accounted for only 23% of the variance among the Texas standards. After reduction, nearest neighbors were used to form recommendations.

5 Evaluation

Five domain experts were selected to conduct an initial evaluation, one representing each of the five disciplines covered by SAS Curriculum Pathways resources. Each expert has subject-specific teaching experience and familiarity with the SAS Curriculum Pathways platform. Recommendations were generated for 20 randomly selected resources from within each discipline (100 total). The top recommendation from each approach was provided for each of the resources, resulting in 600 total recommendation pairs. The pairs were randomly ordered and presented to the evaluators with no indication of which approach was used to generate the recommendation. Evaluators were asked to rate each recommendation using the following guidelines:

- Great Recommendation (1) – "Yes, I believe a teacher who used this resource being interested in the recommendation."
- Could be Relevant (0.5) – "I probably would not have made this recommendation, but a teacher who used this resource might be interested in the recommendation."
- Not at all Relevant (0) – "This is completely unrelated. It is very unlikely that a teacher who used this resource would be interested in the recommendation."

In total, 42% of recommendation pairs were rated as a 'Great Recommendation', 27% were rated as 'Could be Relevant', and 30% were rated as 'Not Relevant'. Using the quantitative scores, a factorial ANOVA was run to identify significant main and interaction effects by recommendation approach and domain. The ANOVA yielded a significant main effect for approach, $F_{(5, 570)} = 7.90$, $p < 0.001$. Post-hoc comparisons with Tukey correction indicated that the normalized usage approach (UB-NOR) had the highest performance with an average score of 0.73 *(SD = 0.37)*. Comparing across all approaches, UB-NOR > (UB-CO, MD-KEY, ST-NC) > (MD-DES, ST-TX). The least effective approaches were those generated from descriptions and Texas standards, with average scores of 0.46 *(SD = 0.42)* and 0.45 *(SD = 0.44)*, respectively. These results indicate that usage-based approaches were more successful at generating acceptable recommendations. This may be because usage behavior reflects actual classroom practices more accurately than expert-generated metadata.

The factorial also revealed a significant main effect for domain, $F_{(4,570)} = 18.7$, $p < 0.001$. Science recommendations had the highest score ($M = 0.75$, $SD = 0.40$), with Spanish having the lowest ($M = 0.35$, SD = *0.37*). Post-hoc comparisons with Tukey correction indicated (science, English language arts) > (math, social studies) > Spanish. To some degree, these results could be explained by the nature of certain domains. Math, social studies, and Spanish curricula generally follow a linear path and these areas are typically more additive over time. On the other hand, science and English language arts subject matter is typically less strictly ordered allowing educators more flexibility in

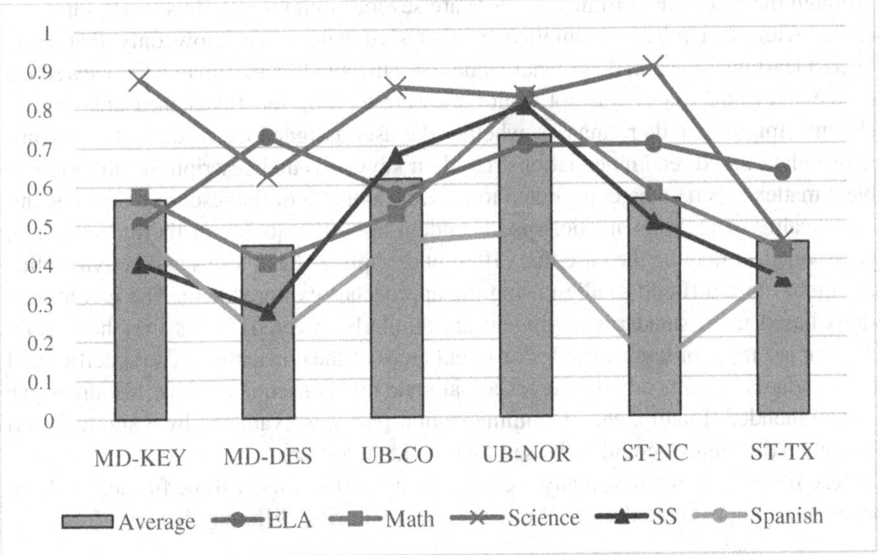

Fig. 1. Performance score average and by discipline

selecting resources. For example, a resource on reading African American poetry is likely to be seen as relevant to a resource on strategies for reading poetry about sports; although, the two resources would likely not be taught in succession. However, a social studies resource on Franklin D. Roosevelt and the New Deal might not be such a good recommendation for a resource about Lincoln and the abolition of slavery even though both concern monumental Presidential legislation and policy.

The factorial ANOVA also indicated significant interaction effect, $F_{(20,570)} = 2.37$, $p < 0.001$. For example, for every discipline except for Spanish, NC standards based recommendations outperformed those from Texas. For Spanish resources, Texas recommendations were rated much higher ($M = 0.38$, $SD = 0.39$) than those from North Carolina ($M = 0.13$, $SD = 0.20$). Perhaps the Texas state standards are more robust for foreign language learning. Additionally, for both English language arts and science metadata driven recommendations performed similarly to those based on usage behaviors. However, for social studies and math, usage behaviors did a better job at selecting appropriate recommendations. This highlights the possibility that different curricular structures (e.g. linear and additive vs. topic based) may require different methods of recommendation generation, and motivates further investigation.

6 Discussion

This work explored six approaches to generating recommendations for a learning object repository. These approaches stemmed from user behavior, expert generated metadata, and academic standard alignment. The top performing approach was based on normalized user agreement of resource pairs. This approach generated excellent recommendations 61% of the time and acceptable recommendations 23% of the time. Three other approaches from each of the data sources also show promise in providing appropriate recommendations of learning objects

Though the results are promising, there are several limitations to this work. First, the user behavior data relied on implicit estimates of value. We know only that users opened a learning object and not what value was attributed. A user may have viewed the resource and found that it was not what they were looking for. Better measures of user preference might include ratings, or whether the user assigned the resource to students. The metadata-based recommendations relied on keywords and descriptions provided by subject matter experts who contributed to the development of the resource. Consequently, the quality of recommendations is dependent upon the quality of the metadata that was provided. It may be the case that different disciplines have terms and activities that make them more difficult to align using the approaches explored here. The recommendations based upon standards alignment are similarly affected. States may have standards that are more or less robust for different areas of the curriculum. The specificity of these standards impacts how resources are aligned and consequently how resources can be recommended. Finally, each recommendation pair was evaluated by a single expert and domain differences could be biased by individual judgment.

These limitations point to many areas for future work. First will be further exploration of more sophisticated algorithms, such as exploring different distance functions for the recommendations based on nearest neighbors. It may also be interesting to explore ensemble methods for combining the multiple data sources for generating recommendations. Another important investigation that has not been explored is whether recommendations to students should differ from those given to teachers. Student accounts are a recent addition to SAS Curriculum Pathways so there is not as much data on their behavior compared to that of teacher users. Consequently, this investigation is expected to be ongoing as student users become more prevalent.

After increased exploration, the top approaches will be deployed to allow user evaluation before a final recommender system is deployed in the main repository. Recommendation quality will be based on how many users access the resources recommended to them. The top approaches are expected to be considered for a future version of the product along with the addition of allowing teachers to rate the quality of resources. Integrations with live recommendations and user ratings will allow for more sophisticated understanding of user interactions with the recommender system and provide increased data to drive future explorations.

References

1. Leachman, M., Mai, C.: Most States Funding Schools Less Than Before the Recession. Center on Budget Policies and Priorities, May 20, 2014
2. Research on the Use of Khan Academy in Schools (2014)
3. DeVries, I.: Evaluating Open Educational Resources: Lessons Learned. Procedia - Soc Behav Sci. (2013)
4. Manouselis, N., Drachsler, H., Verbert, K., Duval, E.: Recommender Systems for Learning. Springer Science & Business Media (2013)
5. Achieve Inc.: State Support for Open Educational Resources: Key Findings from Achieve's OER Institute. Washington D.C. (2013)
6. Koren, Y.: The BellKor Solution to the Netflix Grand Prize (2009)
7. Goldberg, K.: Eigentaste: A Constant Time Collaborative Filtering Algorithm. Inf. Retr. Boston. **4**, 133–151 (2001)
8. Manouselis, N., Sampson, D.: Recommendation of quality approaches for the European quality observatory. In: 4th IEEE International Conference on Advanced Learning Technologies/EQO-Workshop Quality in European E-Learning (2004)
9. Vialardi, C., Bravo, J., Shafti, L., Ortigosa, A.: Recommendation in Higher Education Using Data Mining Techniques (2009)
10. Duffin, J., Muramatsu, B., Logan, N.: OER Recommender: Linking NSDL Pathways and OpenCourseWare Repositories (2008)
11. Verbert, K., Drachsler, H., Manouselis, N., Wolpers, M., Vuorikari, R., Duval, E.: Dataset-driven research for improving recommender systems for learning. In: Proceedings of the 1st International Conference on Learning Analytics and Knowledge - LAK 2011, pp. 44–53. ACM Press, New York (2011)
12. Wang, Y., Sumiya, K.: Semantic ranking of lecture slides based on conceptual relationship and presentational structure. Procedia. Comput. Sci. **1**(2), 2801–2810 (2010)
13. Shen, L.-P., Shen, R.-M.: Learning content recommendation service based-on simple sequencing specification. In: Liu, W., Shi, Y., Li, Q. (eds.) ICWL 2004. LNCS, vol. 3143, pp. 363–370. Springer, Heidelberg (2004)
14. Underwood, J.: Metis: a contentmap-based recommender system for digital learning activities. In: Educational Recommender Systems and Technologies, pp. 24–42 (2012)

Diagrammatic Student Models: Modeling Student Drawing Performance with Deep Learning

Andy Smith(✉), Wookhee Min, Bradford W. Mott, and James C. Lester

Center for Educational Informatics, North Carolina State University, Raleigh, NC 27695, USA
{pmsmith4,wmin,bwmott,lester}@ncsu.edu

Abstract. Recent years have seen a growing interest in the role that student drawing can play in learning. Because drawing has been shown to contribute to students' learning and increase their engagement, developing student models to dynamically support drawing holds significant promise. To this end, we introduce *diagrammatic student models*, which reason about students' drawing trajectories to generate a series of predictions about their conceptual knowledge based on their evolving sketches. The diagrammatic student modeling framework utilizes deep learning, a family of machine learning methods based on a deep neural network architecture, to reason about sequences of student drawing actions encoded with temporal and topological features. An evaluation of the deep-learning-based diagrammatic student models suggests that it can predict student performance more accurately and earlier than competitive baseline approaches.

Keywords: Student modeling · Intelligent tutoring systems · Deep learning

1 Introduction

Diagrams and drawing are fundamental to science learning and understanding. From primary through post-secondary education, students use drawings and graphical representations to make sense of complex systems and as a tool to organize and communicate their ideas to others. Studies have shown that learning strategies centered on learner-generated drawings can produce effective learning outcomes, such as improving science text comprehension and student affect, facilitating the writing process, and improving the acquisition of content knowledge [1] .

Unlike the well studied areas of how people learn from writing text, viewing graphics, and reading, relatively little is known about how generating drawings affects learning. The benefits of drawing arise from actively involving learners in the cognitive processes of selecting, organizing, and integrating the information they have been presented, while also requiring both essential and generative processing to mentally connect multiple representations [2]. The benefits of learner-generated drawing are best realized through supports that constrain and structure the drawing activity [3]. The act of generating a visual representation can be a cognitively demanding task and, as such, requires scaffolds to guard against excessive and extraneous cognitive load [4].

F. Ricci et al. (Eds.): UMAP 2015, LNCS 9146, pp. 216–227, 2015.
DOI: 10.1007/978-3-319-20267-9_18

Examples of effective scaffolds for drawing include providing symbolic drawing elements, guided questioning, and targeted drawing prompts [5].

Intelligent tutoring systems (ITSs) offer a promising approach to addressing the complexity of scaffolding and assessing students' drawing activities. A key feature of many ITSs is the ability to leverage student models that assess knowledge and skills from observed learning activities and support learning based on the predicted competency level in real-time. In this paper, we introduce *diagrammatic student models* that are designed to reason about students' drawing trajectories to generate a series of predictions about their conceptual knowledge based on their evolving sketches. The diagrammatic student modeling framework utilizes deep learning, a family of machine learning methods based on a deep neural network architecture, to reason about sequences of student drawing actions encoded with temporal and topological features. As students draw, an effective diagrammatic student model should be able to not only predict student knowledge but also to weight the contributions of individual drawing actions toward the goal of the sketching activity, as well as monitor student drawing time and efficiency.

To explore diagrammatic student modeling, we have developed a diagrammatic student model for a tablet-based learning environment designed for elementary school science education. In an evaluation, the deep-learning-based diagrammatic student model was compared against multiple baseline models using an annotated corpus of elementary student science drawings. The evaluation shows that the deep-learning-based diagrammatic student model predicts student drawing performance more accurately than baseline models, as well as requires fewer actions to converge on the correct prediction.

This paper is structured as follows. Section 2 discusses related work on analyzing student drawing and predicting student performance. Section 3 describes the tablet-based learning environment that was used to collect the drawing dataset of symbolic sketches from elementary students. Section 4 presents the diagrammatic student modeling framework used for the predictive modeling task as well as the stacked autoencoder pre-training technique used in deep learning. Section 5 describes an evaluation of the system compared to other predictive models.

2 Related Work

Research on student modeling has explored a variety of computational frameworks. Several families of models perform a running estimate of students' skills and knowledge based on their previous performance across multiple problems, including techniques such as Bayesian knowledge tracing [6] and performance factor analysis [7]. Sabourin et al. combined differential sequence mining with a dynamic Bayesian network to perform early prediction of students' self-regulated learning behaviors in an educational game [8]. Chi et al. used reinforcement learning to identify features from student-tutor interactions and induce pedagogical strategies [9]. Other systems have explored features based on analysis of trace logs to predict transfer of inquiry skill [10], predict gaming the system behaviors [11], and predict user goals [12]. Similar to the techniques used in this work, a deep learning technique leveraging denoising autoencoders has been used to accurately identify intermediate player goals in an open-ended science mystery game [13]. The approach presented here utilizes deep learning techniques on the problem of modeling students drawing activities.

Outside of the student modeling community, several efforts have made significant progress on machine understanding of student drawing artifacts. Mechanix uses free-hand sketch recognition capabilities to convert student statics drawings into free-body equations that the system can then compare to a target solution and provide basic forms of feedback [14]. Van Joolingen et al.'s SimSketch system merges free-hand sketching with modeling and simulation of science phenomena by segmenting the drawing into distinct objects that are then annotated by the user with a variety of behaviors, attributes, and labels [15]. Students can then run a simulation based on their drawing and see the results before revising their sketch. SimSketch has been evaluated in a planetarium setting and been shown to be both a useable and engaging system for visitors. Researchers have also investigated CogSketch, an open-domain sketch understanding engine, to compare the drawings of expert and novice users to analyze differences in final drawings, as well as differences in the way the drawings are created [16].

3 The LEONARDO Science Notebook

Recent years have seen a growing interest in introducing science notebooks into elementary science classrooms [17]. Science notebooks capture students' inquiry-based activities in both written and graphical form, potentially providing a valuable source of both diagnostic and prognostic information. However, because elementary school teachers sometimes have limited training in science pedagogy, they often struggle with effectively using science notebooks in classroom learning activities.

For the past four years our laboratory has been developing a digital science notebook for elementary school students, LEONARDO (Figure 1), which runs on tablet computing platforms. LEONARDO integrates intelligent tutoring systems technologies into a digital science notebook that enables students to graphically model science phenomena with a focus on the physical and earth sciences. LEONARDO features a pedagogical agent that supports students' learning with real-time problem-solving advice. LEONARDO is designed for use in the classroom in conjunction with popular science kits, and it is aligned with the Next Generation Science Standards for elementary school science education. It has been used in schools in more than ten states in the US.

Throughout the inquiry process, students using LEONARDO are invited to create symbolic sketches of different types, including electrical circuits. Given the challenges of machine recognition for freehand sketch, as well as concerns of excessive cognitive demand for fourth graders working in such an unstructured space [18], LEONARDO supports symbolic drawing tasks. To preserve the generative processing thought to be of great benefit for learner-generated drawings strategies, each activity begins with a blank workspace so that the representations must be created from scratch. Students then choose from a variety of semantically grounded objects and place them at various points on the drawing canvas. For example, objects for the electricity unit include light bulbs, motors, switches, and batteries. Students can then place wires on the drawing canvas and connect the various objects that together simulate proper electrical behavior. This approach enables students to focus on choosing the appropriate circuit elements and creating the appropriate circuit topology rather than having to concentrate on free-hand sketching complex objects such as motors and switches. Drawing tasks vary in complexity from replicating a picture of a circuit held up by the pedagogical agent, to recreating a circuit made during a physical investigation, to creating more complex circuits designed to increase their understanding of series and parallel circuits.

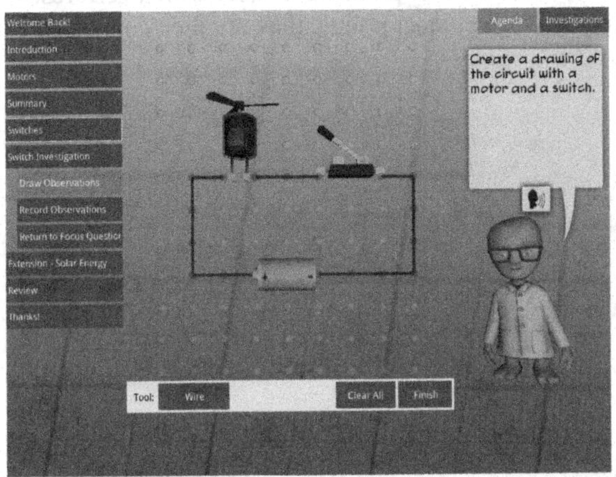

Fig. 1. LEONARDO digital science notebook

4 Diagrammatic Student Modeling

To scaffold and assess drawing activities such as those supported by the LEONARDO digital science notebooks, a *diagrammatic student model* could reason about students' drawing progress and infer students' conceptual knowledge. We introduce diagrammatic student models by first discussing topology-based methods they use to analyze and compare student drawings. We then describe how they can predict student conceptual knowledge based on their drawing trajectories.

To analyze student drawings the diagrammatic student modeling system first translates them into a more abstract representation (Figure 2) [19]. It takes as input trace logs from students' work and extracts student actions at a level of granularity capable of producing replay-quality representations of the activities. From these actions it can reconstruct the state of the student drawing at each point in the activity. After each student action, a topological representation of the drawing is constructed using the set of objects and locations combined with a simulation engine that supports the querying of topological features of the drawing.

These topological features are used to generate a labeled graph representation of the drawing. The first step in the translation from drawings to topological graphs is encoding of the primary elements for the domain. For the domain of circuits, we define this as non-wire circuit elements. Circuit elements are represented as nodes in the graph. Because there are only two points where each node can interact with other objects in the drawing space, each node is connected to two child nodes representing its contact points. Nodes are then labeled by type, for circuits the supported element types are Light bulb, Motor, Switch, or Battery.

After creating the nodes of the graph, edges are generated based on relationships between elements. For this domain the only relationship encoded is electrical connectivity, though for other domains additional relationships could be encoded such as 2D spatial relations such as near/far, overlapping, or containing. For each contact point in the graph, the simulation engine uses a depth first search with resistance as the cost function to return all other contact points reachable with a zero resistance path. If one or more paths exist between contact points, they are then connected with a single edge in the graph.

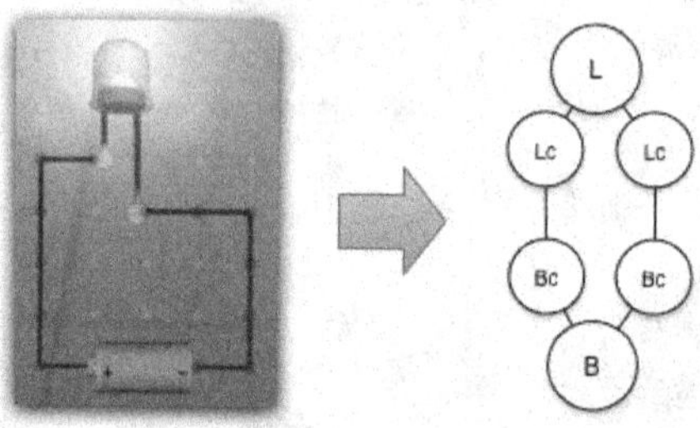

Fig. 2. Circuit encoded as topological graph

Topologies can then be compared using a modified form of edit distance, which determines the number of operations needed to transition from one graph to a target graph. Edit distance measures the number of element additions, element deletions, edge additions, and edge deletions needed to match two topologies. While traditional string edit distances tend to also utilize substitution, we chose to treat this instead as deleting an element, then adding a new one because this is the path students would take to modify their drawing. While edit distance allows an ITS to compare individual drawings, it is also critical for the system to be able to incorporate information about how the student arrived at that point. For example, consider a student with a blank workspace. By assessing only the current state of the drawing, the system would have no idea whether the student is yet to start drawing, or has been attempting unsuccessfully to complete the circuit for several minutes.

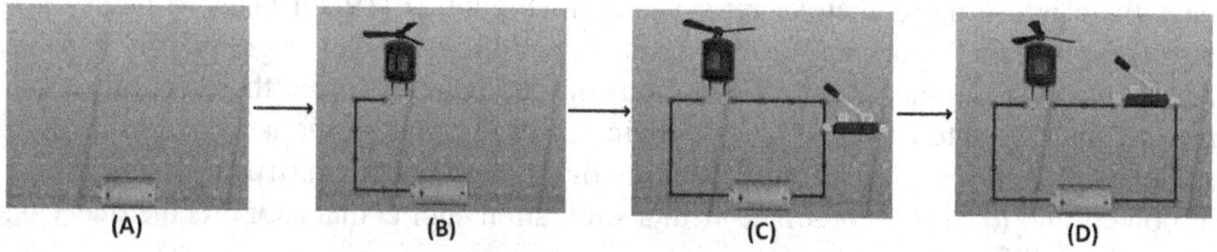

Fig. 3. Sample drawing progression

An important capability of diagrammatic student models is accurately predicting the level of performance a student will attain in a drawing task. For example, using the drawing progression shown in Figure 3, the diagrammatic student modeling system seeks to predict the quality of the final submitted drawing (D), based on each drawing action (e.g., add, remove, rotate, drag). We treat this as a multiclass classification problem, in which the model seeks to predict the most likely student outcome state given a sequence of drawing actions. Outcome states for the diagrammatic student modeling system are defined using a clustering approach previously shown to align with human classification [19]. Students' final drawings are grouped into 3 clusters: Correct, Near-Miss, and Far-Miss. For each drawing action by a student, we aim to predict which of these clusters the final drawing will belong to. The input to the classification task is encoded as a feature vector constructed from the student drawing after every action. The feature vectors consist of 6 features:

- **Time:** Number of seconds from the start of the activity.
- **Action Step:** Number of actions performed by the student thus far.
- **Extra Elements:** Number of superfluous non-wire elements on the workspace.
- **Missing Elements:** Number of required elements missing from the workspace.
- **Extra Topological Connections:** Number of superfluous connections between non-wire elements.
- **Missing Topological Connections:** Number of missing connections between non-wire elements.

The output the diagrammatic student model is a prediction of which cluster the action sequence will culminate in. It is intuitive that predicting student outcomes could benefit from observations based on the sequence of actions preceding the current action. While this information is partly encoded in the drawing features, we further investigated it by augmenting the input feature vector with *n*-gram encodings. For *n*-gram encodings, the feature vector for a given action was combined with the feature vectors of the previous *n*-1 actions. For example, the input feature for a 1-gram encoding would contain 6 elements, the input vector for a 5-gram model would include 30 elements, and a 10-gram model would include 60 elements in total.

For our classifier we leverage deep learning. *Stacked autoencoders* (SAEs), a pre-training technique, are investigated to avoid issues of underfitting that are often encountered when training deep neural networks. The following sections provide background on deep learning in general as well as the specific techniques used in our model.

4.1 Deep Learning Overview

Deep learning (DL) is a family of machine learning techniques that seek to learn multiple levels of higher-level features from lower-level data (e.g., pixels in image classification, acoustic inputs in speech recognition) through deep neural networks. A key advantage of DL is its feature extraction capabilities, which reduces the need for feature engineering by human experts that is often expensive in terms of time and effort. The majority of deep learning techniques and model structures are based on artificial neural networks (ANNs). ANNs' structures are typically based on a collection of nodes, often referred to as neurons, and weighted edges propagating values to neurons in the next layer using both linear and non-linear transformations. ANNs have multi-layered structures that consist of an input layer, one or more hidden layers, and an output layer. As a method of training ANNs, a variety of backpropagation methods have been examined for model optimization, including stochastic gradient descent and batch gradient descent methods. Unfortunately, these algorithms were often not scalable to deep networks with multiple hidden layers. The resulting deep networks often performed worse than single hidden layer networks due to their increased vulnerability to converging on poor local optima during training [20]. DL systems have successfully set state-of-the-art benchmarks in a variety of tasks in fields such as computer vision [21], and sentiment analysis of text [22].

The diagrammatic student models utilize the SAE technique. SAEs operate based on a set of *autoencoders* (AEs) that are characterized by encoding and decoding steps using an unsupervised criterion [20]. The encoding step takes an input vector and projects it onto an output space using an activation function. A decoder step performs the opposite action, in which it decodes the projected output back to the original input with the objective of minimizing the reconstruction error of the input data. By situating an "encoder" and "decoder" in a three-layer network and optimizing the network using backpropagation, one can obtain a set of initialized weights that can be used for the connections between the first two layers. Once a weight configuration is initialized between the first two layers, the hidden layer activations based on the previous AE will be used as the input layer in the next AE training as a part of the larger network. This iterative method of initializing weights between two layers and combining pre-trained weights across all layers is referred to as *stacked autoencoders*. Once the weights for all hidden layers have been pre-trained, the entire network can be optimized using standard backpropagation techniques in a supervised fashion to fine-tune the network for the classification task.

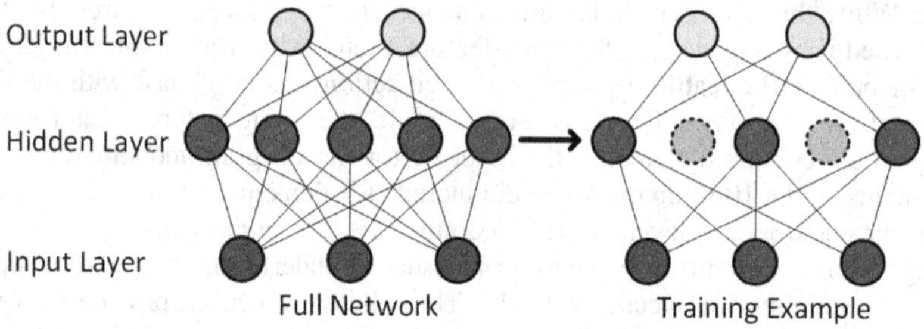

Fig. 4. Dropout training

While significantly improving the predictive performance of multi-layer neural networks, SAEs can induce networks that are highly overfit to the training set resulting in high generalization error. One approach to overcoming this problem would be to train a large number of networks using different portions of the training data and averaging their predictions to classify new data. Unfortunately, this requires a large amount of training data, and greatly increases both the training time, and prediction time for a trained network to an impractical level. Researchers led by Geoffrey Hinton developed a method called dropout to mimic this behavior, while only requiring the training of one network [23]. As illustrated in Figure 4, dropout works by probabilistically removing neurons from the network during training. For each training example, a pre-defined proportion (*p*) of neurons are stochastically dropped from each layer, and both the input and output weights connected to these neurons are correspondingly removed from the network. The weights are then learned for the thinned network using standard backpropagation, and the process is repeated for each training batch. Once training a network is completed, all the weights are downscaled by (1-*p*) as an adjustment process. Empirical analyses demonstrate that a network made up of weights combined from a large number of thinned networks effectively lower generalization error when training deep neural networks [23].

4.2 Model Training and Inference

The open-source DeepLearnToolbox [24] was used to create and test the networks for the diagrammatic student models. While some general guidelines exist, the optimal structure and parameters for a multi-layer network must be determined empirically for each data set. We explored the space of models by conducting a grid search across the following parameters:

- N-grams: 1, 5, 10
- Dropout Rate: 0, .25, .5
- Hidden Layers: 2, 3

All other parameters were fixed for all trials. The number of neurons per hidden layer was set to 150, the activation function was set to the sigmoid function, the back-propagation algorithm was set to stochastic gradient descent over 100 epochs with the learning rate set to .2 for all layers in both the pre-training and fine-tuning steps. Each model contains 3 output nodes that represent class labels (Correct, Near-Miss, and Far-Miss) inferred through this predictive model. To compare models, student-level 10-fold cross validation was conducted using 10 train/test pairs created with data from each student appearing in exactly one of the 10 test sets.

5 Evaluation

To evaluate our model, a corpus of fourth grade symbolic drawings was collected with the LEONARDO system running on iPads in elementary classrooms in North Carolina and California in the spring of 2014. Specifically, the student drawings were from an exercise requiring the students to create a circuit involving a switch, motor, and battery connected in series. After data cleaning, drawings from 403 students were used for the analysis. For this exercise, students spent an average of 4 minutes and 24 seconds in the drawing environment, completing an average of 171 actions. The drawings were automatically scored in comparison to normative models after each action, and the final drawings were clustered using the procedure described in [19]. The clustering process grouped student answers into 3 groups: Correct, Near-Miss, and Far-Miss. Far-Miss was the most common outcome, accounting for 40.01% of final drawings, and 37.34% of total drawing actions. 37.57% of students correctly completed the exercise (30.19% of actions), and 22.42% of student answers were labeled as Near-Miss (32.47% of actions). For each of the actions in the drawing environment, the model attempted to predict the cluster of the final drawing.

The deep-learning-based (DL) diagrammatic student model, which used SAE pre-training, was evaluated against other diagrammatic student models that used a J48 Decision Tree, a Naïve Bayesian classifier, and a Support Vector Machine (SVM) with a Gaussian kernel as well as a most common class baseline. In total 69,979 actions were classified by each model. Each model was trained on a single action based inputs (1-gram encoding), and a sequence of actions based inputs (5 and 10-gram encoding). Because the effectiveness of SVM depends largely on its hyperparameter settings as in deep neural networks, a grid search of C {*.5,1,2,4,8*} and γ {.0625, .125, .25, .5, 1, 2} was conducted for fair comparisons, and the model with the highest accuracy is reported out of models based on all possible hyperparameter combinations within the ranges [25]. All models were evaluated with the same 10 train/test pairs, with the overall accuracies presented below representing the average across the 10 folds.

Table 1. Model accuracy rates

	Accuracy
Most Common Class	37.34%
Naïve Bayes	45.88%
Decision Tree	45.87%
SVM	50.85%
DL	**55.68%**

Table 1 shows the best performing model for each technique. All models performed best using the 10-gram encoding, showing the importance of including previous student actions in the task of predicting students' knowledge based on their evolving sketches. For the SVM model, a C of 4 and a γ of 2 produced the best model. For the DL model, 2 hidden layers and a dropout rate of .5 produced the best model, with an accuracy of 55.68%. Due to our data not conforming to the normal distribution, we computed significance using two non-parametric tests. Both a Friedman test ($p < .05$) and a McNemar post hoc test ($p < .0001$) elicit that the DL model significantly outperformed the top-performing baseline technique (SVM).

While accuracy provides one metric for evaluating classifiers, it is also important to evaluate how quickly and accurately a model converges on a solution. To achieve this, we used two metrics from the goal recognition literature [26]: convergence rate and convergence point. *Convergence rate* (CR) calculates what percentage of students our model had an accurate last prediction for, and thus higher is better for this metric. *Convergence point* (CP) measures how early in the sequence of actions our model was able to converge on the correct prediction, with a lower percentage indicating earlier convergence. Table 2 shows that the DL model outperformed SVM with respect to both CR and CP, and importantly its significantly lower CP score demonstrates DL's effectiveness as an early predictor of student performance.

Overall, the results show that the deep-learning-based diagrammatic student model more accurately predicted student drawing outcomes compared to several competitive models on the corpus of fourth grade circuit drawings. A possible explanation for the

DL model's outperformance compared to the competing techniques is DL's ability to discover high-level representations processed through hierarchical abstraction of low-level data, an attribute closely related to the latent nature of the student modeling task. Further, the model was also able to converge to the correct prediction sooner in the sequence of actions than the baseline models, showing great potential for informing an intelligent tutoring system of student's outcomes early in the drawing process.

Table 2. Convergence rate and convergence point

	Convergence Rate	Convergence Point
SVM	78.3%	68.5%
DL	78.8%	**55.4%**

6 Conclusions and Future Work

Drawing is critical to science learning, and it provides a rich source of diagnostic and predictive information about a student's understanding. However, it has been shown that without proper support, students can be overwhelmed by the process of drawing and fail to experience its benefits. It appears that if ITSs could scaffold the drawing process and perhaps use it as a source for assessment, they could enable students to experience the benefits that drawing appears to offer. To pave the way toward ITSs that support student drawing, we have introduced diagrammatic student models, which analyze student drawing artifacts and use these analyses to predict drawing performance.

In this paper we have reported on the investigation of a diagrammatic student modeling framework based on deep learning. The deep-learning-based diagrammatic student model utilizes temporal and topological features of students' drawing trajectories to predict students' performance from their drawing actions. In an evaluation in which the deep-learning-based framework was compared with several competing models, the deep-learning approach was most accurate, and outperformed the other models on both convergence rate and convergence point. The strong performance of the model suggests that deep-learning-based diagrammatic student modeling offers significant potential for modeling student drawing activities, which will play an increasingly important role in education with the proliferation of tablet computing devices.

The encouraging results suggest several promising directions for future work. First, it will be important to begin experimenting with embedding diagrammatic student models into ITSs that support drawing in order to better evaluate the practical requirements for model accuracy in improving learning outcomes. Similarly, it will be important to develop techniques that allow diagrammatic student models to predict intermediate sub-goals in drawing activities. These techniques will contribute directly to misconception detection functionalities. Finally, it will be important to explore alternative deep learning architecture to support drawing analyses. For example, recurrent neural networks have proven effective for sequential data and hence may perform well in diagrammatic student modeling considering the highest accuracy was achieved by the 10-gram encoded models.

Acknowledgments. The authors thank our colleagues from the LEONARDO project for their contributions to the LEONARDO project: Eric Wiebe, Courtney Behrle, Mike Carter, Angela Shelton, Samuel Leeman-Munk, and Robert Taylor. This material is based upon work supported by the National Science Foundation under Grant No. DRL-1020229. Any opinions, findings, and conclusions or recommendations expressed are those of the authors and do not necessarily reflect the views of the National Science Foundation.

References

1. Van Meter, P., Garner, J.: The Promise and Practice of Learner-Generated Drawing: Literature Review and Synthesis. Educational Psychology Review. **17**, 285–325 (2005)
2. Schwamborn, A., Mayer, R.E., Thillmann, H., Leopold, C., Leutner, D.: Drawing as a Generative Activity and Drawing as a Prognostic Activity. Journal of Educational Psychology **102**, 872–879 (2010)
3. Schmeck, A., Mayer, R.E., Opfermann, M., Pfeiffer, V., Leutner, D.: Drawing Pictures During Learning from Scientific Text: Testing the Generative Drawing Effect and the Prognostic Drawing Effect. Contemporary Educational Psychology **39**, 275–286 (2014)
4. Verhoeven, L., Schnotz, W., Paas, F.: Cognitive Load in Interactive Knowledge Construction. Learning and Instruction **19**, 369–375 (2009)
5. Zhang, H., Linn, M.: Using drawings to support learning from dynamic visualizations. In: Proceedings of the 8th International Conference of the Learning Sciences, Utrecht, The Netherlands, pp. 161–162 (2008)
6. Corbett, A.T., Anderson, J.R.: Knowledge Tracing: Modeling the Acquisition of Procedural Knowledge. User Modelling and User-Adapted Interaction **4**, 253–278 (1994)
7. Gong, Y., Beck, J.E.: Looking beyond transfer models: finding other sources of power for student models. In: Konstan, J.A., Conejo, R., Marzo, J.L., Oliver, N. (eds.) UMAP 2011. LNCS, vol. 6787, pp. 135–146. Springer, Heidelberg (2011)
8. Sabourin, J., Mott, B., Lester, J.: Utilizing dynamic bayes nets to improve early prediction models of self-regulated learning. In: Carberry, S., Weibelzahl, S., Micarelli, A., Semeraro, G. (eds.) UMAP 2013. LNCS, vol. 7899, pp. 228–241. Springer, Heidelberg (2013)
9. Chi, M., VanLehn, K., Litman, D., Jordan, P.: Inducing effective pedagogical strategies using learning context features. In: De Bra, P., Kobsa, A., Chin, D. (eds.) UMAP 2010. LNCS, vol. 6075, pp. 147–158. Springer, Heidelberg (2010)
10. Sao Pedro, M.A., De Baker, R.S.J., Gobert, J.D., Montalvo, O., Nakama, A.: Leveraging Machine-learned Detectors of Systematic Inquiry Behavior to Estimate and Predict Transfer of Inquiry Skill. User Modelling and User-Adapted Interaction **23**, 1–39 (2013)
11. Muldner, K., Burleson, W., Van De Sande, B., Vanlehn, K.: An Analysis of Students' Gaming Behaviors in an Intelligent Tutoring System: Predictors and Impacts. User Modelling and User-Adapted Interaction **21**, 99–135 (2011)
12. Armentano, M.G., Amandi, A.A.: Modeling Sequences of User Actions for Statistical Goal Recognition. User Modelling and User-Adapted Interaction **22**, 281–311 (2012)
13. Min, W., Ha, E.Y., Rowe, J.P., Mott, B.W., Lester, J.C.: Deep learning-based goal recognition in open-ended digital games. In: Tenth Artificial Intelligence and Interactive Digital Entertainment Conference, Raleigh, NC, pp. 37–43 (2014)
14. Valentine, S., Vides, F., Lucchese, G., Turner, D., Kim, H., Li, W., Linsey, J., Hammond, T.: Mechanix: a sketch-based tutoring system for statics courses. In: Proceedings of the Twenty-Fourth Conference on Innovative Applications of Artificial Intelligence, Toronto, Ontario, Canada (2012)

15. van Joolingen, W.R., Bollen, L., Leenaars, F.A.: Using drawings in knowledge modeling and simulation for science teaching. In: Nkambou, R., Bourdeau, J., Mizoguchi, R. (eds.) Advances in Intelligent Tutoring Systems. SCI, vol. 308, pp. 249–264. Springer, Heidelberg (2010)
16. Jee, B., Gentner, D.: Drawing on experience: use of sketching to evaluate knowledge of spatial scientific concepts. In: Proceedings of the 31st Annual Conference of the Cognitive Science Society, Amsterdam, The Netherlands (2009)
17. Ruiz-Primo, M.a., Li, M., Ayala, C., Shavelson, R.J.: Evaluating Students' Science Notebooks as an Assessment Tool. International Journal of Science Education **26**, 1477–1506 (2004)
18. Wiebe, E.N., Madden, L.P., Bedward, J.C., Carter, M.: Examining Science Inquiry Practices in the Elementary Classroom through Science Notebooks. Presented at NARST Annual Meeting, Garden Grove (2009)
19. Smith, A., Wiebe, E., Mott, B., Lester, J.: SketchMiner: mining learner-generated science drawings with topological abstraction. In: Proceedings of the Seventh International Conference on Educational Data Mining, London, UK, pp. 288–291 (2014)
20. Bengio, Y., Lamblin, P.: Greedy Layer-wise Training of Deep Networks. Advances in neural information processing systems **19**, 153 (2007)
21. Krizhevsky, A., Sutskever, I., Hinton, G.: Imagenet classification with deep convolutional neural networks. In: Advances in neural information processing systems, pp. 1097–1105 (2012)
22. Socher, R., Pennington, J., Huang, E.: Semi-supervised recursive autoencoders for predicting sentiment distributions. In: Linguistics, A. for C. (ed.) Proceedings of the Conference on Empirical Methods in Natural Language Processing, pp. 151–161 (2011)
23. Srivastava, N., Hinton, G.: Dropout: A simple way to prevent neural networks from overfitting. The Journal of Machine Learning Research **15**, 1929–1958 (2014)
24. Palm, R.: Prediction as a candidate for learning deep hierarchical models of data. Technical University of Denmark. (2012)
25. Hsu, C., Chang, C., Lin, C.: A Practical Guide to Support Vector Classification. **1**, 1–16 (2003)
26. Blaylock, N., Allen, J.: Hierarchical Goal Recognition. Plan, Activity, and Intent Recognition Theory and Practice, pp. 3–31 (2014)

Lessons Learned – 15 Years of Delivering Real-World Pedagogically Driven Courses Using Experimental Platforms

Athanasios Staikopoulos(✉), Ian O'Keeffe, and Owen Conlan

Knowledge and Data Engineering Group, School of Computer Science and Statistics, Trinity College Dublin, Dublin, Ireland
{Athanasios.Staikopoulos,Ian.OKeeffe,Owen.Conlan}@scss.tcd.ie

Abstract. Advancing research and developing innovative personalization platform whilst at the same time striving to evolve and improve learning experiences for learners, is a challenging prospect. This may be achieved through a longitudinal commitment to developing real-world educational offerings that are used in the daily delivery of learning experiences. This gives the opportunity to continuously apply methods, develop platforms and perform evaluations to realize improvements in the field of user modeling and personalization as well as improving the user experiences they support. In addition, there are specific requirements and obstacles that need to be considered like the robustness and reliability of the experimental platform in order to make this process viable and integrated both with the daily tasks of users and the core business activities of the institution. In this paper, we record our experiences in delivering real-world online courses using experimental platforms that advance personalization and user modeling techniques for over 15 years. We also describe how our research and technology, which is driven by solid pedagogical requirements, has evolved during that time in order to deliver richer learning experiences.

Keywords: Personalization platforms · Challenges using experimental platforms · Improving learning experiences · Pedagogical driven courses · User modelling

1 Introduction

Over the past 15 years the Knowledge and Data Engineering Group in Trinity College Dublin have been building personalisation systems and services. The group have been at the forefront of many innovations in the field of personalisation and adaptation [1]. In order to achieve and maintain this level of research, the group has cultivated and maintained an experimental environment that is grounded in a real-world context with the personalised technology enhanced learning systems developed, having been successfully delivered to over 1000 students. Performing research in this type of environment presents many challenges, but also offers significant advantages. This paper describes the key decisions made and lessons learned over the last 15 years.

F. Ricci et al. (Eds.): UMAP 2015, LNCS 9146, pp. 228–239, 2015.
DOI: 10.1007/978-3-319-20267-9_19

As a research driven educational institution Trinity College, like most universities, has a mandate to deliver high quality educational experiences to our undergraduate and postgraduate learners. A key component of such teaching is to ensure that the learners are engaged in meaningful ways and are offered appropriate opportunities to develop relevant skills. As part of the Computer Science and Computer Engineering undergraduate degree programmes, students take a module in Database Management Systems and Knowledge Engineering. This module is offered to students in the latter years of these programmes; many of the students had already gained some informal exposure to the topics covered through summer work. This was, and still is, particularly true in the case of SQL, a language for accessing and manipulating data within databases. This diversity of experience provides a natural opportunity to offer personalised learning and experiences to these students.

This paper describes the decisions made at the inception of that new form of learning, specifically to deeply embed the resulting system in curriculum and making the decision to have the SQL language taught solely online. It highlights the changes needed to the university's statutes to facilitate such a blended approach to teaching and learning. The paper then focusses on the research systems that were developed and the pedagogical ideals that were adopted to ensure their relevance to the students. Three systems are outlined: the Personalised Learning Service (PLS), the Adaptive Personalised eLearning Service (APeLS) and the Adaptive Media and Service Engine (AMASE). These systems progressively introduced both richer pedagogical approaches and facilitated more ambitious personalisation research to realise them. For example, PLS conceived the idea of narrative-driven personalisation [2], [3], [4], then APeLS introduced a conceptual separation of concepts [3], [5], content and interactive service integration [6], which AMASE expanded on to include rich workflows of services (e.g. peer review) and content [7]. This has resulted in adaptive engines that have become capable of delivering rich pedagogically sound experiences to learners.

This paper starts by outlining our approach and experience through describing each of the systems and their deployment. It then describes how these three generations of adaptive system have been used to deliver pedagogically sound experiences to students as part of blended learning delivery. It then describes the key lessons learned that have enabled this successful merging of research innovation and a real-world context.

2 Approach

In order to ensure that the learners are engaged in meaningful, effective and novel ways, advanced research methods need to be applied and combined from different domains. For example pedagogical strategies and design, adaptation and personalisation of web based systems, user modelling and human computer interaction. The experimental platform also needs to be robust and reliable in order to facilitate research and deliver learning experiences to users on a daily basis. Such requirements, to develop real-word educational offerings, can only be achieved through a longitudinal commitment and when the business activities of the institution are well integrated with the delivery of the course. In this section, based on our 15 years of experience on delivering personalised online courses that are driven by solid pedagogical objectives, we explore the underlining objectives and obstacles. Finally, we highlight and describe the different stages of our approach.

2.1 Objectives

A pedagogical underpinning is a fundamental requirement to the success of a learning course and should be considered when designing and developing learning experiences. However, often that requirement is neglected in favour of the personalisation and user modelling aspects of a course. In our approach, the pedagogy is the main driver of our research and is used to apply best teaching practices and also to improve the student's learning and experience. In particular, we use the power of personalisation and activity based learning to enhance the quality and effectiveness of the pedagogy. In addition, our objective is to embed the learning course in the curriculum of a learner and deliver a truly blended and sound learning experience with clear educational value.

Next, in order to improve and enhance the learner's experience with specific pedagogical requirements we are advancing research. As a result, in our research we combine adaptation and personalisation of web based systems, user modelling, dynamic composition of learning activities, model based systems, rule based systems, learning analytics and narrative visualizations. Finally, we build increasingly powerful platforms in which we apply and evaluate our research methods and deliver real-world personalized and engaging learning experiences.

On the other side, delivering pedagogically driven online courses using complex experimental platforms comes with a high cost, effort and commitment. Therefore to improve the return of investment we need to identify potential funding and industrial opportunities that would allow us to maintain and advance our research plans and agendas. In particular, once the technologies have been initially tested and evaluated, there is a need to engage with industrial partners in order to test our research methods and platforms in alternative settings and uncompromising environments.

2.2 Obstacles

In order to achieve and maintain this level of research using experimental environments, we need to consider and overcome different types of obstacles. Examples include the high cost and risk of such investment as well as the conformance to the underlying institutional regulations. More specifically, delivering personalised and pedagogical driven courses using experimental platforms come with a high cost both in terms of the required resources and the time invested. Significant resources are needed to support research and development as a mixture of different skills and experiences are required. For example to design the pedagogy, provide quality educational material, rich and interactive activities, develop authoring tools as well as integrate the build platforms with other production systems. It also requires a lot of time and energy to design and set authentic case studies, which may need to be repeated in a yearly basis and where an elaborate evaluation is followed to compare results, and identify the benefits or the limitations of the research methods and platforms.

Another obstacle is the high level of risk associated with such investment. Primarily dealing with a research domain there are no guarantees of success and different types of complications may occur. For example, the research methods selected, after an exhaustive evaluation, may appear inappropriate to our context or inferior from other ones. In addition, they may have not been tested in an authentic and realistic setting, the evaluation is subjective, or their technological implementation does not reflect their original potential.

In addition, the platforms and technologies used need to be stable and reliable enough to generate accurate test data that would allow the evaluation of the research methods and the environment. They also need to perform and scale adequately to support multiple concurrent learners and provide a responsive and seamless learning experience. Finally, the experimental platforms may need to be integrated with other existing production systems that could be incompatible or proprietary. All these problems if not addressed, could be reflected back to the learners experience and influence their opinion about the systems and the research methods provided.

Finally, there are specific institutional regulations, e.g. policies, procedures, ethics, with which the pedagogically driven courses need to be aligned and integrated with. Such an example is the delivery of online personalised courses as part of the curriculum.

2.3 Process for Evolving Experimental Platforms

Figure 1 highlights the different stages of our process to deliver and gradually evolve, real-world and pedagogical driven courses using experimental platforms. At each evaluation stage, we determine if our research and system objectives are realised, so accordingly we investigate them more thoroughly, extensively or alternatively. As a result, different research methods and technological artefacts (systems) are developed (evolved) at each iteration stage.

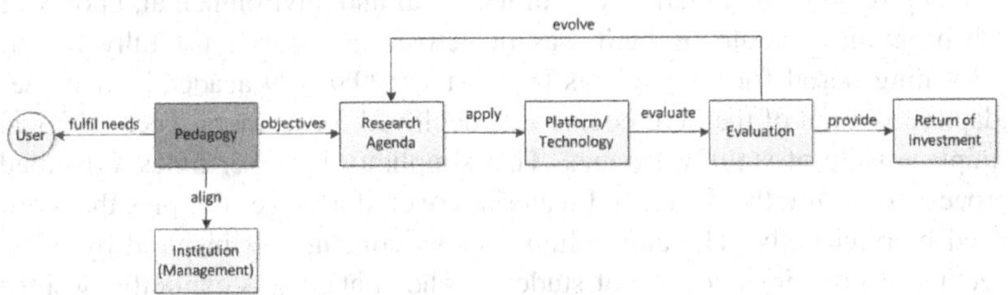

Fig. 1. Delivering and evolving pedagogical-driven courses using experimental platforms

The stages of our approach are described as follows:

Pedagogy: Pedagogy is the main driver of our research and course delivery. Relative research and experienced instructors identify the best teaching practices and techniques to be used in order to improve the learning value and experience of users.

User: We consider users as individual entities having specific learning needs, prior knowledge, skills, preferences and context that need to be reflected and satisfied by the course and the learning experience. Advanced user modelling techniques are used to represent different aspects of a user as accurate as possible.

Institution: Courses and pedagogies are delivered within specific academic institutions, so there is a need to be aligned and integrated with their core business activities, procedures and policies.

Research Agenda: Driven by the pedagogical objectives, the research investigates the best methods and techniques that will support and improve the learning experience of users as well as to make it more efficient and effective.

Platform/Technology: A platform (system) applies the research methods with a specific technology and delivers the learning experience to users. The platform needs to be robust and reliable.

Evaluation: At specific phases our research methods and system are evaluated in order to determine if our goals are met.

Return of Investment: External collaborations and funding opportunities need to be identified that will allows us to further advance our research plans as well as to evaluate the application and the maturity of our research methods and platforms.

3 Delivering Real-Word Courses: SQL Course Evolution

In this section we describe three different generations of adaptive systems, and a precursor non-adaptive deployment, that we have developed in Trinity College Dublin in order to deliver pedagogical driven learning experiences to students.

3.1 Non-adaptive Course

The first step in creating a platform, both technical and environmental, upon which a research programme could be built was in delivering a basic, yet fully functional, online learning portal for the students [8]. In the 1998/1999 academic year the first non-adaptive version of the SQL course was deployed for learners. Technologically it was simply a suite of static webpages. That simplicity however hides a detailed design process to ensure the developed material covered a range of topics that could be organized hierarchically. The curriculum for this content was inspired by what had been lectured to previous cohorts of students. The content was explicitly designed to have both theoretical and practical components. The specification of the practical assignment that the students were required to undertake was only made available through the online SQL course.

From a university statutes perspective the formal description of the module, with which the online course was to be integrated, was changed to indicate that the students were required to undertake a practical assignment (worth 20% of their overall grade) and that it was expected that the students consume certain content online. Pedagogically this was integrated into the lectures by presenting a timeline over which online material would be discussed face-to-face. The online SQL course was assessed through individual interviews with students, which were also used to help assess their practical SQL assignment.

3.2 Personalised Learning Service (PLS)

The second phase in progressing the research programme, which ran from 2000 to 2002, was to include personalisation techniques into the static online course. This necessitated the design and development of a brand new adaptive engine [2] which was capable of reconciling a user model and content model with a narrative model, which was introduced as part of this research [3]. The vision was that the modelling of the user would be used to explicitly assess their prior experience with SQL, through a sequence of questions that mapped to underlying competencies in the SQL domain. This domain model was derived from the online SQL curriculum developed for the non-adaptive course. The content was also reassessed to determine if the granularity was appropriate. It is from this examination that the notion of a pagelet [9] was derived; these are discrete pieces of content with attached metadata that can be composed as part of a narrative execution. The role of the narrative was to provide a set of rules, expressed as domain concepts, that when reconciled with the user's model would provide a conceptual instance of the content to be delivered. These concepts were compared with the metadata of the available pagelets. A navigation structure across the pagelets was then constructed and the resulting course was delivered.

The PLS adaptive engine represented a significant step forward in how such personalization systems were implemented. Deploying this engine in a production environment necessitated using robust, industry scale technologies such as Jakarta Tomcat and Microsoft's Internet Information Service. The services had to have a high uptime over a protracted period of time (October to May in each academic year). This placed an increased onus on engineering relative to most experimental platforms.

The evaluation results for PLS were extremely encouraging [5] with students showing increased performance in both their assessment and examinations. From a research perspective this system provided a baseline to engage with European Commission FP6 funded projects, which offered a mechanism to further advance both the experimental platform and leverage the cohort of students as a use case.

3.3 Adaptive Personalised eLearning Service (APeLS)

PLS demonstrated the benefits of personalization for one category of stakeholder, the learners, but it also highlighted the limitations of the state of the art architectures of that time. The deep integration of the adaptation rules with the content and engine resulted in systems that were complex and expensive to repurpose and did not address the needs of other stakeholders such as adaptive course developers. This led to APeLS [10] and the development of one of the earliest truly reusable, general purpose adaptation engines. APeLS allowed the research team to investigate the separation of concerns in an adaptive hypermedia system through the use of approaches such as the multi-model, metadata driven and candidacy [11] in the context of an existing application, with a proven track record as an educational platform and also as an adaptive system. Evaluating APeLS by migrating the PLS based SQL course and subsequently using it to deliver the same undergraduate degree courses, demonstrated that the model driven approaches embodied by APeLS could be successfully applied without any effect on the adaptive behavior or importantly on the educational outcomes for the learners [5]. APeLS was so successful as a platform that it was used to deliver adaptive courses in TCD for almost 8 years. It that time there were several cosmetic upgrades to the courses delivered to keep up with the constantly evolving trends and increasing expectations of users. This is an important point to note. The long term use of research platforms such as APeLS cannot be considered a once off expense. Even if the core technology goes unchanged, the needs of end users and the changing technologies of the web demand that applications keep with the times.

While the central pillar of the APeLS research program was the undergraduate SQL course, the existence of APeLS allowed the research agenda of the team to grow in its ambitions. In particular, APeLS grew the realization that all stakeholders needed to be considered, especially non-technical authors of adaptive courses. In response, the team began to develop and evaluate authoring tools such as the Adaptive Course Construction Toolkit (ACCT) [12]. The core adaptive engine developed as part of APeLS also lead to other successful stands of research. It continued to evolve as part of the iClass project [13] where service oriented approaches to the architecture of adaptive education systems were investigated. These moved away from the more traditional adaptive hypermedia systems and looked to develop more modular frameworks in which adaptation was a core behavior of a much larger system [13].

A diverse body of research began to form around APeLS with two key themes beginning to emerge. The first was the application of adaptation beyond eLearning with a focus on the wider challenge of global intelligent content as part of the Centre for Global Intelligent Content [14]. The second theme was around the need move beyond content driven adaptive systems towards ones that could deliver more diverse, engaging and interactive experiences. APeLS again formed the basis for research into the integration of user centric services and the management of those services as part of an activity based eLearning platform [15]. This research in turn led to a more comprehensive research program as part of the AMAS project.

3.4 Adaptive Media and Service Engine (AMASE)

In the fourth phase the focus of the research was on investigating new innovative techniques and technologies to provide a more personalised and engaging learning experience to users. As a result, based on our previous experience we designed and developed the Adaptive Media and Service Engine (AMASE). AMASE was developed in the context of the AMAS project [4], [7], [16] and became our more recent experimental platform to apply our research methods and deliver personalized courses to learners. In AMASE the learning experience itself is perceived as a learning activity (workflow) which orchestrates and combines in a unified manner a) rich learning media content that a learner has to study, b) (user centric) tasks that a learner has to complete and c) other automated services that are auxiliary to the learning process and management. This kind of personalized activity-based learning provides sound, interactive, deep and effective learning experiences [7]. In AMASE we had also the opportunity to explore additional challenges around the motivation and engagement of users. As a result, AMASE incorporates advanced monitoring mechanisms that capture and analyze the learner's behavior and interactions with their learning activity and environment. In that way we can get a deeper understanding of the learner's experience. For example, we can determine the level of engagement and progress of students, if they struggle with a specific task, identify potential problems and their behavior trends in their course. Accordingly, the framework will trigger suitable personalized interventions that will guide and motivate the students with their course. After an evaluation, we verified that such forms of personalized interventions can both stimulate and sustain the engagement of students with their course [16].

The AMASE platform and technology was developed, evolved and tested over a 4 year period (2011-2014). The platform itself is based on different modular components which communicate together via an integrated message oriented framework and where their public functionality is exposed via web services. The learning courses are modelled at a higher level of abstraction with authoring tools and they are managed via an administrative portal. In this period, AMASE was used to deliver online courses for a database undergraduate course, a SCRUM training course as well as to serve as an experimental platform to test smaller case studies. The database courses were up and running for long periods (October to May), providing a truly blended learning experience to learners where they could learn and practice their SQL skills, collaborate in group tasks, work on assessments and prepare for their exams. Finally, during the years the system became more robust and reliable.

As before in order to evaluate the AMASE approach and platform the SQL database course was used as an authentic case study. In this phase, the original SQL database course was redesigned and modernized in order to provide a more enhanced and effective learning experience. As a result, the course consisted of rich learning content, interactive tasks, collaborative activities, recommendations, questionnaires, narrative visualizations and automated interventions in the form of motivations, feedback and notifications. During this period our prime objective was to evaluate the students' perception about the quality of their personalized learning experience via a survey. In overall the student responses were positive [7], [16]. Despite the success of the framework a number of potential improvements have also been identified and which are part of our future work. Another primary objective of our evaluation was to investigate if and how the underlying monitoring mechanisms and assistive interventions in AMASE, had increased the level of engagement of students. After comparing the level of engagement of more than 200 students in two consecutive years - the year (2012-13) where no motivations were provided and the year (2013-14) where motivations were provided, we found out that the monitoring and motivations had significantly increased the engagement of students by 8% [16]. In addition, the level of engagement of students in the year (2013-14) was clearly shifted (distributed) towards higher scores. We also confirmed that the monitoring and motivations had improved the progress rate (completion) of the course and its activities and that the received motivations had increased the engagement of students in that period.

So far AMASE was developed and used as a core component of the AMAS project. All this 4 years AMASE was used to deliver personalized online courses and training in particular for a database undergraduate course. The platform allowed us to establish collaborations with main industrial partners from the eLearning Publishing sector. Currently we are in process of licensing the platform and establishing further commercial collaborations with partners for example from the aviation sector - deliver personalized, interactive and responsive training courses. There are also plans the engine to be used or initiate other projects, as well as be used, extended and disseminate knowledge to the CNGL2[1], ADAPT[2] and the Learnovate Centre[3].

3.5 Evolution of Experimental Platforms

In this section we highlight how our research and platforms have evolved over the years in order to improve different aspects of the learner's experience.

The early system offered a very basic blended learning approach, where the learning material was taught online. The course was not adapted and the learning material was solely based on static web pages, which were organized hierarchical in topics. In the next phase, PLS provided a truly personalized learning experience, which was based on simple user modelling, multi models and where the learning material was annotated with metadata to allow the selection and composition of content as part of a narrative execution. Next, APeLS build a more advanced engine, which was more modular and service-oriented and which provided a more dynamic content composition and adaptation. In addition, specific authoring tools were used to facilitate the creation of personalized courses with model abstractions. Finally, with AMASE we led to a truly blended learning experience, which was purely activity based (based on learning paths) combining learning content and tasks seamlessly. The learning experience became more enhanced and engaging by using rich content, collaborative tasks, recommendations, visualizations, automated motivations and feedback as well as the monitoring of the learner's behavior and engagement with the system.

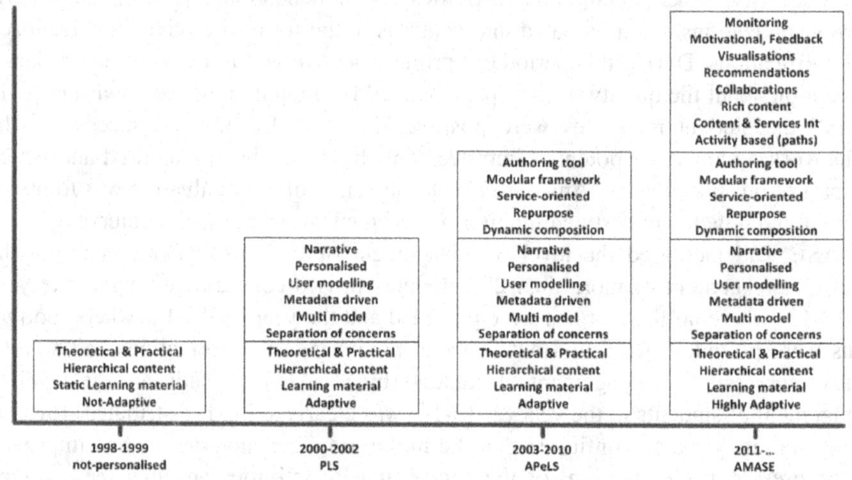

Fig. 2. Towards improving the learner's experience with experimental platforms

[1] CNGL2, refer to http://www.cngl.ie/

[2] ADAPT, refer to http://www.adaptcentre.ie

[3] Learnovate Centre, refer to http://www.learnovatecentre.org/

4 Lessons Learned

4.1 Integrate with User's Daily Tasks and Core Business Activities

One of the key elements when applying adaptive educational systems in the real-world as part of a long term research programme is to ensure that the experimental platform (the adaptive system) is fully integrated into both the daily tasks of the users who will use it and that it aligns with the core business activities of the institution. This is very challenging as the system has to be both reliable and fulfil the needs of the users. This is an issue for most research focussed organisations, which don't often have the resources to invest in the engineering required. Moreover, fulfilling users' needs often requires integrating the experimental system with existing tools and platforms, e.g Blackboard, used in the work environment. Such integration with production systems is highly costly, as it requires an investment of time to develop an in-depth knowledge of those systems and to subsequently implement and maintain good engineering solutions. In order to warrant such investment the research planning is necessarily longitudinal.

In an educational and research institution the above challenges can only be met by embedding the adaptive eLearning systems into the curriculum of the learners. This often necessitates changes to the statutes and regulations of the institution so that the students are made fully aware of the expectations placed on them to engage with such systems as part of their learning and to formalise the obligation placed on the institution to provide the services in an adequate manner.

As the system, which is an experimental platform, is to be used in a production environment its uptime and reliability needs to be high. This is not just to ensure the users have an appropriate level of experience, but also because the platform needs to generate accurate experimental data. By technically integrating the experimental system with the tool the users interact with it becomes more familiar to access and can be evaluated in a more authentic setting. This deep integration into the operation of the institution and the daily activities of the users comes with a high commitment and at a cost. The researchers must plan for a series of experiments, potentially executed on a yearly basis that escalate in their complexity and ambition. This is a challenge as they need to ensure they have the resources to execute the experiments over that period. The cost of failure is quite high: not only will the experiment generate compromised results, but it may also prevent the users in accomplishing their daily tasks. However, these challenges and risks are tempered by the overwhelming benefits that are afforded by the long term planning as they can now execute longitudinal studies.

4.2 Improve User's Experience

The risk of failure is balanced with the potential reward of both improving the experience of users and in the strong experimental findings discovered. In the context of eLearning taking a longitudinal approach has enabled ever increasing pedagogical value to be added to the adaptive systems. The early systems offered a basic blended learning approach, where some material was taught (in a personalised manner) online and the outcomes used to perform classwork and project work. It was important that this was not an artificial experience and that it was embedded with the user's activities. This led to a truly blended experience where the online learning offered in the adaptive systems allowed the researchers to tackle increasingly complex questions.

The early online systems used in Trinity College Dublin facilitated rudimentary personalisation by today's standards. However, as there was a commitment to ensure the system would be year on year there was also a commitment to evolve and improve the user experience. This blended system grew to offer personalised interactive learning activities, personalised collaboration support and tailored motivational support. This led to not only tackling increasingly complex research questions, but also to a better user experience. This user experience, importantly, was assessed using experimental data.

4.3 Advance Research

The final important element to realising such longitudinal research success is in ensuring that the context and environment set up to support the experiments would allow the researchers involved to further their research agendas. As mentioned above, by focussing on improving the user experience the team were able to create increasingly complex adaptive systems without compromising on their delivery. This was only possible through the evolutionary approach to the research that the long term planning afforded. It allowed increasingly more complex problems to be addressed by building on the strong foundation that the proven core research platform provided. Furthermore, as these systems had to work in a live environment the potential to engage with industry partners was greatly increased as they could witness the reliability of the software and more importantly the capability of the researchers to work in uncompromising environments. Having a proven core research platform has also enhanced the research team's ability to engage with funding opportunities as they had strong proof that their experimental systems delivered results. This in turn allowed the team to further advance their research plans, allowing for more powerful adaptive systems to be built, giving an even stronger foundation to build from.

5 Conclusions

Evolving a research programme over 15 years with in excess of 1000 users has been a rewarding and often challenging experience. It has enabled the Knowledge and Data Engineering group in Trinity College to deliver three generations of cutting-edge adaptive systems, namely the Personalised Learning Service (PLS), the Adaptive Personalised eLearning Service (APeLS) and the Adaptive Media and Service Engine (AMASE). Through the deployment of these systems in a real-world live production environment we have gathered strong and authentic evaluation data, whilst delivering a high quality learning experience to our students. This paper has described the evolution of these systems and highlighted three key lessons that were learned in carrying out this exciting research.

Acknowledgements. This research is supported by the Science Foundation Ireland (grant 07/CE/I1142) as part of the CNGL Centre for Global Intelligent Content (www.cngl.ie) and ADAPT (www.adaptcentre.ie) at Trinity College, Dublin.

References

1. Brusilovsky, P.: Methods and Techniques of Adaptive Hypermedia. User Modeling and User Adapted Interaction **6**(2–3), 87–129 (1996)
2. Conlan, O.: Novel components for supporting adaptivity in education systems - model-based integration approach. In: 8th International Conference on Multimedia, pp 519–52 (2000)
3. Conlan, O., Wade, V.P., Bruen, C., Gargan, M.: Multi-model, metadata driven approach to adaptive hypermedia services for personalized elearning. In: De Bra, P., Brusilovsky, P., Conejo, R. (eds.) AH 2002. LNCS, vol. 2347, pp. 100–111. Springer, Heidelberg (2002)
4. Conlan, O., Staikopoulos, A., Hampson, C., Lawless, S., O'Keeffe, I.: The Narrative Approach to Personalisation. New Review of Hypermedia and Multimedia, 132–157 (2013)
5. Conlan, O., Wade, V.P.: Evaluation of APeLS – an adaptive elearning service based on the multi-model, metadata-driven approach. In: De Bra, P.M., Nejdl, W. (eds.) AH 2004. LNCS, vol. 3137, pp. 291–295. Springer, Heidelberg (2004)
6. O'Keeffe, I., Conlan, O., Wade, V.P.: A unified approach to adaptive hypermedia personalisation and adaptive service composition. In: Wade, V.P., Ashman, H., Smyth, B. (eds.) AH 2006. LNCS, vol. 4018, pp. 303–307. Springer, Heidelberg (2006)
7. Staikopoulos, A., O'Keeffe, I., Rafter, R., Walsh, E., Yousuf, B., Conlan, O., Wade, V.: AMASE: A framework for supporting personalised activity-based learning on the web. Computer Science and Information Systems **11**(1), 343–367 (2014)
8. Wade, V., Power, C.: Evaluating the design and delivery of WWW based educational environments and courseware. ITiCSE 1998 **33**(3), 243–248 (1998)
9. Conlan, O.: The multi-model, metadata driven approach to personalised eLearning services, PhD, Department of Computer Science, Trinity College, Dublin (2005)
10. Conlan, O., Hockemeyer, C., Wade, V., Albert, D.: Metadata Driven Approaches to Facilitate Adaptivity in Personalized eLearning Systems. Journal of the Japanese Society for Information and Systems in Education **1**(1), 38–45 (2003)
11. Dagger, D., Conlan, O., Wade, V.: An Architecture for Candidacy in Adaptive eLearning Systems to Facilitate the Reuse of Learning Resources. E-Learn (2003)
12. Dagger, D., Wade, V., Conlan, O.: Personalisation for All: Making Adaptive Course Composition Easy. Educational Technology and Society journal, IEEE IFETS (2005)
13. O'Keeffe, I., Brady, A., Conlan, O., Wade, V.: Just-in-time Generation of Pedagogically Sound, Context Sensitive Personalized Learning Experiences. International Journal on E-Learning (IJeL) **5**(1), 113–127 (2006)
14. Steichen, B., O'Connor, A., Wade, V.: Personalisation in the Wild - providing personalisation across semantic, social and Open-Web Resources. In: HT 2011, pp. 73–82 (2011)
15. O'Keeffe, I., Wade, V.: Personalised web experiences: seamless adaptivity across web service composition and web content. In: Houben, G.-J., McCalla, G., Pianesi, F., Zancanaro, M. (eds.) UMAP 2009. LNCS, vol. 5535, pp. 480–485. Springer, Heidelberg (2009)
16. Staikopoulos, A., O'Keeffe, I., Yousuf, B., Conlan, O., Walsh, E., Wade, V.: Enhancing student engagement through personalised motivations. In: 15th IEEE International Conference on Advanced Learning Technologies, ICALT (2015)

Smartphone Based Stress Prediction

Thomas Stütz[1], Thomas Kowar[1], Michael Kager[1], Martin Tiefengrabner[1], Markus Stuppner[2], Jens Blechert[2], Frank H. Wilhelm[2], and Simon Ginzinger[1(✉)]

[1] Department of Multimedia Technology, University of Applied Sciences Salzburg, Campus Urstein Süd 1, 5412 Puch/Salzburg, Austria
{thomas.stuetz,thomas.kowar,michael.kager, martin.tiefengrabner,simon.ginzinger}@fh-salzburg.ac.at
http://fh-salzburg.ac.at/mmt

[2] Department of Psychology, University of Salzburg, Hellbrunnerstrasse 34, 5020 Salzburg, Austria
{markus.stuppner,jens.blechert,frank.wilhelm}@sbg.ac.at
http://uni-salzburg.ac.at/psychologie

Abstract. Smartphone usage has tremendously increased and most users keep their smartphones close throughout the day. Smartphones have a broad variety of sensors, that could automatically map and track the user's life and behaviour. In this work we investigate whether automatically collected smartphone usage and sensor data can be employed to predict the experienced stress levels of a user using a customized brief version of the Perceived Stress Scale (PSS). To that end we have conducted a user study in which smartphone data and stress (as measured by the PSS seven times a day) were recorded for two weeks. We found significant correlations between stress scores and smartphone usage as well as sensor data, pointing to innovative ways for automatic stress measurements via smartphone technology. Stress is a prevalent risk factor for multiple diseases. Thus accurate and efficient prediction of stress levels could provide means for targeted prevention and intervention.

Keywords: Stress · Prediction · Smartphone sensing · Data analysis · Field study · Observational study

1 Introduction

Stress has become a major concern, as stress-related diseases cause a decrease in life expectancy and in the quality of life, as well as an increase in the number of sick leaves. Stress is a risk factor for a multitude of diseases, also because stress is closely linked to unhealthy behaviour, such as excessive consumption of food and alcoholic beverages [1,21]. Accurate and efficient assessment of unhealthy stress exposure could greatly help to administer timely and appropriate support measures. Smartphones can offer a deep insight in the user's daily life, due to their multitude of sensors, their frequent use in everyday life and their constant

F. Ricci et al. (Eds.): UMAP 2015, LNCS 9146, pp. 240–251, 2015.
DOI: 10.1007/978-3-319-20267-9_20

proximity to the user. Therefore it would be desirable to develop stress indices based on smartphone usage and sensor data.

If subjective stress levels were predictable by these data, health-related smartphone apps can automatically take appropriate actions, such as a notification of the responsible physician or prompts to the user to reduce stress through other means. The main objective of the study is to research the connection between perceived stress and smartphone usage and sensor data. More specifically the objective is to answer the question whether there is a significant correlation between perceived stress scores and smartphone usage and sensor data.

The presented study was part of a broader study on the relation between stress and diet. The study was formally approved by the ethics committee of the University of Salzburg.

A brief overview of related work is given in section 2. The presentation of the study is structured as recommended in [22]. The context of the study is explained in section 3. In section 4 the methodology is presented and in section 5 the results are given, which are discussed in section 6. Finally, we conclude in section 7.

2 Related Work

Initial results on stress detection with smartphones are presented in [4]. Mobile phone usage data of a stressful (exam period) and a normal week is compared in seven subjects. In [20] wrist sensor data and smart phone data has been used to predict high and low levels of stress, as measured by the full PSS questionnaire [7]. Sensor and smart phone usage data of 18 persons was collected for 5 days and 75% accuracy was reported for binary classification (high / low stress). Stress prediction on the basis of sophisticated audio processing is presented in [17]. Stress levels were measured with a GSR (galvanic skin response sensor). In [23] smartphone usage and sensor data collected by a continuous sensing app has been shown to correlate with academic performance and various psychological scores, namely PHQ-9 for depression, PSS for stress, flourishing scale, and UCLA loneliness scale. The study with 48 participants has a broad spectrum and does not focus on stress alone. Compared to our study, stress is measured only before and after the study with the full PSS questionnaire [7].

The influence of weather and mobile phone usage on perceived stress is investigated in [5]. Phone usage data consisted of call logs (no audio properties), sms logs (no content based features), and proximity data (other Bluetooth devices). Stress levels were measured by one direct question with a 7-point Likert scale to answer. Data was collected from 117 persons for almost half a year. For binary classification (stress / no stress) an 72.28% accuracy is reported.

A mobile phone app for depression is presented and analysed in [6]. The application provided self-monitoring via questionnaires and tailored, real-time feedback and intervention. Somewhat similar work for bipolar disorder is presented in [3,11]. The application of smartphones (and processed sensor data) for large scale behaviour change interventions is discussed in [15].

3 Study Context

The study was performed at the department of Psychology at the University of Salzburg and the participants were students of psychology. The smartphone app (TheStressCollector) was developed at the department of MultiMediaTechnolgy at the Salzburg University of Applied Sciences. The study was joint work of the two departments. In the study two smartphone applications were employed. The smartphone app TheStressCollector (TSC) was responsible for logging usage and sensor data, while the commercial framework movisensSX [19] was used to administer the questionnaires. MovisensXS allows non-programming experts to conduct questionnaire-based studies for Android smartphones.

3.1 Mobile App for Smartphone Usage and Sensor Logging

The smartphone app TheStressCollector (TSC), once installed on an Android smartphone, runs permanently in the background and periodically collects smartphone usage and sensor data and uploads the data to a database server (PHP, MySQL). For participants who want to avoid mobile data usage an option to only synchronize via WiFi network is offered.

All collected data were fully anonymized, i.e. the subjects were identified by a random ID. Furthermore only data items that did not allow to trace back a person's identity have been collected.

In the following we give a brief overview of the collected data items (see Fig. 1 as well):

Activity: TSC uses the activity recognition provided by Google Play Services [2]. In the following we list the different activities detected, which were classified into physical versus non-physical activities.

- ON_FOOT: The device is on a user who is walking or running. This is classified as *physical.*
- ON_BICYCLE: The device is on a bicycle. This is classified as *physical.*

Fig. 1. Smartphone Usage and Sensor Logging

- IN_VEHICLE: The device is in a vehicle. This is classified as *non-physical.*
- TILTING: The device angle relative to gravity changed significantly. This is most often the case when the user is using the phone at the moment. This is classified as *non-physical*
- STILL: The device is not moving. This is classified as *non-physical.*
- UNKNOWN: It is not possible to detect the current activity. This is classified as *physical.*

The activity detection interval is set to 20 minutes. More frequent measurements may occur in case another application request more frequent activity updates. Less frequent measurements may occur in case the device is in the STILL state.

App Usage: Due to privacy concerns the TSC app does not save the exact package names of executed apps, but categorizes them into one of the six rough categories Information, System, Health, Social, Entertainment or Work.

Table 1. App categories of TSC and the Google Play Store

Category	Google Play Store Categories
Information	Transportation, Weather, Travel & Local, News & Magazines, Shopping and Lifestyle
System	Libraries & Demo, Personalization, Live Wallpapers, Tools and Widgets
Health	Sports, Medical and Health & Fitness
Entertainment	Photography, Entertainment, Music & Audio, Media & Video, Books & Reference and 19 game categories
Social	Communication and Social
Work	Business, Productivity, Finance and Education

Network Traffic: As a measurement of general smartphone usage intensity, the amount of network traffic (in terms of bytes) was logged as well. TSC splits the traffic into the categories 'Received' and 'Transmitted' as well as 'Mobile Network' and 'Wireless Network'.

Reboot Activity: TSC logs power on and power off events.

Calls: If a call gets active, the microphone input is processed in real-time. The power levels in dB are measured during the call. Measurements were taken every 300 milliseconds. After the call has finished, the minimum, maximum and mean dB-values are saved. Furthermore the call duration is logged. Calls within working hours are counted separately as well (call working count).

Light: The environment brightness as measured by the light sensor was measured. Measurements were taken whenever the screen was on, i.e. when the user was interacting with the smartphone (to avoid meaningless measurements when the smartphone is stored e.g. in a pocket). Each measurement has been classified into 'light' or 'dark' and the frequency summarized in 'light session count' and dark 'session count'.

Messages: TSC logs time stamps for every SMS and MMS received on the smartphone, but neither the content nor the receiver (no privacy incriminating information). Messengers like WhatsApp, Google Hangouts or Facebook Messenger are covered by the app usage tracking and categorized as 'Social'.

Noise exposure: Noise exposure was logged periodically, i.e., the minimum, maximum and mean power in dB of a 20 seconds sample (with a sampling rate of 100 milliseconds) was computed every 20 minutes.

Screen Activity: User session duration was logged. A user session starts when the device screen is powered on and ends if the screen goes off. User sessions during working time are counted separately as well (user session working time) User session percent summarizes the ratio of active smartphone usage and no usage.

4 Methods

We conducted a longitudinal, ambulatory, observational study on smartphone usage, stress, and eating behaviour. The study was conducted in 2014 in the summer semester and included one week in mid-semester (assumed not very stressful) and one week at the end of the semester (assumed stressful due to end-term examinations).

There were no exclusion criteria for participation in the study. Participants installed the app on their private smartphones. Seven times a day questionnaires including the PSS had to be answered, i.e. at 8:00, 9:00, 12:00, 15:00, 18:00, 21:00, and 22:00. Only in the morning a questionnaire on sleeping behaviour was scheduled. At 22:00 an extensive set of questions on eating and stress was scheduled. Throughout the day a short questionnaire on food and drink consumption was asked repeatedly. During the study, the test users had access to a website which provided information about the study and clear instructions regarding what to do before and after the two study weeks. For purpose of installation on the participants' smartphones the TSC app was made available in the Google Play Store.

4.1 Outcome Measures for Perceived Stress

The perceived stress score (PSS) has been introduced in [7]. The original PSS questionnaire consists of 14 questions. For the study the original questionnaire was considered too time-consuming and thus an abbreviated four question version of the PSS was employed. Internal consistency (based on averaged items over all assessment points of week 1) was good (.831). The following four questions were asked repeatedly:

1. Since the last entry: Has something unexpected upset you?
2. Do you feel nervous and stressed?

3. Since the last entry: Have you felt that you were on top of things?
4. Do you feel that you can successfully cope with all upcoming tasks and problems at the moment?

Questions 1, 2, and 4 could be answered on a 7-level Likert scale, while question 3 could be answered on 8-level Likert scale (which was a human error in the setup of the study). Thus for each question the answer is a number in the range of 1 (not at all) to 7 or 8 (extremely). The PSS is simply computed by adding the scores of answers 1 and 2 and the inverted scores of answers 3 and 4. Thus high PSS values (max = 29) correspond to high level of perceived stress and low PSS values (min = 4) correspond to a low level of perceived stress.

4.2 Methods for Data Analysis

Data analysis was conducted in R (version 3.1.2 for Windows). The Pearson correlation coefficient and its significance level [16] were computed with the R-function `cor.test`.

Preliminary results on prediction were generated with the data mining software WEKA (version 3.7 for Windows) [13,24]. The WEKA software was used to evaluate the prediction performance of standard machine learning tools on the collected data. Specifically linear regression and random forests [24] were employed with 5-fold and 10-fold cross validation.

5 Results

PSS and smartphone usage and sensor data from 15 participants (12 women and 3 men) were collected. PSS measurements resulted in 104898 data points; 967 PSS measurements were obtained in the first week, and 754 PSS measurements in the second week. In the first week the average response rate results to 85% with a standard devision of 12%. In the second week the average response rate results to 88% with a standard devision of 13%. The average PSS value in the first week (10.3) wasn slighly lower as compared to the second week (11.0). Detailed information on the participants is summarized in table 2. Initially 28 participants had been recruited for the study. The decrease to 15 participants with associated data ist due to the entry of mismatching identification codes in the TSC and the MovisensSX app, personal smartphones with insufficient free memory (therefore only the MovisensSX app was installed), and privacy concerns. Out of the 15 participants of the first week four participants did not return to the second week. All PSS data from both weeks used in further data analysis is shown in Figure 2. The PSS data is ordered by the time it was received at the server. Table 3 summarizes the correlation and associated p-values of single PSS scores with different collected data items. For the correlations and p-values in table 4 the seven single PSS scores of each day were averaged, while for table 5 all PSS scores of each week were averaged. Figures 3 and 4 show plots of the most significant data items versus average PSS scores.

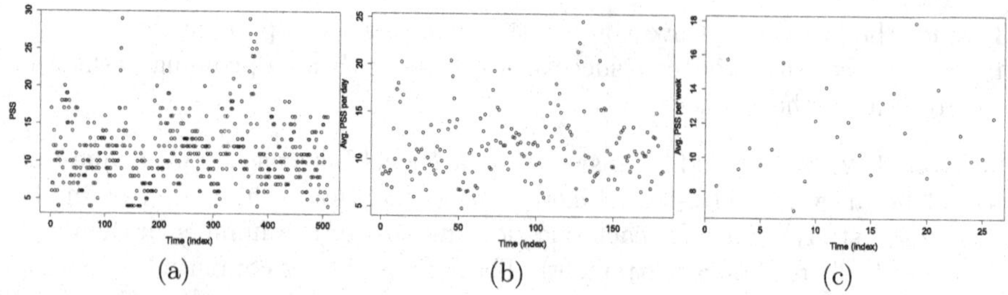

(a) (b) (c)

Fig. 2. PSS values (a), average PSS per day (b), and average PSS per week (c)

Table 2. Participant details

Id	Gender	BMI	Age(years)	Height(cm)	Weight(kg)	Smoker	Diet	Edu
3	female	22.0	23	165	60	no	non-veg.	univ.
5	female	19.1	23	168	54	no	non-veg.	univ.
8	female	21.3	24	162	56	yes	non-veg.	univ.
9	female	25.0	24	165	68	no	non-veg.	univ.
10	female	19.4	22	173	58	no	veg.	univ.
11	female	19.1	21	155	46	no	non-veg.	A-level
12	female	22.9	23	162	60	no	non-veg.	univ.
13	female	19.6	27	178	62	no	non-veg.	univ.
17	female	21.8	24	163	58	no	non-veg.	univ.
18	male	23.3	26	192	86	no	non-veg.	univ.
19	female	24.9	21	169	71	no	non-veg.	A-level
23	female	22.8	27	169	65	no	non-veg.	univ.
25	female	20.2	24	165	55	no	veg.	univ.
26	male	24.2	24	183	81	no	non-veg.	A-level
27	female	21.5	33	178	68	no	non-veg.	univ.

Table 3. Single perceived stress score and Pearson correlation with the 10 most significant data items

Automatically logged data item	Pearson cor	Pearson p-value
noisiness min	0.2024	0.00002
social count	0.1135	0.01033
app mean time cat health	-0.1119	0.01350
call count	0.1022	0.02195
app mean time cat system	-0.1018	0.02465
wifi received	0.0930	0.03578
app sum time cat health	-0.0947	0.03673
noisiness mean	0.0963	0.04309
lighter sessions count	0.1275	0.05400
user session count	0.0958	0.10099

The aim is to predict excessive levels of stress, thus we have employed the collected data as data set for machine learning algorithms. The results, i.e., the correlation of the predicted stress score and the actual stress score, are

Table 4. Daily average of perceived stress scores and Pearson correlation with the 10 most significant data items

Automatically logged data item	Pearson cor	Pearson p-value
noisiness mean	0.3214	0.00001
power on count	0.2841	0.00010
noisiness min	0.2579	0.00047
call max db	0.2840	0.00111
call mean db	0.2833	0.00114
light changes count	0.3105	0.00479
app mean time cat work	0.2082	0.00568
call count	0.2022	0.00730
call sum time	0.2256	0.01014
lighter sessions count	0.2706	0.01456

Table 5. Weekly average of the perceived stress scores and Pearson correlation with the 10 most significant data items

Automatically logged data item	Pearson cor	Pearson p-value
user session percent	0.6506	0.00862
user session sum time	0.6503	0.00867
activity difference (physical - non-physical)	0.6758	0.01124
user session sum working time	0.6065	0.01652
activity nonphysical count	-0.6388	0.01875
user session max time	0.5638	0.02859
power on count	0.3527	0.07718
user session mean time	0.4521	0.09063
noisiness mean	0.3230	0.10755
call working count	0.3113	0.12988

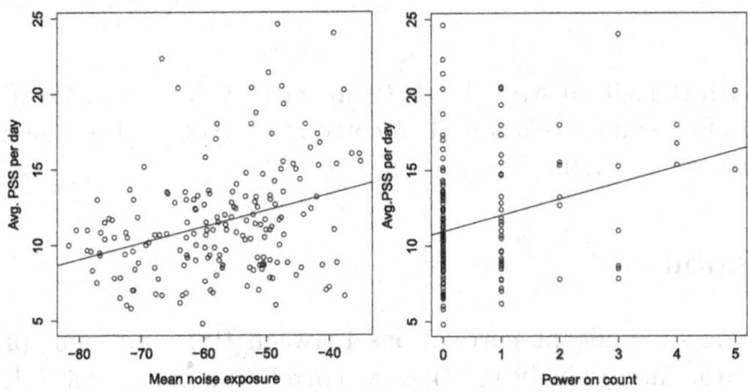

Fig. 3. Daily PSS averages and selected smartphone data

summarized in tables 6 and 7 for linear regression and random forests. The quality of the predicted stress levels (predicted by WEKA's machine learning algorithms) was evaluated in terms mean absolute error (MAE) to and Pearson

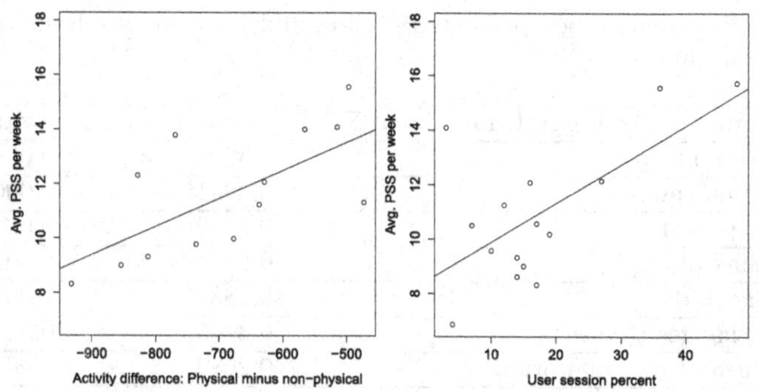

Fig. 4. Weekly PSS averages and selected smartphone data

Table 6. Results for predicting the PSS with linear regression

Dataset	Fold 5			Fold 10		
	MAE	cor	p-value	MAE	cor	p-value
PSS, single (510 instances)	3.7	0.08	0.07448	3.7	0.07	0.10840
PSS, daily average (182 instances)	3.5	0.14	0.06006	3.5	0.14	0.08606
Week (26 instances)	6.7	-0.15	0.45770	9.2	-0.19	0.34750

Table 7. Results for predicting the PSS with random forests

Dataset	Fold 5			Fold 10		
	MAE	cor	p-value	MAE	cor	p-value
PSS, single (510 instances)	3.3	0.15	0.00074	3.3	0.16	0.00043
PSS, daily average (182 instances)	2.4	0.4	1.02e-08	2.4	0.45	2.28e-10
Week (26 instances)	2.0	0.03	0.87530	1.9	0.16	0.42130

correlation with the actual stress levels (using cross validation). We also give the p-value of the Pearson correlation. The correlation plot for the most significant predictor is shown in Figure 5

6 Discussion

The results show significant correlations between PSS and smartphone usage and sensor data. Interestingly the highest correlation coefficient value is found with the weekly PSS average, which indicates that longer periods of high stress exposure could be identified better than short periods. However, the most significant result is not found for weekly average of the PSS, because too few data points are available. The most significant result is found for the daily averages of PSS and the average noise exposure (noisiness mean).

Overall we find significant correlations (p-value < 0.05) for single PSS, daily averaged PSS, and weekly averaged PSS.

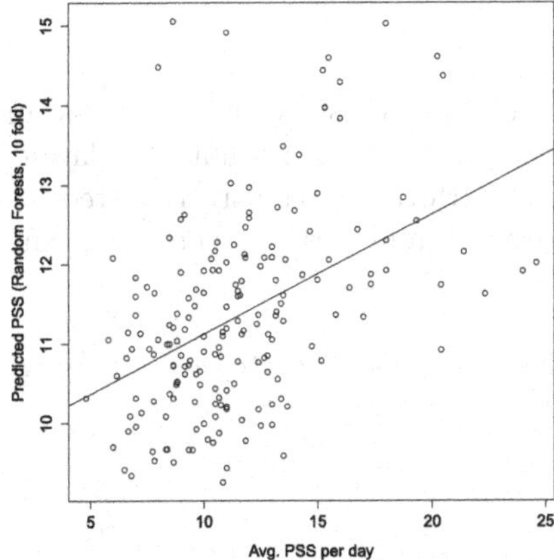

Fig. 5. Correlation Plot for most significant predictor

For a single PSS measurement, recent noise exposure (noisiness min) and social contacts (social count) are most significant influences. Noise exposure is also the most significant influence for the daily average of PSS values. The negative influence of noise and health has been previously reported [12, 18]. Social interactions and stress are discussed in [8] and proprieties of conversations (duration, frequency) have been found to correlate negatively with PSS [23].

The number of times a user has pressed the power on button of his smartphone also shows high correlation with the daily average of PSS (power on count).

For the weekly average of PSS correlation with active usage of the smartphone is most significant. Interestingly there is also a significant correlation with physical activity. This seems to contradict previous findings on activity and mental well-being. Physical activity and mental well-being have been researched in [9, 10, 14], assessing a positive influence of physical activity on mental well-being. However, we believe that our findings reflect the circumstance that students have to go the exams more often in the second week (walking has been counted as a physical activity).

The prediction results show potential, but are not yet very accurate. We believe a bigger data set will lead to better results and that predictions targeted for individual persons could perform better. Our results foster the hope that given sufficient training data automatic stress predictors are feasible.

Despite the small number of participants we achieve highly significant correlations, even as compared to larger studies [23]. Most probably this is due to the focus on stress and the associated evaluation of PSS several times a day.

In future work we plan to extend and improve our app, especially with respect to localization analysis, conversation analysis and sleep. We hope that further improvements in sensor data processing bring us closer to the goal of fully automatic stress prediction.

7 Conclusion

We have conducted an observational study on stress and smartphone usage and sensor data. Our results show significant correlations between stress and smartphone data and outperform previously reported significance levels. Our study encourages future work and further studies on smartphone based stress prediction.

Acknowledgments. This work was supported by the Austrian research promotion agency (FFG), project number 839076.

References

1. Adam, T.C., Epel, E.S.: Stress, eating and the reward system. Physiology & behavior **91**(4), 449–458 (2007)
2. Android: Google play services (August 2014). https://developer.android.com/google/play-services/index.html
3. Bardram, J.E., Frost, M., Szántó, K., Marcu, G.: The monarca self-assessment system: a persuasive personal monitoring system for bipolar patients. In: Proceedings of the 2nd ACM SIGHIT International Health Informatics Symposium, pp. 21–30. ACM (2012)
4. Bauer, G., Lukowicz, P.: Can smartphones detect stress-related changes in the behaviour of individuals? In: IEEE International Conference on Pervasive Computing and Communications Workshops, pp. 423–426. IEEE (2012)
5. Bogomolov, A., Lepri, B., Ferron, M., Pianesi, F., Pentland, A.S.: Daily stress recognition from mobile phone data, weather conditions and individual traits. In: Proceedings of the ACM International Conference on Multimedia, pp. 477–486. ACM (2014)
6. Burns, M.N., Begale, M., Duffecy, J., Gergle, D., Karr, C.J., Giangrande, E., Mohr, D.C.: Harnessing context sensing to develop a mobile intervention for depression. Journal of medical Internet research **13**(3) (2011)
7. Cohen, S., Kamarck, T., Mermelstein, R.: A global measure of perceived stress. Journal of health and social behavior, 385–396 (1983)
8. Coyne, J.C., Downey, G.: Social factors and psychopathology: Stress, social support, and coping processes. Annual review of psychology **42**(1), 401–425 (1991)
9. Dunn, A.L., Trivedi, M.H., O'Neal, H.A.: Physical activity dose-response effects on outcomes of depression and anxiety. Medicine & Science in Sports & Exercise **33**, S587–97 (2001)
10. Fox, K.R.: The influence of physical activity on mental well-being. Public health nutrition **2**(3a), 411–418 (1999)
11. Frost, M., Doryab, A., Faurholt-Jepsen, M., Kessing, L.V., Bardram, J.E.: Supporting disease insight through data analysis: refinements of the monarca self-assessment system. In: ACM international joint conference on Pervasive and ubiquitous computing, pp. 133–142. ACM (2013)
12. Haines, M.M., Stansfeld, S.A., Job, R.S., Berglund, B., Head, J.: Chronic aircraft noise exposure, stress responses, mental health and cognitive performance in school children. Psychological medicine **31**(02), 265–277 (2001)

13. Hall, M., Frank, E., Holmes, G., Pfahringer, B., Reutemann, P., Witten, I.H.: The weka data mining software: An update. SIGKDD Explor. Newsl. **11**(1), 10–18 (2009)
14. Hansmann, R., Hug, S.M., Seeland, K.: Restoration and stress relief through physical activities in forests and parks. Urban Forestry & Urban Greening **6**(4), 213–225 (2007)
15. Lathia, N., Pejovic, V., Rachuri, K.K., Mascolo, C., Musolesi, M., Rentfrow, P.J.: Smartphones for large-scale behavior change interventions. IEEE Pervasive Computing **3**, 66–73 (2013)
16. Lee Rodgers, J., Nicewander, W.A.: Thirteen ways to look at the correlation coefficient. The American Statistician **42**(1), 59–66 (1988)
17. Lu, H., Frauendorfer, D., Rabbi, M., Mast, M.S., Chittaranjan, G.T., Campbell, A.T., Gatica-Perez, D., Choudhury, T.: Stresssense: detecting stress in unconstrained acoustic environments using smartphones. In: Proceedings of the 2012 ACM Conference on Ubiquitous Computing, pp. 351–360. ACM (2012)
18. Matheson, M., Stansfeld, S., Haines, M., et al.: The effects of chronic aircraft noise exposure on children's cognition and health: 3 field studies. Noise and Health **5**(19), 31 (2003)
19. movisensXS: experience sampling for android (August 2014). https://xs.movisens.com
20. Sano, A., Picard, R.W.: Stress recognition using wearable sensors and mobile phones. In: Humaine Association Conference on Affective Computing and Intelligent Interaction, pp. 671–676. IEEE (2013)
21. Schwabe, L., Dickinson, A., Wolf, O.T.: Stress, habits, and drug addiction: a psychoneuroendocrinological perspective. Experimental and clinical psychopharmacology **19**(1), 53 (2011)
22. Talmon, J., Ammenwerth, E., Brender, J., de Keizer, N., Nykänen, P., Rigby, M.: STARE-HI: Statement on reporting of evaluation studies in health informatics. International Journal of Medical Informatics **78**(1), 1–9 (2009)
23. Wang, R., Chen, F., Chen, Z., Li, T., Harari, G., Tignor, S., Zhou, X., Ben-Zeev, D., Campbell, A.T.: Studentlife: assessing mental health, academic performance and behavioral trends of college students using smartphones. In: Proceedings of the 2014 ACM International Joint Conference on Pervasive and Ubiquitous Computing, pp. 3–14. ACM (2014)
24. Witten, I.H., Frank, E.: Data Mining: Practical machine learning tools and techniques. Morgan Kaufmann (2005)

Exploiting Implicit Item Relationships for Recommender Systems

Zhu Sun[1](✉), Guibing Guo[2], and Jie Zhang[1]

[1] School of Computer Engineering, Nanyang Technological University, Singapore, Singapore
{sunzhu,zhangj}@ntu.edu.sg

[2] School of Information Systems, Singapore Management University, Singapore, Singapore
gbguo@smu.edu.sg

Abstract. Collaborative filtering inherently suffers from the *data sparsity* and *cold start* problems. Social networks have been shown useful to help alleviate these issues. However, social connections may not be available in many real systems, whereas implicit item relationships are lack of study. In this paper, we propose a novel matrix factorization model by taking into account implicit item relationships. Specifically, we employ an adapted association rule technique to reveal implicit item relationships in terms of item-to-item and group-to-item associations, which are then used to regularize the generation of low-rank user- and item-feature matrices. Experimental results on four real-world datasets demonstrate the superiority of our proposed approach against other counterparts.

1 Introduction

Recommender systems have become a prevalent tool to help satisfy users' need of personalization over the exponentially increasing amount of information on Web 2.0. Collaborative filtering (CF) is a widely accepted recommendation technique built upon the concept of user (or item) similarity. That is, a user's preference can be inferred by aggregating the taste of similar users. However, CF inherently suffers from the *data sparsity* and *cold start* problems [1].

To address these issues, trust-aware recommender systems [1–5] are emerging with the advent of social networks. Many recently proposed approaches are designed upon the matrix factorization technique [6]. The intuition behind is that social friends share similar preferences and influence each other by recommending items. It has been shown that such additional side information among users is useful to deal with the concerned issues and thus to improve recommendation performance. However, the reliance on social connections may restrict the application of trust-based approaches to other scenarios where social networks are not available or supported. The potential noise and weaker social ties (than trust) in social networks can further hinder the generality of these approaches [7].

Similarly, the side information of items is also exploited for recommender systems, given its effectiveness in improving recommendation performance [6].

F. Ricci et al. (Eds.): UMAP 2015, LNCS 9146, pp. 252–264, 2015.
DOI: 10.1007/978-3-319-20267-9_21

The basic assumption is that users tend to have similar preferences towards a set of *associated* items. For example, a person is likely to enjoy the movie series of *The Lord of the Rings*, and possibly appreciates the associated background soundtracks. A number of approaches [8–10] have been proposed by making use of explicit item relationships such as category, genre, location, etc. However, similar as additional social information, items' side information may be unavailable for some real applications, or it is prohibitively expensive (or time-consuming) to extract the side information due to the large volume of items. Furthermore, only few works [6,11] have considered and demonstrated the value of implicit item relationships for recommender systems.

In this paper, we propose a novel matrix factorization model by exploiting association rule-based implicit item relationships, called *IIR*. It is developed merely based on user-item rating information, and requires no reliance of additional user or item side information. We ascribes this feature to the essential difference from other literature studies. Specifically, we employ an adapted associate rule technique to reveal the implicit item relationships in the form of item-to-item and group-to-item associations, which are then used to regularize the generation of low-rank user- and item-feature matrices in the proposed IIR model. In addition, we design four different strategies to select the most reliable item associations to train the model. Experimental results on four real-world datasets show that our approach achieves superior performance against other counterparts, and that group-to-item associations are more effective than item-to-item associations.

2 Related Work

Additional side information is often incorporated in collaborative filtering to improve recommendation performance. We give a brief overview below regarding such kind of recommendation approaches from the perspectives of users and items, respectively. First, a notable research field is the trust-aware recommender systems which take into account additional user relationships. Many approaches have been proposed to date. Ma et al. [2] propose the *RSTE* approach by linearly combining a basic matrix factorization model and a trust-based neighborhood approach. The same authors later find that using social information as a regularizer works better than using it to decompose the user-item rating matrix [4]. This finding is endorsed by Jamali and Ester [3] where a user's latent feature vector is regularized by those of her trusted users. Therefore, to incorporate item relationships in the IIR model, we follow the same rule to utilize item relationships to regularize the generation of items' latent feature vectors. More recent works consider more aspects of social trust such as implicit trust influence [5,7], etc. However, trust-based approaches may fail to work if being applied to the situations where social networks are not built-in or connected. Our work is intended for a more general case where only user-item ratings exist.

Second, some researchers also attempt to make use of item relationships to enhance recommender systems. In this paper, we classify two kinds of item relationships: *explicit* and *implicit*. Typical examples of explicit item relationships include items' extrinsic properties: category, location and tag, just to name a few. For example, Hu et al. [10] contend that the quality of a business shop has some implicit indication on that of other shops in a certain geographical neighborhood. Shi et al. [9] show that tags can be used to bridge cross-domain knowledge to provide better recommendation. Implicit item relationships refer to the relationships that cannot be explicitly observed between items. A classic example is that a man buying diaper is likely to buy beer as well, though the diaper and beer are distinct items. Kim and Kim [8] apply association rule mining techniques to reveal multi-level item associations in the light of item categories. Our approach also adopts association rule to identify implicit item relationships, but differs in that we do not classify item associations to multiple levels in terms of category. Instead, we consider simple rules (one item indicating another, or item-to-item) and then generalize to group-to-item (a group of items indicating another item) associations. Wang et al. [11] identify item relationships using a similarity measure, and claim that an item's feature vector can be influenced by those of other similar items. However, they build the item-item similarity matrix with some ad-hoc settings when item similarity equals 0 or uncomputable. Another issue is that their model is very time-consuming in training and thus prevents from being applied to large-scale datasets. In this paper, we are more interested in association rule-based item relationships rather than item similarity, the explanation of which is deferred to Section 3.2.

3 Recommendation with Implicit Item Relationships

In this section, we first introduce the IIR recommendation model, and then elaborate how item-to-item associations can be identified by an adapted association rule technique, followed by the generalization to group-to-item associations.

3.1 The IIR Model

Matrix factorization (MF) techniques have been widely applied in recommender systems. The basic assumption is that a user's preference can be characterized by a few number of latent features. In particular, MF models [6] factorize the user-item rating matrix $R \in \mathbb{R}^{m \times n}$ into two low-rank user-feature $U \in \mathbb{R}^{m \times d}$ and item-feature $V \in \mathbb{R}^{n \times d}$ matrices, where m, n are the number of users and items, respectively; and $d \ll \min(m, n)$ is the number of latent features. The rating matrix R is very sparse due to the fact that a user generally only rates a small portion of items. Let $r_{u,i}$ be a rating given by user u on item i, and $\hat{r}_{u,j}$ be a rating prediction for user u on a target item j. We preserve symbols u, v, p for users, and i, j, k for items. The rating prediction $\hat{r}_{u,j}$ can be estimated by the inner product of user-specific feature vector U_u and item-specific feature vector V_j, given by:

$$\hat{r}_{u,j} = U_u^\top V_j,$$

where the matrices U and V can be learned by minimizing the differences between the prediction and the ground truth over all the users and items.

In this paper, we propose the IIR model which focuses on the incorporation of implicit item relationships in order to better factorize the rating matrix R. Assume that two items j, k are implicitly associated with the strength of $s_{j,k}$. In this case, we contend that the two items should be close to each other in terms of feature vectors. Inspired by the usage of social relationships in [4], we devise the implicit item relationships as a regularizer to adjust the decomposition of rating matrix R. Specifically, the IIR model is given as follows.

$$\mathcal{L}=\frac{1}{2}\sum_{u=1}^{m}\sum_{j=1}^{n}I_{u,j}(r_{u,j}-\hat{r}_{u,j})^2+\frac{\alpha}{2}\sum_{j=1}^{n}\sum_{k\in A_j}s_{k,j}\|V_j-V_k\|_F^2+\frac{\lambda_u}{2}\|U\|_F^2+\frac{\lambda_v}{2}\|V\|_F^2 \quad (1)$$

where $I_{u,j}$ is an indicator function that equals 1 if user u rated item j and equals 0 otherwise; $\alpha > 0$ is a regularization parameter to control the importance of regularization by implicit item relationships; $s_{k,j}$ indicates the extent to which item k is associated with item j; A_j is a set of reliable association rules for item j; $\|\cdot\|_F$ is the Frobenius norm; and λ_u, λ_v are regularization parameters to avoid over-fitting. Suppose that we have identified two implicit item relationships from i to j and from k to j, the IIR model will add the following two regularizers:

$$s_{i,j} \parallel V_j - V_i \parallel_F^2 \quad \text{and} \quad s_{k,j} \parallel V_j - V_k \parallel_F^2$$

In other words, the IIR model can indirectly minimize the differences between the feature vectors of related items i and k to some extent. We treat it as an advantage of our model to capture both the influence of direct and indirect implicit item relationships.

Equation 1 indicates that it is necessary for our model to effectively identify the set of item associations A_j and the corresponding strength with other items $s_{k,j}$. We proceed to describe how to achieve them in the next subsection.

3.2 Mining Implicit Item Relationships

Item Similarity. A straightforward method to define implicit item relationships is item similarity. If many users like both items, it indicates that the two items have some similarity in common. This intuition underpins the well-known item-based collaborative filtering. The most popular similarity measures are the Pearson correlation coefficient (PCC) and cosine similarity (COS). However, with the following concerns, we believe that item similarity measures are not suitable for our work. First, a key characteristic of similarity measures is symmetry, i.e., $s_{j,k} = s_{k,j}$. In our case, we would like to distinguish the influence of items j to k from that of items k to j. For example, a man buying beer may not buy diaper, though a man buying diaper is likely to buy beer. Second, the computation of similarity measures is generally based on the overlapping ratings between two rating vectors. However, we argue that the non-overlapping ratings may help define the differences between the two items. Third, PCC and COS may produce misleading similarity measurements as pointed out by Guo et al. [12], especially when the size of overlapping ratings is small. Lastly, similarity measures often consider the correlation between two individual items, whereas we intend to measure more generalized correlations between a group of items and a single item (i.e., group-to-item) other than item-to-item implicit relationships.

Item-to-Item Associations. We define the implicit item relationships as the item associations between a target item and another item or a set of other items. This definition directs us to adopt association rule techniques to measure item associations. The association rule mining is to search the associated item pairs that often co-occur in transaction events. Assume that item i appears frequently together with item j, and an association rule can then be denoted by $l_{i,j} : i \to j$. Note that the occurrence of item j may not frequently indicate the occurrence of item i, i.e., the association is asymmetric as we demand. Generally, an association rule is valid only if its *support* and *confidence* (indicating the usefulness and certainty) are greater than a user-specified minimum support (denoted by *minSup*) and confidence (denoted by *minCon*) thresholds, respectively.

By regarding the rating matrix as a user-item transaction matrix, we can apply association rules to reveal implicit relationships among items. Generally, we need to determine proper values for thresholds *minSup* and *minCon*. The settings are not trivial considering that: (1) higher thresholds will decrease the available number of association rules due to the sparseness of rating matrix; and (2) lower thresholds will result in too many association rules, which may significantly slow the model training and take into account many unreliable association rules. Both issues can greatly deteriorate recommendation performance. Instead of empirically tuning the two parameters, we define a new measure *reliability* as the extent to which a mined association rule is reliable in terms of both support and confidence measures. The reliability of an association rule $l_{i,j}$ is defined as:

$$\text{reliability}(l_{i,j}) = \frac{\text{support}(l_{i,j})}{\text{support}(l_{i,j}) + C} * \text{confidence}(l_{i,j}), \tag{2}$$

where $\text{support}(l_{i,j})$ and $\text{confidence}(l_{i,j})$ are the support and confidence measures of an association rule $l_{i,j}$, respectively; and C is a constant to adapt the importance of association rule support. This formulation produces high reliability only if both support and confidence values are high. Then, we sort all the association rules in the descending order of computed reliability values, and select the top-K most reliable association rules to form the association set A_j for target item j.

Group-to-Item Associations. A natural generalization to item-to-item associations is group-to-item associations. That is, we further consider whether a set of items can be associated with a specific item. We represent such kind of association rules as $l_{G,j} : G \to j$, where G denotes a set of associated items. Similarly, this kind of association rules can be also identified by applying association rule techniques as well as the computation of association rule reliability. Hence, the objective function in Equation 1 can be rewritten as follows:

$$\mathcal{L} = \frac{1}{2}\sum_{u=1}^{m}\sum_{j=1}^{n} I_{u,j}(r_{u,j} - \hat{r}_{u,j})^2 + \frac{\alpha}{2}\sum_{j=1}^{n}\sum_{G\in A_j} s_{G,j}\|V_j - |G|^{-0.5}\sum_{k\in G} V_k\|_F^2 + \frac{\lambda_u}{2}\|U\|_F^2 + \frac{\lambda_v}{2}\|V\|_F^2, \tag{3}$$

where $s_{G,j}$ is the strength (i.e., reliability) of association rule $l_{G,j}$. Note that we represent the characteristic of a group G by the average of all group items' feature vectors. In other words, we constrain that a target item's feature vector should be close to the majority of its associated group.

For simplicity, hereafter we only consider group-to-item associations with group size 2, i.e., $|G| = 2$.[1] This is due to that, $|G| = 0$ indicates no items are associated with item j while $|G| = 1$ implies that group-to-item associations are equivalent with item-to-item associations. Now that there are two kinds of item association rules, we propose the following four strategies to select the association neighborhood of item j, i.e., A_j.

Half: select half a number of group-to-item and the other half a number of item-to-item association rules separately as the baseline strategy.

Mix: select the top-K most reliable association rules after sorting all kinds of association rules in term of reliability values.

Group: select the top-K most reliable group-to-item association rules only, and ignore all item-to-item association rules.

Group+: select the top-K most reliable group-to-item association rules. In case of insufficient rules, we select item-to-item association rules to complement.

Note that we do not incorporate the strategy of *selecting item-to-item association rules only* by setting $|G| = 1$. The reason is that, by definition the strength of item-to-item association rules is generally weaker than that of group-to-item association rules. Hence, incorporating weaker rules will have smaller effect in regularizing the objective function, and result in less-performing recommendations. The experimental results on real-world datasets have also confirmed our intuition (see Section 4.2).

3.3 Model Learning

The stochastic gradient descent (SGD) method is widely used to achieve a local minimum of the objective function given by Equation 3. Specifically, the SGD update rules for variables U_u and V_j of the IIR[2] model are given as follows.

[1] We empirically noted that groups with size greater than 2 did not provide visibly better performance or even provide worse performance sometimes. We are aware that the observed effect may not be the same on other datasets we did not use.

[2] Source code is included in the Librec library at www.librec.net.

Table 1. Statistics of the used datasets

Dataset	#Users	#Items	#Ratings	Sparsity
FilmTrust	1058	2071	35,497	98.86%
MoiveLens	943	1682	100,000	93.70%
Ciao	8000	9749	38,591	99.95%
Epinions	7941	10,000	107,552	99.86%

$$\frac{\partial \mathcal{L}}{\partial U_u} = \sum_{j=1}^{n} I_{u,j}(g(U_u^\top V_j) - r_{u,j})g'(U_u^\top V_j)V_j + \lambda_u U_u,$$

$$\frac{\partial \mathcal{L}}{\partial V_j} = \sum_{i=1}^{m} I_{u,j}(g(U_u^\top V_j) - r_{u,j})g'(U_u^\top V_j)U_u + \lambda_v V_j$$

$$+ \alpha \sum_{G \in A_j} s_{G,j}\Big(V_j - |G|^{-0.5} \sum_{i \in G} V_i\Big) - \alpha \sum_{\substack{M \in A_k, \\ j \in M}} \frac{s_{M,k}}{\sqrt{|M|}}\Big(V_k - |M|^{-0.5} \sum_{g \in M} V_g\Big),$$

where $g(x) = 1/(1 + exp(-x))$ is a logistic function used to bound the value rang of rating prediction into $[0, 1]$, and $g'(x)$ is the derivative of function $g(x)$. To be consistent, we adopt the max-min normalization approach to convert the observed ratings to the same value range $[0, 1]$.

4 Experiments and Results

4.1 Experimental Setup

Datasets. Four real-world datasets are used in our experiments, namely FilmTrust[3], MoiveLens[4], Ciao[3] and Epinions[5]. FilmTrust is a movie sharing website that allows users to assign numerical ratings (scaled from 0.5 to 4.0 with step 0.5) to movies. MoiveLens is a personalized movie recommendation website, where users can rate movies with integers from 1 to 5. The data set has been preprocessed such that each user has rated at least 20 items. Both Ciao and Epinions are product review sites, where consumers can review various products with ratings from 1 to 5 stars. The statistics of our datasets is presented in Table 1.

Comparison Methods. We compare our **IIR** model with the following methods: (1) **PMF** [13] is a basic matrix factorization method without any additional side information. (2) **IR-P** [11] is the item relationship-based approach where PCC is used to compute item similarity.[6] For fair comparison, we remove the influence of social networks from the original model. (3) **IR-I** is a substitute of IR-P by replacing PCC with item-to-item associations. (4) **IIR-C** is a variant

[3] http://www.librec.net/datasets.html
[4] http://www.cs.umn.edu/Research/GroupLens
[5] http://www.trustlet.org/wiki/Epinions
[6] We convert the original PCC value from [-1,1] to [0,1] by function $f(x) = (x + 1)/2$.

of the IIR model which adopts COS to identify implicit item relationships. (5) **IIR-I** is our approach merely based on item-to-item relationships. (6) **IIR-G** is our approach with the incorporation of group-to-item relationships.

Evaluation Metrics. We perform 5-fold cross validation in our experiments. Specifically, we randomly split each dataset into five folds and in each iteration four folds are used as the training set and the remaining fold as the test set. All folds will be tested, and the average results are reported as the final performance. Predictive performance is evaluated by two widely used measures: the mean absolute error (MAE) and root mean square error (RMSE), defined by:

$$\text{MAE} = \frac{\sum_{u,j} |r_{u,j} - \hat{r}_{u,j}|}{N}, \qquad \text{RMSE} = \sqrt{\frac{\sum_{u,j}(r_{u,j} - \hat{r}_{u,j})^2}{N}}$$

where N is the number of test ratings. Smaller MAE and RMSE values imply better predictive accuracy.

Parameter Settings. The number of latent features d is selected in $\{5, 10, 20, 50\}$. We empirically find that the following parameter settings can help achieve the best performance for each comparison method. For **IR-P** and **IR-I**, the importance of item relationship-based rating prediction is set $0.005, 0.01, 0.1, 0.005$ corresponding to FilmTrust, MovieLens, Ciao and Epinions, respectively.[7] All these item relationship-based approaches reach the best performance when the size of association neighborhood is set 50, i.e., $K = 50$. For all the methods, we apply grid search in $\{0.00001, 0.0001, 0.001, 0.01, 0.1\}$ for regularization parameters λ_u, λ_v, and in $\{0.0001, 0.001, 0.01\}$ for the learning rate.

4.2 Results and Analysis

Effect of Parameters C and K. In our approach, C controls the importance of association rule support. We apply a grid search in {0,10,20,50,100,150,200} to find the optimal setting for parameter C. The results are shown in Figure 1, where the best settings are around 100.[8] To select the top-K most reliable association neighbors for each item j (see Equation 3), we tune the value of K from 0 to 100 stepping by 10, where $K = 0$ indicates that no implicit item relationships are considered, i.e., our model is degrading to the basic matrix factorization model. The performance is illustrated in Figure 2.[8] The results show that adding implicit item relationships can help improve predictive performance ($K > 0$), but further improvements tend to be negligible when $K > 50$ across all the datasets. In other words, the top-50 association rules have the most important influence. For the association rules after that, their strength of associations with the target item may be too small to have a visible impact.

[7] Due to space limitation, we do not present the results of tuning this parameter.

[8] For simplicity, we only present the results when $d = 5$, and similar trends are observed on other settings including d values and IIR variants.

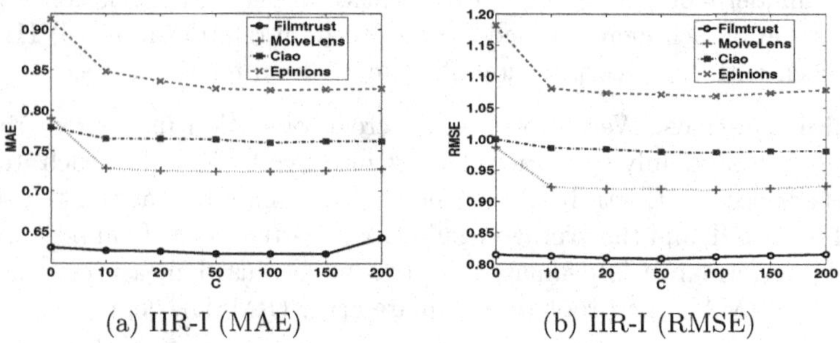

(a) IIR-I (MAE) (b) IIR-I (RMSE)

Fig. 1. The effect of parameter C in our approaches IIR-I ($d = 5$)

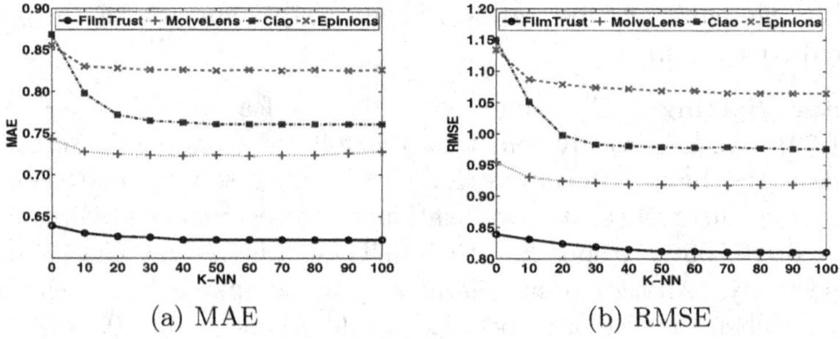

(a) MAE (b) RMSE

Fig. 2. The effect of number of association rules K in our approach IIR-I ($d = 5$)

Effect of Parameter α. The parameter α in Equation 3 controls the importance of item relationship regularization. We apply a grid search in {0.0001,0.001,0.01, 0.1,0.2,0.5,1.0} to find the optimal setting for parameter α. The results are plotted in Figure 3, where the best settings for parameter α are around 0.5 on the Epinions dataset and $0.1 \sim 0.2$ on the other datasets. Note that for the IIR-G method, similar trends are obtained when any one of the four strategies is adopted to select group-to-item association rules (see Section 3.2).

Effect of Four Strategies. We have identified four different association rule selection strategies for our approach IIR-G in Section 3.2, namely Half, Mix, Group and Group+. Table 2 summarizes the performance obtained by applying the four strategies to all the datasets and across the different number of latent features d. The results are consistent across all the cases, and demonstrate that (1) Half reaches the poorest performance; (2) Group works better than Mix; and (3) Group+ achieves the best performance. These results confirm our previous claim, that is, the strength of group-to-item associations is stronger than that of item-to-item associations. When only half of group-to-item associations are used, the performance is the worst; as more group-to-item associations are selected (by Mix, Group and Group+), the performance is improved accordingly. It suggests

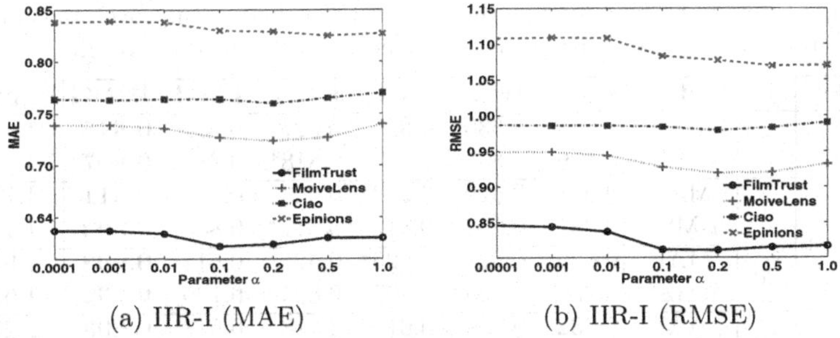

(a) IIR-I (MAE) (b) IIR-I (RMSE)

Fig. 3. The effect of regularization parameter α in our approaches IIR-I

Table 2. The effect of four strategies to select association rules for our approach IIR-G

d	Metrics	FilmTrust				MovieLens			
		Half	Mix	Group	Group+	Half	Mix	Group	Group+
5	MAE	0.621	0.620	0.619	**0.615**	0.724	0.721	0.721	**0.718**
	RMSE	0.809	0.810	0.809	**0.807**	0.914	0.916	0.914	**0.911**
10	MAE	0.615	0.614	0.614	**0.611**	0.720	0.717	0.716	**0.712**
	RMSE	0.804	0.805	0.804	**0.802**	0.909	0.908	0.907	**0.903**
20	MAE	0.611	0.611	0.610	**0.608**	0.718	0.714	0.714	**0.707**
	RMSE	0.798	0.800	0.796	**0.792**	0.906	0.905	0.904	**0.899**
50	MAE	0.610	0.606	0.605	**0.603**	0.716	0.713	0.711	**0.703**
	RMSE	0.794	0.792	0.790	**0.789**	0.904	0.902	0.901	**0.896**

d	Metrics	Ciao				Epinions			
		Half	Mix	Group	Group+	Half	Mix	Group	Group+
5	MAE	0.757	0.754	0.754	**0.750**	0.827	0.824	0.823	**0.820**
	RMSE	0.977	0.976	0.977	**0.969**	1.067	1.066	1.064	**1.063**
10	MAE	0.746	0.746	0.744	**0.741**	0.826	0.823	0.821	**0.817**
	RMSE	0.968	0.970	0.962	**0.960**	1.064	1.063	1.058	**1.056**
20	MAE	0.738	0.739	0.738	**0.732**	0.823	0.820	0.817	**0.816**
	RMSE	0.959	0.960	0.957	**0.952**	1.059	1.056	1.056	**1.053**
50	MAE	0.731	0.731	0.730	**0.728**	0.819	0.816	0.815	**0.812**
	RMSE	0.954	0.956	0.950	**0.946**	1.054	1.050	1.050	**1.050**

that we should always first select stronger group-to-item associations, and adopt relatively weaker associations only if stronger ones do not suffice.

Comparison with Other Methods. Table 3 presents the results of all comparison methods on the four real-world datasets, where the best performance is highlighted in bold and the second best performance among the first four methods[9] is denoted by * symbol. A number of interesting observations can be noted from the present results. First, all the methods exploiting item relationships perform better than the basic PMF method, indicating the usefulness of incor-

[9] We tend to treat IIR-C as a baseline as it uses item similarity-based rather than association rule-based implicit item relationships.

Table 3. The experimental results on the four datasets, where * indicates the best performance among the first four methods, and the column "Improve" indicates the relative improvements that our approaches achieve relative to the * results.

Dataset	d	Metrics	PMF	IR-P	IR-I	IIR-C	IIR-I	IIR-G	Improve
FilmTrust	5	MAE	0.639	0.630	0.627	0.627*	0.622	**0.615**	1.91%
		RMSE	0.839	0.835	0.825	0.818*	0.812	**0.807**	1.34%
	10	MAE	0.638	0.629	0.622*	0.623	0.617	**0.611**	1.77%
		RMSE	0.837	0.832	0.812	0.811*	0.805	**0.802**	1.11%
	20	MAE	0.636	0.625	0.620*	0.621	0.613	**0.608**	1.94%
		RMSE	0.830	0.826	0.807	0.805*	0.799	**0.792**	1.61%
	50	MAE	0.632	0.620	0.617*	0.618	0.618	**0.603**	2.27%
		RMSE	0.824	0.814	0.798*	0.798	0.790	**0.789**	1.13%
MoiveLens	5	MAE	0.743	0.737	0.735	0.734*	0.724	**0.718**	2.18%
		RMSE	0.954	0.951	0.947	0.930*	0.919	**0.911**	2.04%
	10	MAE	0.742	0.737	0.730*	0.732	0.720	**0.712**	2.47%
		RMSE	0.944	0.946	0.935	0.927*	0.913	**0.903**	2.59%
	20	MAE	0.735	0.728	0.725*	0.726	0.715	**0.707**	2.48%
		RMSE	0.935	0.931	0.924*	0.925	0.906	**0.899**	2.71%
	50	MAE	0.733	0.725	0.723*	0.724	0.713	**0.703**	2.77%
		RMSE	0.921	0.924	0.919	0.916*	0.903	**0.896**	2.18%
Ciao	5	MAE	0.868	0.788	0.779	0.770*	0.760	**0.750**	2.60%
		RMSE	1.150	1.101	1.081	0.991*	0.979	**0.969**	2.22%
	10	MAE	0.832	0.785	0.775	0.766*	0.749	**0.741**	3.26%
		RMSE	1.134	1.096	1.078	0.984*	0.970	**0.960**	2.44%
	20	MAE	0.828	0.770	0.765	0.760*	0.740	**0.732**	3.68%
		RMSE	1.126	1.074	1.060	0.978*	0.959	**0.952**	2.66%
	50	MAE	0.823	0.769	0.762	0.754*	0.732	**0.728**	3.45%
		RMSE	1.124	1.067	1.050	0.972*	0.952	**0.946**	2.67%
Epinions	5	MAE	0.855	0.845	0.838	0.836*	0.825	**0.820**	1.91%
		RMSE	1.134	1.130	1.123	1.090*	1.069	**1.063**	2.48%
	10	MAE	0.848	0.843	0.833	0.833*	0.824	**0.817**	1.92%
		RMSE	1.128	1.120	1.112	1.082*	1.063	**1.056**	2.40%
	20	MAE	0.846	0.836	0.826*	0.830	0.822	**0.816**	1.21%
		RMSE	1.117	1.094	1.090	1.075*	1.058	**1.053**	2.05%
	50	MAE	0.839	0.826	0.818*	0.828	0.816	**0.812**	0.73%
		RMSE	1.106	1.070	1.064*	1.065	1.051	**1.050**	1.32%

porating item relationships for recommender systems. Second, IR-I consistently obtains lower values of MAE and RMSE than IR-P, implying that item-to-item associations are more effective than item similarity computed by similarity measures. This is further confirmed by the fact that IIR-I outperforms IIR-C. In Section 3.2, we explained in detail why item similarity may not be suitable to reveal implicit item relationships. Third, among the three variants of the IIR model, IIR-G achieves the best performance from which we may conclude that: group-to-item associations are stronger than item-to-item associations which are then preferred to similarity-based item associations. Last, our approach IIR-G reaches the superior performance to the other counterparts, and the percentages of improvements relative to other baselines are put to the last column in Table 3. On the average, the percentages of relative improvements across different number of latent features are summarized as follows in terms of (MAE, RMSE) pair: (1.97%, 1.30%) on FilmTrust, (2.48%, 2.38%) on MovieLens, (3.25%, 2.50%) on Ciao, (1.44%, 2.06%) on Epinions and (2.29%, 2.06%) over all the datasets. Koren [6] has pointed out that even small improvements in predictive accuracy can have great impact on real applications. Hence, we claim that our approach obtains important improvements by exploiting implicit item relationships.

5 Conclusion and Future Work

This paper proposed a novel matrix factorization model that incorporated the influence of implicit item relationships for recommender systems. We introduced an adapted association rule technique to reveal implicit item relationships, and justified that item similarity may not be a good measure for implicit item relationships. A new measure *reliability* of an association rule was defined to help sort and select item associations. We investigated not only item-to-item associations but also generalized group-to-item associations. Four strategies were designed to choose the most reliable set of association rules, which were used to regularize the generation of low-rank user- and item-feature matrices. Empirical results on four real-world datasets demonstrated that our approach gained important improvements relative to other comparison methods. For future work, we intend to incorporate both explicit and implicit item relationships to further improve recommendation performance.

References

1. Guo, G., Zhang, J., Thalmann, D.: A simple but effective method to incorporate trusted neighbors in recommender systems. In: Masthoff, J., Mobasher, B., Desmarais, M.C., Nkambou, R. (eds.) UMAP 2012. LNCS, vol. 7379, pp. 114–125. Springer, Heidelberg (2012)
2. Ma, H., King, I., Lyu, M.: Learning to recommend with social trust ensemble. In: Proceedings of the 32nd International ACM SIGIR Conference on Research and Development in Information Retrieval (SIGIR), pp. 203–210 (2009)
3. Jamali, M., Ester, M.: A matrix factorization technique with trust propagation for recommendation in social networks. In: Proceedings of the 4th ACM Conference on Recommender Systems (RecSys), pp. 135–142 (2010)
4. Ma, H., Zhou, D., Liu, C., Lyu, M., King, I.: Recommender systems with social regularization. In: Proceedings of the 4th ACM International Conference on Web Search and Data Mining (WSDM), pp. 287–296 (2011)
5. Yang, B., Lei, Y., Liu, D., Liu, J.: Social collaborative filtering by trust. In: Proceedings of the 23rd International Joint Conference on Artificial Intelligence (IJCAI), pp. 2747–2753 (2013)
6. Koren, Y.: Factorization meets the neighborhood: a multifaceted collaborative filtering model. In: Proceedings of the 14th ACM SIGKDD International Conference on Knowledge Discovery and Data Mining (KDD), pp. 426–434 (2008)

7. Guo, G., Zhang, J., Yorke-Smith, N.: Trustsvd: Collaborative filtering with both the explicit and implicit influence of user trust and of item ratings. In: Proceedings of the 29th AAAI Conference on Artificial Intelligence (AAAI) (2015)
8. Kim, C., Kim, J.: A recommendation algorithm using multi-level association rules. In: Proceedings of 2003 IEEE/WIC International Conference on Web Intelligence (WI), pp. 524–527 (2003)
9. Shi, Y., Larson, M., Hanjalic, A.: Tags as bridges between domains: improving recommendation with tag-induced cross-domain collaborative filtering. In: Konstan, J.A., Conejo, R., Marzo, J.L., Oliver, N. (eds.) UMAP 2011. LNCS, vol. 6787, pp. 305–316. Springer, Heidelberg (2011)
10. Hu, L., Sun, A., Liu, Y.: Your neighbors affect your ratings: on geographical neighborhood influence to rating prediction. In: Proceedings of the 37th International ACM SIGIR Conference on Research & Development in Information Retrieval (SIGIR), pp. 345–354 (2014)
11. Wang, D., Ma, J., Lian, T., L., G.: Recommendation based on weighted social trusts and item relationships. In: Proceedings of the 29th Annual ACM Symposium on Applied Computing (SAC), pp. 2000–2005 (2014)
12. Guo, G., Zhang, J., Yorke-Smith, N.: A novel Bayesian similarity measure for recommender systems. In: Proceedings of the 23rd International Joint Conference on Artificial Intelligence (IJCAI), pp. 2619–2625 (2013)
13. Salakhutdinov, R., Mnih, A.: Probabilistic matrix factorization. Advances in Neural Information Processing Systems (NIPS) **20**, 1257–1264 (2008)

The Mars and Venus Effect: The Influence of User Gender on the Effectiveness of Adaptive Task Support

Alexandria Katarina Vail[1](✉), Kristy Elizabeth Boyer[1], Eric N. Wiebe[2], and James C. Lester[1]

[1] Department of Computer Science, North Carolina State University, Raleigh, NC, USA
{akvail,keboyer,lester}@ncsu.edu
[2] Department of STEM Education, North Carolina State University, Raleigh, NC, USA
wiebe@ncsu.edu

Abstract. Providing adaptive support to users engaged in learning tasks is the central focus of intelligent tutoring systems. There is evidence that female and male users may benefit differently from adaptive support, yet it is not understood how to most effectively adapt task support to gender. This paper reports on a study with four versions of an intelligent tutoring system for introductory computer programming offering different levels of cognitive (conceptual and problem-solving) and affective (motivational and engagement) support. The results show that female users reported significantly more engagement and less frustration with the affective support system than with other versions. In a human tutorial dialogue condition used for comparison, a consistent difference was observed between females and males. These results suggest the presence of the *Mars and Venus Effect*, a systematic difference in how female and male users benefit from cognitive and affective adaptive support. The findings point toward design principles to guide the development of gender-adaptive intelligent tutoring systems.

Keywords: Gender effects · Adaptive support · Intelligent tutoring systems · Affect · Engagement · Frustration

1 Introduction

Effective adaptation to users during problem solving and learning is a long-standing goal of the user modeling community [17,22,30]. Adaptive learning environments, specifically intelligent tutoring systems (ITSs), are inspired by the adaptation of human tutors to student learners [5,12]. This intelligent adaptation often focuses on knowledge and skill, relying on user modeling techniques such as knowledge tracing [17], constraint-based modeling [22], or reinforcement learning for strategies [11]. These models, which differentiate users primarily by

F. Ricci et al. (Eds.): UMAP 2015, LNCS 9146, pp. 265–276, 2015.
DOI: 10.1007/978-3-319-20267-9_22

the user-system interactions that unfold rather than by any characteristics of the user, have been proven highly effective not only for ITSs but more broadly within user modeling, e.g., detecting the manner in which learners interact with online content [6], modeling engagement with social games [7], delivering tailored content based on historical data [28], and estimating how much a student learns while browsing online materials [25].

While task characteristics can inform models of user interaction, recent findings suggest that characteristics of the *person* are more indicative of user behavior than characteristics of the *task* [23]. There is a growing body of evidence suggesting that individual characteristics such as personality profile [16,29], cognitive processing ability [4], and level of expertise [13] influence the effectiveness of adaptive support.

Of all the learner characteristics that are known to influence the effectiveness of adaptive support, *gender* is one of the most widely recognized. Female and male students tend to differ in their receptiveness to feedback [1,26], and although users of both genders have been observed to display strong affective responses to adaptive support, female students may particularly benefit from motivational scaffolding [10].

This paper examines the hypothesis that male and female students benefit most fully from different types of adaptive support. We focus on the crucial open question of how to most effectively balance *cognitive* support (pertaining to knowledge and problem solving) with *affective* support (pertaining to motivation, self-confidence, and engagement) [14,27]. Design principles for cognitive and affective feedback have begun to emerge from the literature. For example, in addition to the effectiveness of task-based scaffolding mentioned above, there is evidence that adapting to affective states such as uncertainty [11] and confusion [16] leads to more effective tutoring. However, the results to date do not clearly provide a comprehensive set of design principles for gender-adapted problem-solving support.

Using an intelligent tutoring system that supports introductory computer programming, JavaTutor [21,29], we conducted a study to examine the advantages and disadvantages of different forms of adaptive support for female and male students. Our study used four versions of JavaTutor: the *Baseline* version provided a problem-solving environment with learning tasks that built progressively upon each other, and the other three versions provided the same progressive learning tasks with additional adaptive support. The *Cognitive* version provided problem-solving feedback and hints, the *Affective* version provided motivational and engagement support, and the *Cognitive-Affective* version provided integrated cognitive and affective support. Results show that female and male users diverge in their responses to the different forms of support, particularly with respect to the important outcomes of frustration and engagement (discussed in detail in Section 2). We also compare these human-ITS conditions with a human-human tutorial dialogue condition from previously collected data within the same learning environment. The differences that emerge among these conditions by gender, taken in concert with findings from previous studies, reveal the *Mars and Venus Effect*, in which female and male users benefit differently from cognitive and affective adaptive support. The findings point toward design principles to improve future user-adaptive intelligent tutoring systems.

2 Related Work

This work builds upon related work on a body of empirical findings on gender and adaptive support during learning as well as on cognitive and affective support.

2.1 Gender and Adaptive Support for Learning

Previous studies have demonstrated that male and female students may benefit differently from adaptive support strategies. In a study with a mathematics tutoring system, female students tended to accept more of the tutor's feedback, spend more time referencing available learning aids, and engage in less gaming of the system than male students, especially when provided with an embodied tutorial agent [1]. Female students were also more engaged when provided with motivational scaffolding [2]. In studies with human tutors that work with mostly young adult learners in college, female students engaged longer and in more content-filled discussion with the tutor than their male counterparts [8,26]. A study with learning companions found that female students' self-efficacy improved when the agent provided motivational scaffolding with corresponding nonverbal behaviors. Male students in that study were particularly frustrated when the agent displayed discordant verbal and nonverbal behaviors [10]. These studies have spanned age groups and reveal important conditions in which gender may influence the perception and effectiveness of support.

2.2 Cognitive and Affective Goals

It is widely recognized that the most effective adaptations take into account both cognitive and affective considerations of learners; yet, an inverse relationship has sometimes been observed between these considerations. In one study within a middle school group, as students became more comfortable with the task (an affectively positive outcome), the students learned less content (a cognitively negative outcome) [27]. In another study, the more frustrated a student became with the complexity of the task, the higher the learning gain displayed at the end of the activity [18].

When university students were offered content feedback, progress feedback, both, or neither, the amount of content feedback was directly correlated with the student's learning gain at the end of the session; further, these students tended to display higher levels of frustration and lower levels of engagement [20]. In another study with university students, more tutor encouragement and praise were associated with increased student self-efficacy but lower overall learning [9]. Additionally, students who were offered purely cognitive feedback had the highest learning gains, even over those who were provided both cognitive and motivational feedback.

This body of empirical findings highlights the complex relationship between cognitive and affective concerns. In addition, the categorization of affective states as "positive" or "negative" with respect to learning is not straightforward. There is growing agreement that some amount of student confusion is not detrimental [3], but rather necessary for learning [14]. Theories related to affect in learning provide insight into these phenomena: flow theory suggests that a balance between perceived skill and perceived challenge is the optimal psychological state for student engagement and learning gain [15], and the theory of cognitive disequilibrium proposes that students enter this often-productive state when attempting to understand new ideas [14].

The present study builds upon this body of prior research in order to better understand how to support students of different gender. Male and female students interacted with four different versions of an intelligent tutoring system, which provided cognitive, affective, cognitive plus affective, or no adaptive support. Their resulting learning gain, frustration, and engagement outcomes identify important differences between male and female users and could have far-reaching implications for the design of user-adaptive support.

3 Studies

To investigate gender-specific adaptive strategies, we conducted two studies in which male and female students interacted with one of several versions of a tutorial dialogue system. This section details the two studies. One is a human-human tutorial dialogue study in which human tutors and students interacted through synchronous problem-solving interfaces with textual dialogue. The second is a human-ITS study conducted in the same problem-solving environment with four different levels of automated cognitive and affective support.

We hypothesized that female and male students would respond differently to cognitive and affective support, and moreover, that there would be significant differences between the human-human and human-ITS studies based upon gender. This section presents the results of analyses to investigate these hypotheses. In particular, we examine the relationship between gender and the outcomes of learning gain, frustration, and engagement.

3.1 Participants, Learning Tasks, and Data Sources

In both the human-human and human-ITS studies, participants were undergraduate students recruited from an introductory engineering course in exchange for course credit. No previous computer science knowledge was assumed or required, and students who reported taking a formal computer science course in the past were not included as participants, since our goals were to investigate adaptive support for novices.

Using a problem-solving environment purpose-built for this project (Figure 1), the students completed a series of programming tasks centered on the creation of a simple text-based adventure game. The problem-solving interface displayed the learning tasks in the upper left, a code editing window beneath that, and the results of compilation or execution of the students' program at the bottom. On the right hand side of the interface was the tutorial support window with textual interactions. Students were presented with subtasks in a succession designed to support them in completing the text-based adventure game and in learning the target concepts (e.g., variables, conditional logic, and iteration). There were five separate problem-solving sessions, and the students' solution built on itself from session to session.

Prior to each tutorial session, each student was administered a content-based pretest. The pretest consisted of a set of multiple-choice and free response items closely aligned to the concepts and skills for that day's learning tasks. After working within the problem-solving environment (and receiving adaptive support while doing so if the student was in an adaptive support condition), students completed a posttest identical to the pretest.

After each problem-solving session, the students also completed a post-session survey intended to gauge their engagement and affective outcomes including frustration. The survey included a validated User Engagement Survey [24] and the validated NASA-TLX workload survey [19], which includes an item on frustration. The frustration item within the NASA-TLX workload survey was of particular interest for the current study as prior work has shown that frustration has a significant impact on student learning [3].

3.2 Human-Human Tutoring Study

In the human-human tutoring study, each tutor and student pair interacted through the remote tutoring interface (Figure 1) with problem-solving tasks and textual dialogue. Human tutors ($N = 5$) were primarily graduate students with prior experience in teaching or tutoring introductory programming. Tutors were not constrained to scripts or protocols, but were encouraged to provide problem-solving support for the task at hand as well as broader concept-knowledge support, both of which are types of cognitive scaffolding. The tutors were also encouraged to provide motivational scaffolding whenever they felt that it would be helpful in order to improve the student's engagement, interest, or affective state.

There were 67 students in the human-human tutoring study, 24 of whom (36%) were female. Their average pretest score was 50.87%, and their average posttest score was 76.67%, reflecting a statistically significant learning gain ($p < 0.0001$).

3.3 Adaptive Support Conditions Study

The human-ITS study included 78 novice computer science students, 23 of whom (31%) were female (two students did not report gender, and were excluded from the analyses on gender). Students were randomly assigned to interact with one of the four versions of the system during the same series of five problem-solving sessions that were utilized in the human-human study described previously. The *Baseline* version of JavaTutor consisted only of the problem-solving environment

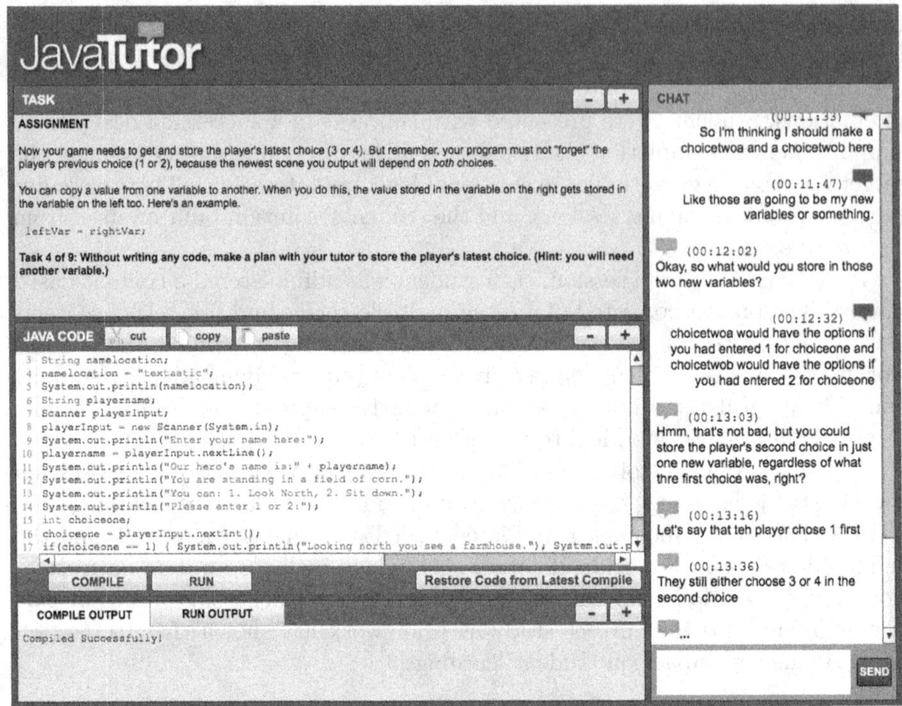

Fig. 1. The web-based interface for introductory Java programming

with its series of subtasks, and no adaptive support; the adaptive support conditions were *Cognitive*, or problem-solving, support; *Affective*, or motivational, support; and a combination of both, which we refer to as the *Cognitive-Affective* condition. All of the adaptive support was delivered as textual utterances within the interface (Figure 1).

The adaptive support in JavaTutor was built over the past several years relying upon a combination of machine-learned models of effective human tutoring from the human-human study described previously, along with handcrafted models of affective support, since the human tutors did not extensively employ affective strategies, as we will discuss later. The timing and content of the support was determined by this suite of machine-learned classifiers and handcrafted policies, triggered by events such as success or failure of the students' program to compile, correct or incorrect programming task actions, or periods of inactivity. Examples of cognitive and affective support offered to the student by JavaTutor are displayed in Table 1.

In the human-ITS study, the average pretest score was 51.08%, and the average posttest score was 65.46%. This difference was highly statistically significant ($p < 0.0001$).

Table 1. Example cognitive and affective scaffolding utterances provided by the JavaTutor ITS to the students

Cognitive Support	Affective Support
The Scanner lines allow you to get input from the player.	Alright, great work! You're doing a great job.
Note that variable names cannot contain spaces.	Congratulations on writing your first program!
There were no errors, so you have completed the task.	Don't give up! You'll get it if you keep trying.
Now, your variable has a value stored in it.	It's okay to make mistakes because each mistake is a chance to learn.

4 Analysis and Results

In order to compare the ways in which male and female students responded to cognitive and affective scaffolding across the conditions, we compared the outcomes between conditions and by gender.

Learning gain was calculated as the difference between a student's posttest score and pretest score for each tutorial session. Frustration score was taken from the Frustration Level scale of the NASA-TLX workload survey [19], administered after each session (Scale 1-100). Engagement scores were calculated as the sum of three sub-scales of the User Engagement Survey [24]: Focused Attention (perception of time passing), Felt Involvement (perception of involvement with the session), and Endurability (perception of the activity as worthwhile) (Scale 1-85). Each student's average learning gain, frustration, and engagement were computed as the average of these values for that student across all five tutoring sessions. The statistical comparisons reported in this section were conducted with the Tukey-Kramer test, which includes a correction for multiple hypothesis testing.

4.1 Learning Gains

The results in Table 2 reveal that students in the human-human tutorial dialogue study learned significantly more overall than in any of the human-ITS conditions ($p < 0.001$). Additionally, the *Cognitive-Affective* condition saw significantly lower learning gains than either the *Cognitive* or *Affective* conditions alone ($p < 0.05$). There was no significant difference in learning gain between genders under any condition ($p > 0.05$).

4.2 Frustration

As shown in Table 2, the human-human condition was significantly less frustrating than any of the human-ITS conditions ($p < 0.0001$). However, mirroring the

Table 2. Student learning gain, frustration, and engagement. Asterisks (*) denote significant differences between conditions; boldface denotes significant differences between genders. *Baseline*, *Cognitive*, *Affective*, and *Cog-Aff* denote type of ITS support; *Human* indicates human tutor support.

	Learning (1-100)		Frustration (1-100)		Engagement (1-85)	
	Female	Male	Female	Male	Female	Male
Baseline	10.14	14.03	***51.87**	**29.01**	63.13	59.69
Cognitive	16.13	15.01	***59.69**	**35.05**	58.47	57.85
Affective	10.86	15.87	31.74	39.42	**63.94**	**59.03**
Cog-Aff	9.42	13.44	27.31	39.24	58.50	56.63
Human	22.82	21.21	**19.54**	***13.30**	*51.61	*53.28
Overall	17.49	17.50	30.91	25.55	56.21	56.13

negative result of the *Cognitive-Affective* ITS condition for learning gain, the *Cognitive-Affective* condition was reported to be the most frustrating of all the ITS conditions ($p < 0.001$).

The results reveal significant differences in frustration across genders. Two of the ITS conditions, *Baseline* and *Cognitive*, as well as the *Human* condition, were more frustrating for females than males ($p < 0.0002$). These ITS conditions are the two in which no adaptive affective support was provided.

Across human-ITS conditions, female students were least frustrated when the automated tutor included affective feedback, that is, in the *Affective* and *Cognitive-Affective* conditions ($p < 0.0001$), while male students found all ITS conditions equal in terms of self-reported frustration ($p > 0.05$).

4.3 Engagement

As shown in Table 2, both male and female students reported lower engagement scores under the human condition than under any of the automated conditions ($p < 0.0001$). Importantly, the lower reported engagement in the human-human condition did not correspond to lower learning (in fact, the opposite was true).

Analogously to the finding with frustration, female students responded more positively to the *Affective* ITS condition than did males ($p < 0.05$), reporting higher engagement. The gender difference on engagement was not observed with the other ITS conditions.

5 Discussion

Results of this analysis confirmed that cognitive and affective support during problem solving were perceived differently by female and male students. First, while there were differences in learning between conditions, there were no significant differences in learning between genders. Male and female students achieved statistically equivalent learning gain in each condition, including all four human-ITS conditions as well as the human-human tutoring condition. The fact that female students learned at the same rate as male students under these conditions is consistent with some findings in previous studies suggesting that males and females may not need different *cognitive* support (e.g., [1]).

The findings are consistent with many prior studies comparing human tutoring to ITSs [17,30]: students learned more with human tutors but also learned significantly with the ITS. However, perhaps counter-intuitively, the *Human* condition was more frustrating for females than males. This finding is likely due in part to the fact that despite encouragement to provide affective and motivational support to students, even our experienced tutors very rarely engaged in utterances that were not task- or concept-related. The scarcity of affective support in the *Human* condition may be the reason that female students were more frustrated with the human tutors than male students were. This notion is supported by the fact that female students found the two ITS conditions that had no affective feedback (*Baseline* and *Cognitive*) to be more frustrating than did male students.

Lower engagement scores were observed for students of both genders when working with human tutors than with ITSs. Human tutors' textual dialogue moves were more varied in nature than those provided by the ITS and therefore may have more easily taken the students' attention from the task, which may have reduced the feeling of involvement and focused attention. Interestingly, students participating in the human-human condition demonstrated a correlation between lower engagement scores and *higher* learning gain. This result, coupled with the lower learning for the *Cognitive-Affective* condition, is consistent with both theory and emerging empirical findings, which suggests that it is challenging to address simultaneously both cognitive and affective concerns. If cognitive scaffolding works, and affective scaffolding works, it is not necessarily the case that combining these two will work better.

The findings highlight important differences between males and females with regard to the importance of adaptive affective support. Female students were significantly less frustrated and significantly more engaged when provided with affective feedback than without. On the other hand, the presence of affective support did not significantly change the male students' frustration or engagement levels.

Design Implications. Although future studies will continue to elucidate the phenomena observed here, the current results suggest a set of design implications for gender-adapted systems. First, the current results taken in concert with prior findings from the literature indicate that in the face of limited resources for adaptive system development, creating separate cognitive support strategies by gender may not be necessary. Second, the results suggest that if system development resources are available to implement affective scaffolding in any form, it should be done: even if this scaffolding is not delivered in a gender-adaptive way, it benefits female users while not negatively impacting male users. Finally, the ideal design of gender adaptation appears to be greater affective scaffolding for females than for males, though identifying the ideal balance and types of support by gender is a crucial area for future study.

6 Conclusions and Future Work

A growing body of findings suggests that user gender should be considered as we design adaptive scaffolding for problem solving. This paper has reported on a study that examined the difference in outcomes, in terms of learning gain, frustration, and engagement, for female and male students engaged in learning to solve computer science problems. The results show that both groups benefited equally from all types of cognitive support studied, but that female students tended to become significantly more frustrated and less engaged than male students in the absence of affective support. The *Mars and Venus Effect* was observed not only with automatically generated ITS support, but also in a study with experienced human tutors. One clear design implication for adaptive systems is that we should take great care to support female students' affective states that are conducive to learning because, while we may measure statistically equivalent learning gain, the perception and memories taken away from the problem-solving experience will likely influence the students in the future.

There are several directions that are important for future work. As indicated by the results presented here, the disproportionate benefit of affective support for females is a phenomenon that is particularly important for future study. The current study has examined different types of affective support related to motivation and self-efficacy, but there are many highly promising types of affective support that hold great promise for users of both genders, and could continue to improve dramatically the effectiveness and personalization of intelligent learning environments. Additionally, along with gender, the community should examine ways in which learning environments can tailor their adaptive support to other influential learner characteristics, such as personality. Given the tremendous increase in at-scale learning and its corresponding collections of "big data" for problem solving, the user modeling field has the opportunity to learn fine-grained adaptive models that reach beyond one-size-fits-all task support and instead adapt highly to each individual. It is hoped that this line of research will tremendously increase the effectiveness of adaptive support for learning.

Acknowledgments. The authors wish to thank the members of the LearnDialogue group at North Carolina State University for their helpful input. This work is supported in part by the Department of Computer Science at North Carolina State University and the National Science Foundation through Grant IIS-1409639 and the STARS Alliance, CNS-1042468. Any opinions, findings, conclusions, or recommendations expressed in this report are those of the authors, and do not necessarily represent the official views, opinions, or policy of the National Science Foundation.

References

1. Arroyo, I., Burleson, W., Minghui, T., Muldner, K., Woolf, B.P.: Gender Differences in the Use and Benefit of Advanced Learning Technologies for Mathematics. Journal of Educational Psychology **105**(4), 957–969 (2013)

2. Arroyo, I., Woolf, B.P., Cooper, D.G., Burleson, W., Muldner, K.: The impact of animated pedagogical agents on girls' and boys' emotions, attitudes, behaviors and learning. In: Proceedings of the 11th International Conference on Advanced Learning Technologies, pp. 506–510. IEEE, Athens (2011)
3. Baker, R.S.J., D'Mello, S.K., Rodrigo, M.T., Graesser, A.C.: Better to Be Frustrated Than Bored: The Incidence, Persistence, and Impact of Learners' Cognitive-affective States During Interactions with Three Different Computer-based Learning Environments. International Journal of Human-Computer Studies **68**(4), 223–241 (2010)
4. Belk, M., Germanakos, P., Fidas, C., Samaras, G.: A personalization method based on human factors for improving usability of user authentication tasks. In: Dimitrova, V., Kuflik, T., Chin, D., Ricci, F., Dolog, P., Houben, G.-J. (eds.) UMAP 2014. LNCS, vol. 8538, pp. 13–24. Springer, Heidelberg (2014)
5. Bloom, B.S.: The 2 Sigma Problem: The Search for Methods of Group Instruction as Effective as One-to-One Tutoring. Educational Researcher **13**(6), 4–16 (1984)
6. Bousbia, N., Rebaï, I., Labat, J.M., Balla, A.: Learners' navigation behavior identification based on trace analysis. User Modelling and User-Adapted Interaction **20**(5), 455–494 (2010)
7. Bouvier, P., Sehaba, K., Lavoué, E.: A trace-based approach to identifying users engagement and qualifying their engaged-behaviours in interactive systems: application to a social game. User Modeling and User-Adapted Interaction **24**(5), 413–451 (2014)
8. Boyer, K.E., Phillips, R., Wallis, M., Vouk, M.A., Lester, J.C.: Balancing cognitive and motivational scaffolding in tutorial dialogue. In: Woolf, B.P., Aïmeur, E., Nkambou, R., Lajoie, S. (eds.) ITS 2008. LNCS, vol. 5091, pp. 239–249. Springer, Heidelberg (2008)
9. Boyer, K.E., Vouk, M.A., Lester, J.C.: The influence of learner characteristics on task-oriented tutorial dialogue. In: Proceedings of the 13th International Conference on Artificial Intelligence in Education, pp. 365–372. IOS Press, Marina Del Rey (2007)
10. Burleson, W., Picard, R.W.: Gender-specific approaches to developing emotionally intelligent learning companions. IEEE Intelligent Systems **22**(4), 62–69 (2007)
11. Chi, M., VanLehn, K., Litman, D.J., Jordan, P.W.: Empirically evaluating the application of reinforcement learning to the induction of effective and adaptive pedagogical strategies. User Modelling and User-Adapted Interaction **21**(1–2), 137–180 (2011)
12. Cohen, P.R., Perrault, C.R., Allen, J.F.: Beyond question answering. In: Strategies for Natural Language Processing, chap. 9, pp. 245–274. Psychology Press, New York (1982)
13. Cordick, A., McCuaig, J.: Adaptive tips for helping domain experts. In: Houben, G.-J., McCalla, G., Pianesi, F., Zancanaro, M. (eds.) UMAP 2009. LNCS, vol. 5535, pp. 397–402. Springer, Heidelberg (2009)
14. Craig, S.D., Graesser, A.C., Sullins, J., Gholson, B.: Affect and learning: An exploratory look into the role of affect in learning with AutoTutor. Journal of Educational Media **29**(3), 241–250 (2004)
15. Csikszentmihalyi, M.: Flow: The Psychology of Optimal Experience. Cambridge University Press, New York (1990)
16. Dennis, M., Masthoff, J., Mellish, C.: Adapting performance feedback to a learner's conscientiousness. In: Masthoff, J., Mobasher, B., Desmarais, M.C., Nkambou, R. (eds.) UMAP 2012. LNCS, vol. 7379, pp. 297–302. Springer, Heidelberg (2012)

17. Desmarais, M.C., Baker, R.S.J.: A review of recent advances in learner and skill modeling in intelligent learning environments. User Modelling and User-Adapted Interaction **22**(1–2), 9–38 (2012)
18. Goldin, I.M., Carlson, R.: Learner differences and hint content. In: Lane, H.C., Yacef, K., Mostow, J., Pavlik, P. (eds.) AIED 2013. LNCS, vol. 7926, pp. 522–531. Springer, Heidelberg (2013)
19. Hart, S.G., Staveland, L.E.: Development of NASA-TLX (Task Load Index): Results of Empirical and Theoretical Research. Advances in Psychology **52**, 139–183 (1988)
20. Jackson, G.T., Graesser, A.C.: Content matters: an investigation of feedback categories within an ITS. In: Proceedings of the 13th International Conference on Artificial Intelligence in Education, pp. 127–134. Los Angeles, California, USA (2007)
21. Mitchell, C.M., Ha, E.Y., Boyer, K.E., Lester, J.C.: Learner characteristics and dialogue: recognising effective and student-adaptive tutorial strategies. International Journal of Learning Technology **8**(4), 382–403 (2013)
22. Mitrovic, A.: Fifteen years of constraint-based tutors: What we have achieved and where we are going. User Modelling and User-Adapted Interaction **22**(1–2), 39–72 (2012)
23. Muldner, K., Burleson, W., Van de Sande, B., VanLehn, K.: An analysis of students gaming behaviors in an intelligent tutoring system: predictors and impacts. User Modeling and User-Adapted Interaction **21**(1–2), 99–135 (2011)
24. O'Brien, H.L., Toms, E.G.: The development and evaluation of a survey to measure user engagement. Journal of the American Society for Information Science and Technology **61**(1), 50–69 (2010)
25. Pirolli, P., Kairam, S.: A knowledge-tracing model of learning from a social tagging system. User Modeling and User-Adapted Interaction **23**(2–3), 139–168 (2013)
26. Rahimi, Z., Hashemi, H.B.: Turn-taking behavior in a human tutoring corpus. In: Lane, H.C., Yacef, K., Mostow, J., Pavlik, P. (eds.) AIED 2013. LNCS, vol. 7926, pp. 778–782. Springer, Heidelberg (2013)
27. San Pedro, M.O.Z., Baker, R.S.J., Gowda, S.M., Heffernan, N.T.: Towards an understanding of affect and knowledge from student interaction with an intelligent tutoring system. In: Lane, H.C., Yacef, K., Mostow, J., Pavlik, P. (eds.) AIED 2013. LNCS, vol. 7926, pp. 41–50. Springer, Heidelberg (2013)
28. Su, J.M., Tseng, S.S., Lin, H.Y., Chen, C.H.: A personalized learning content adaptation mechanism to meet diverse user needs in mobile learning environments. User Modeling and User-Adapted Interaction **21**(1–2), 5–49 (2011)
29. Vail, A.K., Boyer, K.E.: Adapting to personality over time: examining the effectiveness of dialogue policy progressions in task-oriented interaction. In: Proceedings of the 15th Annual Meeting of the Special Interest Group on Discourse and Dialogue, pp. 41–50. Philadelphia, Pennsylvania, USA (2014)
30. VanLehn, K., Graesser, A.C., Jackson, G.T., Jordan, P.W., Olney, A., Rosé, C.P.: When Are Tutorial Dialogues More Effective Than Reading? Cognitive Science **31**(1), 3–62 (2007)

Quiet Eye Affects Action Detection from Gaze More Than Context Length

Hana Vrzakova(✉) and Roman Bednarik

University of Eastern Finland, PO 111, 80101 Joensuu, Finland
{hanav,roman.bednarik}@uef.com

Abstract. Every purposive interactive action begins with an intention to interact. In the domain of intelligent adaptive systems, behavioral signals linked to the actions are of great importance, and even though humans are good in such predictions, interactive systems are still falling behind. We explored mouse interaction and related eye-movement data from interactive problem solving situations and isolated sequences with high probability of interactive action. To establish whether one can predict the interactive action from gaze, we 1) analyzed gaze data using sliding fixation sequences of increasing length and 2) considered sequences several fixations prior to the action, either containing the last fixation before action (i.e. the quiet eye fixation) or not. Each fixation sequence was characterized by 54 gaze features and evaluated by an SVM-RBF classifier. The results of the systematic evaluation revealed importance of the quiet eye fixation and statistical differences of quiet eye fixation compared to other fixations prior to the action.

Keywords: Action · Intentions · Prediction · Eye-tracking · SVM · Mouse interaction · Problem solving

1 Introduction

Understanding users, their interests and actions computationally is key for tapping into user's needs and provision of seamless interactions where the interactive systems *knows user's intentions*. A good interface design gives an impression of being able of anticipating future interactions because designers succeeded in understanding of the model in head and the user's needs. If they succeeded, the interface is perceived as natural, user friendly, responsive, immersive and intuitive.

Everyday experience unfortunately indicates that such user interfaces are still scarce. Current interactive systems typically do not contain mechanisms for prediction of the user's actions, and consequently restrict them from implementing their intentions effectively. It is however not only the designers who have to anticipate the user's actions; the interface itself needs to play an active role and just in time, or even *ahead of time*, adapt to the changing user needs proactively.

There are numerous benefits if an interface is able to *predict* that the user wants to interact with it, but one of the primary motivations is to mitigate

F. Ricci et al. (Eds.): UMAP 2015, LNCS 9146, pp. 277–288, 2015.
DOI: 10.1007/978-3-319-20267-9_23

consequences of interaction errors. For example, when a system assumes the cursor to be located at the respective field for user input – such as when starting to type a search query– a truly proactive interface needs to be able to detect user's *intention to input*. Detection can then trigger automatic assistance to adjust the cursor location to avoid an unintended error. The eventual errors could be avoided if the intention to type was predicted early enough.

This work considers modeling and automatic detection of actions in human computer interaction. All interactive actions begin with an intention to interact. Specifically, the formation of the intention to explicitly interact is a stage preliminary to interactive activity [21] and part of larger planning activities. For instance, to press a button a user has to first internally formulate an intention to interact, then execute the hand movement toward the button, and finally, flex the finger to issue the button press. Finger flexes, however, are not the most reliable indicators of intention, since they embody the post-intention activity that is merely mechanically executed (a button was pressed after an intention to press it occurred). The novelty of this work is to model computationally the stages preliminary to actions. In this work we consider an intention as an entity for action recognition. To access the plan formation activities, we employ eye-movement analysis as a proxy to cognitive processes related to action formation.

Eye movements have for long been established as a window to human cognition, including planning and motor action [12,16,23]. As indicators of voluntary and involuntary attention, eye movements can reveal intention origins and uncover the mechanisms of action planning, execution and evaluation. In this work we examine mouse interaction, we focus on action detection from user's eye-movements and lay down pathways towards interaction design enhanced by user's actions.

1.1 Gaze in Proactive User Interaction

The problem of plan recognition using a computational agent have for long been a central issue in artificial intelligence research [18]. In this work we deal with intention on the level of motor-interactive action. While there are higher- and more sophisticated levels of intentions, such as social intentions (A wants to leave a good impression on B), here we explore intentions at the lower level of action implementation [13]. Our overall goal is to develop a system that would be able to reliably and effectively perform online intention detection.

We employ eye-gaze as a source of intention information since gaze reliably indicates the person's focus of visual attention and can be unobtrusively tracked. Gaze is also proactive as it reflects the anticipated actions when gathering critical information before performing actions [12], and therefore modeling of proactive gaze can potentially lead to prediction of the resulting actions. Understanding this level of interactive action planning is key for implementation of proactive intelligent systems, in particular, for avoidance of interaction slips [21], Midas Touch effect [15], action slips [13] and human errors in interface design [22].

1.2 Eye Tracking in Interaction Modeling

Eye-tracking data can be used to discover user's cognitive states [6,10,24], workload [1,2], expertise [5,11,19] or to predict the context of interaction [9,14] and aspects of learning with intelligent tutoring systems [7,17]. Eye-tracking is also expected to become a ubiquitous interaction technique [8,15,27]. If eye-tracking is indeed going to be a pervasive source of user data, the implicit behavioral information can be used for modeling of user states.

Because of the voluminous eye-tracking stream, current research employed customized machine learning techniques as a feasible modeling approach and achieved acceptable levels of predictions. Existing research reached acceptable predictions in human-computer interaction, such as mind-wandering [6] and cognitive abilities [25].

Starting from the pioneering work that adopted a standard classification method for prediction of problem solving states [5], recent research investigated the nuances of eye-tracking pattern-recognition systems in terms of data preprocessing methods [3] or classifier training approaches [28].

In prior work, we and others explored a machine learning pipeline for eye-tracking data that performs training of a classifier to detect various states and individual characteristics of a user. In [5] we presented a machine learning pipeline for intention detection from gaze. Later, we improved the efficiency of the method [28] and evaluated various options for data processing, such as effect of the data before and after an intention occurs, and simplified classifier training.

Although the eye-tracking pattern-recognition systems presented so far achieve classification accuracies far above the chance levels, there are several technical, methodological, and practical questions that motivate the improvements of the prediction pipeline.

In this work we deal with one of the essential questions, namely, how much information an automated modeling system needs to make a reliable decision?

2 Methods

We explore interactive actions during problem solving and recording framework of 8Puzzle[4]. In the 8Puzzle game (Figure 1), users re-arrange the moving tiles into final configuration using a traditional computer mouse. The interaction in detail consisted of moving the mouse cursor onto the tile to be moved, pressing a button, upon which the tile moved to the empty position. The final mouse click represents the interactive action and was recorded with the timestamp in the gaze signal data and represent the ground truth.

2.1 Experimental Task and Procedure

The task was to arrange the originally shuffled eight tiles into a required target configuration. There were altogether one warm-up trial (data was excluded from the analysis) and three sessions from which data has been collected. On

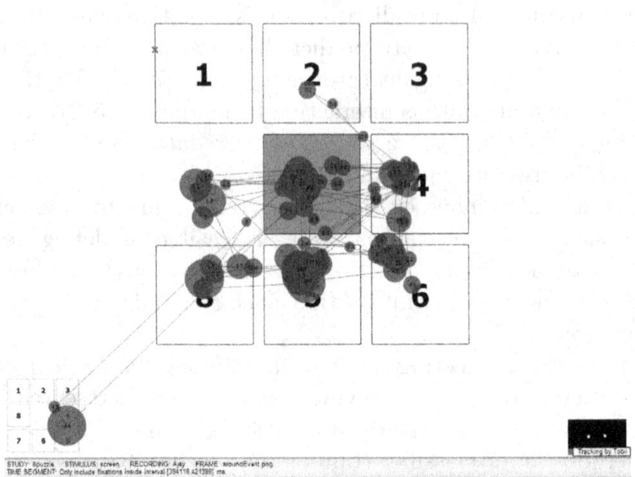

Fig. 1. The interface of 8Puzzle. The shuffled tiles with numbers illustrate a current configuration of the game and the lower left corner the target configuration. Blue circles represent the participant's fixations in sequence; the visualization of the gaze was hidden to the participants during the experiment.

Users	Modality	Experiment					Actions
11		*Calibration*	*Warm-up*	Task 1	Task 2	Task 3	2 595

Fig. 2. Overview of the experimental design

average a session took about five minutes, and participants were instructed to solve the puzzle till the end. Each participant interacted with the interface individually and participants were motivated to think aloud. Figure 2 summarizes the experimental design, number of participants and the size of the collected dataset.

2.2 Participants and Apparatus

The mouse-based experiment consisted of 11 participants (5 male and 6 female) with normal or corrected-to-normal vision, in the 24-47 age range (mean age = 30.36, sd=7.90).

The experiments were conducted in a quiet usability laboratory. Participants' eye movements were recorded binocularly using a Tobii ET1750 eye-tracker, sampling at 50Hz. The default settings of event identification were set for fixation detection (ClearView, fixation radius 30px, minimal fixation duration 100ms).

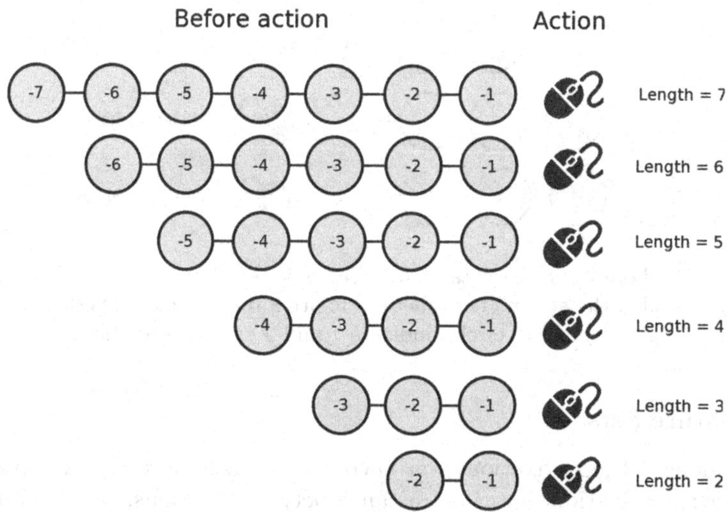

Fig. 3. Scheme of the sequence lengths. The sequence ending right before the mouse click has been annotated as *action*, the rest of sequences before and after the mouse click as *non-action*.

The mouse button press was automatically logged into the stream of eye-tracking data and sets the boundaries for action prediction. The following analysis and classification were performed using custom Python scripts, RapidMiner and SPSS.

2.3 Analysis of Data

To understand how much data is needed to reliably predict the upcoming action, we employ gaze fixations as a unit of analysis. Fixations are indices of cognitive processing, and extracted short and long sequences of gaze fixations captured before the mouse click should correspond to various stages of cognitive activities. Here, we systematically shifted the fixation sampling window through the data and created following datasets, illustrated in Figure 3. All data was sequenced and annotated as either *action* (action happened after the last fixation in the actual sequence) or *non-action* (other sequences where no interaction occurred). The sequences were extracted with one-fixation overlap to emulate fixation processing as implemented in a hypothetical real-time system.

In a real-time scenario when the intelligent system predicts the upcoming action, we would like to answer the question when it is possible to predict the action before it happens. For this purposes, we analyzed sequences of one fixation and two fixations prior to the action, as demonstrated in Figure 4, and evaluated how predictive power changes further from the mouse click. The motivation here is to predict the upcoming action as soon as possible so that the adaptive system can proactively respond.

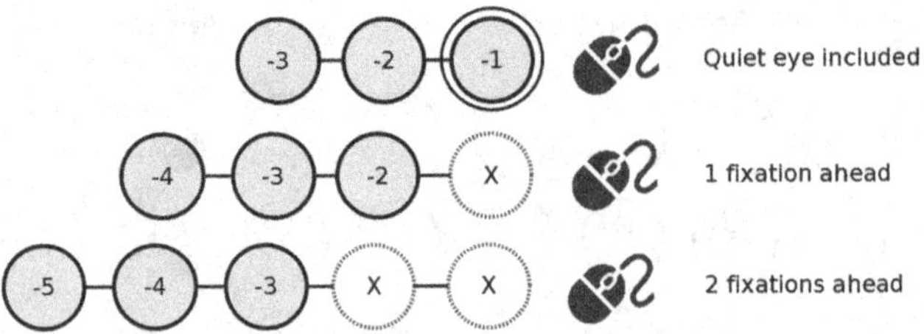

Fig. 4. Analysed datasets: the dataset with the quiet eye fixation (QE), 1-fixation and 2-fixations ahead of the action. The quiet eye fixation (double-circle) is the last fixation before the action. The empty circles indicate 1 and 2 excluded fixations.

2.4 Feature Sets

Each sequence of gaze fixations was encoded into a feature vector represented by gaze events: fixation duration, distance between fixations, saccade duration, saccade orientation, saccade velocity and saccade acceleration. Each gaze event was described by statistical parameters (mean, median, variance, standard deviation, first, last) and ratio-based parameters (ratio of first vs. last fixation). All together each sequence was represented by the 54 gaze features. Datasets of 2-fixation based sequences were represented by 11 gaze features (fixation duration: mean, standard deviation, variance, sum, first, last, ratio of first vs. last, fixation distance, saccade duration, saccade direction and saccade velocity) as there were lacking enough gaze events for other statistical parameters.

We balanced datasets of action and non-action feature vectors. All available action-related sequences were included and non-action feature vectors were randomly sub-sampled. Since the amount of extracted actions slightly differed across datasets (within 10-50 samples), all datasets were evened out to 2500 action and 2500 non-action vectors. The balanced setting allowed to examine optimal setup for classifier training and for cross-study comparison. In real interaction, the proportion of user actions is more imbalanced, the original dataset contained over 2500 actions (12.5%) compared to 17500 non-actions. The search for the optimal class weights for the imbalanced datasets is out of scope of this work.

2.5 Classification Framework

The classification in this study builds on the baseline prediction framework proposed by [5]. A nested parameter grid search employs Support Vector Machine (SVM) as a core classifier with an RBF kernel. Parameter search is the central process in model learning. In the two nested cross-validations (3 x 3-fold), the learning process estimated the most fitting hyperparameters for SVM-RBF (C, Gamma). The remaining settings, such as parameter grid search and SVM classifier, adhered to the classification standards employed in current machine learning studies. Using output SVM.C and SVM.Gamma, the model was built on training data (2/3 of the balanced dataset) and tested on the unseen data (1/3 of the balanced dataset).

3 Classification Results

To understand dependencies between context length (number of fixations in the sequence), context timing (omitting fixations prior to action) and gaze signal, we evaluated 6 sequence lengths (2 up to 7 fixations at once), and compared datasets with quiet eye (QE dataset) and two datasets prior to action; all together 18 datasets were classified using the classification framework introduced above. Here we report on classifier accuracy and Area Under the Curve (AUC), as the primary performance metrics, and training and testing AUCs for all datasets, as measures of classifier generalizability.

3.1 Context Length and Timing

When comparing length of the context, the datasets from longer fixation sequences performed better than the shorter ones. Figure 5 summarize classifier training performance for all timing variants and all sequence lengths. The best performance was reached with sequences of length 5 (accuracy=67.8%, AUC=0.735) and length 7 (accuracy=67.57%, AUC=0.745) in the QE dataset; the dataset 1-fixation-ahead performed best on sequence lengths 6 (accuracy=59.9%, AUC= 0.647) and the dataset 2-fixations-ahead of the action scored the best accuracy with length = 7 (accuracy = 60.6, AUC = 0.653) .

When comparing the effect of sequence length, the original datasets performed similar in all lengths with just slight deviations in accuracy and AUC; the difference between the best and worst performance was 2.6% in the accuracy measure and Δ AUC = 0.026. Both datasets prior to action revealed higher differences between the best and the worst performance than the QE dataset; the difference in the dataset 1-fixation-ahead of the action reached an accuracy of 6.43% (Δ AUC = 0.05) and sequences 2-fixations-ahead differed in the best and the worse accuracy of 9.2% (Δ AUC = 0.075).

The primary difference between QE and prior-to-action datasets was in missing quiet eye fixation [26], therefore we statistically compared durations of the quiet-eye fixation and two previous fixations.

Informally, we observed a moderate decrease in fixation duration towards the action. A one-way ANOVA showed a significant difference between the duration of three fixations: the QE-fixation (M = 243.96, SD=133.69), the previous fixation (M = 253.83, SD = 134.90) and the second last fixation (M = 294.10, SD = 158.92), $F(2, 3213) = 36.99$, $p < .001$). The mean duration of QE fixation was significantly shorter than second last fixation (Shapiro-Wilk test $p < 0.001$).

3.2 Generalizability of Classifier

The classifier generalizability was evaluated using unseen data (1/3 of the whole dataset) in all datasets. Figure 6 captures the AUC rates for training and testing classifications using the QE and prior-to-action datasets. The classifier trained on the QE dataset proved stable performance in line with the training; the testing results outperformed the training performance (mean difference between testing

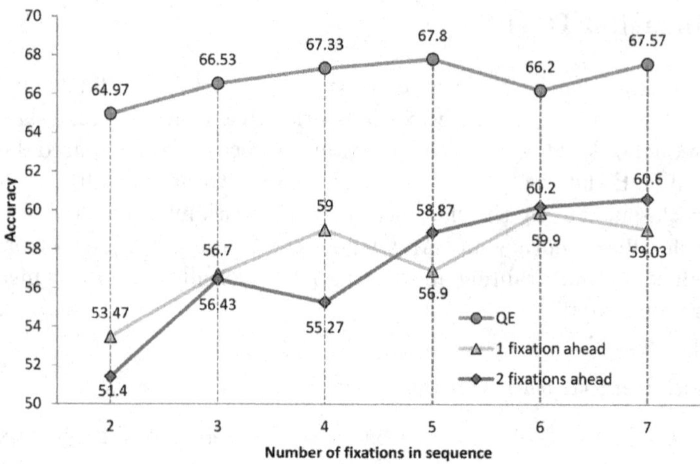

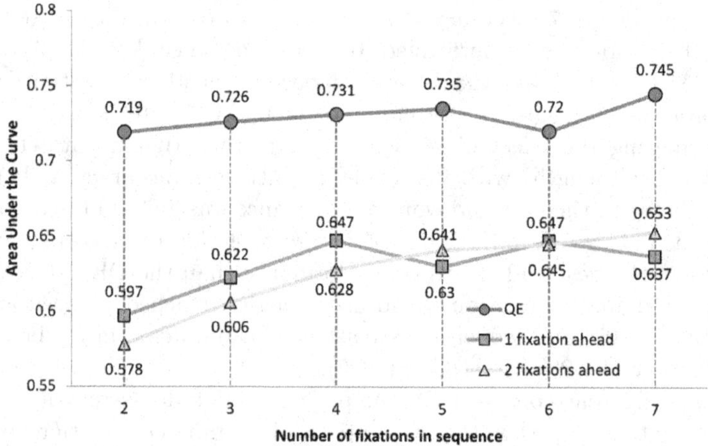

Fig. 5. Performance on datasets with different sequence lengths (number of fixations analyzed in the sequence). Accuracy (top) and Area Under the Curve (bottom).

and training AUC= 0.004, SD = 0.016), suggesting good classifier generalizability on the unseen datasets.

Differences between training and testing AUC for the prior-to-action datasets were also minimal (1-fixation prior to action: mean difference in AUC = 0.008, SD = 0.01) and (2-fixations prior to action: mean difference in AUC = -0.0018, SD = 0.01). The negative value of the difference indicates that training classifier AUC was on average better than the testing one.

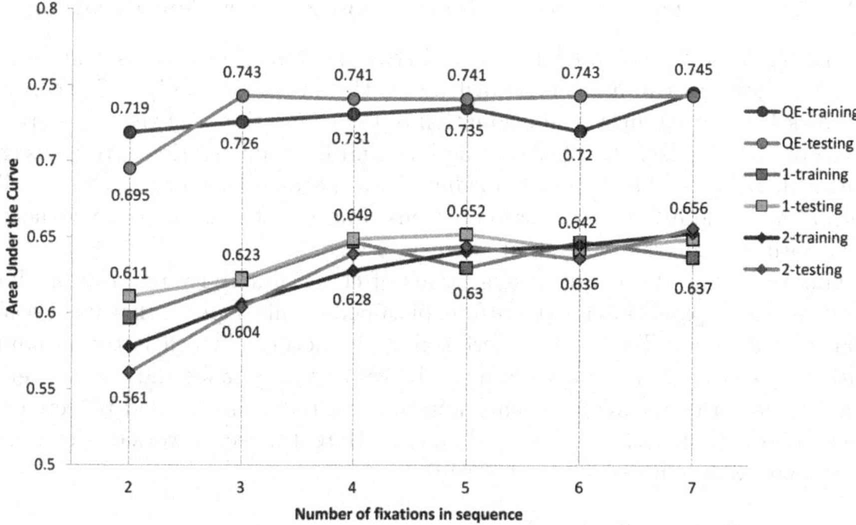

Fig. 6. Comparison of training and testing AUCs for all analyzed datasets

4 Discussion

Detection of user actions remains a persistent challenge in intelligent system design. To tackle the action detection from gaze, we systematically modified context length (number of fixations) and timing (excluding quiet eye fixations and two fixations prior to the action), and classified the sequences with a standard SVM framework. We compared cross-validation and testing results to demonstrate generalizability of the approach. The main novelty is the analysis of the individual fixations and their contribution to the action detection performance.

4.1 Context Length and Timing

When comparing length of the context, the datasets from the longer fixation sequences performed better than the shorter ones. The best scores in terms of accuracy and AUC were received with 5 to 7 fixations in the sequence. However, the number of fixations did not affect the action detection when the quiet eye fixation was included. The systematic evaluation of the fixation sequences revealed minor improvements, the increasing performance was achieved generally with longer sequences. Omitting the quiet eye fixation from the analysis, on the other hand, decreased the classifier performance and highlighted the higher recognition rates in longer sequences.

Quiet eye fixation is the important part in movement programming of targeting tasks [29] and in our experiment, we observed how properties of quiet eye fixations contributed to action recognition. When we compared fixation durations of quiet eye fixations and previous two fixations, the quiet eye fixation was significantly shorter.

4.2 Applications of Action Detection and Further Considerations

In this work we investigated the links between interaction actions and user's gaze, and how one can use such knowledge in the interaction design. The core of the work lies in computational evaluation of the connections between properties of the proactive gaze, the phases of actions and its manifestation. We envisage that such computational model, mediated by machine learning methods, will automatically detect the interaction actions from the stream of eye movements and inform the interactive system about user's goals.

Our work can also extend the systems of classical activity recognition. For example, one explanation for the results obtained in this paper is that users were often multitasking. Thus, while performing the action -?which is the ground-truth for our work-? another planning activities may have taken the place. Therefore, the patterns of eye movements were not entirely constant and reflected at times other activities than action and planing. Here, the recent work on detection of interleaved activities [20] can be utilized.

5 Conclusion and Future Work

Reliable detection of user actions is a fundamental challenge in building intelligent interfaces that interact with the user in a human-like way. Based on the results of our study, it is safe to argue that eye movements reveal interactive actions and that eye-movement patterns around the interactive actions differ from other types of activities. We presented that processing eye movements as signals is a feasible way for detection of interaction actions. We adopted a pattern recognition system and applied it on the dataset from interactive problem solving. In order to evaluate its effects on the classification performance, we varied the contextual information and timing available for the decision, in terms of fixation counts and the analysis ahead of the action.

Our findings pointed out that the context length does not affect the action detection as much when the quiet eye fixation is part of the analyzed sequence. Systematic evaluation of the fixation sequences revealed minor improvements in the classification towards longer sequences. Omitting the quiet eye fixation from the analysis, on the other hand, decreased the classification performance and highlighted higher recognition rates with longer sequences.

Recent research in this domain employed classifiers trained on general population as descriptors and models of individual user behavior. Studies that would focus on personalized classification and performance differences when each participant presents own training and testing environment are however rare. In future work we will compare the performance of the existing system trained for the individual to the one trained for global behavioral data. It is essential that future work will couple both personal and global models, and will assess the contribution of each.

Independently on the type of the adaptation style, the complex domains demand collections of reliable datasets with genuine samples of the ground-truth actions. While in this work the ground-truth was objective, eliciting higher-level actions, for instance an intention to influence a person, will require a careful methodological work.

References

1. Bailey, B.P., Iqbal, S.T.: Understanding changes in mental workload during execution of goal-directed tasks and its application for interruption management. ACM Trans. Comput.-Hum. Interact. **14**(4), 21:1–21:28 (2008)
2. Bartels, M., Marshall, S.P.: Measuring cognitive workload across different eye tracking hardware platforms. In: Proc. of the Symposium on Eye Tracking Research and Applications, ETRA 2012, pp. 161–164. ACM (2012)
3. Bednarik, R., Eivazi, S., Vrzakova, H.: A computational approach for prediction of problem-solving behavior using support vector machines and eye-tracking data. In: Nakano, Y.I., Conati, C., Bader, T. (eds.) Eye Gaze in Intelligent User Interfaces, pp. 111–134. Springer (2013)
4. Bednarik, R., Gowases, T., Tukiainen, M.: Gaze interaction enhances problem solving: Effects of dwell-time based, gaze-augmented, and mouse interaction on problem-solving strategies and user experience. J. of Eye Movement Research **3**(1), 1–10 (2009)
5. Bednarik, R., Vrzakova, H., Hradis, M.: What do you want to do next: a novel approach for intent prediction in gaze-based interaction. In: Proc. of the Symposium on Eye Tracking Research and Applications, ETRA 2012, pp. 83–90. ACM (2012)
6. Bixler, R., D'Mello, S.: Toward fully automated person-independent detection of mind wandering. In: Dimitrova, V., Kuflik, T., Chin, D., Ricci, F., Dolog, P., Houben, G.-J. (eds.) UMAP 2014. LNCS, vol. 8538, pp. 37–48. Springer, Heidelberg (2014)
7. Bondareva, D., Conati, C., Feyzi-Behnagh, R., Harley, J.M., Azevedo, R., Bouchet, F.: Inferring learning from gaze data during interaction with an environment to support self-regulated learning. In: Lane, H.C., Yacef, K., Mostow, J., Pavlik, P. (eds.) AIED 2013. LNCS, vol. 7926, pp. 229–238. Springer, Heidelberg (2013)
8. Bulling, A., Gellersen, H.: Toward mobile eye-based human-computer interaction. IEEE, Pervasive Computing **9**(4), 8–12 (2010)
9. Bulling, A., Roggen, D., Troster, G.: What's in the eyes for context-awareness? IEEE, Pervasive Computing **10**(2), 48–57 (2011)
10. Eivazi, S., Bednarik, R.: Inferring problem solving strategies using eye-tracking: system description and evaluation. In: Proc. of the 10th Koli Calling Int. Conference on Computing Education Research, pp. 55–61. ACM (2010)
11. Eivazi, S., Bednarik, R., Tukiainen, M., von und zu Fraunberg, M., Leinonen, V., Jääskeläinen, J.E.: Gaze behaviour of expert and novice microneurosurgeons differs during observations of tumor removal recordings. In: Proc. of the Symposium on Eye Tracking Research and Applications, ETRA 2012, pp. 377–380. ACM (2012)
12. Flanagan, J.R., Johansson, R.S.: Action plans used in action observation. Nature **424**(6950), 769–771 (2003)
13. Heckhausen, H., Beckmann, J.: Intentional action and action slips. Psychological Review **97**(1), 36–48 (1990)
14. Hradis, M., Eivazi, S., Bednarik, R.: Voice activity detection from gaze in video mediated communication. In: Proc. of the Symposium on Eye Tracking Research and Applications, ETRA 2012, pp. 329–332. ACM (2012)

15. Jacob, R.J.K., Karn, K.S.: Commentary on section 4. eye tracking in human-computer interaction and usability research: ready to deliver the promises. In: The Mind's Eye: Cognitive and Applied Aspects of Eye Movement Research, pp. 573–605. Elsevier Science (2003)
16. Just, M.A., Carpenter, P.A.: A theory of reading: From eye fixations to comprehension. Psychological Review **87**, 329–354 (1980)
17. Kardan, S., Conati, C.: Comparing and combining eye gaze and interface actions for determining user learning with an interactive simulation. In: Carberry, S., Weibelzahl, S., Micarelli, A., Semeraro, G. (eds.) UMAP 2013. LNCS, vol. 7899, pp. 215–227. Springer, Heidelberg (2013)
18. Kautz, H.A., Allen, J.F.: Generalized plan recognition. In: AAAI,vol. 86, pp. 32–37 (1986)
19. Memmert, D.: Pay attention! a review of visual attentional expertise in sport. Int. Review of Sport and Exercise Psychology **2**(2), 119–138 (2009)
20. Modayil, J., Bai, T., Kautz, H.: Improving the recognition of interleaved activities. In: Proc. of the 10th Int. Conf. on Ubiquitous Computing, UbiComp 2008, pp. 40–43. ACM (2008)
21. Norman, D.A.: The Design of Everyday Things. Basic Books, New York (2002)
22. Prabhu, P.V., Prabhu, G.V.: Handbook of Human-Computer Interaction Chapter 22 Human Error and User-Interface Design. Elsevier Science B. V. (1997)
23. Rayner, K.: Eye movements in reading and information processing: 20 years of research. Psychological Bulletin **124**(3), 372 (1998)
24. Simola, J., Salojärvi, J., Kojo, I.: Using hidden markov model to uncover processing states from eye movements in information search tasks. Cognitive Systems Research **9**(4), 237–251 (2008)
25. Steichen, B., Carenini, G., Conati, C.: User-adaptive information visualization: using eye gaze data to infer visualization tasks and user cognitive abilities. In: Proc. of the 2013 Int. Conf. on Intelligent User Interfaces, pp. 317–328. ACM (2013)
26. Vickers, J.N.: Visual control when aiming at a far target. J. of Experimental Psychology: Human Perception and Performance **22**(2), 342 (1996)
27. Vrzakova, H., Bednarik, R.: Eyecloud: cloud computing for pervasive eye-tracking. In: PETMEI 2013, 3rd Int. Workshop on Pervasive Eye Tracking and Mobile Eye-Based Interaction (2013)
28. Vrzakova, H., Bednarik, R.: Fast and comprehensive extension to intention prediction from gaze. In: IUI 2013 Workshop on Interacting with Smart Objects (2013)
29. Williams, A.M., Singer, R.N., Frehlich, S.G.: Quiet eye duration, expertise, and task complexity in near and far aiming tasks. Journal of Motor Behavior **34**(2), 197–207 (2002)

User Model in a Box: Cross-System User Model Transfer for Resolving Cold Start Problems

Chirayu Wongchokprasitti[1(✉)], Jaakko Peltonen[2,3], Tuukka Ruotsalo[2], Payel Bandyopadhyay[4], Giulio Jacucci[4], and Peter Brusilovsky[1]

[1] School of Information Sciences, University of Pittsburgh, Pittsburgh, USA
{chw20,peterb}@pitt.edu

[2] Helsinki Institute for Information Technology HIIT, Aalto University, Espoo, Finland
{jaakko.peltonen,tuukka.ruotsalo}@aalto.fi

[3] School of Information Sciences, University of Tampere, Tampere, Finland

[4] Helsinki Institute for Information Technology HIIT, Department of Computer Science, University of Helsinki, Helsinki, Finland
{pbandyop,giulio.jacucci}@cs.helsinki.fi

Abstract. Recommender systems face difficulty in cold-start scenarios where a new user has provided only few ratings. Improving cold-start performance is of great interest. At the same time, the growing number of adaptive systems makes it ever more likely that a new user in one system has already been a user in another system in related domains. To what extent can a user model built by one adaptive system help address a cold start problem in another system? We compare methods of cross-system user model transfer across two large real-life systems: we transfer user models built for information seeking of scientific articles in the SciNet exploratory search system, operating over tens of millions of articles, to perform cold-start recommendation of scientific talks in the CoMeT talk management system, operating over hundreds of talks. Our user study focuses on transfer of novel explicit *open user models* curated by the user during information seeking. Results show strong improvement in cold-start talk recommendation by transferring open user models, and also reveal why explicit open models work better in cross-domain context than traditional hidden implicit models.

Keywords: Cross-system user modeling · Recommender systems

1 Introduction

Recommender systems often face the *cold-start problem*, where recommendations are required for users for whom not enough preference information is available, because the users have rated few or no items in the system [9]. In this article, we investigate the idea of *user model transfer* to enable warm start in cross-system recommendation scenario. That is, we consider user models that can be established in a *source system* and then used in another *target system*. While this idea

F. Ricci et al. (Eds.): UMAP 2015, LNCS 9146, pp. 289–301, 2015.
DOI: 10.1007/978-3-319-20267-9_24

is not new, past research on user model transfer produced mixed results. Our paper expands earlier research by exploring transferability of *open user models.* We investigate a scenario where user or the source system have the ability to explore and curate their model by visual interaction. We believe that open user modeling approach produces better quality user models that could be especially valuable for cross-system transfer. To assess this hypothesis, we investigate how the cross-system transfer of open user models improves performance of recommender methods both in the extreme cold-start setting when no preferences are available from the user, and over time when some preferences from the user become available. We compare different transfer strategies in an academic information setting where the source system is a search system for scientific papers and the target system is a system for sharing academic talks. The open user models in the source system are built from visual interaction with keywords and other available information includes views and bookmarks of query results; models in the target system are built from ratings of talks.

We believe that our work is the first one to explore the transferability of open user models. Its main contributions are: 1) we show cross-system transfer of open user models greatly improves cold-start recommendation performance, 2) we investigate different ways of transferring open user models from an information seeking system to a talk recommendation system, as well as transfer of more traditional implicit and explicit document information, and show the open user models bring the greatest benefit, for which we provide an explanation by analysis of cross-system similarities of the different information types.

2 Related Work

In recent years, cross-system and cross-domain recommendation research is grown in popularity due to the growing number of personalized system that collect information about the users. It this context, it becomes natural to export information collected about a user in one system and transfer it to another system (maybe in a different domain) to improve the quality of recommendations. It has been argued that this transfer might be most valuable in cold-start context when a recommender system has insufficient information about new users in a target system [8]. Despite the overall interest in this field, there are still very few studies exploring real cross-system user information transfer due to the lack of sizable datasets that have pairs of users in two systems. As a result, a major share of research on cross-domain recommendation focused on transfer learning approaches that do not assume a common user set for different domains [4,6].

According to the most recent review [3], the work on cross-domain recommendation could be split into two large groups - those using collaborative filtering and content-based approaches. The classic examples or collaborative filtering transfer are [1,2]. These papers offered an extensive discussion of cross-domain recommendation problems and suggested interesting generic approaches but were not able to explore these approaches in a true cross-domain context using instead artificial datasets produced by separation of single-domain user movie ratings into subdomains. More recent work explored collaborative transfer approaches in more realistic settings with hundreds of users having ratings in both domains [8]. Content-based cross-domain recommendation appeared to be a harder challenge. No immediate success was reported for simple keyword-based profile transfer approaches. As a result, the majority of research and success in this category focused on using shared semantic-level features such as social tags [11] or Wikipedia [5]. Unfortunately, it leaves open the case where user preference data in the source domain includes no tags and can't be associated with an extensive ontology such as Wikipedia.

In this context, our work attempts to re-examine the prospects of the keyword-level user model transfer across related, but different domains. To fight the known problems of keyword profile transfer, we explored a different kind of profile. While more traditional implicit keyword-level user model is served as a baseline in our studies, main emphasis is on transfer of an explicit model of interest that is open to the users in the source systems and explicitly curated by them.

3 Setting: Two Academic Information Systems

We study cross-system transfer of user models between two recent academic information systems, CoMeT and SciNet.

CoMeT is a system for sharing information about research talks at Carnegie Mellon University and University of Pittsburgh. The system is available online at http://halley.exp.sis.pitt.edu/comet/; it is a collaborative tagging system, which allows any individual to announce, find, bookmark, and tag talks. To help users locate interesting talks, CoMeT includes a content-based recommender system which builds an interest profile of individual users and recommend new talks to users immediately after such talks are posted.

SciNet [7] is an exploratory search system. SciNet indexes over 50 million scientific documents from Thomson Reuters, ACM, IEEE, and Springer. Going beyond text-based queries, SciNet helps users direct exploratory search by allowing them to interact with an *open user model* discussed below. The approach (called "interactive intent modeling" in [7]) significantly improved users? information seeking task performance and quality of retrieved information [7], thus the open user models are promising for cross-system transfer.

Open User Models in SciNet. Unlike traditional information seeking systems, SciNet opens its user model by allowing users to directly see a visual representation of the model and interact with it. User intent is modeled as a vector of interest values over a set of available keywords. The vector can be seen as a bag-of-keywords representation of an "ideal" document containing keywords in proportion to their interest values. Figure 1 shows the interface. The open user model is visualized as a radial layout where the estimated search intent and alternative intents are represented by scientific keywords, organized so that keywords relevant to the user are close to the center and similar intents have similar angles. Users start by typing a query and receive a list of documents which they can bookmark, and then direct the search by interacting with the user model.

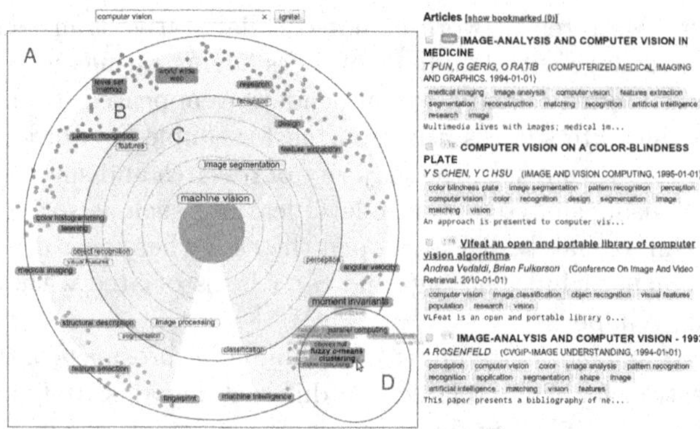

Fig. 1. The SciNet system. The radial display (A) represents the open user model by showing keywords for interaction; inner keywords (C) represent estimated intent and outer keywords (B) represent alternative intents. The user can inspect keywords with a fisheye lens (D) and bookmark documents.

Users can inspect model keywords shown on the radar and *curate* the model by dragging keywords to change their importance. After each iteration, the user model is inferred from the whole set of user actions, documents are searched based on the updated model, and the radial visualization is updated.

Our interest is to use (1) the whole content of the open user model and (2) its curated subset (the keywords the user moved in the process of curation). As a baseline, we also explore transfer of more traditional information: (3) the set of relevant documents selected by the user in the process of search (which could be considered as hidden, implicit user model) and (4) a broader set of all documents retrieved in response to user queries that is a weaker reflection of user interests.

4 Model Transfer for Cross-System Recommendation

The goal of our cross-system setup is to recommend users relevant talks based on features extracted from the description of the talk and their model of interests . Each CoMeT talk is represented by a unigram model, that is, as a vector of word counts in the description of the talk, normalized by the maximum word count, and converted into term frequency–inverse document frequency (TF-IDF) representation. We create a warm start for CoMeT talk recommendation by transferring user models from SciNet. We use two approaches to transfer the explicit *open user model* from SciNet, and two approaches to transfer implicit user models from the SciNet search trace, detailed below.

A. Ranking based on the CoMeT user model alone (denoted 'Baseline'). The baseline method ignores SciNet, and ranking is based only on the CoMeT user model. In the pure cold-start case where no bookmarks are available, the baseline is unable to give recommendations.

B. Transfer the explicit open user model from manipulated keywords (denoted 'ma.keywords'). The SciNet open user model represents the user's interest over keywords. While the model predicts importance over all keywords, a subset of most promising ones are shown for interaction, and a further subset out of those are manipulated by the user. Here we take this last subset: the set of all scientific keywords dragged by the user on the SciNet interface during the search session is treated as a pseudodocument containing the keywords. Each keyword is associated with a weight corresponding to the user's interest (radius where the user dragged the keyword). The pseudodocument is converted into a vector of unigrams by taking each unigram within each keyword (e.g. "support" and "vector" within "support vector"), associating it with the corresponding weight of the keyword (or sum of weights if the unigram occurs in several keywords), and discarding unigrams that do not appear in the CoMeT corpus. This extracts from the SciNet open user model the unigram information common with the CoMeT information space. Since the open user model is represented as a single pseudodocument instead of a corpus, we do not convert the corresponding unigram vector into TF-IDF representation, instead we only normalize it by its maximum value; the corpus of CoMeT talks is then converted into TF-IDF over CoMeT talks only. The resulting unigram vector of the pseudodocument is added into the user's cold-start set of bookmarked CoMeT talks.

C. Transfer the explicit open user model from shown keywords (denoted 'sh.keywords'). The SciNet open user model displays the subset of most important keywords to the user at each search iteration (area A in Figure 1 right). We take the subset in each iteration as a pseudodocument, where each keyword is associated with a weight corresponding to the user interest predicted by SciNet. We convert each such pseudodocument into a vector of unigrams in the same way as in **B**; the user thus gets one vector of unigrams for each search iteration, which together represent the evolution of the user model over the search session. As in **B** this is not a corpus, hence we only normalize each vector of unigrams by its maximum value and CoMeT talks apply TF-IDF weighting over CoMeT talks only. The unigram vectors of the pseudodocument are added into the user's cold-start set of bookmarked CoMeT talks.

D. Transfer an implicit user model from bookmarked documents (denoted 'bm.papers'). Scientific documents bookmarked by the user during the SciNet search session provide implicit information about the user's interests. We convert all bookmarked documents the same unigram representation as CoMeT talks as in **B**. Since the bookmarked documents form a corpus, we convert unigram vectors of CoMeT talks and SciNet documents into a TF-IDF representation computed over both corpuses. For each user we add the resulting unigram vectors of the SciNet bookmarks into the cold-start set of that user's bookmarked CoMeT talks.

E. Transfer an implicit user model from shown documents (denoted 'sh.papers'). We do the same as in **D** but using all documents seen by the user during the SciNet search session (not only bookmarked documents). Note that these documents had been retrieved for the momentary user models during the session; **C** represents the momentary models, whereas **E** represents the momentary best matches to the models in the corpus. Documents as in **E** are available in all interactive search systems whereas keywords in **C** require an open model.

5 User Study for Data Collection

To perform experiments on cross-system model transfer, we had to collect data that capture interests of the same users in the two explored systems. This data was collected through a user study In Section 6 we will perform experiments on cross-system transfer from SciNet to CoMeT, for cold-start prediction of CoMeT talk attendance using information from the SciNet search trace. Before we perform the recommendation experiments, we conduct a task-based user study in a laboratory setting, to collect data for a set of users over both systems:

1. We collected the search trace and open models of the users when they conducted an exploratory search in SciNet for scientific literature corresponding to their research interests. Participants were asked to imagine that they are preparing for a course or seminar on their research interest.
2. We collected user preference in attending academic talks indexed in the CoMeT system. Participants were asked to bookmark interestin talks and rate to what extent they would like to attend it.

Task Descriptions. For SciNet, we chose a search task complex enough that users must interact with the system to gain the information needed to accomplish the task, and broad enough to reveal research interests of users. The task is: "Write down three areas of your scientific research interests. Imagine that you are preparing for a course or a seminar for each research interest. Search scientific documents that you find useful for preparing for the courses or seminars." To determine which documents were relevant to the task, we asked the users to bookmark at least five documents for each research interest. For CoMeT, we used the following rating task: "Please rate all the scientific talks whether you would like to attend the talks or not. If you don't want to attend the talk then just click "no" button and go to next talk. If you want to attend the talk then you click "yes" button and fill the ratings." We provided the following guidelines for ratings:
"5" : This talk matches my research interest and I would definitely attend it.
"4" : This talk matches my research interest and I would likely attend it.
"3" : This talk somewhat matches my research interest and I might attend it.
"2" : This talk somewhat matches my interest, but its unlikely that I attend it.
"1" : This talk somewhat matches the research interest but I wouldn't attend it.

Participants. We recruited 20 researchers (14 male and 6 female) from University of Helsinki to participate in the study. All participants were research staff (10 PhD researchers and 10 research assistants) in computer science or related fields. The participation was limited to researchers because the nature of SciNet and CoMeT required participants having experience in scientific document search and having interest in attending research related talks or seminars.

Prior to the experiment, we conducted a background survey of the participants to ensure that they have conducted literature search before and have also attended research related talks or seminars.

Procedure. The study used a within-subject design in which all the participants performed both the tasks using both the systems alternatively. To minimize the impact of experience in one system on another, we counter balanced the order of system use. Ten participants used the SciNet system first and then used the Comet system while the remaining ten participants used the CoMeT system first and then used the SciNet system. The protocol for each system had two stages: for SciNet the stages were demonstrating the system (7 minutes) and then performing the search task by the participant (30 minutes); for CoMeT the stages were demonstrating the system (7 minutes) and then performing the rating task by the participant (75 minutes).

Data Logging. When the participants were performing the search task in SciNet, we logged all their interactions with the system Data logged from each interaction included details of the scientific documents displayed, keywords for the estimated intent predicted by the system and for alternative intents (areas C and B in the right-hand subfigure of Figure 1), curated keywords, search query of the users, abstracts of scientific documents viewed, scientific documents bookmarked by the users and the corresponding timestamps of all the user interactions. When the participants were performing the rating task in CoMeT, we logged the ratings of the scientific talks or seminars and the ratings of the novelty of the scientific talks or seminars.

6 Cross-System Recommendation Experiment

The user data gathered in Section 5 was used to create experiments on cross-system recommendation of CoMeT talks by transporting user models from Scinet to CoMeT. We compare the four modes of transporting user models described in Section 4. We evaluate both the global impact in a setting with several rated talks available from each user, and performance in the harder cold-start setting.

Data Processing and Demographics. There were 500 CoMeT talks selected from January 10 to February 5, 2013, containing 8,406 unique unigram terms. SciNet indexes over 50 million scientific articles, out of which users see a subset based on their interest and search behavior: there were 9,457 unique SciNet articles returned to our participants with 30,848 unique terms. SciNet also records keywords shown to the user and manipulated by the user; in total the participants were shown 3,474 unique keywords and manipulated 178 unique keywords. Scientific documents and keywords from Scinet and research talks (talk descriptions) from CoMeT were cleaned from html tags, stop words were removed, and words were stemmed by the Krovetz algorithm. In each cross-system transfer approach, the documents, talks, and keywords were converted into unigram vectors with according to term frequency–inverse document frequency (TF-IDF) schemes, as described in Section 4.

6.1 Experiment 1: Global Impact of Cross-System Models

We first consider the traditional (non-cold-start) learning setting where much training data is available within CoMeT, that is, recommendation for users that have used both CoMeT and SciNet for some time. We call this evaluation of global impact of the transfer. We compare the CoMeT-only baseline and four transfer approaches: explicit open user model from manipulated or shown keywords, and implicit user model from bookmarked or shown documents. For each approach we use three methods to make recommendations based on the transported user model: Centroid, k-Nearest Neighbors, and positive-sample-only k-Nearest Neighbors. In all three approaches, We assign equal weight on any vector from either CoMeT or SciNet source.

- **Centroid**: We take the centroid (mean) of the unigram vectors of the user's bookmarked CoMeT talks and any vectors transferred from SciNet. The unigram vectors are extracted from the content of CoMeT talks and SciNet papers (title and abstract) users have bookmarked. Test talks are ranked by cosine similarity of their unigram vector to the centroid.
- **k-Nearest Neighbors (k-NN)**: We treat unigram vectors of bookmarked CoMeT talks and vectors transferred from SciNet as positive samples, and vectors of non-bookmarked CoMeT talks as negative samples. For each test talk we find its k neighbors (nearest positive or negative samples) by cosine similarity of unigram vectors. The k neighbors can be all positive samples or negative ones or combination of them. Test talks are then ranked by $s_{pos} - s_{neg}$, where s_{pos} is the sum of cosine similarities from the test talk to the positive neighbors and s_{neg} is the sum of cosine similarities to the negative neighbors.
- **Positive-Sample-Only k-Nearest Neighbors (denoted k-NN.PO)**: This method is similar to the k-NN approach but we find the k neighbors of a test talk from the positive samples only, and rank the test talk by the sum of cosine similarities from the test talk to the k positive neighbors [10].

We use a ten-fold cross-validation setup: bookmarked and non-bookmarked CoMeT talks of each user were randomly divided into ten equal-size bins, and evaluation was run ten times with each bin in turn held as the test set and the other nine bins as the learning set used to construct user models. SciNet user model data was transferred to each learning set by the transfer approaches to augment the resulting user model. Results (rankings of test talks) are evaluated by mean average precision (MAP): mean of precision values at locations of positive test talks in the ranking, averaged over users and cross-validation folds.

Results of Experiment 1. Table 1 shows the results of global transfer models from Scinet data to CoMeT system. Performance of the CoMeT-only baseline varies by recommendation approach: Centroid and k-NN perform comparably and k-NN.PO is slightly better. For the transfer approaches centroid performs comparably to other approaches; k-NN or k-NN.PO can yield slightly higher MAP but depend on value of k. Overall, in this non-cold-start setting transfer

Table 1. The Mean Average Precision (MAP) of Global Impact from Transferring Models by Transporting Data Methods and by Recommending Algorithms

Mean Average Precision		Centroid	k-NN				k-NN.PO			
			5nn	10nn	20nn	30nn	5nn.po	10nn.po	20nn.po	30nn.po
baseline		0.47	0.45	0.47	0.48	0.46	0.48	0.50	0.50	0.50
Implicit User Model	ex.papers	0.42	0.44	0.45	0.45	0.44	0.43	0.44	0.44	0.44
	im.papers	0.36	0.36	0.36	0.35	0.35	0.36	0.37	0.36	0.36
Explicit Open User Model	ex.keywords	0.48	0.46	0.48	0.48	0.47	0.49	0.51	0.51	0.50
	im.keywords	0.47	0.46	0.48	0.49	0.49	0.48	0.49	0.49	0.48

of SciNet information did not yield much improvement over the CoMeT-only baseline: transferring an implicit model from shown SciNet documents underperformed the CoMeT-only baseline and the other transfer approaches were not significantly different from that baseline. In this non-cold-start situation user profiles in CoMeT had enough data to work well on their own; thus we expect greatest benefit of transfer in the cold-start setting.

6.2 Experiment 2: Cold-Start Recommendation

Here we study the main focus of the paper: cold-start settings. We again transfer four kinds of user models from Scinet (explicit open user models from shown and manipulated keywords, and implicit models from shown and bookmarked documents).

Experimental Setup: Ten-round-ten-fold Cross-Validation. We consider a range of cold-start setups where the user has bookmarked 0-20 CoMeT talks. For each number of bookmarked talks we use a ten-fold cross-validation setup: we divide data into ten bins; in each fold we hold out one cross-validation bin as test data, and from the remaining nine bins we randomly sample a pool of bookmarked talks and a pool of non-bookmarked talks; within each fold we perform that random sampling 10 times (10 "rounds") and report average results over rounds. For each number of bookmarked talks, the number of sampled non-bookmarked talks was chosen to keep the same ratio of bookmarked to non-bookmarked talks as overall in the data of that user. We evaluate results by the same MAP criterion as in the first experiment.

Results of Cold-Start Recommendation. We first tested cold-start recommendation for the CoMeT-only baseline using the three recommendation methods (centroid, k-NN, k-NN.PO as in Table 1). centroid and k-NN.PO models performed equally (results omitted for brevity; essentially no visible difference regardless of the profile size) and outperformed the k-NN models. Given that the centroid model is simpler and faster than k-NN.PO, it was used for all transfer methods in the cold-start recommendation. Figure 2 shows the results of transfer in the cold-start setting. Explicit transfer of the SciNet open user models (ma.keywords and sh.keywords) helped the transition of the new users into the CoMeT system. The MAP results of keyword models are significantly better than the baseline until the user has two bookmarked talks in the Scinet implicit

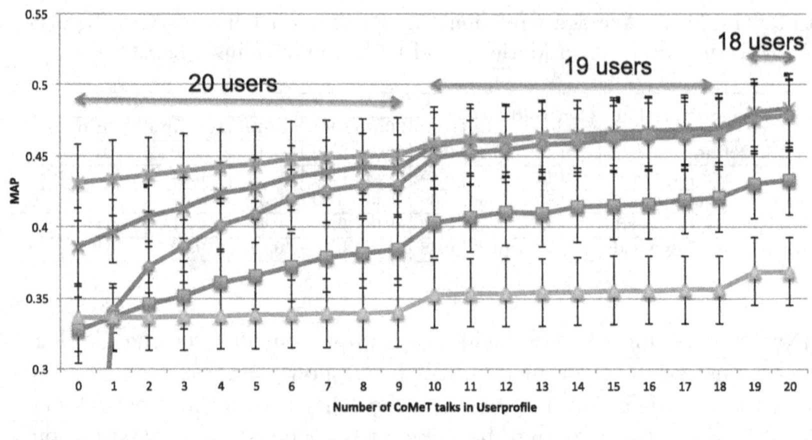

Fig. 2. Cold-start-effect MAP Results of Centroid Models. The MAP is shown for each method and each number of bookmarked CoMeT talks. Error bars show 95% confidence interval of the mean over users and cross-validation folds. "20 users"–"18 users" denote how many users had enough data within cross-validation folds to have the desired number of bookmarked talks.

keyword transfer centroid model, and until five bookmarked talks in the Scinet explicit keyword transfer centroid model. While the transfer of explicit curated models worked well, the transfer of implicit models built from retrieved and bookmarked papers harmed the MAP performance. Even the model built from explicitly selected talks performed poorly comparing to the baseline. We analyze reasons for this performance difference in the next section.

7 Analysis of Cross-System Transfer Performance

As expected, the transfer of explicitly curated user models yielded better results than alternative transfer approaches and the baseline. The reason for the good performance of open curated models can be analyzed by comparing the spaces formed by vectors of the bookmarked and non-bookmarked CoMeT talks with vector spaces of different types of transferred information to the information contained .

The results of this analysis are shown in Figure 3 which plots the distribution across users of average similarities between five representations of user interests – (bookmarked talks in CoMeT and four kinds of models transferred from SciNet) on one side and bookmarked/non-bookmarked CoMeT talks (CP/CN) on the other side. The foure kinds of transferred models are SciNet implicit/explicit keywords (SIK/SEK) and implicit/explicit paper (SIP/SEP). As expected, bookmarked talks in CoMeT are pairwise closer to each other (CP_CP boxplot) than to non-bookmarked ones (CP_CN boxplot). More interesting is that both manipulated SciNet keywords (SEK_CP boxplot) and shown SciNet keywords (SIK_CP

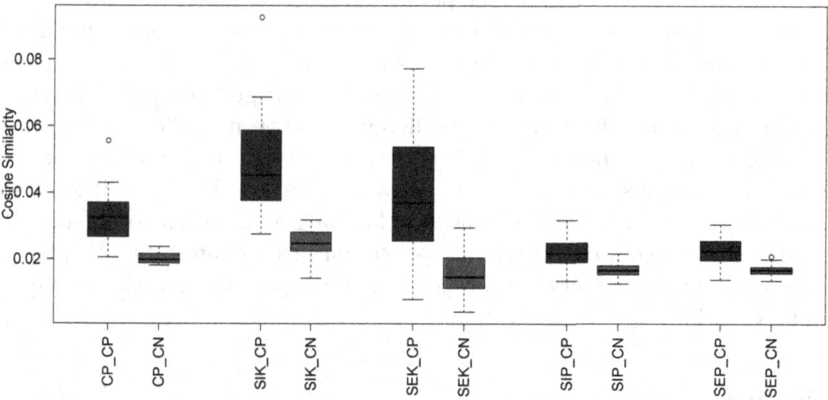

Fig. 3. Distributions of similarities between CoMeT talks five representations of user interests (bookmarked talks and 4 kinds of transfer models). The box-and-whiskers plot shows the median (band inside the box), first and third quartiles (edges of the box), 9th and 91th percentiles (whiskers), and values outside the percentiles as circles. Details for each of plot are in the section 7.

boxplots) are even closer to the space of bookmarked talks, separating them quite well from non-bookmarked ones (SEK_CN and SIK_CN boxplots, respectively). As a result, incorporating open curated keywords into the Centroid model helped alleviate the cold-start problem and improved recommendation performance. In contrast, implicit models built from all shown SciNet papers and bookmarked SciNet papers (SIP_CP and SEP_CP, respectively) are quite far from the space of bookmarked talks and offer poor separation of this space from the non-bookmarked talks (SEP_CN and SIP_CN, respectively). Consequently, implicit models add more noise than value and damage recommendation.

8 Conclusions

This paper explores a novel approach to cross-system personalization based on transferring an explicit, open, and editable user model maintained by one system to another system in a similar, yet different domain. More specifically, we explored whether an open user model maintained by SciNet exploratory literature search system could help recommend relevant research talks to users of CoMeT talk sharing system who have established SciNet interest models. The impact of open model transfer was compared with a baseline case that uses no information from SciNet and with more traditional implicit model transfer based on information about retrieved and marked papers. The comparison examined an overall impact of the transfer as well as its value in a cold-start situation when the user has none or too few talks bookmarked in CoMeT. The results showed that cross-system model transfer is a challenging task. We were not able to register a significant impact of model transfer in a general situation. However, the study demonstrated a significant positive impact of the open model transfer in the *cold-start* case. It also demonstrated that the use of open, explicitly curated user models is critical for the success of user model transfer: the transfer of SciNet data in the form of implicit model damaged the performance of talk recommendation. The analysis of differences between explicit and implicit model hinted that the use of explicitly curated models reduces the noise in modeling user interests. An interesting research question that we will leave for the future work is to what extent machine learning approaches could simulate model curation focusing on better representation of user interests. We plan to explore several feature selection approaches and compare them with the impact of manual curation.

References

1. Berkovsky, S., Kuflik, T., Ricci, F.: Mediation of user models for enhanced personalization in recommender systems. User Modeling and User-Adapted Interaction **18**(3), 245–286 (2008)
2. Cremonesi, P., Tripodi, A., Turrin, R.: Cross-domain recommender systems. In: 2011 IEEE 11th International Conference on Data Mining Workshops, pp. 496–503. IEEE, December 2011
3. Fernadez-Tobis, I., Cantador, I., Kaminskas, M., Ricci, F.: Cross-domain recommender systems: a survey of the state of the art. In: the 2nd Spanish Conference on Information Retrieval
4. Li, B., Yang, Q., Xue, X.: Can movies and books collaborate?: cross-domain collaborative filtering for sparsity reduction. In: Proceedings of the 21st International Jont Conference on Artifical Intelligence, IJCAI 2009, pp. 2052–2057. Morgan Kaufmann Publishers Inc, San Francisco (2009)
5. Loizou, A.: How to recommend music to film buffs: enabling the provision of recommendations from multiple domains. Thesis (2009)
6. Pan, W., Liu, N.N., Xiang, E.W., Yang, Q.: Transfer learning to predict missing ratings via heterogeneous user feedbacks. In: Proc. of the Twenty-Second International Joint Conference on Artificial Intelligence - Volume Three, IJCAI 2011, pp. 2318–2323. AAAI Press (2011)
7. Ruotsalo, T., Peltonen, J., Eugster, M., Głowacka, D., Konyushkova, K., Athukorala, K., Kosunen, I., Reijonen, A., Myllymäki, P., Jacucci, G., Kaski, S.: Directing exploratory search with interactive intent modeling. In: Proceedings of the 22nd ACM International Conference on Conference on Information & Knowledge Management, CIKM 2013, pp. 1759–1764. ACM, New York (2013)
8. Sahebi, S., Brusilovsky, P.: Cross-domain collaborative recommendation in a cold-start context: the impact of user profile size on the quality of recommendation. In: Carberry, S., Weibelzahl, S., Micarelli, A., Semeraro, G. (eds.) UMAP 2013. LNCS, vol. 7899, pp. 289–295. Springer, Heidelberg (2013)

9. Schein, A.I., Popescul, A., Ungar, L.H., Pennock, D.M.: Methods and metrics for cold-start recommendations. In: Proceedings of the 25th Annual International ACM SIGIR Conference on Research and Development in Information Retrieval, SIGIR 2002, pp. 253–260. ACM, New York(2002)
10. Schwab, I., Pohl, W., Koychev, I.: Learning to recommend from positive evidence. In: Proceedings of the 5th International Conference on Intelligent User Interfaces, IUI 2000, pp. 241–247. ACM, New York (2000)
11. Shi, Y., Larson, M., Hanjalic, A.: Tags as bridges between domains: improving recommendation with tag-induced cross-domain collaborative filtering. In: Konstan, J.A., Conejo, R., Marzo, J.L., Oliver, N. (eds.) UMAP 2011. LNCS, vol. 6787, pp. 305–316. Springer, Heidelberg (2011)

Implicit Acquisition of User Personality for Augmenting Movie Recommendations

Wen Wu(✉) and Li Chen

Department of Computer Science, Hong Kong Baptist University, Kowloon Tong, Hong Kong, China
{cswenwu,lichen}@comp.hkbu.edu.hk

Abstract. In recent years, user personality has been recognized as valuable info to build more personalized recommender systems. However, the effort of explicitly acquiring users' personality traits via psychological questionnaire is unavoidably high, which may impede the application of personality-based recommenders in real life. In this paper, we focus on deriving users' personality from their implicit behavior in movie domain and hence enabling the generation of recommendations without involving users' efforts. Concretely, we identify a set of behavioral features through experimental validation, and develop inference model based on Gaussian Process to unify these features for determining users' big-five personality traits. We then test the model in a collaborative filtering based recommending framework on two real-life movie datasets, which demonstrates that our implicit personality based recommending algorithm significantly outperforms related methods in terms of both rating prediction and ranking accuracy. The experimental results point out an effective solution to boost the applicability of personality-based recommender systems in online environment.

Keywords: Recommender systems · User personality · Implicit acquisition · Collaborative filtering

1 Introduction

Nowadays, recommender systems (RS) have been widely adopted in many online applications for eliminating users' information overload and providing personalized services to them. In order to more accurately learn users' preferences, personality has been increasingly recognized as a valuable resource being incorporated into the process of generating recommendations [18,25]. As a typical work, Tkalcic *et al.* [25] adopted users' personality to enhance the measure of nearest neighborhood in collaborative filtering (CF) systems. Hu and Pu demonstrated that personality can be leveraged into solving the cold-start problem of CF [18]. However, existing studies have mostly relied on personality quiz to explicitly acquire users' personality, which unavoidably demands user efforts. From users' perspective, they may be unwilling to answer the quiz for the sake of saving efforts or protecting their privacy. The application of existing personality-based RSs will thus be limited in real life.

F. Ricci et al. (Eds.): UMAP 2015, LNCS 9146, pp. 302–314, 2015.
DOI: 10.1007/978-3-319-20267-9_25

In this paper, we are motivated to study how to implicitly derive users' personality from their behavior data. Specifically, the main contributions of our work are as follows:

(a) We have first identified a set of features that are significantly correlated with users' personality traits, through experimental validation. Among them, some are domain dependent, such as users' preference for movie genre and movies' diversity, watching duration, and watching motives. Some are domain independent, like users' rating behavior and age info.
(b) We have then integrated all of these features into a regression model to infer users' personality. We have concretely tested three different models, Gaussian Process, Pace Regression, and M5 Rules, and found that Gaussian Process performs the best in terms of inference accuracy.
(c) At the last step, we have developed three variations of personality based CF algorithm, for which the personality is implicitly inferred from user behavior in real-life movie datasets. Through experiment, we have demonstrated that the method combining user personality and ratings is most accurate in terms of both rating prediction and ranking accuracy. The results thus highlight the practical merit of our method in augmenting online movie recommendations.

In the following, we first introduce related work on personality-based recommender systems (Section 2). We then present the details of our feature selection process in movie domain, as well as the experiment on personality inference model in Section 3. In Section 4, we describe how the model is incorporated into the CF based recommending framework. We finally conclude the work and indicate its future directions in Section 5.

2 Related Work

How to use user personality for benefiting recommender systems has attracted increasing attentions in recent years. For instance, Tkalcic *et al.* employed personality to enhance the nearest neighborhood measure in a CF-based image recommender system, and demonstrated that the personality based similarity measure is more accurate than the rating based measure [25]. Hu and Pu [18] also incorporated users' personality into the CF framework. Their experiment indicated that personality-based CF methods are significantly superior to the non-personality based approach in terms of solving the cold-start problem. In addition, they proposed a preference-based approach [17], for which a personality-based interest profile is established for each user to reflect the relationship between her/his personality and preference for music genre [23]. The items that best match the user's profile are recommended. A user study revealed that users in this system perceive the recommended items to be accurate for their friends. Elahi *et al.* [7] developed a novel active learning strategy based on personality, for predicting items that users are able to rate before they get recommendations. They concretely implemented an attribute-based matrix factorization (MF) algorithm, where the attributes include users' age, gender, and personality traits. Through a live user study, they proved that involving these attributes, especially users' personality, can significantly increase the number of items that users can rate.

However, the issue of how to obtain users' personality is still not well solved. The existing studies mainly rely on psychological questionnaires (such as IPIP personality quiz [11] used in [25], and TIPI personality quiz [12] in [7,17,18]) to measure users' personality traits, which unavoidably demand a lot of user efforts and hence impede the system's practical application in real life. Lately, there have been endeavors to derive users' personality from their self-generated data. For instance, Gao *et al.* attempted to derive users' personality from their micro blogs [8]. Golbeck *et al.* identified users' personality traits through their Facebook profile, which includes language features, activities, and personal information [9]. But their main focus has been on social networking sites, rather than on social media domains such as movie. Another limitation is that little work has been done on incorporating the implicitly acquired personality into the process of recommendation generation.

We are thus interested in not only exploring proper behavioral features in movie domain that can be used to infer user personality, but also investigating how to improve recommendation accuracy with the inferred personality.

3 Implicit Acquisition of User Personality

A widely used personality model is the so called big-five factor model, which defines user personality as five traits [14][1]: *Openness to Experience (O)*, *Conscientiousness (C)*, *Extroversion (E)*, *Agreeableness (A)*, and *Neuroticism (N)*. In this section, we first describe how we have identified a set of features and experimentally validated their significant correlations with users' personality traits. We then introduce the personality inference model and its accuracy measurement.

3.1 Feature Identification

User Preference for Movie Genre. The psychological researches conducted in movie domain have shown that users' personality can influence their preference for movie genre. For example, both Cantador *et al.* [1] and Chausson [3] pointed out that more imaginative and creative people (with high O[2]) are more inclined to choose comedy movies, whereas people with low O (i.e., cautious and consistent people) and high E (i.e., outgoing and energetic people) tend to choose romance movies. Therefore, in our work, "movie genre" is taken as an important personality feature.

[1] Due to space limit, the description of these five traits can be found in [14].

[2] High O means that the user has high score on the personality trait "Openness to Experience", which is also applied to the other abbreviations.

Users' Watching Duration. Users' watching duration is another feature that we have considered, because it was reported that people with different personality traits may behave differently in terms of time spent on watching TV programs [21]. For instance, those who are more sensitive and nervous (with high N) tend to spend more time in watching. Considering that movie is similar to TV program in that it is also a type of leisure media, we think that users' personality may also influence their movie watching duration.

Users' Motives Behind Watching Movies. Chamorro-Premuzic *et al.* [2] indicated that users' personality traits can affect their motives when choosing movies. Specifically, the motives include emotional factors (like hedonism and sensation seeking) and cognitive factors (like boredom avoidance and information seeking). It was found that those who possess high O tend to select movies for seeking useful information (i.e., cognitive motives), while individuals with high A and E are likely to watch movies for fun (i.e., emotional motives). Thus, in our work, we take "watching motive" as one personality feature.

User Preference for Movies' Diversity. In our previous work [4,27], we found that users' personality can affect their spontaneous needs for the level of diversity within a list of movies that they will select. For instance, people with high N are more likely to prefer movies with diverse directors. Moreover, the personality trait C is significantly correlated with users' preference for movies' overall diversity when all attributes are considered. Formally, a user's preference for diversity in respect of a specific movie attribute (e.g., genre, director) can be determined via the intra-list metric:

$$Div(attr_k) = \frac{2}{|S_u| \times |S_u - 1|} \sum_{m_i \in S_u} \sum_{m_j \neq m_i \in S_u} (1 - Sim(m_i, m_j)) \tag{1}$$

where $attr_k$ is the k-th attribute, S_u is the set of movies selected by the user, and $Sim(m_i, m_j)$ gives the similarity between two movies in terms of $attr_k$ (i.e., $Sim(m_i, m_j) = \frac{|S_{m_i,attr_k} \cap S_{m_j,attr_k}|}{|S_{m_i,attr_k} \cup S_{m_j,attr_k}|}$, where $S_{m_i,attr_k}$ contains all values of $attr_k$, such as all actors, in movie m_i). The user's preference for movies' overall diversity is further measured as:

$$OverDiv = \sum_{k=1}^{n} (w_k \times Div(attr_k)) \tag{2}$$

where w_k indicates the attribute's relative importance to the user ($0 <= w_k <= 1, \sum_{k=1}^{n} w_k = 1$) and n is the total number of attributes.

Users' Rating Behavior. Users' rating behavior might also be indicative of their personality. As shown by Golbeck and Norris [10], two personality traits E and C are both positively correlated with users' ratings on movies. That is, people who are more extrovert, outgoing, cautious, and self-disciplined tend to give higher ratings than others. Besides, Hu and Pu [19] found that C is negatively correlated with the number of ratings that a user gives, which implies that unorganized and impulsive people are likely to rate more items.

Users' Demographic Properties. There are several demographic properties that have been shown related to users' personality. For instance, Chausson [3] found that females usually score higher on personality traits N and A than males. As for age, McCrae *et al.* found that older people have lower scores on E and O, but higher scores on A and C [20]. Regarding education, people with high C (i.e., self-disciplined ones) are more likely to obtain higher education degree [5].

In summary, we have identified six major types of features for implicitly deriving users' personality. Some of them, such as users' rating behavior and demographic properties, can be applied to other domains except for movie, which we call *domain-independent* features, and the others are called *domain-dependent* features.

3.2 Validation Experiment

In order to validate whether the above-mentioned features are truly significantly correlated with users' personality, we have conducted a validation experiment.

User Survey Setup. To do the validation, we first performed a user survey to collect users' interaction behavior with movies and personality values. A total of 148 volunteers (77 females) joined this survey. All of them are Chinese, who are with different education backgrounds (28% with Bachelor, 57% with Master, 7% with PhD, and 8% miscellaneous) and age ranges (61% in the range of 20-25 years old, 32% in the range of 25-30, 4% in the range of 30-40, and 3% in the other ranges).

Each user's personality was assessed via a popular big-five personality quiz that contains 25 questions [14]. Each personality trait's score is the sum of scores on its related 5 questions. For example, one question of assessing *Neuroticism* is *"Do you feel you are always calm or eager?"* which is rated from 1 "calm" to 5 "eager". We also asked each user to freely rate at least 10 movies that s/he has watched by checking movies' information in Douban Movie (movie.douban.com), which is a popular movie reviewing website in China.

Implicit Features. The behavioral features (identified in the previous section) were concretely determined in the following ways. A user's preference for movie genre was obtained by asking her/him to choose three most favorite genres and three least favorite ones (among 15 genres such as action, horror, etc.) in our survey. As for watching duration, we first used the user's answer to the question *"How often do you see a movie?"* (among the options "one week", "one month", "three months", etc.) to represent her/his watching frequency, and then calculated the watching duration by multiplying her/his weekly watching frequency with the movie's average length (i.e., 1.5 hours). The user's main motive behind watching movies was assessed via the question *"At most of times, why do you want to see a movie, for seeking useful information or just for fun?"* In parallel, Eq.1 and Eq.2 were applied to measure the user's preferences for movies' attribute-specific diversity and overall diversity, for which only movies that the user gave positive ratings (i.e., above 3 out of 5) were considered, and attributes' weights (in Eq.2) were obtained through conjoint analysis [13]. Regarding rating behavior, both the average rating and the total number of ratings that a user gave to movies were taken into account.

Correlation Results. The correlations between users' personality traits and their behavioral features were computed via Spearman's rank coefficient because it can be applied to both ordinal and numerical variables [29]. Table 1 shows the results. With respect to user preference for movie genre, it is significantly correlated with all of the five personality traits. For example, people with high O tend to prefer music and animation movies, whereas those who score low on O prefer documentary movies. The genre's preference is also correlated with users' personality traits C, E, A, and N. In terms of watching duration, the personality traits C and A show significantly positive correlations with it, which implies that those who are more organized, patient, friendly and cooperative are more likely to spend more time in watching movies. In addition, those people also tend to watch movies for fun rather than seeking information given the significant correlations between the two traits C and A and users' watching motive. As for rating behavior, people with high C and A are found being more subject to give higher ratings. Furthermore, O and E are significantly negatively correlated with users' preference for movies' diversity w.r.t. genre, indicating that conventional and introvert persons are more inclined to choose diverse genres. The movies' diversity w.r.t country is preferred by suspicious and antagonistic users (with low A). Finally, among users' demographic properties, we observe that age is significantly correlated with O in a negative way, which suggests that young people are more imaginative and creative than elders.

Thus, it can be seen that most of features are empirically proven with significant correlations with users' personality. Particularly, more *domain-dependent* features, such as users' preference for movie genre, their watching duration, and watching motive, exhibit strong correlations, which suggests that the behavioral features related to a specific domain can be more helpful for inferring users' personality. For the next step, we have attempted to combine all of these significant features into a unified inference model.

3.3 Personality Inference Model and Evaluation

Inference Model. We have compared three regression models for inferring users' personality: Gaussian Process, Pace Regression, and M5 Rules. Formally, a standard form of regression model can be represented as $y = f(x) + \varepsilon$, where x denotes an input vector (in our case, it includes the implicit features like user preference for movie genre, the user's watching duration, etc.), y denotes a scalar output (in our case, it gives the inferred big-five personality scores), and ε is the additive noise. Our purpose is then to estimate the regression function $f(\cdot)$.

Gaussian Process (GP) [22] defines a probabilistic regression based on Bayesian theory and statistical learning theory: $f(x) \sim gp(\mu(x), k(x, x'))$, where

Table 1. Correlations between users' personality traits and implicit features ($^{*}p < 0.05$ and $^{**}p < 0.01$)

		Openness to Experience (O)	*Conscien-tiousness (C)*	*Extrover-sion (E)*	*Agreeable-ness (A)*	*Neuroti-cism (N)*
User preference for movie genre		*O*: Music (0.207*), Animation (0.183*), Documentary (-0.167**); *C*: Animation (-0.201*), Comedy (-0.163*), War (0.192**), Science Fiction (0.176*); *E*: Mystery (-0.163*), Crime (-0.18*), Romance (0.136**); *A*: Animation (-0.20*), Science Fiction (0.171*), War (0.192*); *N*: Romance (0.203*), History (-0.173*), Drama (0.184*), Adventure (-0.106*), Animation (0.202*), Documentary (-0.165*).				
Watching duration		-0.043	**0.176***	0.147	**0.175***	-0.094
Watching motive		-0.091	**0.208***	0.001	**0.181***	-0.139
User preference for movies' diversity	Overall div.	0.038	0.033	-0.010	-0.029	-0.051
	Genre div.	**-0.135***	0.057	**-0.176***	-0.072	0.050
	Country div.	0.069	-0.130	0.069	**-0.189***	0.166
	Release time div.	-0.144	-0.040	-0.104	-0.140	0.085
	Actor/actress div.	-0.003	0.025	0.061	0.001	-0.012
	Director div.	-0.037	-0.013	0.050	0.085	-0.053
Rating behavior	Average rating	-0.134	**0.175***	0.082	**0.262****	-0.018
	Number of ratings	-0.145	0.219	0.040	0.217	-0.012
Demographic property	Gender	0.068	-0.070	0.110	-0.049	0.075
	Age	**-0.201***	0.103	0.121	0.082	-0.057
	Education level	-0.033	0.157	-0.002	0.109	-0.137

$\mu(x)$ stands for the mean function and $k(x, x')$ is the covariance function. In practice, GP can handle datasets with small number of samples and/or many input features. Unlike GP, Pace Regression [26] is a typical form of linear regression analysis. It is applicable when some of the input features are mutually dependent. M5 Rules [16] also assumes a linear distribution of the input features, but it is grounded on the separate-and-conquer strategy to build a decision tree. In comparison to the other models, M5 Rules costs less calculation and can deal with small-scale datasets or datasets with missing values.

Evaluation Procedure. We randomly selected 90% of 148 users who participated in our user survey (see Section 3.2) to train each model and tested it on the remaining 10% users. To avoid any biases, we performed 10-fold cross validation, and measured the accuracy via metrics *Root Mean-Square Error (RMSE)* [15] and *Pearson correlation* [15]. Formally, we define a user's personality as a 5-dimension vector $p_u = (p_u^1, p_u^2, ..., p_u^5)^T$, where each dimension p^k represents one personality trait among O, C, E, A, and N.

Evaluation Results. The results are shown in Table 2, in which *RMSE* values that are returned by the three regression models in respect of each personality trait are all within 10% of its real score. Moreover, Gaussian Process obtains a relatively smaller margin of error than Pace Regression and M5 Rules. In terms of *Pearson correlation*, Gaussian Process produces results with higher correlations than Pace Regression and M5 Rules, regarding all of the personality traits. Particularly, the correlations by Gaussian Process are significant regarding personality traits C ($p < 0.01$), A ($p < 0.05$), and N ($p < 0.05$). We further run

Table 2. RMSE and Pearson correlation results of testing three inference models (*note*: the number in superscript indicates that the model significantly ($p < 0.05$) outperforms the referred one in terms of the corresponding metric)

Personality trait	[1]Gaussian Process	[2]Pace Regression	[3]M5 Rules
RMSE			
Openness to Experience (O)	0.0354^{3}	0.0357^{3}	0.0369
Conscientiousness (C)	0.0350^{3}	0.0382^{3}	0.0380
Extraversion (E)	0.0375^{3}	0.0378^{3}	0.0410
Agreeableness (A)	0.0484^{3}	0.0494^{3}	0.0504
Neuroticism (N)	0.0568^{3}	0.0584^{3}	0.0605
Pearson correlation coefficient ($^{*}p < 0.05$, $^{**}p < 0.01$)			
Openness to Experience (O)	$0.1424^{2,3}$	0.0458	0.0537
Conscientiousness (C)	$\mathbf{0.3319}^{**,2,3}$	0.0600	$\mathbf{0.1942}^{*}$
Extraversion (E)	$0.1085^{2,3}$	0.0839	0.0871
Agreeableness (A)	$\mathbf{0.2177}^{*,2,3}$	0.1204	$\mathbf{0.1704}^{*}$
Neuroticism (N)	$\mathbf{0.2634}^{*,2,3}$	0.0553	0.1375

Note: Here, we normalized each personality value into [0-1] scale via the logarithmic form of normalization: $\overline{X} = \frac{\log_{10} X}{\log_{10} max}$, where X is the original score of each personality trait, and max gives the maximum value among all of the samples. Moreover, the standard deviations of the five personality traits at the normalized 0-1 scale are respectively: $\boldsymbol{O}(0.035)$, $\boldsymbol{C}(0.038)$, $\boldsymbol{E}(0.037)$, $\boldsymbol{A}(0.048)$, $\boldsymbol{N}(0.058)$.

a pairwise t-Test to identify the significance level of differences between these models. It shows that Gaussian Process significantly outperforms M5 Rules in terms of both *RMSE* and *Pearson correlation* ($p < 0.05$) in respect of all of the personality traits, and is significantly better than Pace Regression in terms of *Pearson correlation* ($p < 0.05$). Pace Regression is significantly better than M5 Rules in terms of *RMSE* ($p < 0.05$). As for the reason why Gaussian Process performs the best, we think it is because the non-linear relationship between input and output as defined in this model may better fit the characteristic of our data. It also avoids bringing the noise of input to output by performing a probabilistic function.

The above results hence demonstrate that a user's personality traits can be inferred by unifying some implicit features. Given that Gaussian Process shows the best accuracy among the three compared models, we adopt it for the next step of recommendation generation.

4 Recommendation Based on Implicit Personality

The next question we are interested in solving is: *how to employ the implicitly acquired personality for improving the real-life movie recommendation?* In the following, we present our algorithm development and evaluation results.

4.1 Algorithm Development

We first apply Gaussian Process to derive users' personality from their interaction behavior with movies (i.e., implicit features). The inferred personality is then incorporated into the collaborative filtering (CF) process. Concretely, we develop three variations of the personality-based recommending method: pure personality-based CF, and two hybrid CF methods that integrate personality with ratings.

Personality-Based CF. Similar to the approach proposed in [18], we can use personality to calculate user-user similarity. Specifically, we adopt the 5-dimension vector $p_u = (p_u^1, p_u^2, ..., p_u^5)^T$ (derived from the previous step; see Section 3.3) to define a user's personality, and then compute the personality-based similarity between two users u and v via *Cosine* measure:

$$Simp(u,v) = \frac{\sum_{k=1}^{5}(p_u^k \times p_v^k)}{\sqrt{\sum_{k=1}^{5} {p_u^k}^2}\sqrt{\sum_{k=1}^{5} {p_v^k}^2}} \quad (3)$$

The rating predicted to an unknown item i for the target user u is then calculated as:

$$PreScore_{personality}(item_i) = \overline{r_u} + k\sum\nolimits_{v\in\Omega_u} Simp(u,v) \times (r_{v,i} - \overline{r_v}) \quad (4)$$

where $r_{v,i}$ is user v's rating for item i, $\overline{r_u}$ and $\overline{r_v}$ are respectively user u's and v's average ratings, k is equal to $\frac{1}{\sum_{v\in\Omega_u}|Simp(u,v)|}$, and Ω_u is the set of u's neighbors who rated item i (note that the similarity threshold is set as 0.7 in our experiment). We call this method PB.

Hybrid CF. We further implement two hybrid CF methods. One is called $RPBL_{score}$, where users' implicit personality scores and ratings are combined into the CF framework in a linear weighted way:

$$PreScore_{hybrid}(item_i) = \alpha \times PreScore_{rating}(item_i) + (1-\alpha) \times PreScore_{personality}(item_i) \quad (5)$$

where $PreScore_{rating}(item_i) = \overline{r_u} + k\sum_{v\in\Omega_u} Simr(u,v) \times (r_{v,i} - \overline{r_v})$, which returns the predicted rating based on the traditional rating-based similarity measure (i.e., $Simr(u,v) = \frac{\sum_{i\in I}(r_{u,i} \times r_{v,i})}{\sqrt{\sum_{i\in I} {r_{u,i}}^2}\sqrt{\sum_{i\in I} {r_{v,i}}^2}}$), $PreScore_{personality}(item_i)$ is the personality-based rating prediction (Eq.4), and α is a weighting parameter used to control the relative contributions of the two types of prediction (that is tuned through experimental trials).

An alternative hybrid method is called $RPBL_{similarity}$ [18], which emphasizes combining personality scores and ratings for computing user-user similarity:

$$Simpr(u,v) = \beta \times Simr(u,v) + (1-\beta) \times Simp(u,v) \quad (6)$$

where β manipulates the weights of the two kinds of similarity measure, i.e., $Simr(u,v)$ and $Simp(u,v)$. $Simpr(u,v)$ is then used to predict an unknown item i's rating for the target user u (by replacing $Simp(u,v)$ in Eq.4).

4.2 Experiment Setup

In the experiment, we compared the three personality-based approaches, i.e., pure personality-based CF (PB) and two hybrid CF methods ($RPBL_{score}$ and $RPBL_{similarity}$), with the standard rating-based CF [18] (shortened as RB) on two real-life movie datasets: HetRec[3] and Yahoo! Movie[4]. Both datasets contain users' movie ratings, and movies' descriptive information such as their genres, actors, directors, and so on. Yahoo! Movie dataset's rating sparsity level[5] is relatively higher (98.8% vs. 95.5% in HetRec dataset). We performed 10-fold cross-validation to measure each method's performance. Concretely, we split the ratings provided by each user into two parts, 80% used for inferring the user's personality, and 20% for testing the recommendation result.

The implicit features used for constructing the personality inference model (see Section 3.2) are identified through the following ways. To obtain user preference for movie genre, we used the proportion of each genre that appears in movies that a user gave positive ratings (i.e., above 3 out of 5), to represent her/his preference for that genre. As for watching duration, we multiplied the average number of movies that the user has rated per week with the movie's average length. The user's preferences for movies' diversity in respect of genre and country were calculated via Eq.1. We also calculated each user's average rating. As for their age information, it is provided in HetRec dataset, but not in Yahoo! Movie. The feature "watching motive" was not considered in this experiment because it is not available in both datasets. We then adopted Gaussian Process (see Section 3.3) to unify these features for inferring each user's big-five personality traits.

The recommendation accuracy was measured in terms of both rating prediction and ranking performance: 1) *Mean Absolute Error (MAE)* and *Root Mean-Squared Error (RMSE)* [15] for determining the tested method's rating prediction accuracy; and 2) *Normalized Discounted Cumulative Gain (nDCG)* and *Mean Average Precision (MAP)* [28] used for determining the method's top-N ranking accuracy ($N = 10$ in our experiment). Due to space limit, the details of these four metrics are referred to [15,28].

4.3 Results

The optimal values of parameters involved in these algorithms, including the neighborhood size k for each method, α in Eq.5, and β in Eq.6, were identified through experimental trials. Table 3 shows each method's performance (with its optimal parameter value(s)) and the pairwise t-Test statistical analysis results.

It can be seen that the two hybrid CF methods, $RPBL_{score}$ and $RPBL_{similarity}$, both significantly outperform the pure personality-based approach (PB) and the standard rating-based method (RB), in terms of rating prediction (i.e., *MAE* and *RMSE*) in the two datasets. They also achieve significantly higher ranking accuracy (*nDCG-5* and *MAP*) than RB. The

[3] HetRec dataset contains 1,872 users, 10,095 movies, and 848,169 ratings.

[4] Yahoo! Movie dataset contains 800 users, 9,128 movies, and 90,832 ratings.

[5] The rating sparsity level is calculated via $Level_{sparsity} = 1 - \frac{|nonzero_{entries}|}{|total_{entries}|}$ [24].

Table 3. Overall comparison results (*note*: the number in superscript indicates that the method significantly ($p < 0.05$) outperforms the referred one in terms of the corresponding metric; and the value inside the parenthesis indicates the improvement percentage against the baseline RB approach)

HetRec				
	^1RB ($k = 200$)	^2PB ($k = 300$)	$^3RPBL_{score}$ ($\alpha = 0.3$)	$^4RPBL_{similarity}$ ($k = 300$, $\beta = 0.8 * \frac{\vert I_u \cap I_v \vert}{\vert I_u \cap I_v \vert + 0.5}$)
MAE	0.6969	0.6835 (1.92%)	$0.6643^{1,2}$(4.67%)	$0.6738^{1,2}$(3.32%)
RMSE	0.9382	0.9362 (0.21%)	$0.8919^{1,2}$(4.93%)	$0.9038^{1,2}$(3.66%)
nDCG-5 (top-10)	0.8421	0.8475 (0.06%)	$0.8689^{1,2}$(3.18%)	0.8593^{1}(2.05%)
MAP (top-10)	0.5348	0.5509 (3.02%)	0.5639^{1}(5.44%)	0.5578^{1}(4.29%)
Yahoo! Moive				
	^1RB ($k = 150$)	^2PB ($k = 200$)	$^3RPBL_{score}$ ($\alpha = 0.3$)	$^4RPBL_{similarity}$ ($k = 200$, $\beta = 0.8 * \frac{\vert I_u \cap I_v \vert}{\vert I_u \cap I_v \vert + 0.5}$)
MAE	1.0308	1.0089^{1}(2.13%)	$0.9912^{1,2}$(3.84%)	$0.9752^{1,2}$(5.39%)
RMSE	1.5620	1.5515 (0.67%)	$1.4767^{1,2}$(5.46%)	$1.4646^{1,2}$(6.23%)
nDCG-5 (top-10)	0.8178	0.8419 (2.94%)	0.8683^{1}(6.16%)	0.8606^{1}(5.22%)
MAP (top-10)	0.7028	0.7110 (1.17%)	$0.7436^{1,2}$(5.81%)	0.7342^{1}(4.45%)

comparison between $RPBL_{score}$ and $RPBL_{similarity}$ shows that, although they are not significantly different, $RPBL_{score}$ is slightly better as for most measures. The optimal value of weighting parameter α in $RPBL_{score}$ (Eq.5) is always 0.3, suggesting that the personality-based prediction takes more contribution to the final prediction result than the rating based prediction. In comparison, as $RPBL_{similarity}$ emphasizes enhancing user-user similarity by integrating personality with ratings, it is shown that the personality is more helpful for accomplishing its rating prediction task in sparser rating situation (because of the relatively better MAE and RMSE scores in Yahoo! Movie dataset).

Hence, through this experiment, we demonstrate that the personality scores as derived from implicit features can take positive effect on augmenting real-life movie recommendations. In particular, combining them with users' ratings can boost both rating prediction and ranking accuracy to a higher level, relative to the method that considers the implicit personality or users' ratings alone.

5 Conclusion and Future Work

In this paper, we presented an approach to deriving users' personality implicitly from their behavior in movie domain, and furthermore used the derived personality to augment online movie recommendations. Specifically, we first validated the significant correlations between multiple features and users' personality traits through user survey. We then compared three regression models in terms of their ability of unifying these significant features into automatically inferring a user's personality, among which Gaussian Process shows better performance than Pace Regression and M5 Rules. We further implemented three variations of CF method which are all based on the implicitly acquired personality: one is purely based on the inferred personality to enhance user-user similarity in CF process, and the other two combine the personality with users' ratings in either generating the final item prediction score ($RPBL_{score}$) or computing user-user similarity ($RPBL_{similarity}$). The experimental results indicate that the algorithms incorporated with both implicit personality and ratings significantly outperform not only the non-personality approach but also the pure personality-based approach, in terms of both rating prediction and ranking accuracy.

The main limitation of our study is that, as there are not users' explicit personality values in the two real-life movie datasets (HetRec and Yahoo! Movie), it is infeasible to validate our personality inference model with them. We hence plan to investigate other datasets as well as trying to increase the diversity and scale of our user survey's population, so as to further consolidate the recommender approach's practical value. On the other hand, we will investigate more types of behavioral features with the goal of further enhancing our personality inference model. For instance, it may be interesting to study whether people with different personality values would possess different propensity for being influenced by the item's word-of-mouth (WOM) when they give its rating [6]. We will also establish the inference model for other domains, such as music, as motivated by the literatures that show the relationship between music features and user personality [23]. In addition, we believe that our work will be beneficial to solve the cold-start issue in cross-domain recommendation, for which the personality as inferred from user behavior in one domain (e.g., movie) may be used to generate recommendations in another domain (e.g., music).

Acknowledgments. We thank grants ECS/HKBU211912 and NSFC/61272365.

References

1. Cantador, I., et al.: Relating personality types with user preferences in multiple entertainment domains. In: UMAP Workshops (2013)
2. Chamorro-Premuzic, T., et al.: Understanding individual differences in film preferences and uses: a psychographic approach. Journal of the Social Science of Cinema 87 (2014)
3. Chausson, O.: Who watches what?: assessing the impact of gender and personality on film preferences. Paper published online on the MyPersonality project website http://mypersonality.org/wiki/doku.php (2010)
4. Chen, L., et al.: How personality influences users' needs for recommendation diversity? In: CHI Extended Abstracts, pp. 829–834. ACM (2013)
5. De, R.B., Schouwenburg, H.C.: Personality in learning and education: A review. European Journal of Personality **10**(5), 303–336 (1996)
6. Duan, W., et al.: The dynamics of online word-of-mouth and product sales - an empirical investigation of the movie industry. Journal of Retailing **84**(2), 233–242 (2008)
7. Elahi, M., Braunhofer, M., Ricci, F., Tkalcic, M.: Personality-based active learning for collaborative filtering recommender systems. In: Baldoni, M., Baroglio, C., Boella, G., Micalizio, R. (eds.) AI*IA 2013. LNCS, vol. 8249, pp. 360–371. Springer, Heidelberg (2013)

8. Gao, R., et al.: Improving user profile with personality traits predicted from social media content. In: Proc. 7th ACM RecSys, pp. 355–358. ACM (2013)
9. Golbeck, J., et al.: Predicting personality with social media. In: CHI Extended Abstracts, pp. 253–262. ACM (2011)
10. Golbeck, J., Norris, E.: Personality, movie preferences, and recommendations. In: Proc. 5th ASONAM, pp. 1414–1415. ACM (2013)
11. Goldberg, L.R., et al.: The international personality item pool and the future of public-domain personality measures. Journal of Research in Personality **40**(1), 84–96 (2006)
12. Gosling, S.D., et al.: A very brief measure of the big-five personality domains. Journal of Research in Personality **37**(6), 504–528 (2003)
13. Green, P.E., et al.: Thirty years of conjoint analysis: Reflections and prospects. Interfaces **31**(3 suppl.), S56–S73 (2001)
14. Hellriegel, D., Wlldman, R.: Organizational Behavior (Eleventh edition). South-western college, Cincinnati, Ohio (2010)
15. Herlocker, J.L., et al.: Evaluating collaborative filtering recommender systems. ACM Transactions on Information Systems (TOIS) **22**(1), 5–53 (2004)
16. Holmes, G., Hall, M., Prank, E.: Generating rule sets from model trees. In: Foo, N. (ed.) Advanced Topics in Artificial Intelligence. LNCS, vol. 1747, pp. 1–12. Springer, Heidelberg (1999)
17. Hu, R., Pu, P.: A study on user perception of personality-based recommender systems. In: De Bra, P., Kobsa, A., Chin, D. (eds.) UMAP 2010. LNCS, vol. 6075, pp. 291–302. Springer, Heidelberg (2010)
18. Hu, R., Pu, P.: Enhancing collaborative filtering systems with personality information. In: Proc. 5th RecSys, pp. 197–204. ACM (2011)
19. Hu, R., Pu, P.: Exploring relations between personality and user rating behaviors. In: UMAP Workshops (2013)
20. McCrae, R.R., et al.: Age differences in personality across the adult life span: parallels in five cultures. Journal of Developmental Psychology **35**(2), 466 (1999)
21. McIlwraith, R.D.: "I'm addicted to television": The personality, imagination, and TV watching patterns of self-identified TV addicts. Journal of Broadcasting and Electronic Media **42**(3), 371–386 (1998)
22. Rasmussen, C.E.: Gaussian Processes for Machine Learning. MIT Press (2006)
23. Rentfrow, P.J., Gosling, S.D.: The do re mi's of everyday life: the structure and personality correlates of music preferences. Journal of Personality and Social Psychology **84**(6), 1236 (2003)
24. Sarwar, B., et al.: Analysis of recommendation algorithms for e-commerce. In: Proc. 2nd EC, pp. 158–167. ACM (2000)
25. Tkalcic, M., et al.: Personality based user similarity measure for a collaborative recommender system. In: Emotion in HCI Workshops, pp. 30–37 (2009)
26. Wang, Y.: A new approach to fitting linear models in high dimensional spaces. Ph.D. thesis, The University of Waikato (2000)
27. Wu, W., et al.: Using personality to adjust diversity in recommender systems. In: Proc. 24th HT, pp. 225–229. ACM (2013)
28. Yilmaz, E., et al.: A simple and efficient sampling method for estimating AP and NDCG. In: Proc. 31st SIGIR, pp. 603–610. ACM (2008)
29. Zar, J.H.: Significance testing of the spearman rank correlation coefficient. Journal of the American Statistical Association **67**(339), 578–580 (1972)

Harnessing Engagement for Knowledge Creation Acceleration in Collaborative Q&A Systems

Jie Yang(✉), Alessandro Bozzon(✉), and Geert-Jan Houben(✉)

Delft University of Technology, Mekelweg 4, 2628 CD Delft, The Netherlands
{j.yang-3,a.bozzon,g.j.p.m.houben}@tudelft.nl

Abstract. Thanks to reputation and gamification mechanisms, collaborative question answering systems coordinate the process of topical knowledge creation of thousands of users. While successful, these systems face many challenges: on one hand, the volume of submitted questions overgrows the amount of new users willing, and capable, of answering them. On the other hand, existing users need to be retained and optimally allocated. Previous work demonstrates the positive effects that two important aspects, namely engagement and expertise valorisation, can have on user quality and quantity of participation. The magnitude of their effect can greatly vary across users and across topics. In this paper we advocate for a more in-depth study of the interplay that exists between user engagement factors in question answering systems. Our working hypothesis is that the process of knowledge creation can be accelerated by better understanding and exploiting the combined effects of the interests and expertise of users, with their intrinsic and extrinsic motivations. We perform a study over 6 years of data from the `StackOverflow` platform. By defining metrics of expertise and (intrinsic and extrinsic) motivations, we show how they distribute and correlate across platform's users and topics. By means of an off-line question routing experiment, we show how topic-specific combinations of motivations and expertise can help accelerating the knowledge creation process.

1 Introduction

Collaborative Question Answering (CQA) systems (e.g. StackOverflow, Quora, Yahoo Answers) are an important class of Web knowledge repositories [1]. They coordinate practitioners with varying levels of expertise in the creation of evolving, crowdsourced, and peer-assessed knowledge bases, often in a reliable, quick and detailed fashion.

In CQAs users (askers) create questions, counting on topically-defined communities to provide an answer to their needs. Community members can browse existing questions, and decide whether or not to contribute to ongoing discussions. Such decisions are influenced by a multitude of factors, including time constraints, quality and difficulty of the question, and the knowledge of the answerer. Previous work [2,17] shows how engagement elements such as gamifications mechanisms, and expertise valorisation can provide users with the right incentive for participation and collaborative knowledge creation.

F. Ricci et al. (Eds.): UMAP 2015, LNCS 9146, pp. 315–327, 2015.
DOI: 10.1007/978-3-319-20267-9_26

While successful, such factors cannot prevent CQAs from facing several sustainability challenges. The volume of submitted questions overgrows the amount of new users willing, and capable, of answering them; a large portion of questions do not receive good (up-voted) answers, and even well-posed and relevant questions might wait for a long time before receiving a good answer [15,16]. Recent studies have proposed to solve these problems with acceleration mechanisms such as: automatic detection of poorly formulated questions, question editing suggestion [15,16], or question routing [5,8,14,18].

To maximise the effectiveness of such mechanisms, a better comprehension of the mechanisms of knowledge creation in CQAs is needed. Recent research [9,17] shows that engagement and topical expertise are complementary user properties. In this paper we advocate for a more in-depth understanding of the interplay that exists between them, and we aim at demonstrating how they can be used to accelerate knowledge creation in CQA systems.

Our working hypothesis is that the process of knowledge creation is topically dependent, and that is driven by a mix of *intrinsic* motivations, *extrinsic* motivations, and *topical expertise* of CQAs users. We suggest that different topic-specific knowledge needs demand for different types of contributor: intuitively, to generate the best answer, some questions may require active answerers engaged in discussion; others may only need one expert user to directly provide the right answer. To test our hypothesis we focus on `StackOverflow`, a question answering system specialised in programming-related issues. The paper provides the following original contributions:

1. A study, focusing on the relation that exist between intrinsic motivations (e.g. interest), extrinsic motivations (e.g. reward), and expertise in topically-centred communities;
2. An off-line question routing experiment, aimed at verifying the impact of (intrinsic and extrinsic) motivations and expertise in user modelling for question recommendation.

Our work provides novel insights on the mechanisms that regulates knowledge creation in CQA systems. Although the study and the experiment focus on `StackOverflow` data, we believe that our results are of general interest. The study shows the relevant impact that different topics exercise on (intrinsic and extrinsic) motivation and expertise: the results can be used to devise novel engagement and retention mechanisms, aimed at accelerating knowledge creation by maximising the effectiveness of contributors. The experiment presented in the paper provides empirical evidences of how existing CQAs can profit from the adoption of question routing mechanisms that include topical interest, motivations, and expertise as user modelling properties.

The remainder of the paper is organised as follows: Section 2 briefly introduces engagement dimension in CQAs. Section 3 analyses (intrinsic and extrinsic) motivations and expertise in `StackOverflow`, while Section 4 shows how they can improve question routing performance. Section 5 describes related work, before Section 6 presents our conclusions.

2 Engagement Dimensions in CQA Systems

User engagement is defined as "the emotional, cognitive and behavioural connection that exists, at any point in time and possibly over time, between a user and a resource" [3]. Among the attributes that characterise engagement (e.g. aesthetics, endurability, novelty, reputation), *user context* embeds a combination of user- and context-dependent factors that profoundly influence and affect the relation between CQAs and their users. In this work we focus on two factors, namely: the *motivations* driving users' activities; and users' *expertise*, as assessed by their peers, in a given topic of interest.

Motivation. is a precondition for action. To foster user engagement, system designers must understand the reasons why users take a particular action. The Self-Determination Theory [6] differentiates between *intrinsic* and *extrinsic* motivation.
Intrinsic motivations lead individuals to perform an activity because of their personal *interest* in it; or because its execution gives some form of *satisfaction*. Users of CQAs are often intrinsically motivated [12]; they decide to interact with systems and their communities: *a*) To look for existing solutions to their issues; this involves browsing the CQA content, in search for the right formulation of knowledge need and, the answer(s) to it. *b*) To post a new question to the community, when no existing solution can be found. Or, *c*) to get satisfaction from the sense of efficacy perceived when, convinced to possess the skills and competence required to contribute to an ongoing discussion, they provide a new answer, or they comment/vote existing questions and answers.
When *extrinsically motivated*, individuals perform an activity for an outcome different from the activity itself, e.g. to obtain *external rewards*. A typical example of an engagement mechanism that exploits extrinsic motivation is *gamification* [2]. CQA systems often adopt two forms of external rewards: 1) a public *reputation score*, calculated by summing the number of votes obtained by all the posted questions and answers; and 2) a set of *badges*, assigned after achieving pre-defined goals (e.g. complete at least one review task, achieve a score of 100 or more for an answer).

Expertise. An expert can be defined as someone who is recognised to be skilful and/or knowledgable in some specific field [7], according to the judgment of the public, or of peers. In CQAs, social judgement is critical for expert identification. A question is usually answered by a set of users, whose answers are voted up or down by other members of the platform, thus reflecting the a user's capability of applying knowledge to solve problems. Hence, voting from other users can be seen as an unbiased, cyber simulation of social judgement for the answerers' expertise level [17]. Expertise can be seen as an example of intrinsic motivation related to competence. However, we stress the fundamental difference that exists between one's perception of competence (which is self-established, and often biased), and social judgement: by being externally attributed, the latter might not set off the same type of intrinsic triggers. Simply put: being perceived as an expert does not necessarily imply behaving like one. Next section elaborates on this behavioural difference, and provides quantitative support to our classification choice.

3 Analysing Extrinsic Motivations, Intrinsic Motivations, and Expertise in StackOverflow

The first part of our work studies how intrinsic motivations, extrinsic motivations, and expertise manifest themselves in topically-centred CQAs communities. We analyse `StackOverflow`, a popular CQA system launched in 2008 with the goal of becoming a very broad knowledge base for software developers. `StackOverflow` now features more than 2.7M users, 6.5M active questions, 11.5M answers, 26.1M comments, and 35.2K tags used by users to briefly characterise the subjects of the submitted questions. `StackOverflow` periodically releases a public version of the platform database, which can be accessed at https://archive.org/details/stackexchange. Our study is based on data created up until January 2014. Due to space limitations, the following sections report only part of the performed analysis and experiments. An extended description is available at http://wis.ewi.tudelft.nl/umap2015.

To investigate topical diversity, we categorise tags into 14 topics, shown in Table 1. Topics are identified by analysing the tag co-occurrence graph, using the approach described in [4].

Table 1. Topical categorisation of tags, with basic knowledge demand and contributors composition statistics

	Knowledge Demand			Contributor Composition				
Topic	**Tags**	**#Q**	**#A**	**#CU**	**#AU**	**%(AU∩CU)**	**%(CU-AU)**	**%(AU-CU)**
.Net	c#, asp.net, .net, vb.net, wcf	571K	1222K	102K	119K	73.84%	6.40%	19.76%
Web	javascript, jquery, html, css	569K	1181K	146K	149K	85.43%	6.40%	8.17%
Java	android, java, eclipse	566K	1097K	136K	136K	85.84%	7.32%	6.84%
LAMP	php, mysql, arrays, apache	432K	927K	39K	128K	21.10%	6.98%	71.92%
C/C++	c, c++, windows, qt	269K	679K	78K	80K	87.45%	10.19%	12.36%
iOS	iphone, ios, objective-c	262K	441K	59K	57K	79.24%	11.98%	8.78%
Databases	sql, sql-server, database	177K	406K	74K	73K	79.37%	10.68%	9.95%
Python	python, django, list	186K	390K	55K	61K	67.59%	12.00%	20.41%
Ruby	ruby, ruby-on-rails	129K	226K	32K	39K	59.57%	12.89%	27.54%
String	regex, string, perl	99K	264K	47K	57K	57.26%	13.93%	28.81%
OOP	oop, image, performance, delphi	88K	212K	52K	61K	59.51%	14.20%	26.29%
MVC	asp.net-mvc, mvc	50K	98K	23K	29K	54.18%	15.06%	30.76%
Adobe	flex, flash, actionscript	39K	65K	18K	17K	73.98%	14.34%	11.68%
SCM	git, svn	34K	74K	21K	25K	44.31%	21.81%	33.88%

3.1 Topical Influence on Extrinsic and Intrinsic Motivated Actions

Table 1 reports topical knowledge demand statistics. For each topic, we include: the number of submitted questions $\#Q$, as a measure of knowledge demand popularity; the number of answers $\#A$ and the number of comments C, as a measure of community participation. Comments or answers to self-created questions are not considered as extra contributors to the topic. Results highlight great topical diversity for both popularity and participation. It also emerges a topic-dependent distribution of answers and comments, which underlines differences in the type of activities performed by contributors.

The difference is more evident when observing the right-hand side of Table 1, which analyses communities' composition. $\#AU$ and $\#CU$ respectively indicate the number answerers and the number of commenters; $\#AU \cap \#CU$ shows the percentage of contributors who are both commenters and answerers; $\#CU - \#AU$ reports the percentage of contributors that are only commenters, and $\#AU - \#AU$ the percentage of contributors that are only answerers.

The distribution of contributors across topics greatly varies. We observe a general trend towards communities where the number of users acting exclusively as answerers is higher; together with an absolute higher number of answers, these figures suggest a preference for rewarded actions. In the `LAMP` topic the trend is more evident. `iOS` and `Adobe` are exceptions, as the percentage of users that exclusively comment is higher, and the absolute numbers of comments and answers is comparable. We observe no trend related to topics's popularity or participation. For instance, `Web`, `Java`, and `Databases` have a very similar number of commenters and answerers, which are mostly overlapping. Other topics like `.Net`, `Python`, and `Ruby` show a slight predominance of answerers of comments, which is reflected in the uneven composition of contributors.

3.2 Measures of Motivations and Expertise in `StackOverflow`

Given its multi-faceted nature, user engagement has been measured in different ways: from subjective (e.g. user questionnaires) to objective (e.g. subjective perception of time) metrics, each measure is characterised by its own cost of acquisition, generalisation capabilities, and bias.

In this work we consider several objective measures. As common in related literature, we define such measures over the set of `StackOverflow` users' activities available in the public dataset. Namely: posting new questions, answers, or comments; and voting existing question and answers (although votes are only available as aggregates, not as individual actions). Our metrics focus on the 3 engagement factors described in Section 2.

Intrinsic Motivations Metric. The `StackOverflow` dataset does not provide page-access (view) data about individual users, thus making the task of measuring intrinsic motivations more challenging. To account for the missing data, we focus on *comments*, i.e. the only type of activity not rewarded by the scoring mechanism of `StackOverflow`. By being unrewarded, we assume commenting actions to be performed only for personal interest in a question, in its topic, or in the community. Figure 1 (a) plots the distribution of comments and answers for each user participating in the `.Net` topic. As typical in `StackOverflow` [17], user activeness brings a strong bias (0.9 correlation, $p < .01$), as most active users are also more likely to engage in discussions, or provide minor help and criticisms. To compensate for the activeness bias, we use as intrinsic motivation measure $IM_u = \frac{\#C_u}{\#A_u}$, defined as the ratio between the number of comments and

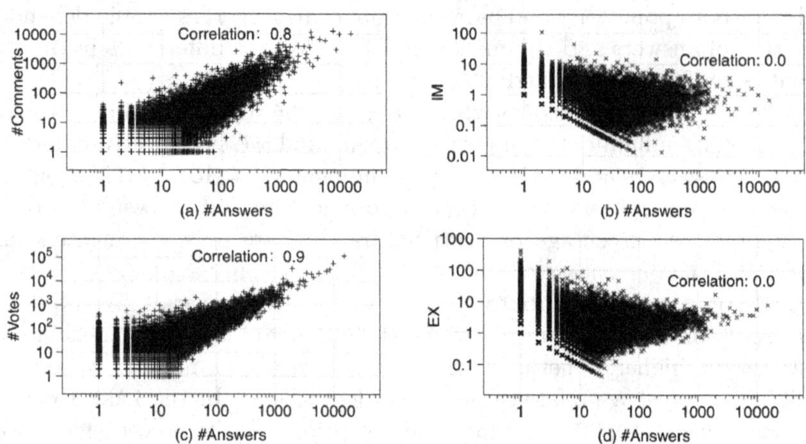

Fig. 1. Distribution of number of comments and votes in the `.Net` without – (a) and (c) – and with – (b) and (d) – activeness correction

the number of answers provided by a user for a given set of topics. Intuitively, IN_u provides a measure of intrinsic motivation by quantifying the self-driven likelihood of a user to contribute to an ongoing discussion. Figure 1 (b) plots the distribution of IN_u, showing its independence from user activeness (0.0 correlation, $p < .01$).

Extrinsic Motivations. External rewards such as reputation score and badges are strictly correlated with user activeness [17] which, in turns, is linearly correlated with the number of provided answers. We therefore use as a measure of extrinsic motivation $EM_u = \#A_u$, i.e. the number of answers provided by a user for questions about a a given set of topics, in a given time frame.

Expertise. In `StackOverflow`, social judgment in expressed in terms of votes assigned to questions or answers provided by users. The number of votes received by other users can be used as a measure of expertise. As for intrinsic motivations, most active users are also more likely to receive more votes for their contributions, as can be seen from Figure 1 (c) ($p < 0.01$). To normalise for user activeness, we use as expertise metric $EX_u = \frac{\#V_u}{\#A_u}$, i.e. the average number of votes received for each answer. Figure 1 (d) plots the distribution of EX_u ($p < 0.01$) for each user in the dataset.

3.3 Topical Relation of Extrinsic Motivation, Extrinsic Motivation, and Expertise

Table 2 reports, for each topic and engagement metric defined in Section 3.2, the mean value (μ), standard deviation (σ) and skewness (γ) of their distributions.

The distributions of users' expertise (EX_u), intrinsic (IM_u) and extrinsic (EM_u) motivations is topically diverse. With metrics of motivation, a general

Table 2. Distribution and correlation of IM_u, EM_u, and EX_u values across topics

Topic	Basic Statistics ($\mu \pm \sigma, \gamma$)			Pearson Correlation		
	EX_u	IM_u	EM_u	EX_u-IM_u	EX_u-EM_u	IM_u-EM_u
.Net	1.65±4.73, 27.25	0.36±0.99, 18.57	10.23±84.17, 86.58	.03($p < .01$)	.02($p < .01$)	.05($p < .01$)
Web	2.06±9.55, 47.37	0.37±9.02, 7.01	7.90±52.35, 40.82	.02($p < .01$)	.00($p = .06$)	.08($p < .01$)
Java	2.30±9.69, 39.92	0.37±1.08, 21.85	8.10±64.61, 64.95	.01($p < .01$)	.00($p = .24$)	.01($p < .01$)
LAMP	1.59±6.09, 53.08	0.41±1.00, 10.42	7.25±44.05, 41.56	.02($p < .01$)	.01($p < .01$)	.08($p < .01$)
C/C++	2.01±6.76, 40.35	0.47±1.17, 9.30	8.41±58.29, 28.47	.03($p < .01$)	.02($p < .01$)	.09($p < .01$)
iOS	2.44±7.81, 18.98	0.38±1.08, 12.65	7.70±39.38, 19.11	.01($p < .01$)	.00($p = .35$)	.05($p < .01$)
Databases	1.69±7.11, 52.15	0.43±0.99, 6.57	5.53±40.94, 41.82	.01($p < .01$)	.01($p = .02$)	.05($p < .01$)
Python	2.43±6.68, 21.68	0.45±1.02, 6.52	6.44±75.77, 48.15	.03($p < .01$)	.02($p < .01$)	.06($p < .01$)
Ruby	2.68±8.44, 24.67	0.37±0.95, 8.27	5.88±27.23, 21.73	.02($p < .01$)	.01($p = .19$)	.06($p < .01$)
String	2.32±10.69, 51.44	0.57±1.21, 6.52	4.65±25.14, 31.61	.01($p < .01$)	.01($p < .01$)	.06($p < .01$)
OOP	2.18±7.54, 30.51	0.54±1.23, 8.18	3.47±16.43, 50.01	.04($p < .01$)	.02($p < .01$)	.07($p < .01$)
MVC	2.08±6.13, 22.34	0.40±0.95, 5.60	3.79±34.27, 132.39	.02($p < .01$)	.01($p = .19$)	.02($p < .01$)
Adobe	1.28±6.88, 77.62	0.24±0.71, 6.41	3.68±19.45, 36.33	.02($p = .03$)	.00($p = .97$)	.07($p < .01$)
SCM	5.51±28.48, 22.99	0.41±0.98, 6.01	2.99±23.64, 87.91	.01($p = .06$)	.00($p = .60$)	.03($p < .01$)

trend can be observed: the averaged EM_u value for very popular topics (e.g., `.Net`) is higher than less popular ones (e.g., `SCM`), while the averaged value of IM_u is lower, meaning that users of these topics are, on average, active in providing answers to gain reputation while less self-interested participating to unrewarded activities. All metrics features very skewed distributions, especially EM_u: this indicates a general trend towards the identification of a small group of users possessing high motivation and/or expertise.

To investigate the relation between engagement factors, for each topic we consider the list of contributing users; we calculate their topical IM_u, EM_u, and EX_u values, and evaluate the pairwise Pearson correlation. Results are reported at the right-hand side of Table 2. Correlation is generally very low, mostly at high level of significance ($p < .01$). Overall, this result validates our choice of measures: in the reference dataset, the three engagement factors are independently observable. $IM_u - EM_u$ correlation is more evident, although still very diverse across topics (e.g. 0.09 in `C/C++`, 0.01 in `Java`). Interestingly, the (low) correlation between extrinsic motivation and expertise is highly not significant in 5 topics. We interpret such lack of statistical support as the result of more homogeneous expertise distributions among very active community members. The phenomenon affects topics at varying levels of popularity and participation, so community size doesn't appear to be a relevant factor. Further investigations are left to future work.

4 Exploiting Extrinsic Motivations, Intrinsic Motivations, and Expertise for Question Routing Optimisation

In this section we provide empirical evidence of how (intrinsic and extrinsic) motivations and expertise can be exploited to improve the knowledge creation process. We employ question routing (i.e. recommendation of questions to the most suitable answerers) as knowledge acceleration mechanism, and compare the performance of different routing model configurations.

4.1 Data Preprocessing and Analysis

We split the dataset into two partitions. We build user profiles by considering actions executed up to Dec 31, 2012; we refer to this data partition as the `Training` partition. Routing performance on question-answering are assessed of the `Testing` partition, which includes 1 year worth of user actions (from Jan 19th 2014). To avoid cold-start problems, we consider only users that performed at least one action in both partitions. As our assessment includes a comparison of answerers rankings, we include in our experiment only questions with at least two answerers. Table 3 reports the resulting dataset figures.

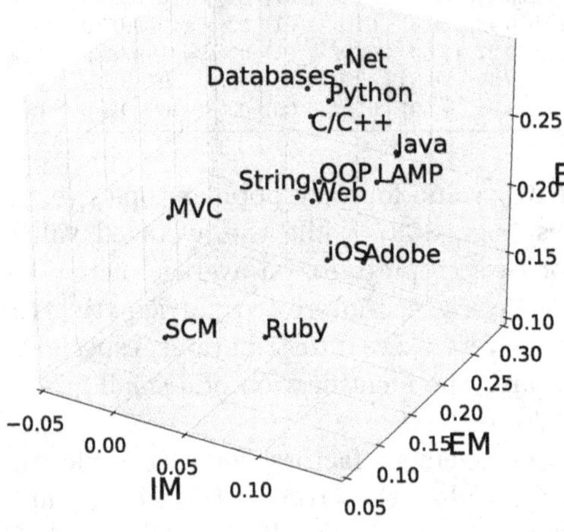

Fig. 2. Pearson correlation of (intrinsic and extrinsic) motivations and expertise w.r.t. answer quality across topics.

Table 3. Users and questions distributions in the `Training`, `Validation`, `Testing` dataset partitions

	`Train`	`Test`	`Valid`	
Topic	**#U**	**#Q**	**#U**	**#Q**
.Net	10,118	37,641	29,357	156,512
Web	13,877	51,267	34,034	180,230
Java	11,679	46,568	40,287	197,688
LAMP	11,305	35,079	35,070	149,487
C/C++	6,114	31,255	19,248	94,409
iOS	4,218	14,508	13,725	70,114
Databases	4,794	16,011	17,488	53,489
Python	4,988	18,380	15,227	55,546
Ruby	2,477	6,640	8,802	30,390
String	4,898	12,805	16,526	39,074
OOP	3,256	4,500	14,059	21,127
MVC	1,435	2,077	5,622	10,613
Adobe	182	267	1,649	4,703
SCM	814	1,546	3,871	7,275

Our working hypothesis is that, by properly weighting different answerers according to their likelihood of being relevant to a given questions, the accuracy of question routing can be optimised. We test how the application of engagement factors in such weighting can lead to better question recommendation performance. To support our hypothesis, we first conduct the following experiment. For each question in the `Testing` set, we order answerers according to the number of votes they received from the community, and evaluate their intrinsic motivations, extrinsic motivations, and expertise measures over the `Training` set. We then calculate the Pearson rank correlations between the answering quality $AQ = \#votes$ and each of the three engagement factors (IM, EM, EX) : results are depicted in Figure 2. Each dot is a topic, and its coordinate indicate the respective correlations.

A higher correlation implies that the corresponding measure is more predictive for answering quality. The plot shows how, in general, intrinsic motivation is a poor predictor of answer quality, while EX and EM are more correlated, although often in a complementary fashion (e.g. `iOS`, `Adobe`). We observe great topical variety in the predictive power of the three engagement features. For instance, expertise in `Java` are more predictive than in `iOS`, while intrinsic motivation for these two topics are similar. Such a diversity calls for a routing model that weights the contributions of engagement properties differently across topics.

4.2 Routing Model

We propose a linear model, defined as follows:

$$S(u, q) = \alpha_{IM}^t IM_u + \alpha_{EM}^t EM_u + \alpha_{EX}^t EX_u,$$

For each question q of topic t in the `Testing` partition, $S(u, q)$ scores the answerer u's answer quality. $\alpha_{IM}^t, \alpha_{EM}^t, \alpha_{EX}^t$ respectively model the topic-specific needs for intrinsic motivated, extrinsic motivated, and expert answerers.

The optimal, topic-specific values for the $\alpha_{IM}^t, \alpha_{EM}^t, \alpha_{EX}^t$ parameters are calculated as follows. We identify a third dataset partition, called `Validation`, defined over the original, unfiltered dataset, and containing two years worth (from Jan 01, 2011 to Dec 31, 2013). Table 3 provides a basic description of the `Validation` partition, where the number of questions higher due to the lack of filtering conditions. We use the Linear Ordinal Regression SVM with L_2 regularization to learn the parameters, such that the profiled users are optimally ranked in the `Validation` partition. To learn more accurate parameters, we exclude the answer pairs in the training phase if the difference of #votes to the answers is less than 2. Such parameters are then used in the routing model to recommend questions to users in the `Testing` partition.

4.3 Experimental Setup

Evaluation Metrics. The routing performance are assessed with three metrics, commonly used in the evaluation of recommender systems: NDCG (normalized discounted cumulative gain) [10], Kendall Tau, and Pearson rank correlation coefficients. The goal is to measure the quality/correlation of the recommended list of potential answerers by comparing it to the ground truth.

The evaluation of NDCG is performed against the #votes received by an answerer in a question. We use **NDCG@1** to assess the quality of the best recommended answerer, while **NDCG** assess the overall quality of the answerer set ranking. Due to the presence of negative voted answers, we exclude from the evaluation questions where the sum of DCGs is negative. Pearson correlation is calculated against #votes to answers, while Kendall Tau only measures similarity in the relative order of answers. Correlation is calculated only for questions where at least one answerer has a unique number of votes in the answer set.

Experimental Configuration. We compare the performance of 5 routing configurations. In the `Rdm` configurations, we randomly order the original answerers in the tested question. This configuration provides a performance baseline, as it measure a purely casual recommendation strategy. In the `Exp`, `Int`, and `Ext` configurations we respectively configure the routing system to return answerers according to their EX, IM and EM scores. These configurations simulate a recommendation strategy based on a single feature of engagement. Finally, Cmb applies the routing model described in Section 4.2, using the topic-specific learned parameters. As a remark, we exclude content-based model (e.g., bag-of-words of user answers) since our preliminary experiment show that it is less effective than configurations (e.g., Ext) that measure user answering activities.

4.4 Results

Table 4 summaries the results of our experiment. As expected, the topic of interest is an important performance diversification element for all the considered engagement factors and evaluation metrics. W.r.t. the numbers reported in Table 4, it is important to highlight how the range of values for NDCG metrics is necessarily narrower than for Pearson and Kendall Tau correlations. This is due to the definition of the metric which, by considering the number of votes received by an answerer, compress results in a more compact spectrum of values[1]. This is also demonstrated by the considerably high performance obtained by the Rdm configuration. Therefore, minor variations in NDCG values entails relevant differences in the quality of the returned answerers list.

As expected, among the configurations of Int, Exp and Ext, Int is the one providing worse results, whereas Exp configuration usually performs better than the others. On the other hand, we observe that Cmb configuration has in general performance better than or comparable with Exp. Small improvements, however, can provide tangible impacts. For instance, in topics such as Web and iOS, Cmb achieves better rankings – for 833 and 167 questions respectively. For some topics Exp could give even slightly better result than Cmb configuration, e.g., Ruby, OOP. Results suggests that the Cmb configuration could leverage different user engagement factors for question routing; however, is many topics, expertise is the most important factor for recommendation quality.

As a final remark, we highlight how the routing performance of Cmb, Exp is generally higher than the ones reported in related literature [18]. This is despite the different targeted dataset, which is more extensive in our setting.

5 Related Work

This section positions our paper in the context of previous work related to user engagement and knowledge creation acceleration in CQA systems.

Although both are factors of user engagement, user motivations and expertise in CQAs have been typically discussed in isolation. In a qualitative study based on interviews with CQA users, [12] finds that altruism, learning and competency are frequent motivations for participation. In addition, previous research shows gamification mechanisms can largely influence users' behaviours [2,4]. Expertise,

[1] **NDCG** = 1 entails a perfect recommendation.

Table 4. Experiment results of question routing with different configurations. Numbers in bold are the highest among all configurations.

Topic	NDCG@1					NDCG					Pearson					Kendall				
	Rdm	Exp	Int	Ext	Cmb	Rdm	Exp	Int	Ext	Cmb	Rdm	Exp	Int	Ext	Cmb	Rdm	Exp	Int	Ext	Cmb
.Net	.572	.687	.589	.676	**.693**	.834	.882	.842	.877	**.884**	.015	.279	.055	.244	**.290**	.014	.266	.054	.231	**.275**
Web	.578	.679	.624	.679	**.689**	.838	.879	.857	.878	**.883**	-.004	.234	.104	.225	**.255**	-.003	.226	.100	.217	**.245**
Java	.572	.665	.602	.647	**.666**	.835	**.873**	.847	.865	**.873**	.007	**.220**	.067	.169	.219	.005	**.210**	.064	.162	.209
LAMP	.579	.675	.602	.664	**.677**	.839	.877	.848	.873	**.878**	-.004	.219	.044	.193	**.228**	-.004	.212	.043	.187	**.220**
C/C++	.568	**.673**	.589	.644	.663	.834	**.878**	.843	.865	.874	.013	**.256**	.056	.181	.233	.015	**.244**	.052	.174	.222
iOS	.569	.644	.605	.650	**.658**	.835	.867	.850	.868	**.871**	-.002	.175	.080	.173	**.204**	.000	.171	.075	.169	**.197**
Databases	.593	.700	.614	.694	**.704**	.847	.889	.855	.886	**.890**	.001	.254	.037	.232	**.259**	.002	.248	.036	.228	**.254**
Python	.582	.682	.605	.684	**.695**	.842	.882	.851	.882	**.887**	.005	.244	.054	.236	**.265**	.005	.235	.052	.229	**.255**
Ruby	.607	**.656**	.628	.651	.651	.853	**.872**	.861	.870	.871	.016	**.141**	.073	.119	.130	.015	**.138**	.071	.119	.130
String	.572	.660	.601	.656	**.663**	.837	.874	.850	.872	**.875**	-.013	.200	.056	.171	**.206**	-.013	.192	.058	.165	**.196**
OOP	.578	**.682**	.614	.672	.680	.840	**.883**	.855	.879	.881	-.011	**.231**	.067	.185	.228	-.005	**.224**	.065	.185	.220
MVC	.623	.692	.613	.697	**.699**	.860	.888	.857	.890	**.890**	.034	.194	-.027	.193	**.214**	.034	.193	-.020	.199	**.208**
Adobe	.60	.663	.654	.649	**.674**	.853	.873	.872	.872	**.879**	-.013	.174	.96	.113	**.184**	-.009	.174	.97	.115	**.186**
SCM	.598	**.663**	.621	.650	.647	.853	**.875**	.861	.873	.871	-.038	**.101**	.010	.078	.083	-.044	**.100**	.008	.079	.081

on the other hand, is mostly studied in the problem expertise identification. Related work typically adopts indicator-based methods such as Z_{score} [19], or graph-based methods such as the adapted PageRank method [11]. A recent study [17] shows how existing metrics of expertise can be heavily biased toward most active users. The normalisation of user activeness in our EX_u metric is inspired by such consideration. Combining expertise and motivation, [13] explores their effect in the specific task of expert finding. W.r.t. literature our work further the understanding of user engagement factors in CQAs, providing new insights about the interplay of user expertise, intrinsic motivation, and extrinsic motivation. We contribute an original and extensive analysis that shows the independent manifestation of these three engagement factors across topical communities.

Knowledge creation acceleration is a topic recently emerged in research related to CQA systems. Typical methods include automatically detection of question quality [15], editing suggestions for poorly formulated questions [16], and active routing of questions to potentially relevant answerers [5,8,14,18]. The latter is the most popular technique, and is the inspiration for our experiment. Previous work typically considers only users' topical activeness[8] as user modelling feature. These works were extended by considering the problem of routing question to a user community, for collaborative problem solving [5,14]. More recently, [18] proposes a question routing user model that includes expertise, providing empirical evidences of its contribution to performance improvement. To the best of our knowledge, our work is the first considering a broader spectrum of engagement factors, and we extensively demonstrate their applicability.

6 Conclusions

The main mechanisms that drive knowledge creation process in CQAs are still to be fully uncovered. In this paper we address the problem of characterising and measuring three engagement factors in `StackOverflow`. The rationale behind our work is simple: to drive participation, thus improving the quality and speed of knowledge creations, we need to better understand the driving forces behind user engagement. Inspired by engagement theory from literature, we focus on intrinsic motivations, extrinsic motivations, and expertise. We propose three metrics, defined over the set of actions available to `StackOverflow` users, and we show how *topic* plays a major role in influencing them. We investigate the relations that exist among these three engagement factors, and demonstrate their independent and decomposable nature. A question routing optimisation experiment confirms the relevant role that engagement can play in knowledge creation acceleration.

Acknowledgments. This publication was supported by the Dutch national program COMMIT. This work was carried out on the Dutch national e-infrastructure with the support of SURF Foundation.

References

1. Anderson, A., Huttenlocher, D., Kleinberg, J., Leskovec, J.: Discovering value from community activity on focused question answering sites: a case study of stack overflow. In: KDD 2012, pp. 850–858. ACM (2012)
2. Anderson, A., Huttenlocher, D., Kleinberg, J., Leskovec, J.: Steering user behavior with badges. In: WWW 2013, pp. 95–106. ACM (2013)
3. Attfield, S., Kazai, G., Lalmas, M., Piwowarski, B.: Towards a science of user engagement. In: WSDM Workshop on User Modelling for Web Applications (2011)
4. Bosu, A., Corley, C.S., Heaton, D., Chatterji, D., Carver, J.C., Kraft, N.A.: Building reputation in stackoverflow: an empirical investigation. In: MSR 2013, pp. 89–92. IEEE (2013)
5. Chang, S., Pal, A.: Routing questions for collaborative answering in community question answering. In: ASONAM 2013, pp. 494–501. IEEE/ACM (2013)
6. Deci, E., Ryan, R.M.: Self-determination Theory. Handbook of Theories of Social Psychology **1**, 416–433 (2008)
7. Ericsson, K.A., Charness, N., Feltovich, P.J., Hoffman, R.R.: The Cambridge Handbook of Expertise and Expert Performance. Cambridge University Press (2006)
8. Guo, J., Xu, S., Bao, S., Yu, Y.: Tapping on the potential of q&a community by recommending answer providers. In: CIKM 2008, pp. 921–930. ACM (2008)
9. Guy, I., Avraham, U., Carmel, D., Ur, S., Jacovi, M., Ronen, I.: Mining expertise and interests from social media. In: WWW 2013, pp. 515–526. ACM (2013)
10. Järvelin, K., Kekäläinen, J.: Cumulated Gain-based Evaluation of IR Techniques. ACM Transactions on Information Systems **20**(4), 422–446 (2002)
11. Liu, J., Song, Y.-I., Lin, C.-Y.: Competition-based user expertise score estimation. In: SIGIR 2011, pp. 425–434. ACM (2011)
12. Nam, K.K., Ackerman, M.S., Adamic, L.A.: Questions in, knowledge in?: a study of naver's question answering community. In: SIGCHI 2009, pp. 779–788. ACM (2009)

13. Pal, A., Farzan, R., Konstan, J.A., Kraut, R.E.: Early detection of potential experts in question answering communities. In: Konstan, J.A., Conejo, R., Marzo, J.L., Oliver, N. (eds.) UMAP 2011. LNCS, vol. 6787, pp. 231–242. Springer, Heidelberg (2011)
14. Pal, A., Wang, F., Zhou, M.X., Nichols, J., Smith, B.A.: Question routing to user communities. In: CIKM 2013, pp. 2357–2362. ACM (2013)
15. Ravi, S., Pang, B., Rastogi, V., Kumar, R.: Great question! question quality in community q&a. In: ICWSM 2014, pp. 426–435. AAAI (2014)
16. Yang, J., Hauff, C., Bozzon, A., Houben, G.J.: Asking the right question in collaborative q&a systems. In: Hypertext 2014, pp. 179–189. ACM (2014)
17. Yang, J., Tao, K., Bozzon, A., Houben, G.-J.: Sparrows and owls: characterisation of expert behaviour in stackoverflow. In: Dimitrova, V., Kuflik, T., Chin, D., Ricci, F., Dolog, P., Houben, G.-J. (eds.) UMAP 2014. LNCS, vol. 8538, pp. 266–277. Springer, Heidelberg (2014)
18. Yang, L., Qiu, M., Gottipati, S., Zhu, F., Jiang, J., Sun, H., Chen, Z.: CQARank: jointly model topics and expertise in community question answering. In: CIKM 2013, pp. 99–108. ACM (2013)
19. Zhang, J., Ackerman, M.S., Adamic, L.: Expertise networks in online communities: structure and algorithms. In: WWW 2007, pp. 221–230. ACM (2007)

Short Presentations

News Recommender Based on Rich Feedback

Liliana Ardissono[(✉)], Giovanna Petrone, and Francesco Vigliaturo

Dipartimento di Informatica, Università di Torino, Turin, Italy
{liliana.ardissono,giovanna.petrone}@unito.it

Abstract. This paper proposes to exploit author-defined tags and social interaction data (commenting and sharing news items) in news recommendation. Moreover it presents a hybrid news recommender which suggest news items on the basis of the reader's short and long-term reading history, taking reading trends and short-term interests into account. The experimental results we carried out provided encouraging results about the accuracy of the recommendations.

Keywords: Hybrid news recommender · Tag-based news specification

1 Introduction

The news domain challenges recommender systems with peculiar issues to be faced with respect to the suggestion of items in online catalogs [1]: e.g., the pool of stories continuously changes; freshness and diversity of recommendations are crucial to keep the reader's interest; moreover, as people are not expected to rate articles, user interests have to be learned unobtrusively; finally, people's interests dynamically change and they can be influenced by reading trends.

Existing news recommendation work tracks page visualization. However modern online newspapers also enable registered users to add comments to news stories and to share them in social networks. Moreover, they support synthetic descriptions of the content of news items based on author-defined tags. In order to investigate the impact of these features on recommendation we developed the Social News Recommender (SAND), which exploits these types of information for the selection of the news stories to suggest. SAND integrates a short-term and a long-term content-based recommender system with a collaborative filtering one to suggest stories on the basis of the user's past history, her/his recent reading history and peers' reading behavior. Moreover the system exploits a popularity-based recommender to enrich suggestions with successful items.

We tested SAND online by involving a small number of readers and using the feeds of newspaper "Il Fatto Quotidiano" (www.ilfattoquotidiano.it/). The test results show that the exploitation of rich information about news items and user actions supports a fairly accurate recommendation of news stories satisfying individual user interests.

Section 2 outlines the related work; Section 3 describes SAND; Section 4 summarizes our test results and Section 5 concludes the paper.

F. Ricci et al. (Eds.): UMAP 2015, LNCS 9146, pp. 331–336, 2015.
DOI: 10.1007/978-3-319-20267-9_27

2 Related Work

Most news recommenders are based on collaborative filtering (e.g., [2,3]), content-based filtering ([4,5]), or integrated approaches ([1,6]). SAND follows this approach but it differs in the following aspects: first, it analyzes new types of user behavior, which were not previously considered (article sharing and commenting), to enhance the estimation of readers' interests. Second, in order to promote recommendations based on rather different principles (with the aim of enhancing diversity, serendipity, etc.), it proposes a fair merging technique to propose the best suggestions identified by each of the integrated recommenders. Furthermore it exploits author-defined tags for characterizing the content of news items in an accurate and scalable way (taking inspiration from [8]) without analyzing the whole text of news stories. Different from our work, semantic news recommenders (e.g., [9]) depend on the definition and maintenance of large ontologies for the representation of concepts and semantic relations. We prefer to adopt a lightweight knowledge representation approach for scalability purposes. Navigation based approaches (e.g., [10]) are complementary to our work: they are suitable for learning interests of anonymous readers; however they only personalize the recommendation of news categories.

3 The SAND Hybrid News Recommender

SAND analyzes the news feeds published by online newspapers and provides personalized recommendations by learning individual user models and by combining different techniques with the aim of enhancing the quality of the suggestions it generates. It can integrate multiple news feeds but, being developed as a web service, it can also be used to enrich an individual online newspaper with personalized news suggestion. The system presents recent stories and recommendations enabling readers to share the stories in a social network and to add comments to them. Our current prototype downloads news stories from the feed of "Il Fatto Quotidiano" (http://www.ilfattoquotidiano.it/feed/). SAND includes two components: a news feed collector which downloads the stories published by the source newspapers and extracts information about their content (see Section 3.1) and a hybrid recommender which analyzes information about user actions on news stories and generates personalized suggestions (Section 3.3). We assume that readers authenticate themselves and can be monitored across sessions.

3.1 Analysis of the Content of News Items

The content of a news item i is represented as a bag of words $BW = \{< k_1, r_1 > \ldots, < k_m, r_m >\}$ where $k_1 \ldots, k_m$ is a set of keywords extracted from i and r_x is the relevance of k_x for the story, computed by applying TF-IDF [11]. The feed collector extracts the list of keywords of a news item from its title and author-defined tags by stop words removal and stemming. Different from previous work, which also uses the summary or the complete text of news items for keyword extraction, SAND uses on title and tags because they focus on the topic of the articles, enabling a fast analysis of news items. We compared the two keyword extraction methods on a dataset from "Il Fatto Quotidiano": for each document we compared the lists including the 5 most similar documents, generated by using title+summary and title+tags. The average intersection between the pairs of lists is about 31%. However, looking at a subset of the dataset in detail we noticed that the documents selected using title+tags are the most similar ones (we obtained comparable results considering the 10 most similar documents).

3.2 Representation of User Interests

The system manages two user models for each registered user U to describe short-term and long-term user interests. The models have the same format but refer to observations collected during the last 10 days / 60 days, respectively.

Each user model is a vector of observations $UM = \{< i_1, e_1, t_1 >, \ldots, < i_n, e_n, t_n >\}$ where $i_1, \ldots, i_n$ are the news items which U inspected during the relevant time interval, e_x is the evidence of U's interest in i_x (inferred by tracking U's behavior), and t_x is the timestamp of U's last observed action concerning i_x. We model evidence as a numerical value in $[0, 1.5]$: (i) Clicking on the title of a news item carries weak information about the reader's interests because it does not prove that (s)he read the story. For this reason, we attribute this type of activity an evidence of interest in the item equal to 0.5. (ii) Sharing a news item in a social network or adding a comment to it do not mean that the actor approves its content but we can interpret these actions as strong evidence of interest towards the story. Thus we attribute them an evidence equal to 1.5.

The system stores in the user model an entry for each news item visualized by the user. The interest value associated to the item is the maximum value which can be attributed on the basis of the user's actions; i.e., 0.5 if (s)he only clicked on it, 1.5 if (s)he also shared/commented it. The timestamps of the observations allow forgetting older ones.

3.3 News Recommendation

According to previous works (e.g., [1,12,13]) recommenders based on collaborative filtering have more chances than content-based ones to suggest variegate items due to the fact that they exploit the ratings provided by other users; moreover they can reflect reading trends. However they tend to suggest highly popular items which the user might not be interested in, and they are affected by the novel item issue. In contrast, content-based recommenders can suggest new entries but they are not sensitive to quality and they tend to recommend items which are rather similar to each other. In order to combine the benefits of both approaches we designed SAND as a hybrid system: the system estimates a user U's interest in the items to be analyzed by merging the suggestions of 4 different recommenders: a collaborative filtering one, a short-time content-based one, a long-term content-based one and a popularity-based one.

Let's consider a fresh item i and vector $interest_i$ representing the evidence values about the interest in i stored in the long-term user models of all the registered readers:

- The collaborative filtering recommender follows the item-to-item approach [12]. It predicts U's preference for i by exploiting U's observed interest in items similar to i from the viewpoint of the other readers' interests:

$$preference_{CF} = \frac{\sum_{j \in N(i)} \sigma(i,j) * e_j}{\sum_{j \in N(i)} \sigma(i,j)} \quad (1)$$

  $\sigma(i,j)$ is the similarity between the interest vectors of i and j, evaluated as the Euclidean distance between the two vectors;[1] e_j is the evidence of interest in j stored in U's long-term user model, and $N(i)$ is the set of neighbors of i, i.e., those news items whose similarity with i is over a threshold.
- The short-term content-based recommender predicts U's preference for i by exploiting her/his recent interests in news stories whose content is similar to that of i. In order to emphasize the impact of individual keywords, which may refer to the occurrence of specific events (e.g., sport ones), the short-term recommender estimates the preference for a fresh news item by directly exploiting the observed interest in news stories having similar keywords. This is done by analyzing the items referenced in U's short-term model and by selecting the most similar ones:

$$preference_{ST} = \sum_{j \in N(i)} \sigma(i,j) * e_j \quad (2)$$

  Given the bag of words representations of i (BW_i) and j (BW_j), $\sigma(i,j)$ is computed as the cosine similarity between BW_i and BW_j. Moreover $N(i)$ is determined by selecting the items whose similarity is over a threshold, and e_j is the evidence of interest in j stored in U's short-term user model.
- The long-term content-based recommender predicts U's preference for i by taking into account U's preferred topics emerging from the keywords which occur in the stories (s)he read in the recent past:
  1. First it estimates U's interest in the keywords associated to the news items which (s)he inspected during the last 60 days by analyzing her/his observed interest in those items. For each keyword k the recommender computes the cumulative evidence of interest of k as follows: $cumulativeEvidence(k) = \sum_{j \in Stories} e(j)$
     $Stories = \{j_1, \ldots, j_h\}$ are the news items in U's long-term model having k as a relevant keyword and $e(j)$ is the evidence of interest for item j.
  2. Then it exploits the 10 keywords having the highest cumulative evidence of interest ($MostInt$) for estimating U's preference for i:

$$preference_{LT} = \sum_{k \in Keywords(i)} score(k) \quad (3)$$

[1] This is the implementation offered by the Apache Mahaut framework exploited for implementing this recommender (http://mahout.apache.org/).

$Keywords(i)$ are the keywords in the bag of words representation of i. $score(k) = cumulativeEvidence(k)$ if $k \in MostInt$ (i.e., the keyword is a most interesting one), 0 otherwise.

- The popularity-based recommender suggests the news items of the current day that received the highest cumulative interest from registered readers.

The contributions of the recommenders are integrated into a list as parallel suggestion flows to include the best items of each flow. Given the lists of items separately ranked by the recommenders, and excluding those which the user has read, the final recommendation list includes 9 entries: typically, 3 items selected by the collaborative filtering one, 3 by the short-term content-based one, 2 by the long-term content-based one and 1 by the popularity-based one. However the first three recommenders start to predict a user's preferences after having collected a minimum amount of evidence about her/his interests (10 user actions). Moreover, the user might be idle for a while and thus the short-term recommender might be unable to estimate her/his interests in that interval. In these cases the contributions of the long-term recommender and of the popularity-based one are extended, enabling them to suggest a larger number of items.

4 Evaluation Results

We evaluated the accuracy of SAND by means of an online test which involved 25 participants (12 males and 13 females; age: min=22, max=55, avg=38.7, median=37) having heterogeneous backgrounds (computer science, humanities, physics, electronics, architecture, social sciences, education science). Participants were asked to overview the news downloaded from the feed of "Il Fatto Quotidiano" for 30 days and they could click on news titles in order to read them; moreover they could make comments or share stories in Facebook. On day 31 the system recommended 9 news stories per participant and asked her/him to specify which ones were very interesting (if any) by clicking on a "Like" button. Moreover the system asked to answer 3 questions (selecting a value in [1, 5] where 1 is the worst value and 5 is the best one) to evaluate whether the recommended news items (i) matched the participant's interests, (ii) dealt with heterogeneous topics, (iii) stimulated her/his curiosity even though they did not correspond to her/his general interests. Furthermore the system offered a free-text field to let participants provide further comments. The test provided the following results:

- 49.5% of suggested stories were evaluated as very interesting by clicking on the "Like button", with an average of 4.5 clicks per user (std. dev. = 1.14).
- The questions aimed at assessing the recommendation accuracy received fairly positive answers: (1) long-term interest matching: 3.8; (ii) topic diversity; 3.7; (iii) stimulate curiosity: 3.7. All values are significant (one-sided T-test with α=0.05).
- The free-text comments revealed that most participants felt that the system suggested relevant articles. The worst evaluations were provided by people who do not like "Il Fatto Quotidiano" because it focuses on topics out of their interests (the newspaper focuses on politics, economics and big events).

These results are encouraging but suggest that other online newspapers should be integrated to improve the diversity of topics and the system's capability of recommending rich pools of news stories. Moreover, an online test with a larger number of readers is needed to collect more extensive feedback and evaluations.

5 Conclusions

We described a hybrid news recommender that exploits information about readers' interaction with news stories and author-defined tags to provide personalized suggestions. The integration of different recommendation techniques in the generation of suggestions has provided encouraging experimental results. In our future work we will extend the analysis of user behavior to further enrich the evidence on user interest which can be collected thanks to the convergence of online newspapers with social networks. Moreover we will carry out further experiments in order to evaluate the recommendation accuracy which can be achieved by employing alternative integration strategies for the recommender systems, and to extend the evaluation to a larger set of users.

References

1. Liu, J., Donlan, P., Ronby Peders, E.: Personalized news recommendation basedon click behavior. In: Proc. of IUI 2010, Hong Kong, China, pp. 31–40 (2010)
2. Resnick, P., Iacovou, N., Suchak, M., Bergstrom, P., Riedl, J.: Grouplens: an open architecture for collaborative filtering of netnews. In: Proc. of CSCW 1994, pp. 175–186. ACM, Chapel Hill (1994)
3. Das, A., Datar, M., Garg, A., Rajaram, S.: Google news personalization: scalable online collaborative filtering. In: Proc. of WWW 2007, Banff, pp. 271–280 (2007)
4. Billsus, D., Pazzani, M.: A hybrid user model for news story classification. In: Proc. 7th Int. Conf. on User Modeling, Banff, Canada, pp. 99–108 (1999)
5. Kompan, M., Bieliková, M.: Content-based news recommendation. In: Buccafurri, F., Semeraro, G. (eds.) EC-Web 2010. LNBIP, vol. 61, pp. 61–72. Springer, Heidelberg (2010)
6. Doychev, D., Lawlor, A., Rafter, R., Smyth, B.: An analysis of recommender algorithms for online news. In: Proc. of CLEF 2014, Sheffield, UK (2014)
7. Agrawal, R., Karimzadehgan, M., Zhai, C.: An online recommender system for social networks. In: Proc. of ACM SIGIR Workshop on Search in Social Media (2009)
8. Gemmel, J., Schimoler, T., Mobasher, B., Burke, R.: Resource recommendation in social annotation systems: a linear-weighted hybrid approach. Journal of computer and system sciences **78**, 1160–1174 (2012)
9. Cantador, I., Castells, P., Bellogin, A.: An enhanced semantic layer for hybrid recommender systems: Application to news recommendation. Int. Journal on Semantic Web and Information Systems **7**(1), 44–77 (2011)
10. Garcin, F., Dimitrakakis, C., Faltings, B.: Personalized news recommendation with context trees. In: Proc. of (RecSys 2013), Honk Kong, China, pp. 105–112 (2013)
11. Salton, G.: Automatic text processing. Addison-Wesley (1989)
12. Desrosiers, C., Karypis, G.: A comprehensive survey of neighborhood-based recommendation methods. Recommender systems handbook, pp. 107–144. Springer (2011)
13. Lops, P., de Gemmis, M., Semeraro, G.: Content-based recommender systems: state of the art and trends. Recommender systems handbook. Springer (2011)

News Recommenders: Real-Time, Real-Life Experiences

Doychin Doychev([✉]), Rachael Rafter, Aonghus Lawlor, and Barry Smyth

Insight Centre for Data Analytics,
University College Dublin Belfield, Dublin 4, Ireland
{doychin.doychev,rachael.rafter,aonghus.lawlor,
barry.smyth}@insight-centre.org
http://www.insight-centre.org/

Abstract. In this paper we share our experiences of working with a real-time news recommendation framework with real-world user and data.

Keywords: Real-life experiences · News Recommender Systems

1 Introduction

Recommender systems have become an essential part of our daily lives. In this work we present our early experiences when it comes to a real-world news recommendation task in the guise of the 2014 NewsREEL challenge [6]. NewsREEL participants respond to recommendation requests with their suggestions and, crucially, received live-user feedback in the form of click-through data, providing an opportunity for a large-scale evaluation of recommender systems *in the wild*.

In contrast to other domains (books, movies, etc.), news has a greater item churn [2,4] and users are much more sensitive to article recency [4]. Furthermore, user profiles are typically constrained to the current session [11] or at best defined by browser cookies [7]. Moreover, it is atypical for users to evaluate articles explicitly and feedback is commonly collected implicitly by observing user behaviour [8]. Finally, there is a low consumption cost associated with reading a news article which can result in a larger than normal diversity of the consumed items [10].

Within the context of the NewsREEL challenge [5] (formerly, The News Recommender System Challenge (NRS'13)), Said et al. [9] study the performance of similarity- and recency-based algorithms. They find that both types perform slightly better when recommending in general news sites than in more topic focussed sites. Others [4,5] recommend representing a news article using a combination of metadata and contextual features; see [7] for a full list of such features available for the NewsREEL challenge.

2 System Architecture and Recommender Algorithms

In NewsREEL, we operate with live-stream data [7], coming from a number of German websites, provided by the Plista Open Recommender Platform

F. Ricci et al. (Eds.): UMAP 2015, LNCS 9146, pp. 337–342, 2015.
DOI: 10.1007/978-3-319-20267-9_28

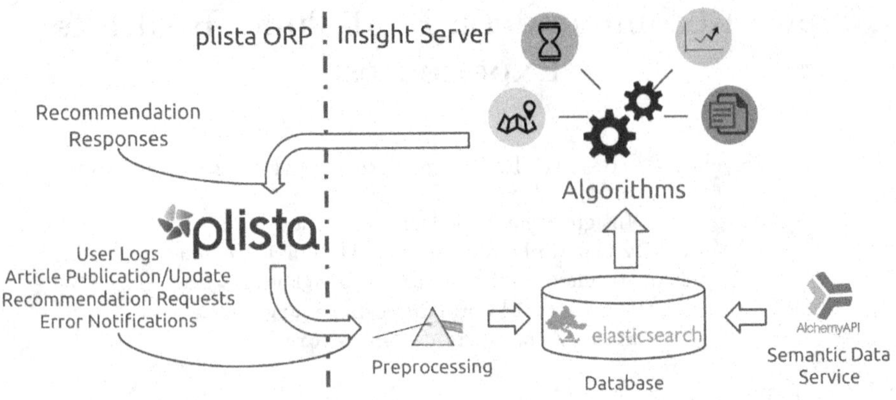

Fig. 1. System Architecture

(ORP) [1]. There are four data types: i) *User Activity Logs* ii) *Article Publication/Update*; iii) *Recommendation Requests*; and iv) *Error Notifications.* Plista requires us to respond to recommendation requests within 100ms.

Our system architecture, shown on Fig 1 is designed for scalability, speed and extensibility. For each of our recommendation algorithms, we have a long running process which continually reads the latest events and articles from the database to recompute and build its recommendations. With this offline approach, there is a danger that we might send back a recommendation which contains outdated, non-recommendable articles, during the time it took to compute the recommendations. To minimise the possibility of recommending outdated articles, we update our recommendations in the background as frequently as possible; the typical refresh time is less than 5 minutes.

We present 12 algorithms, 6 popularity-based algorithms and 6 similarity-based algorithms (see Table 1). The algorithms are applied to each site. Then, we filter out those articles the user has already seen, and those marked by Plista as out-of-date.

Popularity-based recommenders rank the candidate set (CS), i.e. the subset of articles considered for recommendation before any ranking is applied, by the visit count of each article.

Content-based similarity algorithms use standard vector space model with TF-IDF. We should note that Plista only provides titles, leads[1] and publisher defined, keywords of an article. Hence to apply `similarity_full_body` and `similarity_entities_alchemy` algorithms we extract the full body text using Boilerpipe[2] and named entities using AlchemyAPI[3], respectively.

[1] The lead is the first sentence or two of an article, often in bold font, which typically summarises the key points.

[2] https://code.google.com/p/boilerpipe/

[3] http://www.alchemyapi.com

Table 1. Our 12 algorithms - 6 popularity- and 6 similarity-based

Rank By	Filter/Source	Description
Popularity	No Filter	CS - all items in the dataset
	Geolocation	CS - all items read by users in a geolocation
	News Category	CS - all items whose category intersects with the target article's category
	Day of Week	CS - all items that have been seen in the same day of the week as the target article.
	Hour of the Day	CS - all items that have been seen in the time range [*current hour* - 1, *current hour* + 1], where current hour is the hour in which we provide the recommendation.
	Positive Implicit Feedback	CS - all items that have been successfully recommended to users in the past (i.e. clicked). Then we rank them by the number of times they've been successful.
Similarity	Title	Represents articles by terms in their title.
	Lead	Represents articles by terms in their lead.
	Title + Lead	Represents articles by terms in their titles and lead.
	Full Body	Represents articles by terms in their title, lead and full text body.
	Keywords	Represents articles by keywords
	German Entities	Represents articles by German named entities.

3 Evaluation

We evaluate the performance of our 12 algorithms (see Table 1) on the Plista data from 21/12/14 to 31/12/14, focusing on click-through rate (CTR) as a measure of relevance. Table 2 shows some statistics about the 7 German websites contained in the dataset.

Table 2. News sites description, including number of articles $N(A)$, number of unique users $N(U)$, number of visits $N(V)$, number of recommendations $N(R)$

Website Name	Description	$N(A)$	$N(U)$	$N(V)$	$N(R)$
channelpartner.de	Business, Marketing & E-commerce Company	1.26k	21k	47k	13.6k
computerwoche.de	Technology & Business	1.1k	93k	240k	70k
gulli.com	IT & Technology	163	415k	1.14M	270k
ksta.de	Regional news	18k	407k	2.81M	224k
sport1.de	National sports	2.2k	1.05M	4.73M	1.35M
tagesspiegel.de	National news	11k	795k	2.88M	613k
tecchannel.de	Computer Hardware & Software news	418	110k	317k	92k

We use a round-robin approach when responding to recommendation requests, so that each algorithm has a reasonable chance of being observed equally across the 7 websites. Each algorithm must return up to 6 recommendations per recommendation request.

4 Results

Fig. 2 shows the *recommendation rate* for each algorithm. We can see that the popularity-based algorithms respond with recommendations for 98-100% of

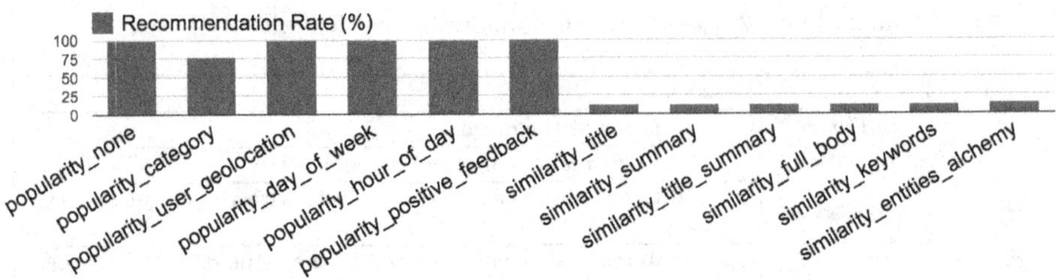

Fig. 2. Recommendation rate of different algorithms

Plista requests with exception of `popularity_category`, which has a recommendation rate of 75% due to there being absent category data in some 25% of requests. By comparison, the similarity-based algorithms have recommendation rates of only about 10% since in the rest, up 90%, of the recommendation requests information about the target article, such as title, lead and url, is not provided to us. Note, this varies considerably by news site with *guilli.com* where the recommendation rate is only about 2% compared to 60% for *tecchannel.de.* This is unfortunate, as it means we have less data on which to evaluate our similarity-based algorithms compared to our popularity-based algorithms. In the future we will adapt our round-robin mechanism, so that we give more weight to similarity-based algorithms for recommendation requests where all the data needed for them to operate is present.

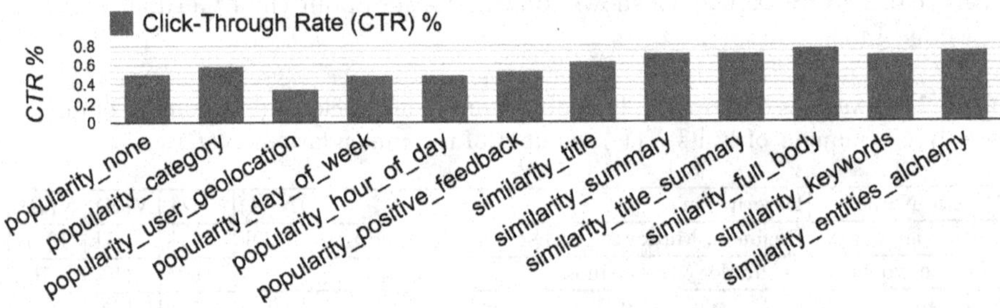

Fig. 3. Overall CTR performance of different algorithms

Fig. 3 shows the average CTR per algorithm. In general the similarity-based approaches attain better CTRs than the popularity-based approaches indicating that they are generating more relevant recommendations. This suggests that users appreciate so called *more-like-this* recommendations, i.e. recommendations of articles that are strongly related to the article they are currently reading, more so than recommendations of articles that are highly popular, yet not necessarily related to the current article.

Surprisingly, we find that geo-location performs comparatively poorly, even though one might expect users to have a special interest in local news. Unfortunately, we cannot investigate this further as the geo-location information in

Plista is only represented numerically, and we cannot resolve it to actual locations. Therefore, this result may be because the geo-location data is imprecise or has low granularity.

It is interesting to note the high CTR for the `popularity_category` algorithm, suggesting that readers are responsive to popular articles so long as they are from the current target article category [3]. This would be in keeping with the fact that similarity-based algorithms perform better than popularity-based algorithms, as category information can be seen as a weaker form of article similarity.

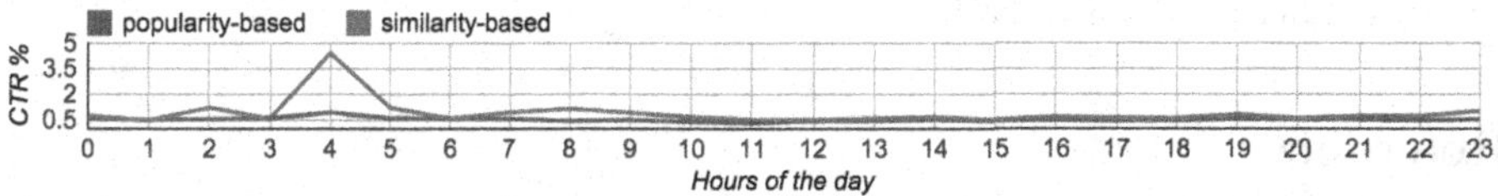

Fig. 4. Hourly CTR of popularity- and similarity-based algorithms

Fig. 4 highlights how the CTR changes during the daily news cycle, peaking significantly at 4AM. The similarity-based algorithms achieve a higher average CTR (4.42%), compared to popularity-based algorithms - 0.93% CTR, suggesting that people are more focussed at 4AM in the subject area they read.

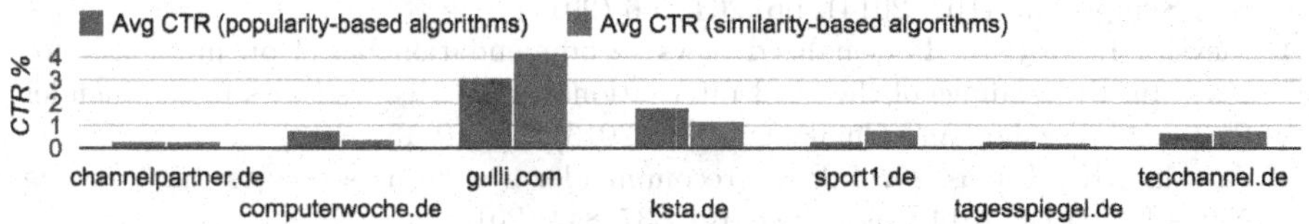

Fig. 5. Average CTR performance across websites

Fig. 5 shows the average CTR across the different news sites, which clearly displays very different CTR characteristics. Both types of algorithm perform particular well on sites like *gulli.com* and *ksta.de*. For technology (*gulli.com*, *tecchannel.de*) and sport (*sport1.de*) sites topic segregation seems to be more important to the user, hence the better performance of similarity-based algorithms, whereas in general news sites (*ksta.de* and *tagspiegel.de*) current and fresh content is preferred over related articles, shown by the better performing popularity-based algorithms. This indicates that readers of the different websites have very different reading behaviours and suggests that this distinction merits further investigation.

5 Conclusions

We present our initial investigation on the CTR performance of a suite of popularity- and similarity-based algorithms over a number of German news sites in an 11 day period. On technology and sport sites we notice the importance of topic segregation for users, hence similarity-based algorithms perform better. Popularity-based algorithms perform better in general news (*ksta.de* and *tagesspiegel.de*), where the freshness of the article is more important. There is a boost in CTR around 4AM, which is especially pronounced for similarity-based algorithms which could point to a particular kind of topic-focussed reading behaviour at that time. In the future we plan to experiment with more complex ensemble algorithms based on these results.

Acknowledgments. This work is supported by Science Foundation Ireland under Grant Number SFI/12/RC/2289

References

1. Brodt, T., Hopfgartner, F.: Shedding light on a living lab: the CLEF NewsREEL open recommendation platform. In: Proceedings of the 5th Information Interaction in Context Symposium (IIiX 2014), pp. 223–226 (2014)
2. Das, A., Datar, M., Garg, A., Rajaram, S.: Google news personalization : scalable online collaborative filtering. In: Proceedings of the 16th International Conference on The World Wide Web (WWW 2007), pp. 271–280 (2007)
3. Esiyok, C., Kille, B., Jain, B., Hopfgartner, F., Albayrak, S.: Users' reading habits in online news portals. In: Proceedings of the 5th Information Interaction in Context Symposium (IIiX 2014), pp. 263–266 (2014)
4. Ilievski, I., Roy, S.: Personalized news recommendation based on implicit feedback. In: Proceedings of the 2013 International ACM RecSys News Recommender Systems Workshop and Challenge (NRS 2013), pp. 10–15 (2013)
5. Jaroslav, K., Tomás, K.: InBeat: recommender system as a service. In: Working Notes for CLEF 2014 Conference, pp. 837–844 (2014)
6. Kille, B., Brodt, T., Heintz, T., Hopfgartner, F., Lommatzsch, A., Seiler, J. : Overview of CLEF NewsREEL 2014: news recommendation evaluation labs. In: Proceedings of the 5th International Conference of the CLEF Initiative (CLEF 2014) (2014)
7. Kille, B., Hopfgartner, F., Brodt, T., Heintz, T.: The plista dataset. In: Proceedings of the 2013 International ACM RecSys News Recommender Systems Workshop and Challenge (NRS 2013) (2013)
8. Liu, J., Dolan, P., Pedersen, E.: Personalized news recommendation based on click behavior. In: Proceedings of the 15th International Conference on Intelligent User Interfaces (IUI 2010), pp. 31–40 (2010)
9. Said, A., Bellogín, A., Lin, J., de Vries, A.: Do recommendations matter?: news recommendation in real life. In: Proceedings of the Companion Publication of the 17th ACM Conference on Computer Supported Cooperative Work & Social Computing (CSCW Companion 2014), pp. 237–240 (2014)
10. Said, A., Lin, J., Bellogín, A., de Vries, A.: A month in the life of a production news recommender system. In: Proceedings of the 2013 Workshop on Living Labs for Information Retrieval Evaluation (LivingLab 2013), pp. 7–10 (2013)
11. Trevisiol, M., Aiello, L.M., Schifanella, R., Jaimes, A.: Cold-start news recommendation with domain-dependent browse graph. In: Proceedings of the 8th ACM Conference on Recommender Systems (RecSys 2014), pp. 81–88 (2014)

On the Use of Cross-Domain User Preferences and Personality Traits in Collaborative Filtering

Ignacio Fernández-Tobías(✉) and Iván Cantador

Universidad Autónoma de Madrid, 28049, Madrid, Spain
{ignacio.fernandezt,ivan.cantador}@uam.es

Abstract. We present a study comparing collaborative filtering methods enhanced with user personality traits and cross-domain ratings in multiple domains on a relatively large dataset. We show that incorporating additional ratings from source domains allows improving the accuracy of recommendations in a different target domain, and that in certain cases, it is better to enrich user models with both cross-domain ratings and personality trait information.

Keywords: Collaborative filtering · Personality · Cross-domain recommendation

1 Introduction

Most recommendation services exploit user preferences obtained explicitly (e.g., by means of ratings) or implicitly (e.g., by mining click-through and log data). Effective hybrid recommendation approaches have been proposed that also exploit auxiliary data, such as user demographics, item metadata, and contextual signals. Recently, new sources of side information have been explored to enrich user models for collaborative filtering (CF). In particular, it has been shown that people with similar personality traits are likely to have similar preferences [3, 9], and that correlations between user preferences and personality traits allow improving personalized recommendations [8, 12]. Moreover, cross-domain recommendation methods [4] have been shown to be effective in target domains, by exploiting user preferences in other source domains [1, 2, 10]. Previous studies have investigated these sources of auxiliary information, focusing on particular approaches and domains, and in general using relatively small datasets. In this paper, we evaluate various CF methods enhanced with user personality traits and cross-domain ratings. Our empirical results on 22,289 Facebook user profiles with preferences for items in several domains –movies, TV shows, music and books– show that incorporating additional ratings from other domains improves recommendation accuracy, and that in certain cases, it is better to enrich user models with both cross-domain rating and personality trait information.

2 Related Work

2.1 User Personality in Personalized Services

Among the different models proposed to represent human personality, the Five Factor model (FFM) is considered one of the most comprehensive, and has been the mostly used to build user personality profiles [8]. This model establishes five dimensions

F. Ricci et al. (Eds.): UMAP 2015, LNCS 9146, pp. 343–349, 2015.
DOI: 10.1007/978-3-319-20267-9_29

(traits) to describe personality: *openness*, *conscientiousness*, *extraversion*, *agreeableness* and *neuroticism*. Recent research has shown that correlations between user preferences and personality factors exist in certain domains [3, 9], and that these correlations can be used to enhance personalized recommendations [7]. For instance, Hu and Pu [8] presented a method in which user similarities are computed as the Pearson's coefficient of their FF scores, and combined this approach with rating-based similarities to improve CF. Tkalčič et al. [12] evaluated three user similarity metrics for heuristic-based CF, and showed that approaches using FF data perform statistically equivalent or better than rating-based approaches, especially in cold-start situations.

In this paper, we also integrate personality information into the user-based nearest-neighbors algorithm, but we explore additional similarity functions besides Pearson's correlation, and evaluate the quality of the recommendations in several domains.

2.2 Cross-Domain Recommendation

Cross-domain recommender systems aim to generate personalized recommendations in a target domain by exploiting knowledge from source domains [4]. This problem has been addressed by means of user preference aggregation in user modeling [1, 2, 10], as a potential solution to the cold-start and sparsity problems in recommender systems [11], and as a practical application of knowledge transfer in machine learning [6]. We distinguish between two main types of approaches: those that *aggregate* knowledge from various source domains, for example, user preferences [1], user similarities [10], and rating estimations [2], and those that *link* or *transfer* knowledge between domains to support recommendations in a target domain [11].

In this paper, we analyze how *aggregating* ratings from different domains can help improving recommendations in a target domain. Furthermore, we empirically compare cross-domain user preferences and personality traits as valuable sources of auxiliary information to enhance heuristic-based CF methods. Approaches based on knowledge transfer are postponed for future investigation.

3 Integrating Personality in Collaborative Filtering

As done in [8], we integrate personality information into heuristic-based CF methods via the user similarity function. Specifically, we focus on the user-based k nearest-neighbors method for unary/binary user feedback (*likes*, *thumbs up/down*), in which ratings are predicted as:

$$\hat{r}(u,i) = \sum_{v \in N(u)} sim_{pref}(u,v) \cdot \mathbb{I}\big(i \in I(v)\big) \tag{1}$$

where $N(u)$ is the user's neighborhood, $I(v)$ is the set of items rated by user v, and the function $\mathbb{I}(p) = 1$ if p is true, and 0 otherwise. A popular user similarity function in this setting is the Jaccard's coefficient:

$$sim_{pref}(u,v) = \frac{|I(u) \cap I(v)|}{|I(u) \cup I(v)|} \tag{2}$$

This metric is considered as baseline in our experiments. To complement it with user personality information we use a linear combination, analogously to [8]:

$$sim(u,v) = \lambda \cdot sim_{pref}(u,v) + (1-\lambda) \cdot sim_{pers}(u,v) \quad (3)$$

where $\lambda \in [0,1]$ controls the influence of user preferences and personality on the recommendation process. For λ values close to 1, user preferences are more relevant, while for λ values close to 0, personality profiles get higher relevance.

We study several formulations of $sim_{pers}(u,v)$ that yield the compared personality-based CF methods, namely cosine similarity (COS), Pearson's correlation (PEA), Spearman's correlation (SPE), and Kendall's correlation (KEN). When combined with the preference-based similarity as in equation (2), we call the methods as COS-λ, PEA-λ, SPE-λ, and KEN-λ. When $\lambda = 0$, we use COS-pers (respectively PEA-pers, etc.) to name the methods, since only personality information is used in the computation of the user similarity. We refer to [5] for more details on the implementation of the above similarities.

4 Integrating Cross-Domain Ratings in Collaborative Filtering

Cross-domain recommender systems aim to exploit knowledge from source domains $\mathcal{D}_S$ to perform recommendations in a target domain $\mathcal{D}_T$. Without loss of generality, we can consider two domains $\mathcal{D}_S$ and $\mathcal{D}_T$ –the definitions are extensible to more source domains. Let U_S and U_T be their sets of users, and let I_S and I_T be their sets of items. The users of a domain are those who expressed preferences (e.g., ratings, tags) for the domain items.

In our study, we are interested in comparing the effects of cross-domain ratings and personality traits as auxiliary user information in the CF framework. Hence, we focus on the data itself and use the same recommendation algorithm as in Section 3, user-based k nearest-neighbors, in order to provide a fair comparison. Assuming $I_S \cap I_T = \emptyset$, we distinguish between two different scenarios of user overlap:

- *User overlap.* There are some common users who have preferences for items in both domains, i.e., $U_S \cap U_T \neq \emptyset$. This is the case, for instance, where some users rated both movies and books. Recommendations of items in $\mathcal{D}_T$ are generated exploiting user similarities based on preferences for items in $\mathcal{D}_S$ and $\mathcal{D}_T$:

$$sim_{pref}(u,v) = \frac{|I_S(u) \cap I_S(v)| + |I_T(u) \cap I_T(v)|}{|I_S(u) \cup I_S(v)| + |I_T(u) \cup I_T(v)|} \quad (4)$$

- *No overlap.* There is no overlap between users and items in the domains, i.e., $U_S \cap U_T = \emptyset$. Recommendations of items in $\mathcal{D}_T$ are generated by exploiting user similarities based only on user preferences for items in $\mathcal{D}_S$.

$$sim_{pref}(u,v) = \frac{|I_S(u) \cap I_S(v)|}{|I_S(u) \cup I_S(v)|} \quad (5)$$

In both cases, recommendations are generated for users in the target domain $\mathcal{D}_T$.

5 Experiments

5.1 Dataset

The dataset used in our experiments was obtained by the myPersonality project (`http://mypersonality.org`). Due to the size and complexity of the database, in this paper we restrict our study to a subset of its items. Specifically, we selected all likes (ratings) associated to items belonging to movie genres, music genres, book genres, and TV genres. Thus, for instance, selected items belonging to the movie genre category are `comedy`, `action`, `star wars`, and `james bond`. Table 1 shows some statistics about the users, items and ratings in the four considered domains.

Table 1. Statistics of the used dataset

domains	users	items	ratings	rating sparsity	user overlap
movies	16,168	268	27,921	99.36%	N/A
music	17,980	1,175	66,079	99.69%	N/A
books	15,251	305	23,882	99.49%	N/A
TV	4,142	111	4,612	98,99%	N/A
movies + music	22,012	1,443	94,000	99.70%	55.13%
movies + books	21,410	573	51,803	99.58%	46.75%
movies + TV	17,671	379	32,533	99.51%	14.93%
music + books	22,029	1,480	89,961	99.72%	50.85%
music + TV	19,201	1,286	70,691	99.71%	15.21%
books + TV	16,766	416	28,494	99.59%	15.67%

5.2 Evaluation Setting

In our experiments we empirically compared the performance of the user-based CF method extended with user cross-domain ratings and personality traits, respectively. We also tested different single-domain baselines in order to analyze the effect of the additional data on the quality of the recommendations.

- **Most popular**. Non-personalized approach that recommends the most liked items.
- **iMF**. Matrix factorization for positive-only feedback. The number of latent factors is set to 10, as we did not observe significant differences with respect to other values in preliminary tests.
- **Item kNN**. Item-based nearest neighbors using Jaccard's similarity. In our experiments, we set $k = \infty$ and considered all similar items rated by the target user.
- **User kNN**. User-based nearest neighbors using Jaccard's similarity. In our experiments, we set $k = 50$. When extended with cross-domain preferences, we used equations (4) and (5) to compute user similarities.
- **Personality-based CF**. User-based nearest neighbors extended with user personality information, using different instances of the similarity in equation (3) with COS, PEA, SPE, and KEN, and $\lambda \in \{0, 0.1, 0.2, \ldots, 0.9\}$. Note that $\lambda = 1$ corresponds to standard User kNN. We also combined these methods with cross-domain preferences, inserting similarities in equations (4) and (5) into equation (3).

These methods were evaluated in terms of MAP, F@5, and coverage, measured as the number of users for which recommendations could be generated. All results were averaged using 5-fold cross validation. For both single- and cross-domain recommendations, the test sets were composed of ratings for items in the target domain, and were never used for computing user similarities.

5.3 Results

Table 2 shows the results of the best performing baseline and personality-based methods (in terms of MAP), in both user overlap and non-overlap cross-domain scenarios. Results for single-domain recommendation are reported in rows where source and target domains match. The best values for each scenario are in bold, and the overall best for each target domain are underlined. Significant differences (Wilcoxon signed rank test, $p < 0.05$) are marked as follows: ▲ against single-domain baseline, * against cross-domain User kNN with same source and overlap configurations, and † for user overlap against no overlap, i.e., by rows.

Table 2. Recommendation performance in single- and cross-domain scenarios

Target domain	Source domain	No overlap Method	MAP	F@5	Coverage	User overlap Method	MAP	F@5	Coverage
Books	Books	Item kNN	0.2822	0.1801	**0.4353**				
		PEA-0.1	0.2679	0.1632	0.4175				
	Movies	User kNN	0.4859▲	0.2387▲	0.3567	User kNN	0.4907▲	0.2271▲	0.3189
		KEN-0.8	**0.4927***	**0.2429***	0.3565	KEN-0.9	**0.4952**	**0.2288**	0.3193
	Music	User kNN	0.2526	0.1669	0.3362	User kNN	0.2674†	0.1684	0.3311
		SPE-0.9	0.2565	0.1674	0.3360	PEA-0.7	0.2736*†	0.1716*†	**0.3348**
	TV	User kNN	0.3680▲	0.2038▲	0.1095	User kNN	0.3830▲†	0.2029▲	0.0980
		COS-0.9	0.3726	0.2084	0.1095	COS-0.9	0.3847	0.2037	0.0979
Movies	Movies	Item kNN	0.5303	0.2716	**0.4994**				
		KEN-0.1	0.5341	0.2655	0.4678				
	Books	User kNN	**0.6940**▲	0.3228▲	0.3853	User kNN	**0.6845**▲	**0.3122**▲	0.3412
		COS-0.2	0.6918	**0.3229**	0.3853	COS-0.9	0.6817	0.3115	0.3412
	Music	User kNN	0.5311	0.2797▲	0.4030	User kNN	0.5502▲†	0.2715	0.3941
		COS-0.1	0.5343	0.2806	0.4030	SPE-0.5	0.5587†	0.2820*†	**0.4024**
	TV	User kNN	0.5530	0.2776	0.1048	User kNN	0.5785▲†	0.2785	0.0933
		SPE-0.9	0.5757	0.2893*	0.1047	PEA-0.8	0.5856†	0.2844*	0.0945
Music	Music	Item kNN	**0.3225**	**0.2335**	**0.5348**				
		KEN-0.9	0.3054	0.2249	0.4293				
	Books	User kNN	0.2207	0.1736	0.3458	User kNN	0.3032†	0.2207†	0.3424
		COS-0.3	0.2277*	0.1780*	0.3458	COS-0.8	0.3036†	0.2207†	0.3424
	Movies	User kNN	0.2504	0.1890	0.3871	User kNN	0.3201†	0.2338†	0.3802
		SPE-0.8	0.2541*	0.1920*	0.3867	COS-0.9	**0.3209**†	**0.2339**†	**0.3803**
	TV	User kNN	0.1880	0.1572	0.0942	User kNN	0.2651†	0.2070†	0.0941
		COS-0.7	0.1971*	0.1646*	0.0942	COS-0.8	0.2661†	0.2082†	0.0941
TV	TV	Most popular	0.4174	**0.2320**	**0.9766**				
		COS-pers	0.3686	0.2106	0.1492				
	Books	User kNN	0.4375	0.2143	0.1201	User kNN	0.4426	0.1961	0.1045
		PEA-0.8	0.4561	0.2176	0.1201	KEN-0.9	0.4591	0.2047	0.1043
	Movies	User kNN	0.4322▲	0.2022	0.1075	User kNN	**0.4645**▲†	0.1998	0.0891
		PEA-0.9	**0.4682***	0.2217*	0.1075	PEA-0.8	0.4618	0.2076	0.0915
	Music	User kNN	0.3882	0.2248	0.1160	User kNN	0.3537	0.1966	0.1123
		COS-0.3	0.4073*	0.2284	0.1160	SPE-0.4	0.3817	**0.2191***	**0.1160**

In the **books** domain, the best personality-based method PEA-0.1 performs worse than the best baseline, Item kNN. Methods exploiting cross-domain preferences from movies and TV shows achieve better performance, although with the latter the coverage drops drastically. We find that this behavior is repeated in the other target domains, and argue that it is due to their low user overlap with the TV shows domain (Table 1). Combining personality traits and cross-domain ratings slightly improves the performance. In the **movies** domain, the improvement achieved by personality is not significant enough, while cross-domain preferences, especially from the books domain, provide much better precision. In this case, however, the user coverage drops roughly 10%. In the **music** domain, the best single-domain baseline is unbeaten, and neither personality nor cross-domain ratings are useful. This seems to indicate that the users' choices on music are only determined by their preferences on this domain. Finally, in **TV shows** domain the same trend as with books and movies is observed: the popularity baseline outperforms the best personality-based method in single-domain recommendation, whereas cross-domain ratings prove to be more valuable. In this case, in contrast, it would be best to stick with the baseline, since it offers a much better coverage and overall tradeoff with accuracy.

In general, even though personality does not outperform a strong single-domain baseline, it allows for further improving cross-domain methods. Also, results in the user overlap cross-domain scenario are just slightly better than in the non-overlap case. This is somewhat unexpected and counterintuitive, and we argue that it may be due to the fact that items represent genres (not items) in our dataset, and users with similar preferences in the source domain are likely to also share similar preferences in the target domain, with possibly the exception of music, as we conjectured before.

On a final note, Item kNN consistently outperformed iMF and User kNN as single-domain baselines. Again, this is likely caused by the fact that in our dataset we are dealing with genres, which can be considered as very popular items with many ratings. Item kNN takes advantage of this by computing more robust item to item similarities.

6 Conclusions and Future Work

We have preliminary compared the suitability of user cross-domain preferences and personality traits as auxiliary information to improve CF. We evaluated a number of personality-aware and cross-domain methods on the top-N recommendation task in various domains. From the achieved empirical results, we conclude that in general it is more valuable to collect user preferences from related domains than personality information to improve the quality of book and movie recommendations. Nonetheless, user personality can be exploited to further enhance cross-domain methods, most notably in the TV domain.

We plan to extend our study using larger datasets. In this paper we tested a large amount of user personality profiles, but focused on preferences for item genres. We want to analyze whether personality and cross-domain ratings can improve recommendation performance when dealing with particular movies, TV shows, music albums, or books.

Acknowledgements. This work was supported by the Spanish Ministry of Economy and Competitiveness (TIN2013-47090-C3). We thank Michal Kosinski and David Stillwell for their attention regarding the dataset.

References

1. Abel, F., Helder, E., Houben, G.-J., Henze, N., Krause, D.: Cross-system User Modeling and Personalization on the Social Web. UMUAI **23**(2–3), 169–209 (2013)
2. Berkovsky, S., Kuflik, T., Ricci, F.: Mediation of User Models for Enhanced Personalization in Recommender Systems. UMUAI **18**(3), 245–286 (2008)
3. Cantador, I., Fernández-Tobías, I., Bellogín, A.: Relating Personality Types with User Preferences in Multiple Entertainment Domains. EMPIRE 2013 (2013)
4. Fernández-Tobías, I., Cantador, I., Kaminskas, M., Ricci, F.: Cross-domain Recommender Systems: A Survey of the State of the Art. CERI **2012**, 187–198 (2012)
5. Fernández-Tobías, I., Cantador, I.: Personality-aware collaborative filtering: an empirical study in multiple domains with facebook data. In: Hepp, M., Hoffner, Y. (eds.) EC-Web 2014. LNBIP, vol. 188, pp. 125–137. Springer, Heidelberg (2014)
6. Gao, S., Luo, H., Chen, D., Li, S., Gallinari, P., Guo, J.: Cross-domain recommendation via cluster-level latent factor model. In: Blockeel, H., Kersting, K., Nijssen, S., Železný, F. (eds.) ECML PKDD 2013, Part II. LNCS, vol. 8189, pp. 161–176. Springer, Heidelberg (2013)
7. Hu, R., Pu, P.: A study on user perception of personality-based recommender systems. In: De Bra, P., Kobsa, A., Chin, D. (eds.) UMAP 2010. LNCS, vol. 6075, pp. 291–302. Springer, Heidelberg (2010)
8. Hu, R., Pu, P.: Enhancing Collaborative Filtering Systems with Personality Information. RecSys **2011**, 197–204 (2011)
9. Rentfrow, P.J., Goldberg, L.R., Zilca, R.: Listening, Watching, and Reading: The Structure and Correlates of Entertainment Preferences. Journal of Personality **79**(2), 223–258 (2011)
10. Shapira, B., Rokach, L., Freilikhman, S.: Facebook Single and Cross Domain Data for Recommendation Systems. UMUAI **23**(2–3), 211–247 (2013)
11. Shi, Y., Larson, M., Hanjalic, A.: Tags as bridges between domains: improving recommendation with tag-induced cross-domain collaborative filtering. In: Konstan, J.A., Conejo, R., Marzo, J.L., Oliver, N. (eds.) UMAP 2011. LNCS, vol. 6787, pp. 305–316. Springer, Heidelberg (2011)
12. Tkalčič, M., Kunaver, M., Košir, A., Tasič, J.F.: Addressing the New User Problem with a Personality Based User Similarity Measure. UM4Motivation 2011 (2011)

Understanding Real-Life Website Adaptations by Investigating the Relations Between User Behavior and User Experience

Mark P. Graus(✉), Martijn C. Willemsen, and Kevin Swelsen

Human-Technology Interaction Group, Eindhoven University of Technology, IPO 0.20, 5600 MB Eindhoven, The Netherlands
{m.p.graus,m.c.willemsen}@tue.nl, kevin@netprofiler.nl

Abstract. We study how a website adaptation based on segment predictions from click streams affects visitor behavior and user experience. Through statistical analysis we investigate how the adaptation changed actual behavior. Through structural equation modeling of subjective experience we answer why the change in behavior occurred. The study shows the value of using survey data for constructing and evaluating predictive models. It additionally shows how a website adaptation influences user experience and how this in turn influences visitor behavior.

Keywords: Online adaptation · Visitor behavior · User experience · Online behavior · Online segmentation · Structural equation modeling

1 Introduction

Individual visitor differences in terms of interests or goals [8] allow website owners to use segmentation to personalize their website. This increases visitors' engagement with the website. As in many advertising pricing models costs are calculated per ad impression, enhancing visitor engagement can increase ad revenues.

The current study investigates on a live website to what extent an algorithm can deduce a visitor's interest from navigation behavior and how an adaptation can be used to increase visitor engagement. Linking visitor behavior to user experience allows for not only indicating how engagement is influenced, but also why.

2 Theoretical Background

2.1 Segmentation

Segmentation is a widely accepted technique originating from marketing [10]. Online segmentation[7] purports to segment the audience of a website into groups of similar visitors to implement adaptations that cater to the needs and interests

Currently working for NetProfiler.

F. Ricci et al. (Eds.): UMAP 2015, LNCS 9146, pp. 350–356, 2015.
DOI: 10.1007/978-3-319-20267-9_30

of these different groups.Hauser [4] investigated the effects of segmenting websites to match visitors' cognitive styles. Tuning to these styles allegedly improves the accessibility of information and improves the visitor experience. Their model based on questionnaire data to infer cognitive styles of website visitors allowed to adapt the website to increase the purchase probability.

2.2 User Experience

To better understand the effect of online adaptations on behavior, evaluation should be grounded in user experience measurements. When considering only behavior, one runs the risk of incorrectly interpreting certain changes in behavior positively (e.g., the number of videos watched in a video browsing service was not positively, but negatively correlated with user satisfaction[6]). We will employ a user-centric evaluation framework [5] to triangulate behavior and user experience. Similarly, Ekstrand et al. [3] used this framework to test how different recommender algorithms were experienced in terms of novelty, diversity and overall user satisfaction and indentified what objective performance metrics correlated to these subjective user experience constructs, thus informing in what direction to develop algorithms.

2.3 Research Questions

The current study will address two main research questions. 1) Can visitor segments be reliably inferred from navigation behavior? and 2) How are visitors affected by a segment-based adaptation in terms of behavior and user experience and how are experience and behavior related?

3 Study

This study was performed jointly with http://www.hardware.info, a content website that provides news, reviews, forums, and price comparisons on electronic hardware. This content originally comprised hardware components (HC for short, e.g. motherboards, video cards, processors), but in recent years expanded to cover content on end user products (EUP for short, e.g. GSM, TV, tablets, laptops). Hardware.info conjectured that they served two types of visitors, HC or EUP interested, and wondered if a personalized adaptation could prevent visitors from the EUP segment being overwhelmed by HC content.

3.1 Procedure

For two weeks in December 2012 the navigation behavior of visitors to the website was measured, consisting of information on URL, content category (EUP or HC) with product group, and page type (news, reviews, etc.) together with a unique user ID stored in a persistent cookie for each pageview. In addition the referrer

URL (if applicable), OS and browser type were stored. After the visitor viewed 5 pages[1] an element was added to the sidebar with links to additional content.

The sidebar element showed, per visitor at random, either HC or EUP content or a mix of both. Depending on the inferred visitor segment the resulting experimental conditions were 'congruent' (content matches the predicted segment), 'incongruent' (content does not match predicted segment) and 'neutral' (content has matching and non-matching items). Clicks made on the links in the new element were measured and a link to a questionnaire to measure user experience was displayed in the header of the website. As an incentive, respondents could enter a raffle for either SSD storage (HC) or a smartphone (EUP).

3.2 Participants

A total of 102350 visitors was exposed to the adaptation. The average number of pageviews was 21.59 (SD: 38.88) over 4.20 (SD: 6.32) visits. 2.45% of visitors interacted with the adaptation. 3234 visitors completed the survey. They engaged with the website more, with on average 67.26 pageviews (SD: 93.18) over 11.81 visits (SD: 13.39) and 8.50% interacted with the adaptation. Demographic information was only available for the survey respondents. Only 39 (1.2%) of them were female. Average age was 32.68 years (median: 28, SD: 14.35). Most visitors stated they were single (51.6%). Education degrees ranged from lower than vocational (11.5%), vocational (39.9%), to undergraduate degree (35.3%) and graduate degree (10.7%). Most participants were returning visitors, only 2.7% indicated to be first time visitors.

3.3 Measurements

The behavior was expected to be influenced in a number of ways. For conditions with congruent content we expect an increase (relative to the neutral and incongruent conditions) in the number of clicks on the adaptation, the number of pageviews (as more relevant content is available) and potentially the number of visits (as the user experience is improved).

A questionnaire was constructed following Knijnenburg et al.[5] to measure how the content of the sidebar element was perceived in terms of accuracy (5 items, e.g. "The items in the sidebar were well chosen"), variety (7 items, e.g. "The items in the sidebar were very diverse"), effectiveness (7 items, e.g. "I'm saving time by using the sidebar") and appeal (6 items e.g. "The sidebar is well designed"). All items were submitted as categorical variables to an exploratory factor analysis using Mplus[9]. A number of items was removed due to high residual correlations with other items resulting in the constructs: perceived accuracy (3 items), experienced appeal (3 items), perceived variety (3 items) and experienced efficiency (4 items). Additionally we asked visitors to express their interest for content from either segment on two 5-point Likert scales.

[1] In a prior analysis based on server logs 5 pages was established as providing a right balance between proportion of visitors exposed to the adaptation and prediction accuracy.

3.4 Analysis of Results

In our first analysis we construct a model that can be used to infer visitor segments based on their navigation behavior. In the second part we use the model output to investigate the effects of the adaptation on visitor behavior, visitor experience and how they relate.

Predictive Modeling. Two different approaches for labeling visitors were tested. Firstly labels were based on the proportion of HC versus EUP content throughout an entire visit. Visits with at least 10 pageviews (51970 visitors did not meet this requirement) were labeled as from one category when viewing twice as much content in that category, resulting in a set of 23874 HC (47.4%), 14461 EUP (28.7%) and 12048 unknown (23.9%) instances. Secondly, labels were based on interest as measured in the survey, taking the category visitors indicated to be most interested in. The resulting dataset consists of 3231 rows, with 1227 HC (38.0%), 476 EUP (14.7%) and 1528 unknown (those with equal interest)(47.3%).

Negative binomial regressions[2] were used to test which type of labeling could best predict user behavior. Testing model fit using Akaike Information Criterion (AIC)[1], we find that AIC was higher for models based on labels from expressed interest (from the survey) than from proportion of EUP/HC pages. This holds for the number of clicks on the adaptation (26,910.6 vs. 26,832.5), number of pages (834,821.3 vs. 832,555.5) and number of visits (517,453.3 vs. 514,761.0). Thus model predictions based on survey data better capture the actual visitor segment than the labels produced by looking at behavior alone, despite the fact that it uses data from just over 3000 users to predict behavior in all ($> 100k$) visits.

Thus, predictive modeling of EUP/HC segment was done through multinomial logistic regressions trained on the dataset based on expressed interest. The final selection was based on the accuracy metrics and confusion matrices, with the final model having an adequate fit. In addition the odds-ratios of the regression model were investigated, which were in the expected direction (e.g. people that were referred to the website from social networks were 26% more likely to be EUP, while people being referred from other external domains had a 12% increase of probability of being a HC visitor).

Visitor Behavior. Regression analysis was performed on the behavioral measures (clicks in the adaptation, number of pageviews, number of sessions), with the predicted segment (from the model) and congruency (match between predicted and shown segment) as predictors. The regression models show that HC visitors have higher values on each measure than the EUP visitors. Other statistically significant coefficients (only for adaptation clicks) were congruency ($\beta = -0.191, p < .05$) and the interaction between congruency and HC ($\beta = 0.574, p < .001$), showing that congruency increases clicks for HC visitors,

[2] A negative binomial model is a generalization of the Poisson model best suited for count/frequency data [2].

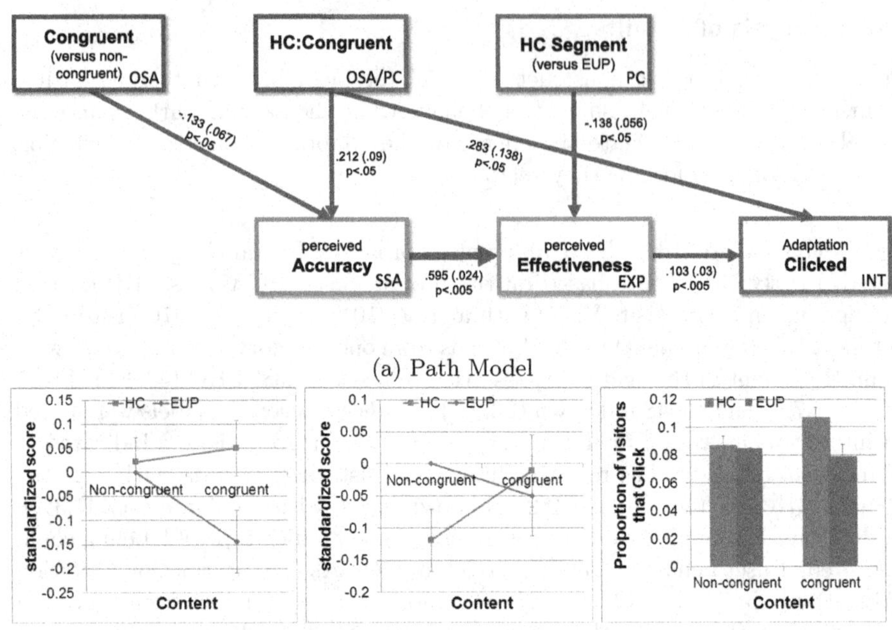

(b) Perceived Accuracy (c) Perceived Effectiveness (d) Adaptation Clicks

Fig. 1. Path model (top) and estimated means for latent constructs and adaptation clicks (bottom). The path model was constructed of the SEM with EUP non-congruent as baseline. The color of the blocks denote different types of construct. The numbers on and thickness of the arrows represent the strength of the relations. Standard errors (between parentheses) and statistical significance are included. (See [5] for a complete overview on how to interpret the path model).

but decreases clicks for EUP visitors. These effects are small due to the (minor) sidebar manipulation. We do not find other effects for pageviews or visits. Furthermore, in all the models there is no difference between the effects of neutral and incongruent content. Therefore these conditions will be collapsed into a new condition 'non-congruent' for the remainder of the result section.

User Experience. A path model using structural equation modeling was built from the constructs described in section 3.3 to investigate how the adaptation was experienced. Measures and constructs that were not affected were removed from the model. The path model in Fig. 1 showed good model fit ($\chi^2(39) = 83.101$, $p < .001$, CFI = .998, TLI = .998, RMSEA = .019). The structural part of the model tells us that a perceived accuracy of the sidebar content increases the perceived effectiveness of the sidebar, which in turn increases the likelihood of adaptation clicks.

Congruency affects accuracy negatively ($\beta = -0.133$) for the baseline EUP visitor segment but not for the HC segment (see the positive interaction of HC:congruent of 0.212). HC visitors find the adaptation less effective ($\beta = -0.138$) on average than EUP visitors. In addition, there is a direct effect of the HC:Congruent interaction on clicks in the adaptation, indicating that accuracy and effectiveness only partially mediate the effect of congruency.

The marginal means in Fig. 1 further illustrate the effects found in the path model. HC visitors do not perceive accuracy differences due to congruency (Fig. 1b), whereas EUP visitors surprisingly find congrument content less accurate. In terms of effectiveness the HC segment experiences higher effectiveness from congruent content, whereas the EUP segment is less influenced by congruency (Fig. 1c). The end result is an increase of adaptation clicks but only for HC visitors that receive congruent content (Fig. 1d).

The combination of visitor behavior and user experience shows us that visitors from different segments react differently to the adaptation. EUP visitors that have lower engagement are less enticed to interact with the adaptation, while HC visitors find the adaptation more accurate and effective if content is congruent and consequently use it more. This demonstrates that a higher perceived accuracy in provided content will lead to more clicks.

4 Conclusion and Discussion

Incorporating the user experience in this study added value over considering behavior alone in three ways. Firstly it allowed us to construct a better prediction model. Secondly the user experience showed what caused the observed change in behavior. Finally it showed us that the adaptation caused an increased user perception and subsequent increased interaction for only one segment. Contrary to the initial intuition of the hardware.info website owners, EUP visitors did not suffer from incongruency, while HC visitors did benefit from congruency.

A limitation to this study is the nature of the adaptation, which was kept minimal to minimize a possible negative impact on business. As a result only the behavior related to the adaptation was influenced without affecting overall visitor engagement (in terms of pageviews and visits).

In conclusion, this study showed that measuring the visitor experience is an inexpensive way to gain valuable additional understanding over user behavior data alone when implementing and evaluating website adaptations.

Acknowledgments. The authors would like to thank hardware.info for providing the resources to perform this study and Bart Knijnenburg for his assistance in conducting the structural equation modeling.

References

1. Akaike, H.: A new look at the statistical model identification. IEEE Transactionson Automatic Control **19**(6), 716–723 (1974)
2. Cohen, J., Cohen, P., West, S.G., Aiken, L.S.: Applied Multiple Regression/Correlation Analysis for the Behavioral Sciences, 3rd edn. Routledge, August 2002
3. Ekstrand, M.D., Harper, F.M., Willemsen, M.C., Konstan, J.A.: User perception of differences in recommender algorithms. In: Proceedings of the 8th ACM Conference on Recommender systems - RecSys 2014, pp. 161–168 (2014)
4. Hauser, J.R., Urban, G.L., Liberali, G., Braun, M.: Website Morphing. Marketing Science **28**(2), 202–223 (2009)
5. Knijnenburg, B., Willemsen, M., Gantner, Z., Soncu, H., Newell, C.: Explaining the user experience of recommender systems. User Modeling and User-Adapted Interaction **22**(4–5), 441–504 (2012)
6. Knijnenburg, B.P., Willemsen, M.C., Hirtbach, S.: Receiving recommendations and providing feedback: the user-experience of a recommender system. In: Buccafurri, F., Semeraro, G. (eds.) EC-Web 2010. LNBIP, vol. 61, pp. 207–216. Springer, Heidelberg (2010)
7. Moe, W.W., Fader, P.S.: Dynamic Conversion Behavior at E-Commerce Sites. Management Science **50**(3), 326–335 (2004)
8. Moe, W.W., Fader, P.S.: Which visits lead to purchases? Dynamic conversion behavior at e-commerce sites. University of Texas, February, 2001
9. Muthén, L.K., Muthén, B.O.: Mplus User's Guide (2012)
10. Smith, W.R.: Product differentiation and market segmentation as alternative marketing strategies. The Journal of Marketing **21**(1), 3–8 (1956)

Modelling the User Modelling Community (and Other Communities as Well)

Dario De Nart[(✉)], Dante Degl'Innocenti, Andrea Pavan, Marco Basaldella, and Carlo Tasso

Artificial Intelligence Lab Department of Mathematics and Computer Science, University of Udine, Udine, Italy
{dario.denart,carlo.tasso}@uniud.it,
{dante.deglinnocenti,pavan.andrea.1,basaldella.marco.1}@spes.uniud.it

Abstract. Discovering and modelling research communities' activities is a task that can lead to a more effective scientific process and support the development of new technologies. Journals and conferences already offer an implicit clusterization of researchers and research topics, and social analysis techniques based on co-authorship relations can highlight hidden relationships among researchers, however, little work has been done on the actual content of publications. We claim that a content-based analysis on the full text of accepted papers may lead to a better modelling and understanding of communities' activities and their emerging trends. In this work we present an extensive case study of research community modelling based upon the analysis of over 450 events and 7000 papers.

1 Introduction

Tracking the activity of research communities and discovering trends in research activity is a complex task which can produce great benefits for future research and is essential for research evaluation. Most commonly used evaluation techniques rely on Social Network Analysis (herein SNA), more specifically on the analysis of the co-authorship relation between scholars. Such methods can lead us to interesting insights about existing research communities and their evolution over time; however we believe that a more semantic approach can lead us to even more interesting insights about the actual topics dealt by a community, the emerging research themes and buzzwords, and also the existence of complementary research communities. Since SNA does not take into account the actual content of papers (which is the reason behind a collaboration) it does not allow discovering communities that deal with the same topics but do not know each other yet. On the other hand, knowing the content of research papers can lead to such information. Manually reading and understanding all the literature produced by a community such as the Computer Science one is simply not feasible due to huge amount of time and resources required. On the other hand, there exist automatic knowledge extraction tools able to extract meaningful concepts from unstructured text with enough precision for this purpose [3]. We claim

F. Ricci et al. (Eds.): UMAP 2015, LNCS 9146, pp. 357–363, 2015.
DOI: 10.1007/978-3-319-20267-9_31

that their combined usage with traditional SNA techniques can better model the research community, achieving a better description of its sub-communities and their relationships. In this paper we present in Sec. 3 an innovative approach towards modelling and discovery of research communities based on the combination of SNA and content-based analysis on the accepted contributions. Our approach is then used in Sec. 4 to analyse over 450 events and 7000 papers spanned over three years of activity of the Computer Science and ICT community. Due to copyright and data access restrictions, the analysis is limited to the proceedings published by *ceur-ws*[1]. Ceur-ws provides open access to a large number of Workshop, Poster session, and conference proceedings of events held all over the world, but mostly in Europe.

2 Related Work

The study of the connections between people and groups has a long research tradition of at least 50 years [1]. SNA is a highly interdisciplinary field whose traditional approach consists in selecting a small sample of the community and to interview the members of such sample. This approach has proved to work well in self contained communities such as business communities, academic communities, ethnic and religious communities and so forth [8]. However the increasing digital availability of big data allows to use all the community data and the relations among them. A notable example is the network of movie actors [12], that contains nearly half a million professionals and their co-working relationship [9]. Academic communities are a particularly interesting case due to the presence of *co-authorship* relations between their members. Several authors in the literature have analysed the connections between scholars by means of co-authorship: in [8] [9] a collection of papers coming from Physics, Biomedical Research, and Computer Science communities are taken into account in order to investigate cooperation among authors; in [1] a data set consisting of papers published on relevant journals in Mathematics and Neuroscience in an eight-year period are considered to identify the dynamic and the structural mechanisms underlying the evolution of those communities. *VIVO* [7] is a project of Cornell University that exploits a Semantic Web-based network of institutional databases to enable cooperation between researchers and their activities. In [6] the problem of content-based social network discovery among people who appear in *Google News* is studied: probabilistic Latent Semantic Analysis [5] and clustering techniques have been exploited to obtain a topic-based representation. The authors claim that the relevant topic discussed by the community can be discovered as well as the roles and the authorities within the community. The authors of [10] perform deep text analysis over the Usenet corpus. Finally the authors of [11] introduce a complex system for content-based social analysis involving NLP techniques which bears strong similarities with our work. The deep linguistic analysis is performed in three steps: (i) concept extraction (ii) topic detection

[1] http://ceur-ws.org/

using semantic similarity between concepts, and (iii) SNA to detect the evolution of collaboration content over time. However the approach relies on a domain ontology and therefore cannot be applied to other cases without extensive knowledge engineering work, whereas our work relies a domain-independent approach.

3 Proposed Method

In order to support our claims a testbed system was developed to provide access to CEUR volumes, integrate the concept extraction system presented in [2], and aggregate and visualize data for inspection and analysis. The SNA part of our study is performed in the following way: all contributing authors are considered as features of an event and form a vector-space model in which it is possible to estimate the similarity between events by means of *cosine similarity*. Non-zero similarity values are then considered to create, for each event, a neighborhood of similar events; such connections are then represented as a graph (*Author Graph* - AG). Communities of similar events in the AG are then identified with the Girvan-Newman clustering algorithm [4] which allows to cluster events corresponding to well connected communities. The Content-based part of the study, instead, is performed in a novel way: the usage of an automatic knowledge extraction tool allows us to finely model the topics actually discussed in a conference and to group events according to semantic similarities. Such topics are represented by means of *keyphrases* (herein KPs), i.e. short phrases of 1 to 4 words that represent a particular concept. Our knowledge extraction tool associates to each relevant KP a score named *keyphraseness* which is intended as an estimation of the actual relevance of a concept inside a long text such as a scholarly paper. By extracting a sufficient number of relevant KPs we can obtain a detailed representation of the main topics of a paper as well as the relevant entities therein mentioned, where more relevant concepts are associated to higher keyphraseness. For each CEUR event, all its papers are processed creating a pool of *event keyphrases*, where each KP is associated to the *Cumulative Keyphraseness* (*CK*) i.e. sum of all the keyphraseness values in the corresponding papers. By doing so a topic mentioned in few papers, but with an high estimated relevance (keyphraseness), may achieve a higher CK than another one mentioned many times but with a low average estimated relevance. For each KP an *Inverse Document Frequency* (*IDF*) index is then computed on event basis, namely we compute the logarithm of the number of considered events divided by the events in which the considered KP appears, as broadly used in Information Retrieval. Then, for each KP in each event, a CK-IDF score is computed by multiplying the IDF with the corresponding CK. This measure behaves in a manner that closely resembles the well known TF-IDF measure; however there is a substantial difference: the CK part of the formula takes into account features more complex than just term frequency[2]. All extracted topics, with their related CK-IDF values, are considered as features of an event and form a vector-space model in which is possible to estimate the semantic similarity between events by means of *cosine similarity*. Due to the high number of non-zero values, only the highest 10% of these similarity values is considered. Within such

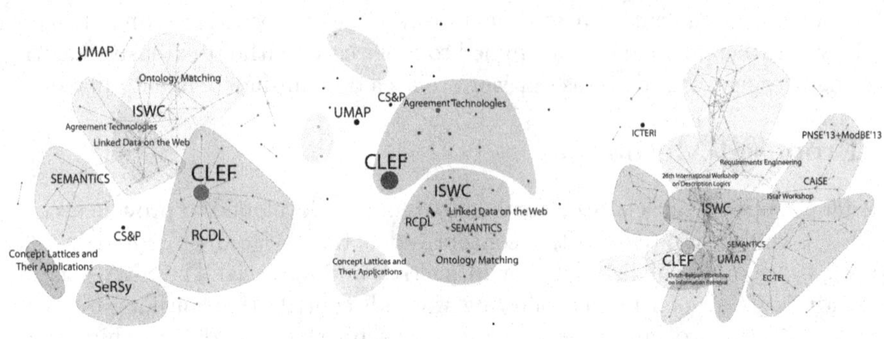

Fig. 1. 2012 AG **Fig. 2.** 2012 TG **Fig. 3.** 2013 AG

a value range, for each event a neighborhood of significantly similar events is identified; such connections are then represented as a graph named *Topic Graph* (herein TG). Communities of similar events in the graph are then identified, as in the previous scenario, with the Girvan-Newman clustering algorithm. Finally, complementary communities analysis is performed by comparing the AG and the TG: events that are connected in the TG and have no direct connections in the AG are potentially complementary communities. To detect such situations a simple metric called *Complementarity*, evaluated as the difference between topic similarity and author similarity, is proposed. Positive values suggest that the considered events bear a strong topic similarity and a low author similarity, meaning that, even though the topics discussed are similar, the contributing authors have little or no overlap.

4 Results

In this section we present and compare the results of our analysis on the last three years of CEUR volumes. Only proceedings available in CEUR were considered, therefore, for conferences such as UMAP, ISWC, and CAiSE we are considering only the part of their proceedings published on CEUR (usually poster and demo sessions, workshops, and doctoral consortia). Fig. 1 and Fig. 2 represent our model of the 2012 events whose proceedings were published on CEUR. The clusters obtained in the AG and in the TG are notably different: in the AG there are several clusters, while in the TG most of the events belong to two large clusters with one of them clearly including all Semantic-Web related events. Fig. 3 and Fig. 4 represent our model of the 2013 events. Again, the AG presents more clusters than the TG, however the four clusters found identify different groups of events: compared to Fig. 4 the upper one includes Data Science related events, the lower one Software Engineering related events, the right one E-Learning related events, and the left one theoretical Computer Science related

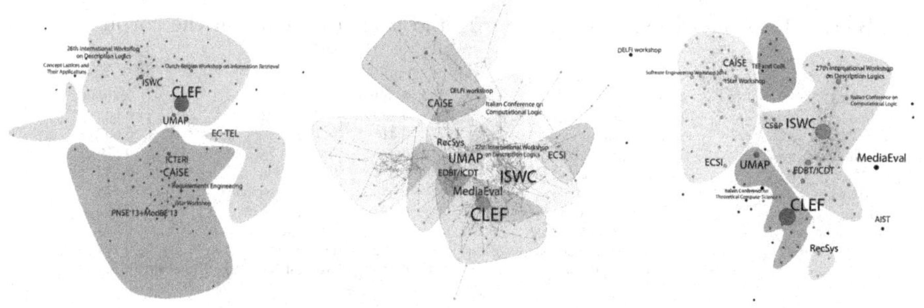

Fig. 4. 2013 TG **Fig. 5.** 2014 AG **Fig. 6.** 2014 TG

events. Finally, Fig. 5 and Fig. 6 represent our model of the 2014 events. Due to the large number of 2014 events published on CEUR it was possible to identify more clusters, however, there are still more clusters in the AG than in the TG. In both graphs is clearly recognizable a large Semantic-Web related cluster, which in the TG includes also theoretic Computer Science events. The comparative analysis of the 2012, 2013, and 2014 models of CEUR events can provide insights on the evolution of the involved research communities. For instance, we can observe how CLEF and ISWC always attract different authors communities, even though there has been some topic overlap in the history of such events; moreover, we can observe how UMAP, in the considered period, was thematically closer to CLEF than ISWC, but it attracted part of the ISWC community as well. Another interesting insight about what research communities actually debate can be obtained by looking at the extracted concepts with the lowest IDF, which means the most widely used in the considered data set (listed in Table 1). The term "Semantic Web" appears in all the three considered years of CEUR proceedings on a large part of the published papers (spanning from 20% to 35% of the considered proceedings) which is far larger than the part covered by the identified Semantic Web event cluster. Finally, the complementary communities analysis highlights how every considered event has at least a potentially complementary event. Since listing all the pairs of potentially complementary events would require too much space, we are only reporting, in Table 2 the potentially complementary events for the UMAP community held in 2014.

5 Conclusions and Future Work

In this paper we presented a new approach towards scientific communities modelling based on a twofold view with the aim of discovering shared interests, spotting research communities and, hopefully, help scientist to address the problem of finding the right venue for their work. The ability of identifying potentially complementary communities is, in our opinion, the most notable feature of our approach: traditional SNA can detect existing communities, but is unlikely to

Table 1. Most widespread buzzwords and their frequency in the corpus

2012		2013		2014	
buzzword	frequency	buzzword	frequency	buzzword	frequency
system	0.30	system	0.521	system	0.662
data	0.291	data	0.416	model	0.607
computer science	0.261	model	0.385	data	0.576
model	0.246	computer science	0.378	information	0.533
information	0.231	information	0.335	computer science	0.478
ontology	0.201	Semantic Web	0.248	Semantic Web	0.355
knowledge	0.201	ontology	0.242	research	0.294
Semantic Web	0.201	Natural Language Processing	0.192	language	0.294
Natural Language Processing	0.134	Software	0.186	Natural Language Processing	0.282

Table 2. Most complementary events to UMAP 2014

Event	Complementarity score
the Workshops held at Educational Data Mining 2014	0.267
the Workshops of the EDBT ICDT 2014 Joint Conference	0.238
the 16th LWA Workshops KDML IR and FGWM	0.235
Workshop on Semantic Matching in Information Retrieval	0.223

identify communities that should talk each other, meet or join. On the other hand, our approach exploits state of the art knowledge extraction techniques to investigate the topics actually dealt by a community and can easily identify communities that deal with the same topics, but have little or no social overlap at all. Our future work includes extending our models of the research community activity with more data coming from different sources than CEUR, as well as employing our modelling techniques to other domains and with different goals. Finally, we believe that the presented modelling technique can be exploited to provide personalized services, for instance scientific papers or conference recommender systems.

References

1. Barabsi, A., Jeong, H., Nda, Z., Ravasz, E., Schubert, A., Vicsek, T.: Evolution of the social network of scientific collaborations. Physica A: Statistical Mechanics and its Applications **311**(34), 590–614 (2002)
2. Degl'Innocenti, D., De Nart, D., Tasso, C.: A new multi-lingual knowledge-base approach to keyphrase extraction for the italian language. In: Proc. of the 6th Int.l Conf. on Knowledge Discovery and Information Retrieval. SciTePress (2014)
3. Gangemi, A.: A Comparison of Knowledge Extraction Tools for the Semantic Web. In: Cimiano, P., Corcho, O., Presutti, V., Hollink, L., Rudolph, S. (eds.) ESWC 2013. LNCS, vol. 7882, pp. 351–366. Springer, Heidelberg (2013)
4. Girvan, M., Newman, M.E.: Community structure in social and biological networks. Proceedings of the National Academy of Sciences **99**(12), 7821–7826 (2002)
5. Hofmann, T.: Probabilistic latent semantic indexing. In: Proc. of the 22nd Annual International ACM SIGIR Conf. on Research and Development in Information Retrieval, SIGIR 1999, pp. 50–57. ACM, New York (1999)

6. Joshi, D., Gatica-Perez, D.: Discovering groups of people in google news. In: Proceedings of the 1st ACM International Workshop on Human-Centered Multimedia, pp. 55–64. ACM (2006)
7. Krafft, D.B., Cappadona, N.A., Caruso, B., Corson-Rikert, J., Devare, M., Lowe, B.J., et al.: Vivo: Enabling national networking of scientists. In: Proceedings of the Web Science Conference 2010, pp. 1310–1313 (2010)
8. Newman, M.: Scientific collaboration networks. network construction and fundamental results. Phys. Rev. E **64**, 016131 (2001)
9. Newman, M.: The structure of scientific collaboration networks. Proc. of the National Academy of Sciences 98(2), 404–409 (2001)
10. Sack, W.: Conversation map: a content-based usenet newsgroup browser. In: From Usenet to CoWebs, pp. 92–109. Springer (2003)
11. Velardi, P., Navigli, R., Cucchiarelli, A., D'Antonio, F.: A new content-based model for social network analysis. In: ICSC, pp. 18–25. IEEE Computer Society (2008)
12. Watts, D.J., Strogatz, S.H.: Collective dynamics of "small-world" networks. Nature **393**(6684), 440–442 (1998)

Personality Correlates for Digital Concert Program Notes

Marko Tkalčič(✉), Bruce Ferwerda, David Hauger, and Markus Schedl

Department of Computational Perception, Johannes Kepler University, Altenberger Strasse 69, Linz, Austria
{marko.tkalcic,bruce.ferwerda,david.hauger,markus.schedl}@jku.at
http://www.cp.jku.at

Abstract. In classical music concerts, the concert program notes are distributed to the audience in order to provide background information on the composer, piece and performer. So far, these have been printed documents composed mostly of text. With some delay, mobile devices are making their way also in the world of classical concerts, hence offering additional options for digital program notes comprising not only text but also images, video and audio. Furthermore, these digital program notes can be personalized. In this paper, we present the results of a user study that relates personal characteristics (personality and background musical knowledge) to preferences for digital program notes.

Keywords: Classical music · Digital program notes · Personality

1 Introduction

Classical music has long resisted the temptation of introducing new devices, such as smartphones or tablets into the live concert experiences. However, things started to change recently. Two efforts are being made in this direction, one within the FP7 Phenicx project[1] and the other by the Philadelphia Orchestra[2], both of them developing a mobile application for supporting the live classical concert experience. Both of these applications feature the program notes in a digital form. Within the Phenicx project we are developing a system that would support personalized digital program notes based on the user profile. The personalization is going to be done of the level of the preferred multimedia type in the notes (music, text or audio) and its length. In order to develop the personalization method we first need to identify the relationships between the users' personal characteristics (in terms of personality and musical background) and the preferences for the supporting multimedia material in the digital program notes. In this paper, we present the results of a user study that was carried out in order to identify these relationships. To be more concrete, we addressed the following research questions

[1] http://phenicx.upf.edu/

[2] https://www.philorch.org/introducing-livenote%E2%84%A2-nights#/

F. Ricci et al. (Eds.): UMAP 2015, LNCS 9146, pp. 364–369, 2015.
DOI: 10.1007/978-3-319-20267-9_32

1. Do the user's preferences for the digital program notes correlate with the user's personality
2. Do the user's preferences for the digital program notes correlate with the user's musical background

2 Related Work

Personality and Learning Styles. The purpose of the program notes is to provide additional information about the concert in terms of the historical background on the piece, the composer and the performer. Similar educational processes, outside the classical music live experience domain, have been investigated in terms of personalization. Research based on learning styles, as a subset of personality, has been done [6] and models for personalizing course materials have been proposed [3].

Personality and User Preferences. Personality has been gaining popularity in research on personalized services. It has been used to alleviate the cold-start problem in recommender systems [4,15]. Research has been carried out to understand how personality relates to user preferences in multiple domains [1]. Special attention has been given to music, where strong relations have been found (i) between personality and genre preferences [14] (ii) between personality and the way people use music (e.g. rationally versus for mood regulation [2]) and (iii) between personality and the way users organize music [5]. However, to the best of our knowledge, there has been no research done on the relations between classical music and personality, except for the aforementioned genre preferences.

Implicit Acquisition of Personality. For a long time, the only way of assessing the user personality has been through extensive questionnaires, such as the Big-Five Inventory (BFI) [9]. There has been an increasing interest for detecting unobtrusively the user personality from various sources. Related work has been done especially on using social media (e.g. facebook or twitter) to infer the personality in the Five Factor Model (FFM) personality space [7,10,13]. These methods can be useful in scenarios when a user logs in an online system with her/his social media account.

3 Usage Scenario

Within the Phenicx project, we are developing technologies for improving the classical concert experience. One of the use cases we focus on is the *digital program notes* scenario, where *automatically generated, tailor-made multimedia editorials are offered to prospective audience members, introducing the concert that will take place with the purpose of informing, educating and pre-engaging users, supporting concert anticipation* [11]. The concrete scenario we foresee is a user (the attendee of a classical concert) having a mobile device (e.g. a smartphone or a tablet device) with a mobile application that supports the scenario. The user logs in the application with her/his social media account (e.g. twitter or facebook). Using some of the aforementioned methods for inferring the user's personality from the social media stream, the application can use this information to tailor the digital program notes to the user's needs. The strategy for personalizing the digital program notes is going to be based on the outcomes of the study we present in this paper.

4 Materials and Methods

We conducted a user study to collect the data needed. We gathered the participants through Amazon Mechanical Turk. In total we had 165 participants aged from 20 to 76 (mean 37, stdev 11), 93 females and 72 males. The participants first filled in a set of background questionnaires: a questionnaire about their musical background, a questionnaire about their musical preferences in general (according to 18 genres) and the Ten-items Personality Inventory (TIPI) questionnaire [8]. The participants were then shown various supporting multimedia content that could fit in an interactive digital program note. For the chosen classical music concert (the piece *La Mer* by the French composer *Claude Debussy* performed by the *Royal Concertgebouw Orchestra*) we prepared multimedia material (text, images and audio) for the composer, piece and performer. Furthermore, each pair (e.g. composer-text) was presented in a long and short version (for images and audio clips *short* meant one item and *long* meant several items). In total we presented the participants 14 combinations of content. For each content combination, the participants gave three ratings: (i) amount of consumption of the content (on the scale *none/some/half/most/all*), (ii) interestingness of the content (on a scale from 1 to 5) and (ii) novelty of the content (on a scale from 1 to 5).

5 Results

As can be seen from Tab. 1, personality traits were correlated with the subjects' musical background. Openness and extraversion were positively significantly correlated to three variables, agreeableness had a negative significant correlation with two variables while conscientiousness had a positive correlation only with the *attending classical concerts* variable. Neuroticism was not significantly correlated with any of the musical background variables.

Personality also appears to be correlated with how much the subjects like classical music as a genre (see Tab. 2). Openness, extraversion and agreeableness have a positive significant correlation with liking classical music, while conscientiousness and neuroticism are not significantly correlated.

We observed several significant correlations among variables that can be useful in a personalized system. Personality did correlate with with the answers provided by the subjects on the consumption, interestingness and novelty of the multimedia material. For example, people who score high on openness, agreeableness, conscientiousness and extraversion tend to show a positive correlation with consumption, interestingness and novelty, hence meaning that they prefer

Table 1. Correlations between personality traits and musical background variables

personality trait	musical background variable	correlation	p value
openness	listening to classical music	0.26	0.0007
	studying an instrument	0.16	0.03
	attending classical concerts	0.19	0.01
extraversion	playing an instrument	0.21	0.008
	attending classical concerts	0.3	0.00009
	attending non-classical concerts	0.24	0.002
agreeableness	listening to non-classical music	−0.22	0.005
	studying an instrument	−0.23	0.003
conscientiousness	attending classical concerts	0.17	0.02

Table 2. Correlation between personality traits and the preferences for the classical music genre

personality trait	correlation	p-value
openness	0.17	0.03
extraversion	0.21	0.006
agreeableness	0.33	0.00001
conscientiousness	0.11	0.16
neuroticism	−0.14	0.06

to consume more of the material, find it interesting and novel. On the other hand, subjects who score high on neuroticism tend to consume less of the material, find it less interesting or novel. Our data show no correlation or negative correlations for neuroticism and the observed answers (see Fig. 1). Similarly, the music background variables showed generally positive correlations with consumption, interestingness and novelty of the multimedia material.

6 Conclusions and Future Work

The analysis of our data showed that there are many significant correlations between personal characteristics (personality and musical background) and preferences for the supporting multimedia content. However, further analyses should be carried out to determine how these personal characteristics relate with various types of material (text/images/audio) or length. The most important step we need to take is to use machine learning techniques to predict the preferred type of digital program notes based on the users' personalities. We plan to use logistic regression for individual binary variables and multinomial logistic regression for individual Likert scale ratings. Furthermore, we plan to use a rule-based algorithm for inferring the preferred modality and length.

We are currently in the process of designing a new user study where we will have better control over the text variance. The text will be curated by musicologists and we will use different levels of complexity (in terms of vocabulary).

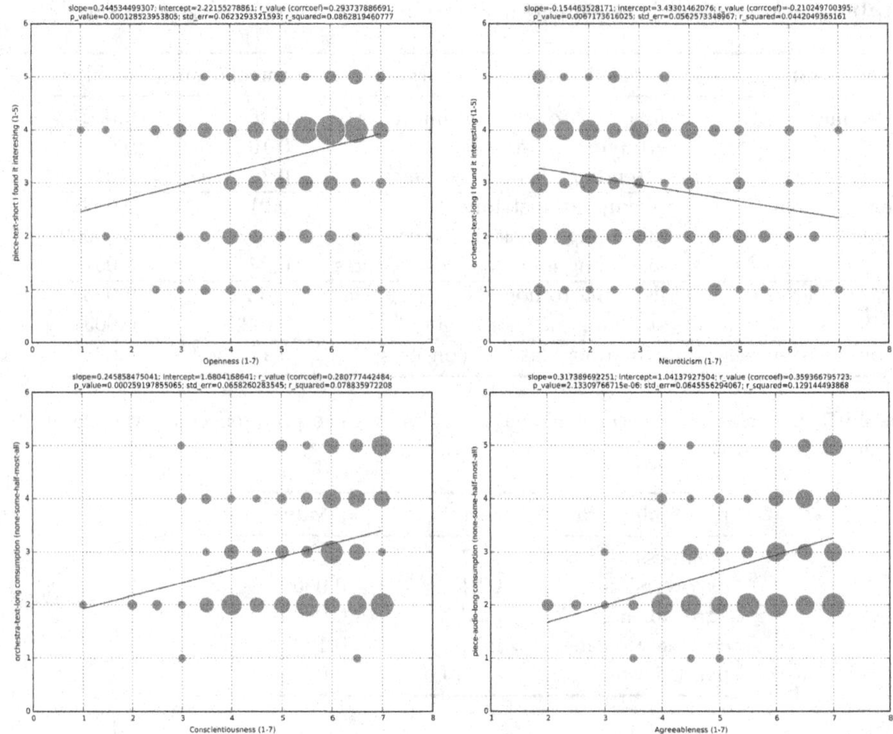

Fig. 1. Bubble plots with correlations between personality and content preferences. In the presented four cases all independent variables (x axis) are on the scale from 1 to 7, while the dependent (y axis) are on the scale from 1 to 5. The top-left figure is the relation between openness and the preference for the short description of the piece (slope $b_1 = 0.24$, correlation $r = 0.29$, p-value $p = 0.0001$). The top-right figure is the relation between neuroticism and the preference for a long description about the orchestra ($b_0 = 0.15, r = -0.21, p = 0.007$). The bottom-left figure is the relation between conscientiousness and the degree of consumption of the long orchestra description ($b_0 = 0.25, r = 0.28, p = 0.003$). The bottom-right figure is the relation between agreeableness and the degree of consumption of the long audio ($b_0 = 0.32, r = 0.36, p = 2 \cdot 10^{-6}$).

Furthermore, we will use the Goldsmiths Music Sophistication Index (MSI) [12] to assess the musical background of the users (the MSI instrument was published after we already carried out the study presented here).

Acknowledgments. This research is supported by the European FP7/2007-2013 programme through the PHENICX project under grant agreement no. 601166 and by the Austrian Science Fund (FWF): P25655.

References

1. Cantador, I., Fernández-Tobías, I., Bellogín, A.: Relating personality types with user preferences in multiple entertainment domains. In: EMPÌRE 1st Workshop on Emotions and Personality in Personalized Services, June 10, 2013, Rome (2013)
2. Chamorro-Premuzic, T., Furnham, A.: Personality and music: can traits explain how people use music in everyday life? British Journal of Psychology (London, England: 1953) **98**(Pt 2), 175–185 (2007)
3. El-Bishouty, M.M., Chang, T.-W., Graf, S., Chen, N.-S.: Smart e-course recommender based on learning styles. Journal of Computers in Education **1**(1), 99–111 (2014)
4. Elahi, M., Braunhofer, M., Ricci, F., Tkalcic, M.: Personality-based active learning for collaborative filtering recommender systems. In: Baldoni, M., Baroglio, C., Boella, G., Micalizio, R. (eds.) AI*IA 2013. LNCS, vol. 8249, pp. 360–371. Springer, Heidelberg (2013)
5. Ferwerda, B., Yang, E., Schedl, M., Tkalčič, M.: Personality traits predict music taxonomy preference. In: CHI 2015 Works-in-Progress (2015)
6. Furnham, A.: The big five versus the big four: the relationship between the Myers-Briggs Type Indicator (MBTI) and NEO-PI five factor model of personality. Personality and Individual Differences **21**(2), 303–307 (1996)
7. Golbeck, J., Robles, C., Edmondson, M., Turner, K.: Predicting personality from twitter. In: 2011 SocialCom and PASSAT Conference Proceedings, pp. 149–156. IEEE, October 2011
8. Gosling, S.D., Rentfrow, P.J., Swann, W.B.: A very brief measure of the Big-Five personality domains. Journal of Research in Personality **37**(6), 504–528 (2003)
9. John, O.P., Srivastava, S.: The big five trait taxonomy: history, measurement, and theoretical perspectives. In: Pervin, L.A., John, O.P. (eds.) Handbook of Personality: Theory and Research, vol. 2, 2nd edn, pp. 102–138. Guilford Press, New York (1999)
10. Kosinski, M., Stillwell, D., Graepel, T.: Private traits and attributes are predictable from digital records of human behavior. In: Proceedings of the National Academy of Sciences, pp. 2–5, March 2013
11. Liem, C.S.S., Van Der Sterren, R.: Innovating the classical music experience in the PHENICX project : use cases and initial user feedback. In: 1st International Workshop on Interactive Content Consumption (WSICC) at EuroITV 2013 (2013)
12. Müllensiefen, D., Gingras, B., Musil, J., Stewart, L.: The musicality of non-musicians: an index for assessing musical sophistication in the general population. PloS One **9**(2), e89642 (2014)
13. Quercia, D., Kosinski, M., Stillwell, D., Crowcroft, J.: Our twitter profiles, our selves: predicting personality with twitter. In: 2011 SocialCom and PASSAT Conference Proceedings, pp. 180–185. IEEE, October 2011
14. Rentfrow, P.J., Gosling, S.D.: The do re mi's of everyday life: The structure and personality correlates of music preferences. Journal of Personality and Social Psychology **84**(6), 1236–1256 (2003)
15. Tkalcic, M., Kunaver, M., Košir, A., Tasic, J.: Addressing the new user problem with a personality based user similarity measure. In: Proceedings of the DEMRA 2011 and the UMMS 2011 Workshops, Girona, Spain (2011)

Integrating Context Similarity with Sparse Linear Recommendation Model

Yong Zheng(✉), Bamshad Mobasher, and Robin Burke

School of Computing, Center for Web Intelligence, DePaul University, 243 South Wabash Ave, Chicago, IL 60604, USA
{yzheng8,mobasher,rburke}@cs.depaul.edu

Abstract. Context-aware recommender systems extend traditional recommender systems by adapting their output to users' specific contextual situations. Most of the existing approaches to context-aware recommendation involve directly incorporating context into standard recommendation algorithms (e.g., collaborative filtering, matrix factorization). In this paper, we highlight the importance of context similarity and make the attempt to incorporate it into context-aware recommender. The underlying assumption behind is that the recommendation lists should be similar if their contextual situations are similar. We integrate context similarity with sparse linear recommendation model to build a similarity-learning model. Our experimental evaluation demonstrates that the proposed model is able to outperform several state-of-the-art context-aware recommendation algorithms for the top-N recommendation task.

Keywords: Context · Context-aware recommendation · Context similarity

1 Introduction and Background

Recommender systems are an effective way to alleviate information overload in many application areas by tailoring recommendations to users' personal preferences. Context-aware recommender systems (CARS) emerged to go beyond user preferences and also take into account the contextual situation of users in generating recommendations.

The standard formulation of the recommendation problem begins with a two dimens-ional (2D) matrix of ratings, organized by user and item: *Users* × *Items* → *Ratings*. The key insight of context-aware recommender systems is that users' preferences for items may be a function of the context in which those items are encountered. Incorporating contexts requires that we estimate user preferences using a multidimensional rating function – *R*: *Users* × *Items* × *Contexts* → *Ratings* [1].

Context-aware recommendation algorithms, such as context-aware matrix factorization [2], seeks to incorporate context into the traditional recommendation framework without considering the relationships among contextual conditions. In this paper, we position the importance of context similarity, where

F. Ricci et al. (Eds.): UMAP 2015, LNCS 9146, pp. 370–376, 2015.
DOI: 10.1007/978-3-319-20267-9_33

the assumption behind is that the recommendation lists should be similar if their contextual situations are similar. Furthermore, we propose the Similarity-Learning Model (SLM) which attempts to integrate context similarity with the sparse linear recommendation model. We explore different ways to represent and model the context similarity in order to build SLM and evaluate these methods using multiple data sets.

2 Similarity-Based Contextual Recommendation

In this paper, we use *contextual dimension* to denote the contextual variable, e.g. "Time". The term *contextual condition* refers to a specific value in a dimension, e.g. "weekday" and "weekend" are two conditions for "Time". A *context* or *contextual situation* is, therefore, a set of contextual conditions, e.g. {*weekend, home, family*}.

We consider the context-aware recommendation task to be a top-N recommendation problem, where a ranked list of items should be recommended to a user in specific contextual conditions (i.e., the input is a pair <user, context>). Therefore, the recommendation list should be updated accordingly if the contextual conditions are changed. Previous work [7] has incorporated contextual deviation into the sparse linear recommendation model and demonstrated its effectiveness. In this paper, we switch to integrate context similarity with the sparse linear method, and propose the similarity-learning model (SLM) which avoids similarity calculation by learning context similarity directly while optimizing the ranking score in the algorithm. Previous research has found that similarity calculations relying on existing ratings, yield unreliable results if the rating space is sparse. In SLM, simply, a ranking score prediction function for <user, item, context> is required in which the similarity between contexts is an integral part. The algorithm learns context similarity by minimizing the ranking score error and provides contextual recommendations to the end user based on the predicted ranking score.

In this paper, we choose the Sparse LInear Method (SLIM) [4] as our base algorithm, where SLIM is a ranking-based recommendation algorithm aggregating users' ratings with item coefficients. And the General Contextual Sparse LInear Method (GCSLIM) [7] is our previous work which integrates the contextual deviations. Alternatively, we try to modify the GCSLIM and replace the rating deviation term by the context similarity in this work. More specifically, the goal in GCSLIM is to create a prediction function shown in Equation 1 to estimate the ranking score, $\widehat{S}_{i,j,k}$, for u_i on item t_j in contexts c_k. t_h is an item in the set of items rated by u_i ($h \neq i$), and c_m is the contextual situation where u_i placed rating on t_h (note: it is allowed that $c_m = c_k$). $R_{i,h,m}$ is one contextual rating placed by u_i on t_h under context c_m. Assume there are L contextual dimensions in total, thus $c_{m,l}$ denotes the contextual condition in the lth dimension in context c_m. The function *Dev* measures the contextual rating deviation between two contextual conditions – it is zero if $c_{m,l} = c_{k,l}$. Meantime, $W_{j,h}$ measures the coefficient between item t_j and t_h. Simply, GCSLIM learns the coefficients between items and the contextual rating deviations, where the optimization goal is to minimize the ranking score prediction error and the loss function can be generated accordingly by using gradient descent [7].

$$\widehat{S}_{i,j,k} = \sum_{\substack{h=1 \\ h \neq i}}^{N} (R_{i,h,m} + \sum_{l=1}^{L} Dev(c_{m,l}, c_{k,l}))W_{j,h} \tag{1}$$

Inspired by GCSLIM, it is also possible to incorporate the notion of context similarity into the model to formulate the SLM by replacing the deviation term in Equation 1:

$$\widehat{S}_{i,j,k} = \sum_{\substack{h=1 \\ h \neq j}}^{N} R_{i,h,m} \times Sim(c_k, c_m) \times W_{j,h} \tag{2}$$

In SLM, we aggregate the ranking score by the contextual rating score $R_{i,h,m}$ with the similarity between c_k and c_m multiplying by the coefficient between item t_j and t_h. Note that we set $h \neq j$ to avoid bias by using u_i's other contextual ratings on t_j. This strategy will ensure that we learn the coefficients between as many different items as possible. The loss function and parameter updating rules can be generated accordingly by using gradient descent. However, the form of the similarity term will vary if the context similarity is represented in different ways. The remaining challenge is how to represent or model the similarity of contexts in the prediction function shown in Equation 2. In this paper, we introduce four ways to represent similarity of contexts.

2.1 Independent Context Similarity (ICS)

	Time=Weekend	Time=Weekday	Loc=Home	Loc=Cinema
Time=Weekend	1	0.54	N/A	N/A
Time=Weekday	0.54	1	N/A	N/A
Loc=Home	N/A	N/A	1	0.82
Loc=Cinema	N/A	N/A	0.82	1

Fig. 1. Example of a similarity matrix

Table 1. Sample of Contexts

	Time (W_T)		Location (W_L)	
	Weekend	Weekday	Home	Cinema
c_k	1	0	1	0
c_m	0	1	1	0

An example of a similarity matrix can be seen in Table 1. With ICS, we only measure the similarity between two contextual conditions when they lie on the same dimension. Each pair of contextual dimensions are assumed to be independent. Assuming there are L contextual dimensions in total, the similarity represented by ICS can be depicted by Equation 3, where l is the index of context dimension.

$$Sim(c_k, c_m) = \prod_{l=1}^{L} similarity(c_{k,l}, c_{m,l}) \tag{3}$$

These similarity values (i.e., $similarity(c_{k,l}, c_{m,l})$) can be learned by the optimization process in SLM. The risk of this representation is that some information may be lost, if context dimensions are not in fact independent, e.g., if users usually go to cinema to see romantic movies with their partners, the "Location" (e.g. at cinema) and "Companion" (e.g. partners) may have significant correlations as a result.

2.2 Latent Context Similarity (LCS)

As noted earlier, contextual rating data is often sparse, since it is unusual to have users rate items repeatedly within multiple situations. This poses a difficulty when new contexts are encountered. For example, the similarity between a *new pair* of contexts <"Time=Weekend", "Time=Holiday"> may be required in the testing set, but it may not have been learned from the training data, while the similarity for two *existing pairs*, <"Time=Weekend", "Time=Weekday"> and <"Time=Weekday", "Time=Holiday">, may have been learned. In this case, the representation in ICS suffers from the sparsity problem. Alternatively, we represent each contextual condition by a vector of weights over a set of latent factors (we use 5 latent factors in our experiments), where the weights are initialized at the beginning and learnt by the optimization process. Even if the newly observed pair does not exist in the training data, the vectors representing the two individual conditions (i.e., "Time=Weekend" and "Time=Holiday") will be learned over *existing pairs*, and the similarity for the *new pair* can be computed by the dot product of those two updated vectors. Then context similarity can be computed as in Equation 3. We call this approach the *Latent Context Similarity* (LCS) model, and we learn the vectors representing contextual conditions, which may increase computational costs in contrast to ICS.

2.3 Weighted Jaccard Context Similarity (WJCS)

Another approach to calculate context similarity is to associate weights with each dimension. An example is shown in the Table 1, where weight W_T is associated with the dimension *Time*, and W_L is assigned to *Location*. This representation of contextual similarity is an adaptation of the differential context weighting algorithm [5].

The weight is used as part of similarity computation only when the conditions within a dimension match. The similarity can be calculated by Equation 4, where l denotes the index of contextual dimension. Given the example in Table 1, only the conditions in *Location* are the same, therefore, the similarity of c_k and c_m is calculated as $\frac{W_L}{W_T+W_L}$.

$$Sim(c_k, c_m) = \frac{\sum_{l \in c_{k,l} \cap c_{m,l}} W_l}{\sum_{l \in c_{k,l} \cup c_{m,l}} W_l} \tag{4}$$

When all the conditions in the same dimension are different, we assign a small fixed value (e.g., 0.01) to the similarity to avoid the zero values being used in the prediction function. In WJCS, the weights for each contextual dimension are the ones to be learned in the optimization process. The computational cost is correlated with the number of contexts in the data set – the more dimensions, the more weights to be learned. However, the number of contextual dimensions can be reduced by a pre-selection process.

2.4 Multidimensional Context Similarity (MCS)

In the multidimensional context similarity model, we assume that contextual dimensions form a multidimensional coordinate system. An example is depicted in Figure 2.

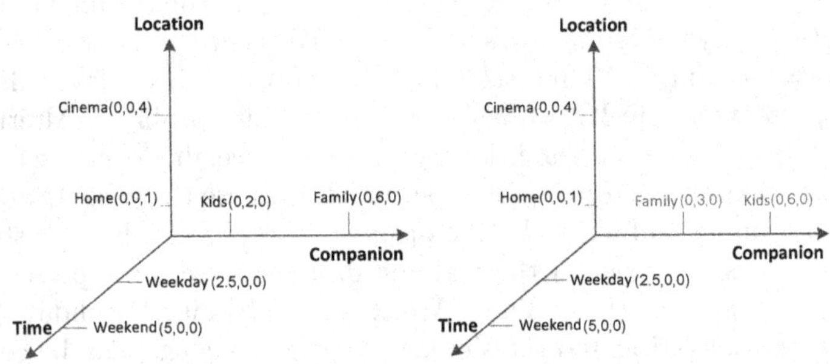

Fig. 2. Example of Multidimensional Coordinate System

Let us assume that there are three contextual dimensions: time, location and companion. We assign a real value to each contextual condition in those dimensions, so that each condition can locate a position in the corresponding axis. In this case, a contextual situation can be viewed as a point in the multidimensional space. Accordingly, the distance between two such points can be used as the basis for a similarity measure. In this approach, the real values for each contextual condition are the parameters to be learned in the optimization process. For example, the values for "family" and "kids" are updated in the right-hand side of the figure. Thus, the position of the data points associated to those two contextual conditions will be changed, as well as the distance between the corresponding two contexts. The similarity can be measured as the inverse of the distance between two data points. In our experiments, we use Euclidean distance to measure the distances, though other distance measures can also be used. The computational cost is directly associated with the number of contextual conditions in the data set, which may make this approach the highest-cost model. Again, the number of contextual conditions can be reduced by context selection, as with WJCS.

3 Experimental Evaluation

In our experiments, we use three context-aware data sets: the Restaurant, Music and Tourism data sets where the data descriptions can be found in [7]. We use a five-fold cross validation, performing top 10 recommendation task evaluated by precision and mean average precision (MAP). The algorithm proposed in this paper is build upon the GCSLIM; therefore, we choose the best performing deviation-based GCSLIM (denoted by "Deviation Model") [7] as baseline. In addition, we compare our approach to the state-of-the-art context-aware recommendation algorithms, including context-aware splitting approaches (CASA) [6], context-aware matrix factorization (CAMF) [2] and tensor factorization (TF) [3]. We vary different parameters for those algorithms and present the best performing one in this paper, which is the same setting used in [7].

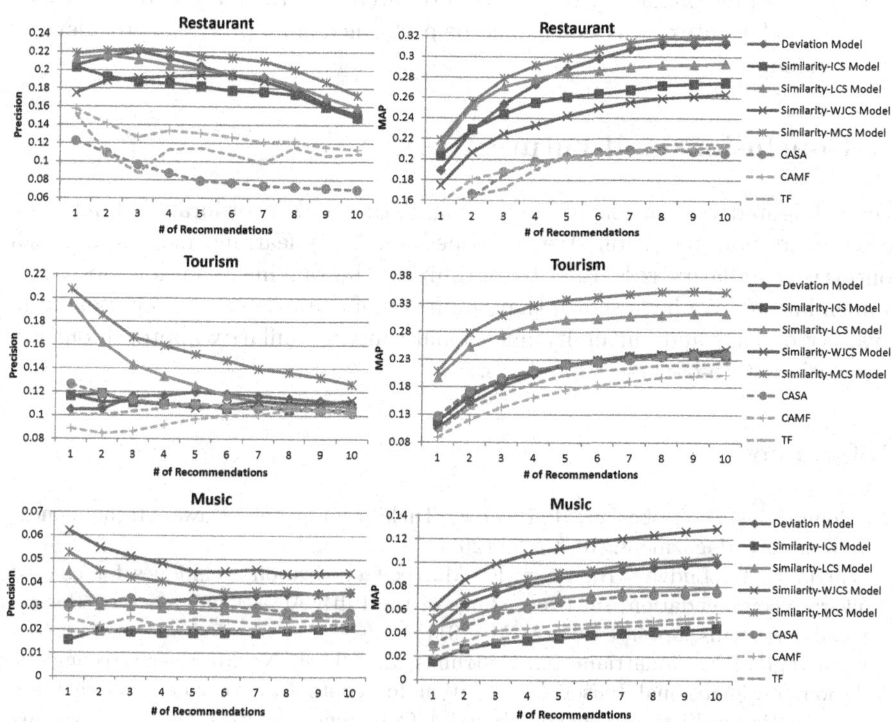

Fig. 3. Results in Precision and MAP @ Top-10 Context-aware Recommendations

The experimental results can be described by the Figure 3. We see that the MCS model outperforms all the baselines for the restaurant and tourism data, and the WJCS model is the best similarity model for the music data set. Note that the LCS model usually outperforms the ICS model. We can conclude that the latent factor approach is able to alleviate the sparsity problem suffered in ICS and improve performance.

The WJCS model has inconsistent performance. It is worse than the deviation-based baseline on the restaurant data, achieves comparable results to the deviation model with the tourism data, and is the best performer on the music data. We would expect the performance of the WJCS model to be influenced by a number of factors. The first is the number of contextual dimensions – more dimensions, more weights to be learned. This requires the rating profiles to be dense enough so that the weights for each dimension can be fully learned.

The second factor is the density of contextual ratings inferred by the data statistics reported in [7]. Based on those two factors, we can see that there are many more dimensions in the Tourism data, and the density in the restaurant data is pretty low, which explains the poor performance of WJCS model in these two data sets.

The multidimensional model seems to be an excellent representation. However, the computational cost is directly correlated with the number of conditions in this model. Context selection should be performed in preprocessing to alleviate this problem.

4 Conclusions and Future Work

We highlighted the notion of context similarity and incorporated it into the recommendation algorithm. We developed similarity-learning models in which contextual similarity is learned by optimizing the ranking score for top-N recommendations. We have shown that similarity of contexts can be represented in a variety of ways and our multidimensional context similarity approach outperforms other state-of-the-art baselines.

References

1. Adomavicius, G., Mobasher, B., Ricci, F., Tuzhilin, A.: Context-aware recommender systems. AI Magazine **32**(3), 67–80 (2011)
2. Baltrunas, L., Ludwig, B., Ricci, F.: Matrix factorization techniques for context aware recommendation. In: Proceedings of the Fifth ACM Conference on Recommender Systems, pp. 301–304. ACM (2011)
3. Karatzoglou, A., Amatriain, X., Baltrunas, L., Oliver, N.: Multiverse recommendation: n-dimensional tensor factorization for context-aware collaborative filtering. In: Proceedings of the Fourth ACM Conference on Recommender Systems, pp. 79–86. ACM (2010)
4. Ning, X., Karypis, G.: SLIM: sparse linear methods for top-n recommender systems. In: 2011 IEEE 11th International Conference on Data Mining, pp. 497–506. IEEE (2011)
5. Zheng, Y., Burke, R., Mobasher, B.: Recommendation with differential context weighting. In: Carberry, S., Weibelzahl, S., Micarelli, A., Semeraro, G. (eds.) UMAP 2013. LNCS, vol. 7899, pp. 152–164. Springer, Heidelberg (2013)
6. Zheng, Y., Burke, R., Mobasher, B.: Splitting approaches for context-aware recommendation: an empirical study. In: Proceedings of the 29th Annual ACM Symposium on Applied Computing, pp. 274–279. ACM (2014)
7. Zheng, Y., Mobasher, B., Burke, R.: Deviation-based contextual SLIM recommenders. In: Proceedings of the 23rd ACM Conference on Information and Knowledge Management, pp. 271–280. ACM (2014)

Doctoral Consortium

Modeling Motivational States Through Interpreting Physical Activity Data for Adaptive Robot Companions

Elena Corina Grigore(✉)

Department of Computer Science, Yale University, New Haven, CT 06520, USA
elena.corina.grigore@yale.edu

Abstract. This research aims to develop an adaptive human-robot interaction system that works with users over long periods of time to achieve a common goal that is beneficial to the user. The particular scenario I focus on is that of a robot companion interacting with adolescents, helping them succeed at achieving daily physical activity goals. To develop such a system, I propose a method of modeling the user's motivational state and employing this model in order to adapt motivational strategies best suited for each user. The proposed system uses both physical activity data obtained from wearable sensors (such as wristband devices) and information acquired by the robot from its interaction partners.

1 Problem and Motivation

The benefits of physical activity are well known, as research shows that daily physical activity has wide-ranging benefits, from improving cognitive and academic performance to helping with bone development and health [17]. My work seeks to sustain these benefits with robot home companions through personalized, data-driven coaching.

The U. S. Department of Health and Human Services comprehensive guidelines on physical activity for individuals ages 6 and older state that children and adolescents should aim to accumulate at least 60 minutes of moderate- or vigorous-intensity aerobic physical activity on most days of the week, preferably daily [1]. Current evidence shows that levels of physical activity among youth remain low, and that levels of physical activity decline dramatically during adolescence [2]. These data show the importance of developing methods to keep adolescents on track to achieving daily-recommended levels of physical activity. With this in mind, I seek to develop a human-robot interaction system that motivates adolescents to engage in physical activity on a daily basis.

2 Background and Related Work

There exists a great deal of work concerning health and well-being applications, such as commercial systems that use motivational strategies to help users stay

F. Ricci et al. (Eds.): UMAP 2015, LNCS 9146, pp. 379–384, 2015.
DOI: 10.1007/978-3-319-20267-9_34

engaged in physical activity, or that support goal-setting and reflection for the user [14], [9]. Other prior work explores tracking of long term goals along with factors that have an important role in goal-setting theory [5].

In the field of human-computer interaction (HCI), wearable sensors are being used in the development of persuasive technologies that motivate healthy behavior. Work in this area is wide, ranging from activity recognition systems that employ this information to keep users engaged in physical activity [7] to how such applications should be evaluated [11].

Social robots have also been used to promote and keep users engaged in physical activity within the field of human-robot interaction (HRI). Work in this area touches on investigating the role of praise and relational discourse [8], as well as on how to create a long-term interaction for help with weight loss [10].

The user model I am building employs an ontology-based approach. Ontologies are defined as explicit accounts of shared understanding in a given subject area, and bolster communication between users, experts, and technology systems [18]. Since ontologies are extremely useful in providing a formalism that specifies and clarifies concepts in a domain and the relationships among them, their value for health applications has been recognized by different lines of research. Such research includes the investigation of computational models of dialogue trying to simulate a human health counselor [6] and that of computerized behavioral protocols that help individuals improve their behaviors [13].

Although the work presented above is wide-ranging, the current paper aims to link all the components important in maintaining physical activity motivation into one system by leveraging human-robot interaction techniques together with the benefits of wearable sensors.

3 Research Questions and Intended Main Contributions

The key research questions I am investigating within this context are as follows. *How can I develop an ontology-based user model of people's motivational states by employing long-term human-robot interaction to gather information needed for the model? How can I then use this interpretation of the user's motivational state in order to create an adaptive robot companion that chooses appropriate motivational strategies to help the user stay on track to achieving daily physical activity goals?* The contributions expected from answering these two research questions consist of the following.

The first contribution represents the ontology-based user model, validated via expert interviews. The model makes use of long-term human-robot interaction by acquiring data from the user about his or her motivational state each interaction, and also acquires contextual information about external factors from online sources (e.g. weather). The second contribution represents an adaptive algorithm based on Q-Learning that uses both the output of the user model and the physical activity data collected from the wristband device. Its output consists of choosing the most appropriate motivational strategy the robot companion employs for a user each day.

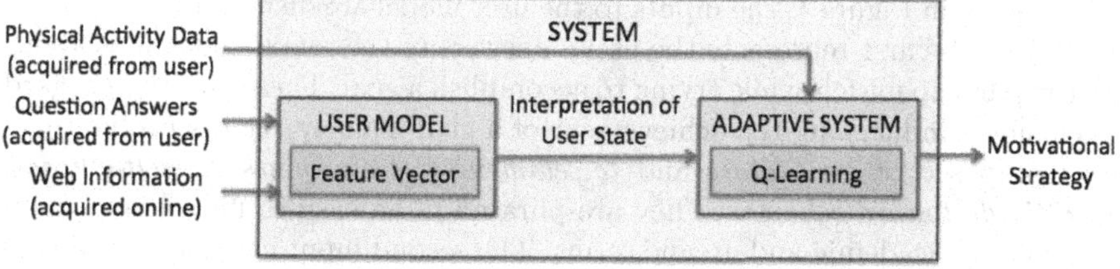

Fig. 1. System Diagram

Such a system would lie at the intersection of HRI, HCI, user modeling, and applied machine learning. Although there are a multitude of applications related to well-being and physical activity, there is no system to date that ties together continuous remote monitoring of user physical activity obtained from wearable sensors with an assistive robot for daily, long-term interactions.

4 Progress to Date and Plan of Further Research

4.1 Methodology and Design of the System

The robot platform chosen for this research is Keepon, a non-mobile platform with four degrees of freedom, designed to interact with children [12]. The adolescent wears a wristband device that keeps track of the number of steps taken throughout the day. He or she interacts with a robot once daily, both directly and via a phone application. The application presents an avatar for the robot with simple, 2D animations.

The system is depicted in Figure 1 above. When the adolescent interacts with the robot, the back-story of the robot unfolds in order to keep the user engaged in the long-term interaction. The robot asks the user a series of questions meant to obtain information about his or her motivational state, as well as acquires external information from online sources (e.g. weather information). This data is fed into the user model. The adaptive system then takes the user model output, together with the physical activity data from the wearable sensor, and outputs an appropriate motivational strategy for the user. This strategy is used to shape the new physical activity goal the adolescent needs to accomplish the next day.

4.2 User Model

The ontology my model relies upon needs to represent core concepts related to creating a profile of a user and keeping track of how this changes over time. Thus, I have initially performed extensive literature review in order to identify the key elements influencing the achievement of a goal. These are factors long studied in goal setting theory [15], social cognitive theory [4], and theory of planned behavior [3], and are introduced below. Since these key elements are part of the ontology-based model, the creation and validation of this model does not rely solely on literature review, but it is also heavily based on expert interviews.

As shown in Figure 1, the inputs to the user model are dichotomized into two categories. The first represents the user's answers to the robot's questions about how the participant felt while trying to accomplish a goal. These questions regard key elements influencing the achievement of a goal, namely *socio-structural factors* (composed of *facilitators* and *impediments*), *social pressure*, *self-efficacy*, and *attitude toward behavior*. They are phrased in an easy to understand manner, avoiding academic and arcane terms. The second input category represents external information acquired by the system online about factors that might have influenced the achievement of a goal, e.g. daily weather, school schedule changes. This information is fed into the socio-structural factors, into either the facilitators or impediments feature. All of these core factors make up the feature vector for a user, which contains numerical values based on the user's responses during the interaction with the robot.

The output of the user model is an interpretation of the user's state. It represents the state of the world (the state the user is in) at each time step (each day). The numerical value of each feature is mapped onto one of three discrete categories representing intensity levels, namely low, neutral, and high. This mapping is applied to reduce the state space size and produce a more intuitive interpretation of the user's state. For example, a value of 7 on a 1-to-7 scale for self-efficacy would be assigned to the "high" level. The interpretation thus consists of a feature vector with intensity levels for each feature.

To validate the user model and create an ontology that links the core elements modeling a user to motivational strategies employed by experts (e.g. health and physical activity counselors, physical education teachers, personal trainers), I utilize a formal interview process. This aims to validate and identify missing main concepts in the domain of physical exercise motivation and the relationships among them. The interview is structured in two parts, as follows.

The first part asks the expert to list (1) important factors for keeping students engaged in physical activity (*corresponding to the main concepts used in the ontology*), (2) techniques used by experts to identify the students' motivational state (*used to create a mapping from users' answers to the state space*), (3) information about students that helps the expert interpret the students' success or failure (*used to validate the user model's output*), and (4) strategies and techniques employed by the expert to keep students engaged in physical activity (*corresponding to motivational strategies*).

The second part presents the expert with the same categories, but with given answers (drawn from literature). The expert is asked to indicate how much he or she agrees with the specific answer, using a Likert scale. This part aims to check if experts indeed use concepts identified in literature as key factors, acquire new key factors used in practice, and acquire the basis for creating an ontology linking the user model to the motivational strategies used by experts.

4.3 Adaptive System

My adaptive human-robot interaction system chooses a motivational strategy based on the user model's interpretation of "why" and "how" the user was (un)successful at his or her previous goal, i.e. the interpretation of the user's state. This is possible since the motivational strategies identified from literature (such as cooperative and competitive strategies, making the user aware of the importance of engaging in physical activity, autonomy support, structure, and involvement) are associated with factors present in the user model, e.g. "Intrinsic motivation is associated with the desire to master a task and the satisfaction that comes with that, whereas extrinsic motivation refers to completing tasks solely as an ego boost, be it beating peers in a competition, or receiving praise from a parent, teacher or colleague" [16].

My system adapts to an individual user by following a Q-learning approach. In the current work, the actions the "agent" (in our case the robot) can take are the different motivational strategies mentioned above, $a \in \{m_1, m_2, m_3, ...\}$, which are to be finalized after concluding expert interviews. The states of the world are the interpretations of a user's state (the output of the user model). Thus, a state is a feature vector representing the interpretation of the user's state, and is defined as $intrp_t = [f_1\ f_2\ f_3\ f_4\ f_5]$, where the f_is represent the features discussed above that take values associated with intensity levels. The reward for a particular state is the difference between the number of steps taken by the user and the number of steps set as the goal, $r_t = \#steps_{taken} - \#steps_{goal}$.

At time step t, the algorithm observes the current state $intrp_t$, chooses an action a_t among the motivational strategies based on an ϵ-greedy policy, takes the action, observes the reward r_t as well as the new state $intrp_{t+1}$, and then updates the Q-value for the state using the observed reward and the maximum reward possible for the next state. The update is performed based on the following formula: $Q(intrp_t, a_t) = Q(intrp_t, a_t) + \alpha[r_t + \gamma \max_{a_{t+1}} Q(intrp_{t+1}, a_{t+1}) - Q(intrp_t, a_t)]$, where α and γ are both set between 0 and 1 and specify how quickly learning occurs and how much future rewards matter, respectively. The algorithm will thus work toward finding an optimal policy, in order to maximize the expected return, i.e. positive reward or small values for negative rewards.

4.4 Future Work

Future work involves finishing the expert interview process in order to validate the ontology-based user model. The system itself is to be validated as part of two user studies. An initial month-long, in-home study is planned for data collection. Participants are assigned to either the robot or the wristband-only condition. The data from this study is to be employed to train the adaptive system used in a second similar study. This second study will employ the adaptive human-robot interaction system (adaptive robot condition) vs. a non-adaptive system that interacts with adolescents in the same manner, daily, but without adapting to the user (non-adaptive robot condition).

I am a third year Ph.D. student in the Social Robotics Lab, Computer Science Department, at Yale University. I have been working on better defining the currently proposed work, thinking through the details of the user model and the machine learning technique I am intending to apply as part of my adaptive system, and starting to conduct expert interviews in order to obtain data for creating an ontology-based user model. My background is in Computer Science, and I have been continuously involved in HRI research since my undergraduate years.

References

1. 2008 physical activity guidelines for americans. Tech. rep., U.S. Department of Health and Human Services (2008)
2. Physical activity guidelines for americans midcourse report: Strategies to increase physical activity among youth. Tech. rep., U.S. Department of Health and Human Services (2013)
3. Ajzen, I.: The theory of planned behavior. Organizational Behavior and Human Decision Processes **50**(2), 179–211 (1991)
4. Bandura, A.: Social cognitive theory of self-regulation. Organizational Behavior and Human Decision Processes **50**(2), 248–287 (1991)
5. Barua, D., Kay, J., Kummerfeld, B., Paris, C.: Modelling long term goals. In: Dimitrova, V., Kuflik, T., Chin, D., Ricci, F., Dolog, P., Houben, G.-J. (eds.) UMAP 2014. LNCS, vol. 8538, pp. 1–12. Springer, Heidelberg (2014)
6. Bickmore, T.W., Schulman, D., Sidner, C.L.: A reusable framework for health counseling dialogue systems based on a behavioral medicine ontology. Journal of Biomedical Informatics **44**(2), 183–197 (2011)
7. Consolvo, S., McDonald, D.W., Toscos, T., Chen, M.Y., Froehlich, J., Harrison, B., Klasnja, P., LaMarca, A., LeGrand, L., Libby, R., et al.: Activity sensing in the wild: a field trial of ubifit garden. In: Proceedings of the SIGCHI Conference on Human Factors in Computing Systems, pp. 1797–1806. ACM (2008)
8. Fasola, J., Matarić, M.J.: Socially assistive robot exercise coach: motivating older adults to engage in physical exercise. In: Desai, J.P., Dudek, G., Khatib, O., Kumar, V. (eds.) Experimental Robotics. STAR, vol. 88, pp. 463–479. Springer, Heidelberg (2013)
9. HealthMonth: Healthmonth - live healthier, for fun! (2014). https://www.healthmonth.com/
10. Kidd, C.D.: Designing for long-term human-robot interaction and application to weight loss (2008)
11. Klasnja, P., Consolvo, S., Pratt, W.: How to evaluate technologies for health behavior change in hci research. In: Proceedings of the SIGCHI Conference on Human Factors in Computing Systems, pp. 3063–3072. ACM (2011)
12. Kozima, H., Michalowski, M.P., Nakagawa, C.: Keepon. International Journal of Social Robotics **1**(1), 3–18 (2009)
13. Lenert, L., Norman, G.J., Mailhot, M., Patrick, K.: A framework for modeling health behavior protocols and their linkage to behavioral theory. Journal of Biomedical Informatics **38**(4), 270–280 (2005)
14. Lifetick: Lifetick - goal setting the way it should be (2014). https://www.lifetick.com/
15. Locke, E.A., Latham, G.P.: Building a practically useful theory of goal setting and task motivation: A 35-year odyssey. American Psychologist **57**(9), 705 (2002)
16. Nicholls, J.G.: Achievement motivation: Conceptions of ability, subjective experience, task choice, and performance. Psychological Review **91**(3), 328 (1984)
17. Trudeau, F., Shephard, R.J.: Physical education, school physical activity, school sports and academic performance. International Journal of Behavioral Nutrition and Physical Activity **5**(1), 10 (2008)
18. Uschold, M., Gruninger, M.: Ontologies: Principles, methods and applications. The Knowledge Engineering Review **11**(02), 93–136 (1996)

Privacy-Enhanced Personalisation of Web Search

Anisha T.J. Fernando

School of Information Technology and Mathematical Sciences,
University of South Australia, Adelaide, Australia
anisha.fernando@mymail.unisa.edu.au

Abstract. In personalised search, user information needs captured through cookies and Web search history for example, make it possible to infer personal or sensitive information about a person. Although prior studies have established sources of privacy leakage on the Web, there is a need for identifying the sources of data leakage concerning personalised search, its impact on users and on the broader privacy laws and regulations. This research study firstly explores the significance of attributes impacting personalised search and considers whether the extensive collection of personal data is necessary for personalised search results through a series of experiments measuring the impact of personalisation and sources of data leakage. These findings will then be evaluated two-fold: through a qualitative study of users, and assessed for its applicability in the Australian context as per the Australian Privacy Principles. Further, the outcomes from the experimental and user studies will be used to develop a Privacy-Enhancing Technology (PET) that will provide users with options to control personal data leakage whilst searching on the Web and enable proactive protection of individual user privacy.

Keywords: Personalisation · Web search · Data leakage · Search query parameters · Experimental study · Privacy

1 Introduction and Motivations

Personalisation in Web search occurs when search results are adapted to the needs of an individual user [1]. Personalised search results enhance the user experience by providing results tailored to a user's information needs [2]. As commercial search engines are profit-oriented with advertising based revenue models, personalisation addresses a secondary goal of providing relevant audiences for advertisers [3]. To personalise search results, users are profiled through behavioural tracking of a user's interests, characteristics and prior online history [4]. Hence, a personalisation-privacy trade-off is created as personal data is used for personalisation, but raises issues of its relevance to personalised search results for users.

Data leakage occurs both implicitly (i.e. without the user's knowledge) and explicitly in Web search through behavioural tracking methods [5, 6]. The transfer of personal and contextual data through search parameters is one example and the focus of this research study. Personal data is now more accessible to Web users who can further analyse it using readily available technologies [7]. Poor awareness and control over collection of personal data adds to the pervasiveness of implicit data leakage. Implicitly leaked personal data can lead to inaccurate inferences or misinterpretation

F. Ricci et al. (Eds.): UMAP 2015, LNCS 9146, pp. 385–390, 2015.
DOI: 10.1007/978-3-319-20267-9_35

of a person's identity, linkability of users, excessive collection of user data, poor control over personal data, and behavioural profiling [8]. Through behavioural tracking methods, personal data may be accessible to not just advertisers (first-party tracking), but other third-parties with access to that data [9]. These implications contribute to a potential loss in anonymity and integrity of a user's identity on the Web.

The personalisation-privacy trade-off and the role implicit data leakage plays underpin the motivation for the current research work. The motivation of this research study also stems from privacy concerns relating to national privacy laws and privacy requirements at different levels such as personal, institutional and national.

2 Related Work

Data Leakage Methods on the Web. Prior research studies have investigated dynamic Web environments to identify sources of leakage and user tracking mechanisms on the Web or variances in personalisation [10, 11]. Commercial search engines collect longitudinal user data by monitoring and tracking user browsing activities of primary and related users [12]. Third-party agents use stateful tracking methods via persistent supercookies and stateless tracking through fingerprinting via both active and passive techniques [13]. Passive fingerprinting concerns leakage of browser-related information including those explored in this experimental study, namely IP address, user-agent and HTTP headers. Recent studies explored the impact of new tracking mechanisms through session hijacking personalised recommendations, canvas fingerprinting, evercookies and cookie syncing and the subsequent privacy loss and risks posed by these techniques [14]. The ability to make inferences about a person is further enhanced through these persistent tracking mechanisms and raises the issue of protecting the identity of users online and the option of being anonymous.

Data Leakage Methods in Web Search. When users search online, search query, browser environment and user details are sent both explicitly (i.e. the query term the user types) and implicitly (i.e. various search query parameters consisting of the HTTP headers, GET/POST parameters and cookies). Typically personalisation may occur through account login and anonymously as in Google's case where personalisation is provided through a cookie that may remain on the user's Web browser for up to 180 days [15]. Personalisation may include contextual factors such as location, language and seasonality and data unique to users such as the MAC address of a user's machine. It is difficult to differentiate data that may personally identify a user, as contextual data when aggregated across different contexts may reveal sensitive or private data about a user.

Privacy Laws and User Privacy Concerns Relating to Personalised Search. In a typical situation, an individual's consent must be obtained before collection of sensitive personal information occurs. This information must only be collected if it is necessary for a function or a process of an organisation and must be destroyed once its purpose has been fulfilled [16]. Similar guidelines are evident in the European Union's Data Protection Directive.

The Australian Privacy Principles mandate controls on the use of people's personal data. Personal data transferred through search queries could be aggregated to profile users, raising concerns surrounding this secondary use of data collection. In a survey conducted on search engine use in 2012, 65% of respondents viewed personalised search as a "bad thing" as it would limit information seen online, whilst 73% were of the view that personalised search was an invasion of privacy [17]. This further raises the importance of upholding privacy and confidentiality of personal user data.

3 Problem Statement and Research Goals

The risks associated with the unauthorised access, collection, release and misuse of personal data may be irreparable and instantaneous damage, most often with a user's reputation at stake. Further, the use of pervasive methods of tracking user activities whilst searching makes it imperative to minimise the leakage of personal data through the different media. It is therefore, important to consider methods of preventing leakage of personal data before the act occurs to minimise the loss associated with the unauthorised access, release and misuse of personal data and protect the identity or anonymity of users on the Web. Hence, this experimental research study explores the data (i.e. the search query parameters including GET and POST Parameters, HTTP headers, cookies and IP address) transferred implicitly whilst users search on the Web and its impact on personalisation. The key research problem underpinning this research is: do search query parameters that contain user data transferred implicitly whilst searching, improve the relevance of results for users or only serve as a potential source of data leakage and thereby, impact user privacy?

A set of research questions to address this research gap are summarised as follows:
RQ 1. How is personalisation achieved by commercial search engines in relation to implicit data leakage?
RQ 2. How does the personalisation performed by commercial search engines impact privacy? Specifically: what personal data appears to be passed to search engines, its impact on personalised search results and how do users perceive this?
RQ 3. Does suppression of personal data released to search engines impact the relevance of results?
RQ 4. How relevant are search results through client-end personalisation or through collaborative personalisation by giving the user a means to control and censor their personal data being released to the search engine?

4 Approach and Current Progress

Experiment Methodology - Stage 1 (nearing completion): This research study consists of three main phases (*see Figure 1*). Currently the research study is progressing towards completing Research Question 1 (RQ 1).

Stage 1. The study commenced with efforts aimed at identifying how personalisation of Web search occurs (RQ 1). Using the experimental research technique, the researcher submitted a series of search queries using a sample of 29 significant search terms across 4 widely used search scenarios (browser search bar; search engine page with and without account login; a newly created control account). The result sets of search query parameters were identified and analysed to verify if they appear to carry possible sources of personal data, and to determine if these are used to achieve personalisation or for data collection purposes. Software tools such as Fiddler (an http intercepting proxy to identify search query parameters) and developed scripts using cURL and PHP were used for this task.

Preliminary results of the experiment on Google were published in the ACM SIGIR PIR Workshop [18]. Location data was found to impact personalisation more than the personalisation parameter 'pws' which is said to turn personalisation on/off. Subsequently after refining the experiment method from the workshop feedback, the full experiment was run on Google and StartPage. Findings from this in-depth experiment are currently under review. Key findings from this experiment include: Personalisation on Google was impacted more by location, query type, type of browser (user-agent) and the method of searching, but not necessarily by personally-identifiable data. Personalisation on StartPage was impacted by location and the query term.

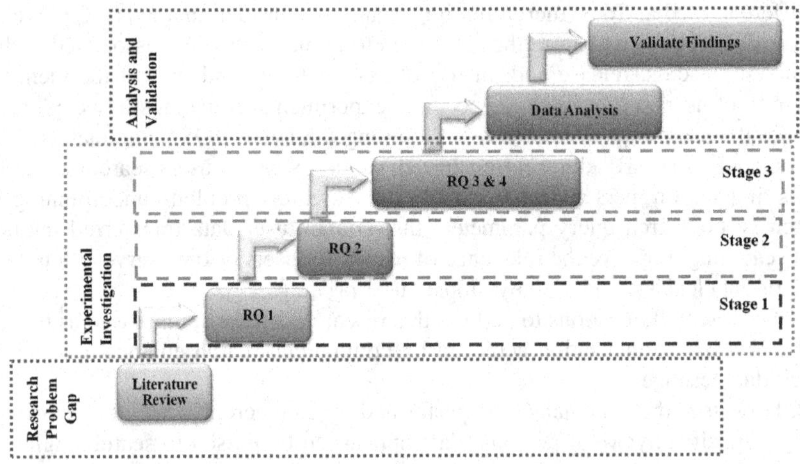

Fig. 1. Overall Research Study Approach

5 Future Work and Contributions

Stage 2. The next stage would be to investigate how personalisation of Web search impacts privacy (RQ 2). This will be done using focus groups for a sample of 25 participants. Participants will be pre-screened using a survey instrument [19], which measures privacy concerns so as to group together participants with similar privacy concern levels (positive, neutral, negative) and limit bias. Each focus group discussion will revolve around the participants' experiences with Web search, personalisation, privacy concerns and the impact on relevance of personal data in Web search personalisation. A post-discussion questionnaire will be used to obtain the participants feedback about the discussion topics. A conceptual model using the Contextual Integrity framework by Nissenbaum and privacy-by-design principles will be created to guide development of the technologies in Stage 3 [7].

Stage 3. The third stage will involve setting up experiments based on four different personalisation scenarios (RQ 3 & 4) to investigate the impact on user privacy and relevance of personalised search results to users. Each personalisation scenario (completely-clear search; control scenario - typical usage; client-end; controlled leakage) is chosen to represent a distinct variation of personal data control and leakage. Evaluation of relevance of personalised search results and the impact of implicit data leakage and privacy concerns will be assessed by users performing simulated search tasks for each scenario and answering pre and post task questions.

The research study aims to address a gap in understanding how personalised search impacts implicit data leakage and privacy. The study has significant implications as privacy laws vary across different jurisdictions or countries, yet users cross these jurisdictions routinely when searching on the Web.

The main contributions of this research study are:

1. A contribution to the understanding of how search engines collect data, and whether the data collected is used for generating personalised results or for other data-collection purposes. Further, the significance of these findings will be compared against privacy legislation in the Australian context namely, the Australian Privacy Principles.
2. A contribution to the understanding of privacy concerns associated with implicit data collected in personalised search and an analysis of the privacy-personalisation trade-off in the personalised search context through qualitative user studies.
3. A contribution to advancing the technological efforts associated with providing users the option to control implicit data leakage in personalised search.
4. Also, importantly this research study will provide the user with the option of being in control of their data privacy, through developing a local personalisation technique as a Privacy-Enhancing Technology (PET). It would empower users to be aware and in more control of the amount of personal data divulged through using online Web search services. The research aims to provide the knowledge and tools needed for individuals to achieve a satisfactory level of personalisation in their search results while controlling the release of their personal data.

Specific Research Aims for Discussion at the UMAP Doctoral Consortium:

- To present current research findings and obtain critique of the experiment method and findings to further efforts to investigate implicit data leakage in this context.
- To have a collaborative and constructive discussion with the assigned mentor and experts in the field regarding the issues of identifiability and anonymity, and privacy concerns for users regarding implicit data leakage of personalised search. This would enable me to further my learning and development in the area.

Background. Currently, I'm a second-year doctoral student at the University of South Australia with research interests in personalised search and user privacy.

Acknowledgements. My advisors: Principal Supervisor: Assoc. Prof. Helen Ashman and Associate Supervisor: Dr. Tina Du. We acknowledge the contributions from the .auDA Foundation for funding this research work.

References

1. Berendt, B., Teltzrow, M.: Addressing users' privacy concerns for improving personalization quality: towards an integration of user studies and algorithm evaluation. In: Mobasher, B., Anand, S.S. (eds.) ITWP 2003. LNCS (LNAI), vol. 3169, pp. 69–88. Springer, Heidelberg (2005)

2. Steichen, B., O'Connor, A., Wade, V.: Personalisation in the wild: providing personalisation across semantic, social and open-web resources. In: Proceedings of the 22nd ACM Conference on Hypertext and Hypermedia, pp. 73-82. ACM, Eindhoven (2011)
3. Feuz, M., Fuller, M., Stalder, F.: Personal Web Searching in the Age of Semantic Capitalism: Diagnosing the Mechanisms of Personalisation. First Monday. **16**(2), 1–8 (2011)
4. Castelluccia, C., Narayanan, A.: Privacy considerations of online behavioural tracking. ENISA Report (2012)
5. Micarelli, A., Gasparetti, F., Sciarrone, F., Gauch, S.: Personalized search on the world wide web. In: Brusilovsky, P., Kobsa, A., Nejdl, W. (eds.) Adaptive Web 2007. LNCS, vol. 4321, pp. 195–230. Springer, Heidelberg (2007)
6. Kobsa, A.: Privacy-enhanced web personalization. In: Brusilovsky, P., Kobsa, A., Nejdl, W. (eds.) Adaptive Web 2007. LNCS, vol. 4321, pp. 628–670. Springer, Heidelberg (2007)
7. Nissenbaum, H.: Privacy in Context: Technology, Policy, and the Integrity of Social Life. Stanford University Press, Stanford (2010)
8. Toch, E., Wang, Y., Cranor, L.F.: Personalization and privacy: a survey of privacy risks and remedies in personalization based systems. User Model. User-Adapt. Inter. **221**(2), 203–220 (2012)
9. Castelluccia, C., Kaafar, M.-A., Tran, M.-D.: Betrayed by your ads! Reconstructing user profiles from targeted ads. In: Fischer-Hübner, S., Wright, M. (eds.) PETS 2012. LNCS, vol. 7384, pp. 1–17. Springer, Heidelberg (2012)
10. Malandrino, D., Scarano, V.: Privacy leakage on the Web: Diffusion and countermeasures. Computer Networks. **57**(14), 2833–2855 (2013)
11. Hannak, A., Sapiezynski, P., Kakhki, A.M., Krishnamurthy, B., Lazer, D., Mislove, A., Wilson, C.: Measuring Personalisation of Web Search. In: Proceedings of the 22nd International Conference on World Wide Web, pp. 527–538. IW3C2, Rio De Janeiro (2013)
12. Krishnamurthy, B., Wills, C.E.: Privacy diffusion on the web: a longitudinal perspective. In: Proceedings of the 18th International Conference on World Wide, pp. 541–550, WWW, Madrid (2009)
13. Mayer, J.R., Mitchell, J.C.: Third-party web tracking: policy and technology. In: Proceedings of the 2012 IEEE Symposium on Security and Privacy, pp. 413–427, SP 2012. IEEE, San Francisco (2012). doi:http://dx.doi.org/10.1109/SP.2012.47
14. Castelluccia, C., De Cristofaro, E., Perito, D.: Private information disclosure from web searches. In: Proceedings of the 10th International Symposium on PETS 2010, pp. 38–55. PETS 2010, Berlin, Germany (2010)
15. Google: Personalized Search – YouTube (2013). https://www.youtube.com/watch?v=EKuG2M6R4VM
16. Office of the Australian Information Commissioner: Australian Privacy Principles and National Privacy Principles-Comparison Guide. Australian Government, Canberra (2013)
17. Purcell, K., Brenner, J., Rainie, L.: Search Engine Use 2012, Pew Research Center - Internet & American Life Project (2012). http://pewinternet.org/Reports/2012/Search-Engine-Use-2012.aspx
18. Fernando, A.T.J., Du. J.T., Ashman, H.: Personalisation of web search: exploring search query parameters and user information privacy implications – the case of google. In: Proceedings of the 1st International Workshop on Privacy-Preserving IR: When Information Retrieval Meets Privacy and Security – ACM SIGIR Conference, pp. 31–36. ACM SIGIR PIR, Gold Coast (2014). http://ceur-ws.org/Vol-1225/
19. Earp, J.B., Anton, A.I., Aiman-Smith, L., Stufflebeam, W.H.: Examining Internet privacy policies within the context of user privacy values. IEEE. Trans. Eng. Manage. **52**(2), 227–237 (2005)

From Artifact to Content Source: Using Multimodality in Video to Support Personalized Recomposition

Fahim A. Salim(✉)

CNGL/ADAPT Centre, Trinity College Dublin, Dublin, Ireland
salimf@tcd.ie

Abstract. Video content is being produced in ever increasing quantities. It is practically impossible for any user to see every piece of video which could be useful to them. We need to look at video content differently. Videos are composed of a set of features, namely the moving video track, the audio track and other derived features, such as a transcription of the spoken words. These different features have the potential to be recomposed to create new video offerings. However, a key step in achieving such recomposition is the appropriate decomposition of those features into useful assets. Video artifacts can therefore be considered a type of multimodal source which may be used to support personalized and contextually aware recomposition. This work aims to propose and validate an approach which will convert a video from a single artifact into a diverse query-able content source.

Keywords: Personalization · Multimodality · Video analysis · Paralinguistic · User engagement

1 Introduction

The variety and amount of content users consume has increased exponentially. Video content is a strong example of this. Over 6 billion hours of video are watched each month on YouTube . The set of videos available on this platform are very diverse, with one hundred hours of new video being added every minute[1]. Videos are one of the richest forms of content in terms of multimodality we consume on a regular basis and thanks to high speed internet we consume them in enormous quantities.

It is safe to say that it is very difficult if not impossible for users to see every piece of video which could be useful or even important for them. It is therefore desirable to deliver the content in a more intelligent manner. By delivering con-tent intelligently, we mean that the consumer should be able to get more value out of content without wasting too much time. But to decide what is valuable in con-tent is highly subjective, since engagement with content is context

[1] https://www.youtube.com/yt/press/statistics.html

F. Ricci et al. (Eds.): UMAP 2015, LNCS 9146, pp. 391–396, 2015.
DOI: 10.1007/978-3-319-20267-9_36

dependent [1]. Users consume different content in different scenarios, users may also consume the same or similar content differently on different occasions. Their engagement with the same piece may vary depending on the type of device they are using or the situation they are in at that moment. Therefore what is of value in a piece of video content at one time may not be of much value for the same user at a different time.

Videos provide an interesting challenge and opportunity for that. Generally a video is considered a single artifact, but we believe that it is a more diverse multimodal content source; a source which can be exploited for recomposition purposes to perform contextual and personalized search queries in a multimodal manner. This paper discusses, the early stage of PhD work for decomposing video content for the purpose of personalized recomposition.

2 Background

There are many ways in which video content can be recomposed. Recomposing a video to generate a video summary attracts a lot attention in research. Most comprehensive multimodal feature extraction to generate video summary can be seen in [6] as authors take advantage of all three visual, audio and linguistic modalities to create video summaries. [3] recompose videos by dividing them in segments based on PowerPoint slides and index those segments using ontologies to perform complex queries. [8] use face name pairs to extract relevant footage form large video archives and presents those recomposed video segments to the user using a specially created application. [18] create a summarization from multiple videos using aesthetic evaluation.

There are other ways as well by which researchers recompose video content e.g. [7] recompose video by altering it in both time and spatial domain, while [13] recompose video by generating 3D content from 2D footage.

In terms of video personalization, creating recommender systems for users based on their viewing habits and commenting patterns also attracts a lot of inter-est. For example, in [17] authors use heterogeneous data from different sources to create a better recommender system based on user video preferences. In [4] authors attempt to predict user movie preferences by clustering movie subtitles, low level visual features and ratings given by users. In [2] authors tried to categorize videos in different categories based on their features.

Video categorization and video recommendation are both interesting and useful problems. But they tend to focus too much on recommending items to the user. We believe that multimodal features in videos can be harvested to extract much more profound knowledge then simple yes no or like or dislike predictions.

Moreover, while a lot of research is done in extracting features from different modalities within video content, the focus of that is still creating a new artifact form another artifact i.e. a video summary etc. instead of harnessing video as a diverse content source. Although [3] and [8] do make some progress towards this goal, however [3] rely too much on the slide structure within the presentation to make each slide within a video more searchable, while [8] focus more on the user experience with the end user interface. The potential of decomposing a video with temporal information for recomposition purposes, to be consumed by heterogeneous entities is under investigated. This work aims to investigate that potential.

3 Proposed Contribution

The main hypothesis of this work is "It is possible to extract and index multimodal signals from video content in order to support personalized and contextually-aware summarization and recomposition, thereby transforming it from an artifact into a diverse queryable content source."

By multimodal signals we mean the characteristics or features within the different modalities by which a video delivers its message to the viewer. There is the visual modality i.e. anything visually interesting or engaging to the viewer, e.g. visual features like camera close up or visual aid, etc. the paralinguistic modality i.e. the audio features, e.g. laughter, applauses and other audio features, and the linguistic modality, i.e. the spoken words, also any text with in the video as well as any supporting resources e.g. human written synopsis etc.

By multimodal content source we mean that a user may not necessarily always need to consume video content as a video artifact. For example, it might be more appropriate for a person to view a video at home on a big screen as it is visually (i.e. video stream) stunning or, it might be more useful to listen to just the audio on their mobile devices, as it is possible that for some videos all of the valuable content is carried by the speaker's voice. For some video, he/she might want to skip some parts and for others he/she may want to skip the video and just watch a summary, which would necessitate recomposing that summary from relevant segments. A recomposed summary may not need be a video summary, it could very well be just audio or a text summary generated from transcript or a human written summary together with some images extracted from the video.

Based on this thesis we envision an approach described in Fig. 1 which is capable of providing personalized and contextually relevant segments form a video collection based on a query. We believe that this research will help harness the potential within videos as diverse content sources thanks to their multimodal nature.

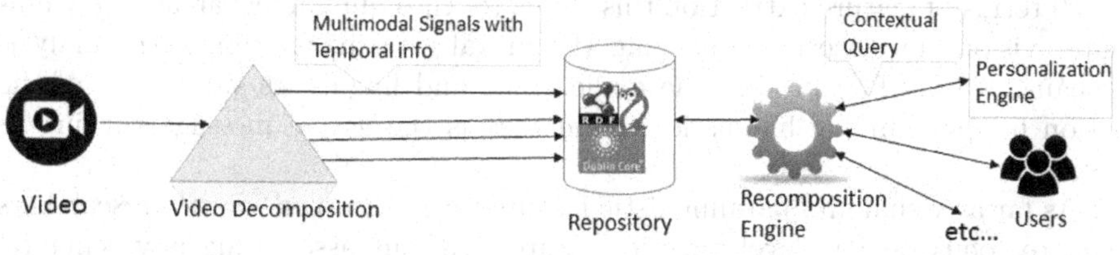

Fig. 1. High level system overview

The approach of this thesis is about delivering content in an intelligent and personalized manner like the AMAS system [15], GALE [14] and the CULTURA system [16]. All these system are end to end approaches investigating all the aspects from content authoring and creation to user modeling and end user experience. Since this approach specifically targets the decomposition of video content. It can, apart from being a standalone solution, could potentially be a part of any of these systems or input to heterogeneous personalization engines to substantially enhanced user's media consumption experience.

Let us consider one specific type of video, i.e. presentations. A video presentation involves typically one speaker presenting a topic, often accompanied by supporting media, such as still images or further video. This form of video may be seen as both simple and sophisticated at the same time. Presentations are simple in the sense that there is usually just one person continuously talking to an audience with or without audio/visual aids; they are sophisticated in the sense that they can deliver semantically diverse kinds of messages to their viewers and engage them in a variety of ways. From video lectures to general-purpose video presentations, we have an enormous amount of video presentations available to us.

TED [2] talks have become very successful with over 1,900 talks as of February 2015, since they were first published online in June 2006 [3]. Imagine a user who would like to know more about economics, there are dozens of talks related to economics on TED website (103 to be precise at the time of this writing) with hours and hours of video content. Consider that recent events had made him/her curious about new economic models which are better for society in general by going beyond traditional capitalism and hyper consumerism. The same user also loves charts and statistics, enjoys a laugh and cares for common good. The above mentioned approach could definitely help a personalization engine provide such relevant content to the user. Virtual conference systems such as one described in [11] can also be greatly enhanced by using video as a personalizable content source.

4 Progress to Date and Future Plans

Since this thesis is combinatory in nature and we need to perform a number of steps to achieve our goal. Therefore progress needs to be reported in terms of each aspect in addition to the overall progress.

In terms of feature extraction this thesis touches quite a few areas, e.g. Computer vision since we are analyzing the visual stream, paralinguistic analysis be-cause we need to process the audio track and linguistics since most of the action happens in the linguistic stream that is the actual message within the talk.

As far as visual and paralinguistic features are concerned, mostly researchers tend to focus on low level generic features without associating any semantic

[2] www.ted.com

[3] http://en.wikipedia.org/wiki/TED_(conference)

meaning to it [6]. This is useful for detecting scene change detection and similar things. Since we are looking at presentations, we do not come across many visual scene changes. We instead adopted somewhat similar approach as in [9] and [8] by taking higher level visual and paralinguistic features.

In terms of linguistic analysis the approach we are planning to use is based primarily on the work presented by [10] called Slicepedia, which focuses on content agnostic slicing.

All the extracted features along with their timestamp information will be in-dexed using Resource Description Framework (RDF), to make the content more queryable, thanks to its wide adaptability and its logical foundation [5]. We believe that storing them using RDF will allow us to use different ontologies [3] and array of diverse tools to create our system. However the details of the meta-data structure and query mechanism still remains an open question for us.

In order to see the effectiveness of our proposed approach and the value it brought to the user's video consumption experience, we need a qualitative analysis of it. Therefore we need a definition of engagement for our context. We believe that, the elaborate feedback system of TED website can give us that. Since it is voluntarily information by users in terms of semantically positive and negative words, it provides good basis to analyze relevant factors of engagement described in [12].

A preliminary experiment with, correlation of multimodal features and user feedback gave us encouraging results. In that experiment we extracted visual features such as close-up shots and distant shots of the speaker together with paralinguistic features such as laughter and applauses within TED talks and saw their impact on how users rated and thereby engaged with the video. We analyzed 1340 TED talks and their corresponding ratings, using machine learning algorithms the classification improved with the introduction of visual features com-pared to paralinguistic features alone. Apart from becoming an initial step in our proposed video decomposition approach, the experiment gave the preliminary statistical evidence of our thesis about the value within different modalities of video content.

All extracted features will be fed into a model to create multimodal segments in a personalized and contextually aware manner, although features, e.g. semantic extraction from the audio track, will most likely prove more valuable in recomposition.

The next step is to examine, the state of the art in adaptive and personalization technologies to further stream line the decomposition and indexing of the video content to get a full video content consumption pipeline. This will help us evalu-ate and demonstrate the capabilities of the proposed approach.

Acknowledgments. This research is supported by the Science Foundation Ireland (grant 07/CE/I1142) as part of the CNGL Centre for Global Intelligent Content (www.cngl.ie) and ADAPT (www.adaptcentre.ie) at Trinity College, Dublin.

References

1. Attfield, S., Piwowarski, B., Kazai, G.: Towards a science of user engagement. WSDM Workshop on User Modelling for Web Applications, Hong Kong (2011)
2. Anwar, A., Salama, G.I., Abdelhalim, M.B.: Video classification and retrieval using arabic closed caption. In: ICIT 2013 The 6th International Conference on Information Technology VIDEO (2013)
3. Dong, A., Li, H.: Ontology-driven Annotation and Access of Presentation Video Data. Estud. Econ. Apl **26**, 840–860 (2008)
4. Brezeale, D., Cook, D.J.: Learning video preferences using visual features and closed captions. IEEE Multimed. **16**, 39–47 (2009)
5. Bruijn, J.D., Heymans, S.: Logical foundations of RDF (S) with datatypes. J. Artif. Intell. Res. **38**, 535–568 (2010)
6. Evangelopoulos, G., Zlatintsi, A., Potamianos, A., Maragos, P., Rapantzikos, K., Skoumas, G., Avrithis, Y.: Multimodal saliency and fusion for movie summarization based on aural, visual, and textual attention. IEEE Trans. Multimed. **15**, 1553–1568 (2013)
7. Guttmann, M., Wolf, L., Cohen-Or, D.: Content aware video manipulation. Comput. Vis. Image Underst. **115**, 1662–1678 (2011)
8. Haesen, M., Meskens, J., Luyten, K., Coninx, K., Becker, J.H., Tuytelaars, T., Poulisse, G.-J., Pham, P.T., Moens, M.-F.: Finding a needle in a haystack: an interactive video archive explorer for professional video searchers. Multimed. Tools Appl. **63**, 331–356 (2011)
9. Hosseini, M.-S., Eftekhari-Moghadam, A.-M.: Fuzzy rule-based reasoning approach for event detection and annotation of broadcast soccer video. Appl. Soft Comput. **13**, 846–866 (2013)
10. Levacher, K., Lawless, S., Wade, V.: Slicepedia: Content-agnostic slicing resource production for adaptive hypermedia. Comput. Sci. Inf. Syst. **11**, 393–417 (2014)
11. Nautiyal, A., Kenny, E., Dawson-Howe, K.: Video adaptation for the creation of advanced intelligent content for conferences. Irish Machine Vision and Image Processing Conference (2014)
12. OBrien, H.L., Toms, E.G.: Examining the generalizability of the User Engagement Scale (UES) in exploratory search. Inf. Process. Manag. **49**, 1092–1107 (2013)
13. Park, M., Luo, J., Gallagher, A.C., Rabbani, M.: Learning to produce 3D media from a captured 2D video. IEEE Trans. Multimed. **15**, 1569–1578 (2013)
14. Smits, D., De Bra, P.: GALE: A Highly Extensible Adaptive Hypermedia Engine. In: HT 2011 - Proc. 22nd ACM Conf. Hypertext Hypermedia (Eindhoven, Netherlands, June 6–9, 2011), pp. 63–72 (2011)
15. Staikopoulos, A., OKeeffe, I., Rafter, R., Walsh, E., Yousuf, B., Conlan, O., Wade, V.: AMASE: A framework for supporting personalised activity-based learning on the web. Comput. Sci. Inf. Syst. **11**, 343–367 (2014)
16. Steiner, C.M., Steiner, C.M., Hillemann, E.C., Conlan, O., Orio, N., Ponchia, C., Hampson, C., Nussbaumer, A., Albert, D.: Evaluating a Digital Humanities Research Environment: The CULTURA Approach. Int. J. Dig. Libr. **15**, 53–70 (2014)
17. Tan, S., Bu, J., Qin, X., Chen, C., Cai, D.: Cross domain recommendation based on multi-type media fusion. Neurocomputing **127**, 124–134 (2014)
18. Zhang, Y., Zhang, L., Zimmermann, R.: Aesthetics-Guided Summarization from Multiple User Generated Videos. ACM Trans. Multimed. Comp. Comm. Apl. **11** (2014)

Exploiting Item and User Relationships for Recommender Systems

Zhu Sun(✉)

School of Computer Engineering, Nanyang Technological University, Singapore, Singapore
sunzhu@ntu.edu.sg

1 Research Challenges

Recommender systems have become a prevalent tool to cope with the information overload problem. The most well-known recommendation technique is collaborative filtering (CF), whereby a user's preference can be predicted by her like-minded users. *Data sparsity* and *cold start* are two inherent and severe limitations of CF.

To address these issues, many researchers have conducted research on leveraging user relationships to improve the accuracy of recommender systems. A number of trust-aware recommender systems [1–6] are emerging due to the advent of social networks. Significant improvements have been achieved up to date. However, these approaches suffer from several issues. First, social information may be unavailable for some real application. Second, some users may only have few friends, or even not be active in the social networks, i.e., cold start is also a problem of social networks. Third, the potential noise and weaker social ties (than trust) in social networks may also produce negative effects on the generality of these approaches [6].

Similarly, the side information of items can also be exploited for recommender systems. Based on the assumption that users tend to have similar preferences towards a set of *associated* items, several approaches [7,8] have been proposed by making use of explicit item relationships such as category, genre, location, etc. However, explicit item relationships are mostly leveraged in a straightforward way and not well analysed in these approaches. Considering the free formats of item attributes/contents across different applications, we argue that more abstract-level item associations should be exploited to enhance both the performance and generality of recommenders. More importantly, the item relationships should not be restricted to the explicit ones based on item attributes, but also implicit ones based on user-item interactions.

In summary, the research challenges of my research can be depicted by: first, how to leverage implicit item relationships to improve the accuracy of recommender systems; second, how to design a unified model that can incorporate both explicit and implicit item relationships; last, how to further integrate user relationships into the unified model for better recommendation.

F. Ricci et al. (Eds.): UMAP 2015, LNCS 9146, pp. 397–402, 2015.
DOI: 10.1007/978-3-319-20267-9_37

2 Related Work

Many approaches have been proposed to date by taking into account additional user relationships. Guo et al. [1] propose a simple method by incorporating trusted neighbors to alleviate *data sparsity* and *cold start* problems. Ma et al. [2] propose the *RSTE* method to linearly combine a basic matrix factorization model with a trust-based neighborhood model. The same authors [4] later design a matrix factorization model with social information as a regularizer to further improve recommendation performance. After that, Jamali and Ester [3] build a model (*SocialMF*) based on the assumption that a user's latent feature vector is regularized by those of her trusted users. Yang et al. [5] devise a hybrid method (*TrustMF*) which combines both a truster model and a trustee model from the perspectives of trusters and trustees. Recently, Guo et al. [6] propose a new model (*TrustSVD*) to comprehensively take the explicit and implicit influence of both ratings and trust into consideration. However, these approaches may fail to work if being applied to the situations where social networks are not built-in or connected.

Typically, there are two types of item relationships: *explicit* and *implicit*. Many researchers attempt to leverage explicit item relationships to enhance recommender systems. For example, Hu et al. [8] contend that the quality of a business shop can be influenced by that of other shops in a certain geographical neighborhood. Shi et al. [7] show that tags are also helpful to enhance recommendation performance. Implicit item relationships refer to the relationships implicitly involved between items. A classic example is that a man buying diaper is likely to buy beer as well, though the diaper and beer are distinct items. Kim and Kim [9] apply association rule mining techniques to reveal multi-level item associations in the light of item categories. Both Wang et al. [10] and Ma [11] make use of the similarity measure (PCC) to identify implicit item relationships. However, the inherent limitations of PCC dramatically degrade recommendation performance of both approaches. Lastly, as we stated earlier, user relationships are also useful resources for recommender systems, while only a few works [10,11] take into account both of them.

3 Progress to Date

The first scenario we look into is the item relationship implicitly involved in user-item rating patterns. Till now, we have proposed a novel matrix factorization model by exploiting association rule-based implicit item relationships, called *IIR* [12]. It is merely based on user-item rating. We are currently working on a unified model that additionally makes use of explicit item information.

3.1 Incorporating Implicit Item Relationships

The work is mainly composed of two parts, including how to mine the implicit item relationships from ratings, and then how to accommodate the mined item relationships in a matrix factorization model.

Mining Implicit Item Relationships. Item similarity is a straightforward method to define implicit item relationships. Pearson correlation coefficient and cosine similarity are the most widely used measures. However, they suffer from inherent weaknesses which have been pointed out by [12,13]. Hence, we adopt association rule techniques to measure item associations as the implicit item relationships. If item i appears frequently together with item j, an association rule can be denoted by $l_{i,j} : i \to j$. A key characteristic of association rule is that $l_{i,j}$ is different from $l_{j,i}$, i.e., the association is asymmetric as we demand. By regarding the rating matrix as a user-item transaction matrix, we apply association rule to mine two types of item relationships: item-to-item and group-to-item associations. We present these two kinds of association rule as $l_{i,j} : i \to j$, and $l_{G,j} : G \to j$ respectively, where G denotes a set of associated items.

Note that proper values for thresholds minimum support and minimum confidence should be determined when using association rule. However, either higher or lower thresholds can greatly deteriorate recommendation performance. We thus define a new measure *reliability* for association rules (see details in [12]). Then, we sort all the association rules in the descending order of computed reliability values, and select the top-K most reliable association rules. Lastly, we propose five different strategies to select the top-K association neighborhoods of a target item, and find that the strategy Group+, i.e., select the top-K most reliable group-to-item association rules, where we select item-to-item association rules to complement in case of insufficient rules, performs best.

Designing IIR Model. After properly defining the implicit item relationships, we proceed to design the recommendation model, i.e., the IIR model based on matrix factorization (MF) techniques. In particular, MF models [14] factorize the user-item rating matrix $R \in \mathbb{R}^{m\times n}$ into two low-rank user-feature $U \in \mathbb{R}^{m\times d}$ and item-feature $V \in \mathbb{R}^{n\times d}$ matrices, where m, n are the number of users and items, respectively; and $d \ll \min(m, n)$ is the number of latent features. Let $r_{u,i}$ be a rating given by user u on item i, and $\hat{r}_{u,j}$ be a rating prediction for user u on a target item j. The rating prediction $\hat{r}_{u,j}$ can be estimated by the inner product of user-specific feature vector U_u and item-specific feature vector V_j.

We posit that two items should be close to each other in terms of feature vectors if they are implicitly associated with each other. Similar to the usage of social relationships in [4], we design the IIR model which leverages the implicit item relationships as a regularizer to adjust the decomposition of rating matrix R. The IIR model is shown in Equation 1, where $I_{u,j}$ is an indicator function that equals 1 if user u rated item j and equals 0 otherwise; $\alpha > 0$ is a regularization parameter to control the influence of implicit item relationships; A_j is a set of reliable association rules for item j; $s_{G,j}$ is the reliability value of association rule $l_{G,j}$, which indicates the extent to which item j is associated with items included in G (note that given the item-to-item relationships, $|G| = 1$); $\|\cdot\|_F$ is the Frobenius norm; and λ_u, λ_v are regularization parameters to avoid over-fitting problem. Here we contend that a target item's feature vector should be close to the majority of its associated group and hence adopt the average of all group items' feature vectors as the characteristic of a group G. A local optima of Equation 1 can be achieved by the stochastic gradient descent (SGD) method.

$$\mathcal{L} = \frac{1}{2}\sum_{u=1}^{m}\sum_{j=1}^{n} I_{u,j}(r_{u,j} - \hat{r}_{u,j})^2 + \frac{\alpha}{2}\sum_{j=1}^{n}\sum_{G\in A_j} s_{G,j}\|V_j - |G|^{-0.5}\sum_{k\in G} V_k\|_F^2 + \frac{\lambda_u}{2}\|U\|_F^2 + \frac{\lambda_v}{2}\|V\|_F^2, \quad (1)$$

We evaluate the effectiveness of our model via four real-world datasets (FilmTrust, MoiveLens, Ciao, Epinions) in terms of predictive accuracy. Experimental results show that our method achieves superior performance over other counterparts.

3.2 Incorporating Explicit and Implicit Item Relationships

Explicit item relationship has been reported as an important additional resource for recommender systems. Different from the implicit item relationships, explicit connections among items are beneficial to help explain items to recommend. For example, for the users who are interested in disaster movies, they are likely to prefer Poseidon Adventure given that they have watched Titanic. Hence, we are considering to design a unified model which incorporates both explicit and implicit item relationships.

The usage of social relationships in [15] gives us some inspirations to design our model. The authors proposed a trust-aware recommendation approach. First decomposing the original single-aspect trust information into four general trust aspects. Then incorporating these aspects into the probabilistic matrix factorization model for rating prediction with the support vector regression technique. Similarly, suppose there are N types of explicit item's information (e.g. category, location, brand etc.), we can design a linear or nonlinear predicted function to predict the item relationships, then incorporate the predicted function into matrix factorization model to generate recommendations. However, more challengingly, we have no ground truth of the strength of item relationships. We will look into unsupervised learning methods to solve the problem.

3.3 Model Evaluation

Proper datasets and metrics should be adopted for the purpose of model evaluation. In particular, due to the usage of explicit item relationships (see Section 3.2) and user relationships (involved in the last research challenge), we choose the datasets with additional item or user information to evaluate the effectiveness of our model. A number of real-world datasets are available. For instance, MoiveLens[1] is a personalized movie recommendation website, where users can rate movies with integers from 1 to 5. It contains moives' genres and tags, as well

[1] http://www.cs.umn.edu/Research/GroupLens

as users information. Epinions[2] and Ciao[3] are product review sites, where consumers can review products with ratings from 1 to 5 stars. In addition, the two datasets involve the information of item category and social trust information. These datasets are widely used for evaluation in the literature. For evaluation metrics, we focus on the accuracy of recommendations in this research. These metrics can be broadly classified into two categories: (1) predictive accuracy metrics, such as mean absolute error (MAE) and root mean square error (RMSE), which are the most widely used metrics for rating prediction; (2) ranking accuracy metrics for top-N item recommendation, such as precision, recall and normalized discount cumulative gain (NDCG), etc. Among these metrics, ranking-based measures are superior to the prediction-based ones since item recommendation is a more optimal task than rating prediction in reality. Hence, we will focus more on the evaluation of item recommendation.

4 Future Research

In our research, we mainly adopt item relationships to improve recommendation performance. The intuition is that item relationships are amenable to explain the inference behind recommendations. This is because users are more familiar with items previously preferred than those allegedly like-minded users. So far, we have proposed the IIR model by leveraging the implicit item relationships involved in the user-item ratings and significant improvements have been achieved. Typically, in real e-commerce applications products can be either alternative or complementary. For example, a user who wants to buy a dress may be fond of two dresses that are similar in style, and a user who have bought a dress may desire to buy heels to match her dress. In the former case, the two dresses are alternative, and in the latter case, the dress and heels are complementary. What we aim to study is more generalized, i.e., how one item can be associated with another, explicitly or implicitly. We will study different kinds of item association.

The future work will be accomplished in two steps. For the first step, we will design a unified model that accommodates both explicit and implicit item relationships for better recommendation performance. This is the research direction we are currently working on. Another way to use explicit item information is to build a heterogeneous information network among items, whereby two items in a distance can be connected. Their correlation can be measured by some graph-based approaches, for example, meta-path similarity. For the second step, we will incorporate user relationships into the model previously devised. For example, we can construct the heterogeneous information networks with both users and items. In this ways, we can not only measure user-user and item-item correlations, but also user-item correlations, i.e., the interaction patterns among users and items. This may also give us some indication how user relationships can be integrated into our unified model.

[2] http://www.trustlet.org/wiki/Epinions
[3] http://www.librec.net/datasets.html

References

1. Guo, G., Zhang, J., Thalmann, D.: A simple but effective method to incorporate trusted neighbors in recommender systems. In: Masthoff, J., Mobasher, B., Desmarais, M.C., Nkambou, R. (eds.) UMAP 2012. LNCS, vol. 7379, pp. 114–125. Springer, Heidelberg (2012)
2. Ma, H., King, I., Lyu, M.: Learning to recommend with social trust ensemble. In: Proceedings of the 32nd International ACM SIGIR Conference on Research and Development in Information Retrieval (SIGIR), pp. 203–210 (2009)
3. Jamali, M., Ester, M.: A matrix factorization technique with trust propagation for recommendation in social networks. In: Proceedings of the 4th ACM Conference on Recommender Systems (RecSys), pp. 135–142 (2010)
4. Ma, H., Zhou, D., Liu, C., Lyu, M., King, I.: Recommender systems with social regularization. In: Proceedings of the 4th ACM International Conference on Web Search and Data Mining (WSDM), pp. 287–296 (2011)
5. Yang, B., Lei, Y., Liu, D., Liu, J.: Social collaborative filtering by trust. In: Proceedings of the 23rd International Joint Conference on Artificial Intelligence (IJCAI), pp. 2747–2753 (2013)
6. Guo, G., Zhang, J., Yorke-Smith, N.: Trustsvd: collaborative filtering with both the explicit and implicit influence of user trust and of item ratings. In: Proceedings of the 29th AAAI Conference on Artificial Intelligence (AAAI) (2015)
7. Shi, Y., Larson, M., Hanjalic, A.: Tags as bridges between domains: improving recommendation with tag-induced cross-domain collaborative filtering. In: Konstan, J.A., Conejo, R., Marzo, J.L., Oliver, N. (eds.) UMAP 2011. LNCS, vol. 6787, pp. 305–316. Springer, Heidelberg (2011)
8. Hu, L., Sun, A., Liu, Y.: Your neighbors affect your ratings: on geographical neighborhood influence to rating prediction. In: Proceedings of the 37th International ACM SIGIR Conference on Research & Development in Information Retrieval (SIGIR), pp. 345–354 (2014)
9. Kim, C., Kim, J.: A recommendation algorithm using multi-level association rules. In: Proceedings of 2003 IEEE/WIC International Conference on Web Intelligence (WI), pp. 524–527 (2003)
10. Wang, D., Ma, J., Lian, T., Guo, L.: Recommendation based on weighted social trusts and item relationships. In: Proceedings of the 29th Annual ACM Symposium on Applied Computing (SAC), pp. 2000–2005 (2014)
11. Ma, H.: An experimental study on implicit social recommendation. In: Proceedings of the 36th International ACM SIGIR Conference on Research and Development in Information Retrieval, pp. 73–82. ACM (2013)
12. Sun, Z., Guo, G., Zhang, J.: Exploiting implicit item relationships for recommender systems. In: Proceedings of the 23th International Conference on User Modeling, Adaptation and Personalization (UMAP) (2015) (under edit)
13. Guo, G., Zhang, J., Yorke-Smith, N.: A novel bayesian similarity measure for recommender systems. In: Proceedings of the 23rd International Joint Conference on Artificial Intelligence (IJCAI), pp. 2619–2625 (2013)
14. Koren, Y., Bell, R., Volinsky, C.: Matrix factorization techniques for recommender systems. Computer **42**(8), 30–37 (2009)
15. Bao, Y., Fang, H., Zhang, J.: Leveraging decomposed trust in probabilistic matrix factorization for effective recommendation. In: Proceedings of the 28th AAAI Conference on Artificial Intelligence (AAAI) (2014)

Author Index

Printed in the United States
By Bookmasters

Printed in the United States
By Bookmasters